THE BEST PLAYS OF 1972-1973

THE
BURNS MANTLE
YEARBOOK

THE
BEST PLAYS
OF 1972-1973

EDITED BY OTIS L. GUERNSEY JR.

*Illustrated with photographs and
with drawings by* HIRSCHFELD

○ ○ ○ ○ ○ ○

DODD, MEAD & COMPANY
NEW YORK · TORONTO

EDITOR'S NOTE

IN THE season of 1972-73 as in other recent years, the diverse origin of our best work points up the New York stage's increasing dependence on far-flung sources of inspiration. It's still true that a playscript hasn't really made it until it has appeared in New York, but the road to success no longer necessarily leads through the office of the Broadway impresario with the view of the Artcraft signs through his window, as we've seen so often in the movies. Today the New York hit may have come straight from a London triumph (*Butley*), or from London via regional theater production (*The Changing Room, Green Julia*), or directly from regional theater, or up from the experimental ranks (*The Hot l Baltimore*).

To keep up with these widening circles of theater activity, in this new *Best Plays* volume we continue to expand our coverage of London, of off off Broadway and of regional theater without in any way attenuating our traditionally thorough factual report on all the professional productions on and off Broadway. This year's list of London shows has been expanded to almost 500 entries, thanks to the supremely diligent efforts of our European Editor, Ossia Trilling, and his assistant, Susan Harrow, with much-appreciated help from the British publications *Time Out* and *Fringe Theater/Experimental Theater*. Also in this year's London listing we introduce a new feature, Trilling's Top Twenty, the 20 best shows of the season as selected by our European Editor, listed with full casts and complete credits. Additionally, our coverage of the London theater in this 1972-73 volume is introduced by two articles, one written from the point of view of the creative artist by the distinguished British playwright Frank Marcus and the other, Mr. Trilling's resume, from the point of view of the critic. Our European coverage also includes Mr. Trilling's comprehensive review of activity in the Continent's major theater capitals, as well as his listing of Paris productions.

On the national scene, too, we continue to broaden our coverage in *The Best Plays of 1972-73*. Ever more new scripts are having their first stagings in the cross-country playhouses, and Ella A. Malin's "Directory of Professional Regional Theater" records each of these world or American premieres in a complete cast-and-credits listing, along with the hundreds of basic reference entries for the production of ancient and modern classics, not only throughout the United States but also in the major Canadian theater centers. We have the honor this year to introduce our national coverage with an article by Arvin Brown, the distinguished artistic director of New Haven's Long Wharf Theater, whose production of *The Changing Room* towered over Broadway this season and won the Critics Award.

Locally, our Broadway and off-Broadway listings are complete, as always.

Where distinctions between off and off off Broadway are blurred, we have included all borderline cases. As the experimental activity in New York's little lofts and arenas grows from year to year, so does our list of leading off-off-Broadway production groups, with a reference entry for each of their major productions (bearing in mind that much of this activity is experimental work in progress and the focus of our interest is the butterfly, not the worm). An article by Jeff Sweet, a musical author-composer as well as a critic, reports on the highlights and trends of the 1973 off-off-Broadway year.

As our New York hits settle in for long runs or set forth in touring companies across the English-speaking theater world from Piccadilly to Sunset Boulevard, no major casting escapes the scrutiny of Stanley Green, author of *Ring Bells! Sing Songs!* (a history of Broadway musicals in the 1930s) and the recent *Starring Fred Astaire* (an illustrated biography of the film great), and compiler of our section on cast replacements. Expertise, patience and dedication to the project are prominent characteristics of all the members of the *Best Plays* team: Rue Canvin (necrology, publications and recordings), Jonathan Dodd of Dodd, Mead and Company, Inc., which has been publishing this volume annually for 54 years, and the editor's toiling and longsuffering wife.

On behalf of the reader who is the ultimate beneficiary of their efforts, we warmly thank the many who helped in providing and acquiring material for these pages: Henry Hewes, Bernard Simon of *Simon's Directory,* Mimi Horowitz of *Playbill,* Hobe Morrison of *Variety,* Clara Rotter of the New York *Times,* Ralph Newman of the Drama Book Shop, as well as the many people in the production offices whose help was essential in collecting accurate information about stage productions. Al Hirschfeld's drawings are a genuine adornment to the text; so are the examples of the year's outstanding designs by Tony Walton, Theoni V. Aldredge and Patricia Zipprodt, and the photographs of theater in New York and across the country by Martha Swope, Inge Morath, Van Williams, Friedman-Abeles, William L. Smith, Bert Andrews, Cosmos, Terence Le Goubin, Nat Messik, George E. Joseph, Raimondo Borea, Diane Gorodnitzki, Andy Hanson, Greenburg May Productions, David Robbins, Daniels, William Baker and others.

We are grateful most of all to the playwrights for their devotion and persistence in giving us yet another fabulous theater season, and to their representatives and publishers who annually cooperate in arranging for the Best Plays synopses. What these playwrights, composers, librettists and lyricists have accomplished we are applauding, so to speak, in the form of this 1972-73 theater yearbook. We hope they will accept this volume as a form of admiration of all their work. We thank them for the events of New York production, successful or otherwise, and for the memory that is treasured in these pages.

OTIS L. GUERNSEY Jr.

June 1, 1973

CONTENTS

Drawings by HIRSCHFELD

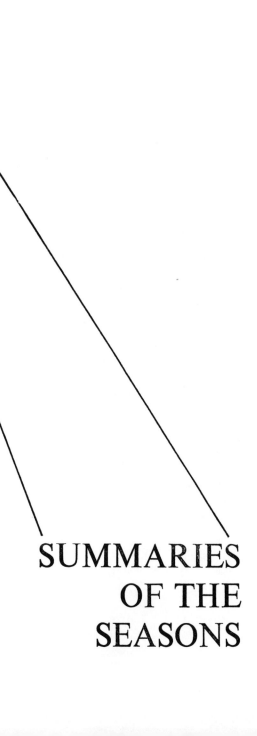

SUMMARIES
OF THE
SEASONS

THE SEASON IN NEW YORK

By Otis L. Guernsey Jr.

ANTICIPATION . . . disappointment . . . surprise . . . anticipation . . . disappointment . . . surprise . . . that's the roller-coaster rhythm of every New York theater season. Yearly, great expectations are aroused by the announced shows. For example, in September 1972 we knew we were going to get new scripts by Tennessee Williams, Arthur Miller, Neil Simon, Stephen Sondheim, Jean Kerr, Paul Zindel and Gerome Ragni. In accordance with the laws of human nature, we anticipated not merely new delights from these richly gifted dramatists, but masterpieces on the order of *A Streetcar Named Desire, Death of a Salesman, The Odd Couple, A Funny Thing Happened on the Way to the Forum, Mary, Mary, The Effects of Gamma Rays on Man-in-the-Moon Marigolds* and *Hair*—and all in the same season, naturally.

Disappointment must always follow as inevitably as September becomes October and November and December. Early in the year even the successes seem less than fulfilling, not yet having taken on that larger-than-life magnification which comes partly from the repetition of the title day after day in capital letters in the newspapers' alphabetized listings. Disappointment is January's other name. The lamentations of the drama critics fall upon the pages like snow, celebrities badmouth the theater on all the talk shows, and parodists compose a new verse for Jerry Herman's "Oh, What a Lovely Theatrical Season We've Had."

And then, surprise . . . a couple of scripts jostle the imagination in a new way, and/or a spring musical suddenly gives Broadway the polish and excitement it needs to make all its other shows look attractive. Surprise . . . all at once, the shows that have managed to live through the winter suddenly seem better than anyone has a right to expect from the creative artists of one performing-arts form in a single season.

Last year it was *That Championship Season, Sticks and Bones* and the vibrating musicals based on the black experience that finally produced the surprise of a good showing. In 1972-73 it was Joseph A. Walker's off-Broadway-to-Broadway-commuting *The River Niger* and Lanford Wilson's off-off-Broadway-to-off-Broadway-commuting *The Hot l Baltimore,* together with the Stephen Sondheim-Hugh Wheeler musical *A Little Night Music,* that finally brought the shining rabbit out of the battered hat. And, true to form, Neil Simon's *The Sunshine Boys,* Arthur Miller's *The Creation of the World and Other Business* and Jean Kerr's *Finishing Touches* grow increasingly worthy

3

The 1972-73 Season on Broadway

PLAYS (16)

That Championship Season (transfer)
6 RMS RIV VU
The Lincoln Mask
The Secret Affairs of Mildred Wild
THE CREATION OF THE WORLD AND OTHER BUSINESS
The Last of Mrs. Lincoln
THE SUNSHINE BOYS
Look Away
Let Me Hear You Smile
FINISHING TOUCHES
Status Quo Vadis
Out Cry
42 Seconds From Broadway
THE RIVER NIGER (transfer)
No Hard Feelings

MUSICALS (13)

Dude
Hurry, Harry
Pippin
Lysistrata
Dear Oscar
Ambassador
Via Galactica
Tricks
Shelter
A LITTLE NIGHT MUSIC
Seesaw
Cyrano
Smith

REVUES (2)

Jacques Brel Is Alive and Well and Living in Paris (transfer)
Nash at Nine

HOLDOVER SHOWS WHICH BECAME HITS DURING 1972-73

Don't Bother Me, I Can't Cope
Grease
Jesus Christ Superstar
The Prisoner of Second Avenue

FOREIGN PLAYS IN ENGLISH (4)

BUTLEY
The Jockey Club Stakes
No Sex Please, We're British
THE CHANGING ROOM

FOREIGN-LANGUAGE PRODUCTIONS (2)

From Israel With Love
Pacific Paradise

SPECIALTIES (3)

Here Are Ladies
Bunraku
Marcel Marceau

REVIVALS (16)

Man of La Mancha
Lincoln Center Rep
Enemies
The Plough and the Stars
The Merchant of Venice
A Streetcar Named Desire
Much Ado About Nothing (transfer)
Circle in the Square
Mourning Becomes Electra
Medea
New Phoenix
The Great God Brown
Don Juan
Purlie
Don Juan in Hell
Irene
Emperor Henry IV
The Women
The Play's the Thing (transfer)

Categorized above are all the plays listed in the "Plays Produced on Broadway" section of this volume.
Plays listed in CAPITAL LETTERS have been designated Best Plays of 1972-73.
Plays listed in **bold face type** were classified as hits in *Variety's* annual list of hits and **flops** published June 6, 1973 or judged likely to become hits.
Plays listed in *italics* were still running June 1, 1973.

of a major place in the canons of their illustrious authors as we reflect upon them, "blossoming even as we gaze."

In 1972-73 as in other recent seasons we enjoyed the added distinction of fine British scripts, most notably David Storey's *The Changing Room,* Simon Gray's *Butley* and, off Broadway, Paul Ableman's *Green Julia.* Add in a successful playwriting debut—Bob Randall's with *6 Rms Riv Vu*—and you certainly have an admirable 1972-73 Best Plays list which breaks down as follows: seven Broadway productions and three off Broadway; nine plays and one musical; seven American scripts and three British; nine by experienced playwrights and one debut. Others in close contention for places on the 1972-73 best list were, on Broadway, James Prideaux's *The Last of Mrs. Lincoln,* Paul Zindel's *The Secret Affairs of Mildred Wild,* the Galt MacDermot Christopher Gore-Judith Ross musical *Via Galactica* and the Stephen Schwartz-Roger O. Hirson musical *Pippin;* and, off Broadway, Alice Childress's *Wedding Band,* Ron Whyte's *Welcome to Andromeda,* Phillip Hayes Dean's *Freeman* and Steve Tesich's *Baba Goya.*

The number of shows produced on Broadway in 1972-73 dropped only very slightly to 54 from an overall total of 56 (including "limited" and "middle" productions) last year and 56 in 1970-71—thus maintaining some sort of plateau after a dropoff from 68 in 1969-70, 76 in 1968-69 and 84 in 1967-68 (at the end of the season David Merrick voiced his opinion that Broadway production will probably maintain its present level in the foreseeable future). Of this 1972-73 Broadway total, 16 were new American plays and 13 were new musicals as compared with totals of 19-13, 14-11, 21-14, 24-12 and 25-10 in previous seasons (so that the number of musicals is slightly up, even with production costs astronomically increased). There was a sharp decline in the off-Broadway production of new American playscripts from 43 last year to 28 in 1972-73, probably a result of the changing character of the off-Broadway environment from informal and experimental to a more formal and ever more expensive "little Broadway."

Ticket prices stayed about the same as they have in recent seasons since reaching but not exceeding that $15 Broadway musical top, $9 for a Broadway play and around $7.50 for a hot off-Broadway ticket if there was such a thing this year. Production costs were continuing to rise like the price of everything else, and it was whispered that one of the Broadway musicals actually cost as much as $1 million. In this context, *Variety*'s annual summary of the Broadway season contained both good and bad news. First, the good news: for the ninth straight year the combined 52-week New York and road-company gross for all legitimate stage attractions was more than $100 million ($100,431,571 according to *Variety*'s figures), with the road's share of this total a whopping, record-breaking $55,532,992, going over the $50 million mark for the first time. Now, the bad news: the total 52-week Broadway gross had shrunk to $44,898,579, the lowest in 10 years, down from $52.3 million last year, $54.9 million in 1970-71 and way under 1967-68's record $59 million.

In the all-important matter of playing weeks, which measure the activity of the Broadway stage (if 10 shows play 10 weeks, that's 100 playing weeks), the total dropped to 878, the lowest since *Variety* began keeping these figures in the late 1930s, down from last year's 1,092 and way below the plateau of 1,200 in the late 1960s. Paradoxically—*Variety* noted—there were more box office successes this year than last. Furthermore, by mid-May 1973 there seemed to be arising in the theater a feeling of optimism, an instinct that some nadir had been passed, some corner turned, as *Irene* and *A Streetcar Named Desire* set new weekly gross records and brave new productions were being announced for 1974.

There is another footnote that should be added to the 1972-73 summary. Those massive $50-million-plus Broadway grosses and 1,000-plus playing week totals of recent years were accomplished with the very considerable help of a group of smash-hit holdovers playing year after year in some of the longest runs in history, comfortably padding the annual statistics. These included *Hello, Dolly!, Fiddler on the Roof, Man of La Mancha, Hair, Promises, Promises, 1776* and *Oh, Calcutta*—all of which added greatly to the activity and grosses of other seasons but none of which played for any appreciable segment of 1972-73. We can at least hope that beneath the low tide of numbers Broadway is taking a leaf out of Neil Simon's book. When a bunch of his hits closes, Simon gets busy on a stack of new ones, and there's not much wrong with Broadway that it couldn't cure in a big hurry by doing likewise.

Ups and Downs

With the shadow of these generally downbeat statistics, there were shining highlights as well as black holes. This was the year that *Fiddler on the Roof* topped *Life With Father's* record June 17 with its 3,225th performance and went on to establish an all-time Broadway long-run record of 3,242 performances before finally closing on July 2 (and meanwhile, off Broadway, *The Fantasticks* played through another year of the longest continuous run of record in the American theater, reaching its 5,443d performance at season's end). According to *Variety* estimates, *Fiddler* has returned $8,347,500 *net* profit on its original $375,000 investment and has sold more than 2,000,000 cast albums, an impressive showing albeit only a fraction of *Hair's* 4,000,000 or *My Fair Lady's* 8,000,000.

Sleuth's success story was a steady pulse beat of rising profits amounting to more than ten times its $15,000 investment. The release of the movie version in late December didn't adversely affect the Broadway box office receipts. *No, No, Nanette's* take is still a matter of conjecture; *Variety* has declined to estimate its exact net thus far but did term it substantial. *Man of La Mancha* earned $103,514 in 18 weeks at the Vivian Beaumont. *Pippin,* which trimmed its original budget from $700,000 to $500,000, was sailing its taut little ship into the black. *Grease* continued its steady progress, achieving new status as a Broadway hit which has paid off its production cost. And from the hinterlands came word to *Variety* that *Luv* (remember *Luv?*) has so far earned $674,000 on its original $90,000 Broadway investment (remember $90,000?).

But then there was *Dude,* which spent more than $100,000 to remodel the Broadway Theater to suit its unique form and personality, and then folded to the tune of $900,000; and *Via Galactica,* nicknamed "daughter of *Dude"* because it had the same composer, Galt MacDermot, and suffered a similar fate, a $900,000 loss after a minuscule run. These two musicals plus *Ambassador, Lysistrata, Tricks* and *Shelter* lost their backers a total of over $3 million. Under the perverse economic conditions of the contemporary stage it would be a mistake to assume that all these shows fell as far short artistically as they did financially; in this game, quality and success don't always play on the same team. One of our landmark musicals, *Follies,* lost $674,443 of its $792,596 cost in its Broadway run and increased its deficit to $700,000 before ending an unsuccessful road tour prematurely in Los Angeles.

Last season's best play, David Rabe's *Sticks and Bones,* not only failed to find an audience in its transfer to Broadway but was cancelled in a scheduled TV version on CBS March 9, presumably because it might have offended viewers oversensitized to its Vietnam War theme at a time when the prisoners were coming home (and also probably because it offended some of the network affiliate programmers, who previewed it on closed-circuit TV and were put off by its highly imaginative, split-level dramatic form). The tribulations of *Sticks and Bones* are doubly ironic because of the great success of its Public Theater stablemate, Jason Miller's *That Championship Season,* which was a big box-office hit in *its* move to Broadway and added to its 1972 Drama Critics Award the 1973 Tony and Pulitzer Prize.

Arthur Miller's fine, if not widely popular, *The Creation of the World and Other Business* was a $250,000 straight-play loser on Broadway. So was *Status Quo Vadis,* Donald Driver's satire on the stratification of American society, with each character wearing the number of his station in the tale of a brash Number 5 who dares to love a haughty Number 1. A big success in its original Chicago production, *Status Quo Vadis* was unenthusiastically received on Broadway and closed after only one performance $235,000 in the red. Other 1973 Broadway productions which gave up after only one viewing were Don Petersen's *The Enemy Is Dead, Let Me Hear You Smile* by Leonora Thuna and Harry Cauley and starring Sandy Dennis, Jerome Kilty's *Look Away* (one of the season's three plays about Mary Todd Lincoln), Louis Del Grande's *42 Seconds From Broadway* and the Sam Bobrick-Ron Clark comedy *No Hard Feelings* starring Eddie Albert and Nanette Fabray. The year's hapless one-night stands off Broadway were three musicals (*Crazy Now, A Quarter for the Ladies Room* and *Buy Bonds, Buster*), three plays (*Blue Boys* by Allan Knee, *Echoes* by N. Richard Nash and *A Phantasmagoria Historia of D. Johann Faust,* etc. by Vasek Simek) and the revival of *We Bombed in New Haven*—thus making a total of 13 unlucky shows in the 1973 New York professional theater which lasted only a single performance. Another off-Broadway musical called *Smile, Smile, Smile,* about the inept ruler of a desert island paradise, lasted a whole 7 performances but drew the shortest review of the year from Clive Barnes of the New York *Times,* only three sentences long. The first identified the who, what, when, where of the production. The last two were: "It was called *Smile, Smile, Smile.* I didn't, I didn't, I didn't."

Stars were receiving strong inducements to twinkle on Broadway by producers waving contracts offering them a percentage of both the gross and net profits (Debbie Reynolds, Maureen Stapleton, Julie Harris) or percentage deals of other kinds (Melina Mercouri, Alan Bates, Eva Marie Saint, Jerry Orbach, Christopher Plummer and many others). The list of outstanding, sometimes memorable, acting contributions on New York stages this season is a long one and should include at least Jack Albertson and Sam Levene as doddering vaudevillians (and not overlooking Lewis J. Stadlen as the nephew) in *The Sunshine Boys* . . . Alan Bates as the disintegrating Butley and Hayward Morse as his inscrutable companion . . . Wilfrid Hyde-White with Robert Coote and Geoffrey Sumner as dedicated aristocrats in *The Jockey Club Stakes* . . . Ben Vereen and Leland Palmer in the foreground of *Pippin* and the late Irene Ryan in the background . . . The diffident lovers of *6 Rms Riv Vu,* Jerry Orbach and Jane Alexander . . . Barnard Hughes's Dogberry, Sam Waterston's Benedick and Kathleen Widdoes's Beatrice in *Much Ado About Nothing* . . . Colleen Dewhurst's powerful O'Neill matron in *Mourning Becomes Electra* . . . John McMartin's Sganarelle in *Don Juan* . . . Julie Harris's often bewildered but always gallant Mary Todd Lincoln (with Leora Dana as her sister) in *The Last of Mrs. Lincoln,* and for that matter Eva Marie Saint's (with Fred Gwynne as Lincoln) in *The Lincoln Mask* and Geraldine Page's (with Maya Angelou as her black companion) in *Look Away* . . . George S. Irving and Patsy Kelly backing up Debbie Reynolds in *Irene* . . . Marcia Rodd upstaging the computer in *Shelter* . . . Keene Curtis as a head without much body and Raul Julia as vice versa in *Via Galactica* . . . Rene Auberjonois's commedia dell'arte Scapin in *Tricks* . . . Stacy Keach's potent Hamlet . . . Maureen Stapleton's movie fantasies in *The Secret Affairs of Mildred Wild* . . . Hume Cronyn and Jessica Tandy doing Beckett in the Forum . . . Barbara Bel Geddes and Robert Lansing overcoming middle-aged madness in *Finishing Touches* . . . Ruby Dee and James Broderick towering over bigotry in *Wedding Band* . . . Fred Grandy and John Pleshette playing *Green Julia's* game of words, like a fast set of tennis . . . Rosemary Harris as Portia and Blanche Du Bois at Lincoln Center . . . Christopher Plummer's memorable *Cyrano* and Leigh Beery's appealing Roxana . . . Kathryn Walker's unloved wife in *Alpha Beta* . . . Roderick Cook as the centerpiece of *Oh, Coward!* . . . Michele Lee's Gittel Mosca in *Seesaw* . . . Rex Harrison bringing his customary flair to Pirandello in *Emperor Henry IV* . . . David Clennon as the intense young invalid of *Welcome to Andromeda* . . . The entire acting ensembles of *The Changing Room, A Little Night Music, The River Niger* and *The Hot l Baltimore,* with not an emphasis out of place nor a point missed.

The directors came on strong in 1973, which in musicals was a vintage year for the directing choreographer (Bob Fosse of *Pippin,* Michael Kidd of *Cyrano,* Gower Champion of *Irene,* Michael Bennett of *Seesaw,* Donald Saddler of *Berlin to Broadway With Kurt Weill*). Among other notable stints of staging were A.J. Antoon's of *Much Ado About Nothing,* Alan Arkin's of *The Sunshine Boys,* Michael Rudman's of *The Changing Room,* Harold Prince's of *A Little Night Music,* Joseph Anthony's of *Finishing Touches,* Roderick Cook's of *Oh, Coward!,* Richard Foreman's of *Doctor Selavy's Magic Theater,* Douglas Turner Ward's of *The River Niger.* The producer of the year was Joseph Papp—who else?—with his two transfers *That Championship Season* and *Much Ado About Nothing* and his takeover of Lincoln Center. As far as his regular indoor season at the Public Theater was concerned, however, it wasn't quite as interesting overall as that of American Place. Another in the forefront of 1973 production was Robert Whitehead with two of the ten Best Plays, the Arthur Miller and the Jean Kerr. For Mr. Broadway himself, David Merrick, it was an off year. He was dabbling in motion pictures and just barely touched home base with his production of Tennessee Williams's *Out Cry.*

After a writing-directing triumph in the movies, Frank D. Gilroy returned to the theater with *Present Tense,* a short-lived off-Broadway program of four experimental playlets, contemporary skirmishes in the never-ending war between men and women. Other former Pulitzer Prize winners who had difficulty finding their feet in the theater this season were Tennessee Williams, Paul Zindel and Abe Burrows. Their problems were not the season's most conspicuous, however. That distinction is the sole property of the *Hair* team of authors, Gerome Ragni, James Rado and Galt MacDermot, who separately and in pairs came up with three new musicals which managed only 51 performances combined. Besides *Dude* and *Via Galactica,* there was *Rainbow* off Broadway with James Rado-authored book (in collaboration with his brother Ted), music and lyrics. *Rainbow* was a musical fantasy of a Vietnam casualty's life after death, almost a sequel to *Hair.* A king-sized collection of rock compositions and pastiches, it poured out 42 numbers in youthful indignation at a universe that isn't as loving as it should be. It was as ardent as *Hair,* and very imaginative, but it lacked *Hair's* coherence both in style and substance.

Much the same could be said about *Dude.* With book and lyrics by Gerome Ragni and music by Galt MacDermot, it didn't so much probe the meaning of existence as strike at it with a sledgehammer in the hope that it might reveal itself in shattering. It, too, was an ardent show, vibrating with rock rhythms, spilling all over a specially-rebuilt theater so that its symbolic characters could descend on wires from symbolic heaven or roam all over the symbolic earth in search of truth, climbing a "mountain" in the balcony aisles or wandering the deep "forest" of the orchestra pit area (the stage itself was placed about where fifth row center should have been). For all its effort and aggressive imagination, *Dude* like *Rainbow* was more of an experience for the performers than for the audience.

Finally from a *Hair* contributor there was *Via Galactica,* opening the new, cavernous and uncomfortable (for the show) Uris Theater with a musical fantasy of the world 1,000 years from now. It was an almost operatic musical, all sung to the music of Galt MacDermot (who, by the way, was additionally represented this year by the musical interludes in Rochelle Owens's *The Karl Marx Play*), with words by Christopher Gore and Judith Ross. As one of only four, or 40, or perhaps 400 theatergoers who enjoyed this show, I find myself slowly forgetting its faults and remembering its glowing MacDermot score (including a notable rock ballad, "Children of the Sun") and its entertaining comic-book concept (the comic-book form doesn't seem to do well on the New York stage—c.f. *Superman, Status Quo Vadis, Warp I,* etc.—but there are those of us who enjoy its bright primary dramatic colors). Its "book" was both fantastic and relevant: if you felt threatened in 1972 you would hate 2972 when all human beings have become happy but will-less robots controlled by a headpiece attached at birth, except for a handful of rebellious individualists who plan to escape to another solar system where they can be free. The brains of the outfit is a disembodied head riding around on a mobile heart-lung machine (played by Keene Curtis with great relish) and the brawn is a space adventurer, played by Raul Julia. Peter Hall staged the action with space ships hovering over the audience and with a trampoline-covered stage on which the actors' bounces suggested a low-gravity environment, thus making the most of the show's adventure-comic ambiance. The climax was an ironic reversal of the United States Cavalry charge we all grew up on, with a spidery, villainous space cruiser with aluminum belly marked "U.S.A." threatening to doom the rebels at the last second. *Via Galactica* lasted only 7 woe-begone performances, and, come to think of it, I do remember one of its flaws: the orchestra was playing so loudly at the performance I attended that it was hard to hear what was being sung. People in the balcony began shouting to the orchestra to tone down so they could hear the words. They were obviously caught up in the show or they wouldn't have cared what the characters were saying—or, rather, singing. Maybe some of them would agree that *Via Galactica* was one of the most satisfyingly *theatrical* concepts of the season, and that MacDermot's excellent score balanced out some of this year's shortcomings of the *Hair* collaborators.

We anticipated . . . in some cases, particularly at the beginning of the season, we were disappointed . . . but finally the surprises came along and the season ended on a rising pitch of accomplishment and optimism. Viewed in perspective, the 1973 New York professional theater season was a sculptural, stationary attraction of line and form, rather than of kinetic energy. It lacked thrust, drive, purpose, boldness. Last year the effort to experiment with new kinds of theater side-by-side with well-made structures of the old form was vividly exemplified in 1972's two outstanding American plays—the challenging, difficult, triple-tiered *Sticks and Bones* and the conventional *That Championship Season,* both dramas. They symbolized the growing split in the form and among audiences of the modern theater art; a split which was weakening the theater commercially, perhaps, but which was producing a dynamic tension among creative artists which frequently proved inspiring.

This season it was as though someone had pulled out the plug connecting this dynamo of invention to its energy source. 1972-73 never ventured beyond *Pippin* or *Shelter*—absurdist Broadway rock musicals—in experimental concept. Except for an occasional *succes d'estime* and the institutional productions, there was hardly anything doing off Broadway, let alone any thrust of experimentation, while on Broadway—symbolically—the creators of the bittersweet musical milestone *Follies* were toying, skillfully but conservatively, with operetta. It was that kind of a year; a year of musicals and comedies; entertaining and restful, an intermission in the artistic abrasion of the recent past.

Broadway

A "hit" in the true Broadway meaning of the word isn't merely a show that is hard to get into on a Friday night in December, but a show which pays off its production cost and starts making a profit (it may be easy to get into but become a "hit" by virtue of a movie sale or a profitable road tour). Recently, however, the word "hit" has been losing a lot of its magic. Production costs are so high that hardly any show, however popular, is expected to reach the break-even point in the season it was produced. And very often Broadway doesn't have either the first or last word on a playscript, as it once did. Plays now come to Broadway with their prominent position in world theater already established in foreign or regional theater production. A good script ignored on Broadway for some special reason may take on an illustrious life of its own elsewhere on world stages or in other media. So we make no special point in this resume about which 1972-73 offerings were "hits" and which were "flops" except that this information is recorded in the one-page summary of the Broadway season accompanying this article.

The ultimate insignia of New York professional theater achievement (we insist) isn't the instant popularity of the hit list, but selection as a Best Play in these volumes. Such selection is made with the script itself as the primary consideration, for the reason (as we have stated in previous volumes) that the script is the very spirit of the theater, the soul in its physical body. The script is not only the quintessence of the present, it is most of what endures into the future.

The Best Plays of 1972-73 were the following, listed in the order in which they opened (an asterisk * with the performance number signifies that the play was still running on June 1, 1973):

6 Rms Riv Vu
(Broadway; 247 perfs.)

Butley
(Broadway; 135 perfs.)

Green Julia
(off Broadway; 147 perfs.)

*The Creation of the World
and Other Business*
(Broadway; 20 perfs.)

The River Niger
(off B'way & B'way; 195* perfs.)

The Sunshine Boys
(Broadway; 187* perfs.)

Finishing Touches
(Broadway; 128* performances)

A Little Night Music
(Broadway; 109* perfs.)

The Changing Room
(Broadway; 100* perfs.)

The Hot l Baltimore
(off Broadway; 80* perfs.)

The 1973 best of these bests, in the opinion of this volume's editor, was the play imported from London by the Long Wharf Theater in New Haven, David Storey's *The Changing Room.* In this new script, as in *Home,* Storey's purpose is to fashion an exact copy of a time, place and circumstance, without much decorative overlay of "plot" or underlay of "theme." In *Home* Storey zeroed, or maybe Xeroxed, in on two less-than-distinguished old men struggling feebly in a web of senility; in *The Changing Room* the object of the playwright's scrutiny is a less-than-distinguished North Country professional rugby team in its locker room before, during and after a game. This is not the rugby of the green playing fields of Eton, but a merciless, brutish form of the game having a special appeal to fans who are only a generation or two removed from the merciless, brutish life of a Victorian-era coal miner. Storey, who himself was once a rugby player of professional ability, has keenly observed the team and its hangers-on, as one by one the men drift into the locker room to peel off their street clothes together with whatever gentling values their outside world may possess. They put on clean uniforms and a special set of values for the duration of the game: the obligatory extra effort, the need to work together as a team, the endurance of pain in bone-crushing action to take place on a frozen field, the urge to demonstrate some kind of commitment to one another in locker room byplay and jokes. There is no conflict except the game in *The Changing Room,* no resolution except the passage of time. The players get themselves "up" for the opening whistle; they collapse between the halves; for a few moments they are rambunctiously elated by victory, then slowly they deflate as they put on their street clothes and street manners and depart individually.

In its effort to produce an exact copy without any retouching, *The Changing Room* was performed with physical reality, without any encumbrance of modesty. That is to say, the players changed into and out of their uniforms as casually as they would in a real locker room as men among men. They let it all hang out, and it is to the great credit of Michael Rudman's staging that the cast performed this aspect of the play without either hesitation or exploitation. This rare example of total mass male nudity on a Broadway stage was so far from being shocking, so fluent a part of the stage action, that most members of the audience didn't become conscious of it until after it was well under way. The Long Wharf production of Storey's British play was cast with American actors (whose North Country accents sounded fine to these inexperienced ears), and to single out any one of this coordinated group of artists would seem to slight the others (though John Lithgow won a Tony and a Drama Desk Award for his portrayal of a battered, sobersided veteran). They were an admirable ensemble in an admirable play which received seven of the 20 first-choice votes in the New York Drama Critics Circle balloting and won their consensus and their 1973 award for the best play of the season regardless of category. It was the eighth foreign script to win the Critics' best-of-bests in the decade, with only *The Subject Was Roses* and *The Great White Hope* taking top honors for American playwriting in their respective seasons in the ten years beginning with John Osborne's *Luther* in 1963-64.

The best American play of the year, other opinions to the contrary notwith-standing, was Neil Simon's *The Sunshine Boys,* a study of human beings on the threshold of senility so amazingly sensistive, with a touch so light and yet so accurate, you hardly realized how good a play it was until you'd had time to reflect on it. Where *The Changing Room* was a kind of stunt, *The Sunshine Boys* was a finely disciplined work (and in every important respect the other play's peer) about two crotchety old show-biz pros, once-famous comedians, trying to solve the problem of getting along with each other long enough to do one of their old skits on a TV special. It was spare but wholly sufficient, with just enough humor, just enough pathos, just enough caricature but not an ounce more than enough for a comment on the aging process that was both deeply felt and highly entertaining. I wouldn't presume to try to identify Alan Arkin's direction apart from the other contributions; the play seemed to be driven forward by its own inner logic, which in itself is evidence of Arkin's skill. If there were performances this year that seemed better than Jack Albertson's and Sam Levene's as the septuagenarian vaudevillians and Lewis J. Stadlen's as the nephew who hero-worships them, it must have been because there were juicier roles. Simon has labeled *The Sunshine Boys* a "comedy." Whatever you call it, it is a superbly crafted piece of theater. Simon may have written funnier plays, but never one that demonstrated such total mastery of his art.

The 1973 season was a year of comedies, to be sure, but not all of them called themselves by this name. On Broadway, for example, only five scripts were self-styled comedies (and, perversely, a Broadway-bound musical which called itself *Comedy* folded out of town). A Best Play selection whose author did *not* identify his work as a comedy was *6 Rms Riv Vu* (the title being an abbreviation in the style of an apartment-to-let classified ad) by Bob Randall, who made his professional playwriting debut with this tale of a youngish mid-dle-class New York couple, very much married to two other people, meeting by chance while inspecting an empty apartment and inevitably gravitating into a brief encounter. This was a very small concept very well realized in Randall's characterization of two people who can have this unique fling but never a real affair. The sexual revolution is not for them, they fall between the stools of the generations; they were brought up on Wonder Woman comics and the last scraps of 19th-century morality, and if they go on from this empty apartment to a real hotel-room rendezvous the first thing she would do, instinctively, would be to wash his socks. The playwright's inventiveness, together with that of the director, Edwin Sherin, and Jerry Orbach and Jane Alexander as the couple, sustained a play physically limited most of the time to two characters in a cavernously empty set, but expansively comic in its observation of two peo-ple who can make love but never be lovers, who can change their luck but never their stripes.

Arthur Miller's *The Creation of the World and Other Business* was far from a bundle of laughs, but certainly its approach was comedic rather than dra-matic, even though it was not specifically labeled a comedy in its Broadway billing. The author of *After the Fall* here peruses the relationship between man (and woman), God and the Devil at the time of the Fall. Miller's Garden of Eden is a place where paradox commands more attention than principle. The puzzle of the coexistence of good and evil is the concern of this work, setting forth its theme in a subtitle for the play's first act: "Since God made everything and God is good—why did He make Lucifer?" Miller looks and often writes like an Old Testament prophet, but in *The Creation* he is in a Shavian humor, not pointing morals or sounding alarms but fashioning irc ˙ ˑs which are very closely reasoned behind their highly-polished facets, like the electric moment at which God places His accusatory and at the same time protecting mark on the murderer Cain. As he so often does in these tales, Lucifer (George Grizzard) stole most of the scenes from God. The production was uneven, with the characters sometimes failing to come to grips with one another, following changes of directors in the midstream of preparation. But Miller's *The Creation* is a muscular comedy which will undoubtedly live on in future productions around the globe and even in New York.

Another Best Play and Robert Whitehead production was Jean Kerr's *Finishing Touches,* a comedy in fact and name. In this one, Mrs. Kerr's laugh-laden subject is the onslaught of middle age. Her idiom continues to be the American suburban (but intellectually oriented) family, viewed through that unremitting sense of humor which makes it so much fun to go to any of Mrs. Kerr's plays. In this one, father (Robert Lansing) is a professor perplexingly infatuated with a pretty girl in his class, and very much in need of a hoped-for promotion as an incentive for going on with his life. Mother is still handsome, still full of the take-charge instinct, still witty, still Barbara Bel Geddes. Three sons scaled from 22 to 11 make all those amusing comments which Mrs. Kerr hears around her house all the time but which, oddly, no one else's children ever seem to come up with. It's all in fun, of course; there is, finally, no place for Lucifer at Mrs. Kerr's table, not even for the harmless consummation of a *6 Rms Riv Vu.* In Mrs. Kerr's family stories the world is a constantly troubled place where, thanks to a modicum of common sense and the persistent influence of the eternal verities, things nevertheless work out. There is no danger that the New York stage will be tainted in some way by her optimism, because no one else writing for the theater today can draw her kind of conclusion so adroitly, so warmly, so convincingly, let alone so entertainingly.

Other scripts billed as comedies on Broadway in 1973 included Paul Zindel's *The Secret Affairs of Mildred Wild,* about an overblown housewife living drably above a candy store in a clutter of movie magazines, escaping from her various crises by fantasizing herself into scenes from 1930s movies, imagining that she is Shirley Temple or, in a particularly aggravating moment of family strife, Fay Wray in the clutches of King Kong. The fantasy scenes created by Zindel and directed by Jeff Bleckner were more valid comically than the straight husband-and-wife involvement from which they sprang, even with Maureen Stapleton's firm grasp on the title role.

A more satisfying comic fancy was the imported *The Jockey Club Stakes* by William Douglas Home, a London comedy of good and bad manners of that vanishing mannered breed, the British aristocrat. In it, three lordly cronies who run the Jockey Club are investigating a charge of race-fixing, at first in stern and righteous judgment; and then, when it develops that one of their own class is the culprit, conniving at a smooth, plausible cover-up. The three rascally old patricians were played by Wilfrid Hyde-White, Robert Coote and Geoffrey Sumner as though W.S. Gilbert were prompting from the wings. He would have been as gratified by their comic skill as was the black-tie theater audience which apparently still hides away somewhere and was brought out by this play. The amusing antics onstage were almost outdone by the absurd performances of a few critics who tried to pin a tail of social significance on this play, attacking it as decadent, but succeeded only in pinning asses' ears on themselves. *The Jockey Club Stakes* is no more significant socially than the bubbles in a glass of champagne, and its existence is totally justified for identical reasons: it tastes good, it's fun. Such was not the case, alas, with a second imported British comedy, *No Sex Please, We're British,* with Maureen O'Sullivan as a respectable matron whose home is flooded with unwanted porn literature because of a mistake in communications. Now, *that's* socially significant.

Turning from comedy to drama on 1973 Broadway, one turns and turns again, scanning and re-scanning a space which, if not quite a void, is a thinly-settled line of country. Not until very late in the season did Broadway get an American drama of Best Play quality, and like last year's *Sticks and Bones* and *That Championship Season* it was a transfer from off-Broadway institutional production. The closest rival of *The Sunshine Boys* as the best American play of 1973, Joseph A. Walker's *The River Niger* was a standout in its articulate sensitivity to the special circumstances of a black family living in today's Harlem. Originated off Broadway by the Negro Ensemble Company and then moved to Broadway for a continuing run, this was certainly the best all-around production in the six-year history of the Douglas Turner Ward-Robert Hooks group, a cut above its two previous standouts *Ceremonies in Dark Old Men* and *The Sty of the Blind Pig.* Some scripts about the contemporary black condition dissipate their energy hammering away at the enemy like Punch with the alligator, but not this one, which hardly ever mentions "whitey" or "the man" and never "Mr. Charlie." It seeks to define battlefields, not enemies, in its closeup of a Harlem father, a poet forced to paint houses for a living. He is a good provider, a loving husband and a devoted parent, somewhat alcoholic but above all a man of great courage and wisdom who is not going to start his war of rebellion until he is sure the terrain suits him. His son is a U.S. Air Force trainee, and his father is proud of him; but the son rejects the white man's uniform just as he rejects the black man's street militancy, and he chooses the law and law school as his battlefield. An excellent ensemble of NEC actors portrays this family and their friends. Douglas Turner Ward played the father as he directed the play, with strong feeling, and the same is true of the performances of Roxie Roker as his wife, Les Roberts as their son, Graham Brown as a West Indian doctor friend of the family, and all others on their periphery. *The River Niger* is the title of a Walker poem about the life force of the black people, its imagery linking the Niger to the Mississippi and the Hudson, as well as of the play itself, which is at its best in dealing with the poetry of the black experience and at its worst in flashes of red melodrama which provide a convenient ending but are not in key with the delicacy of Walker's writing at its best. Walker is the author of two previous NEC-produced plays—*Ododo* and *Harangues*—and this early promise has flowered in *The River Niger,* which received five first-choice votes, as many as any of the other contenders, on the Critics Circle first ballot for Best American Play.

Two other distinguished scripts with fairly serious thrust were the British imports *The Changing Room* and *Butley*—though if either of their authors insisted on calling his work a comedy, we would raise no serious objection. In contrast to the ensemble-performed slice-of-life Storey play, Simon Gray's *Butley* was a star turn by the brilliant Alan Bates in the season's best performance by an actor. His role was that of a college professor whose character has been eaten away by termites of sexual dissatisfaction and academic disillusionment long before the play begins. What we see on the stage is the day the whole structure of his life collapses. The younger man who has been sharing his office, his apartment and his life goes off with another, more solid companion; his ex-wife has decided to marry a rival professor whom he considers a clown and a clod; he cannot seem to relate to his students or perform his academic duties; he cannot pick up a simple object from his desk without dropping it; he has even cut himself shaving. Finally he has nothing left except the intellectual prop of quoting nursery rhymes as though they contained the wisdom and poetry of the ages. He has not a shred of confidence or self-respect, and Bates's performance shows every leaking seam, every chipped surface, every frayed nerve connection. Hayward Morse, too, was particularly good as the smooth, ambitious, unflappable young professor who keeps his cool under assault from Butley's eccentricities but also coolly leaves him for a better man. The original London direction was by Harold Pinter, and one must assume that James Hammerstein followed it as closely as he could in staging the play here. Anyhow, there is distinction enough to go all the way around among the contributors to this richly rewarding show.

Elsewhere in drama on Broadway in 1973 there were the three scripts about Mary Todd Lincoln and a kind of theatrical experiment by Tennessee Williams. James Prideaux's *The Last of Mrs. Lincoln* studied the tortured widowhood of this ill-fated woman who, after the murder of the President, watched one son die and the other seemingly betray her with cruelty disguised as kindness, suffered agonies of penury, and choked on the poisoned air of the asylum before finding a kind of peace on her deathbed. Julie Harris gave us an impassioned portrait of Mary Todd, in the year's best performance by an actress, in a strong play in the mournful atmosphere of William Ritman's settings. V.J. Longhi's *The Lincoln Mask* was a more philosophical work, set at Ford's Theater on the night of the assassination and flashing back over the career of Lincoln (Fred Gwynne) as a man so fanatically devoted to a cause—the concept of equality and abolition of slavery—that he will ultimately decide to stake and sacrifice millions of lives in an effort to achieve his grand and noble purpose; a paradox with obvious modern overtones. In this one, Eva Marie Saint's

Mary Todd was a Southern belle devoted to Lincoln's cause but grief-stricken at its impact on her world. The last of the three Mary Todd Lincolns was played by Geraldine Page in Jerome Kilty's *Look Away,* on the eve of the President's widow's departure from the asylum, discussing the past with a loyal black confidante.

The Tennessee Williams experiment, *Out Cry,* was a re-working of a Williams script entitled *The Two-Character Play,* previously produced several times on this continent and abroad. It was an exorcism of emotion rather than an evocation of it, in which a brother and sister, performers stranded by their troupe, put on a two-character play which is in reality some kind of parable of their real emotional stresses and guilt feelings. It was philosophically curious but dramatically unsound, a real disappointment in comparison to Williams's triumphant *Small Craft Warnings* last year.

Leading the season's parade of 13 Broadway musicals was—as usual—a Harold Prince show, *A Little Night Music,* with Stephen Sondheim at the top of his virtuosity, and with a beguiling book by Hugh Wheeler based on Ingmar Bergman's film *Smiles of a Summer Night* (as you probably don't remember, it was about the ways of love on a Swedish country estate on Midsummer's Eve, when the sun never sets and the characters from both drawing room and scullery wander in pairs among the birch trees throughout the long, warm twilight). This show took an operetta form, not as a pastiche but in a very high style. These northern midnight follies concern themselves with a middle-aged husband (Len Cariou) who is enduring an unconsummated marriage with a teenaged wife (Victoria Mallory), meanwhile amusing himself with his onetime mistress (Glynis Johns), all guests at the country estate of an elderly chatelaine (Hermione Gingold) who couldn't care less who does what to whom as long as the dinner table conversation sparkles. All colors of burlesque were screened out by the Sondheim-Wheeler-Prince treatment, which filtered through a sophistication as delicate and provocative as the lighting of the midnight sun (an off-white mauve, or perhaps ivory). Sondheim's waltz score insists gently, with a consistent lilt but never a blare. His lyrics scale the show's every peak, most notably in Miss Johns's show-stopping blues number "Send in the Clowns." They are also marvellously acrobatic when they feel like it ("raisins" rhymed with "liaisons," "virgin" with "submerge in," "women" with "indis*crimin*-ate"). Every major element of this show including Prince's direction, Boris Aronson's grove of phallic birch trees, Florence Klotz's elegant costumes, Tharon Musser's lighting, the starring and supporting performances including the maid (D. Jamin-Bartlett), the butler (George Lee Andrews) and a wooden soldier (Laurence Guittard) ranks among the best that the Broadway theater has to offer.

Broadway also owed much to *Pippin,* which came along early in the year and played a lone hand for many weeks as the only new musical interest of 1973. With book by Roger O. Hirson and a Stephen (*Godspell*) Schwartz score, this was a theater-of-the-absurd concept about a young man trying to "find" himself in the heat of battle, romance, revolution and other turbulences, but in the long run discovering nothing worth finding out about himself or the world around him, and finally settling rather cheaply for domestic ease. The young hero happened to be called Pippin or Pepin, son of Charlemagne, and the show had a period atmosphere in the extremely attractive and imaginative sets by Tony Walton and costumes by Patricia Zipprodt, but history was not to be studied here. This was a free-swinging, free-dancing show under Bob Fosse's energetic direction, not a period piece, as Pippin's career was acted out like a series of vaudeville sketches by a group of clowns (shades, at least, of commedia dell'arte) led by Ben Vereen's notable presence as the Leading Player and commentator who maintains contact with the audience. The cast also included Irene Ryan, the nationally beloved Grandma of TV's *The Beverly Hillbillies,* in the role of an elderly cut-up (it was her last; she died during the run of the show). In a year of little experiment and less musical appeal until *Night Music* came along at the end of February, *Pippin* was a standout entertainment and a stand-in for the dormant avant garde.

A couple of plays were set to music with quite considerable success, though you would scarcely think of them as "musicals" in the rich, full-bodied sense of that term. Edmund Rostand's *Cyrano de Bergerac,* in a new Anthony Burgess adaptation, turned up as a *soi-disant* musical entitled *Cyrano,* but in spite of the ruffles and flourishes the play remained very much the thing here. Christopher Plummer played Cyrano expertly as a poet, a bit of a roisterer and a cosmically persuasive lover, with panache as long as his nose. In this version of the play, Plummer pauses once in a while to express himself in song—this is a "musical," after all—as in "No Thank You," about Cyrano's insistence on being independent of all forms of patronage and control, and "I Never Loved You" to Roxana as he is dying, trying to maintain his masquerade to the very end. Plummer reached the heart with the thrust of his performance, side-by-side with the music, whose peak moment occurred when Leigh Beery (Roxana) stopped the show with a lyric "You Have Made Me Love"—but Michael Kidd's direction didn't stress musical moments. He enhanced Cyrano's presence with manner and movement as though the whole world were an adjunct to the waving white plume on the Gascon's hat, in a thoroughly handsome show with sets by John Jensen and costumes by Desmond Heeley.

William Gibson's play *Two for the Seesaw* also was musicalized. The score by Cy Coleman and Dorothy Fields heightened the New York flavor with Broadway and barrio numbers, but here again the play predominated under the direction of Michael Bennett, who also took over the writing of the book in the late stages of *Seesaw's* production. Michele Lee was every inch the Second Avenue gamine Gittel Mosca, the warm-hearted dancer who comes to rue the day she permitted herself to fall in love with that lonesome lawyer from Nebraska. The latter role, the Henry Fonda part in the 1958 straight play, was played by blonde Ken Howard with such uncanny resemblance to New York's then Mayor John V. Lindsay that it was inevitable that the fun-loving chief executive of Fun City would be asked to take a turn in the show—and accept. On March 23 Lindsay came onstage in place of Howard in the Broadway scene, in which he is accosted by hookers and asked to move on by a police-man (and of course these bit players were provided with special lines of dia-logue for the occasion). Both Lindsay and Howard were good in the part, in a show indigenous to and comfortable in the New York scene.

The revival of *Irene* starring Debbie Reynolds got a mixed notice from Pres-ident Nixon when it played Washington. The President called it "A great show . . . . . a good family show . . . . . a lot of fun" but predicted that it might not be popular with New Yorkers. It was well received when it finally reached Broadway, however, with Miss Reynolds, George S. Irving, Patsy Kelly and Peter Gennaro's dances receiving Tony nominations. *Irene* opened the new Minskoff Theater in the skyscraper which has replaced the Astor Ho-tel on Broadway, and though the show was technically a revival it must be viewed as a contemporary effort in any consideration of the 1973 musical scene. Its book about a male coutourier and a beautiful piano tuner in the carefree days of 1919 was re-worked by Hugh Wheeler (his second hit li-bretto of the season) and Joseph Stein from an adaptation by Harry Rigby (*Irene's* producer, who had previously helped revive *No, No, Nanette*) and more songs were added (some of them by Charles Gaynor and Otis Clements) than were retained from the original Harry Tierney-Joseph McCarthy score. Certainly *Irene* was offered by its collaborators and accepted by its audience as a show for now, not an antique. Stanley Green, the musical theater historian and critic (who does the "Cast Replacements and Touring Companies" sec-tion of this volume), commented at a symposium that there are a great many old musicals with wonderful scores that are not easily revivable because of their dated books. *Irene*, like *No, No, Nanette*, is a good example both of the problem stated by Mr. Green and its successful solution. In May, *Irene* set a new all-time record Broadway gross for a non-holiday week of $143,567.

Elsewhere on the musical stage the rewards were only partial. *Shelter*, with book and lyrics by Gretchen Cryer and music by Nancy Ford, was an am-bitiously inventive, modern-idiom fairy tale about a TV writer who lives in a Tony Walton vision of a TV studio set, with background projections of any-where on earth he wants to be, in company with a computer named Arthur and occasional visits from beautiful women. As done by Marcia Rodd and Terry Kiser in the leads under Austin Pendleton's direction, *Shelter* seemed to have been shaped by warm hands but a cold heart. In another part of the musical forest, Rene Auberjonois's rendering of Scapin in *Tricks*, a musical version of the Molière comedy brought up from regional production by the Actors Theater of Louisville, Ky. where it originated, was a commedia dell'-arte design of great virtuosit, disembodied in a nervously ineffectual show. Melina Mercouri blazed briefly in a Michael Cacoyannis-Peter Link adapta-tion-with-music of Aristophanes's anti-war comedy *Lysistrata*. Howard Keel escorted Danielle Darrieux onto the New York stage for a brief hour in *Am-bassador*, based on a Henry James novel and defying the fates by coming to New York against the strong current of an unsuccessful tryout on the London stage last year. *Smith* put forward Don Murray in a pleasant but short-lived fable about a square who becomes trapped in a dream that he is the hero of a stage musical. Two other ill-fated Broadway musical efforts were *Hurry, Harry,* like *Pippin* about an overprivileged young man trying to find a life worth living, and *Dear Oscar,* an attempt to musicalize the life and conflicts of Oscar Wilde. Additionally, there was one new musical revue, *Nash at Nine,* paying homage to Ogden Nash and his writings, some of them set to music by Milton Rosenstock, with E.G. Marshall in the center spotlight.

The first of many distinguished visitors to 1973 Broadway was also a revue, the long-run off-Broadway cabaret production *Jacques Brel Is Alive and Well and Living in Paris,* which moved uptown for a limited engagement before going on tour. Israel sent over the revue *From Israel With Love,* a production of their Army entertainment groups. Maori folklore played the Palace in *Pacific Paradise,* a New Zealand compendium of songs, dances and games. New York audiences were also treated to Siobhan McKenna in her portraits of women in Irish literature (*Here Are Ladies*), Marcel Marceau's miming and the Bunraku Puppets of the National Puppet Theater of Japan, all three in return engagements, all incomparable special talents.

From *Irene* to *Mourning Becomes Electra,* revival production was an extremely important part of the 1973 Broadway package and will be taken up in the next section of this report. Meanwhile, here is where we list the *Best Plays* choices for the top individual achievements of 1972-73. In the acting categories, clear distinctions among "starring," "featured" or "supporting" players cannot possibly be made on the basis of official billing, in which the actor's agent may bargain him into a contract as a "star" following the title (which is not true star billing), or as an "also starring" star, or any of the other typographical gimmicks. Here in these volumes we divide the acting into "primary" and "secondary" roles, a primary role being one which carries a major responsibility for the play; a role which might some day cause a star to inspire a revival in order to appear in that character. All others, be they vivid as Mercutio, are classed as secondary.

Here, then, are the *Best Plays* bests of 1972-73:

PLAYS

BEST PLAY: *The Changing Room* by David Storey
BEST AMERICAN PLAY: *The Sunshine Boys* by Neil Simon
ACTOR IN A PRIMARY ROLE: Alan Bates as Butley in *Butley*
ACTRESS IN A PRIMARY ROLE: Julie Harris as Mary Todd Lincoln in *The Last of Mrs. Lincoln*
ACTOR IN A SECONDARY ROLE: Fred Grandy as Robert Lacey in *Green Julia*
ACTRESS IN A SECONDARY ROLE: Mari Gorman as Jackie in *The Hot l Baltimore*

DIRECTOR: Michael Rudman for *The Changing Room*
SCENERY: William Ritman for *The Last of Mrs. Lincoln*
COSTUMES: Theoni V. Aldredge for *Much Ado About Nothing*

MUSICALS

BEST MUSICAL: *A Little Night Music* by Hugh Wheeler
MUSIC: Stephen Sondheim for *A Little Night Music*
LYRICS: Stephen Sondheim for *A Little Night Music*
ACTOR IN A PRIMARY ROLE: Christopher Plummer as Cyrano de Bergerac in
  Cyrano
ACTRESS IN A PRIMARY ROLE: Michele Lee as Gittel Mosca in *Seesaw*
ACTOR IN A SECONDARY ROLE: Ben Vereen as Leading Player in *Pippin*
ACTRESS IN A SECONDARY ROLE: Hermione Gingold as Madame Armfeldt in
  A Little Night Music
DIRECTION: Harold Prince for *A Little Night Music*
SCENERY: Tony Walton for *Pippin* and *Shelter*
COSTUMES: Patricia Zipprodt for *Pippin*
CHOREOGRAPHY: Bob Fosse for *Pippin*

Revivals on and off Broadway

Writing in the New York *Times Magazine* about the then-doubtful situation at the Lincoln Center theater facility, Walter Kerr observed that the versatile New York stage is a whole repertory theater already in being, and maybe that's why it's so hard to establish another separate one in the same city. This season the New York theater did indeed put on a huge repertory of 35 revival productions, 16 on and 19 off Broadway. From Maxim Gorky to Cole Porter, the season wore a coat of many familiar colors, some of them antique and some of them as modern as a re-staging of Joseph Heller's *We Bombed in New Haven,* Richard Kiley in *Man of La Mancha,* or *Purlie* stopping in for a brief revisit.

This was the season in which Jules Irving finally gave up trying to establish a sort of repertory operation in New York. Like a prime minister faced with the fact that he cannot form a viable government, Irving resigned as director of the Repertory Theater of Lincoln Center before the season had begun. Irving had led the organization to many an achievement but no discernable long-range purpose. Ironically, his post-resignation season was one of his most successful, beginning with Maxim Gorky's 1906 play *Enemies* about fragmenting Russian society, never before mounted in a full-scale New York production like this one with Joseph Wiseman, Nancy Marchand and the Lincoln Center company under Ellis Rabb's direction, in a Maharam Award-winning setting by Douglas W. Schmidt. This was followed by a production of Sean O'Casey's *The Plough and the Stars* whose drama of the Easter Rebellion in Dublin is a kind of parable of modern Irish troubles, and by an Ellis Rabb-modernized version of *The Merchant of Venice,* setting it in the now era of *la dolce vita,* dresed in Pucci, with Portia (Rosemary Harris) living on a yacht and Shylock (Sydney Walker) as a dark-suited counting-house square—but nevertheless raising the usual controversy over Shakespearean anti-Semitism.

Jules Irving's last program at the Vivian Beaumont Theater was certainly one of his finest hours, a revival of Tennessee Williams's powerful drama *A Streetcar Named Desire* with James Farentino as Stanley Kowalski and Rosemary Harris as Blanche Du Bois, again under Rabb's direction. It was so well received by Lincoln Center subscribers and others in the theatergoing public that its engagement had to be extended, and in May it broke the house record for a non-musical at the Beaumont with a week's gross of $60,797.

Meanwhile, at Lincoln Center Repertory's smaller theater, the Forum, a season of new experimental works by several well known playwrights, contemplated if not actually scheduled, was canceled after the opening program. This Forum finale too was one of the more rewarding efforts of Irving's tenure, a series of four Samuel Beckett one-acters, three seen previously (*Happy Days, Krapp's Last Tape* and *Act Without Words 1*) and one world premiere (*Not I,* a monologue of a woman talking desperately and effusively in an effort to stave off death), performed by Hume Cronyn, Jessica Tandy and Henderson Forsythe under Alan Schneider's direction.

The Forum's season was curtailed for the same reason Jules Irving resigned: the Lincoln Center Board couldn't raise enough money to finance either the Beaumont or the Forum adequately. Irving's regime always operated in a state of near-beggary and at the same time under continuous fire from critics, present company included, demanding that Lincoln Center Rep serve this or that high purpose. If Walter Kerr's observation about repertory theater in New York is correct, and I believe that it is, then to attempt to create a separate one here is to attempt the near-impossible. New York is one of the world's great financial capitals, however, so presumably it *is* possible to raise large sums of money here for noble arts enterprises—witness the Beaumont's next-door neighbor, the Metropolitan Opera. If Irving's departure from Lincoln Center marks the end of the dream of a large-scale permanent repertory company in New York, probably for a decade or a generation, then our loss is to be blamed more upon the board's shortcomings in pursuit of the possible than on those of Irving and his collaborators in the producing and acting company in pursuit of the impossible.

Joseph Papp, who will take over both Lincoln Center theaters next year, repeated the New York Shakespeare Festival's 1972 *Two Gentlemen of Verona* success with yet another streamlined Shakespearean production which moved on from summer in Central Park to Broadway in winter. Papp's *Much Ado About Nothing* was staged as though it had been written by Booth Tarkington, set in the America of the early 1900s and clothed by Theoni V. Aldredge in ice cream suits and Gibson Girl dresses. The wooing of Beatrice (Kathleen Widdoes) and Benedick (Sam Waterston) was as disarming as the brass-band rags and oom-pah-pah music written by Peter Link and Scott Joplin. The show floated pleasantly along despite the weight of one of Shakespeare's least workable comic subplots. The New York Shakespeare summer season at the Delacorte also presented a potent *Hamlet* by Stacy Keach under Gerald Freedman's direction and a new musical folk fable, *Ti-Jean and His Brothers,* a symbolic affirmation of life by the West Indian poet Derek Walcott. During the winter season downtown at the Public Theater, New York Shakespeare staged *The Cherry Orchard* with James Earl Jones and Gloria Foster heading a cast which was all black, for whatever reason and to no special effect.

Speaking of Shakespeare, the entry of Papp's musical version of *Two Gentlemen of Verona* on the longest-runs list at 627 performances marks the first time that a Shakespeare title has appeared on this honor roll of shows that have played more than 500 performances of record in a single production in the New York professional theater. The Bard has never made it on his own, and unless we've overlooked something, his works have appeared there only four additional times in musical versions more or less loosely based on his plays, as follows: *Kiss Me Kate* (1,070 perfs.), *West Side Story* (732 perfs.), *Your Own Thing* (933 perfs.) and the off-Broadway revival of *The Boys From Syracuse* (500 perfs.)

Two other institutions mounted revivals in Broadway theaters: T. Edward Hambleton's New Phoenix Repertory Company which, like its mythical namesake, rises triumphant from the flames of each new burning circumstance; and Circle in the Square in its uptown phase at the brand new, massively-named Circle in the Square Joseph E. Levine Theater. John McMartin and Paul Hecht headed the Phoenix company in two outstanding productions in repertory: Eugene O'Neill's *The Great God Brown,* with its examination of an artist's spiritual dichotomy set in a new time frame of 1916-1936 and directed by Harold Prince successfully disguised as a straight-play director; and Molière's *Don Juan* (sometimes known as *Dom Juan*) as adapted and directed by Stephen Porter. The Circle in the Square came to grips with O'Neill, too, in the *Mourning Becomes Electra* trilogy cut to three and a half hours, with Colleen Dewhurst under Theodore Mann's direction; followed by Irene Papas playing Euripides's *Medea* in a version adapted and staged by Minos Volanakis. All these revivals offered the New York playgoer valuable new acquaintance and sometimes new insight into important segments of the theatrical past.

The 1973 "New York Repertory Theater" also included three large-scale Broadway revivals individually produced as star vehicles. *Emperor Henry IV* was the Pirandellian context of a Rex Harrison portrait of a dreamer dazed in an accident and suffering for many years the delusion that he is an 11th-century monarch, a delusion supported by his faithful retainers who dress up in costume and play the game with him. Even after he regains his senses, the object of all this attention continues to pretend even to himself that he is Henry IV because he prefers a life of vivid illusion to one of boring reality—one of Pirandello's famous variations on this theme. Harrison was both whimsical and commanding in this highly intellectual diversion, a Hurok concert of a stage production.

A clutch of stars turned out in a period revival of Clare Boothe Luce's once daring, now rather ingenuously disarming, study of the feminine gender in its 1936 manifestation, *The Women,* starring (in alphabetical order) Rhonda Fleming, Kim Hunter, Dorothy Loudon, Myrna Loy and Alexis Smith, with Leora Dana and Doris Dowling also in the cast. The men had their innings in a revival of George Bernard Shaw's *Don Juan in Hell,* performed as a staged reading in the style designed by Charles Laughton in 1952, also an exercise of intellectual brilliance ably served by Paul Henreid (the Commander), Ricardo Montalban (Don Juan) and Edward Mulhare (the Devil), with Agnes Moorehead playing Dona Ana as she did in the original production.

The final Broadway revival program of the season was *The Play's the Thing,* a transfer from off Broadway produced and performed by the Roundabout Theater Company, a group which continues to defy the law of repertory gravity in New York City. Its curve is ever upward as it annually presents a series of programs with a top-notch repertory cast, usually under Gene Feist's elucidating direction. This year the Roundabout presented *Right You Are* (still another Pirandello illusion-and-reality puzzle), Beatrice Straight as the guest star in a starkly effective staging of Ibsen's *Ghosts* and an ebullient, accent-on-comedy staging of the Molnar work which eventually wound up on Broadway. The Roundabout's 1973 season also included a program of Chekhov readings and, as in 1972, one program of new material, *American Gothics,* a compendium of four moody one-acters by Donald Kvares. This organization seems to have changed its name this season from the Roundabout *Repertory* Company to The Roundabout *Theater* Company, but there has been no change in the continuing high level of its aspiration and performance. We *have* a professional resident company in New York, the Roundabout, in 1973 stretching its well-disciplined muscles and extending its influence north toward Broadway.

Still another off-Broadway repertory company was fledged this year: City Center Acting Company, a group of players who made up the Julliard Acting Ensemble a year ago and now, having graduated from school, sticking together in an effort to find a lasting place in the New York theater scene. With John Houseman as artistic director, they presented a large, versatile and uniformly creditable program which included Sheridan's *The School for Scandal,* Paul Shyre's adaptation of John Dos Passos's *U.S.A.,* the Jacobean tragedy *Women Beware Women* by Thomas Middleton and Maxim Gorky's *The Lower Depths,* as well as Brendan Behan's *The Hostage* and James Saunders's *Next Time I'll Sing to You.* The troupe will further justify its name next April in a scheduled two-week engagement at City Center's 55th Street Theater.

Also in revival off Broadway was the Gertrude Stein-Virgil Thomson work *The Mother of Us All,* a 25-year-old operatic composition presented at the Guggenheim Museum but far from a museum piece in its celebration of the life and times of Susan B. Anthony, the noted 19th-century suffragette whose struggle was a deep root of Women's Lib. Cole Porter's *You Never Know* surfaced for a brief moment in a shaky production. Ayn Rand's famous gim-

mick play, *Night of January 16th,* a courtroom drama in which the jury is selected from the audience and there are two endings depending on its verdict,
was resurrected for a short time under the title *Penthouse Legend.* And *Spoon
River Anthology,* the Edgar Lee Masters works of Americana adapted for
staged reading by Charles Aidman, was seen in a return engagement.

Add to this imposing list of revivals the specialty programs like The Bil
Baird Marionettes' popular perennials *Winnie the Pooh* and *Davy Jones'
Locker,* the one-man program of readings and songs *Shay Duffin as Brendan
Behan,* or The Everyman Players version of *The Pilgram's Progress,* and you
have an ever-widening circle of renewed acquaintance with the distinguished
past. In 1973 alone the New York repertory theater in the Walter Kerr sense
brought us productions of Gorky, O'Casey, Shakespeare, Tennessee Williams,
O'Neill, Euripides, Shaw, Molière, Ibsen, Joseph Heller, Sheridan, Behan,
Thomas Middleton, James Saunders, Beckett, Chekhov and others. What
could another so-called permanent repertory company do for an encore?

Off Broadway

The numbers tell quite a lot of the off-Broadway story: there was a sharp
drop in the number of straight-play programs in English to 37 from 52 last
year, down even from the 45 produced in 1970-71 and only a little more than
half of 1969-70's 64.

Of these, only 28 were new American plays, as compared with 43 last year,
39 the year before and more than 50 in each of the two previous years.

The production of musicals, on the other hand, jumped to 16 (18 if you
count a couple of revues heavily oriented to their scores; see the one-page
summary accompanying this report), up from 10 last year and 13 the year
before, back to the 16 musicals produced in 1969-70. And when we say that
the numbers tell quite a lot of the story, we mean also that in a distressingly
large proportion of these cases the shows were just statistics, here today and
gone into the column of figures tomorrow. Of all the musicals—excepting the
revues—there was only one solid success (*Doctor Selavy's Magic Theater*).
Among straight plays, the off-Broadway output, which last season shared the
Best Plays list evenly with Broadway, produced only three Best Plays in 1972-
73, and two of these were brought in from outside. One—Paul Ableman's
Green Julia—came from the London stage and another—Lanford Wilson's
The Hot l Baltimore—from off off Broadway.

There was seldom any mood of experimentation, any thrust of innovation
in the smaller playhouses this season. The creative style of even the best work
tended to be conservative. Shrinking straight-play and expanding musical volume . . . reluctance to experiment, with a consequently lower level of invention . . . rising production costs and substantial ticket prices . . . if all of this
seems *deja vu,* it is, we saw it all happen before on Broadway. Off Broadway
appears to be changing from a free-swinging adventure into some sort of mini-
commercial theater, inheriting all the problems which have for so long bur-

The 1972-73 Season off Broadway

PLAYS (28)

Public Theater 1972
The Corner
Present Tense
Coney Island Cycle
Public Theater 1973
Wedding Band
The Children
Siamese Connections
The Orphan
American Place
The Kid
Freeman
The Karl Marx Play
Baba Goya
American Gothics
F.O.B.
Blue Boys
Negro Ensemble
THE RIVER NIGER
Please Don't Cry and
Say No
Mystery Play
The White Whore and
the Bit Player
Welcome to Andromeda
& Variety Obit
The Tooth of Crime
Brother Gorski
An Evening With the
Poet-Senator
*THE HOT L
BALTIMORE*
(transfer)
Echoes

MUSICALS (16)

Buy Bonds, Buster
Joan
Ti-Jean and His
Brothers
Safari 300
Aesop's Fables
Speed Gets the
Poppies
Crazy Now
Lady Audley's Secret
Lady Day; A Musical
Tragedy
Doctor Selavy's Magic
Theater
The Contrast
The Bar That Never
Closes
Say When
Rainbow
Thoughts
Smile, Smile, Smile

REVUES (7)

They Don't Make 'Em
Like That Anymore
Berlin to Broadway
With Kurt Weill
Oh Coward!
A Quarter for the
Ladies Room
*National Lampoon's
Lemmings*
Hot and Cold Heros
*What's a Nice Coun-
try Like You Doing
in a State Like This?*

SPECIALTIES (8)

The Sunshine Train
Baird Marionettes
Winnie-the-Pooh
Davy Jones' Locker
Band-Wagon
Anton Chekhov's
Garden Party
Shay Duffin as
Brendan Behan
Fly Chelsea to
Brooklyn
The Pilgrim's
Progress

REVIVALS (19)

N.Y. Shakespeare
Hamlet
Much Ado About
Nothing
Roundabout
Right You Are
The Play's the
Thing
Ghosts
We Bombed in New
Haven
City Center Company
The School for
Scandal
U.S.A.
The Hostage
Women Beware
Women
Next Time I'll Sing
to You
The Lower Depths
Lincoln Center Forum
Happy Days & Act
Without Words 1
Krapp's Last Tape
The Mother of Us All

Penthouse Legend
Public Theater 1973
The Cherry Orchard
You Never Know
Spoon River
Anthology

FOREIGN-
LANGUAGE
PRODUCTIONS (8)

Jewish of Bucharest
The Dybbuk
The Pearl Necklace
Yerma
Die Brücke
Der Frieden
Woyzeck
The Grand Music Hall
of Israel
*El Grande de
Coca-Cola*
Le Médecin Malgre
Lui

FOREIGN PLAYS
IN ENGLISH (9)

Chelsea Theater
Sunset
Kaspar
GREEN JULIA
Not I
The Trials of Oz
L'Eté
Crystal and Fox
Alpha Beta
Owners

Categorized above are all the plays listed in the "Plays Produced off Broadway" section of this volume.
Plays listed in CAPITAL LETTERS have been designated Best Plays of 1972-73.
Plays listed in *italics* were still running June 1, 1973.

dened Broadway. New York City's crime-in-the-streets publicity affects off Broadway even more adversely than it does the Times Square area because its little theaters are scattered in many dark corners of a Manhattan many of whose residents are reluctant even to venture forth on broad avenues in broad daylight. The truth is that the theater areas both on and off Broadway are as close to 100 per cent secure at show time as anywhere in any city in the world, but ballyhoo counts more than truth in matters like this. The fact remains that in 1972-73 off Broadway was suffering all of Broadway's ills on top of those uniquely its own, with only the organizations like the Public Theater, Negro Ensemble, American Place and Chelsea seeming to have any sort of viable answer to the double dilemma.

By the term "off Broadway" in this volume we mean those productions offered in houses of 299 seats or less, usually under the organizational umbrella of the League of Off-Broadway Theaters, which have Equity casts, plan to play regular full-week schedule of performances open to the public and to public scrutiny by means of reviews. A few others which don't qualify technically are included at the editor's discretion, usually because they are visitors from abroad or have found their way onto other major but less precise lists of "off-Broadway" shows and therefore would be expected to appear on this one.

The only bona fide unsubsidized, independent off-Broadway production to make the Best Plays list this year was *Green Julia,* a British comedy by Paul Ableman first produced in 1965 at the Edinburgh Festival by the Traverse Theater. It was its author's first full-length play, and when it was brought in to London in the season of 1965-66 it was selected by Ossia Trilling as one of the year's outstanding new British works. *Green Julia* had its American premiere at the Washington, D.C. Theater Club under Davey Marlin-Jones's direction May 9, 1968 and was still a long time coming to New York. It was well worth waiting for, like a good tune that finally catches on. Ableman's script is a song of youth, a "Gaudeamus Igitur" for an era when sentiment is out of fashion and emotional manifestation of student brotherhood is frowned upon. The play's flood of mocking, parodistic words and poses exchanged between two college roommates breaking up housekeeping after graduation is camouflage for their real (but not clearly perceived even by themselves) feelings of sadness and loneliness at their imminent parting. Their studies completed, they are poised on the threshold of great adventure, one as a botanist and one as an economist, and they are making a pretense of celebrating the event with champagne and a lady friend (Julia, who dawdles in a bar downstairs and never shows up). Underneath this surface is a premonition that they have grown too close together for comfort as individuals in the outside world. These two roommates are *Moonchildren* at the end of their graduate studies, three or four years older but still insecure, playing a private game of charades and assuming the characters of priests, doctors, soldiers, etc. and improvising dialogue as a ritual to ward off reality for an hour . . . a minute . . . a second more. But reality will finally intrude, and when it does there is a moment of mutual hatred at their interdependence. As the more vulnerable of the two— the botanist—Fred Grandy gave a performance which was surely the begin-

ning of an important acting career. The other, more dominant role was originally played by Moonchild James Woods, a fine actor whose performance
nevertheless couldn't have been any better than that of his replacement, John
Pleshette, who took over the part shortly after the opening. In every department including the direction by William E. Hunt, *Green Julia* was one of the
engrossing evenings of theater in 1972-73.

The best of bests off Broadway this season, we feel, was Joseph A. Walker's
compelling *The River Niger,* about a Harlem family. The only full-scale program produced by the Negro Ensemble Company in 1972-73, it was an instant success and was later brought to Broadway and has already been described in the Broadway section of this report. The third off-Broadway Best
Play, Lanford Wilson's *The Hot l Baltimore* (the missing "e" in the title is
meant to be a letter missing in the dilapidated sign of a run-down hotel), was
a transfer upward from its original production off off Broadway by the Circle
Theater Company. It won the New York Drama Critics Circle Award as the
best American play of 1972-73 and an Obie best-play citation, and it is worthy
of these distinguished honors (though I am compelled to add that I personally
admire *The Sunshine Boys* and *The River Niger* more; *The Hot l Baltimore*
is deeply and sincerely felt, but somewhat out of focus). A detailed description of this Lanford Wilson prizewinner appears in Jeff Sweet's report on the
off-off-Broadway season elsewhere in this volume. So, by the way, does a detailed report on Sam Shepard's *The Tooth of Crime,* a Performance Group
production at the Performing Garage which greatly enlivened this all-too-list-
less season in the tributary theater.

American Place had an outstanding season in its new Sixth Avenue home
in a skyscraper's basement, with its *Freeman* and *Baba Goya* ranking close to
the top ten, and with Robert Coover's *The Kid* and Rochelle Owens's *The
Karl Marx Play* (which included a musical score by the ubiquitous Galt Mac-
Dermot) making their tart comments on idolatry of heroes and philosophers.
Phillip Hayes Dean's *Freeman,* like his *The Sty of the Blind Pig* last year, was
a commentary but not a diatribe on the black condition, presenting a conformist black family making it in the middle class but unable to persuade their
aggressively independent misfit son to go along.The son tries first to use, then
to subvert "the system," and he follows that different drummer stubbornly to
his doom.

In a lighter treatment of the argument for doing your own thing no matter
what, Steve Tesich's *Baba Goya* brightened up the final weeks of American
Place's season with another disharmoniously funny view of a way-out American home like his previous full-length play *The Carpenters* (also produced by
American Place). In *Baba Goya* we have a mother (Olympia Dukakis) who
has been through three or four husbands and several children and is hungry for
more—more children, preferably adopted orphans, to replace those who have
grown up, and another husband to replace the current one when he dies, which
he and she believe will be soon. During most of the play a malefactor of Japanese extraction is chained to a radiator, and an old guy runs around insisting
on *not* being called "grandpa"—this is the kind of thing that goes on in Tesich

plays and is incapable of brief explanation. This playwright has a knack of welding bits of the absurd into fairly naturalistic situations, a trick which is entertaining but maybe not yet quite as intriguing as it will be when he perfects it.

The season at Joseph Papp's Public Theater produced no blockbusters on the scale of 1972's *Sticks and Bones* and *That Championship Season,* but there was never an idle moment down on Lafayette Street. The Public led off with Alice Childress's *Wedding Band,* a reflection on the black American South in the recent past. The time is the summer of 1918, the place is a seaside community in South Carolina, and the matter to be dramatized is a love affair which crosses a color line sharply drawn and primly observed by both factions. Ruby Dee and James Broderick played the ill-fated lovers who know they can't win but will insist harder and hold out longer than most, in a Ming Cho Lee representation of the cozy and homogenized black world of adjoining back yards—the real world (Miss Childress seems to be saying in her play) where real values are established and observed, regardless of what parades may be going by in the street out front. Co-directed by its author and Joseph Papp, *Wedding Band* was the leading attraction of a Public Theater season which included Michael McGuire's *The Children,* a nightmare fantasy of family relationships; Dennis J. Reardon's *Siamese Connections,* about a bad apple in the basket of a family which has lost another son in Vietnam; and, finally, a new David Rabe script, *The Orphan,* about an individual doomed in advance by the established circumstances and preconditions of the world around him, like Rabe's Pavlo Hummel and his blinded Vietnam veteran in last year's prizewinning drama. His new protagonist was an Orestes re-enacting his story as a parable of our own era. It was creditable but not memorable, like the Public Theater's season as a whole, marking time and getting in trim for next year's great leap forward when Joseph Papp will take over the Lincoln Center facilities.

Fly Chelsea to Brooklyn was the title of one of Chelsea Theater Center's programs this year; and, indeed, Chelsea has been both a vehicle and a destination for cultural adventure across the river at the Academy of Music. Whether reviewing the life and times of Billie Holiday as portrayed by Cecelia Norfleet in the musical *Lady Day: A Musical Tragedy,* or looking back on the special world of Jewish Russia early in the century in Isaac Babel's *Sunset,* the Chelsea's programs are always reaching, always challenging. This year's peak was *Kaspar,* by the avant garde German playwright Peter Handke, about a 16-year-old boy in an animal condition, unable to speak or walk, suffering the spiritual agonies of slowly being trained and transformed into a human being, with particular attention to the function of language as a humanizing force. The role of Kaspar (which means "clown"), played by Christopher Lloyd, was the perpetual center of the play's concentration through 15 closed-circuit TV screens as well as in the flesh onstage. The final Chelsea program, the first named, was a portmanteau invitation to a mini-festival of guest attractions put on by theater groups which flew into Brooklyn from the mid-West and West.

Elsewhere on the list of straight plays, Terrence McNally's *Whiskey,* about a booze-ridden touring troupe of Western performers, was an amusing collection of black comedy skits. Jean-Claude van Itallie appeared with an even blacker but not quite so comic script, *Mystery Play,* an absurdist murder yarn in which all the characters are killed off (the trouble was, they were all easily expendable and the play seemed to improve as the stage emptied). Van Itallie's return to the mainstream theater after his long sojourn off off Broadway, during which his only work of record was the brilliant *The Serpent,* was an important event regardless of any one script, and we earnestly hope he has come out to stay out. Tom Eyen's *The White Whore and the Bit Player,* a famous off-off-Broadway piece based somewhat on the life of Marilyn Monroe, surfaced in a production at St. Clement's (whose status as a production center for this, McNally's *Whiskey* and other plays is now a borderline case between off and off-off). *The Children's Mass,* about transvestism and the New York City sex and drug scene, was a promising playwriting debut for the actor Frederick Combs.

Green Julia was much the best of the English-speaking imports off Broadway this season, but not the only one of at least passing interest. Brian Friel's *Crystal and Fox* was a dark but rather effective play about a brooding showman, the leader of a third-rate touring Irish entertainment troupe, bent on the destruction of himself and of those around him. E.A. Whitehead's *Alpha Beta* was a relentlessly abrasive two-character study of a marriage going from bad to worse over a period of almost a decade, with Laurence Luckinbill in a flashy performance as the husband and Kathryn Walker slowly but finally and firmly stealing the show with her portrait of an indomitable woman caught in a domestic trap and determined both to do her duty and to see that others perform theirs toward her. *The Trials of Oz,* a semi-documentary play about the British trial of the editors of the magazine *Oz* for obscenity aimed deliberately at school children, should also be classed as an import because it was previously presented in London in a Royal Shakespeare Company reading, though never fully produced there.

The off-Broadway season also brought a number of foreign-language visitors: The Jewish State Theater of Bucharest with *The Dybbuk* and *The Pearl Necklace,* Spain's Nuria Espert Company in a production of *Yerma,* Germany's Die Brücke with *Der Frieden* and *Woyzeck,* The Grand Music Hall of Israel and France's Le Jeune Théâtre National. Finally, delightfully (and probably not quite accurately classified as a foreign-language production), there was *El Grande de Coca-Cola,* a multi-national endeavor written for the British stage by members of its cast, with an American (Ron House) in top authorship billing. This zany show was set in Honduras, where the owner of a run-down night club is trying to con customers with a fake "Parade of Stars," and it was performed in a sort of Spanish, fractured with most other leading languages of the Western world, but understandable and appealing to all in its short but sweet one-hour context.

The miniature pleasures of the one-act-play form seemed less and less comfortable in the New York stage environment this season. The old days of the Albee, Pinter and Beckett programs were days of bold experimentation off

Broadway, which once was especially hospitable to the imaginative one-act statement. Now that off Broadway is being tainted with cost problems and their attendant hit-psychology syndrome, however, the one-act play programs have attenuated in both number and stature. Lincoln Center Repertory's Forum Theater schedule of Samuel Beckett one-acters was a distinguished exception, including as it did the world premiere of *Not I*. The year's best new short play (albeit performed with an intermission) was Ron Whyte's *Welcome to Andromeda* about a bedridden young cripple (David Clennon) overprotected by his mother and trying to induce his nurse to put him out of his misery while his mother is out of the house—presented on the same program with Whyte's one-acter *Variety Obit,* a frivolous musical bit about a show-business family. The season brought only five other one-act programs, all off Broadway: *The Corner,* a Public Theater production of plays by Ed Bullins, Oyamo and Clay Goss; and four one-playwright programs, Frank Gilroy's *Present Tense,* Peter Schuman's *Coney Island Cycle* done by the Bread and Puppet Theater, a Donald Kvares program of four plays produced by the Roundabout under the portmanteau title *American Gothics,* and Townsend Brewster's *Please Don't Cry and Say No.* This is quite a change from only five seasons ago, when there were 20 off-Broadway programs of one-acters including the Best Play *Adaptation/Next.*

On the musical side off Broadway in 1973, revues took a major share of the bows. The hit of the year was *Oh, Coward!,* Roderick Cook's compendium of Noel Coward songs interspersed with word passages from his plays and prose writings. The filaments of Coward's wit still carried their powerful charge in a show which could have been viewed as a sort of swan song and eulogy for its author, a posthumous tribute to one of the century's most sparkling literary lights who died last winter at his home in Jamaica. In fact, the show was intended as nothing of the sort. It was produced with only pleasure in mind long before Coward died, and Coward came to see it during a New York visit. Like everybody else, he enjoyed it. His fragile tunes making their highly sophisticated observations, meant for a time when amusing one's self was a serious part of the business of living, have retained their power to entertain and even move the audiences of this battered era.

The late Kurt Weill was also roundly celebrated in a popular off-Broadway revue, *Berlin to Broadway With Kurt Weill,* billed as "a musical voyage" through shows like *The Threepenny Opera, Knickerbocker Holiday, Lady in the Dark* and *Lost in the Stars,* stopping to revisit about 40 song numbers. It was a melodic bonanza. On the subject of revues, a comic bonanza arrived at the Village Gate late in the season, *National Lampoon's Lemmings,* co-written and assembled by its producer-director Tony Hendra (like David Frost a graduate of England's TV hit *That Was the Week That Was*) as a sort of theatrical spin-off from the humor magazine named in the title. With music by Paul Jacobs and Christopher Guest, it fired away at all the usual topical revue targets like sex and politics and especially the world of pop music, peaking in its version of "The Woodchuck Festival of Peace, Love and Death" as a young people's mass-suicide ritual.

Of the 16 book musicals off Broadway in 1973, only one attracted a sizeable audience: *Doctor Selavy's Magic Theater,* conjured up by Richard Foreman as a parody of a case history in a madhouse (proving once again that you can make a musical out of almost *anything*), with a versatile score by Stanley Silverman and Tom Hendry. It was a clever raising of the eternal question about who is sane and who crazy, which the reality and which the delusion. Another book show of more than routine interest was *Joan,* a musicalization of the Joan of Arc story by Al Carmines, that prolific off-off-Broadway composer whose work often adorns and/or challenges the professional theater. Still another musical of note was Derek Walcott's *Ti-Jean and His Brothers,* a folk fable by the Trinidadian poet about three brothers symbolic of affirmative human attributes like strength and intellect, pitted against the Devil, with music by Andre Tanker, the first new, modern work presented by the New York Shakespeare Festival in its Central Park seasons. Other lesser efforts in this busy but not very productive musical season off Broadway, which began with the single-performance *Buy Bonds, Buster* and ended similarly with *Smile, Smile, Smile,* included a William Russo rock musical rendition of *Aesop's Fables* and others of *Lady Audley's Secret* and Royall Tyler's *The Contrast* (produced in New York in 1787, the first comedy of record by an American playwright). A gospel program entitled *The Sunshine Train,* assembled and staged by William E. Hunt and featuring The Gospel Starlets, Clara Walker and the Carl Murray Singers, proved to be one of the season's more popular off-Broadway attractions.

The contractual experiments in so-called "middle theater" or "limited gross Broadway agreement" seem to have virtually disappeared in 1973—maybe for somewhat the same reasons that Lincoln Center Repertory couldn't find a place for itself in the New York theater scene. Maybe New York doesn't need a middle theater because it already *has* a middle theater, or is growing one. Off Broadway is looking more and more like a "middle" Broadway, a $7.50 farm league for the big $9-$15 league uptown. In the past few seasons, off Broadway has fed *Two Gentlemen of Verona, Sticks and Bones, That Championship Season* (a Critics Award and Pulitzer Prize winner), *Much Ado About Nothing, The River Niger, The Play's the Thing* and *The Trial of the Catonsville Nine* into Broadway houses. It is now developing a suction of its own, pulling *The Hot l Baltimore* and other works up from the ferment of off-off. Off Broadway seems to be bent on occupying the middle ground between experimentation and super-commercialism, becoming a place for tryout instead of way-out theater whose success will ultimately be measured not by the number of its own indigenous hits but by the number of shows it feeds out to Broadway and the world.

Offstage

The behind-the-scenes story of the year began the last week in October when Jules Irving confirmed reports of his resignation as director of the

Repertory Theater of Lincoln Center. The story ended—or, rather began again—with the announcement tentatively put forward March 7 and finally confirmed in May that Joseph Papp's New York Shakespeare Festival would take over at the Vivian Beaumont and Forum Theaters, using the former to house mostly new plays and the latter as a year-round showcase for the plays of William Shakespeare.

These events had roots in the Elia Kazan-Robert Whitehead era when the Lincoln Center Repertory board, apparently refusing to understand the function of a permanent repertory company, dismissed Kazan and Whitehead and replaced them with Jules Irving and Herbert Blau from the West Coast. Having failed one set of gifted impresarios, the board then failed the second. In all the years of the Irving regime, this board never provided the financing necessary, let alone appropriate, to a first-class repertory operation. They nearly permitted the Forum to slide into the oblivion of motion picture re-runs; they nearly permitted an intrusion into Lincoln Center Repertory's affairs by interests alien and maybe even antipathetic to the legitimate theater; they nearly permitted the irrevocable dismantling of the facility's specially-designed storage space for repertory productions. They did permit the financing to fall into disarray, so that there were no funds to continue the Forum's season beyond the Beckett repertory and barely enough to carry out the Beaumont's 1973 schedule.

This and other major policy problems left Irving with no alternative but to resign. The board appointed a committee to study the situation, and at first it was thought that the Beaumont could be booked for a series of outside attractions in 1973-74 (the touring *Man of La Mancha* had enjoyed a very profitable run there during the summer of 1972). At one point David Merrick wanted to lease the Forum for a three-year period of experimental production of about a half-dozen plays a season but was unable to reach a satisfactory agreement which did not also include the Beaumont, in which he had no interest. Then, on March 7, came the announcement that many had hoped for but few really expected: Joseph Papp would take over at Lincoln Center, not instead of but in addition to operations at the Public and Delacorte Theaters, if adequate financing was available. Just as there is New York Shakespeare Festival Public Theater, there is now also to be New York Shakespeare Festival at Lincoln Center, and *Joseph Papp's board will replace the Lincoln Center board*. The personnel of this Papp board of trustees was as follows as of the 1973 season: George C. Scott chairman, Joseph Papp president, Charles M. Grace, Mrs. LuEsther T. Mertz vice presidents, Mrs. Samuel Parkman Peabody secretary-treasurer, Mrs. Martin Brody, George T. Delacorte, Leo J. Fidler, Aaron R. Frosch, Monroe Goldwater, Stanley H. Lowell, Paul Martinson, Jerome A. Newman, Mrs. Arthur F. Schiff, Mrs. Guedaliahou Shiva, Alfred A. Strelsin.

The arrangement was contingent on raising money for operations, and Papp immediately and boldly doubled the anticipated, budgeted, annual Beaumont-Forum deficit from the previous $750,000 to $1.5 million. Of this, $500,000 was to be raised by the Shakespeare Festival board and the rest from other sources. Papp made it clear that he expected a firm commitment to a five-year deficit of $7.5 million, but he declared himself officially go for the full mission after Mrs. Samuel I. Newhouse presented him with a $1 million donation, following a $350,000 grant from the Rockefeller Foundation. Mrs. Newhouse's magnificent gift was of momentous importance, not only because of its size but also because of its unusual character. It was earmarked for operations, for putting on plays, not putting up a building with the donor's name on a brass plaque. Mrs. Newhouse has donated life itself to the theater art form, and the urge to put up a plaque anyway in honor of this rarely discerning patron is irresistible.

Papp's policy at Lincoln Center will be exactly the same as at the Public Theater and exactly the opposite of Lincoln Center Rep's: he will present new plays, not classics. "We are coming in as a contemporary force in what is basically a classic constituency," Papp told the *Times,* and he is also coming in with complete artistic, managerial and financial autonomy. If the present 25,000 Beaumont subscribers don't like the kind of plays he produces (Papp said), he'll try to find an audience that does. Off the top of his first thoughts he rather views the Public Theater as a continuing showcase for the more experimental kind of plays and the Beaumont Theater for more finished ones, though the distinction will not be sharply drawn.

Asked why he wanted to take on so vast an added responsibility, Papp replied, "For personal aggrandizement and to establish a cultural power base here in New York so as to take over the rest of the repertory theaters in the country, and create a liaison with Russia and China." Then he took his tongue out of his cheek and indicated that Lincoln Center represented, like Everest to Mallary, a challenge he and his New York Shakespeare Festival colleagues found they simply had to accept.

It was a troubled year for the theater, and its capital T Trouble was crime in the streets—not so much that which actually occurred but more troublingly that which was imagined *might* occur, in the ballooning image of New York City as a lawless jungle, an image relentlessly inflated by TV comedians, feature writers and others to whom sensation is a valuable commodity. From Scarsdale to Sacramento the theater's glamorous appeal was tarnished by the mistaken belief that theatergoing was an unsafe pastime—a falsehood which nevertheless had its effect on attendance. Certainly there has been an increase in street crime in this decade in New York as in other cities all over the world. But with the help of a special ongoing effort by the city government and its police force, all fully aware of the theater's value to the city's culture and economy, there are few safer places than the New York theater areas during show time.

Another growing sociological threat to the theater in 1973 was the porno industry in both its fleshly and its vicarious forms. Prostitutes and their pimps were crowding the edges of the theater district, some of whose legitimate playhouses were reportedly on the verge of takeover by porno flick operators, while massage parlors and peep shows were outbidding legitimate enterprises for rentable space. Early in the season the Shubert organization rattled the saber, hinting it might start selling off theaters if the cheapening of the Times Square area was allowed to continue unchecked. The city moved in to eliminate the porno nuisance wherever it impinged on theatergoing. Efforts to acquire the Bijou, Ritz and Little Theaters for the porno circuit were thwarted. A concerned theater industry is working with a concerned city government to maintain a glamorous environment for enjoying the theater. They have gone a long way toward pushing out crime and porno, and they will keep on working until theatergoing is as it should be in image as well as in fact.

The Shubert organization itself was troubled in 1973. In a power shift, three executive directors—Gerald Schoenfeld, Bernard B. Jacobs and Irving Goldman—took over the active management of the company from Lawrence Shubert Lawrence, the late Lee Shubert's grand-nephew, who was named chairman of the board. Differences between the troika and Lawrence soon came to the surface in the form of court proceedings, in which Lawrence attempted to oust the executive directors and regain control of the organization and the Shubert Foundation. The suit was unsuccessful and has been appealed.

The Tony Awards were troubled by a dispute between the American Theater Wing, which originated them, and the League of New York Theaters, which now administers them and arranges for their presentation at a nationally televised ceremony. During negotiations between the League and the Wing over the Tony arrangement, the Wing president, Isabelle Stevenson, let it be known that in her opinion the Tonys were becoming "tarnished." A proposed special award to *Playbill,* the theater program magazine, was an element of the controversy, and a *Playbill* executive roiled the waters further with a statement that "the firm may cease or drastically revise publication of the free program for Broadway theaters." The League decided to present its own special "Theater Awards" the night of the Tonys but entirely apart from them. The 1972-73 recipients of Theater Awards were Mayor John V. Lindsay, the Actors Fund of America and the Shubert organization. *Variety* reported, "It's figured that the Theater Award may be the first step in a new setup" of annual award-giving on Broadway, but this didn't happen; the League-Tony arrangement is on again for next season, with the awards night scheduled for April 21. Meanwhile, back at *Playbill,* a $400,000 annual deficit was causing some long thoughts about whether to charge the playgoer a small sum for the program in future, or whether some kind of financial palliative could be arranged with the help of the League.

Trouble with the musicians' union caused *Pippin* to cancel its tryout booking at the Kennedy Center Opera House in Washington, D.C., until the musicians agreed to compromise as to the number of men employed and their salaries, and *Pippin* rescheduled the booking. As always in the course of a long, hotly creative theater season, some shows had director trouble including *The Creation of the World and Other Business* which started with Harold Clurman and ended with Gerald Freedman; *Irene* which started with John Gielgud and ended with Gower Champion (and there is a lesson in *that* somewhere); and *Cyrano* which started with Michael Langham and ended with Michael Kidd. The directors as a group raised a specter when their organization, the Society of Stage Directors and Choreographers (SSD & C) negotiated a contract with the producers (represented as always by the League of New York Theaters) which, in SSD & C's own words in a notice to its members, "established the principle that directors and choreographers have property rights. The League has agreed that they will not authorize publication in any form of the 'work' of the director or choreographer. In immediate practical terms this means that the final prompt script of a Broadway production may not be published without the consent of the director or choreographer who has staged the production."

In reality it meant nothing of the sort; it meant only that the SSD & C was waving its plume above the parapet, with the producers whistling and looking up at the sky, playing innocent bystanders. The Dramatists Guild, the organization of playwrights, composers, librettists and lyricists, who do in fact own the written material, was never a party to any such agreement and promptly advised its members to be on guard against and resist any encroachment upon their property. The SSD & C members are paid for what they do, the Dramatists Guild pointed out, and their work belongs to the production whose script, in turn, belongs to the playwright (who is compensated, not by any salary, but by a share of the box office receipts when and if—a very big if—they begin coming in). A lot of words were exchanged but no material issue joined in this matter in the 1972-73 season, and it looked as though the whole controversy might vanish in a slow dissolve.

Even the new and apparently very successful 7:30 p.m. curtain time was in trouble this season. The restaurateurs felt that their business, hurt, they say, by the early curtain, would be greatly improved by pushing the curtain back to at least 8 o'clock. The League considered doing this—in exchange for a promotional boost by the restaurants—but it didn't happen this season.

For the critics, the year was relatively untroubled. When the New York Drama Critics Circle met to vote its annual awards on May 23, 1973, the meeting opened with the Circle president, Henry Hewes, questioning his own eligibility to vote. Hewes's magazine, *Saturday Review,* had just suspended publication with the announced intention of merging with *World.* In these special circumstances, similar to a situation where a critic's publication might be on strike, it was up to the members to rule whether or not Hewes should be considered an active critic with full voting rights. Douglas Watt made a motion that Hewes be so considered, and the motion was passed unanimously.

Some critics complained openly that producers were catering to Clive Barnes of the *Times,* sometimes shifting opening dates to suit his convenience (he has a particularly tight reviewing schedule since he covers dance as well as theater), regardless of the inconvenience to other critics. And inside the Critics Circle there were indigestive rumbles about *Variety's* publishing the intimate and sometimes controversy-ridden details of the group's private meetings. But with David Merrick mostly absent from the theater scene in 1972-73, there was no one to goad the critical fraternity into excesses of righteous indignation individually or in combination, so that the pundits maintained a fairly low profile.

There was a positive sign of growth in 1973 in the completion and putting-into-operation of new theaters built into high-rise office structures, a fruition of the city's program to give developers in the Broadway area valuable concessions in the building regulations if they will include theaters within their skyscraper designs. The first of these was American Place's new home below ground level at 46th Street and Sixth Avenue, opened last season, an intimate, efficient and pleasant environment for experimental activity (but one hypersensitive and dissenting playwright commented, "I don't like it, I can feel that whole building weighing down on top of me"). In contrast, the word for the three new Broadway houses which opened this season is cavernous. The Uris, the Minskoff and the Circle in the Square Joseph E. Levine Theaters seem to have been designed as though bigness had the same value in stage housing as it does in office buildings. *Via Galactica* managed to fill the Uris, but they needed a space ship and an amplified rock band to do it; *Seesaw* seemed to shrink in its vastness. The Minskoff opened with the expansive *Irene,* but even so there were complaints about a feeling of remoteness in the balcony. The Circle in the Square's new uptown arena-stage facility is great for the massive emotional content of O'Neill and Euripides, but a Yankee Stadium for an intimate presentation like Siobhan McKenna's *Here Are Ladies.*

On the plus side, these theaters are more comfortable, with much more width and breadth of individual seating room than in the Shubert-era Broadway houses (and the slight inconvenience of the so-called "continental" aisleless seating arrangement, with access to the seats laterally through the wider-spaced rows, is small in comparison to the pleasure of the increased *lebensraum*). Also, these new theaters *are,* they exist, and they are a great deal better than nothing—which is what we might have been left with, were it not for the Mayor Lindsay administration's concern for the future of the legitimate theater and its district. In another housing matter, a move to have the Lyceum Theater on the east side of Broadway at 45th and 46th Streets named a landmark by the state commission was under way as the season ended. The Lyceum was built in 1902 by Daniel Frohman and is about a generation older than other Broadway houses, the oldest New York City theater devoted to legitimate stage attractions (two theaters are older, but one is now a warehouse and one a movie house).

On a personal note, Stephen Sondheim was elected to succeed Robert Anderson as president of the Dramatists Guild, the fourth time a dramatist from the musical side has been named to lead this authors' organization (the other three were Richard Rodgers, Alan Jay Lerner and the late Oscar Hammerstein II). Harvey B. Sabinson announced his resignation from the public relations firm of which he is a partner, Solters, Sabinson & Roskin, Inc., together with his intention to leave theatrical press agentry and go into another field, possibly teaching (he has served as a visiting professor at Yale Drama School). A gifted and widely respected member of his profession, Sabinson will be missed both sorely and affectionately. Another unexpected resignation in 1973 was that of Angus Duncan as executive secretary of Actors Equity, a post which he had held since 1952.

Alexander H. Cohen produced another good Tony TV show and made a good point in a letter to *Variety* about "the custom of allowing the marquees of shows which have closed to remain standing on Broadway theaters until an incoming production displaces them." He pointed out that leaving the name of an unsuccessful show on the marquee of an empty theater turns Broadway into a "Street of Flops" which have strutted and fretted their brief hour upon the stage and then, instead of being heard of no more, continue having their titles blazoned on Broadway's prime promotional space, like names on elaborate tombstones. Cohen asked in his letter, "Would any other industry trumpet its mistakes in this fashion? It is of course regrettable that most of the shows in question didn't find acceptance and that the theaters they played in are dark. But must we continue to remind the public of their fate?" He urged that marquee signs be taken down as soon as a show closes and, while the theater remains vacant, the space be used to promote living hits.

All the organized efforts to aid and promote the theater continued as before, some of them in ever-widening circles of influence. The Theater Development Fund had given out $105,795 in direct production subsidy and $191,825 in ticket purchases in 1972 and continued in 1973 with a new program of stimulating off-off-Broadway attendance by underwriting part of the cost of a ticket. Direct assistance was received by *Much Ado About Nothing, Doctor Selavy's Magic Theater, The Mother of Us All* and *The Trials of Oz*. Efforts to set up some kind of center for the last-minute sale of unsold tickets at reduced prices were suspended at the beginning of the season, then picked up again and brought to fruition under the auspices of the New York City Cultural Council and the Office of Midtown Planning and Development, together with the Theater Development Fund. A Ticket Center was set up in a booth in Duffy Square offering unsold tickets to Broadway and off-Broadway shows at cut-rate prices, on the day of the performance only. And also locally, a Theater Hall of Fame has been established in the spacious lobby of the Uris Theater and the first group of 90 names of theater greats from the period 1860-1930 are now permanently affixed. Five more names are to be added each year.

Those who look back over the 1972-73 drama season seeking signs and portents are apt to find more than they can conveniently interpret. Something is happening to the theater in this decade, all right—but what? Off Broadway seems to be middling and Broadway, unable to middle with any degree of commercial viability, is concentrating on the big, conventional theater concepts—does that augur good or bad? New theaters are being built in New York, but the season's gross is down considerably, but road grosses are at an all-time high. The audience, harassed by social unrest, is just barely maintaining a constant numerical level, but when Theater Development Fund offered 25,000 cut-rate ticket vouchers to off-off-Broadway shows, the offering was oversubscribed by 30,000. Our contemporary playwrights are trying like alchemists to transsubstantiate the theater form—but not this year, when the most radical show was a Broadway musical. The regional theater stole the show in 1973 with the Long Wharf Theater's *The Changing Room* winning the Critics Prize for best-of-bests and thus symbolizing the growing decentralization of the American theater—but it was a production of a British script.

One of the prime movers of the 1970s, Joseph Papp, is certainly bullish on the New York theater and the American playwright's ability to keep its stages full of excitement. Papp voices his confidence in the continuing strength of the *Broadway* theater when he says that shows which prove popular at the Public or the Beaumont are to be "summarily moved to higher ground," that is, transferred to Broadway, which obviously he expects will retain its firm, large-scale commercial eminence. David Merrick, the leading Broadway producer of the era, interviewed in the New York *Times* at the end of a 1973 season in which he scarcely participated at all, voiced his conviction that Broadway production will stabilize at about the present level. "I think things are improving now," he said, and he intends to come on strong next year with a play and two musicals.

Most would agree with Papp and Merrick that even with all its perplexing 1972-73 symptoms, the theater still looks like an art form for the millenia, adaptable, enduring, endlessly inventive. Even if we can't read all the signs clearly, at least we know that the New York theater is still in action, in motion, and we have a pretty clear idea of where it is bound. If it can live down its particular problems of urban blight, rising costs, artistic dichotomy, developmental encroachment and critical tyranny; if it can shake off all the minor afflictions of the age like traffic jams and power blackouts, then all that remains for it to do is merely to devise entertainments to fascinate and astonish not only its regulars—who have already seen everything the theater has been able to offer since the 1920s—but also attract audiences of a new generation which is bored with walking on the moon.

THE 1972-73 OFF-OFF-BROADWAY SEASON

By Jeff Sweet

Off-off-Broadway critic and author-composer

Any attempt to cover the entire off-off-Broadway season is immediately doomed to failure from a purely statistical point of view. The Theater Development Fund has on file over one hundred self-described off-off-Broadway companies, each of which may present anywhere from one to several dozen productions a season. The weekly listing of off-off-Broadway events in *The Village Voice* usually crowds a large page with tiny type; a typical listing from the October 19, 1972 issue heralded the presentation of 67 productions. The grand total for the year is anybody's guess. Clearly, comprehensive coverage is physically impossible. But the off-off-Broadway spirit is "What-the-hell-gung-ho" in the face of impossibility, so onwards—keeping in mind that one man's view is necessarily limited by what he can see, and apologizing to those involved in the dozens of undoubtedly worthy and important efforts missed owing to the nature of the task.

Generalizations about off-off-Broadway activity are also risky because of the sheer diversity of material presented. After noting that the bulk of the companies play to houses of well under 200 seats and that they are presented on shoestring budgets, one throws up one's hands trying to find commonly-shared characteristics. Off off Broadway, not being subject to the same kinds of financial pressures as the commercial theater, has less reason to try appealing to a general audience. This is the area of special-interest groups. One company may specialize in absurdist farce, another in classical revivals. One may be geared to a black audience, one to a gay audience, one to children, others to virtually any and every other minority group one can name. This may be the ultimate value of off off Broadway: its responsiveness to the needs and interests of its patrons. This responsiveness, this relevance (to use a much-abused term) lies at the heart of the excitement of the off-off-Broadway experience.

If the patronage of any one offering is limited, the interest in off off Broadway in general would seem to be wide—wider perhaps than one might have guessed. At the beginning of the season, the Theater Development Fund announced a new program under which those on the T.D.F. mailing list were offered vouchers in sets of five for $2.50 (or 50 cents a voucher). Each voucher entitled the user to admission, or a $2.00 discount off regular admission price, to any off-off-Broadway organization on the T.D.F. list of one hundred plus. The theaters would then redeem their vouchers at T.D.F. at the rate of $2.00 each. Initially, some 25,000 vouchers, representing $50,000 in direct aid, were made available. No sooner had the word gone out than T.D.F. was deluged with orders. One office worker estimated that for every voucher order filled, four others had to be returned unfilled because of the shortness of the supply; certainly an indication of public interest in what off off Broadway has to offer.

This season, a number of organizations sprang up within the chaos. One of these, the Off-Off-Broadway Alliance (O.O.B.A.), initiated a series of bi-monthly newsletters of member theaters' productions. As the listing had to be at the printer's a month before publication, the producing organizations frequently found themselves in the position of having to predict their activities as much as three months in advance. Understandably, the resulting calendars were not a model of accuracy. In an effort to deal with this problem, beginning with the 1973-1974 season, the Alliance hopes to bring out the newsletters on a monthly basis. In addition to informing the theater public, O.O.B.A. hopes to serve as a central communication agency for its members. One of the aspects of this agency would be the establishment of a script-referral service which would channel promising scripts to the appropriate companies.

Meanwhile, not one but two separate writer's organizations were formed this season and have begun activities: The Playwrights' Cooperative, composed of Claire Burch, Helen Duberstein, Nancy Fales, Richard Foreman, Mario Fratti, Guy Gauthier, Byrd Hoffman School of Byrds, Arthur Kopit, William Kushner, Donald Kvares, Victor Lipton, Oscar Mandel, Christopher Mathewson, Sally Ordway, Robert Patrick, Jean Reavey, Arthur Sainer, Sharon Thei, Nancy Walter and Susan Yankowitz; and the New York Theater Strategy, composed of Kenneth Bernard, Julie Bovasso, Ed Bullins, Rosalyn Drexler, Tom Eyen, Maria Irene Fornes, Paul Foster, Robert Heide, William M. Hoffman, Adrienne Kennedy, Charles Ludlam, Terrence McNally, Murray Mednick, Leonard Melfi, John Ford Noonan, Rochelle Owens, Robert Patrick (again), Sam Shepard, David Starkweather, Ronald Tavel, Megan Terry, Jean-Claude van Itallie and Lanford Wilson. In an interview, Maria Irene Fornes, a member of the latter's executive committee, explained that the Strategy's festival this season is only the starting point of a larger dream: a subsidized touring agency for theater. Ideally, New York would be one of many stops on the tour for packages of Strategy members' plays, the other stops generally being at college campuses. To make the packages more attractive, the playwrights would travel with their plays and be available for discussion with their audiences. The plan is certainly ambitious, but judging from the quality of the Strategy's initial presentations and the enthusiastic response with which it has been greeted so far, it would seem to stand a good chance of succeeding.

The dynamism of off off Broadway is attracting an increasing number of "name" talents from the commercial theater. It gives them opportunities to test themselves in ways that commercial theater, for financial reasons, does not. This is particularly true of well-known actors who turn up not only as performers but also as directors and writers. Among those who contributed their talents this year were David Cryer, Marcia Rodd, Geraldine Fitzgerald, James Broderick, Doris Roberts, Austin Pendleton, Fritz Weaver and Mildred Dunnock. Apparently the appeal of alternative theater's artistic challenges outweighs the lack of financial remuneration. Part of the availability of such talent may also be attributed to the sad fact that the commercial theater was not able to employ some of its finest artists this season.

Quite a few of the playwrights who got their starts off off Broadway returned from notable careers in commercial theater and films to present new works on their old stamping grounds. Among them were Israel Horovitz, Terrence McNally, Sam Shepard and Lanford Wilson.

Horovitz' play, *Dr. Hero,* presented by the Shade Company, chronicles the life of a combination Everyman-Sammy Glick. By lying, cheating and exploiting those around him, he finally attains the status of World's Greatest Man, never finding true fulfillment and finally expiring in a Home for Aging

Charismatics. The play means to make a statement on the soul-destroying properties of competition, decrying a society in which style has come to count for more than substance. Unfortunately, in light of the dramatic choices Horovitz made, one is tempted to respond, "Judge not lest ye yourself be judged." The play's best scene shows the title character leading a group of advertising agency types in the planning of a campaign for a product of no value. In performance, the scene is undeniably funny. Under the lightning-paced direction of Edward Berkeley, it made short work of advertising jargon and graphically illustrated the contempt for public intelligence which lies at the heart of the profession. But the employment of the advertising world as a metaphor for the falsity of American values is hardly an original idea. Much as his hucksters conspire to promote a useless product with razzle-dazzle slogans and packaging, Horovitz attempts to sell a cliche with razzle-dazzle style. The theater has need of stylists of Horovitz's ability, but style cannot salvage the stale. I look forward to a play in which Horovitz employs his craft to enhance a fresh perception.

The title character of Terrence McNally's *Whiskey,* which had its premiere at the Theater at St. Clements under the direction of Kevin O'Connor, is the star of a hit TV series who happens to be an unusually ornery horse. The play concerns the last hours of the animal's human co-stars, a droll quintet of alcoholics called the Lush Thrushes. After a disastrous live appearance at the Houston Astrodome, the five—three men and two women—get plastered in a hotel room and, oblivious to the fire consuming the building, ruminate about the implications of their failure and lurch down memory lane. McNally has created five engaging characters, but the work seems aimless. The characters come to no new awarenesses during the course of the play, and there isn't sufficient investigation of them as figures of public prominance to indicate that he meant to make a statement on the quality of those we tend to embrace as folk heroes. Still, the play made possible a set of fine performances by Beeson Carroll, Charlotte Rae, Tom Rosqui, Michael Sacks, and most particularly, Susan Browning, whose portrayal of the desperately-schizoid Southern Comfort displayed a range and skill which she has had too little opportunity to call upon previously. Within weeks of *Whiskey*'s premiere, the New York Theater Strategy presented an excerpt from McNally's *Bad Habits,* a work-in-progress. The playwright has requested it not be reviewed in its present form, but on the basis of this sample, it seems safe to predict that *Bad Habits* will prove to be among the best of this significant American dramatist's works.

Sam Shepard's *The Tooth of Crime* was given its New York premiere by Richard Schechner's Performance Group. Taking note of the myths surrounding rock stars, the American tendency to romanticize murderers, and the influence popular culture has over lifestyle and language, Shepard cooked up a vision of the future in which rock star and murderer become one, making the word "hit" ring with double meaning. Hoss, who has worked his way to the top of the charts through the established system, finds himself challenged by Crow, a young "gypsy" killer who works outside of the system. In a contest of style, the two combatants battle each other with jive composed like raunchy guitar solos. One of Shepard's favorite themes is the inevitability of the young seizing power from the old; true to form, Crow emerges victor. But Shepard implies that he will hold onto this rank only until the day when someone younger and with faster footwork comes along and dethrones him in a similar fashion. Especially striking is Shepard's creation of a whole new system of jargon which rolls off his characters' tongues so naturally that one could well accept it as an accurate prophecy of the language that will come into common use within the next few generations. As befitted an unconventional script, the Performance Group gave *The Tooth of Crime* a most unconventional mounting. The environment by Jerry Rojo was so constructed that there was no single place where one could perch and see it all. In order to follow the action of the play, one had to truly *follow* the action, one way of fighting complacency on the part of the theatergoer. The danger of techniques such as this is that they tend to be employed to cover up lack of discipline and training on the part of the performers. Such was emphatically not the case in this production, however. Rather than camouflage, the staging proved to be a challenge to the company, and it met that challenge with gusto. Particularly impressive were Spalding Gray as Hoss and Stephen Borst in two roles—Hoss' astrologer-adviser and his "doctor."

But it was Lanford Wilson's *The Hot l Baltimore,* under Marshall W. Mason's skillful direction, which proved to be the most highly regarded new play of the off-off-Broadway season. Describing a day's activity in the lobby of a soon-to-be-razed, once-quality-but-now-shabby hotel, *Baltimore* weaves together the lives and fading dreams of its seedy tenants. But unlike Wilson's *Balm in Gilead,* a similarly structured look at low life in an inner-city greasy-spoon diner, *Baltimore's* tone is not dispassionate and clinical but intensely romantic, a poignant salute to the illusions we build to act as buffers against the intrusion of reality. The characters are easily-identifiable prototypes—a grumpy old geezer, sentimental hookers, a belligerent young man on the run from the law and a batty old lady who claims contact with ghosts—but under Wilson's pen they become fresh and vital once more. After enthusiastic notices in the local and national press and a consistently sold-out extended engagement in the Circle Theater's loft on the Upper West Side, the production was moved to a regular commercial run off Broadway at the Circle-in-the-Square Downtown, garnering another slew of enthusiastic notices, picking up a handful of awards for writing, direction and performances including the Critics Award for Best American Play, and becoming eligible for selection as a Best Play. Regional theaters across the country sensed a classic in the making, and even before the off-Broadway transfer was accomplished a Chicago production was in rehearsal and negotiations for Los Angeles, London and (of course) Baltimore productions were in progress. The Circle production featured what was, in my opinion, the performance of the season—Mari Gorman as Jackie, the tough little health nut and petty thief. Stephanie Gordon contributed another standout performance as Suzy, the dumb, dyed-blonde prostitute who compulsively rushes into bad situations.

Another off-off-Broadway "hit" was *The Dragon Lady's Revenge,* the program credits for which read "written, directed, designed, composed, built, costumed, staged, painted, publicized, performed by the San Francisco Mime Troupe." First presented in the parks of the San Francisco Bay area, the production was scheduled for a limited run at the Washington Square Methodist Church, but the response was so enthusiastic that it stayed in town for several additional weeks, traveling from theater to theater as the houses' schedules dictated. Several producers were eager to transfer the work to a commercial run, but the Troupe turned down all offers on the ideological grounds that such a move would compromise its function as a peoples' theater. The company's credo is "Good Art Entertains, Tells the Truth and is Freely Available." Certainly *The Dragon Lady* entertained. In a style made up of one part vaudeville, one part grade B movie and one part Brecht, the piece begins with the murder of a G.I. in a back alley in Long Pinh, a city somewhere in Southeast Asia. Expiring in the arms of one Lieutenant Clyde Dillsworth Junker III, the victim utters a few cryptic last words which send the idealistic if somewhat dim lieutenant off on a mission to unmask the archfiend behind the local heroin trade, a man known only as—what else?— Mr. Big. Our hero has many adventures and brushes with death before the final confrontation, encountering on the way secret agents, B-girls and the kind of villain Sessue Hayakawa used to portray. At the end, Mr. Big is revealed to be the lieutenant's own father, the U.S. ambassador to the Viet Nam-ish country in question. Whether or not one chose to accept the troupe's contention that the United States is supporting heroin trade in Southeast Asia as a means of political control, the evening was undeniably a vital and important one. Michael Christensen made the most of a flashy part which called on him to impersonate a mumber of characters including a malevolent nun and a mysterious fencing instructor. General Rong Q, the country's dictator, was played with great spirit by Sharon Lockwood in an inspired bit of transsexual casting.

Trans-sexual casting was also featured to good advantage in Joseph Renard's *A Boy Name Dog* and Charles Ludlam's *Corn. A Boy Name Dog,* presented at the Workshop of the Players Art, was a parody of a leading American playwright's plays and a lifestyle which alternated between moments of hilarity and tedium. Much of the former was supplied by James Hilbrandt's wonderfully subtle performance as Schulamaith Beauregard, a grey-haired little old "Big Mama" with fond memories of the good old days in the family manse and a taste for mint julips.

Corn was also played for laughs. Presented by the Ridiculous Theatrical Company, it was a blatantly silly concoction about the efforts of a country-Western singer named Lola Lola to resolve a Hatfield-McCoy-style feud. The tall and gangly John D. Brockmeyer was especially funny as the matriarch of one of the broods. Between the scenes of high camp and low comedy, a group called the Lucky Stars sang songs by Virgil Young which were to country-Western what the score of *Grease* was to rock 'n' roll.

Any discussion of off off Broadway must include mention of Al Carmines, who, besides being a minister at the Judson Memorial Church, has staked a credible claim to being the king of the off-off-Broadway musical. The anti-thesis of Broadway's Stephen Sondheim, who may labor for weeks perfecting a single song, Carmines regularly turns out one or more numbers a day. His aim is not the precision and subtlety of expression which characterize a Sondheim song, but a kind of gleeful messiness—rough, puckish, giving the illusion of great spontaneity. Working as swiftly as he does, each year he produces a fresh batch of full-length shows for the Judson Poets' Theater, guiding his frequently enormous casts through performances from his piano and, more often than not, singing a song or two himself. Among his premieres this year was *The Life of a Man,* which followed the central character, well-played by Judson regular Raethel Bean, from birth to death. Having chosen to do a show on the life cycle, Carmines inevitably echoes images seen many times in other similarly-themed shows. For the most part, however, he brings to the overly-familiar concept a fresh spirit. For instance, in the section deal-ing with the central character's education, he introduces a dreamy Einstein who announces, "I'm in love!" The boys asks him with whom. "I don't know," the mathematician replies. "You're in love with something you don't know?" asks the boy, puzzled. "Exactly," beams Albert, "I'm in love with something I don't know," then launches into a romantic ballad on his quest for knowl-edge.

Also featured this season was a revival of Carmines's *Christmas Rappings,* in which he set the Bible's account of the Nativity to music colored by such diverse influences as folk songs, vaudeville turns and operatic arias. How natural it seems for the "No room at the inn" scene to be sung as a gentle country waltz! His attempts to musicalize Gertrude Stein's novel, *The Making of Americans,* and to investigate the homosexual subculture in *The Faggot,* were, in my opinion, less rewarding. But even when he misfires, Carmines gives ample evidence that his is one of the most creative and original minds in musical theater today.

A pair of musicals were notable among the La Mama Experimental Theater Club's productions this year. *Everything for Anybody,* with book and lyrics by Louisa Rosa and fine music by Tom Mandel, took a clown-whited "Any-body" through a series of scenes centering on the gap between sex and love and the irony of being alone in a crowded city. Adding spice to the evening were three dramatized "erotic fables" by Marco Vassi dealing with the ridicu-lous lengths to which people may go in search of sexual fulfillment. Occasion-ally, the tone of the piece threatened to cross the thin line separating poig-nance from bathos, but the overall effect was strong enough to warrant its transfer to an off-Broadway run under the title *The Bar That Never Closes.*

Thoughts by Lamar Alford, with a little help from contributing lyricists Joe Tapia and Megan Terry, also found its way to off Broadway after an enthusiastic reception at La Mama. I had some quibbles with the show structurally. It seems to me that a production needs to have more than songs to qualify for the term "musical." The form requires more in the way of characterization and dramatic development than was offered in *Thoughts,* a loose collection of musical sketches drawn from Alford's youth as a black in the South. Weak as I believed the work to be in this respect, however, the score and the performances proved more than ample justification for its production. Time and time again, the rhythms of gospel and soul roused the audience to hand-clapping, foot-stomping enthusiasm, a high point being Mary Alice's rendition of "Sunshine."

The other off-off-Broadway musicals I attended this year proved to be a discouraging lot. Without detailing the faults and merits of individual offerings, generally speaking it seems that the plotted musical is in disfavor, as is true character writing in the lyrics. Unfortunately, it would appear that the rejection of the traditionally-crafted musical is motivated not so much out of the urge to explore new forms as the desire to avoid the discipline the old form requires. Writers with the desire to truly apply themselves to the task of creating articulate and disciplined theater songs seem to be rare, though not altogether absent. The numbers in a musical revue at the Manhattan Theater Club called, appropriately, *The Revue,* featured wryly succinct lyrics in disarmingly melodic settings, the handiwork of an up-and-coming songwriter named Ed Kleban.

Talented women writers and directors were in ample evidence this season. Louisa Rosa, author of *Everything for Anybody,* has already been mentioned. At St. Clements, *Moon Mysteries* featured Jean Erdman's exciting dance interpretations of three William Butler Yeats plays, the result being one of the most highly-praised productions of 1972-73. *Canadian Gothic* and *American Modern,* a double bill of one-acts by Joanna Glass, directed by Austin Pendleton at the Manhattan Theater Club, were quietly moving looks at two households troubled by the inability of their inhabitants to truly touch each other. Harlene Kim Friedman staged a Whitman's Sampler of new feminist stage humor called the *Wicked Woman Revue,* featuring material written by members of the Westbeth Feminist Collective. An off-Broadway version is said to be in the offing.

Three companies of New York University drama alumni, all working from an improvisational approach, premiered new works. Andre Gregory's Manhattan Project followed up its internationally-successful retelling of *Alice in Wonderland* with an offbeat production of Samuel Beckett's *Endgame.* The Shaliko Company presented *Children of the Gods,* a chronology-scrambled collage based on Aeschylus's and Euripedes's chronicles of the fall of the House of Atreus. Of the N.Y.U. companies, however, my favorite is Section Ten. Under the direction of Omar Shapli and Andrea Balis, this group of talented young actors developed two unusual works, *The New York Monster Show* and *Great Hoss Pistol.* The former is a grimly humorous look at various aspects of city life; a series of sketches connected by impressionistic movement and sound and lighting effects. At one moment an actor may be in the middle of a scene about a hostile employment agency; the next, he may be playing a giant cockroach in a nightmare; and the next, he may be portraying the fender of an ambulance. *Great Hoss Pistol* is an intriguing look at the power struggle between Thomas Jefferson, Alexander Hamilton and Aaron Burr. This brand of highly-physicalized improvisationally-created theater is usually most effective in making observations on external behavior and societal situations as opposed to the internal working of the human heart, but in this case I was particularly impressed with the depth of characterization which transformed the textbook issues into the drama of three complex and remarkable men in conflict. I emerged with the hope that Section Ten will continue its exploration of American history as source material.

This season also saw the birth of the American Indian Theater Ensemble. Formed by playwright Hanay Geiogamah, with the assistance of La Mama's Ellen Stewart, the 25-member company presented a triple bill at La Mama, consisting of a segment of Indian music and dance, a dramatic version of a Navajo myth called *Na Haaz Zan,* and Geiogamah's play *Body Indian.* After a warm welcome by the press, the company began a cross-country tour, with heavy emphasis on stops where Indian audiences would be reached.

Black writers were well represented this season. In the fall, the Afro-American Studio for Acting and Speech presented three one-acts by Imamu Amiri Baraka (LeRoi Jones) in repertory. Baraka was also represented by the premiere of an early play called *A Recent Killing* at the Henry Street Settlement Playhouse. Another black play presented at the Playhouse, *Dudder Love* by Walter Jones, was also warmly received. Another Baraka play, *The Baptism,* appeared on a double bill with Ed Bullins's *Street Sounds* as part of a festival of black theater at the Players Workshop. Also part of the festival were a revival of Lonne Elder III's *Ceremonies in Dark Old Men* and Richard Wesley's *The Black Terror.*

Off off Broadway offered many other exciting evenings this season. At the top of my list would be Phillip Lam's *The Uncle,* four related scenes from the life of an apartment agent. The portrayal of the central character was not particularly sympathetic, nor were the situations overtly dramatic or the language remarkable. Nonetheless, with its rich subtext and its sadly ironic tone, *The Uncle* was one of the best plays of the season. Based on the classic H.G. Wells science fiction tale *The Island of Doctor Moreau,* Joel Stone's *The Horrors of Doctor Moreau* at the Jean Cocteau Theater dealt with a scientist's attempt to create men out of animals through surgery. The point that there is animal potential within all of us was made with something less than subtlety, but the piece offered Marc Kaplan, Eleanor Schlusselberg, Deborah Nadel and David Sternberg in bravura performances as the Beast People. John Steinbeck's *Of Mice and Men* got a fresh treatment in Charles Briggs' production at St. Clements. Featuring a white George and a black Lennie, the interracial casting brought out new values in the script. Joe Fields's Lennie was particularly fine. The Bread and Puppet Theater stopped in New York to present *That Simple Light Should Rise Out of Complicated Darkness,* summoning up a series of arresting images, the puppets, shrouded figures and eerie music coming together in an epic of symbolic pageantry. And, at this writing, the Open Theater is working on what has been announced will be the troupe's last presentation before it disbands.

Theater of every persuasion is lighting up lofts and basements, addressing its audiences in a variety of styles and languages. The seats (when there are seats) may not be as comfortable as those in the Booth or the Morosco, but if your luck is with you, you may find yourself in the presence of tomorrow's Tennessee Williams or Eugene O'Neill. Or, for that matter, today's Lanford Wilson or Terrence McNally.

THE SEASON AROUND THE UNITED STATES

with

A DIRECTORY OF PROFESSIONAL REGIONAL THEATER

○
○
○

INTRODUCTION: CASTING A SHADOW ON NEW YORK

By Arvin Brown

Artistic director of the Long Wharf Theater, New Haven, Conn.

TIME was when "Stick with me kid—I'll take you off Main Street and put you on Broadway" was one of the greatest seduction lines in the land. But no more. Even the most wide-eyed Arkansas honey blondes, desperate to break into Show Biz, have probably read an article somewhere about Broadway, "the fabulous invalid," and the lecherous producers of the 1970s have had to find themselves a new approach. Broadway is dead, Broadway is dying, no one in the theater holds out the slightest ray of hope. Yet this season the most successful drama on Broadway, David Storey's *The Changing Room,* came direct from the Long Wharf Theater in New Haven, its production intact and praised as a major theatrical event, and in that transfer I for one find more than a grain of optimism.

The Changing Room is not the first of its kind. It is one of a string of important plays which found their beginnings in what, for want of a better term, we'll call America's "regional" theaters: *The Great White Hope* and *Indians* from Washington's Arena Stage, *The Trial of the Catonsville Nine* from the Mark Taper Forum, *The Effect of Gamma Rays on Man-in-the-Moon Marigolds* from Houston's Alley Theater, *A Whistle in the Dark* again

49

from Long Wharf, the current musical version of *Cyrano* from the Guthrie Theater in Minneapolis—one could go on and on. And the better productions from the regional theaters deserve their success; they often possess a vitality and integrity long missing from the Broadway scene. The interested theater-goer might well ask to what these theaters owe their energy, and Broadway might well learn from the answer.

First of all, let's take a long, hard look at the word "regional." The reason most of us working in the theater outside of New York hate the term is that it connotes all the naive simplicity, the rural hick charm of the country mouse before his visit to his cousin in the city; culture in "the sticks," barefoot but with good intentions. Few stop to think that the theater's origins were in ritual, that ritual celebrates an active and energetic sense of *community,* and that community is most often the result of a common home, a "region." Jack Kroll, in a review of *The Changing Room,* had the good sense to praise the Long Wharf audience, and by so doing highlighted one of the major factors in the theater's success. A subscription audience feels increasingly "at home" as the season progresses, the faces at intermissions are familiar, and if the work on stage has been compelling, a bond of shared emotional experience has been created. That bond leads the "regional" audience slowly but inevitably toward the center of the theatrical event—participation. The stage is a unique medium in an era of passive response to the arts. Films and TV supply many things but never a dialogue; try shouting back at a televised hearing, or letting them know on the 6 o'clock news that you think the world is coming to an end. In the theater, response is the core of the experience, and the more sense of identity the audience has, the more intelligent and spontaneous its response will be. The Broadway audience too often has only one thing in common—the exorbitant price of a ticket—and only one shared emotion—the demand that the show be worth what they paid for it. Small wonder that many plays open in New York tender and flawed but interesting, only to die in days from a lack of give and take. The audience watches, scowling, thinking $12.50 or $15 and wishing it had what it always has handy at home—the knob that turns the whole thing off.

If a play needs a mature relationship with an audience in order to survive its perilous infancy, performances are no less fragile in their earlier stages. A lot has been written about "ensemble" acting, much of it silly, but there is no question that good acting is a team sport. Broadway talks about teams but is really much more interested in the lone survivor. Nothing thrills Broadway more than the aging lady film star who suddenly reappears in a musical, not only surprising all her former fans who thought she was dead, but delighting everyone who hopes to be able to kick above his head at 55. The Broadway success story is the old American dream of the rugged individualist, and while a single great performer is one of the true excitements of the theater, important plays are usually written about relationships, about man as a social family animal.

The "regional" theater once again has the advantage in creating a team. An ensemble is built on trust, and on that rare ability of actors to give freely and generously to each other on stage when there are no pressures to make them feel that their openness is dangerous. Actors are only human, and when they happen also to be Americans, it is naive to imagine that they will be free of the drives and goals which our society implants in all of us. A Broadway opening night can be the pot of gold at the end of the rainbow, or it can be the cobra in the woodpile—you get rich or you die, and the whole world will know which the following morning. It is an unnatural event, based on an assumption that the performance an actor gives before an audience of international critics bears some relationship to the performance he gave the night before, or will give the night after. In the years I have spent directing in the "regional" theater I have had so little contact with the time-honored actor tricks for gaining unfair attention—upstaging, moving on someone else's laugh line, etc.—I used to wonder if I'd recognize the phenomenon when I saw it. Directing in New York, as opening night approaches, I've watched great actors unconsciously maneuver for the spotlight and subtly coarsen what might have been in rehearsal the most detailed and generous of performances. "Regional" theaters have opening nights, too, but they are followed by a guaranteed run, not instant oblivion, and that simple fact colors the whole rehearsal process. I honestly believe that camaraderie which all critics have extolled in *The Changing Room,* and which is so convincing because it is genuine, could never have developed if the production had begun on Broadway; as it was, the Long Wharf actors during the weeks preceding the New York opening had to clamp their jaws and hang on like bulldogs to the structure and the spontaneity they had found in New Haven.

I know the many other reasons for the degeneration of New York as a home for serious theater—demands of the unions, rising costs, the urban crime problem, etc.—but they have been written about too often to go into here. I am also aware of the notable survivors of the New York malaise; the Chelsea Theater Center, for example, and of course Joseph Papp. Papp has created in the Public Theater the closest thing New York has known to a regional community, and he has done it by beating Broadway on its own terms: he has been meaner than Merrick, tougher than Cohen, and he is the greatest upstager in theater history. But what happens now? The Broadway ethic is more ingrained than we know, and it's hard to play the power game without being corrupted by its rules. Can any actor work at the Public today with the same freedom he had four years ago? Can any playwright put his first play on for Papp, even in worshop, without the terrible dread that he might not be found worthy of his illustrious ancestors, Jason Miller and David Rabe? No, Papp notwithstanding, New York is still the most difficult atmosphere in the country for the development of the kind of theater which celebrates not the individual but the human condition, and which can prove itself over and over again as one of the most flexible media we have for the revelation of man's relationship to his fellow man.

Broadway will always be with us, not just because there must be a place for costly musicals and star-studded comedies in the scheme of things, but because Americans love a center, a place where fortunes can be made or lost in a single night, and where judgments can be formed by the experts before any individual theatergoer dare give his own opinion an airing. But that cultural inferiority complex which has plagued America since its beginnings is perhaps more of a problem now in New York than anywhere else. In a few places out there in the hinterlands, the sticks, audiences and actors are finding their voices and beginning to talk to each other, and Broadway can only benefit from all the possibilities of that new and exciting dialogue.

A DIRECTORY OF PROFESSIONAL REGIONAL THEATER

*Including selected Canadian programs
and selected programs for children*

Compiled by Ella A. Malin

Professional 1972-73 programs and repertory productions by leading resident companies around the United States, plus major Shakespeare festivals including that of Stratford, Ontario (Canada), are grouped in alphabetical order of their locations and listed in date order from late May, 1972 to June, 1973. This list does not include Broadway, off-Broadway or touring New York shows, summer theaters, single productions by commercial producers or college or other non-professional productions. The directory was compiled by Ella A. Malin for *The Best Plays of 1972-73* from information provided by the resident producing organizations at Miss Malin's request. First productions of new plays—American or world premieres—in regional theaters are listed with full casting and credits, as available. Figures in parentheses following title give number of performances and date given is opening date, included whenever a record of these facts was obtainable from the producing managements. A plus mark (+) with the performance number signifies the show was still running on June 1, 1973.

Augmented reports on other than regional theater production in Los Angeles by Rick Talcove and Washington, D.C. by Jay Alan Quantrill are included under those cities' headings in this listing.

Summary

This Directory lists 341 productions of 354 plays (including one-acters and worshop productions) presented by 40 groups in 59 theaters in 36 cities (31 in the United States and 5 in Canada) during the 1972-73 season. Of these, 151 were American plays in 122 full productions and 29 workshop

Jack Albertson, Lewis J. Stadlen and Sam Levene in *The Sunshine Boys*

Alan Bates as Ben Butley in *Butley*

Julie Harris as Mary Lincoln in *The Last of Mrs. Lincoln* (FAR RIGHT)

Debbie Reynolds as Irene O'Dare in *Irene* (FAR LEFT)

Ben Vereen as Leading Player in *Pippin*

Jerry Orbach as Paul Friedman in *6 Rms Riv Vu*

Barbara Bel Geddes as Katy Cooper in *Finishing Touches* (FAR RIGHT)

Hermione Gingold (FAR LEFT) as Mme. Armfeldt and Glynis Johns as Desirée Armfeldt in *A Little Night Music*

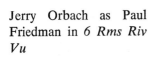

Michele Lee as Gittel Mosca in *Seesaw*

Christopher Plummer as Cyrano de Bergerac in *Cyrano* (FAR RIGHT)

Fred Grandy as Robert "Bradshaw" Lacey in *Green Julia* (FAR LEFT)

Mari Gorman as Jackie in *The Hot l Baltimore*

Douglas Turner Ward as Johnny Williams in *The River Niger*

R o s e m a r y Harris as Blanche Du Bois in *A Streetcar Named Desire* (FAR RIGHT)

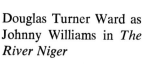

Colleen D e w h u r s t as C h r i s t i n e Mannon in *Mourning Becomes Electra* (FAR LEFT)

Rex Harrison as "Henry IV" in *Emperor Henry IV*

THE CHANGING ROOM
—The locker room in David Storey's award-winning play is as *above*, with the coach (George Ede) haranguing his rugby players between the halves of the game. *At left*, a badly injured player (John Lithgow) is restrained by his coach and trainer (Alan Castner)

Above, Hayward Morse and Alan Bates in Simon Gray's *Butley*

Below, Zoe Caldwell, Bob Dishy and George Grizzard in Arthur Miller's *The Creation of the World and Other Business*

The Williams family of Harlem in Joseph A. Walker's *The River Niger*: *left,* Douglas Turner Ward (father) and Graham Brown (friend); *below,* Roxie Roker (mother), Lee Roberts (son) and Frances Foster (grandmother)

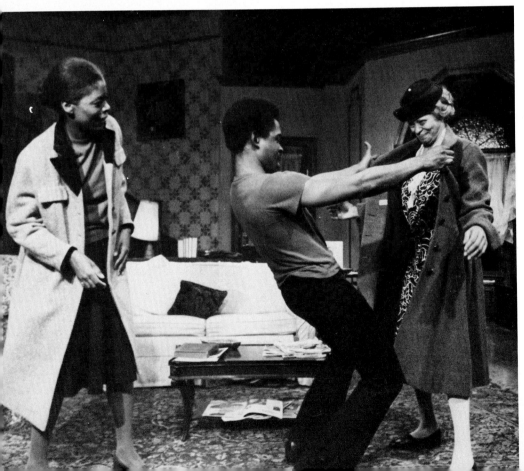

FAMILIES ON THE STAGE

The Cooper family of an eastern university town in Jean Kerr's *Finishing Touches*: Scott Firestone (youngest son), Barbara Bel Geddes (mother), Oliver Conant (middle son) and Robert Lansing (father)

6 RMS RIV VU — *Right*,
Jerry Orbach and Jane Al-
exander in the play by Bob
Randall

*THE JOCKEY CLUB
STAKES* — *Below*, Robert
Coote, Wilfrid Hyde-White
and Geoffrey Sumner in the
British comedy by William
Douglas Home

MARY TODD LINCOLN

Mrs. Lincoln was played by three actresses on Broadway this season: *above left* as the wife by Eva Marie Saint of the President (Fred Gwynne) in V. J. Longhi's *The Lincoln Mask*; *directly above* as a widow by Julie Harris in James Prideaux's *The Last of Mrs. Lincoln*; and *left* also as a widow by Geraldine Page in Jerome Kilty's *Look Away*

THE SECRET AFFAIRS OF MILDRED WILD — *Above,* Maureen Stapleton (*center*) imagines herself in a Shirley Temple movie in Paul Zindel's play

STATUS QUO VADIS—Above, Gail Strickland and Bruce Boxleitner in Donald Driver's satire

OUT CRY—Cara Duff-MacCormick and Michael York in a scene from the two-character play by Tennessee Williams

MUSICALS

PIPPIN—Above, Ben Vereen and the company; *below,* samples of Patricia Zipprodt's costume sketches for the Roger O. Hirson-Stephen Schwartz musical (Tony Walton's *Pippin* scene designs appear on the next page)

TONY WALTON
DESIGNS

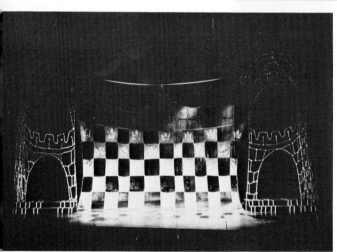

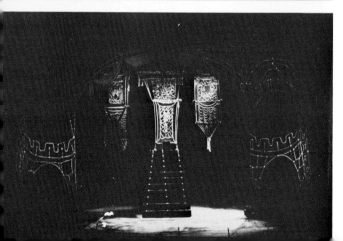

The evolution of the *Pippin* set design is illustrated on this page. *At top*, the ideas are developing in three trial sketches attempting to get away from what Walton calls "the Camelot look." Finally, *directly above,* Walton hits upon a design he decides to use. *At left* are two photos of the actual *Pippin* set with curtain drawn and open

Above, Terry Kiser and Marcia Rodd in a scene from *Shelter,* the Nancy Ford-Gretchen Cryer show also designed by Walton

In designing the set for *Shelter,* Walton used a model (*above*) representing a TV studio with changing projections, some drawings and some photographs, in the background. Walton also designed the costumes for *Shelter;* two of his sketches are pictured *at right*

CYRANO—Christopher Plummer (*opposite right*) in the duel scene of the Anthony Burgess-Michael J. Lewis musical based on Rostand

SEESAW—Giancarlo Esposito, Ken Howard and Michele Lee in the "Spanglish" number of the Michael Bennett-Cy Coleman-Dorothy Fields musical based on William Gibson's *Two for the Seesaw*

TRICKS—*Below*, Christopher Murney and Rene Auberjonois (as Scapin) in the musicalization of Molière's *Les Fourberies de Scapin*

Authors of *Hair* contributed to the three musicals pictured on this page: *above, Via Galactica* (music by Galt MacDermot); *right*, members of the cast racing along the balcony aisle in *Dude* (music by MacDermot, book and lyrics by Gerome Ragni); *below*, *Rainbow* (music and lyrics by James Rado, book by Rado and his brother Ted)

THE HOT L BALTIMORE—In the hotel-lobby setting of Lanford Wilson's award-winning play are, *in foreground,* Mari Gorman and Antony Tenuta and, *in background,* Zane Lasky, Jonathan Hogan (in shadow), Trish Hawkins, Rob Thirkield and Helen Stenborg

GREEN JULIA—*Left* and *below,* Fred Grandy (at left in both photos) with James Woods (photo at left), later replaced by John Pleshette (photo below), in Paul Ableman's two-character play

BERLIN TO BROADWAY WITH KURT WEILL—*Below*, Hal Watters, Judy Lander, Margery Cohen, Jerry Lanning and Ken Kercheval in a scene from the musical revue of Weill numbers

CHELSEA CLOSEUPS — *Left*, Cecelia Norfleet (as Billie Holiday) and Roger Robinson in *Lady Day: A Musical Tragedy*; *below*, Christopher Lloyd as Peter Handke's *Kaspar*, both at Chelsea Theater Center

WELCOME TO ANDROMEDA — David Clennon and Bella Jarrett as patient and nurse in Ron Whyte's play

PUBLIC THEATER PORTRAITS—
Left, Ruby Dee and Robert Loggia in
Wedding Band by Alice Childress; *below*, Marcia Jean Kurtz, Rae Allen and
W. B. Brydon in David Rabe's *The Orphan*, both produced at the Public
Theater by Joseph Papp

OH COWARD!—Roderick
Cook, Barbara Casen and
Jamie Ross in the Noel
Coward revue

THE TOOTH OF CRIME
—*Right*, a scene from Sam Shepard's play at the Performing Garage

EL GRANDE DE COCA-COLA—*Below*, Sally Willis, Ron House and Diz White in the multi-lingual comedy from London

Right, a scene from *Doctor Selavy's Magic Theater*, conceived by Richard Foreman

Left, Will Hare and Rue McClanahan as an Irish actor-manager and his wife in Brian Friel's drama *Crystal and Fox*

Right, Bil Baird's interpretation of "The Dying Swan" in the Baird Marionettes show *Band Wagon*

IRENE—An updated version of the 1919 Broadway musical, with a revised book by Hugh Wheeler and Joseph Stein and with many musical numbers added to the original score, starred Debbie Reynolds in the title role (center in photo above, with Ted Pugh)

MUCH ADO ABOUT NOTHING—The time and place of Shakespeare's play were changed to America early in this century in Joseph Papp's N.Y. Shakespeare Festival production. *Above* and *on opposite page* are some of Theoni V. Aldredge's costume designs. *Below,* a scene from the show with April Shawhan (as a bride), Jerry Mayer (in uniform), Douglass Watson and Glenn Walken

EMPEROR HENRY IV—Eileen Herlie, Rex Harrison
and David Hurst in a scene from the Pirandello play

SWAN SONG AT LINCOLN CENTER —
The distinguished final season of Lincoln Center Repertory under Jules Irving's direction included, *above left*, Nancy Marchand, Barbara Cook, Frances Sternhagen and Joseph Wiseman in Gorky's *Enemies*; *above right*, Hume Cronyn in Samuel Beckett's *Act Without Words 1* (in the Forum Theater); and Rosemary Harris as Blanche Du Bois in *A Streetcar Named Desire* (*below, left,* with Philip Bosco) and as Portia in *The Merchant of Venice* (*right*)

PHOENIX REPERTORY — *Above*, Paul Hecht and John McMartin in Molière's *Don Juan*; *right*, John Glover and Katherine Helmond in O'Neill's *The Great God Brown*

CIRCLE IN THE SQUARE—*Above*, Irene Papas as Euripides's *Medea*; *below*, Siobhan McKenna in *Here Are Ladies*

ROUNDABOUT THEATER COMPANY — The 1972-73 season of plays under the direction of Gene Feist included (*above*) Wesley Addy, Victor Garber and Beatrice Straight in Ibsen's *Ghosts*

CITY CENTER ACTING COMPANY—John Houseman's Juilliard spin-off group's season included *The School for Scandal* (*above*, with David Ogden Stiers and Patti LuPone) and Behan's *The Hostage* (*right*, with Mary Joan Negro, Dakin Matthews and Mary Lou Rosato)

A SAMPLING
OF NEW PLAYS
IN REGIONAL
THEATERS

DALLAS — *Right, Jabber-wock* by Jerome Lawrence and Robert E. Lee at Dallas Theater Center

PROVIDENCE — *Below, Feasting With Panthers,* a musical by Adrian Hall and Richard Cumming, at Trinity Square Playhouse

BUFFALO—*Left*, Jeanne De Baer and Earl Milton Forrest in *The Saving Grace* by John Tobias at Studio Arena Theater

HARTFORD — *Right*, Eda Reiss Merin and Richard Pilcher in *Nightlight* by Kenneth H. Brown at the Stage Company

WASHINGTON, D.C. — *Below*, a scene from Dennis Turner's *The Rapists* at the Washington Theater Club

CINCINNATI—*Above,* a scene from *Baboon,* conceived by Word Baker, Dan Early, Maria Irene Fornes, Milburn Smith, Sherman F. Warner and the company at the Playhouse in the Park

SPRINGFIELD, MASS.—*Below,* a playwright (Paul G. Enger, *left*) is pleased with a scene from his *The Good News* at Stage West

NEW HAVEN — Scenes from William Styron's *In the Clap Shack* (*above*) and Eric Bentley's *Are You Now or Have You Ever Been* at Yale Repertory Theater

LOS ANGELES—*Below,* Joe Flynn, Ann Morgan Guilbert and Jane Dulo in Jules Tasca's *The Mind With the Dirty Man* at Mark Taper Forum

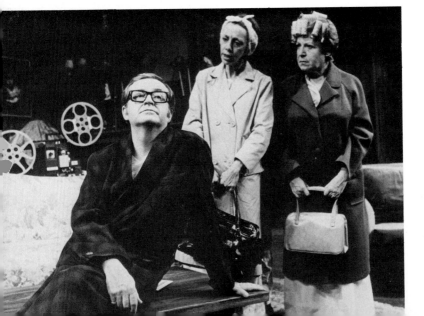

productions. 73 were world premieres, 15 were American or North American continental premieres.

Frequency of production of individual scripts was as follows:

1 play received 9 productions (*Old Times*)
1 play received 6 productions (*The Crucible*)
2 plays received 4 productions (*Butterflies Are Free, A Streetcar Named Desire*)
7 plays received 3 productions (*Child's Play, Summer and Smoke, One Flew Over the Cuckoo's Nest, As You Like It, The Effect of Gamma Rays on Man-In-The-Moon Marigolds, The House of Blue Leaves, A Midsummer Night's Dream*)
28 plays received 2 productions
315 plays received 1 production

Listed below are the playwrights who received the greatest number of productions. The first figure is the number of productions; the second figure (in parentheses) is the number of plays produced, including one-acters.

Shakespeare	31 (21)	Fry	3 (2)
Pinter	10 (2)	Albee	3 (2)
Williams	8 (6)	O'Casey	3 (2)
Arthur Miller	8 (3)	Behan	3 (2)
Molière	6 (5)	Brecht	2 (3)
Simon	4 (4)	Stoppard	2 (3)
Ibsen	4 (3)	Strindberg	2 (2)
Wilde	4 (3)	Beckett	2 (2)
Orton	4 (2)	Shaw	2 (2)
Feydeau	3 (3)	Singer	2 (2)
Shepard	3 (3)		

ABINGDON, VA.

Barter Theater

LAST OF THE RED HOT LOVERS (21). By Neil Simon. June 6, 1972. Director, Owen Phillips; scenery, Bennet Averyt; lighting, Stuart Richman; costumes, Evelyn Moricle. With Haskell Gordon, Jennifer Warren, Ellen March, Dorothy Marie.

THE COUNTRY GIRL (15). By Clifford Odets. June 20, 1972. Director Rae Allen; Scenery, Richard Davis; lighting, Stuart Richman; costumes Evelyn Moricle. With Ann Buckles, Robert Blackburn, George Nahoom.

BUTTERFLIES ARE FREE (40). By Leonard Gershe. July 4, 1972. Director, Kristina Callahan; scenery, Bennet Averyt; lighting, Stuart Richman; costumes, Evelyn Moricle. With Milton Tarver, Caryll Coan, Nancy Coleman, Joe Russo.

HARVEY (19). By Mary Chase. July 18, 1972. Director, Owen Phillips; scenery, Richard Davis; lighting, Stuart Richman; costumes; Evelyn Moricle. With Robert Blackburn, Nancy Coleman, Beth Dixon.

SUMMER AND SMOKE (24). By Tennessee Williams. August 22, 1972. Director, George Touliatos; scenery, Bennet Averyt; lighting, Stuart Richman; costumes, Evelyn Moricle. With Sheila Russell, Milton Tarver, Richard Sanders, Marcia Bennett.

DEAR LIAR (16). By Jerome Kilty; adapted from the correspondence of George Bernard Shaw and Mrs. Patrick Campbell. Director, Owen Phillips; lighting, Stuart Richman; costumes, Evelyn Moricle. With Michaele Myers, Dalton Dearborn.

YOU KNOW I CAN'T HEAR YOU WHEN THE WATER'S RUNNING (24). By Robert Anderson. October 10, 1972. Director, John Going; lighting, Stuart Richman. With Milton Tarver, Caryll Coan, Joe Russo, Richard Sanders, Jo Henderson.

SPOON RIVER ANTHOLOGY (28). By Charles Aidman, adapted and arranged from Edgar Lee Masters's poems. April 9, 1973. Director, Rex Partington; lighting, David Mazikowski; costumes, Marianne Powell-Parker.

With David Darlow, Eda Zahl, George Hosmer, Barbara Tarbuck, Mary Gallagher, Richard Leigh.

THE COMEDY OF ERRORS (21). By William Shakespeare. April 30, 1973. Director, Owen Phillips; scenery, Bennet Averyt; lighting, David Mazikowski; costumes, Marianne Powell-Parker. With David Darlow, Michael Tolaydo, Josef Warik, Charles Thomas Harper, Eda Zahl.

ASHLAND, ORE.

Oregon Shakespearean Festival: Elizabethan Theater

THE TAMING OF THE SHREW (27). By William Shakespeare. June 24, 1972. Director, Robert Benedetti; scenery, Richard L. Hay; costumes, Jean Schultz Davidson. With Jim Edmondson, Elizabeth Cole, Alice Rorvik, Jeffrey Brooks.

LOVE'S LABOUR'S LOST (26). By William Shakespeare. June 25, 1972. Director, Laird Williamson; scenery, Richard L. Hay; lighting,

Jerry Glenn; costumes, Jean Schultz Davidson. With Elizabeth McAninch, Tom Donaldson, Michael Winters, Philip Davidson.

HENRY IV, PART 2 (25). By William Shakespeare. June 26, 1972. Director, William Roberts; scenery, Richard L. Hay; costumes, Jean Schultz Davidson. With Powers Boothe, Garry Moore, Alice Rorvik, Diana Bellamy.

Oregon Shakespearean Festival: Angus Bowmer Theater

TROILUS AND CRESSIDA (25). By William Shakespeare. July 1, 1972. Director, Jerry Turner; scenery, Richard L. Hay; lighting, Steven Maze; costumes, Jean Schultz Davidson. With Janie Atkins, Joel Colodner, Richard Allan Edwards, Laird Williamson, Tom Donaldson.

THE CRUCIBLE (24). By Arthur Miller. July 2, 1972. Director, Pat Patton; scenery, Richard L. Hay; lighting, Steven Maze; costumes, Jean Schultz Davidson. With Edna Sterling, Stephanie Voss, Garry Moore, Elizabeth Cole, Philip Davidson.

UNCLE VANYA (23). By Anton Chekhov; adapted by Larry Oliver. July 4, 1972. Director, Larry Oliver; scenery, Richard L. Hay; lighting, Steven Maze; costumes, Jean Schultz Davidson. With Elizabeth Cole, Michael Winters, Laird Williamson, Shirley Patton, Mary Turner.

THE IMPORTANCE OF BEING EARNEST (12). By Oscar Wilde. March 9, 1973. Director Jim Edmondson; scenery, Richard L. Hay;

lighting, Steven Maze; costumes, Jean Schultz Davidson. With Garry Moore, Peter Silbert, le Clanche du Rand, Elizabeth Cole, Denene von Glan.

OUR TOWN (11). By Thornton Wilder. March 10, 1973 (matinee). Director, Pat Patton; scenery, Richard L. Hay; lighting, Steven Maze; costumes, Jean Schultz Davidson. With Jim Edmondson, Michael Winters, Margit Moe, Aldena Leonard, Will Huddleston, Karen Seal, Philip Davidson.

OTHELLO (11). By William Shakespeare. March 10, 1973 (evening). Director, Jerry Turner; scenery, Richard L. Hay; lighting, Steven Maze; costumes, Jean Schultz Davidson. With Ernie Stewart, Laird Williamson, Denene von Glan, Elizabeth Cole.

THE ALCHEMIST (10). By Ben Jonson. March 11, 1973. Director, Laird Williamson; scenery, Richard L. Hay; lighting, Steven Maze; costumes, Jean Schultz Davidson. With Jim Edmondson, Richard Leonard, Karen Seal, Ernie Stewart, Michael Winters.

BALTIMORE

Center Stage

ONE FLEW OVER THE CUCKOO'S NEST (28). By Dale Wasserman, based on the novel

by Ken Kesey. October 24, 1972. Director, Harvey Medlinsky; designer, Raymond C.

Recht; costumes, Mary Strieff. With George Shannon, Millie Slavin, Manu Tupou, Robert Chamberlain.

DANDY DICK (28). By Arthur Wing Pinero. November 28, 1972. Director, John Stix; scenery and costumes, John Boyt; lighting, Ray Recht. With Henry Strozier, Betty Sinclair, Carl Shurr, Richard Dix.

TWO SAINTS: GIMPEL THE FOOL by Isaac Bashevis Singer; adapted by Larry Arrick; lyrics by Barbara Damashek and ST. JULIAN THE HOSPITALER by Gustave Flaubert; adaptation and lyrics by Kenneth Cavander (28). January 2, 1973. Director, Larry Arrick; scenery and lighting, Raymond C. Recht; costumes, Juliellen Weiss; music, Barbara Damashek. With C. David Colson, Barbara Damashek, Nancy Franklin, Wil Love, Carl Shurr, Henry Strozier, Shana Sullivan.

JULIUS CAESAR (28). By William Shakespeare. February 6, 1973. Director, Mitchell Nestor; designer, Raymond C. Recht. With Henry Strozier, Lane Smith, Wil Love, Bert Houle, Richard Dix, Jan Rothman, James Tokan.

THE PETRIFIED FOREST (28). By Robert E. Sherwood. March 13, 1973. Director, John Stix; scenery and lighting, Bennet Averyt; costumes, Mary Strieff. With Edward Bell, Liz Kemp, Lane Smith, Henry Strozier.

THE ME NOBODY KNOWS (28). By Robert H. Livingston and Herb Schapiro, based on a book of the same name; music, Gary William Friedman; lyrics, Will Holt. April 10, 1973. Director, Robert H. Livingston; musical director, John Sichina; choreography, Gerri Dean; designer, Raymond C. Recht; costumes, Mary Strieff. With Hector Mercado, Margaret Stuart-Ramsey, Charlotte Johnson, Jean Thaxton, Cheryl Brown, Troy McQuaige, Ronnie Duncan.

BOSTON

Theater Company of Boston

PLAY STRINDBERG (16). By Friedrich Duerrenmatt; translated from the original German by James Kirkup. December 5, 1972. Director, F.M. Kimball; scenery and costumes, Franco Colavecchia; lighting, Richard Lee. With Paul Benedict, Larry Bryggman, Stockard Canning.

RICHARD III (20). By William Shakespeare. February 3, 1973. Director, David Wheeler; scenery, Michael Anania; lighting, Cameron Forbes; costumes, Marsha MacDonald. With Al Pacino, Penelope Allen, Paul Benedict, Jan Egleson, Lance J. Henriksen.

OLD TIMES (25). By Harold Pinter. March 6, 1973. Directors, David Wheeler and William Young; scenery, Lance J. Henriksen and Jan Egleson; lighting, Cameron Forbes and Maureen Gibson. With Paul Benedict, Roberta Collinge, Linda Selman.

BUFFALO

Studio Arena Theater

ROBERTA (30). Book and lyrics by Otto Harbach, based on a story by Alice Duer Miller; music by Jerome Kern; additional lyrics by Dorothy Fields. October 12, 1972. Director, William Gile; musical director, William R. Cox; choreography, Bick Goss; scenery, Larry Aumen; lighting, David Zierk; costumes, Duane Andersen. With Lilia Skala, Michael Beirne, Bonnie Franklin, Tricia O'Neil, Lee Roy Reams, Michael Prince.

SITTING and THE SAVING GRACE (30). By John Tobias. November 9, 1972 (world premiere). Director, Leland Ball; scenery, Karl Eigsti; lighting, Peter J. Gill; costumes, Evelyn Lea Moricle.
Sitting

Man .... John Newton
Boy .... Winifred Williams III
Mrs. Box .... June Squibb
First Workman .... Ric Mancini
Second Workman .... Samuel Barton
The Saving Grace
Godbrother; Moon .... Samuel Barton
Suburban Negro-
Mendesilo .... Earl Milton Forrest
Policeman .... Ric Mancini
The Girl .... Jeanne De Baer
Osgood Whitelaw .... Rod Browning
Miss Rackley .... June Squibb
Two acts.

PETER PAN (30). Book by James M. Barrie; music by Mark Charlap; music by Carolyn Leigh; additional music by Jule Styne; additional lyrics by Betty Comden and Adolph Green. December 7, 1972. Director and choreographer, Bick Goss; musical director, Lawrence J. Blank; scenery, Kenneth Foy; lighting, Peter J. Gill; costumes, Evelyn Lea Moricle. With Bonnie Franklin, Stephen Arlen, Mary Jane Houdina, Marsha Kramer, Mary Woman . . . . Dorothy Chace Meikelham, Craig Bundy.

RING-A-LEVIO (30). Book by Donald Ross; music by Lance Mulcahy; lyrics by Jason Darrow. January 4, 1973 (world premiere). Director, Paul Aaron; musical director, Rod Derefinko; orchestrations, Arthur B. Rubinstein; choreography, Tony Stevens; scenery and lighting, David F. Segal; costumes, Karen Laurie Roston.

Reuben Fraser . . . . Harvey Evans
Rocky . . . . Susan Campbell
Mrs. Fraser . . . . Camila Ashland
Old Man; Guide . . . . Bernard Erhard
LeRoy . . . . Alan Brasington
Butch . . . . Paul Farin
Irene . . . . Merry Flershem
Sally . . . . Mary Jane Houdina
Willie . . . . Erik Robinson
Brenda . . . . Renee Semes
Charlotte . . . . Mychelle Smiley
Harold . . . . Bob Spencer
    Time: The Present. Place: The city. Two acts.

BUTTERFLIES ARE FREE (32). By Leonard Gershe. January 30, 1973. Director, Elizabeth Caldwell; scenery, Douglas F. Lebrecht; lighting, Peter J. Gill. With Celeste Holm, Kipp Osborne, Erin Connor, Raymond Cole.

THE TAMING OF THE SHREW (30). By William Shakespeare. March 1, 1973. Director, Warren Enters; scenery, Douglas F. Lebrecht; lighting, Peter J. Gill; costumes, Lurena McDonald. With Richard Green, Linda Carlson, Kathleen Doyle, Paul Milikin.

CHILD'S PLAY (30). By Robert Marasco. April 5, 1973. Director, Warren Enters; scenery, Douglas F. Lebrecht; lighting, Peter J. Gill; costumes, Pearl Smith. With Donald Moffat, Ronald Bishop, Dale Helward.

BERLIN TO BROADWAY WITH KURT WEILL (22). Music by Kurt Weill; lyrics by Maxwell Anderson, Bertolt Brecht, Michael Feingold, Paul Green, Alan Jay Lerner, George Tabori, Marc Blitzstein, Jacques Deval, Ira Gershwin, Langston Hughes, Ogden Nash. May 3, 1973. Director, Richard Landon; musical director and conductor, Robert Rogers; text and format, Gene Lerner; arrangements, Newton Wayland; scenery, Douglas F. Lebrecht; lighting, Mark Kruger; costumes, Christine Cotter. With Stephen Arlen, Susan Campbell, Margery Cohen, Dale Helward, Hal Watters.

BURLINGTON, VT.

Champlain Shakespeare Festival: University of Vermont Arena Theater

THE MERRY WIVES OF WINDSOR (14). By William Shakespeare. July 26, 1972. Director, Edward J. Feidner; scenery and lighting, William M. Schenk; lighting, Gregory MacPherson; costumes, Julie Schwalow. With Maxim Mazumdar, Rob Evan Collins, Jeanne De Baer, Anastasia Lyman.

AS YOU LIKE IT (13). By William Shakespeare. July 28, 1972. Director, Ernest Cabrera; scenery, William M. Schenk; lighting,

Gregory MacPherson; costumes, Julie Schwalow. With Jeanne De Baer, William Lyman, Rob Evan Collins, Susan Freeman.

TITUS ANDRONICUS (11). By William Shakespeare. August 2, 1972. Director, Edward J. Feidner; scenery, William M. Schenk; lighting, Gregory MacPherson; costumes, Julie Schwalow. With Randy Kim, Maxim Mazumdar, Jeanne De Baer.

CHICAGO

The Goodman Theater Center: Goodman Memorial Theater

OLD TIMES (44). By Harold Pinter. October 8, 1972. Director, Michael Kahn; scenery, Marjorie Kellogg; lighting, G. E. Naselius. With Donald Madden, Tudi Wiggins, Sharon Laughlin.

SCENES FROM AMERICAN LIFE (44). By A. R. Gurney Jr. November 26, 1972. Director, Harold Stone; scenery, David Jenkins;

lighting, Beverly Emmons; costumes, Alicia Finkel; musical director, Bill McCauley. With Chet Carlin, Susan Merson, Anthony Mockus, Gretchen Oehler, Roy K. Stevens, Marcy Vosburgh, Tudi Wiggins, Jerry Zafer.

IN THE MATTER OF J. ROBERT OPPENHEIMER (44). By Heinar Kipphardt; translated by Ruth Speirs. January 7, 1973. Director, Gene Lesser; scenery and visual effects, Robert U. Taylor; lighting, William Mintzer; costumes, Virgil Johnson. With William Prince, Maurice D. Copeland, Charles Randall, Jerome Dempsey, Michael Granger.

TWENTIETH CENTURY (44). By Ben Hecht and Charles MacArthur, with Bruce Milholland. February 18, 1973. Director, William Woodman; scenery and lighting, Clarke Dunham; costumes, Virgil Johnson. With Merwin Goldsmith, Ken Parker, Jerome Dempsey, Jan Farrand.

THE LADY'S NOT FOR BURNING (44). By Christopher Fry. April 1, 1973. Director,

Stephen Porter; scenery and costumes, Alicia Finkel; lighting, G. E. Naselius. With John Cullum, Tudi Wiggins, Merwin Goldsmith, Roy K. Stevens.

PAL JOEY (44+). By John O'Hara; music by Richard Rodgers; lyrics by Lorenz Hart. May 13, 1973. Director, Melvin Bernhardt; musical director, Daryl Wagner; choreographer, Joyce Trisler; scenery and costumes, Alicia Finkel; lighting, G. E. Naselius. With Anthony S. Teague, Nancy Marchand, Marti Rolph, Barbara Erwin.

Goodman Theater: Guest Production

GILGAMESH (8). Adapted and directed by Larry Arrick. November 14, 1972. Scenery, David Hays; lighting, John Gleason; costumes, Fred Voelpel. With Bernard Bragg, Edmund

Waterstreet, Joseph Sarpy, Mary Beth Miller and members of the National Theater of the Deaf Company.

Goodman Theater: Children's Theater Company

SLEEPING BEAUTY or THE GREAT ROSE TABOO (18). Book and lyrics by Barbara Fried; music by Norman Sachs. October 1, 1972 (world premiere). Director and choreographer, Kelly Danford; scenery, David Emmons; lighting, Paul Gregory; costumes, Martha Ferrera.

Sorceror ....R. J. Frank
Good Fairy ....Phyllis Ward
Bad Fairy ....Angeliki Stathakis
Queen ....Susan Brashear
King ....David Brenton
Prince Charming ....Gisli Bjorgvinnson
Fairy Godfather ....John Bannick
Princess Beauty ....Sarah Frutig
Guinevere ....Sharon Lea Standler
Anastasia ....Krisha J. Fairchild
Alphone ....Brian Clare
Leopold ....Anson Downes
    Place: Far away. Time: Long ago. The action takes place in a clearing outside the Good Fairy's house; at the castle; outside Prince Charming's palace; and in a magic wood.

LITTLE RED RIDING HOOD (18). By Eugene Schwartz; translated by George Shail. November 19, 1972. Director, Libby Appel; music, Phillip Kusie; choreography, Beth Caldwell; scenery, Vincent Faust; lighting, James F. Highland; costumes, Julie Nagel; animal puppets, David Emmons. With Sandra Gray, Susan

Wolfson, Peter Zopp, Timothy Hagen.

THE THREE MUSKETEERS (22). By Brian Way; adapted from the novel by Alexandre Dumas. January 28, 1973. Director, John Medici; choreography, Estelle Spector; scenery, William Schmiel; lighting, Marsha Hardy; costumes, Pepper Ross. With Donald Smith, Steven Fletcher, Daniel Goodring, Philip Kusie.

THE COMICAL TRAGEDY or TRAGICAL COMEDY OF PUNCH AND JUDY (25). By Aurand Harris. March 25, 1973 (world premiere). Director, Ned Schmidtke; composer and arranger, David Beaird; choreography, Estelle Spector; scenery, Jeffrey Masters; lighting, Phillip A. Evola; costumes, Julie Nagel.

Toby ....Edward Wass
Punch ....Yancy Bukovec
Musician ....Sharon Lea Standler
Judy ....Kathy Deligianis
Puppets:
Professor; Policeman;
    Guard ....Anson Downes
Hector; Devil ....Sydney Skipper
Hector; Hangman ....Kip Gillespie
Doctor; Guard ....Tim Oman
Ghosts ....Sharon Lee Standler,
                       Kathy Deligianis

Note: The Goodman Theater Center Professional Touring Company presented *Speed Gets the Poppies,* an anti-drug musical melodrama for young people and *It Certainly Isn't Baked Beans,* a dramatic anthology based on children's literature, adapted and starring Bob Gibson. Also, in association with the Museum of Science and Industry and made possible through a grant from the National Science Foundation, *Lamp at Midnight* by Barrie Stavis, directed by Kelly Danford, November 6, 1972 (7); *Dr. Dan: A Pioneer in Heart Surgery* by Tom Zito, directed by Kelly Danford, April 26, 1973 (7).

CINCINNATI

Playhouse in the Park: Robert S. Morse Theater

SHELTER (22). Book and lyrics by Gretchen Cryer; music by Nancy Ford, June 1, 1972 (world premiere). Director, Word Baker; musical directors, George Broderick, Worth Gardner; scenery, Ed Wittstein; lighting, David F. Segal; costumes, Caley Summers; properties, Tom Oldendick.

Penelope; Maud .... Marcia Rodd
Michael .... Keith Charles
Wednesday November ...... Susan Browning
Gloria .... Anne Murray
Arthur (not seen) .... Charles Collins
Director (not seen) .... Philip Kraus
 TV Crew: Mark Brown, Maureen Flanigan, David Holbrook, Richard Jaffe, Richard Michaelson, Richard Loder, Linda Nolan, Charlotte Patton, Nancy Scanlon, Connie Shutt, Margo Bourgeois, Marja Scheeres.

THE PLAY'S THE THING (22). By Ferenc Molnar. July 6, 1972. Director, Word Baker; scenery, Tom Oldendick; lighting, John McLain; costumes, Caley Summers. With Rene Assa, Charles Berendt, Sirin Devrim, Philip Minor.

SENSATIONS OF THE BITTEN PARTNER (14). By Milburn Smith. August 3, 1972 (world premiere). Director, Word Baker; scenery, William F. Matthews; lighting, John McLain; costumes, Caley Summers; properties, Tom Oldendick.

Ann .... Swoosie Kurtz
Michael .... T. Richard Mason
Janet .... Karin Patterson
Mrs. Young .... Anne Shropshire

THE RIVALS (14). By Richard Brinsley Sheridan. September 7, 1972. Directors Word Baker, Donald L. Brooks; scenery, William F. Matthews; lighting, John McLain; costumes, Caley Summers. With Dorothy Chace, Jack Gwillim, Flair Bogan.

THE CRUCIBLE (14). By Arthur Miller. September 21, 1972. Directors, Word Baker, Dan Early; scenery, Paul Shortt; lighting, John McLain; costumes, Caley Summers. With T. Richard Mason, Patty Romito, Jack Gwillim, Frank Raiter, Georgia Spelvin, Flair Bogan.

BABOON!!! (14). Conceived by Word Baker with Dan Early, Maria Irene Fornes, Milburn Smith, Sherman F. Warner and the company. October 5, 1972 (world premiere). Director, Word Baker. With Adrian Berwick, Flair Bogan, George Brengel, Thomas Burke, Dorothy Chace, Debby Deguire, Dan Early, Laura Edwards, Jonathan Fairbanks, Tony Gaetano, Sally Gensler, Jack Gwillim, Dana Hibbard, Philip Kraus, Richard Loder, David Mack, T. Richard Mason, Paul Milikin, Georgia Neu, Charlotte Patton, Frank Raiter, Patty Romito, Marja Scheeres, Oliver Schwab, Anita Trotta, David Wiles, Gene Wolters, Edward Zang.

A DELICATE BALANCE (22) By Edward Albee. February 1, 1973. Director, Harold Scott; scenery, Stuart Wurtzel; lighting, John Gleason; costumes, Caley Summers. With Jill Andre, Carolyn Coates, James Noble, Patricia Falkenhain, Robert Gerringer, Katherine Rao.

LONG DAY'S JOURNEY INTO NIGHT (22). By Eugene O'Neill. March 1, 1973. Director, Harold Scott; scenery, Stuart Wurtzel; lighting, Arden Fingerhut; costumes, Caley Summers. With Robert Gerringer, Carolyn Coates, James Noble, Benjamin Masters, Enid Kent.

A STREETCAR NAMED DESIRE (22). By Tennessee Williams. March 29, 1973. Director, Glenn Jordan; scenery, Stuart Wurtzel; lighting, John Gleason; costumes, Caley Summers. With Carrie Nye, Barbara Eda Young, Lloyd Battista, James Ray.

INCIDENT AT VICHY (22). By Arthur Miller. April 26, 1973. Director, Harold Scott; scenery, Stuart Wurtzel; lighting, Arden Fingerhut; costumes, Caley Summers. With James Noble, James Ray, Gene Wolters, Henry Winkler.

A RAISIN IN THE SUN (22). By Lorraine Hansberry. May 24, 1973. Director, Edmund Cambridge; scenery, Tom Oldendick; lighting, John Gleason; costumes, Caley Summers. With Harold Scott, Michele Shay, Gertrude Jeannete, Hannibal Penney, Jr., Sylvia Soars.

CLEVELAND

The Cleveland Play House: Euclid-77th Street Theater

A YARD OF SUN (24). By Christopher Fry. October 13, 1972 (American premiere). Director, José Ferrer; scenery, Richard Gould; lighting, William J. Plachy; costumes, Estelle H. Painter.

Angelino Bruno ....Edmund Lyndeck
Roberto ....Jonathan Farwell
Luigi ....John Buck Jr.
Edmondo ....John David
Giosetta Scapare ....Evie McElroy
Grazia ....Carolyn Younger
Alfio ....Douglas Jones
Franco ....Robert Snook
Ana-Clara ....Brenda Curtis
Ettore ....Dale E. Place
Piero Martini ....William Burnett
Cesare Scapare ....George Touliatos
Men of the Town: Candace Ann Corr, Eugene Hare, Daniel Morris, Ralph Neeley, Michelle Reilley
Time: July 1946. Place: The courtyard of the Palazzo del Traguardo, Siena. Two acts.

THE SHORT MAGICAL MINISTRY OF THE REVEREND DOCTOR JOHN FAUST (17). By J. Ranelli; concept developed in rehearsal by the company. November 17, 1972 (world premiere). Director, J. Ranelli; scenery, Richard Gould; lighting, William J. Plachy; costumes, Bernadette O'Brien, Estelle H. Painter.
John Faust ....Jonathan Farwell

Curate ....William Burnett
The Girl; Laura ....Carolyn Younger
Professor Wolders ....Robert Allman
Mephistopheles ....John Buck Jr.
Lucifer ....Robert Snook
Chantress ....Michelle Reilley
Celeris ....Julia Curry
Vannus ....Dale E. Place
Asmodeus ....John Bergstrom
Beelzebuth ....Allen Leatherman
Ephemera, Jean Barrett, Brenda Curtis, Candace Ann Corr, Bill Jones, Bob Moak, Daniel Morris, Ralph Neeley, Marcus Smythe, George Touliatos.
The action of the play is continuous and takes place on Easter Eve.

BUTTERFLIES ARE FREE (36). By Leonard Gershe. December 15, 1972. Director, George Touliatos; designer, Richard Gould; costumes, Harriet Cone. With Douglas Jones, Julia Curry, Peggy Roeder, John Bergstrom.

ONE FLEW OVER THE CUCKOO'S NEST (35). By Dale Wasserman, based on the novel by Ken Kesey. February 17, 1973. Director, Larry Tarrant; scenery, Richard Gould; lighting, Larry Jameson; costumes, Harriet Cone. With Victor Carroll, Jo Farwell, Bob Moak, Norm Berman, John Buck Jr.

The Cleveland Play House: Drury Theater

THE SHOW-OFF (17). By George Kelly. October 20, 1972. Director, Jonathan Bolt; scenery, Richard Gould; lighting, John Rolland; costumes, Harriet Cone. With Bob Moak, June Gibbons, Allen Leatherman, Robert Allman, John Bergstrom, Jo Farwell.

JOHNNY NO-TRUMP (12). By Mary Mercier. November 24, 1972. Director, Jonathan Bolt; scenery, Richard Gould; lighting, John Rolland; costumes, Harriet Cone. With Richard Oberlin, Douglas Jones, Evie McElroy, Richard Halverson, Dorothy Paxton.

SHERLOCK HOLMES (28). By William Gillette; adapted by Dennis Rosa. December 22, 1972. Director, Dennis Rosa; scenery and lighting, Richard Gould; costumes, Estelle

H. Painter. With Jonathan Farwell, Robert Snook, Robert Allman, Brenda Curtis, Edith Owen.

THE LOVES OF CASS McGUIRE (23). By Brian Friel. February 23, 1973. Director, Edmund Lyndeck; scenery, Richard Gould; lighting, John Rolland; costumes, Harriet Cone. With June Gibbons, Robert Allman, Richard Halverson, Margaret Hilton, Ibby Hardies.

ROMEO AND JULIET (13). By William Shakespeare. April 6, 1973. Director, Dennis Rosa; scenery, Richard Gould; lighting, William J. Plachy; costumes, Jo Dale Lunday. With Douglas Jones, Brenda Curtis, John Bergstrom, Evie McElroy.

The Cleveland Play House: Brooks Theater

RICHARD MORSE MIME THEATER (18). February 9, 1973. With Richard Morse, Pilar

Garcia.

In repertory:

THE CARETAKER (20). By Harold Pinter. November 30, 1972. Director, Richard Morse; designer, Barbara Leatherman. With Jonathan Bolt, John David.

OLD TIMES (20). By Harold Pinter. December 1, 1972. Director, Evie McElroy; designer, Barbara Leatherman. With Edmund Lyndeck, Myrna Kaye, Jo Farwell.

THE RABINOWITZ GAMBIT (23). By Rose Leiman Goldemberg. April 13, 1973 (world premiere). Director, Jonathan Farwell; scenery, Richard Gould; lighting, Larry Jameson; costumes, Estelle H. Painter.

Irving Rabinowitz	Norm Berman
Blitz	Richard Morse
Jerry	Ralph Neeley
Niele Teague	Kerry Slattery
The Etcetera	Richard Halverson

Time: New Year's Eve. Place: In and around a hotel room in mid-Manhattan. Three acts.

DALLAS

Dallas Theater Center—Kalita Humphreys Theater

THE HOUSE OF BLUE LEAVES (27). By John Guare. June 6, 1972. Director, Sally Netzel; scenery, Nancy Levinson; lighting, Linda Blase; costumes, Patricia Lobit. With Synthia Rogers, Mona Pursley, Ryland Merkey.

WIND IN THE BRANCHES OF THE SASSAFRAS (33). By Rene De Obaldia; translated by Joseph Foster. July 11, 1972 (American premiere). Director, Ryland Merkey; designer, John Henson; lighting, Sally Netzel; music, John Lee Nowlin.

John Emery	
Rockefeller	James Nelson Harrell
Tom	Randolph Tallman
Caroline	Lynn Trammell
Dr. William Butler	Michael Dendy
Pamela	Cindy Holden
Partridge Eye and	
Lynx Eye	Carlos Gonzalez
Carlos	Chelcie Ross

Time: The beginning of the 19th century. Place: The frontier cabin of the Rockefellers, a pioneer family in Kentucky. Three acts.

THE EFFECT OF GAMMA RAYS ON MAN-IN-THE-MOON MARIGOLDS (19). By Paul Zindel. September 12, 1972. Director, Michael Dendy; designer, Yoichi Aoki; lighting, Allen Hibbard. With Sally Netzel, Margaret Tallman, Ellen Lynskey.

THE HAPPY HUNTER (27). By Georges Feydeau; English adaptation by Barnett Shaw. October 24, 1972 (American premiere). Director, John Reich; scenery, David Pursley; lighting, Robyn Flatt; costumes, John Henson; lyrics for *The Hunting Song* by Barnett Shaw.

Roussel	Randy Moore
Yvonne Chandel	Carol Teitel
Chandel	Ryland Merkey

Babette	Martha Robinson Goodman
Pierre	John Figlmiller
Senor Castillo	Preston Jones
Madame de Latour	Judith Davis
Inspector Duval	Barry Hope
1st Policeman	John A. Black
2d Policeman	B.J. Theus

Time: Around 1900. Place: Paris. Act I: Afternoon, the Chandel's study. Act II: Evening, Roussel's love nest at 35 Avenue Gambetta. Act III: Morning, same as Act I. One intermission after Act II.

LIFE WITH FATHER (33). By Howard Lindsay and Russel Crouse. November 28, 1972. Director, David Pursley; scenery and costumes, Kathleen Latimer; lighting, Sam Nance. With Chelcie Ross, Louise Mosley, Allen Hibbard, Kerry Newcomb, John Stevens, Claudia Latimer.

SUMMER AND SMOKE (33). By Tennessee Williams. January 16, 1973. Director, Mary Sue Jones; scenery, Yoichi Aoki; lighting, Randy Moore; costumes, David Pursley. With Robyn Flatt, John Figlmiller, Michael Dendy, Lynn Trammell, Cecilia Flores, Gary Moore.

JABBERWOCK (33). By Jerome Lawrence and Robert E. Lee; adapted from the life and writings of James Thurber. March 6, 1973 (world premiere). Director, Jerome Lawrence; scenery, David Pursley; lighting, John Henson; costumes, Margaret Tallman.

Jamie Thurber	Steven Mackenroth
Herman Thurber	Michael Russell
Charley Thurber	John Hallowell Jr.
Roy Thurber	John Bundy Bratcher
Mary Agnes Thurber	Mary Sue Jones
Grandpa Fisher	Randy Moore
Doc Marlowe	Ken Latimer
Georgiana	Martha Robinson Goodman
General Littlefield	Barry Hope

Get-Ready-Man ....Brian O'Reilly
Mrs. Bodwell;
   War Bond Girl ....Judith Rhodes
Mr. Bodwell;
   Carpenter; Moving Man ....James Smith
Professor Welch;
   ROTC Band ....Randolph Tallman
Dr. Ridgeway ....John Henson
Dr. Quimby ....Joseph Nilson
Mr. Briscoe ....William Landry
Police Sergeant ....Chelcie Ross
1st Policeman ....Tom Cantu
2d Policeman ....Richard Carlson
3d Policeman;
   Electrician ....Allen Hibbard
Reporter; Recruiting Sgt. ......Lyle Maurer
Draftee ....Michael Mullen
A Swarm of Aunts:
   Aunt Esther ....Elfriede Russell
   Aunt Belinda ....Judy Dockrey
   Aunt Ida ....Suzanne Theus
   Aunt Fanny ....Daryl Conner
   Aunt Minnie ....Mary Rohde
   Aunt Charlotte ....Synthia Rogers

Aunt Bessie ....Cindy Holden
Aunt Sarah ....Nancy Krebs
A Pride of Maids:
   Dora ....Deborah Mogford
   Mrs. Weir ....Sally Netzel
   Lily Loomis ....Denise Waters
   Gertie Straub ....Judith Davis
Moving Man ....Terry Clotiaux
Place: The Thurber menage in Columbus, Ohio; also various haunts above, below and beyond High Street. Act I: When Woodrow Wilson was keeping us out of war. Act II: When Woodrow Wilson, Mary Agnes, Grandpa and others were making the world safe for democracy. Two acts.

HOW THE OTHER HALF LOVES (33). By Alan Ayckbourn. April 17, 1973. Director, Sally Netzel; scenery, John Henson; lighting, Allen Hibbard; costumes, Bonnie Stroup. With David Pursley, Mona Pursley, Randolph Tallman, Linda Daugherty, Brian O'Reilly, Margaret Tallman.

Dallas Theater Center: Down Center Stage

THE ANNIVERSARY—EL ANIVERSARIO and THE MARRIAGE PROPOSAL—PROPUESTA DE MATRIMONIO (10). By Anton Chekhov; adapted by Leo Lavandero into English and Spanish. October 5, 1972. Director, Leo Lavandero; scenery, Judith Ann Cuesta; lighting, Linda Blase; costumes, Linda Daugherty.

ENDGAME (18). By Samuel Beckett. November 9, 1972. Director, Ken Latimer; scenery, Allen Hubbard; lighting, Sam Nance; costumes, Yoichi Aoki. With Randolph Tallman, Herman Wheatley, T. Alan Doss, Linda Daugherty.

TO BE YOUNG, GIFTED AND BLACK (15). By Robert Nemiroff; adapted from the work of Lorraine Hansberry. December 21, 1972. Director, Judith Davis; scenery and photography, Linda Blase; lighting, John Henson; costumes, Gloria Bernal-Guinn. With Larry Kennedy, Chequita Jackson, Johanna Clayton, Reginald Montgomery, Steven Mackenroth, Mona Pursley, Norma Moore, Sharon West.

OLD TIMES (15). By Harold Pinter. February 1, 1973. Director, Ryland Merkey; designer, Nancy Levinson; lighting, Russell Guinn. With Preston Jones, Mona Pursley, Jacque Thomas.

MOON ON A RAINBOW SHAWL (15). By Errol John. March 15, 1973. Director, Reginald Montgomery; scenery, Sam Nance; lighting, Barry Hope; costumes, Chequita

Jackson. With Larry Kennedy, Ronni Lopez, Sharon West, Greg Poe, Gerald Jines.

IF YOU SEE ANY LADIES by James Crump; THE NOVITIATES by Denise Chavez; QUINCUNX by Celia Karston (12). May 3, 1973 (world premiere).
If You See Any Ladies
John Tudor ....Daniel Turner
Martin ....Robert Duffy
"Senator" Paul Webb ....Bryant J. Reynolds
Gil Kyson ....John Hallowell Jr.
Jay Lindsley ....Bob Dickson
Julia Chance ....Diana Shriner
Vision ....Denise Waters
   Director, Yoichi Aoki; scenery, Gerald Jines; lighting, Russell Guinn; costumes, Judith Rhodes.
The Novitiates
Alex ....Richard Carlson
Chris ....Suzanne Theus
Grandma ....Marilyn Goss
Cast of Thousands ....Keith Dixon
   Director, Kerry Newcomb; scenery, Gerald Jines, lighting, Russell Guinn; costumes, Jacque Gavin.
   Place: Bedrooms.
Quincunx
Aries ....William Landry
Libra ....Cindy Holden
Taurus ....Mary Rohde
Sagittarius ....Michael Mullen
Pisces ....Gloria Bernal-Guinn
   Director, Kevin Kelley; scenery, Gerald Jines; lighting, Russell Guinn; costumes, Mary Rohde.

Dallas Theater Center: Children's Theater

HEIDI (8). By Lucille Miller, adapted from the novel by Johanna Spri. October 28, 1972. Director, Steven Mackenroth; scenery, Russell Guinn; lighting, Gerald Jines; costumes, Daryl Conner. With Susan Anderson, Paul Callihan.

WINNIE THE POOH (13). By A.A. Milne; adapted for the stage by Kristin Sergel. December 16, 1972. Director, Sally Netzel; scenery, Bonnie Stroub; lighting, Russell Guinn; costumes, Sallie Laurie. With John Bundy Bratcher, Joseph Wilson.

THE RED SHOES (8). By Robin Short; based on the fairy tale by Hans Christian Andersen. January 27, 1973. Director, Bryant J. Reynolds; scenery, Linda Daugherty; lighting, Bob Dickson; costumes, Sherry Reynolds; choreography, Margaret Tallman. With Ellen Lynskey, Randolf Pearson.

THE ADVENTURES OF RAGGEDY ANN AND RAGGEDY ANDY (9). Basic script by Kevin Kelley. March 31, 1973. Directors, John Stevens, Robyn Flatt; scenery, Dandy Pearson; lighting, Tommy Duplissey; costumes, Peter Lynch.

Note: The Dallas Theater Center also presented a 1972 summer season of the Janus Players in the Lay Studio and the Kalita Humphreys Theater. *Ceremonies in Dark Old Men* (15) by Lonne Elder III, directed by Reginald Montgomery; *Frankenstein's Monster* (10) by Sally Netzel, adapted from the novel by Mary Shelley, directed by Judith Davis; *La Conquista De Mexico* (9) adapted and directed by Cecilia Flores.

HARTFORD

Hartford Stage Company

THE MISANTHROPE (44). By Molière; English verse translation by Richard Wilbur. October 6, 1972. Director, Paul Weidner; scenery, John Conklin; lighting, Larry Crimmins; costumes, Victoria Zussin. With Chris Sarandon, Ted Graeber, David O. Petersen, Pamela Gilbreath.

A STREETCAR NAMED DESIRE (44). By Tennessee Williams. November 24, 1972. Director, Jacques Cartier; scenery, Santo Loquasto; lighting, Larry Crimmins; costumes, Linda Fisher. With Tony Musante, Angela Thornton, Lynn Milgrim, Richard Greene.

NIGHTLIGHT (44). By Kenneth H. Brown. January 12, 1973 (world premiere). Director, Paul Weidner; scenery, Lawrence King; lighting, Larry Crimmins; costumes, Kathleen Ankers.

Rae ....Eda Reiss Merin
Goose ....Richard Pilcher
E.W. ....John Dignan
Ferri ....Eve Collyer
The Reb ....Alan Gifford
Time: The present. Place: New York City. Three acts.

OLD TIMES (44). By Harold Pinter. April 6, 1973. Director, Paul Weidner; scenery, Lawrence King; lighting, Larry Crimmins; costumes, Carola Meleck. With James Broderick, Barbara Caruso, Maureen Quinn.

JUNO AND THE PAYCOCK (44). By Sean O'Casey. May 18, 1973. Director, Paul Shyre; scenery, Lawrence King; lighting, Peter Hunt; costumes, Linda Fisher. With Peg Murray, Alan Gifford, Bernard Frawley, Paddy Croft.

HOUSTON

Alley Theater: Large Stage

PANTAGLEIZE (32). By Michel de Ghelderode. October 15, 1972. Directors, Nina Vance and Beth Sanford; scenery, William Trotman; lighting, Jonathan Duff and William Trotman; costumes, Jerry Williams. With Joseph Maher, Philip Fisher, I.M. Hobson, Woody Skaggs.

LIFE WITH FATHER (44). By Howard Lindsay and Russel Crouse. November 30, 1972. Director, Jack Westin; scenery and costumes, Jerry Williams; lighting, Jonathan

Duff. With Betty Fitzpatrick, William Trotman, Anthony Auer, David Cindric, Christopher Newlin, David Folwell.

THE HOSTAGE (36). By Brendan Behan. January 18, 1973. Director, Robert E. Leonard; scenery and costumes, Jerry Williams; lighting, Jonathan Duff; musical director, Paul Dupree. With Rutherford Cravens, Joann Rose, William Hardy, Lillian Evans.

COLETTE (36). Adapted from her autobiographical writings by Elinor Jones. March 1, 1973. Director, Beth Sanford; scenery, William Trotman; costumes, Jerry Williams; special music and lyrics by Harvey Schmidt and Tom Jones; musical director, Paul Dupree. With Jeannette Clift, Darlene Conley, Jonathan Kidd, Woody Eney.

SCHOOL FOR WIVES (36). By Molière; verse translation by Richard Wilbur. April 12, 1973. Director, Robert E. Leonard; scenery and costumes, Jerry Williams; lighting, Jonathan Duff. With William Hardy, Judy Mueller, Michael Parish, Jonathan Kidd.

JACQUES BREL IS ALIVE AND WELL AND LIVING IN PARIS (48). By Eric Blau and Mort Shuman; based on Brel's lyrics and commentary; music by Jacques Brel. May 24, 1973. Director, Beth Sanford; musical director, Paul Dupree; scenery, Jerry Williams; lighting, Jonathan Duff. With Denise Le Brun, J.T. Cromwell, Judy Rice, Sheldon Epps, Renae Pickens.

Alley Theater: Arena Stage

HAPPY BIRTHDAY, WANDA JUNE (42). By Kurt Vonnegut Jr. November 24, 1972. Director, Robert E. Leonard; scenery, William Trotman; lighting Jonathan Duff; costumes, Karen Kinsella. With Woody Eney, Barbara Barnett, Lee Smith, Philip Fisher.

ALL OVER (16). By Edward Albee. January 23, 1973. Director, Nina Vance; scenery, William Trotman; lighting, Jonathan Duff; costumes, Jerry Williams. With Jeannette Clift, Darlene Conley, William Trotman, Woody Skaggs, Glynis Bell.

Alley Theater: Children's Theater

YELLOW BRICK ROAD (2). By Iris Siff, adapted from *The Wizard of Oz*. Music by George Morganstern. February 3, 1973.

KANSAS CITY, MO.

Missouri Repertory Theater

MURDER IN THE CATHEDRAL (15). By T.S. Eliot. June 29, 1972. Director, Robert Speaight; scenery, John Ezell; lighting, Charles Weeks; costumes, Janet Warren. With Steven Gilborn, Art Ellison, Michael Mertz, Robert Scogin, John Vitale, Robin Humphrey.

CAT AMONG THE PIGEONS (15). By Georges Feydeau; translated by John Mortimer. July 6, 1972. Director, John O'Shaughnessy; scenery, John Ezell; lighting, Charles Weeks; costumes, Janet Warren. With Kathryn Grody, Robert Scogin, Steven Ryan, Harriet Levitt, John Vitale.

BAREFOOT IN THE PARK (15). By Neil Simon. July 13, 1972. Director, William Glover; scenery, John Ezell; lighting, Charles Weeks; costumes, Judy Dolan. With Kathryn Grody, Steven Ryan, Harriet Levitt, John Q. Bruce Jr.

LONG DAY'S JOURNEY INTO NIGHT (15). By Eugene O'Neill. July 20, 1972. Director, Patricia McIlrath; scenery, John Ezell; lighting Charles Weeks; costumes, Janet Warren. With John Brandon, Robin Humphrey, Steven Gilborn, Holmes Osborne, Sally Mertz.

THE HOUSE OF BLUE LEAVES (14). By John Guare. August 3, 1972. Director, William Glover; scenery, John Ezell; lighting, Charles Weeks; costumes, Janet Warren. With John Q. Bruce, Jr., Kathryn Grody, Sally Mertz, Robert Scogin.

BORSTAL BOY (16). By Brendan Behan; adapted by Frank McMahon. August 10, 1972. Director, Vincent Dowling; scenery, Tomas MacAnna; lighting, Charles Weeks; costumes and songs from original Abbey Theater production. With Robert Elliott, John Brandon, Eden Lee Murray, J. Morton Walker, Steven Gilborn, Robert Scogin.

Note: Missouri Repertory Theater, as the Missouri Vanguard Theater, toured two productions in 22 cities in Missouri: *Charley's Aunt* by Brandon Thomas, directed by Thomas Gruenewald and *The Fourposter* by Jan de Hartog, directed by J. Morton Walker.

LAKEWOOD, OHIO

Great Lakes Shakespeare Festival

THE MERRY WIVES OF WINDSOR (19). By William Shakespeare. July 7, 1972. Director, Lawrence Carra; scenery, Warner Blake; lighting, Frederic Youens; costumes,

William French. With Susan Willis, Dimitra Arliss, Robert Machray, George Vafiadis, Kermit Brown.

THE BEGGAR'S OPERA (21). By John Gay. July 12, 1972. Director, Lawrence Carra; scenery, Warner Blake; lighting, Frederic Youens; costumes, Susan Irene Thomas. With Bruce Gay, Robert Allman, Susan Willis, Maureen Moore, Keith Mackey, Norma Joseph.

RICHARD III (16). By William Shakespeare. July 26, 1972. Director, Lawrence Carra; scenery, Warner Blake; lighting, Frederic Youens; costumes, William French. With Lawrence Carra, Susan Willis, Robert Allman,

George Vafiadis, David Little, Dimitra Arliss.

COLLAGE VERSION OF HAMLET (16). By Charles Marowitz. August 9, 1972. Director, Charles Marowitz; scenery and lighting, Frederick Youens; costumes, William French. With Gregory Lehane, Susan Willis, Keith Mackey, John Milligan, Maureen Moore, David Little.

ELECTRA (12). By Sophocles; translated by H. D. F. Kitto. August 23, 1972. Director, George Vafiadis; scenery and lighting, Frederick Youens; costumes, William French; choral director, Jane Vafiadis; music, Takis Georgiou. With Dimitra Arliss, David Little, Susan Willis, Norma Joseph, John Milligan.

LOS ANGELES

Center Theater Group: Mark Taper Forum

DONT BOTHER ME I CANT COPE (54). By Micki Grant. August 10, 1972. Director, Vinnette Carroll; musical director, H. B. Barnum; choreography, Claude Thompson; scenery, H. R. Poindexter; lighting, Ken Billington; costumes, Noel Taylor. With Paul Kelly, Emily Yancy, Alan Weeks, Isaiah Jones Jr.

HENRY IV, PART 1 (54). By William Shakespeare. October 26, 1972. Director, Gordon Davidson; scenery, Ming Cho Lee; lighting, Martin Aronstein; costumes, Lewis Brown. With Kristoffer Tabori, Victor Buono, Penny Fuller, Al Alu, William Devane.

MASS (54). By Leonard Bernstein, with text from the Liturgy of the Roman Mass and additional texts by Stephen Schwartz and Leonard Bernstein; music by Leonard Bernstein. January 4, 1973. Director, Gordon Davidson; musical director, Maurice Peress; choreography, Donald McKayle; scenery, Peter Wexler; lighting, Gilbert V. Hemsley Jr; costumes, Frank Thompson. With Michael Hume, Gilbert Price, Carolyn Dyer, Lee Hooper.

THE MIND WITH THE DIRTY MAN (54). By Jules Tasca. March 15, 1973 (world premiere). Director, Edward Parone; scenery, Robert O'Hearn; lighting, Donald Harris; costumes, Noel Taylor.

Dianne Dracman	Jane Dulo
Father Jerome	James Flavin
Lucrecia Conwell	Ann Morgan Guilbert
Alma Stone	Allyn Ann McLerie
Wayne Stone	Joe Flynn
Clayton Stone	Peter Strauss
Divina	Barra Grant

Time: The present. Place: Living room of the Stone home, Buckram, Md. Act I: A day in spring. Act II: A week later. Act III: That evening.

FORGET-ME-NOT-LANE (54). By Peter Nichols. May 31, 1973. Directed by Arvin Brown; scenery, Elmon Webb and Virginia Dancy; lighting, Tharon Musser; costumes, Pete Menefee. With John McMartin, Donald Moffat, Beaulah Garrick, Charlotte Moore.

Center Theater Group: Mark Taper Forum—New Theater For Now

THE MIND WITH THE DIRTY MAN (6). By Jules Tasca. July 12, 1972 (experimental production). Director, Edward Parone; lighting, Donald Harris; costumes, Marianna Elliott. With Allyn Ann McLerie, Kathleen Freeman, Helen Page Camp, John Fiedler, Joe Flynn, Peter Strauss, Timothy Blake.

REVOLUTION (4). By Eric Monte. October 4, 1972 (world premiere). Director, Robert Greenwald; scenery, Russell Pyle; lighting, Donald Harris; costumes, Terence Tam Soon.

Willa Mae	Margaret Avery
Mama	Brunetta Barnett
Sheriff; K.K.K.; Cop	Paul Carr
Mr. Reed; K.K.K.	Lee Corrigan
Sarah Green	Ja'Net DuBois
Ralph	Danny Goldman
Civil Rights Worker; Marie	Gloria Jones
Mr. Jesse	Jim Millsap
Civil Rights Worker; George	Eric Monte
Sam	Glynn Turman
James	Spence Wil-Dee
Fighting Youth; Lonnie; Cop.	Bill Woodard

Act I, Scene 1: The South, 1955. Scene 2: The same, two weeks later. Act II, Scene 1: The South, 1961. Scene 2: The morning after the march. Act III, Scene 1: Watts, 1965. Scene 2: The same, immediately following.

A BOOTH CALLED WAR (3). By Leonard Horwitz. October 7, 1972 (world premiere). Director, Wallace Chappell; scenery, Russell Pyle; lighting, Donald Harris; costumes, N. Ted Shell.
Dree ....Mary Ann Beck

Sly ....Dennis Redfield
Wanda (Child) ....Ellen Sommers
Curry ....Rudy Solari
Groom ....John D. Garfield
Wanda (Adult) ....Barra Grant
Act I, Scene 1: Dree's apartment. Scene 2: The ferryboat. Scene 3: A network TV show. Scene 4: The skating rink. Scene 5: Dree's apartment. Scene 6: The Greenhouse. Act II, Scene 1: Dree's apartment. Scene 2: The Greenhouse. Scene 3: Dree's apartment.

Note: The Mark Taper Forum presents a Forum Laboratory which had workshop productions of *Help* by Michael McGuire; *What Are You Doing After The War?*, by Merrick Talcove; *Here I Am* by Ted Graham; *Soon* by Scott Fagan; *Harvey Perr's Scandalous Memories* by Harvey Perr in collaboration with Jack Rowe; *Rainbows For Sale* by John Ford Noonan; *Superman in the Bones II* by John Dennis; *The Women of Trachis* by Sophocles, based on a translation by Ezra Pound; *Tales of Oncle Jo* by Harold Oblong.

Center Theater Group: Ahmanson Theater

THE PRISONER OF SECOND AVENUE (40). By Neil Simon. October 17, 1972. Director, Mike Nichols; scenery, Richard Sylbert; lighting, Tharon Musser; costumes, Anthea Sylbert. With Art Carney, Barbara Barrie, Jack Somack, Jean Barker, Ruth Jaroslow, Roslyn Alexander.

THE CRUCIBLE (48). By Arthur Miller. December 5, 1972. Director, Joseph Hardy; scenery and lighting, H. R. Poindexter; costumes, Noel Taylor. With Charlton Heston, Inga Swenson, James Olson, Beah Richards, Donald Moffat, Gale Sondergaard, Ford Rainey.

A MIDSUMMER NIGHT'S DREAM (48). By William Shakespeare. Jan. 23, 1973. Director, Peter Brook; designer, Sally Jacobs. With Alan Howard, Gemma Jones, Robert Lloyd and the Royal Shakespeare Company. Guest production.

A STREETCAR NAMED DESIRE (48). By Tennessee Williams. March 20, 1973. Director, James Bridges; scenery, Robert Tuler Lee; lighting, H. R. Poindexter; costumes, Theadora Van Runkle. With Jon Voight, Faye Dunaway, Earl Holliman, Lee McCain.

The Season Elsewhere in Los Angeles

By Rick Talcove

Theater critic of the Van Nuys, Calif. *Valley News* and author of the play *What Are You Doing After the War?*, produced this season in the Forum Laboratory

Los Angeles theater? It's surviving, even flourishing, but on a somewhat cautionary basis. If nothing else, the 1972-73 season proved that, despite the best intentions, nothing is ever *too* solid in the local theatrical scene. Thus, in one year's time, the ever-reliable Century City Playhouse ceased operation; the ever-rebellious Company Theater split into two separate producing factions, and the long-awaited relief from a rigid Equity 8-performance limitation on acting workshops produced virtually the same kind of material on virtually the same limited-run basis.

Still, there were plenty of bright spots. For instance, in July the long-awaited Shubert Theater finally opened its doors with Harold Prince's admirable but controversial *Follies,* complete with Alexis Smith, a $750,000 production cost, and deep resentment on the part of some theatergoers who went expecting more Ziegfeld than Freud. *Follies* lasted 11 weeks. The reasons for its not "taking off" were many. One must mention the fact that the show had booked no substantial theater parties because, as a New York-based press agent commented, "Everyone's out of town until September." What then of the flourishing audiences at the Civic Light Opera's attractions at the Music Center's Pavilion and Ahmanson? Obviously, it's a different ball game in Los Angeles, where residents go to the beach and mountains within an hour's drive, then return for an evening of entertainment.

As a matter of record, the Shubert had an extremely spotty opening semester. Following two months of darkness after *Follies,* Dory Previn's *Mary C. Brown and the Hollywood Sign* managed all of one week of previews before producer Zev Bufman courageously canceled the entire production. Following *another* two months' darkness, the Theater Guild began booking touring shows, and the Shubert had Rex Harrison, Alan Bates and Sada Thompson playing their latest triumphs. Hopefully, it's onward and upward from now on.

Don't Bother Me, I Cant Cope did everything *Follies* was supposed to do: it kept theaters filled, first at the Mark Taper Forum for a limited run and then at the Huntington Hartford where extention followed extention. Despite a modest New York reputation, *Cope* unquestionably found its audience and hung on to it. Vinnette Carroll's concept and direction made good use of the dynamic Paula Kelly.

Film studio facilities used legitimate theater for the first time with Universal's new Amphitheater offering *Jesus Christ Superstar,* considerably scaled down from its Broadway counterpart. Goldwyn Studios leased one of its sound stages to launch temporarily Ray Bradbury's space-age variation of *Moby Dick,* retitled *Leviathan 99.* William Inge and Norman Corwin also premiered new works in Los Angeles.

On the small theater scene, two organizations bent on promoting this unique area of stagecraft came into being: the League of Los Angeles Theaters and the Professional Actors League. Positive results? Forthcoming.

A young producer-director named William S. Bartman Jr. took hold of the Oxford Playhouse and soon had three stages turning out admirable productions. A West Coast counterpart of Joseph Papp? Time will tell.

The following is a selection of the most noteworthy Los Angeles productions staged during the year. The list does not include the numerous touring shows nor the Center Theater Group productions at the Ahmanson and the Mark Taper (see the Regional Theater listing above). A plus sign (+) with the performance number indicates the show was still running on June 1, 1973.

JESUS CHRIST SUPERSTAR (77). Music by Andrew Lloyd Webber; lyrics by Tim Rice. June 26, 1972. Director, Tom O'Horgan; scenery, Robin Wagner; costumes, Randy Barcelo; lighting, Jules Fisher. With Ted Neeley, Heather MacRae, Carl Anderson, Bruce Scott. At the Amphitheater, Universal Studios.

CANVAS (27). By David Roszkowski. July 7, 1972 (world premiere). Director, Alistair Hun-

ter; scenery and lighting, Allan Rabinowitz; costumes, Jonathan Foster. At Scorpio Rising Theater.

Morey J. Blunden	Richard Cottrell
Actor 1	Jonathan Foster
Actor 2	Tom Stitzel
Actor 3	Allan Rabinowitz
Actor 4	Chuck Logue
Actress 5	Bennett Wright

No intermission.

CAESAREAN OPERATIONS (9). By William Inge. October 6, 1972 (world premiere). Director, Milton Selzer; scenery and lighting, Donold Harris. At Theater West.

Al .... Roy Stuart
Ron .... Charles Tachovsky
Olive .... Claudette Nevins
Fred .... Charles Aidman
Roger .... Dick Van Patten
No intermission.

LEVIATHAN 99 (15). By Ray Bradbury. November 24, 1972 (world premiere). Director, Charles Rome Smith; scenery and lighting, Michael Shere. At Samuel Goldwyn Studio.
The Captain .... William Marshall
Ishmael .... Dennis Robertson
Quell .... Ronald Feinberg
Two Acts.

ENDGAME (36). By Samuel Beckett. November 24, 1972. Director, Gar Campbell; scenery and lighting, Russell Pyle. With Gar Campbell, Lance Larsen, Arthur Allen, Nancy Hickey. At Company Theater.

THE ODYSSEY OF RUNYON JONES (17). Book by Norman Corwin; music and lyrics by Jay Livingston and Ray Evans. December 16, 1972 (world premiere). Director, Norman Corwin; scenery, Tad Anheier; costumes, Sylvia Moss; lighting, Jerry Grollnek. At the Valley Music Theater.
Runyon Jones .... Johnny Whitaker
B.Z.L. Bubb .... John Myhers
Mother Nature .... Jeanne Arnold
Father Time .... William Schallert
Wick .... Michael Evans
Voom .... Byron Webster
Chief .... Earle MacVeigh
Space Clown .... Johnny Silver
Two Acts.

DOES A TIGER WEAR A NECKTIE? (24). By Don Petersen. February 16, 1973. Director, Willard Rodgers; scenery, Robert G. Hunt, Gammy Burdett; costumes, Midge; lighting, Gregg Wynne. With Ron Thompson, Margaret Avery, Wally Taylor. At the Zodiac Theater.

THAT WAS LAURA BUT SHE'S ONLY A DREAM (27+). By David Zane Mairowitz. March 24, 1973 (world premiere). Director, Herbert Davis-Stein; scenery and lighting, John Banicki. At the Onion Company/Horseshoe Theater.
Lydia .... Nada Rowand
Elena .... Jessica Jurney
Lilianna .... Shirley Dion
Madame Nhu .... Dianne Carter
Two Acts.

FATHER'S DAY (24). By Oliver Hailey. March 30, 1973. Director, Tom Troupe; scenery, Dale Barnhart. With Carole Cook, Gwynne Gilford, Jacquelyn Hyde, Jordan Rhodes, Paul Kent, Paul Mantee. At the Melrose Theater Association.

OEDIPUS (14+). By Seneca; adapted by Ted Hughes. April 13, 1973 (American premiere). Director, William S. Bartman Jr.; choreographer, Carol Zeitz; scenery, lighting and costimes, Robert W. Zentis. At the Oxford Playhouse.
Oedipus .... Richard Hoffman
Jocasta .... Elizabeth Brandlin
Creon .... Steve Marshall
Manto .... Deborah Klose
No intermission.

THE HASHISH CLUB (27+). By Lance Larsen. April 28, 1973. (world premiere). Directed by the actors; scenery and lighting, Russell Pyle. At the Company Theater.
First .... Gar Campbell
Second .... Lance Larsen
Third .... Dennis Redfield
Fourth .... Michael Stefani
A Girl .... Trish Soodik
Two Acts.

CHIPS WITH EVERYTHING (2+). By Arnold Wesker. May 28, 1973. Director, Peter Wight; scenery, Conrad Penrod; costumes, Linda Taylor; lighting, Grant Morrill. With Christopher Mears, Alan Simon, Bill Coleman, Michael Murphy, Don Summerfield, Jac Mcanelly, Dennis Woodall, John Town, Philip Simms, John Quinn, James Antekier, Jason Carlisle, Eric Holmes. At the New Mercury Players/Hollywood Center Theater.

LOUISVILLE, KY.

Actors Theater of Louisville: Macauley Theater

A MAN FOR ALL SEASONS (27). By Robert Bolt. October 19, 1972. Director, Jon Jory; scenery, Paul Owen; lighting, Geoffrey T. Cunningham; costumes, Kurt Wilhelm. With Max Gulack, Victor Jory, Angela Wood, Max Howard.

YOU CAN'T TAKE IT WITH YOU (27). By Moss Hart and George S. Kaufman. November 16, 1972. Director, Victor Jory; scenery, Paul Owen; lighting, Geoffrey T. Cunningham; costumes, Kurt Wilhelm. With Jean Inness, Max Gulack, Sandy McCallum, Leslie Barrett.

THE PIRATES OF PENZANCE (33). By W. S. Gilbert and Arthur Sullivan. December 14, 1972. Director, Frank Wicks; musical director, Alan Rafel; scenery, lighting, costumes, Paul Owen. With Patrick Tovatt; John Wylie, Danny Sewell, Donna Curtis.

KENTUCKY (33). By Daniel Stein. January 18, 1973 (world premiere). Director, Patrick Tovatt; scenery, Paul Owen; lighting, Geoffrey T. Cunningham; costumes, Kurt Wilhelm; properties, Diann Fay; musical consultant, Wil Greckel.
With The Company: G. W. Bailey, Nathan Cook, Donna Curtis, Patrick Gorman, Max Howard, Susan Cardwell Kingsley, Sandy McCallum, Michael McCarty, Anne Shropshire, Falvia Smith, Patrick Tovatt, Jim Webb, John Wylie.
Two acts.

IN FASHION (27). Book, Jon Jory; music, Jerry Blatt; lyrics, Lonnie Burstein. February 22, 1973 (world premiere). Director, Jon Jory; costumes, Kurt Wilhelm; lighting, Geoffrey T. Cunningham; properties, Diann Fay; choreography, Judith Haskell; musical arrangements, Peter Howard.

Etienne	John Wylie
Yvonne	Lu Ann Post
Moulineaux	Daniel Davis
Bassinet	Patrick Tovatt
Madame Aigreville	Carmen Mathews
Suzanne	Pamela Hall
Aubin	Sandy McCallum
Abdul Hassim	G. W. Bailey
Madame Brigot	Lee Anne Fahey
Rosa	Donna Curtis

Musicians: Cello Reed E. Drews, french horn Denny Hallman, Piano Eileen LaGrange Paris, just after the turn of the century. Three acts.

MACBETH (27). By William Shakespeare. March 22, 1973. Director, Jon Jory; scenery, Paul Owen; lighting, Geoffrey T. Cunningham; costumes, Kurt Wilhelm. With David Canary, Carol Teitel, Max Howard, Sandy McCallum.

WHAT THE BUTLER SAW (27). By Joe Orton; April 19, 1973. Director, Jon Jory; scenery, Paul Owen; lighting, Geoffrey T. Cunningham; costumes, Kurt Wilhelm. With John Wylie, Lee Anne Fahey, Donna Curtis, Patrick Gorman, Max Howard, Patrick Tovatt.

MILWAUKEE

Milwaukee Repertory Theater Company: Todd Wehr Theater

THE TWO GENTLEMEN OF VERONA (50). By William Shakespeare. October 6, 1972. Director, Nagle Jackson; scenery, Grady Larkins; lighting, Ken Billington; costumes, James Edmund Brady. With Davis Hall, Jim Baker, Robert Ground, Fredi Olster, Mary Wright.

SCENES FROM AMERICAN LIFE (50). By A. R. Gurney Jr. November 24, 1972. Director, Charles Kimbrough; scenery and lighting, Christopher M. Idoine; costumes, Pamela Scofield. With Candace Barrett, Raye Birk, Robert Ground, Ric Hamilton, Mary Jane Kimbrough, William McKereghan, Josephine Nichols, Fredi Olster, Penelope Reed, Jack Swanson, Jeffrey Tambor.

THE PLAY'S THE THING (50). By Ferenc Molnar; adapted by P. G. Wodehouse. January 12, 1973. Director, Rod Alexander; scenery Stuart Wurtzel; lighting, Ken Billington; costumes, James Edmund Brady. With William McKereghan, Charles Kimbrough, Jack Swanson, Elizabeth Franz.

STICKS AND BONES (50). By David Rabe. April 20, 1973. Director, Robert Risso; scenery and lighting, Christopher M. Idoine; costumes, James Edmund Brady. With Jack Swanson, William McKereghan, Mary Jane Kimbrough.

ALL TOGETHER (50). Book by Nagle Jackson, Jeffrey Tambor and members of the MRT Company; music and lyrics by G. Wood. June 8, 1973 (world premiere). Director, Nagle Jackson; musical director, Edmund Assaly; scenery and lighting, Christopher M. Idoine; costumes, James Edmund Brady; musical numbers staging, William Reilly.

Horace	G. Wood
George Kay	Charles Kimbrough
Betty Lou Kay	Mary Jane Kimbrough
Simon	Raye Birk
Edith	Judith Light
Philip	William McKereghan
Naomi	Josephine Nichols
Mr. Green	Jeffrey Tambor
Charlie	Fredi Olster
Dick	Ric Hamilton
Gerta	Martha J. Tippin

The play is set in a Greenwich Village loft in which an encounter group meets.

Note: *Adaptation* by Elaine May and *The Golden Fleece* by A. R. Gurney Jr. were presented throughout Wisconsin at college, civic, cultural and fraternal organizations from April 17, 1973 through June 3, 1973.

MINNEAPOLIS

The Guthrie Theater Company: Guthrie Theater

A MIDSUMMER NIGHT'S DREAM (51). By William Shakespeare. July 7, 1972. Director, John Hirsch; scenery, John Jensen; lighting, Gil Wechsler; costumes, Carl Toms. With Frank Langella, Roberta Maxwell, Linda Carlson, Dianne Wiest.

OF MICE AND MEN (42). By John Steinbeck. July 10, 1972. Director, Len Cariou; scenery and costumes, John Jensen; lighting, Gil Wechsler. With Richard Ramos, Peter Michael Goetz, Eric Fredricksen, Michelle Shay.

THE RELAPSE (36). July 12, 1972. By John Vanbrugh. Director, Michael Langham; scenery, John Jensen; lighting, Gil Wechsler, costumes, Carl Toms. With Frank Langella, Roberta Maxwell, Edward Zang, Bernard Behrens, Robert Pastene, Katherine Ferrand.

AN ITALIAN STRAW HAT (30). By Eugene Labiche and Marc-Michel; English version by David Feldshuh and David Ball. September 12, 1972. Director, David Feldshuh; scenery and lighting, John Jensen; costumes, Hal George. With Peter Michael Goetz, Paul Ballantyne, Katherine Ferrand.

OEDIPUS THE KING (40). By Anthony Burgess; translated and adapted from Sophocles. October 24, 1972 (world premiere). Director, Michael Langham; scenery and costumes, Desmond Heeley; lighting, Richard Borgen; composer, Stanley Silverman; conductor, Dick Whitbeck; choral coach, Fran Bennett.

Oedipus ....Len Cariou
Jocasta ....Patricia Conolly
Creon ....James Blendick
Tiresias ....Robert Pastene
Messenger ....Paul Ballantyne
Philocles ....Bernard Behrens
Officer ....Leon Pownell
Child ....Ellin Gorky
Antigone and Ismene ....Linda Frailich, Nancy L. Joseph

Representatives of the People of Thebes: James J. Lawless (Chorus Leader), Peter Michael Goetz, Ivar Brogger, David Monasch. Citizens of Thebes: Fran Bennett, Barbara Bryne, Carey Connell, Lance David, Tovah Feldshuh, Katherine Ferrand, Erik Fredricksen, Mary Hitch, J. Warren Johnson, Katherine Lenel, Roberta Maxwell, Robert John Metcalf, Michele Shay. Officers, Farmers: William Metcalf, Terry Hill, Thomas Jasorka, Jean-Paul Mustone, Gerald J. Quimby, Craig Smith. Children: Trent Brunier, Paul Dallin, Jeffrey Eisenberg, Joseph Hughes, Greg Kassmir.

The action takes place before the palace of King Oedipus in Thebes. Two acts.

CYRANO (24). Book and lyrics by Anthony Burgess, based on Cyrano de Bergerac by Edmond Rostand; music by Michael J. Lewis. January 23, 1973 (world premiere). Director, Michael Langham; musical director, Joseph Klein; orchestrations, Eddie Sauter; musical staging, Rhoda Levine; scenery, John Jensen; lighting, Gilbert V. Hemsley Jr.; costumes, Desmond Heeley.

Theater Caretaker ....Shawn McGill
Doorman ....Joseph Della Sorte
Foodseller ....Tova Feldshuh
Nobleman ....Michael Vita
Pickpocket; Monk ....Geoff Garland
Pickpocket's Apprentice ....James Richardson
Citizen ....Richard Curnock
Citizen's Son ....Tim Nissen
1st Marquis ....Alexander Orfaly
2nd Marquis ....William Tynan
Ligniere; Journalist ....Arnold Soboloff
Christian de Neuvillete ....Mark Lamos
Madame Aubry; Lise ....Betty Leighton
Madame de Guemene ....Janet McCall
Barthenoide; Sister Claire .....Patricia Roos
Felizerie ....Judith Ross
Urimedonte ....Mary Straten
Ragueneau ....Bruce MacKay
Le Bret ....James Blendick
Roxana ....Leigh Beery
Roxana's Chaperone;
  Sister Marthe ....Anita Dangler
Count de Guiche ....Louis Turenne
Viscount de Valvert ....J. Kenneth Campbell
Actors ....Anthony Inneo, Neal Jones
Actresses ....Dee Martin, Jill Rose
Montfleury;
  Spanish Officer ....Patrick Hines
Cyrano de Bergerac ....Christopher Plummer
Jedelet ....Michael Goodwin

Candle Lighters, Musketeers, Bakery Staff, Boys, Poets, Gascon Cadets, Spanish Soldiers, Nuns, Pages, etc.: Paul Thompson, Christopher Klein, Michael Nolan, Donovan Sylvest, Paul Berget, Richard Curnock, J. Kenneth Campbell, Tovah Feldshuh, Geoff Garland, Patrick Hines, Janet McCall, Shawn McGill, James Richardson, Patricia Roos, Mary Straten, Tim Nissen, Joseph Della Sorte, Michael Goodwin, Anthony Inneo, Neal Jones, Alexander Orfaly, William Tynan, Michael Vita, Dee Martin, Jill Rose, Judith Ross.

Place: A theater, Paris, 1640; Ragueneau's bakery, Paris; The balcony of Roxana's house, Paris; a battle camp near Arras; a convent, Paris, 1655. Two acts.

Note: In addition to the main season, the Guthrie Theater presented a special Christmas-week story-theater production of Charles Dickens's A Christmas Carol (10), December 18, 1972, as well as a 15-city tour of *Of Mice and Men*, in Minnesota, North and South Dakota, Wisconsin, Nebraska and Iowa from January to March 1973.

NEW HAVEN

(Comments on the Long Wharf Theater by its artistic director, Arvin Brown, appear in this section's introductory article.)

Long Wharf Theater

THE LADY'S NOT FOR BURNING (33). By Christopher Fry. October 14, 1972. Director, Kent Paul; scenery, Marjorie Kellogg; Judy Rasmuson; costumes, Bill Walger. With Joyce Ebert, George Hearn, John Lithgow, Louis Beachner, Ruby Holbrook.

THE CHANGING ROOM (33). By David Storey. November 17, 1972 (American premiere). Director, Michael Rudman; scenery, David Jenkins; lighting, Ronald Wallace; costumes, Whitney Blausen.

Harry ....Louis Beachner
Patsy ....Douglas Stender
Fielding ....Rex Robbins
Morley ....Jack Schultz
Kendal ....John Lithgow
Luke ....Jake Dengel
Fenchurch ....William Rhys
Jagger ....John Tillinger
Trevor ....George Hearn
Walsh ....Tom Atkins
Sandford ....John Braden
Copley ....Paul Rudd
Stringer ....Richard D. Masur
Atkinson ....James Hummert
Spencer ....Mark Winkworth
Clegg ....Ron Siebert
Moore ....Alan Castner
Owens ....Robert Murch
Crosby ....George Ede
Tallon ....Peter DeMaio
Thornton ....William Swetland
Mackendrick ....Emery Battis
  Place: The changing room of a Rugby League Team in the North of England. Act I: 3:30 p.m. Act II: 35 minutes later. Act III: After the game.

WHAT PRICE GLORY? (33). By Laurence Stallings and Maxwell Anderson. December 22, 1972. Director, Arvin Brown; scenery, John Conklin; lighting, Ronald Wallace; costumes, Linda Fisher. With Charles Cioffi, Tom Atkins, Suzanne Lederer.

TRELAWNY OF THE "WELLS" (33). By Arthur Wing Pinero. January 26, 1973. Director, Max Stafford-Clark; scenery, Elmon Webb and Virginia Dancy; lighting, Ronald Wallace; costumes, Bill Walker. With Mildred Dunnock, Suzanne Lederer, John Lithgow, Emery Battis, Rex Robbins, George Ede.

JUNO AND THE PAYCOCK (33). By Sean O'Casey. March 2, 1973. Director, Arvin Brown; scenery, Marjorie Kellog; lighting, Judy Rasmuson; costumes, Bill Walker. With Geraldine Fitzgerald, Joseph Maher, Emery Battis, Joyce Ebert, Richard Mathews, Ruby Holbrook.

FORGET-ME-NOT-LANE (33). By Peter Nichols. April 6, 1973 (American premiere). Director, Arvin Brown; scenery, Elmon Webb, Virginia Dancy; lighting, Ronald Wallace; costumes, Whitney Blausen.

Frank ....Joseph Maher
Young Frank ....Thomas Leopold
Ursula ....Joyce Ebert
Young Ursula ....Suzanne Lederer
Charles ....Ralph Drischell
Amy ....Geraldine Fitzgerald
Ivor ....Clyde Burton
Miss 1940 ....Astrid Ronning
Mister Magic ....Henry Thomas
  Two acts.

DANCE OF DEATH and MISS JULIE (33). By August Strindberg. May 11, 1973. Director, Austin Pendleton; scenery, Steven Rubin; lighting, Ronald Wallace; costumes, Bill Walker. With Joseph Maher, Joyce Ebert, Emery Battis, Roberta Maxwell, Christopher Walken.

Long Wharf Theater: Children's Theater

SLEEPING BEAUTY (8). Book and Lyrics by Barbara Fried; music by Norman Sachs. October 21, 1972. Director, Peter Brouwer; scenery, Gary Finkel; lighting, George Hedges; costumes, Jania Szatanski. With Evalyn Baron, James Erickson, Alice Nagel, Bradford O'Hare, Gene Parseghian, Susan Wefel, Alice White, Paul Zegler.

RAPUNZEL, LET DOWN YOUR HAIR! (12). Book by Charles Richard; music and lyrics by Terrence Sherman. December 2, 1972 (world premiere). Director, George Spalding; scenery, David Snyder; lighting, George Hedges; costumes, Jania Szatanski.

Betty Bertha ....Peggy Cosgrave
Rolland ....James Erickson

Rapunzel .... Alice Nagel
Burford .... Bradford O'Hare
Grayson .... Paul Zegler

KALEIDOSCOPE (8). Conceived and directed by Craig Anderson. January 27, 1973. Scenery, Astrid Ronning; lighting, George Hedges; costumes, Jania Szatanski. With Melanie Chartoff, Peggy Cosgrave, Jeremy Lawrence, Bradford O'Hare, John Swanson, Alice White.

JASON AND THE ARGONAUTS (8). Adapted and translated by Kenneth Cavander from the original Greek myths. March 10,

Yale Repertory Theater

THE BOURGEOIS GENTLEMAN (19). By Molière; translated by Michael Feingold. October 6, 1972. Director, Alvin Epstein; scenery and costumes, Steven Rubin; lighting, Nathan L. Drucker. With Leonard Frey, Elizabeth Parrish, Amandina Lihamba, John V. Shea, Deborah Mayo.

A BREAK IN THE SKIN (19). By Ronald Ribman. October 13, 1972 (world premiere). Director, Arthur Sherman; scenery, Michael H. Yeargan; lighting, William B. Warfel; costumes, Enno Poersch.
Dr. Murray Zeller .... Leonard Frey
Paul Holliman .... Stephen Joyce
Phil .... Bill Gearhart
Mrs. Osborne .... Elizabeth Parrish
Mr. Crow .... Jonathan Marks
Julie Holliman .... Janet Ward
Mary Holliman .... Robin Pearson Rose
Dr. Karamanos .... Joseph G. Grifasi
Mr. Humm .... Jeremy Geidt
    Place: Southeast Texas from one night to the next. Three acts.

ARE YOU NOW OR HAVE YOU EVER BEEN (19). By Eric Bentley. November 10, 1972 (world premiere). Director, Michael Posnick; scenery and costumes, Steven Rubin; lighting, Barb Harris.
Sam G. Wood .... Tom Haas
Edward Dmytryk .... Paul Schierhorn
Ring Lardner Jr.;
    Elia Kazan .... William Peters
Larry Parks .... Stephen Joyce
Sterling Hayden .... Nicholas Hormann
Abe Burrows .... Allan Miller
Tony Kraber; Marc Lawrence . Michael Gross
Jerome Robbins .... Michael Quigley
Elliott Sullivan .... John McAndrew
Martin Berkeley .... Joseph G. Grifasi
Lillian Hellman .... Elizabeth Parrish
Lionel Stander .... Leonard Frey
Zero Mostel .... Jeremy Geidt
Paul Robeson .... Al Freeman Jr.
Stenographers ..... Marycharlotte Cummings,
                              Deborah Mayo

1973. Director, Kenneth Cavander; scenery and lighting, George Hedges; costumes, Jania Szatanski. With Charles Bartlett, Jeremy Lawrence, Bradford O'Hare, Andrew Potter, Linda Rubinoff, Alice White, Jamil Zakkai.

AESOP'S FABLES (8). Adapted by Gitta Honegger. April 14, 1973. Director, Gitta Honegger; costumes, Jania Szatanski; lighting, George Hedges; choreography, Joe Hayes; music arranged and performed by Timothy Ryan. With Kim Ameen, Charles Bartlett, Peggy Cosgrave, Jeremy Lawrence, Andrew Potter, Alice White.

All spoken material edited from transcripts in the Congressional Record of testimony given before the House Un-American Activities Committee. Two acts.

IN THE CLAP SHACK (19). By William Styron. December 15, 1972 (world premiere). Director, Alvin Epstein; scenery and costumes, Richard L. Roswell; lighting, D. Edmund Thomas.
Lineweaver .... Nicholas Hormann
Stancik .... Joseph G. Grifasi
Dadario .... Michael Gross
Schwartz .... Eugene Troobnick
Clark .... Hannibal Penny Jr.
Magruder .... Miles Chapin
Dr. Glanz .... Jeremy Geidt
Capt. Budwinkle .... Paul Schierhorn
Chaplain .... Bill Gearhart
Wilkins .... Thomas E. Lanter
McDaniel .... William Ludel
Chalkley; Marine Corporal ... Steven Robman
    Three acts.

THE MIRROR (19). By Isaac Bashevis Singer. January 19, 1973 (world premiere). Director, Michael Posnick; music, Yehudi Wyner; choreography, Carmen de Lavallade; scenery and costumes, Steven Rubin; lighting, Nathan L. Drucker.
Zirel .... Marcia Jean Kurtz
Yenta .... Elizabeth Parrish
Abraham .... Jeremy Geidt
Shloimele .... Nicholas Hormann
Hurmizah .... Richard Venture
Yoetz .... Eugene Troobnick
Dalfon .... Jonathan Marks
Naamah .... Carmen de Lavallade
Briri .... Michael Gross
Shabriri .... Bill Gearhart
Zluchah .... Deborah Mayo
    Demons: Marycharlotte Cummings, Amandina Lihamba, Michael Quigley, Robin Pearson Rose.
    Act I: Krashnik, a small town in Poland. Act II: Sodom.

BAAL (19). By Bertolt Brecht; translated by William E. Smith and Ralph Manheim. February 16, 1973. Director, Tom Haas; scenery and costumes, John Beatty; lighting, D. Edmund Thomas; music, Walton Jones, Carol Lees, Paul Schierhorn. With Bob Balaban, Stephen Joyce, Carmen de Lavallade, Elizabeth Parrish.

MACBETT (19). By Eugene Ionesco; translated by Charles Marowitz. March 16, 1973 (American premiere). Directors, William Peters, John McAndrew, Alvin Epstein; scenery, Enno Poersch; lighting, Ian Rodney Calderon; costumes, Maura Beth Smolover; music, Gregory Sandow; sound, Carol M. Waaser.

Glamis; Sick Person	John McAndrew
Cawdor; Sick Person	William Peters
Banco	Stephen Joyce
Macbett	Alvin Epstein
Duncan	Eugene Troobnick
Lady Duncan	Carmen de Lavallade
Lady-in-Waiting	Deborah Mayo
Macol	Stephen Joyce

Ensemble: Michael Quigley, Amandina Lihamba, Michael Gross, Paul Schierhorn, John McCaffrey, Joseph G. Grifasi.

Two acts.

LEAR (19). By Edward Bond. April 13, 1973 (American premiere). Director, David Giles; scenery, Ming Cho Lee; lighting, William B. Warfel; costumes, Jeanne Button; sound, David Jonathan Ward.

The Cast: Foreman, Prison Guard, Convoy Escort, Prison Commandant, Soldier at the House—Jonathan Marks; Workman, Ben (Prison Orderly), Prison Guard—John McAndrew; Workman, Prisoner—Bill Gearhart; Soldier at the Wall, Soldier at the House, Farmer's Son—Michael Quigley; Lear—Donald Davis; Bodice—Elizabeth Parrish; Fontanelle—Carmen de Lavallade; Warrington, Judge—Alvin Epstein; Old Councillor, Wounded Rebel Soldier—Eugene Troobnick; Engineer, Prisoner—Mark McCarthy; Firing Squad Officer, Thomas—Nicholas Hormann; Duke of North, Carpenter—Michael Gross; Duke of Cornwall, Prison Guard—Paul Schierhorn; Private, John—John V. Shea; Gravedigger's Boy—Bob Balaban; Gravedigger's Boy's Wife—Linda Gates; Sergeant, Old Sailor, Prison Guard, Farmer—Joseph G. Grifasi; Soldier at the House, Prison Guard, Convoy Escort—William Peters; Usher, Prisoner—Robert Gainer; Old Prison Orderly, Small Man—Jeremy Geidt; Bodice's Aid (Major Pellet)—Stephen Robman; Convoy Escort—Larry Strichman; Prisoner (M.O.), Officer—Stephen Joyce; Prison Guard—Bill Ludel; Farmer's Wife—Marycharlotte Cummings; Susan—Robin Pearson Rose; Boy—Raphael Sbarge.

Three acts.

Yale Repertory Theater: Experimental Theater

MAD DOG BLUES by Sam Shepard, directed by Robert Gainer, February 1-4, 1973; TWO ONE-ACTS BY YALE PLAYWRIGHTS, directed by Bill Ludel and Steven Robman, March 8-10, 1973.

Yale Repertory Theater: Sunday Series

ALBERTA RADIANCE by Robert Auletta, January 28, 1973; THE TRANSFIGURATION OF BENNO BLIMPIE by Albert Innaurato and THE AMERICAN WAR MOTHERS by Roma Greth, February 18, 1973; ANGEL, HONEY, BABY, DARLING, DEAR by Robert Patrick, March 4, 1973. Under the artistic direction of Michael Feingold.

Note: The Yale Repertory Theater and Drama School also presents Children's Theater, Yale Cabaret, Studio Projects and Main Stage Productions with students, members of the Repertory Theater and faculty members.

PRINCETON, N. J.

McCarter Theater

AGAMEMNON (8). By William Alfred. October 26, 1972 (world premiere). Director, Hohvannes I. Pilikian; scenery, John Conklin; lighting, John McClain; costumes, Elizabeth Covey; sound, Cathy MacDonald.

Agamemnon	Dolph Sweet
Iphegeneia; Xanthis; Slaver	Wanda Bimson
Moeris	Karl Light
Philo	Jerome Dempsey
Dipsas	Joseph Leon
Gnatho	Gene Gross
Eubolus of Crete	Al Corbin
Cassandra	Cara Duff-MacCormick
Guard	David Duhaime
Greek Soldier	Dwight Schultz
Another Soldier; Scamandrus Helenus	Franklin Getchell

Meno; Herald ....Peter Blaxill
Aegisthus ....Clifford David
Clytemnestra ....Nan Martin
Handmaiden ....Anne Louise Hoffmann
Aegon ....Nicholas Kepros
Mainos ....Anne Sheldon
  Place: From the council chamber of Aga-
memnon's palace, to Argos, to the deck of his
ship, to his private chamber, to Meno's coun-
try residence, back to the council chamber and
private chamber. Two acts.

THE TOOTH OF CRIME (8). By Sam Shep-
ard. November 9, 1972 (American premiere).
Director, Louis Criss; scenery, David Jenkins;
lighting, John McClain; costumes, Linda Fisher;
sound, Abe Jacobs.
Hoss ....Frank Langella
Becky ....Gloria Maddox
Star-Man ....William Myers
Galactic Jack ....Clarence Felder
Cheyenne ....Dale Helward
Doc ....John Scanlan
Crow ....Mark Metcalf
Referee ....Gray Gage

Musicians:
  Drummer ....Steeler
  Guitar ....Michael Metz
  Two acts.

THE TEMPEST (8). By William Shakespeare.
March 1, 1973. Director, Louis Criss; scenery,
David Jenkins; lighting, John McClain; cos-
tumes, Elizabeth Covey. With Nicholas Kepros,
Tom Brannum, Francesca Norsa, Clarence Fel-
der, Dwight Schultz.

LOOT (8). By Joe Orton. March 15, 1973, Edward Payson Call; scenery, Philip Gilliam;
lighting, John McClain. With James Gallery,
Jeanette Landis, Jess Richards, Donald Warfield, MacIntyre Dixon, Julian Lopes-Morillas,
Judy Parton.

ROSMERSHOLM (8). By Henrik Ibsen. March
29, 1973. Director, Louis Criss; scenery, David
Jenkins; lighting, John McClain; costumes,
Elizabeth Covey. With Mark Lenard, Lauri
Peters, I. M. Hobson, Ed Zang.

PROVIDENCE, R. I.

Trinity Square Repertory Company: Trinity Square Playhouse

OLD TIMES (22). By Harold Pinter. Septem-
ber 24, 1972. Director, Jacques Cartier; scenery,
Eugene Lee; lighting, Roger Morgan. With
Gerardine Arthur, Paul Benedict, Angela
Thornton.

LADY AUDLEY'S SECRET (87). By Douglas
Seale, adapted from the novel by Mary Elizabeth Braddon; music by George Goehring;
lyrics by John Kuntz. November 21, 1972 (re-
opened March 22, 1973). Director, Word
Baker; musical director, Richard Cumming;
scenery, Robert D. Soule; lighting Roger Morgan; costumes, Sunny B. Warner. With Barbara
Orson, Richard Kavanaugh, George Martin,
Ann Sachs.

THE ROYAL HUNT OF THE SUN (57). By
Peter Shaffer. January 10, 1973. Director,
Adrian Hall; scenery, Eugene Lee; lighting,
Roger Morgan; costumes, A. Christina Gian-
nini; armor and masks, Robert D. Soule. With
Richard Kneeland, James Eichelberger, George
Martin, Richard Loder.

THE SCHOOL FOR WIVES (25). By Molière,
English verse translation by Richard Wilbur.
February 28, 1973. Director, Adrian Hall;
scenery, Robert D. Soule; lighting, Roger
Morgan; costumes, A. Christina Giannini.
With George Martin, Richard Kavanaugh,
Jobeth Williams, William Damkoehler, Mina
Manente.

FEASTING WITH PANTHERS (39). By
Adrian Hall and Richard Cumming; music and
lyrics by Richard Cumming. April 18, 1973
(world premiere). Director, Adrian Hall; scen-
ery, Eugene Lee; lighting, Shirley Prendergast;
costumes, Betsey Potter; puppets and fantasy
costumes, Robert D. Soule.
  The Cast: Oscar Wilde, John Worthing,
Lord Henry Wotton, Herod Antipas—Richard
Kneeland; Governor of the Prison, Isaacson,
Lady Bracknell, Edward Carson, the Devil—
George Martin; 1st Warder, Sir Edward Clarke,
Triton—David Kennett; 2d Warder, Pawtucket
Toastmaster, Young Fisherman—Richard Jen-
kins; Critic, Lord B, Narraboth, Witch, Fish-
erman's Soul—Robert Black; Lady Agatha,
Marquess of Queensbury, Merchant, Witch—
Robert J. Colonna; Lady Wilde, Lady B, Ada
Leverson (the Sphinx), Young Witch—James
Eichelberger; Critic, Sir A, Justice Wills, Priest
—David C. Jones; Dorian Gray, Salome, Tri-
ton—Richard Kavanaugh; Critic, Lord C, Lord
Alfred Douglas (Bosie), Triton—T. Richard
Mason; Critic, Lute Player, Narraboth's Friend,
Harlequin—Daniel Von Bargen; Constance
Wilde, Sibyl Vane, Little Mermaid—Jobeth
Williams; Frank Harris—Timothy Crowe;
Robert Ross; Basil Hallwark; Jokanaan; Tri-
ton—William Damkoehler.
  Time: The late Victorian era, ranging for-
ward and backward between 1880 and 1900.
Place: Reading Gaol and the mind, memory,
imagination, fantasy and work of Oscar Wilde.
Two acts.

ROCHESTER, MICH.

Oakland University Professional Theater Program: Meadow Brook Theater

THE FRONT PAGE (29). By Ben Hecht and Charles MacArthur. October 12, 1972. Director, Charles Nolte; scenery and lighting, Richard Davis; costumes, Mary Schakel. With William Le Massena, Jim Oyster, Elaine Browne.

INHERIT THE WIND (29). By Jerome Lawrence and Robert E. Lee. November 9, 1972. Director, Charles Nolte; scenery and lighting, Richard Davis; costumes, Mary Schakel. With Booth Colman, Fred Thompson, James D. O'Reilly, David Himes, Kirstin Mooney.

THE TORCH-BEARERS (20). By George Kelly. December 7, 1972. Director, Terence Kilburn; scenery and lighting, Richard Davis; costumes, Mary Schakel. With Elaine Browne, James D. O'Reilly, Louise Kirtland, Dee Victor, Robert Englund, Dorothy Blackburn, John Brandon.

THE MIRACLE WORKER (29). By William Gibson. January 4, 1973. Director, Warren Enters; scenery and lighting, Richard Davis; costumes, Mary Schakel; With Jennifer Harmon, Kerri LuBell, Debra Mooney, James D. O'Reilly.

RIGHT YOU ARE IF YOU THINK YOU ARE (29). By Luigi Pirandello. February 1, 1973. Director, Terence Kilburn; scenery and lighting, Richard Davis; costumes, Mary Schakel. With William LeMassena, Dee Victor,

Katherine Squire, J. D. Dahlmann, David Sabin, Ivar Bragger, Debra Mooney.

THE COUNTRY GIRL (29). By Clifford Odets. March 1, 1973. Director, Michael Sinclair; scenery, Richard Davis; lighting, Dan T. Willoughby; costumes, Mary Schakel. With Elizabeth Orion, Bill Moor, Jean-Pierre Stewart.

BEDTIME STORY by Sean O'Casey and A DOCTOR IN SPITE OF HIMSELF by Molière (29). March 29, 1973. Director; Terence Kilburn; scenery and lighting, Richard Davis; costumes, Mary Schakel, David Warda. With Robert Casper, Judith Jordan, Anthony McKay, Debra Mooney, William LeMassena, James D. O'Reilly.

COUNT DRACULA (29). Adapted by John Ulmer and the Meadow Brook Company from the novel by Bram Stoker. April 26, 1973 (world premiere). Director, John Ulmer; scenery, Richard Davis; lighting, Dan T. Willoughby; costumes, Mary Schakel.

Sybil Seward	Elizabeth Orion
Hennessey	Phillip Mallet
Dr. Arthur Seward	James D. O'Reilly
Renfield	Fred Thompson
Wesley	Mark Bennett
Jonathan Harker	Anthony McKay
Mina	Lynn Ann Leveridge
Count Dracula	Eric Tavaris
Heinrich Van Helsing	William LeMassena

SAN FRANCISCO

American Conservatory Theater: Geary Theater

CYRANO DE BERGERAC (38). By Edmond Rostand; translated by Brian Hooker; Adapted by Dennis Powers. October 28, 1972. Director, William Ball; scenery, Robert Blackman; lighting, F. Mitchell Dana; costumes, Robert Fletcher. With Peter Donat, Marc Singer, Paul Shenar, Donald Ewer, Marsha Mason

THE HOUSE OF BLUE LEAVES (26). By John Guare. October 31, 1972. Director, Edward Hastings; scenery, Ralph Funicello; lighting, F. Mitchell Dana; costumes, Robert Morgan. With Ed Flanders, Barbara Colby; Joy Carlin, E. Kerrigan Prescott.

THE MERCHANT OF VENICE (12). By William Shakespeare. November 14, 1972. Director, Robert Bonaventura; scenery, lighting and projections, James Tilton; costumes, Ann Roth. With Joseph Bird, Paul Shenar, Barbara Colby, Marsha Mason.

THE MYSTERY CYCLE (24). Compiled and adapted by Nagle Jackson. December 5, 1972. Director, Nagle Jackson; scenery, Robert Blackman; lighting, Fred Kopp; scenery, James Brady. With Janie Atkins, Joseph Bird, John Hancock, Elizabeth Huddle, E. Kerrigan Prescott, Ray Reinhardt, Mary Wickes.

A DOLL'S HOUSE (25). By Henrik Ibsen; translated by Allen Fletcher. January 9, 1973. Director, Allen Fletcher; scenery, Ralph Funicello; lighting, Fred Kopp; costumes, Robert Blackman. With Marsha Mason, Barbara Colby, Peter Donat, Paul Shenar.

YOU CAN'T TAKE IT WITH YOU (26). By George S. Kaufman and Moss Hart. January 30, 1973. Director, Jack O'Brien; scenery and costumes, Robert Blackman; lighting, Fred Kopp. With Mary Wickes, William Paterson,

Marc Singer, Marsha Mason, Elizabeth Huddle, E. Kerrigan Prescott.

THAT CHAMPIONSHIP SEASON (37). By Jason Miller. February 20, 1973. Director, Allen Fletcher; scenery, Ralph Funicello; lighting, Fred Kopp; costumes, J. Allen Highfill. With Paul Shenar, Ray Reinhardt, Ed Flanders, Ramon Bieri, Dana Elcar.

THE CRUCIBLE (19). By Arthur Miller. April 3, 1973. Director, William Ball; scenery, Robert Blackman; lighting, F. Mitchell Dana; costumes, Lewis Brown, Walter Watson. With Peter Donat, Barbara Colby, Janie Atkins, Marsha Mason, Mary Wickes, Ray Reinhardt, Paul Shenar.

American Conservatory Theater: Guest Production

A MIDSUMMER NIGHT'S DREAM (23). By William Shakespeare. March 6, 1973. Peter

Brook's Royal Shakespeare Company.

American Conservatory Theater: Marines' Memorial Theater

GODSPELL. Conceived by John-Michael Tebelak, music and new lyrics by Stephen Schwartz, based on the Gospel According to St. Matthew. June, 1972. Director, Nina Faso; music director, Steve Reinhardt; lighting, Spencer Moss;

costumes, Susan Tsu. With Jon Buffington, Angela Ruth Elliott, Laurie Faso, Lois Foraker, Patti Mariano, Stephen Nathan, Kitty Rea, Tom Rolling, Craig Schaefer, Cle Thompson.

Note: American Conservatory Theater "plays in progress" program presented the following between December 1972 and May 1973: *The Tunes of Chicken Little* by Robert Gordon, directed by Edward Hastings; *Hagar's Children* by Ernest A. Joselovitz, directed by Robert Bonaventura; *The Kramer* by Mark Medoff, directed by Paul Blake; *The Roots* by McCarthy Coyle, directed by Allen Fletcher; *Bursting Out* and *Blessing* by Joseph Landon, directed by Paul Blake.

SARASOTA, FLA.

Asolo Theater Festival: The State Theater Company

WAR AND PEACE (21). By Erwin Piscator, Alfred Neumann, Guntram Fuller; from the novel by Leo Tolstoy. June 30, 1972. Director, Eberle Thomas; scenery, Henry Swanson; lighting, James Meade; costumes, Catherine King. With Philip LeStrange, Penelope Willis, Bradford Wallace, Barbara Redmond, Walter Rhodes, Robert Lanchester, William Leach.

THE TIME OF YOUR LIFE (11). By William Saroyan, July 28, 1972. Director, Richard G. Fallon; scenery, Henry Swanson; lighting, James Meade; costumes, Catherine King. With William Leach, Eberle Thomas, Kathleen O'Meara Noone, Walter Rhodes, Robert Strane.

PYGMALION (31). By George Bernard Shaw. February 15, 1973, re-opened May 29, 1973. Director, Richard G. Fallon; scenery, Rick Pike; lighting, Martin Petlock; costumes, Catherine King. With Robert Strane, Corie Sims, Bradford Wallace, Walter Rhodes, Philip LeStrange.

ANGEL STREET (25). By Patrick Hamilton. February 17, 1973. Director, Howard Millman; scenery, Rick Pike; lighting, Martin Petlock; costumes, Catherine King. With Barbara Reid McIntyre, Patrick Egan, William Leach.

THE PHILADELPHIA STORY (23). By Philip Barry. February 23, 1973. Director, Eberle Thomas; scenery, Rick Pike; lighting, Martin Petlock; costumes, Catherine King. With Penelope Willis, Devora Millman, Bradford Wallace.

THE CRUCIBLE (25). By Arthur Miller. March 2, 1973. Director, Bradford Wallace; scenery, Rick Pike; lighting, Martin Petlock; costumes, Flozanne John. With Patrick Egan, Barbara Redmond, Corie Sims, Isa Thomas, Philip LeStrange, William Leach.

HOTEL PARADISO (18). By Georges Feydeau and Maurice Devallieres; English translation by Peter Glenville. April 6, 1973. Director, Robert Strane; scenery, Rick Pike; lighting, Martin Petlock; costumes, Catherine King. With Bradford Wallace, Isa Thomas, Barbara Reid McIntyre, Eberle Thomas, Richard Hopkins, Penelope Willis.

THE EFFECT OF GAMMA RAYS ON MAN-IN-THE-MOON MARIGOLDS (18). By Paul Zindel. May 4, 1973. Director, Richard D. Meyer; scenery, Rick Pike; lighting, Martin Petlock; costumes, Mary Gibson. With Isa Thomas, Penelope Willis, Corie Sims.

LITTLE MARY SUNSHINE (29). Book, music and lyrics by Rick Besoyan. May 25, 1973. Director, Peter J. Saputo; scenery, Rick Pike; lighting, Martin Petlock; costumes, Flozanne John; music director, Deena Kaye Lange. With Walter Rhodes, Eberle Thomas, Bradford Wallace, Barbara Reid McIntyre, Isa Thomas.

Asolo Theater Festival: Children's Theater

KING STAG (18). By Eberle Thomas, based on the commedia dell'arte fable *Il Re Cervo* by Carlo Gozzi. August 4, 1972 (world premiere). Director, Moses Goldberg; designer, Rick Pike. With Morris Matthews, Danny Koren, Doug Kaye, Rita Grossberg, Patricia Richardson.

BIG KLAUS AND LITTLE KLAUS (5). By Dean Wenstrom; adapted from the story by Hans Christian Andersen. March 11, 1973. Director, Richard Hopkins; scenery, Rick Pike; costumes, Paige Sosnoski. With Burton Clarke, Henson Keys, Vicki Casarett.

ALADDIN (4). Created by Moses Goldberg. April 7, 1973. Director, Moses Goldberg; designer, Rick Pike. With Morris Matthews, Richard Jacobs, Kerry Shanklin.

Note: During the 1972-73 season, Asolo toured *Two Pails of Water* by Aad Greidanus and the old English fairy tale *Jack and the Beanstalk* from December 18 to December 31, 1972 to schools in 20 counties.

SEATTLE

Seattle Repertory Theater

MACBETH (20). By William Shakespeare. October 25, 1972. Director, Duncan Ross; scenery, Jason Phillips; lighting, Steven Maze; costumes, Lewis D. Rampino. With Peter Coffield, Susan Clark, Ted D'Arms, Judith Light, Clayton Corzatte.

CAMINO REAL (21). By Tennessee Williams. November 22, 1972. Director, Duncan Ross; scenery, Jason Phillips; lighting, Steven Maze; costumes, Lewis D. Rampino. With James Tripp, Rita Gam, Laurence Hugo, Eve Roberts, Michael Keenan, Elizabeth Cole.

CHARLEY'S AUNT (22). By Brandon Thomas. December 13, 1972. Director, Mario Siletti; scenery, Jason Phillips; lighting, Steven Maze; costumes, Lewis D. Rampino. With Robert Moberly, James Jansen, Judith Light, Bonnie Hurren, Eric Sinclair, June Gibbons.

CHILD'S PLAY (22). By Robert Marasco. January 3, 1973. Director, Edward Payson Call; scenery, Jason Phillips; lighting, Steven Maze; costumes, Lewis D. Rampino. With Donald Woods, James Cahill.

ALL OVER (22). By Edward Albee. January 24, 1973. Director, Duncan Ross; scenery, Jason Phillips; lighting, Steven Maze; costumes, Lewis D. Rampino. With Pippa Scott, Nina Foch, James Cahill, Gwen Arner, Tom Carson.

THE TAVERN (22). By George M. Cohan. February 14, 1973. Director, Clayton Corzatte; scenery, Jason Phillips; lighting, Steven Maze; costumes, Lewis D. Rampino. With Donald Moffat, Gwen Arner, Michael Lewis, James Jansen, Gun-Marie Nilsson.

PROMENADE ALL! (22). By David V. Robison. March 6, 1973. Directors, Hume Cronyn, Jessica Tandy; scenery, Jason Phillips; lighting, Steven Maze; costumes, Lewis D. Rampino. With Hume Cronyn, Jessica Tandy, Biff McGuire, Rusty Thacker.

Note: In addition to student matinees and special community performances, Seattle Repertory Theater presented its second Rip 'n' Rap 40-performance summer tour in a potpourri of James Thurber.

STRATFORD, CONN.

American Shakspeare Festival

JULIUS CAESAR (30). By William Shakespeare. June 22, 1972. Director, Michael Kahn; scenery, Robin Wagner; lighting, Marc B. Weiss; costumes, Jane Greenwood. With Bernard Kates, James Ray, Paul Hecht, Josef Sommer, Joseph Maher, Ruby Holbrook, Sharon Laughlin.

ANTONY AND CLEOPATRA (29). By William Shakespeare. June 23, 1972. Director, Michael Kahn; scenery, Robin Wagner; lighting, Marc B. Weiss; costumes, Jane Greenwood. With Paul Hecht, Salome Jens, Philip Kerr, William Larsen, Sharon Laughlin, Madelon Thomas.

MAJOR BARBARA (29). By George Bernard Shaw. June 27, 1973. Director, Edwin Sherin; scenery, William Ritman; lighting Marc B. Weiss; costumes, Jane Greenwood. With Jane Alexander, Lee Richardson, Jan Miner, Peter Thompson.

Note: The American Shakespeare Festival Theater also has a new playwrights series. Among the new plays presented were *Sanctum* and *An Especially Private Place* by Joseph Maher, directed by Gene Nye.

SYRACUSE

Syracuse Repertory Theater

CHILD'S PLAY (13). By Robert Marasco. October 20, 1972. Director, Rex Henriot; scenery and lighting, James Singelis; costumes, Marilyn Skow. With Jay Lanin, Jack Collard, William Newman.

MISS LONELYHEARTS (19). By Howard Teichmann, from the novel by Nathanael West. November 10, 1972. Directors, Jack Collard, Rex Henriot; scenery, Leonard Dryansky; lighting, James Paoletti; costumes, Marilyn Skow. With Stephen Keep, Susan Hunter Harney, William Newman, Jack Collard, Rex Henriot, Anna Kathleen White.

BYE BYE BIRDIE (8). Book by Michael Stewart; music by Charles Strouse; lyrics by Lee Adams. December 1, 1972. Director and choreographer, David Gold; musical director, Martha Reed Boughner; scenery and lighting, Robert Lewis Smith; costumes, Marilyn Skow. With Carolyn Kirsch, Mike Penna.

GALILEO (8). By Bertolt Brecht; adapted by Charles Laughton. March 2, 1973. Director Gerard E. Moses; scenery, Leonard Dryansky; lighting, James Paoletti; costumes, Jane

McGillivray. With Howard Da Silva, Ted Lillys, Maria Wida, David Wyeth.

THE SECRET LIFE OF WALTER MITTY (13). Book by Joe Manchester, based on the story by James Thurber; music by Leon Carr; lyrics by Earl Shuman. March 16, 1973. Director, Rex Henriot; musical director, Tony Riposo; choreography, Mallory Graham; scenery, Robert Lewis Smith; lighting, Walter Uhrman; costumes, Jane McGillivray. With Richard Blair, Mitchell Edmunds, Joan Maniscalco.

THE GINGERBREAD LADY (13). By Neil Simon. April 6, 1973. Director, Rex Henriot; scenery and lighting, James Singelis; costumes, Jane McGillivray. With Kathryn Loder, Adale O'Brien, James Carruthers, Gerard E. Moses.

DEAR LIAR (13). By Jerome Kilty, adapted from the letters of George Bernard Shaw and Mrs. Patrick Campbell. April 27, 1973. Director, Rex Henriot; scenery and lighting, Robert Lewis Smith; costumes, Jean Levine. With John Heffernan, Adale O'Brien.

WALTHAM, MASS.

Brandeis University: Spingold Theater

GUYS AND DOLLS (14). Book by Jo Swerling and Abe Burrows, based on a story and characters by Damon Runyon; music and lyrics by Frank Loesser. October 17, 1972. Director, Peter Sander; musical director, Herman Weiss; choreography and musical numbers staging, Billy Wilson; scenery, Gerry Hariton; lighting, J.M. Bald; costumes, Ralph Dressler. With Jack Sevier, David S. Howard, Lisa Brailoff, Elizabeth Sarason, Sam Weisman.

THE HAPPINESS CAGE (14). By Dennis J. Reardon. December 6, 1972. Director, Ted

Kazanoff; scenery, Marilyn Reed; lighting, Beth Morgan; costumes, Charles Flaks. With John Zurick, Douglas R. Nielsen, Randall Merrifield, Jack Sevier, David Palmer, Claudia Zahn.

AS YOU LIKE IT (14). By William Shakespeare. February 6, 1973. Director, John O'-Shaughnessy; scenery, Charles Otis Sweezey; lighting, Joanna Hill; costumes, Lorraine Bege. With Jessie Natovitz, Janet Lewis, Mitchell Block, Rex D. Hays, Ian McElhinney, Douglas R. Nielsen, Jay Drury.

THE CRUCIBLE (14). By Arthur Miller. March 27, 1973. Director, Ted Kazanoff; scenery, J.M. Bald; lighting, Ralph Dressler; costumes, Joanna Hill. With Rex D. Hays, Barbara Teitelbaum, Joseph Warren, Lucy Chudson, Shelley Wyant.

THE PREVALENCE OF MRS. SEAL (14). By Otis Bigelow. May 9, 1973 (world premiere). Director, Peter Sander; scenery, Lorraine Bege; lighting, Marilyn Reed; costumes, John Kenny.

Graves .... David Palmer
Mrs. Norma-Jean Pilgrim .. Eugenia Dromey
Mr. Murdstone .... Joseph Warren
Harry .... Ian McElhinney
Belinda Seal .... Felicity Russell
Mr. Smith .... Randall Merrifield
Dr. Wolfgang Porteous .... Amiel Schotz
Igor .... Gil Schwartz
Mrs. Seal .... Mary Jane Wells
    Place: The Great Hall of Seal Castle, Sussex, between midnight and dawn. Two acts.

Note: New plays in the Laurie Premier Theater were *Passover* by Lloyd Gold and *The Last of the Marx Brothers Writers* by Louis Phillips.

WASHINGTON, D.C.

Arena Stage: Kreeger Theater

THE HOSTAGE (40). By Brendan Behan. November 1, 1972. Director, Norman Gevanthor; scenery, John Conklin; lighting, Vance Sorrells; costumes, Marjorie Slaiman; musical preparation, Alan Rafel; dances, Virginia Freeman. With Leslie Cass, Robert Prosky, Dianne Wiest, Gary Bayer.

A PUBLIC PROSECUTOR IS SICK OF IT ALL (40). By Max Frisch; translated by Michael Bullock. January 31, 1973 (American premiere). Director, Zelda Fichandler; scenery, Santo Loquasto; lighting, William Mintzer; costumes, Linda Fisher; original score, David Horowitz.
Public Prosecutor ...... Shepperd Strudwick
Elsa .... Dorothea Hammond
Hilde; Coco; Inge .... Dianne Wiest
Murderer .... Max Wright
Dr. Hahn .... Stanley Anderson
Warder; Gendarme .... Gene Gross
Inge's Mother .... Leslie Cass
Inge's Father;
    Police Inspector .... George Ebeling
Signor Mario .... Richard Bauer
Asst. Hotel Manager ...... Richard Sanders
Taxi Driver .... Terrence Currier
Director of Banking .... William Myers
Minister of Interior .... Howard Witt
General of the Army .... Glenn Taylor
Student .... Gary Bayer
Convict 112 .... Wendell Wright

Arena Stage: Arena Theater

THE FOURSOME (33). By E.A. Whitehead. November 3, 1972 (American premiere). Director, Alan Schneider; scenery, Robert U. Taylor; lighting, Hugh Lester; costumes, Gwynne Clark.
Harry .... John Horn
Tim .... Munson Hicks
Marie .... Lynn Ann Leveridge

Patrons of the
    Arts......... Leslie Cass, Richard Bauer
Frau Hoffmeier .... Halo Wines
Aged President .... Robert Pastene
    Hotel Guests: William Myers, Melvin Bruce, Vladimir Chernozemsky, Leslie Cass, Bellhops: Jan Greenfield, Bruce Kaiden. Waiters: David Reinhardsen, Daniel Diggles, Michael Haney, Robert Cumberledge.
    Time: 2 a.m. Place: Close to a frontier, the study of a Public Prosecutor's Villa in a small, cold country. A crime story in ten scenes: 1. The study (A Public Prosecutor is sick of it all); 2. A cell (The Murderer); 3. A hut in the forest (The Public Prosecutor gets his axe); 4. The study (The first news arrives); 5. A hotel lobby (The axe); 6. The cell (A Murderer is lucky); 7. A cavern in the sewers. The Count is called upon to give himself up); 8. A hall in the residency (Masters of the situation); 9: An attic bedroom (The Murderer is unlucky); 10. The study again (Law and order are restored). Two acts.

ONE FLEW OVER THE CUCKOO'S NEST (40). By Dale Wasserman; based on the novel by Ken Kesey. May 2, 1973. Director, Norman Gevanthor; scenery, David Jenkins; lighting, William Mintzer; costumes, Gwynne Clark. With Richard Bauer, Manu Tupou, Leslie Cass, Howard Witt.

Bella .... Barbara Dana
    Place: A hollow in the sandhills near Liverpool, England. Act I, Scene 1: Morning. Scene 2: Midday. Act II: Late afternoon.

OUR TOWN (33). By Thornton Wilder. December 20, 1972. Director, Alan Schneider; scenery, Ming Cho Lee; lighting, Hugh Lester;

costumes, Marjorie Slaiman. With Robert Prosky, Leslie Cass, Howard Witt, Jane Groves, Terence Currier, Dianne Wiest, Gary Bayer.

A LOOK AT THE FIFTIES (19). Book, Music and Lyrics by Al Carmines. February 14, 1973. Director, Lawrence Kornfeld; musical director, Susan Romann; choreography, Dan Wagoner; scenery, Robert U. Taylor; lighting, William Mintzer; costumes, Marjorie Slaiman. With Michael Petro, Scott Mansfield, Boni Enten, Stuart Silver, Frank Coppola, Essie Borden.

ENEMIES (33). By Maxim Gorky; English version by Kitty Hunter-Blair and Jeremy Brooks. March 21, 1973. Director, Alan Schneider; scenery, Robert U. Taylor; lighting, William Mintzer; costumes, Marjorie Slaiman. With Howard Witt, Dorothea Hammond, Ken Ruta, Gloria Maddox, Robert Pastene, Gene Gross.

RAISIN (33). Book by Robert Nemiroff and Charlotte Zaltzberg, based on Lorraine Hansberry's *A Raisin in the Sun;* music by Judd

Washington Theater Club

SPREAD EAGLE PAPERS (30). Compiled and edited by Sue Lawless from material developed by the company. September 27, 1972 (world premiere). Director, Sue Lawless; musical direction and arrangements, Richard De Mone; scenery, John H. Paull; lighting, Michael J. Rosati; costumes, Danica Eskind. With Ann Clements, Lynn Grossman, Mickey Hartnett, William McClary, Ken Olfson, Ronn Robinson, Renny Temple. Two acts.

THE RAPISTS (30). By Dennis Turner. November 8, 1972 (world premiere). Director, Stephen Book; scenery, Michael Stauffer; lighting, Michael J. Rosati; costumes, Danica Eskind.
Gerte .... Dempster Leech
Frederick .... Bruce Hall
Erich .... Robert La Tourneaux
The Boy .... Henry Carter Shaffer
Edna .... Lenka Peterson
The Guard .... Mark Robinson
The Lieutenant .... Ronn Robinson
Schimke .... Louis Edmonds
Mellman .... William McClary
Kurt .... Edward Clinton
Dieter .... Robert Dannenberg
The action takes place in postwar Germany: Munich, 1945, and a concentration camp outside Remagen, 1943. Two acts.

THE BOYS FROM SYRACUSE (30). Book by George Abbott, based on William

Woldin; lyrics by Robert Brittan. May 23, 1973 (world premiere). Director and choreographer, Donald McKayle; musical director, Joyce Brown; scenery, Robert U. Taylor; lighting, William Mintzer; costumes, Bernard Johnson; dance music, Dorothea Freitag; orchestrations, Al Cohn.
Ruth Younger .... Ernestine Jackson
Travis Younger .... Ralph Carter
Mrs. Johnson .... Helen Martin
Walter Lee Younger .... Joe Morton
Beneatha Younger .... Shezwae Powell
Lena Younger .... Virginia Capers
Willie Harris; Orator; Pastor ..Herb Downer
Bibo .... Ted Ross
Cobra .... Eugene Little
Travis's Friend .... Kofi Burbridge
Joseph Asagai .... Robert Jackson
African Drummer .... Aristide Pereira
Karl Lindner .... Richard Sanders
People of the Southside: Loretta Abbott, Deborah Allen, Hinton Battle, Lettie Battle, Elaine Beener, Eugene Little, Al Perryman, Zelda Pulliam, Chuck Thorpes. Moving Men: Al Perryman, Chuck Thorpes.
Time: The 1950's. Place: Chicago. Two acts.

Shakespeare's *The Comedy of Errors;* music by Richard Rodgers; lyrics by Lorenz Hart. December 13, 1972. Director, Pirie MacDonald; music director, Richard De Mone; choreography, Judith Haskell; scenery, Michael Stauffer; lighting, Michael J. Rosati; costumes, Danica Eskind. With Gary Dontzig, Kelly Walters, Susan Long, Samuel D. Ratcliffe, Art Ostrin, Karen Shallo.

CEREMONIES IN DARK OLD MEN (30). By Lonne Elder III. January 17, 1973. Director, Bette Howard; scenery, John H. Paull; lighting, Michael J. Rosati. With Frank Adu, Jerry Bell, Ensley-Everett, Jimmy Hayeson, Bette Howard, La Voncye Howard, Thurman Scott.

THE ENCLAVE (30). By Arthur Laurents. February 21, 1973 (world premiere). Director, Arthur Laurents; scenery, Michael Stauffer; lighting, John H. Paull; costumes, Danica Eskind.
Eleanor .... Rochelle Oliver
Bruno .... Don Gantry
Cassie .... Peg Murray
Donnie .... Jack Betts
Ben .... Hal Linden
Wyman .... Tom Happer
Oliver .... Larry Hugo
Roy .... Charles Turner
Janet .... Ann Sweeny
Two acts.

SCENES FROM AMERICAN LIFE (30). By A.R. Gurney Jr. March 28, 1973. Director, Stephen Aaron; scenery and lighting, John H. Paull, Michael Stauffer; costumes, Danica Eskind. With Laurinda Barrett, Oliver Malcolmson, Art Vasil, Justin Taylor.

THE ECSTASY OF RITA JOE (30). By George Ryga. May 2, 1973 (American premiere). Director, Harold Stone; scenery and lighting, John H. Paull, Michael Stauffer; costumes, Danica Eskind.

Singer Guitarist	Giulia Pagana
Magistrate	Roger DeKoven
Rita Joe	Frances Hyland
Constable	John Jackson
Jaimie Paul	Henry Bal
Eileen Joe	Kathy Gittel
Father Andrew	Philip Baker Hall
Miss Donohue	Laurinda Barrett
Young Indian Man	Mike Halsey
Chief David Joe	Chief Dan George
Indian Woman	Billie Lyon

Indian Men	John Tiger, Mike Halsey
Mr. Homer	Pat Corley
Schoolboard Official;	
Clerk's Voice	Bruce MacDonald

White Men: Richard DeAngelis, Ronn Robinson, Bruce MacDonald. Indian Men: John Tiger, Mike Halsey. Music Ensemble: Joel Eigen recorder, Doug Shear bass guitar, Dave Cole percussion.

Time: The present. Place: A Canadian city and an Indian Reservation. Two acts.

SOMETHING WILD: THE LADY OF LARKSPUR LOTION, THE LAST OF MY SOLID GOLD WATCHES, 27 WAGONS FULL OF COTTON (30). By Tennessee Williams. June 6, 1973. Director, Dennis Brite; scenery, Michael Stauffer; lighting, John H. Paull; costumes, Danica Eskind. With Mary Jo Catlett, Alfred Hinckley, George Hillman, Joseph Palieri, Mimi Norton Salamanca.

The Season Elsewhere in Washington

By Jay Alan Quantrill

Drama critic of radio station WAVA and *Woodwind* magazine

In Washington in 1972-73, three theaters opened and a fourth unveiled its new marquee. One closed three days after its opening (a 1,100-seat film house trying a two-a-day program of matinees of *The Me Nobody Knows* six days a week, for youngsters). Another has been stumbling along (the *Jacques Brel Is Alive and Well and Living in Paris* cabaret opus set too formally at the Mayflower Hotel). Another was the culmination of two years' planning by Robert Hooks and Carolynne Jones, the D.C. Black Repertory at another old film house, now called the Last Colony (350 seats). It opened with a vivid new play, *Coda,* by Evan Walker. A program of three one-acters by Howard University's playwright-in-residence, Clay Goss, alternated with dance presentations for the rest of the season.

The fourth new theater venture is the American Theater (originally L'Enfant Theater, 860 seats, film) which will be Washington's second completely commercial theater—all others except the National are government- or foundation-supported in some way. The American plans a program of off-Broadway-scale productions and one-man shows.

Godspell, still running, has played over 14 months, surpassing the previous longest run in Washington: *Hair,* five months. *Godspell* and *The Me Nobody Knows* are the long and short of it in a town that exists mainly on subscription engagements of two to six weeks.

The Washington Theater Club emerged from its organizational problems to renewed vigor under the artistic direction of Steve Aaron, who replaced Davey

Marlin-Jones, the Club's director for seven years. The most successful productions were *Ceremonies in Dark Old Men,* Arthur Laurents's *The Enclave* with Hal Linden, and the American premiere of the Canadian *The Ecstasy of Rita Joe* by George Ryga. The National had a shaky year of many touring post- and pre-Broadway productions, ending with Carol Channing in a sadly rickety vehicle, *Lorelei,* on a year-long pre-Broadway tour.

Arena Stage's quality is unquestionable and its value to the Washington theater scene inestimable. It is soon to gain international fame as the first American theater company to play the Soviet Union, at the invitation of the State Department. Its finest show of the season was a dazzling production of *One Flew Over the Cuckoo's Nest,* directed by Norman Gevanthor. The Folger met with some success: *Total Eclipse* (by Christopher Hampton), about the poets Verlain and Rimbaud, gave Armand Assante an opportunity to show off his consummate acting skills, and *The Complete Works of Studs Edsel* by Percy Granger was pretentiously verbal but possessed some value.

The Kennedy Center had a busy year. Summer in the Eisenhower saw the Shaw Festival of Canada's delicious production of *Misalliance.* This was followed by *The Pleasure of His Company* with Douglas Fairbanks Jr. and then a spurt of tryouts. As spring approached, *The Enchanted* was assembled with Elizabeth Ashley, but all plans of touring were quickly abandoned when the results became obvious. The fifth annual American College Theater Festival took place in late spring. In the Opera House, *Mass* was re-mounted and sent on tour in June. The four musicals planned for the fall-to-spring season dwindled to one, *Pippin.*

Olney's summer 1972 season presented the American premiere of Hugh Leonard's Dublin hit, *The Patrick Pearse Motel.* At Catholic University's Hartke, Mercedes McCambridge was appalling as Medea, but Ruby Holbrook, Nancy Reardon and a fine cast made *Vivat! Vivat Regina!* a sweeping historical pageant. Wolf Trap Farm Park for the Performing Arts presented its first theatrical production, a dated re-mounting of *The King and I.*

Aside from the major productions, the capital has gained a non-professional but highly successful Playwrights' Theater of Washington that brought a number of authors to the public's attention. Another group, Back Alley Theater presented some socially-oriented experimental productions, most notably *A Torture of Mothers* under the direction of Glenda Dickerson, about the Harlem Six. Arena presented one performance of *The New Theater (TNT),* an evening of poetry and scenes by Gerald Hiken and Paul E. Richards.

Offstage, the summer of 1972 saw the death of the *Daily News,* leaving only two dailies, the *Post* with Richard L. Coe as its drama critic and the *Star-News* with David Richards. As the season ended, a new bi-weekly on the performing arts, *The First Folio,* came into being.

This year, Washington gained an awareness of itself as a theater town. As for overall quality, there is no reason for exultation. We are on the threshold of forming a creative center, and we still depend on outside productions for a large portion of our attractions. But we look forward to a new season with great anticipation, sure now that it isn't a dream, but a true, steady and solidly-based growth of the theatrical arts.

Catholic University: Hartke Theater

MEDEA (18). By Euripides, adapted by William H. Graham and Mercedes McCambridge. January 5, 1973. Directed by William H. Graham; scenery and lighting, James D. Waring; costumes, Joseph Lewis. With Mercedes McCambridge, Jack Gwillim, Eda Seasongood, Peter Vogt, Tom Roland, Frank Pope.

VIVAT! VIVAT REGINA! (18). By Robert Bolt. May 4, 1973. Directed by James D. Waring; scenery, Rolf Beyer; lighting, James D. Waring; costumes, Joan E. Thiel; musical consultant, Emerson Meyers. With Ruby Holbrook, Nancy Reardon, Edward McPhillips, Peter Vogt, Tom Roland, Ralph A. Byers Jr., Tedd Rubenstein, Nicholas Cosco, Dan Diggles.

D. C. Black Repertory: Last Colony Theater

CODA (20). By Evan Walker. December 8, 1972 (world premiere). Directed by Motojicho; scenery, James Hooks; lighting, Eric Hughes; costumes, Lynn C. Smith.

Mama Sally ....Dee Porter/Louise Robinson
Josha Duncan ..John Bell/Robert T. Whitson
William Duncan ....Charlie Brown/Le Tari
Sara Kincaid .....Joy Hooks/Jenifer Baker
Lonnie Duncan ....Robert Whitson
Smokey Jackson ....Smokey/Moon
Fullerman ....Le Tari/Ed De Shae

Entire production double cast for this engagement only. A three-act drama concerning a black Vietnam veteran returning to the dilemma of the black uprisings in the late 1960s.

THREE DISHES: HOME COOKIN, SPACES IN TIME and OF BEING HIT (20). By Clay Goss. February 28, 1973. Directed by Sati Jamal; scenery and lighting,

Eric Hughes; costumes, Motojicho; projections, Ron Anderson.

Of Being Hit
Hollie ......Robert McFadden/Clark Brown
Duncan ....Robert T. Whitson
Wilson ....Michael Hodge

One-act play based on the life of a fighter named Holly Mims, one-time contender for the middleweight championship title who died three years ago in D.C. as a janitor.

Spaces in Time
Staged poetry performed in ensemble by the company.

Home Cookin'
Robert ....Charles Brown/Kene Holiday
Clay ....Elvin Benjamin
Homosexual ....Robert T. Whitson/Le Tari

Concerns itself with destinations, when two young men who knew each other as youngsters meet years later on a subway train heading towards their future.

Folger Library Theater Group

TOTAL ECLIPSE (35). By Christopher Hampton. October 17, 1972 (American premiere). Director, Louis W. Scheeder; scenery, William F. Riley; lighting, Michael Lodick; costumes, Olivia McElroy. With Peter Vogt, Armand Assante.

THE COMPLETE WORKS OF STUDS EDSEL (28). By Percy Granger. December 12, 1972. Director, David Margulies; scenery, Paul Hastings; lighting, Michael Lodick; costumes, Olivia McElroy. With Jo Henderson, Demo DiMartile.

THE WINTER'S TALE (28). By William

Shakespeare. February 6, 1973. Director, Louis W. Scheeder; scenery, Jason Rubin; lighting, Michael Lodick; costumes, Olivia McElroy. With Kathleen Klein, Edmund Day, Stuart Pankin, Michael Gabel.

BARTHOLOMEW FAIR, or THE STAPLE OF NEWS (28). By Ben Jonson. April 10, 1973. Directed by Robert Maudel; scenery, William G. Mickley Jr; lighting, Jack Carr; music, Robert Dennis; choreography, Virginia Freeman. With Barbara Meyer, Stuart Pankin, Kene Holliday, Earle Edgerton, Herman O. Arbeit.

John F. Kennedy Center: Eisenhower Theater

MISALLIANCE (16). By George Bernard Shaw. June 26, 1972. Director, Paxton Whitehead; scenery, Maurice Strike; lighting, Lynne Hyde; costumes, Hilary Corbett. With Ronald Drake, Noel Howlett, Tom Kneebone, Angela Wood. A Shaw Festival production from Niagara-on-the-Lakes, Ontario, Canada.

THE PLEASURE OF HIS COMPANY (40). By Samuel Taylor and Cornelia Otis Skinner. July 11, 1972. Director, Neil Kenyon; scenery, Donald C. Beman; wardrobe, Louise Allen. With Douglas Fairbanks Jr., June Travis, Fawne Harriman, Wallace Rooney. A Kennedy Center Productions, Inc., production which moved to Los Angeles for two weeks.

YERMA (8). By Federico Garcia Lorca. October 9, 1972. The Nuria Espert Company production on a tour of the U.S.

THE PHILANDERER (16). By George Bernard Shaw. January 2, 1973. Director, Tony Van Bridge; scenery, Maurice Strike; lighting, Donald Acaster; costumes, Tiina Lipp. With Patricia Gage, Paxton Whitehead, James Valentine. A Shaw Festival of Canada production.

THE ENCHANTED (35). By Jean Giraudoux. March 2, 1973. Director, Stephen Porter; scenery, Robert O'Hearn; lighting, Tom Skelton; costumes, Peter Joseph; incidental music, Francis Poulenc. With Elizabeth Ashley, Fred Gwynne, Stephen McHattie, Richard Venture, Eugenia Rawls, Eleanor Phelps, Joe Ponazecki.

THE AMERICAN COLLEGE THEATER FESTIVAL. Two-week festival of ten college productions selected from all over the U.S., plus one foreign guest production, brought to the Kennedy Center annually. THE STY OF THE BLIND PIG (2) by Phillip Dean. April 23, 1973. California State University. ANTIGONE (2) by Sophocles. April 24, 1973. Gallaudet College. AN EVENING OF KABUKI (2) Classic Japanese Theater. April 25, 1973. Pomona College. KABUKI TRAINING STUDENTS (2), music, song, acting, acrobatics, and theater from Japan. April 26, 1973. National Theater of Japan. A MAN'S A MAN (2) By Bertolt Brecht. April 27, 1973. Hanover College. JACQUES BREL IS ALIVE AND WELL AND LIVING IN PARIS, musical revue by Jacques Brel. April 28, 1973. University of Miami. VOLPONE (2) by Ben Jonson. April 30, 1973. University of Virginia. KABUKI TRAINING STUDENTS (2), another program of Kabuki. May 1, 1973. National Theater of Japan. HEAD OF STATE (2) by John Ahart, May 2, 1973 (world premiere). University of Illinois. LONG DAY'S JOURNEY INTO NIGHT (2) by Eugene O'Neill. May 3, 1973. Fordham University. CANTERBURY TALES (2) by Martin Starkie, Nevill Coghill, Richard Hill and John Hawkins. May 4, 1973. University of Massachusetts. DAMES AT SEA (2) musical by George Haimsohn, Robin Miller and Jim Wise. May 5, 1973. Purdue University/Fort Wayne Campus.

THE BLACKS (5+). By Jean Genet. May 26, 1973. Directed by Robert Hooks; scenery, James Hooks; lighting, Jim Albert Hobbs; costumes, Quay Truitt; movement, Mike Malone; music, Clyde Jacques Barrett. With members of the D.C. Black Repertory Company and the Anthony Booker Singers.

Note: The season at Kennedy Center also included tryouts or touring companies of Broadway and other productions of (at the Eisenhower Theater) *The Creation of the World and Other Business, The Jockey Club Stakes, Finishing Touches, A Midsummer Night's Dream, Story Theater, Out Cry* and (at the Opera House) *Pippin, The Last of Mrs. Lincoln, Emperor Henry IV, Bunraku, Marcel Marceau* and a 20-performance revival of *Mass* 6/1/72-6/17/72.

The Mayflower Theater

JACQUES BREL IS ALIVE AND WELL AND LIVING IN PARIS (84+). By Eric Blau and Mort Shuman; based on lyrics and commentary by Jacques Brel; music by Jacques Brel. March 3, 1973. Directed by Moni Yokim; lighting, Tom Field Associates.

With Joe Maisell (replaced by Robert Guillaume), Betty Rhodes (replaced by Judy Lander), Annette Pirrone, Jackie Cronin, Shawn Elliott. Produced by Chandler-Nash and Robert M. Lang Jr. (succeeding Frank Sugrue and Jerome Rosenfeld).

National Theater

LORELEI (11+). Musical based on *Gentlemen Prefer Blondes;* book by Anita Loos and Joseph Fields; music by Jule Styne; lyrics by Leo Robin; new book by Kenny Solms and Gail Parent; new music by Jule Styne; new lyrics by Betty Comden and Adolph Green. May 15, 1973. Directed by Betty Comden and Adolph Green; scenery, John Conklin; lighting, John Gleason; costumes, Alvin Colt; musical direction, Milton Rosenstock; orchestrations, Philip J. Lang, Don Walker; additional choreography, Ernie Flatt. Entire production staged by Joe Layton.

Lorelei Lee .... Carol Channing
Henry Spofford .... Lee Roy Reams
Mrs. Ella Spofford .... Dody Goodman
Lord Francis Beekman .... Brooks Morton
Lady Phillis Beekman .... Jean Bruno
Josephus Gage .... Brandon Maggart
Dorothy .... Tamara Long
Gus Esmond .... Peter Palmer

Bartender; Announcer ....Ray Cox
Frank; Maître D ....David Roman
George ....Bob Daley
Pierre ....Ray Cox
Charles ....Ken Ploss
Lobster ....Gia de Silva
Caviar ....Angela Martin
Pheasant ....Aniko Farrell
Salade ....Donna Monroe
Dessert ....Carol Channing
Zizi ....Katherina Hull Mineo
Fifi ....Maureen Crockett
Master of Ceremonies ....Robert Riker
Announcer ....Ray Cox
Engineer ....Ken Sherber
Mr. Esmond ....David Neuman
  Bridesmaids: Gia de Silva, Aniko Farrell,
Angela Martin, Donna Monroe. Ship's Per-
sonnel, Passengers, Tourists, Olympic Team
Members, Waiters, Wedding Guests: Joyce
Chapman, Georgia Dell, Peggy Marie Haug,
Linda Lee MacArthur, Penny Pritchard, Chris

Bartlett, Bob Fitch, Casey Jones, Howard
Leonard, Jonathan Miele, John Mineo,
Richard Natkowski, Robert Riker.
  Act I, Prologue: The pier of the Ile de
France. Scene 2: The deck of the Ile de
France. Scene 3: Lorelei's suite on the Ile
de France. Scene 4: The Eiffel Tower. Scene
5: Lorelei's suite, Ritz Hotel, Paris. Act II,
Scene 1: The Pre-Catalan night club. Scene
2: On the way home. Scene 3: The Central
Park Casino, New York. Epilogue.
  Musical Numbers: Act I—"Looking Back,"
"It's High Time," "Lorelei," "Little Rock,"
"I'm A-Tingle, I'm A-Glow," "I Love What
I'm Doing," "A Girl Like I," "Paris," "I
Won't Let You Get Away," "Keeping Cool
With Coolidge," "Men." Act II—"Coquette,"
"Mamie Is Mimi," "Lorelei" (Reprise),
"Homesick," "We're Just a Kiss Apart,"
"Button Up With Esmond," "Diamonds Are
a Girl's Best Friend."

Olney Theater, Olney, Md.

THE EFFECT OF GAMMA RAYS ON
MAN-IN-THE-MOON MARIGOLDS (21).
By Paul Zindel. June 20, 1972. Directed by
Leo Brody; scenery, and lighting, James D.
Waring; costumes, Marguerite Mayo. With
Kathryn Baumann, Meg Myles, Jennifer
Harmon, Vivienne Schub.

TARTUFFE (21). By Molière. July 11,
1972. Direction, scenery and lighting by
James D. Waring; costumes, Veronica Gustoff.
With John McGiver, Laurinda Barrett, Vivienne Schub, Gloria Maddox, Jack Gwillim.

HOME (21). By David Storey. August 1,
1972. Direction, scenery, and lighting by
James D. Waring; costumes, Marguerite

Mayo. With Jack Gwillim, Sydney Walker,
Pauline Flanagan, Anita Daugler.

PATRICK PEARSE MOTEL (21). By Hugh
Leonard. August 22, 1972 (American pre-
miere). Directed by Leo Brady; scenery and
lighting, James D. Waring; costumes, Mar-
guerite Mayo.
Dermot Gibbon ....Richard Bauer
Grainne Gibbon ....Halo Wines
Fintan Kinnore ....Robert Symonds
Nianh Kinnore ....Pauline Flanagan
James Usheen ....Patrick Bedford
Miss Manning ....Anita Dangler
Hoolihan ....Sydney Walker
  Domestic farce in two acts set in and
around present-day Dublin.

Summer Shakespeare Festival

TROILUS AND CRESSIDA (30). By William Shakespeare. July 18, 1972. Directed by
Ellie Chamberlain; scenery and lighting, John

Doepp; costumes, Tony Eikenbary; music,
Greg A. Steinke. With Johanne Leister, Dalton Cathey, Howard Green, Tedd Rubenstein.

The Virginia Theater, Alexandria, Va.

THE ME NOBODY KNOWS (6). Based on
the writings of students, collected by Stephen
M. Joseph; adapted by Robert H. Livingston
and Herb Schapiro; music, Gary William
Friedman; lyrics, Will Holt; additional lyrics,
Herb Schapiro. May 1, 1973. Directed by

Herb Schapiro; scenery and lighting, Michael
Hotopp; costumes, Myra Turley; musical
direction, Danny Rocks. With Darren Green,
Joe Mydell, Mel Johnson, Sharita Hunt, Carol
Anne Ziske. Entire production supervised by
George Patterson.

Wolf Trap Farm Park of the Performing Arts

THE KING AND I (6). By Richard Rodgers
and Oscar Hammerstein II. July 20, 1972.
Directed by Jerome Eskow; scenery, (no

credit); lighting, Don Abrams; costumes,
Brooks-Van Horn Costumes, New York.
With Roberta Peters, Michael Kermoyan.

WATERFORD, CONN.

Eugene O'Neill Theater Center: Playwrights Conference

THE GENERAL BRUTUS (2). By Jeff Wanshel. July 12, 1972 (world premiere).

Lord Fauntleroy	Benjamin Masters
Gravedigger	J.T. Walsh
Brutus	John Harkins
Atrocius	Kevin O'Connor
Ignominius	Roger Robinson
Plagier	Robert Christian
Artemidorus	Norman Rose
Informer	Ken Swiger

Senators and Footsoldiers: David Berman, Carl Bradshaw, Vaughan Crosskill, Timothy Scanlon, Tom Doran, Patrick Graybill, Richard Kendall, Benjamin Masters, Glenn Morrison, Bev Randell, Norman Rose, Joseph Sarpy, Gilbert Shasha, Ken Swiger, Joe Taffe, Cotyn Thompson, J.T. Walsh, Alan Woolf. Messengers: David Berman, Tom Doran, Bev Randell, Gilbert Shasha, Ken Swiger, J.T. Walsh, Alan Woolf.

PORCELAIN TIME (2). By Ronald Cowen. July 14, 1972 (world premiere). Director, James Hammerstein; dramaturg, Edith Oliver.

Donald	Lenny Baker
Ricki	Michael Sacks
Walter	Andrew Backer
Maggie	Geraldine Sherman
Florrie	Margaret Hall.

AND THE OLD MAN HAD TWO SONS (2). By Elizabeth Levin. July 15, 1972 (world premiere). Director, Hal Scott; dramaturg, Dan Sullivan.

Rachel	Tandy Cronyn
Julie English	Jacqueline Brookes
Uncle John; Old Man	Norman Rose
Silkie	Jeanne Ruskin
Jakie	David Berman
Dr. Karl	John Harkins
Thomas Manther	Peter Turgeon
Charles Manther	J.T. Walsh
Messenger	Alan Woolf
Peter Manther	Benjamin Masters
Bartender; Policeman; Doctor	Gil Rogers
Linder	Peggy Pope

PRODIGAL IN BLACK STONE (2). By Lennox Brown. July 18, 1972 (world premiere). Director, Dennis Scott; dramaturg, Edith Oliver.

Stewardess	Beth Hyde
Husband; Lalsingh	Glen Morrison
Wife; Shouter Woman	Grace McGhie
Perpetual Immigrant; Maraval	Carlton Bradshaw
Black American Tourist; Borbon	Bob Christian
British Gentleman; Achong	Vaughan Crosskill

Joseph Drayton	Joe Taffe
Captain Blackaron	Bev Randell
Mrs. Drayton	Melrose Randell

THE EXECUTIONERS (2). By Charles Kespert. July 19, 1972 (world premiere). Director, Tunc Yalman; dramaturg, Dan Sullivan.

1	William Rhys
2	Roger Robinson
3	Kevin O'Connor
4	Andrew Backer
5	J.T. Walsh
6	Lenny Baker
7	Gil Rogers

CASANOVA AND HIS MOTHER (2). By Danny Lipman. July 20, 1972 (world premiere). Director, James Hammerstein; dramaturg, Samuel Hirsch.

Carla	Geraldine Sherman
Philip	Michael Sacks

PROFESSOR GEORGE (2). By Marsha Sheiness. July 21, 1972 (world premiere). Director, Hal Scott; dramaturg, Edith Oliver.

John Wilson	Ben Masters
Elizabeth Oliver	Deloris Gaskins
Shirley Preston	Peggy Pope
Philip Richards	Roger Robinson
Joseph Grazzio	William Rhys
Professor George	John Harkins

ARTISTS FOR THE REVOLUTION (2). By Eric Thompson. July 22, 1972 (world premiere). Director, J. Ranelli; dramaturg, Samuel Hirsch.

Francoise Nevers	Margaret Hall
Anne Letourniez	Carol Flemming
Philippe Fabre	Lenny Baker
Edouard Ecousse	Peter Turgeon
Maximilien Robespierre	Gil Rogers
Paul Letourniez	Bob Christian
Auguste Dinville	J.T. Walsh
Rene Chappe	Norman Rose
Jean-Nicolas Houchard	Andrew Backer
Street Vendor	Kevin O'Connor

People of Paris: Leon Calanavin, Karen Carroll, Pat Carroll, Fred Cohen, Tom Doran, Louise Legue, Jack Neville, Camille Ranson, Zena Shervin, Gerda Schwartz, Pat Taggert.

THE WEB (2). By Trevor Rhome. July 25, 1972 (world premiere). Director, Dennis Scott; dramaturg, Dan Sullivan.

Martha	Melrose Randell
Harry	Vaughan Crosskill
Althea	Grace McGhie
Arthur	Joe Taffe

Carol ....Beth Hyde
Uncle Frankie ....Bev Randell

A DISTURBANCE OF MIRRORS (2). By
Pat Staten. July 25, 1972 (world premiere).
Director, Tunc Yalman; dramaturg, Edith
Oliver.
Anna ....Tandy Cronyn
Ellen ....Geraldine Sherman
Sydney ....Jeanne Ruskin
John ....Michael Sacks
Brian ....Benjamin Masters

THE BREAKOUT (2). By Oyamo. July 27,
1972 (world premiere). Director, Hal Scott;
dramaturg, Edith Oliver.
Slam ....Roger Robinson
Feet ....Bob Christian
Private Hack ....Reginald Johnson
Sgt. Hack .....................J.T. Walsh
Cpl. Hack ....Tom Doran
Rev. J.P. Jackson .............J.A. Preston
Cat ....Bill Cobbs
Woman Reporter ....Deloris Gaskins
1st Reporter ....Joe Taffe
3d Reporter ....Leon Calanquin
Dollarbill ....Carlton Bradshaw
Malcolm X; 2d Reporter ..Vaughan Crosskill

THE CRETAN BULL (2). By Kenneth H.
Brown. July 27, 1972 (world premiere). Di-
rector, J. Ranelli; dramaturg, Samuel Hirsch.
Rothcroft ....John Harkins
Browder ......................J.T. Walsh
Wanda ....Peggy Pope

WARREN HARDING (2). By Steven Shea.
July 29, 1972 (world premiere). Director,
James Hammerstein; dramaturg, Samuel
Hirsch; composer, Michael Posnick.
The Narrator ....Lenny Baker
Warren Harding ....Kevin O'Connor
Harry Daugherty ....Peter Turgeon
Nan Britton ....Tandy Cronyn
Sen. Lodge;
  Robert LaFollette ....Norman Rose
Mrs. Harding ....Jacqueline Brookes
Mme. Marcia; Red Fox;
  E.L. Doheny ....Michael Sacks
Texas Guinan ....Margaret Hall
Jess Smith ....Gil Rogers
Carrie Phillips ....Jeanne Ruskin
Albert Fall ....William Rhys
Gaston Means ....Andrew Backer
Roxy Stinson ....Geraldine Sherman
Girl ....Marianna Houston
Piano Player ....Michael Posnick
  Chorus of Senators: Joy Javitz, Charles
Kespert, Danny Lipman, Michael Sacks,
Gerda Schwartz, Jeff Wanshel.

STUCK (2). By Sandra Scoppettone. July 31,
1973 (world premiere). Director, Tunc Yal-
man; dramaturg, Edith Oliver.
Kitty Linden ....Margaret Hall
Anabelle Werner ....Peggy Pope
Young Woman ....Jeanne Ruskin
Fred Werner ....Peter Turgeon
Jim Linden ....John Harkins
Place: The Linden front porch and the
Werner front porch. Three acts.

TALES OF THE REVOLUTION AND
OTHER AMERICAN FABLES (2). By Jane
Chambers. August 3, 1972 (world premiere).
Director, J. Ranelli; dramaturg, Martin Esslin.
Lennie .......................J.T. Walsh
Bob ....Hal Scott
Barbara ....Tandy Cronyn
Mel ....Gil Rogers
Dyke ....Margaret Hall
Female ....Jeanne Ruskin
Lena; Old Woman ......Jacqueline Brookes
Man ....Bob Christian
Henry ....Benjamin Masters
Marty ....Michael Sacks
Andy ....Tom Doran
John ....David Berman
Dum-Dum ....Bob Christian
Sally ....Carol Flemming
Ruby ....Christine Vadnals
Kitty ....Beth Hattub
Lucy ....Linder Hookey
  Act I, Scene 1: A mixed gay bar in the
city, late Halloween night. Scene 2: The living
room of an old farmhouse. Act II, Scene 1:
Fancy hotel room overlooking amusement
park. Scene 2: Photographer's studio in
Manhattan.

ALFRED THE GREAT (2). By Israel Hor-
ovitz. August 4, 1972 (world premiere). Di-
rector, James Hammerstein; dramaturg, Mar-
tin Esslin.
Margaret ....Peggy Pope
Alfred ....Lenny Baker
Will ....Kevin O'Connor
Emily ....Geraldine Sherman
  This is the primary play in a trilogy called
The Wakefield Mystery Plays. Three acts.

SMILE ORANGE (3). By Trevor Rhone.
August 5, 1972 (world premiere). Director,
Dennis Scott.
Ringo ....Carl Bradshaw
Joe ....Joseph Taffe
Miss Brandon ....Grace McGhie
Cyril ....Glen Morrison
O'Keefe ....Vaughan Crosskill
Martha ....Beth Hyde
Bud ....Bev Randell
  Two acts.

WEST SPRINGFIELD, MASS.

Stage/West Theater

HEDDA GABLER (20). By Henrik Ibsen. November 10, 1972. Director, John Ulmer; designer, Charles G. Stockton. With Lucy Martin, Curt Williams, Edward Holmes, Margery Shaw.

TEN LITTLE INDIANS (20). By Agatha Christie. December 8, 1972. Director, William Guild; designer, Charles G. Stockton; costumes, Susan Glenn Harvuot. With Ted Graeber, Harry Ellerbe, Virginia Payne, Peter Blaxill.

THE GOOD NEWS (20). By Paul G. Enger. January 5, 1973 (world premiere). Director, William Guild; designer, Charles G. Stockton; costumes, Susan Glenn Harvuot.

Mme. Alpha Voldt	Virginia Payne
Malford Clay Hansen	Ted Graeber
Duane Folstad	Anthony McKay
Mona	Betty Williams
Patrolman Disantis	Jim Caporale
John	Edward Clinton

Time: The present, Tuesday night of Holy Week through Easter Sunday morning. Place: the first floor of a down-at-the-heels apartment building on Manhattan's West Side. Three acts.

THE EFFECT OF GAMMA RAYS ON MAN-IN-THE-MOON MARIGOLDS (20). By Paul Zindel. January 19, 1973. Director, John Ulmer; designer, Charles G. Stockton; costumes, Susan Glenn Harvuot. With Michaele Myers, Mary Gallagher, Paula Wagner.

THE IMPORTANCE OF BEING EARNEST (20). By Oscar Wilde. February 16, 1973. Director, John Ulmer; designer, Charles G. Stockton; costumes, William Schroeder. With Jeremiah Sullivan, Michaele Myers, John Colenback, Peter Blaxill, Charlotte Jones.

OLD TIMES (20). By Harold Pinter. March 16, 1973. Director, John Ulmer; designer, Charles G. Stockton; costumes, Susan Glenn Harvuot. With Ed Bardo, Michaele Meyers, Patricia Peardon.

BUTTERFLIES ARE FREE (20). By Leonard Gershe. April 13, 1973. Director, William Guild; designer, Charles G. Stockton; costumes, Susan Glenn Harvuot. With Edward Clinton, Joy McConnochie, Michaele Myers, Terry Burgler.

CANADA

HALIFAX

Neptune Theater: Main Stage

THE MISER (20). By Molière. July 10, 1972. Director, Jean-Louis Roux; designer, Mark Negin; lighting, Rae Ackerman. With David Dodimead, Dean Harris, Diane D'Aquila, David Renton, Jerry Franken.

WHAT THE BUTLER SAW (21). By Joe Orton. July 18, 1972. Director, Robert Sherrin; designer, Mark Negin; lighting, Jan Boland. With Eric House, Peggy Mahon, Ann Morrish, Jerry Franken, David Renton, Tom Celli.

COLOR THE FLESH THE COLOR OF DUST (15). By Michael Cook. November 16, 1972 (world premiere). Director, Robert Sherrin; designer, Robert Doyle; lighting, Rae Ackerman; music, Alan Laing.

Willie	Dean Harris
Ben	Peter Rogan
Sean; French Officer; English Officer	R.D. Reid
Lt. Mannon	James Hurdle
Marie	Diane D'Aquila
Biddies	Joan Orenstein, Joan Hurley
James Tupper	Eric House
Boy	Ian Deakin
Mrs. McDonald	Florence Paterson
Magistrate Neal	David Renton
Spokesman	Don Allison
Patrick	Bruce Armstrong
Kevin	Dean Smith
Lawrence	Lionel Simmons
Gert	Margot Sweeny
Capt. Gross	Rowland Davies
Fisherman	Donald Meyers
French Soldier; English Soldier	George Henderson
Percussionist	Brian Furlott
Fiddler	Leo Doublet

Time: The spring and fall of 1762. Place: St. John's, Newfoundland. Two acts.

LISTEN TO THE WIND (15). By James Reaney, with poems by Charlotte and Emily Brontë. January 18, 1973. Director, Keith Turnbull; design coordinator, Nancey Pankiw; lighting, Bennet Averyt. With Jerry Franken, Nicola Lipman, Nancy Beatty, Blair Brown, Tom Carew, Bryan Stanion, Edgar Wreford, Joan Orenstein, Rowland Davies, Diana D'Aquila.

LOOT (21). By Joe Orton. February 8, 1973. Director, Christopher Newton; designer, Maurice Strike; lighting, Hugh Jones. With Bob Cartland, Patricia Ludwick, Dean Harris, Tom Carew, David Renton, Robert D. Reid.

Neptune Theater: Second Stage

THE MAN WITH SEVEN TOES by Michael Ondaatje and BABEL created by the St. Francis Xavier University Performing Group (9). July 6, 1972. Director, John Rapsey; lighting, Jane Boland; costumes, Candy Sweet, Bob Doyle. With David Miller, Cecile O'Connor, Barry Reynolds, Denise Golemblaski, Mary Tramley. Patrick Dunne, Allan Meuse.

KRAPP'S LAST TAPE (6). By Samuel Beckett. July 17, 1972. With Terence G. Ross.

In repertory:

CRABDANCE (14). By Beverley Simons. August 6, 1972. Director, Michael Mawson; lighting, Jane Boland. With Joan Orenstein, Barry Minshull, John Garrett, Howard D'Arcy.

GORILLA QUEEN (11). By Ronald Tavel. August 15, 1972. Director, Keith Turnbull; lighting, Jane Boland. With Bob Martyn, Diane D'Aquila, Ewan Sutherland, Bruce Wilson.

3000 RED ANTS by Lawrence Ferlinghetti and ONE MAN MASQUE by James Reaney (10). September 6, 1972. Director, Michael Mawson. With Lionel Simmons, Margot Sweeny, Ian Deaken, John Dunsworth, Patricia Ludwick, Allan Meuse, Suzanne Turnbull.

THE DEATH OF FIELDING (9). By Tom Lackey. September 21, 1972. Director, Keith Turnbull. With Hans Boggild, Richard Donat, Robert Reid, Michael Hartley-Robinson, Dean Smith.

REVELATIONS (11). Adapted from The Seventh Seal by Ingmar Bergman. November 1, 1972. Director, Michael Mawson. With members of the Company.

THE COLLECTED WORKS OF BILLY THE KID (11). By Michael Ondaatje. November 21, 1972. Director, Michael Mawson; music, David Hellyer. With Jerry Franken, Nicola Lipman.

THE FOURSOME (10). By E. A. Whitehead. January 31, 1973. Director, Michael Mawson. With Nick Mancuso, Richard Donat, Suzanne Turnbull, Susan Little.

Note: Neptune Theater special Christmas show, The Magical Guitar (16) by Janet MacEachen, directed by Robert Sherrin, was produced December 26, 1972.

MONTREAL

Centaur Theater

LEAVING HOME (33). By David French. November 11, 1972. Director, Bill Glassco; scenery, Dan Yarni, Stephen Katz; costumes, Vicky Manthorpe. With Maureen Fitzgerald, Frank Moore, Mel Tuck, Sean Sullivan, Lyn Griffin, Anne Butler, Les Carlson.

DEATH OF A SALESMAN (33). By Arthur Miller. December 16, 1972. Director, Joel Miller; scenery, Feliz Mirbt; lighting, Vladimir Svetlovsky; costumes, Erla Gliserman. With Maurice Podbrey, Joyce Campion, Gary Reineke, Alan Royal, Griffith Brewer.

CREEPS (26). By David Freeman. January 3, 1973. Director, Maurice Podbrey; scenery, Feliz Mirbt; lighting, Vladimir Svetlovsky; costumes, Erla Gliserman. With James Hurdle, Robert Sime, George Dawson, Gary Reineke, Allan Royal, Sheila Haney.

THE REAL INSPECTOR HOUND, directed by Michael Sinelnikoff and AFTER MAGRITTE, directed by Joel Miller (33). By Tom Stoppard. January 31, 1973. Scenery, Michael Eagan; lighting, Vladimir Svetlovsky; costumes, Erla Gliserman. With Gary Reineke, Scotty

Bloch, Myra Benson, James Hurdle, George Dawson.

AUTUMN AT ALTENBURG (26). By Ronald Garrett. March 7, 1973 (world premiere). Director, Henry Tarvainen; scenery and costumes, Michael Eagen; lighting, Vladimir Svetlovsky.
Capt. Frederick K. Haller ......James Hurdle
John Eugen Haller ....Booth Harding Savage
Ernest Haller ....George Dawson
Mrs. Alison Haller ....Scotty Bloch
Maj. Gen. Victor Haller ......Stan Mallough
Father Eric Junhens ....Nicholas Simons
Rev. Dr. Jessop ....Barrie Baldaro
Gervase ....Leo Phillips
Lt. Vivian ....Campbell Smith
Mrs. Ullmans ....Sheila Haney
Johannes Oswald ....Fred Doederlein

McGregor ....Griffith Brewer
Mungo ....Ardon Bess
The action takes place in 1931 at Altenburg in the County of Lunenburg, Nova Scotia. Three acts.

MANDRAGOLA (26). By Niccolo Machiavelli; English version by Eric Bentley. April 4, 1973. Director, Henry Tarvainen; scenery and costumes, Jean Pierre Carbonneau; lighting, Vladimir Svetlovsky. With Booth Harding Savage, George Dawson, James Hurdle, James Edmund, June Keevil, Sheila Haney.

OLD TIMES (33). By Harold Pinter. May 2, 1973. Director, Elsa Bolam; scenery and costumes, Michael Eagan; lighting, Vladimir Svetlovsky. With Maurice Podbrey, June Keevil, Elizabeth Shepard.

STRATFORD, ONT.

Stratford Festival: Festival Theater

AS YOU LIKE IT (34). By William Shakespeare. June 5, 1972. Director, William Huff; designer, Alan Barlow; lighting, Gil Wechsler. With Carole Shelley, Pamela Brook, William Needles, Edward Atienza, Nicholas Pennell, Barry Macgregor.

LORENZACCIO (22). By Alfred de Musset; English version by John Lewin. June 6, 1972 (world premiere). Director, Jean Gascon; designer, Michael Annals; lighting, Gil Wechsler; music, Gabriel Charpentier.
Lorenzo de Medici ....Pat Galloway
Alessandro de Medici ....Kenneth Welsh
Maria Soderini ....Mary Savidge
Caterina Ginori ....Pamela Brook
Bindo Altoviti; Mafio ....Barry MacGregor
Scoronconcolo ....Michael Liscinsky
Giomo ....Jack Roberts
Giuliano Salviati ....Stanley Coles
Cosimo de Medici ....John Innes
Felippo Strozzi ....Powys Thomas
Pietro ....Daniel Davis
Tomaso ....Don Sutherland
Leone ....Blaine Parker
Luisa ....Krysia Read
Francesco Pazzi ....William Webster
Baptista Venturi ....Joseph Rutten
Cardinal Cibo ....Roland Hewgill
Countess Cibo ....Elizabeth Shepherd
Agnolo ....Colin Bernhardt
Cardinal Valori ....Joel Kenyon

Signor Maurizio ....Mervyn Blake
Silk Merchant ....William Needles
Goldsmith ....Erik Donkin
Tebalde Freccia ....Nicholas Pennell
Maffio ....Barry MacGregor
German Officer ....Carl Gall
1st Lady ....Trudy Cameron
2d Lady ....Mary Barton
Citizens of Florence, Servants, Soldiers, Exiles, Strozzi Clan, Monks, Council of Eight: Colin Bernhardt, Theodore Britton, Dan Conley, Nicole Evans, Christine Foster, Roy Frady, Edward Henry, Maureen Lee, Charles Northcote, Raymond O'Neill, Thomas Stebing, Allan Stratton, Joseph Totaro, David Wells, Jack Wetherall.
Time: 1537. Place: Florence. Two acts.

KING LEAR (35). By William Shakespeare. June 7, 1972. Director, David William; designer, Annena Stubbs; lighting, Gil Wechsler; music and sound, Louis Applebaum. With Edward Atienza, William Hutt, Daniel Davis, Pat Galloway, Carole Shelley, Elizabeth Shepherd.

SHE STOOPS TO CONQUER (20). By Oliver Goldsmith. July 25, 1972. Director, Michael Bawtree; designer, Desmond Heeley; lighting, Gil Wechsler. With Mary Savidge, Tony Van Bridge, Alan Scarfe, Carole Shelley, Nicholas Pennell, Barry MacGregor, Powys Thomas.

Stratford Festival: Avon Theater

THE THREEPENNY OPERA (35). Book and lyrics by Bertolt Brecht; music by Kurt Weill; English adaptation by Marc Blitzstein. June 30, 1972. Director, Jean Gascon; music director, Alan Laing; designer, Robert Prevost; lighting, Gil Wechsler. With Jack Creley, Lila Kedrova,

Anton Rodgers, Monique Leyrac, Marilyn Gardner.

LA GUERRE, YES SIR! (35). By Roch Carrier; translated by Suzanne Grossman. August

4, 1972. Director, Albert Millaire; designer, Mark Negin; lighting, Gil Wechsler; songs, Garbriel Charpentier. With Bernard Assiniwi, Danielle Roy, Albert Millaire, Jacques Thisdale, Roger Garand, Lucille Cousineau.

Stratford Festival: Third Stage

MARK (13). By Betty Jane Wylie. July 19, 1972 (world premiere). Director, William Hutt; designer, Art Pension; lighting, Ian Johnson.

Mark .... Antony Parr
Anna .... Christine Bennett
Kate .... Sylvia Shore
Tom .... Doug McGrath
  Time: The Present, spanning one season,

from fall to winter, about six weeks. Two acts.

PINOCCHIO (19). By John Wood; adapted from the stories of Carlo Collodi. August 2, 1972. Director, John Wood; designer, John Ferguson; lighting, F. Mitchell Dana; music, Alan Laing. With Michael Burgess, Sean Sullivan, Giuseppe Condello.

Note: There was also a guest appearance by Tony Van Bridge as G.K.C. (*The Wit and Wisdom of Gilbert Keith Chesterton*) on August 27, 1972.

VANCOUVER

The Playhouse Theater Company: Mainstage

FORTY YEARS ON (24). By Alan Bennett. October 16, 1972. Director, Paxton Whitehead; scenery, Cameron Porteous; lighting, Frank Masi; costumes, John Fenney. With Patrick Boxill, Graeme Campbell, Paxton Whitehead, Marjorie Le Strange.

HOW THE OTHER HALF LOVES (24). By Alan Ayckbourn. November 13, 1972. Director, Richard Ouzounian; scenery, Stephen Geaghan; lighting, Frank Masi; costumes, John Fenney. With Barbara J. Gordon, Paxton Whitehead, Patricia Gage, Graeme Campbell, Owen Foran, Shirley Broderick.

TREASURE ISLAND (24). By Robert Louis Stevenson; adapted by Bernard Miles. December 11, 1972. Director, Patrick Crean; designer, Cameron Porteous; lighting, Frank Masi. With Graeme Campbell, John Pozer, Michael Ball, Derek Ralston.

LULU STREET (24). By Ann Henry. January 15, 1973. Director, Robert Clothier; scenery and costumes, Jack Simon; lighting, Frank Masi. With Derek Ralston, Walter Marsh, Marti Maraden, Daphne Goldrick, Roger Norman.

OLD TIMES (24). By Harold Pinter. February 9, 1973. Director, Tom Kerr; scenery and costumes, Cameron Porteous; lighting, Frank Masi.

With Bruno Gerussi, Anni Lee Taylor, Patricia Gage.

PILLAR OF SAND (24). By Eric Nicol, with Peter Church and Thomas Barbour. March 12, 1973 (world premiere). Director, Malcolm Black; scenery and costumes, Brian Jackson; lighting, Lynne Hyde; music, Arnold Black.

Daniel .... Jace Van Der Veen
Medeah .... Sam Moses
Titus .... Peter Church
Leo I .... Thomas Barbour
Eudoxia .... B.J. Gordon
Niobe .... Angela Gann
Theodore .... Paxton Whitehead
Hero .... Wayne Robson
Basiliscus .... Neil Dainard
  Soldiers: Jeffrey Jones, Thomas Hauff, Allan Lysell. Pilgrims: Michael Curtis, Gary Griffiths, Beatrice Hicks, Melody Horbulyk, Ed Astley, Eric Stine.
  Time: The 5th century. Place: A desert a few miles outside Constantinople. Act I, Scene 1: Dawn. Scene 2: Later in the morning. Scene 3: Midnight the same day. Act II, Scene 1: The following morning. Scene 2: Sunset the same day.

ARMS AND THE MAN (24). By George Bernard Shaw. April 9, 1973. Directors, Paxton Whitehead, Ron Nipper. Scenery and costumes, Cameron Porteous; lighting, Frank Masi. With B. J. Gordon, Neil Dainard, Jeffrey Jones.

Note: In addition, Playhouse Theater Company's Youtheater presented an evening of Oscar Wilde, including *The Happy Prince*, letters and poems, and *The Nightingale and the Rose*. The Studio Theater presented *Cowboys #2* by Sam Shepard, *The Dutchman* by Leroi Jones, *Love Mouse* by Sheldon Rosen, *The End of the Picnic* by David Campton.

WINNIPEG

Manitoba Theater Center: Main Stage

A STREETCAR NAMED DESIRE (24). By Tennessee Williams. October 2, 1972. Director, Edward Gilbert; designer, Peter Wingate; lighting, Robert Reinholdt. With Debra Mooney, Anthony Palmer, Dana Ivey, Kenneth Pogue.

SLEUTH (24). By Anthony Shaffer. October 30, 1972. Director, David Giles; scenery and lighting, William Ritman. With Douglas Rain, David Buck, Eric Rogers, Robin Mayfield, Maurice K. Schwartz.

A THURBER CARNIVAL (24). By James Thurber. November 27, 1972. Director, Biff McGuire; designer, Peter Wingate; lighting, Robert Reinholdt. With Tony Aylward, Jay Garner, Christian Grant, Budd Knapp, Ben Yafee, Tandy Cronyn, Rita Howell, Dana Ivey, Marijane Maricle.

HEDDA GABLER (24). By Henrik Ibsen. January 8, 1973. Director, Edward Gilbert; designer, Joseph Scelenyi; lighting, Robert Reinholdt. With Martha Henry, Douglas Rain, John Neville, Terry Tweed, Roland Hewgill.

GUYS AND DOLLS (24). Book by Jo Swerling and Abe Burrows, based on a story and characters by Damon Runyon; music and lyrics by Frank Loesser. February 5, 1973. Director, John Hirsch; musical director, Alan Laing; musical staging and dances, Marvin Gordon; scenery, Eoin Sprott; lighting, F. Mitchell Dana; costumes, Jack Edwards. With Gordon Pinsent, Rik Colitti, Judy Armstrong, Denise Fergusson, Joseph Palmieri.

Manitoba Theater Center: Main Stage (in repertory)

HAMLET (24). By William Shakespeare. March 19, 1973. Director, Edward Gilbert; designer, Peter Wingate; lighting, Robert Reinholdt. With Alan Dobie, Maurice Good, Denise Fergusson, Edgar Wreford, Deborah Kipp.

ROSENCRANTZ AND GUILDENSTERN ARE DEAD (24). By Tom Stoppard. March 20, 1973. Director, Douglas Rain; designer, Peter Wingate; lighting, Robert Reinholdt. With Bernard Hopkins, Terry Wale, Alan Dobie, Deborah Kipp, Maurice Good, Denise Fergusson, Edgard Wreford.

Manitoba Theater Center: Warehouse Theater

THE PROMISE (12). By Aleksei Arbuzov. October 25, 1972. Director, Tibor Feheregyhazi; designer, Ralph McDermid; lighting, Bill Williams. With Deborah Kipp, David Schurmann, Hardee T. Lineham.

EN PIECES DETACHÉES (12). By Michel Tremblay; translated by Allan Van Meer; adapted for the stage by Andre Brassard. January 17, 1973 (English language premiere). Director, Andre Brassard; designer, Real Ouellette; lighting, Kent McKay.

Helene	Dana Ivey
Robertine	Irene Hogan
Claude	Heath Lamberts
Francine	Margaret Bard
Henri	Michael Donaghue
Mado; Lucille	Liza Creighton

The action of the play takes place a few years ago in Montreal. No intermission.

JACQUES BREL IS ALIVE AND WELL AND LIVING IN PARIS (19). By Eric Blau and Mort Shuman; based on Brel's lyrics and commentary; music by Jacques Brel. February 2, 1973. Director, Richard Ouzonian; musical director and conductor, Roger Perkins; scenery, Glenn MacDonald; lighting, Kent McKay; costumes, Margaret Ryan. With Diane Stapley, Pat Rose, Ruth Nichol, Brent Carver.

WEDDING IN WHITE (12). By William Fruet. May 9, 1973. Director and designer, Alan Dobie; lighting, Kent McKay. With Richard Farrell, John Boylan, Doris L. Petrie, Hardee T. Lineham, Nancy Beatty.

Note: Manitoba Theater Center also presented The Dancing Donkey by Eric Vos, a Christmas play for children; Tony Van Bridge as G.K. Chesterton; and Libby Morris in Women's Libby.

THE SEASON IN LONDON

PROBLEMS OF AN ENGLISH PLAYWRIGHT

By Frank Marcus

Author of the Best Play *The Killing of Sister George* and other scripts including *Mrs. Mouse, Are You Within?, The Window, The Formation Dancers, Notes on a Love Affair, Blank Pages* and *Christmas Carol* and drama critic of London's *The Sunday Telegraph.*

TO THE unproduced playwright, there exists only one problem: to get his play on the stage. The stench of decay emanating from a rejected, ignored or abandoned playscript lying in a desk drawer can be poisonous and overwhelming. To such a writer, the cries of woe of established dramatists must sound presumptuous, indeed impertinent.

By "established" I mean a writer who has had his plays performed at a reasonably high professional level, has achieved some success and critical approbation (not to mention publicity) and can therefore be said to have a "reputation." He, at least, has the satisfaction of knowing that any completed play of his will be considered sympathetically at the highest level. There is never a *guarantee* of production, and the allegiance of critics is as fickle as that of audiences. The writer who is tenuously or even contractually bound to a producing management or, say, a provincial repertory theater—the "house" dramatist—is in a fractionally more favorable position. He might feel that he is writing to order, but with the illustrious examples of Shakespeare and Molière before him, he need not consider himself to be a hack. On the other hand, commissioned plays often have a habit of not turning out well: it could be that a deep sense of self-contempt on the part of the author causes him to inject an agent of destruction into his work.

I am on nodding terms of acquaintance with most of my playwriting contemporaries, and bound in friendship to some, and never cease to be intrigued by why they write or what they write at any given time. Our problems tend to be similar and, irrespective of whether or not we like each other's plays, there is a deep and almost tangible bond between us. I am speaking now of the mature writer, who is about to enter, or has entered, middle age. The first explosion of talent has been spent: the early, therapeutic, fiercely introspective

92

cries of anguish have resounded from the stage; the golden visions have been communicated. What happens next?

The first and most striking impression is the almost universal desire to avoid writing at all. They will act, direct, adapt, teach, lecture in American universities, get involved in politics, make films, and—heaven help me— become theater critics, in their search for alibis. A symposium of dramatists' wives would provide illuminating information on the subject.

Yet, there will be a spate of new plays from distinguished sources this year; their inspiration is predictably varied. Two plays—by Christopher Hampton and by Peter Shaffer—owe their existence to newspaper reports. Hampton read about a massacre of Brazilian Indians and was moved to travel to Brazil and to write *Savages*; Shaffer's *Equus* stemmed from a psychiatric case history about a homosexual teenager, whose seduction by a girl in a stable made him blind the horses. History, with its rich opportunities for analogy, has turned David Storey's attention to *Cromwell,* and Peter Barnes, who, incidentally, worked for two years from 9 to 5 (Saturdays included) at the British Museum, rummaging among the more obscure works of the Jacobeans, has surfaced with a monumental play of his own on the subject of the Spanish Succession. John Osborne, in his obsessive search for self-identification with heroes and heroines of literature, has moved from *Hedda Gabler* (a straight translation) to *Coriolanus,* rendered in modern paraphrase. Edward Bond has essayed a bizarre comedy; Tom Stoppard has the contented look about him of a man who obtains satisfaction from constructing intricate games and puzzles for his own amusement. Arnold Wesker, after sitting in as observer (no pun intended) on *The Sunday Times,* came up with a panoramic view of the press which has yet to be seen.

Marriage retains its popularity—as a subject for plays, that is, if not as an institution. Peter Nichols is reputedly dissecting it in a new work; John Mortimer, emulating the lucrative practise of his ex-wife, has mined their turbulent union for yet another piece of fiction, *Collaborators,* in which the somewhat mildewed facts are covered frantically in verbal glitter. The literary uses of experience are carried to their ultimate degree by Charles Wood: first he wrote a screen play, then he wrote a play about the making of the film, and now, proceeding on the principle of a Russian doll, he has written a play about the staging of the play.

The outside world rarely impinges. There was the expected, shrill, polemical piece about Northern Ireland from Mr. and Mrs. John Arden, but to most of us the very idea of politics is totally dispiriting. A most distinguished dramatist, who has recently experimented with formal innovations with the desperation of a blind man lost in a labyrinth, said to me on the telephone last week: "I feel completely drained. I think in future I'll just stick to adaptations." I remembered the anguished words from John Whiting's diary: "I suppose nothing is going to make me angry or sad enough to write a new play. Sitting in the weak sunshine it seems as unimportant to me as it would seem to anyone else. Perhaps it really is the climate. In a little over a year I shall be 40. All the people who urged me to write for the theater ten years ago have husbands and children now, and are not concerned with anger or sadness. I am becoming petulant, but it has no irritant value, except to others."

Well, writers, too, have families. That is why I admire to the point of veneration the industry of all the writers mentioned above—irrespective of the outcome. A West End success—which, in practical terms means a run of some six months, followed by provincial and overseas productions—will buy a playwright two or three years of freedom, but not freedom from anxiety. A 60-minute television play will earn him not much more than 1,000 pounds. He would have to write four or five television plays a year in order to make a modest living.

The recent death of Noel Coward, who had enjoyed an active working life of 50 years, brought an avalanche of assessments. Most of them agreed that, like Oscar Wilde, he had produced one indisputable masterpiece and three or four comedies with a chance of survival. Measured in the perspective of history, that is enough. We all want to strike sparks, and naturally we hope that one or two of them will not be extinguished by time. In the meantime, we have to provide fodder for the ever-increasing number of theaters, now that it appears to have been officially decided that culture in general and the theater in particular is "a good thing."

To the aspirant playwright, we are objects of envy; to the public, incredibly, we are objects of glamor; to our families, we are neurotic nuisances that have to be tolerated. Most of us feel precarious and unnecessary, haunted not by fears of failure—that is inevitable—but by the possibility that our creative urge might suddenly dry up. We could probably bluff our way for a few years longer, sustained by skill and cunning, but sooner or later we would be found out. That's why it is a good thing to have a reserve occupation. It is not greed or an unquenchable desire for publicity, nor a sign of Herculean energy. Most of us are *nice* people. My agent once said to me sagaciously that she thought we were nice because we were able to express all our nastinesss in our plays. The Literary Adviser of one of our major Companies remarked the other day about one of our best playwrights: "If that man didn't write plays, he'd be Jack the Ripper!".

And yet, is it not a matter for regret that we should be such depleted human beings? A cracker I pulled last Christmas contained not the usual feeble joke, but the extraordinary and frighteningly apt pronouncement: "How vain it is to sit down to write when you have not stood up to live." I have kept that slip of paper—next to my typewriter. And I remember with a shudder that the self-disgust and emptiness that constitutes the tragicomic condition of the creative writer was the subject of my last play. Clearly, I am beyond redemption.

REVIEW OF THE LONDON SEASON

By Ossia Trilling

Author, critic, lecturer, broadcaster; member of the Council of the Critics' Circle; president of the International Theater Critics' Association; European Editor of *Best Plays*

THE BEST theatrical news this year was the decision of the various people who run the affairs of the National Theater to take the bull by the horns and entrust to Peter Hall the virtual management of the entire enterprise at the side of Laurence Olivier, whose position as sole director has long been under criticism. There was first Olivier's illness which has certainly taken its toll of him even if his strength is unimpaired. But also the delays in completing the new complex on the South Bank, with its three auditoriums now not expected to be ready until 1975, would have meant that his successor would have occupied a subsidiary position for far too long a time. As a result, Peter Hall joined Olivier as co-director on April 1 with a view to taking over entirely in November 1973. Olivier remains as an acting member of the company. In the spring of 1974 he is to withdraw completely, returning only as an actor when the new building begins to function. Operating the two main auditoriums, the "Olivier," seating 1,150, with its amphitheater, and the "Lyttelton," seating 900 with its proscenium-stage, and the 200-seat flexible studio theater a glimpse of which was obtained during the "topping-out" ceremony on May 2, will require early planning resources, so that already a new directorate that includes Michael Blakemore, Jonathan Miller, Harold Pinter, John Schlesinger and John Russell Brown has been formed. Kenneth Tynan, literary manager and the former director's right hand from the foundation of the company ten years ago, is due to be replaced at the end of the season.

To give Olivier his due, his swan-song year was marked by remarkable artistic and box-office successes, which wiped out last year's deficit, and the internal dissensions seem to have been ironed out. So now, in another 24 months, Londoners may look forward to the final realization of Effingham Wilson's 1848 dream of the creation of a National theater in body as well as in spirit. Meantime, speculation grew rife about the future relations between the National Theater and the Royal Shakespeare Company, of which Mr. Hall remains a director, at least until the latter's new home in the Barbican Center in the City of London is ready for it, perhaps in 1978. It was officially admitted that secret talks had been going on between the two and possible forms of collaboration, if not a total merger, were examined.

The acquisition of Michael Blakemore last year proved a godsend to the National's fortunes. He was responsible for directing a British "first," that of the Hecht-MacArthur *The Front Page,* which was both colorful and fast-moving and displayed many hitherto unsuspected talents among the company. If it proved disappointing to some American visitors, that was only because of the lack of authentic American accents among the English players. His handling of *Macbeth* revealed in a more enthralling way than ever before the versatility and dynamic personality of Diana Rigg as Lady Macbeth playing opposite Anthony Hopkins's somewhat dour Macbeth. Hopkins was reported to have overworked himself and was given leave of absence from the company for the second time in two years, but as he cropped up in a film studio soon afterwards, his recovery must have taken an unexpectedly rapid turn. His role in Macbeth was taken over by Denis Quilley, a late developer who has been improving immensely and stretching his considerable talents most agreeably ever since, most recently as a self-consciously jovial Lopahin in Mr. Blakemore's ingeniously cheerful and inventive *The Cherry Orchard*—inventive without offending against Chekhov's comic intentions, except in the very last moment, when the illusion of reality so painstakingly built up was shattered in a single blow by an ill-advised piece of technical trickery.

Among the season's most memorable successes was the new commissioned version of Molière's *The Misanthrope,* by the 36-year-old Yorkshire poet Tony Harrison, which John Dexter (who retains his connection with the company under Mr. Hall as occasional director) situated in present-day Paris with considerable comic flair. It provided two scintillating comic performances in Alec McCowen's atrabilious (the epithet is Mr. Harrison's) Alceste, and Diana Rigg's outrageously self-revealing Célimène. Miss Rigg also played the insidious Hippolita in *'Tis Pity She's a Whore* with the National Theater's newly-formed touring company, appearing a few hundred yards downstream of the Old Vic Theater under canvas in Sam Wanamaker's first Festival Season at the makeshift site of the projected Bankside Globe Playhouse on the South Bank.

The Old Vic Theater itself was offered to the Royal Court Theater (with its newly-appointed manager Oscar Lewenstein) for occupation after the National Theater company eventually moves out. At the Young Vic, across the road, Frank Dunlop's company were preparing to cut the umbilical cord that had bound them to the parent company and to operate as a wholly independent organization. Among the season's highlights was Frank Dunlop's own production of Ben Jonson's *The Alchemist,* updated to modern times and unveiled not in London at all but at the Vienna Festival, where it raised as many eyebrows among theatergoers with traditional predilections as had Dexter's *The Misanthrope* in the case of a small number of dedicated, mostly French, Molière fans. A welcome newcomer to the company was Peter McEnery, not only as an actor but also as director, notably of Ted Hughes's poem *The Wound,* a singularly moving piece of drama which, I hope, will tempt the author to return to the theater with another play of his own and in his own language.

At the Royal Shakespeare Company's London home, the Aldwych Theater, Trevor Nunn opened the season by presenting some of the previous season's Stratford successes, with a few necessary cast changes. These included John Barton's partly updated *Othello,* with Brewster Mason as a stolid Christian blackamoor, surrounded by a posse of Muslim Mediterranean servants, and a curiously soft-toned *The Merchant of Venice* that featured Susan Fleetwood as a sly, not to say devious, Portia. Terry Hands worked wonders with T. S. Eliot's old dramatic warhorse, *Murder in the Cathedral,* and breathed new life into it by lifting the only scene with any comic relief into the realm of contemporary music-hall, a device that would surely have gladdened the poet's heart. David Jones's noble but clumsy effort to get English actors to impersonate Russians convincingly in Gorky's *The Lower Depths* fell far short of the success he had obtained with the previous year's *The Enemies.* With his subsequent production Jones succeeded far better. This was the four-hour-long new epic drama, inspired by the legends and stories of King Arthur, to which the authors, John Arden and his wife Margaretta D'Arcy, had given the title of *The Land of the Mighty* and in which the traditional romantic trappings were stripped away to reveal the brutal violence and self-seeking interests that held sway at the time, much as they have done in more recent days. A taut and gripping production of an overlong text and virtually unmanageable flood of dramatic ideas and language was rewarded at the eleventh hour by the public protests of the two cantankerous authors who accused their director, and the R.S.C., of betraying their political message and their dramatic purpose by turning an anti-imperialist poetic drama into its opposite. A less than tactful reply in the press by Nunn and Jones caused the resignation of one right-wing member of the board, who should have known better. The Ardens stomped the sidewalks outside the theater with banners and slogans protesting their case. They failed to give it coherence, if only because of the contradictions and inconsistencies in their pronouncements, but got some valuable publicity in the process. They got more publicity when a person claimed he had been libeled by them in a play about the Irish question called *The Ballygombeen Bequest,* when this moved from the Edinburgh Festival to London, but this did not help them financially, since a legal injunction, or at any rate the threat of one, caused the producer to cut short the run.

A similar fate nearly befell Frank Norman's satirical comedy *Costa Packet,* which was one of several enterprising new plays staged at the Theater Royal in Stratford, East by Joan Littlewood to celebrate the 20th anniversary of the foundation of Theater Workshop. He alleged that she had rewritten and changed his play beyond recognition, but his justified anger was finally allayed by the mounting box-office returns. A birthday celebration at Miss Littlewood's theater brought together a large number of friends and former members of one of Britain's best-loved and most influential theatrical groups, many of whom, prominent today on stage and screen, had made their forgotten debuts under her wing.

The Royal Court both before and after Lewenstein took over continued its unique policy of encouraging new drama, both on its large stage and at the tiny Theater Upstairs, under the eves. John Dexter staged the world premiere of Arnold Wesker's latest realistic comedy called *The Old Ones* here, a play that harked back to the characters the author knows and depicts so convincingly from the Anglo-Jewish working-class immigrant milieu from which he himself stems. Here, too, the problem of mastering the authentic accents proved insuperable, but otherwise the comedy moved nimbly from one family situation to another in Wesker's characteristically sympathetic vein. John Osborne's adaptation of Ibsen's *Hedda Gabler* was a misguided, if well-intentioned, attempt to find an acceptable colloquial idiom for a modern production; but the styles used were too disparate and the occasional Americanisms suggested that Osborne had not had the home market in mind alone when turning his hand to this version. Osborne's introduction in the published version contained a most ungenerous, not to say ill-mannered, comment on Ingmar Bergman and his very special and idiosyncratic view of the tragedy, that indirectly supported my view of Osborne's insensitivity to the original work. His own play *A Sense of Detachment* was far more satisfactory, for, though its intellectual level was no higher than might be expected, the witty handling of the actors (greatly assisted by Frank Dunlop's hilarious production) was as masterfully done as in any previous play in which Osborne's pet aversions have come under fire. A marvellous performance by Billie Whitelaw as The Mouth in *Not I,* coupled with Albert Finney's as the old codger in *Krapp's Last Tape,* made a fascinating double turn for Beckett fans. There was a new play by Edna O'Brien and a first full-length one by Caryl Churchill, a promising newcomer (upstairs, this time), to show that the example set by Anne Jellicoe at this theater had not been forgotten, and yet another collectively-written piece about the "throubles" in Ulster. But the greatest satisfaction came from two new works by Christopher Hampton and Edward Bond. The former's *Savages,* based on an investigation into the criminal, genocidal and anti-democratic policies of the present authoritarian regime in Brazil, found little favor with orthodox critical opinion, in my submission quite unjustifiably. One critic who opined that he didn't wish to be preached to about the world's ills reminded me of the supporter of theatrical censorship who is said to have objected to a theater that depicts rape, arson, sodomy, adultery, drug addiction, *et al.,* on the grounds that he could "get all that in his own home". It seems, then, that Hampton's critical shafts may have hit their mark. Certainly Paul Scofield gave one of the most efficiently mannered and persuasive characterizations of his entire career as the kind of woolly-minded British liberal diplomat who would have been quite capable of uttering the sentiments I have just quoted. In my view, Hampton's play is not only his best; it is also among the most important contributions to the contemporary political theater repertory. Almost the same might be said of Bond's *The Sea,* except that the political message, which is as broadly humanitarian as Hampton's, is less directly preached. Bond's philosopher spokesman may be naive and even perplexing in his pronouncements, but the central theme, which utterly exposes and condemns a society encouraging hypocrisy, servility, despotism and violence, is unimpeachable.

Quite a few new and promising writers surfaced in outlying theaters, like those at Stratford, East, Greenwich or Hampstead; and even the Shaw Theater unexpectedly offered a sizable new work of great merit in a regional dramatist's fascinating attempt to reconstruct the atmosphere of the struggling young Scottish labor movement half a century and more ago: Bill Bryden's *Willy Rough.* A new regime in Greenwich under Robin Phillips proved itself with James Saunders's *Hans Kohlhaas,* a Brechtian parable play about despotism and class injustice set in historical times but with a clear present-day moral in it, plus Tom Stoppard's new English version of Lorca's *The House of Bernarda Alba,* and, above all, in the perceptiveness of its realistic playing, against a stylized background setting, of Ibsen's *Rosmersholm,* a fitting vehicle for Joan Plowright's return to the London stage (as Rebecca West) after too long an absence. The Mermaid rediscovered Noel Coward in *Cowardly Custard,* a medley of his songs, sketches and other writings, that ironically caught the public fancy in the year of his death, the very year in which a commercial revival of *Private Lives* also scored a public triumph with the former National Theater players Robert Stephens and Maggie Smith in the parts created by Coward and Gertrude Lawrence. The bill of fare at the Hampstead Theater Club was enlivened by the British premiere of Tennessee Williams's *Small Craft Warnings,* featuring American guest star Elaine Stritch and offering a number of startling cameo portraits of human frailty, not the least memorable among them the sexually aberrant Violet of Frances de la Tour. There were new plays by Howard Barker (*Alpha Alpha* at the Open Space), David Rudkin (*The Filth Hunt* at the Almost Free Theater), William Trevor (a few impressively written one-acters), David Mercer (*Let's Murder Vivaldi,* a former TV playlet, at The King's Head), and others, to justify the continued existence of these experimental stages and lunchtime theaters. The Act Inn closed its doors through lack of state support, and the lunchtime theater movement as a whole had to draw its belt in, but somehow these efforts were of a kind to keep most of them going, if not quite as going concerns. Clearly they fulfill a need, but equally clearly much of what is done is of purely ephemeral quality. If they do no more than give some actors who might otherwise be forced to earn their living in less congenial surroundings an opportunity to practise their chosen profession, however, no matter how restricted the space or depressing the physical circumstances, they perform a positive and useful service.

A precarious situation is not the monopoly of the small fringe theaters alone. The threat of demolition is hanging over several well-established West End theaters which occupy valuable land that could be more profitably exploited by property dealers and speculators. The authorities are alive to the dangers, and propaganda campaigns organized by the acting profession have not fallen on deaf ears. Nevertheless, the future is uncertain and will be even more uncertain so long as the private sector operates under disabilities that do not affect the subsidized theaters. Private managers have at long last persuaded the authorities to introduce a system which would assist ailing but deserving productions of worthwhile new plays and possibly revivals, too, over the first hurdle, that of public apathy; in short, to supply the cash which would "nurse" the laggards during the early period. A production investment corporation, similar to that which the government created to assist an ailing film industry, is envisaged. This would certainly benefit authors, players and technicians and might indeed help to keep keen young producers out of the bankruptcy courts. In the meantime, in the established commercial theater, despite rising costs and the introduction of the new Value Added Tax which has led to the raising of theater ticket prices, the successful shows increase in number and the length of the runs increases. London has even acquired a brand new theater, the New London, which is supposed to be the most modern and best equipped technically in the capital, and which Peter Ustinov's *The Unknown Soldier and His Wife* has been packing daily at each and every performance. Since this theater (built on the site of the old Winter Garden Theater) opened, the New Theater (owned by the Albery family) has been renamed the Albery after the late Sir Bronson Albery. Here the smash hit was *Joseph and the Amazing Technicolor Dreamcoat,* a musical by the authors of *Jesus Christ Superstar,* staged by Frank Dunlop.

The numerous popular American imports included *Applause, Two Gentlemen of Verona, Gypsy* and *No, No, Nanette,* though the last named, with an all-English cast, provided far too many embarrassing moments. I suppose that among American imports should be included *Jesus Christ Superstar* and the polished Hillard Elkins production of *A Doll's House,* though the authors of each are European. But not only American fare draws the crowds. Commercial success has been the order of the day whether the entertainment has been light, as in the case of William Douglas Home's *Lloyd George Knew My Father* or Alan Ayckbourn's *Time and Time Again,* each given polished productions and impeccable acting; or, in the case of more serious stuff like John Mortimer's family drama, *Collaborators* (and even his *I Claudius* which was far better in conception and execution than it was given credit for), or Frank Harvey's *The Day After the Fair,* which brought Deborah Kerr back to the London stage, or Ronald Mavor's study of English snobbery and class prejudice, *A Private Matter,* which I am told was better done when tried out in a regional theater a year ago (though I can't imagine how), or Alan Bennett's bittersweet study of the neuroses associated with encroaching disease and death, perversely titled *Habeas Corpus,* with its splendid starring role for Alec Guinness, or, finally, though perhaps to class it with the more serious stuff is a mark of my own perverseness, the two-handed *Behind the Fridge,* by Britain's funniest clowns, Peter Cook and Dudley Moore.

And then, of course, there are the foreign imports, which grow in numbers every year, and among which I include the plays of Athol Fugard from South Africa; or the plays of Irish writers like Brian Friel and Brendan Behan (whose posthumous *Richard's Cork Leg* was brought to London from the Dublin Festival); and those brief exposures given mostly on the fringe to the new European drama, that possibly nobody would have looked at twice had it not been for the influence of consecutive World Theater Seasons, for which their founder and artistic director, Peter Daubeny has earned our undying thanks, as well as our wishes both for a speedy recovery during his forthcoming enforced twelve months of absence from the theater and for a quick return to take up where he left off.

Highlights of the London Season

Selected and compiled by Ossia Trilling, who has designated his choice of the 20 best productions of the 1972-73 London season. These 20 appear within the listing in expanded entries, with full casts and credits.

TRILLING'S TOP TWENTY
(listed from left to right in the order of their opening dates)

Lloyd George Knew My Father	*The Front Page*	*Habeas Corpus*
The Old Ones	*Time and Time Again*	*Cowardy Custard*
Private Lives	*The Day After the Rain*	*Murder in the Cathedral*
A Sense of Detachment	*The Unknown Soldier and His Wife*	*Behind the Fridge*
Small Craft Warnings	*Joseph and the Amazing Technicolor Dreamcoat*	*Krapp's Last Tape & Not I*
A Doll's House	*Hans Kohlhaas*	*The Misanthrope*
Savages		*The Sea*

OUTSTANDING PERFORMANCES

RALPH RICHARDSON as General Boothroyd in *Lloyd George Knew My Father*	DENIS QUILLEY as Hildy Johnson in *The Front Page*	DAVID WARNER as Claudius in *I Claudius*
TOM COURTENAY as Leonard in *Time and Time Again*	MAGGIE SMITH as Amanda in *Private Lives*	DEBORAH KERR as Edith in *The Day After the Fair*
MIRIAM KARLIN as Nova Scrubbs in *Alpha Alpha*	WENDY HILLER as Queen Mary in *Crown Matrimonial*	POLLY JAMES as Victoria in *I and Albert*
DIANA RIGG as Lady Macbeth in *Macbeth*	CLAIRE BLOOM as Nora in *A Doll's House*	EILEEN ATKINS as Suzanna Andler in *Suzanna Andler*
PAUL SCOFIELD as Alan West in *Savages*	ALEC GUINNESS as Arthur Wicksteed in *Habeas Corpus*	JOAN PLOWRIGHT as Rebecca West in *Rosmersholm*

OUTSTANDING DIRECTORS

DAVID JONES *The Island of the Mighty*	JEROME SAVARY *The Last Lonely Days of Robinson Crusoe*	JOHN DEXTER *The Misanthrope*

OUTSTANDING DESIGNERS

FARRAH *Murder in the Cathedral*	TANYA MOISEIWITSCH *The Misanthrope*	NADINE BAYLIS *Joseph and the Amazing Technicolor Dreamcoat*

OUTSTANDING NEW BRITISH PLAYS

(D)—Playwright's London debut. Figure in parentheses is number of performances; plus sign (+) indicates play was still running on June 1, 1973

I CLAUDIUS by John Mortimer. Based on Robert Graves's life of the Roman emperor. With David Warner, Sarah Kestelman, Warren Clarke, Freda Jackson. (71)

THE OLD ONES by Arnold Wesker. Produced by the English Stage Company at the Royal Court Theater. Opened August 8, 1972. (Closed September 9, 1972) (38)

Emmanuel .... Max Wall
Gerda .... Amelia Bayntun
Boomy .... George Pravda
Teressa .... Wanda Rotha
Millie .... Rose Hill
Sarah .... Patience Collier
Rosa .... Susan Engel
Martin .... James Hazeldine
Rudi .... Leonard Fenton
Jack .... George Tovey
Three Youths .. Terry Burns, Stephen Grives, Martin Skinner

Directed by John Dexter; scenery, Douglas Heap; costumes, Harriet Geddes; lighting, Andy Phillips.

The quarrels, the hopes, the fears and the special relationships of a group of Jewish immigrants and their children in a London rooming house, as they look back on the past and forward to an uncertain future.

TIME AND TIME AGAIN by Alan Ayckbourn. Produced by Michael Codron at the Comedy Theater. Opened August 16, 1972. (Closed March 3, 1973) (229)

Leonard .... Tom Courtenay
Graham .... Michael Robbins
Joan .... Cheryl Kennedy
Anna .... Bridget Turner
Peter .... Barry Andrews

Directed by Eric Thompson; scenery and costumes, Alan Tagg; lighting, Mick Hughes.

Place: Graham and Anna's conservatory and garden. Act I, Scene 1: Spring. Scene 2: A few weeks later. Act II, Scne 1: Autumn. Scene 2: The next day.

Leonard, a whimsical young English middle-class non-conformist and Graham, his conventional married brother-in-law, think they both fancy the same girl; and so does her fiance, Peter.

THE ISLAND OF THE MIGHTY by John Arden and Margaretta D'Arcy. New treatment of the Arthurian legend as Britain's national theme. With Patrick Allen, Emrys James, Estelle Kohler, Beatrix Lehmann, Richard Pasco. (29 in repertory)

THE UNKNOWN SOLDIER AND HIS WIFE by Peter Ustinov. Produced by Alexander H. Cohen. Presented by Bernard Delfont. Opened January 11, 1973. (161+)

Television Engineer .... Peter Abbott
Sergeant .... Mark Kingston
Bugler (35914) ...... David Rhys Anderson
General .... Brian Bedford
Rebel .... Brett Usher
Wife .... Tamara Ustinov
Archbishop .... Peter Ustinov
14768 .... Stuart Mungall
71696 .... Christopher Munckle
Unknown Soldier .... Miles Anderson
94343 .... David Quilter
Enemy Leader .... Jeffry Wickham
Inventor .... Tony Jay
Woman .... Margaret Robertson
Reinforcements .... Peter Abbott, Alan Granville, Barry McGinn, Ronald O'Neill

Directed by Peter Ustinov; scenery and costumes, Motley; music, David Shire; lighting, Robert Ornbo; production supervisor, Jerry Adler; produced by Hildy Parks.

Music under the direction of Raymond Bishop; trumpet Michael Hinton; percussion Joe Watson; piccolo, flute, clarinet John Sands; organ Raymond Bishop.

Revival of satirical comedy about man's inability to avoid war abroad and strife at home. The play was originally produced by Alexander H. Cohen for the Lincoln Center Festival 7/6/67 and thereafter moved to Broadway where it opened 9/18/67. It was presented at the Chichester Festival 5/22/68.

WILLIE ROUGH by Bill Bryden (D). Guest visit by the Royal Lyceum, Edinburgh, company in a play about the Clydeside strike of World War I days. With James Grant, Fulton Mackay, Eileen McCallum, Clark Richards. (12)

A PRIVATE MATTER by Ronald Mavor (D). Cambridge professor tries to write a General's biography. With Alastair Sim, Dorothy Reynolds, Derek Fowlds, Peter Collier. (113+)

HANS KOHLHAAS by James Saunders. Produced by the Greenwich Theater. Opened February 22, 1973. (Closed March 22, 1973) (25)

Hans Kohlhaas .... Richard Moore
Sternbald .... Peter Gordon
The Tollkeeper; Martin Luther;
Elector of Brandenburg .... Frank Gatliff
The Steward; Henkel; Hinz .... John Rogan
Von Tronka .... Jonathan Elsom
Elizabeth .... June Jago
Lawyer; Elector of Saxony ... Trevor Baxter
Gov. of Brandenburg; Kunz .... Alan Helm
Sheriff of Wittenburg;
Prince Meissen .... Charles Dance
Count Wrede .... Peter Howell

Directed by Frederick Proud; scenery and costumes, John Hallé.

Time: Mid-16th century in Brandenburg.

Based on Kleist's novel about the chain of momentous events following a 16th-century German horse-dealer's bid to get redress against an injustice suffered at the hands of a willful aristocrat. This play was originally staged by an amateur company at the Questors Theater.

SAVAGES by Christopher Hampton. Produced by the English Stage Company at the Royal Court Theater. Opened April 12, 1973. (Closed May 19, 1973) (32)

Alan West	Paul Scofield
Mrs. West	Rona Anderson
Carlos	Tom Conti
Crawshaw	Michael Pennington
General	Leonard Kavanagh
Attorney-General;	
Investigator	Gordon Sterne
Ataide Pereira	Glyn Grain
Major Brigg	A. J. Brown
Chief; Bert	Frank Singuineau
Elmer Penn	Geoffrey Palmer
Kumai	Terence Burns
Pilot	Leonard Kavanagh
Co-pilot	Glyn Grain

Indians: George Baizley, Lynda Dagley, Thelma Kidger, Donna Louise, Eddy Nedari, J.C. Shepherd.

Directed by Robert Kidd; costumes and scenery, Jocelyn Herbert and Andrew Sanders; lighting, Andy Phillips.

Time: Most of the play is set in 1970-71 in Brazil.

Semi-documentary story of genocide and pauperization of the natives, seen through the eyes of a kidnaped British diplomat.

COLLABORATORS by John Mortimer. Battle of wits of an estranged married couple. With Glenda Jackson, John Wood, Joss Ackland, Gloria Connell. (51+).

HABEAS CORPUS by Alan Bennett. Produced by Michael Codron in association with Stoll Productions Ltd., at the Lyric Theater. Opened May 10, 1973. (25+).

Arthur Wicksteed	Alec Guinness
Muriel Wicksteed	Margaret Courtenay
Dennis Wicksteed	Christopher Good
Constance Wicksteed	Phyllida Law
Mrs. Swabb	Patricia Hayes
Canon Throbbing	Roddy Maude-Roxby
Lady Rumpers	Joan Sanderson
Felicity Rumpers	Madeline Smith
Mr. Shanks	Andrew Sachs
Sir Percy Shorter	John Bird
Mr. Purdue	Mike Carnell

Directed by Ronald Eyre; scenery, Derek Cousins; costumes, Daphne Dare; lighting, Robert Ornbo; music, Carl Davis; movement, Eleanor Fazan.

Place: In and around the Wicksteed house in Hove.

"Now get you to my lady's chamber, and tell her, let her paint an inch thick, to this favour she must come; make her laugh at that"—Hamlet, Act V, Scene 1.

THE SEA by Edward Bond. Produced by the English Stage Company at the Royal Court Theater. Opened May 22, 1973. (10+).

Willy Carson	Simon Rouse
Evens	Alan Webb
Hatch	Ian Holm
Louise Rafi	Coral Browne
Jessica Tilehouse	Gillian Martell
Hollarcut	Mark McManus
Thompson	Simon Cord
Carter	Anthony Langdon
Mafanwy Price	Susan Williamson
Jilly	Adrienne Byrne
Rachel	Barbara Ogilvie
Vicar	Jeremy Wilkin
Rose Jones	Diana Quick
Davis	Margaret Lawley

Directed by William Gaskill; scenery and costumes, Deirdre Clancy; lighting, Andy Phillips.

The bizarre reaction of the people of a seaside town to the death at sea of a local boy.

LIMITED RUNS OF INTERESTING NEW BRITISH PLAYS

MAGIC FOR THE MILLION by Margaret Gibb. The story of a down-at-heel magician. With the Unicorn Theater company. (12)

PRETTY BOY by Stephen Poliakoff. Back in his childhood home, Benny strives ferociously for fulfilment. With Michael Pennington, Tony Steedman, Elizabeth Sladen. (1)

THE TWO OF THEM by Raymond Bantock. Two flat-mates compare notes. With Gillie Graham, Jean Fergusson. (12)

NINETY-FIVE PER CENT MAN-MADE FIBER by Alan West (D). Apathy in an American hospital. With Kate Beswick. (5)
PLAYS FOR RUBBER GO-GO GIRLS by

Chris Wilkinson. Modern attitudes knocked. With Diana Patrick, Emma Williams. (22)

CANDLELIGHT AND BABYLON by Don Roberts. Bitter-sweet but humorous comment on one man's life. With Philip Wright, Sheila Sorley, David Lorraine. (4)

HANS KOHLHAAS by James Saunders. With the Questors Theater company. (12) (See its entry under "Outstanding New British Plays").

HITLER DANCES by Howard Brenton. Revised version of the author's examination of the myths and residue of war. With the

Edinburgh Traverse Workshop Theater company. (12)

ANIMALS UNDER CANVAS by Jackie Skarvellis, the destruction of the hero; and THE HIDDEN ARTHUR by William Dumaresq, Jackie Skarvellis, and Alan West, Jack's adventures in Wonderland serialized. With Michael Sadler, Roy Martin. (10)

JINKS by Amos Mokadi (D). A first play by an Israeli Londoner set in Israel and in the characters' imagination. With Peter Cartwright, Margaret Robertson, Inigo Jackson. (18)

NAKED ON A TRAMPOLINE. Double bill comprising LIFELINE by Frank Wyman, a study of loneliness; and LOU by Hilton Root, a sexual recollection. With Donal Cox, Karin Dominic. (9) *Lifeline* revived with Leo Dolan, Eileen Pollock. (13)

TIME, LIFE, SEX AND YOU KNOW WHAT by James Hepburn. Intellectual absurdist entertainment, by an American Londoner, with David Gower, Mike Moriarty; and THE TIME-KEEPER by Tony Gariff, a couple look at their past and their future, with Peter Small, Pat Harris. (5)

SWIMMING POOLS AND CHANDELIERS by Peter King. Triangular comedy with a sociological core. With Alex Marshall, Michael McClain, Michael Harbour. (12)

THE INHABITANTS by Olwen Wymark. American-born British author's play on "endless analyzing." With David Neville, Patricia Perry, Edmund Thomas. (2)

TI KIN by Katy Hounsel-Robert. A tale of a Vietnamese mother. With Rowan Stuart, Barry Whittaker, June Lewis, Frank Lyons. (9)

WAS HE ANYONE? by N.F. Simpson. A rich, funny look at the mysterious values of established philanthropy. With Yvonne Antrobus, Stanley Lebor. (22)

LEAVE US ALONE by James Hanley. A mother and her two sons receive an unexpected caller. With Maggy Maxwell, James Fagan, Mike Hadley, Roger Kemp. (10)

PLEASE DON'T SHOOT ME WHEN I'M DOWN by William Morrison. The failure of a would-be assassin. With Ian Thompson, Michael Richmond. (12)

A MATTER OF CONVENIENCE by Richard Moss. The Camden Town *Clochemerle*. With Laurence Davies, Andy Pantelidou. (17)

THE WOUND by Ted Hughes (D). An injured soldier's determination to survive. With Peter McEnery, Brenda Hartill Moores. (16 in repertory)

LUNCH DUTY by Rony Robinson. Sheffield Crucible Vanguard Theater company production about pupil power and its troubles. With Maggie McCarthy, Garry McDermott, Ray Ashcroft, Dicken Ashworth. (12)

STILL LIFE: MAN IN BED by David Edgar. A rebel tries fruitlessly to switch off. With James Locker, Annie Irving, Murray Noble, Jill Richards. (10)

THERE'S NO BUSINESS . . . by Frank R. Long. Humorous look at the seamy side of show biz. With Gillie Gratham, Jon C.P. Mattocks. (10)

PLUGGED IN by John McGrath. Three plays from the Liverpool Everyman Theater: ANGEL IN THE MORNING, man versus girl-guerrilla; PLUGGED IN TO HISTORY, misunderstanding on a park bench; and THEY'RE KNOCKING DOWN THE PIE-SHOP, clash of right and left in an urban setting. With Robert Hamilton, Anthony Haygarth, Gillian Hanna, Elizabeth MacLennan, Cliff Corker, Iain Sylvester. (16)

THE CONSERVATIONIST by T.C. O'Brien. A stall-keeper's demise. With Richard Merson, Alan Stirling, Timothy Welch. (12)

MALCOLM by Lewis Nkosi and THE PROSECUTION by J.A. Maimane. Two plays by South Africans about color prejudice in London circles. With Patricia Cutts, Horace James, Carmen Munroe. (8)

FOCO NOVO by Bernard Pomerance. By American author living in U.K., guerilla kidnappings and class warfare in South America. With Stephen Bradley, Mona Hammond, Judy Monyhan. (19)

TRAINS by Alan West. A mother's faith in an ex-convict son. With Richard Marson, Eve Raine, Stephen Williams. (10)

THE CRICKETER AND THE CARPENTER by Richard Franklin, a loner seeks gratification, with John Ruskin, Jonathan Sherwood, Elizabeth Connor; and AN EVENING WITH MARCEL PROUST by Patrick Williams, a TV-breakdown causes a family crisis, with David Taylor, Felicity Welson, Chetwynd Townsend. (12)

HE, SHE AND IT by Roger Milner. Rich husband is fired, to his wife's surprise. With Gay Soper, Robin Parkinson. (12)

WITH ALL MY LOVE I HATE YOU by Lynda Marchal. Two-handed battle of female wits. With Petronella Ford, the author. (12)

INTRUSIONS comprising THE DAY THEY CAME, the Martians are here!; and A NIGHT OUT FROM THE GHOSTS, a new horror story, both by Billy Hamon. With Mathew Guinness, Michael Kitchen. (17)

YOU KNOW ME by Alan Drury. Analysis of a friendship. With Timothy Block, Paul Ratcliffe. (6)

THE BALLYGOMBEEN BEQUEST by John Arden and Margaretta D'Arcy. Edinburgh Festival production of documentary drama about personal and political "troubles" in Ireland. With Valerie Lilley, Vari Sylvester, Stephen Rea, John Joyce. (9)

STRETCH by Tudor Gates. Should a communist defector be granted asylum? With Peter Geddes, Michael Shannon. (12)

MRS. PRINCESS, adaptation of a Celtic fairy-story; WHAT ABOUT THE CROCODILE, adventure in London today, both by Madeleine Sotheby. With the Unicorn Theater company. (9)

MONSIEUR ARTAUD by Michael Almaz. The creator of Theater of Cruelty dramatized. With Fiona Moore, David Mouchter-Samorai. (6)

THE GREATEST NURSERY RHYME by William Martin. Based on 1970 Bristol U.N. Community Care Conference. With Richard Gofton, Pauline Siddle, Robert Spiers, Ivan Vander. (12)

PANDEMOLIUM by David Fisher. A nonsense play about words for the kiddies. With the Unicorn Theater company. (16)

YOU PARALYSE ME by Peter King. Devious psycho-sexual variant on the eternal triangle. With Joy Harrison, Michael McIain, Michael Watkins. (10)

EVIDENCE OF INTIMACY by Gabriel Josipovici. An investigation into the affairs of an adulterous couple. With Warren Clarke, David Foxxe, Linda Lisles, John Muirhead. (17)

SURVIVORS by Jackie Scarvellis. Two victims of a nuclear holocaust fail to hit it off. With Jo Speller, Nicholas Lakes. (13)

BETTER DAYS, BETTER KNIGHTS by Stanley Eveling. The travails of a chivalrous would-be knight errant. With Peter Gordon, Elizabeth Roud. (12)

ENGLAND'S IRELAND by seven writers: A.M. Bicht, Howard Brenton, Brian Clark, David Edgar, Francis Fuchs, David Hare, Snoo Wilson. Current events in Ireland seen through English and Irish eyes. With Tim Curry, Timothy Davies, Fidelma Murphy, Finnuala O'Shannon. (9)

A COUPLE WITH A CAT by Tony Connor. The misleadingly realistic relationship of a married couple. With Paul Ratcliffe, Anthea Holloway, Alex Sobin. (10)

LOOK FORTH WITH LOVE by Harcourt Nicholls. Interracial drama set in Greenwich Village. With Kerry Francis, Mark Heath, Patricia Perry. (10)

REJECTION by Niall Quinn. Jesuit-Irish novice versus his teacher. With John Boswall, Lawrence Douglas. (12)

TRIANGLE by James Saunders. Soul-searching monologue. With Michael Graham Cox. (10)

PARENTS by Peter King. An unmarried couple and their view of their respective parents. With Heather Stoney, the author. (12)

THE SENSATION SEEKERS by Bernard Goss. The "comic paper" world of children. With the Young Vic Studio company. (22)

BACKFIRE, OR THE TRIALS OF STANELEY by Andrew Hilton. The automobile presented to 7 to 12 year olds. With the Molecule Club company. (12)

THE COMING OF THE KINGS by Ted Hughes, a new treatment of the nativity theme; and THANKS TO PARKINSON by Joan Macalpine, a funny tale about Penelope, Parkinson, and Co. With songs by Joan Macalpine and Peter Durrant. With the Unicorn Theater company. (17)

THE POT PLANT by Charles Gray. An aged couple's nostalgic bickering. With Julie Martin, John Rutland. (12)

THE WEEKEND GUEST by Alan C. Taylor. Change your clothes, change your character. With Robert Swales, Susan Edmonstone, David Shackleton. (12)

FORGOTTEN DREAMS, a schoolteacher's daydreams; and END OF THE ROAD, two oldsters at the end of their road, both by Patrick Broughton. With Angela Pleasance, Ken Colley. And with the world premiere of a late-night showing of THE ART AND CRAFT OF PORNOGRAPHY by Dr. Horn-berg and J. Brad Cutrara, with Vass Anderson, Steve Kimber.

WHO SINS MOST? by James Scott. Macabre comedy of a gay couple. With John Fahey, Lawrence Harrington. (10)

OUT OF THE BOX, INTO THE BOX by Brian Raith and Martin V. Haselberg. Mobile art gallery with the Kipper Kids. (8)

THE MAXI-BAR TRAGEDY by William Dumaresq. Music by Galt MacDermot. A trio in a bar. With Howard Wakeling, Joan Geary, Peter Farrell. (18)

MONOGRAMS, comprising WHY MRS. NEUSTADTER ALWAYS LOSES by Colin Spencer, the confessions of an American divorcee, with Patricia Cutts; and BLANK PAGES by Frank Marcus, the frustrations of a would-be diarist, with Julia Foster. (8)

COMIC PICTURES by Stephen Wright. A family at the seaside. With Betty Alberge, Larry Noble, Georgina Melville, Richard Franklin. (18)

HOPSCOTCH by Norris Harvey. Man proposes, woman disposes. With Susan Tracey, Roger Brierley. (10)

MORITURI by David Mowat. An oldster's defeatist death wish. With Leonard Fenton, Tamara Hinchco, Susan Drury. (12)

OWNERS by Caryl Churchill (D). The cruelties of ownership. With Stephanie Bidmead, Kenneth Cranham. (20)

THE FILTH HUNT by David Rudkin. Skit on the Longford Report on Pornography. With Lord St. George, Jane Wood. (12)

SCHREIBER'S NERVOUS ILLNESS by Caryl Churchill. Medical reports on an aberrant onetime German legal luminary. With Kenneth Haigh, the author. (10)

BEOWULF adapted for the stage by Liane Aukin from the classic. With the Freehold company. (8)

TABLE SERVICE by Ron Hart. A waitress and her dream customer. With Pamela Merrick, Alan Hay. (12)

CHRISTMAS CAROL by Frank Marcus. World premiere of dialogue between a whore and her visitor. With Catherine Kestler, Michael David. (10)

ABOUT THIS NEW TEAPOT . . . by Joseph Delaney. A glimpse of the lives of six laboratory workers. With Peter Sergeant, Brendan Price, Jon Glover, Richard Everett. (16)

HENRY PILK'S MADHOUSE by and with Ken Campbell's Road Show company. A crazy show featuring the absent Henry Pilk. With Jennifer Watts, Phillip Schreibman, Bob Dermer, Andy Jones. (16)

LORD MOUNTLADY AND THE MORTAL ODORS, OR THE DALAI LAMA LIES DEAD IN THE ROAD by Jim Hiley. Skit on the permissive society. With Terence Brook, Henry Goodman, Ian Marten. (16)

CLAUDE by Leo J. Heaps. Based on the Claude Eatherley case history. With Michael Duggan, James Locker. (11)

A FART FOR EUROPE by Howard Brenton and David Edgar. Riposte to the British government's "Fanfare for Europe" festival. With Hugh Hastings, Jeremy Child, Alun Armstrong. (10)

RULE BRITANNIA by Howard Barker. Political allegory of the British class system. With Judy Geeson, Neil Cunningham, David Schofield, Tony Milner. (2).

BLACK BLAST by Lindsay Barnett. The story of the blacks. With Ray Blair, Yemi Agibadi, Elvanj Zirimu, Basil Winzira, Eddie Tagoe, Merdell Jordine, Yulisa Maddy, Leslie S. Palmer. (4)

OTTO'S INTERVIEW by Tony Connor. Why do we lie, cheat and deceive? With Donald McIver, Rosemary MacVie, Frank Dux. (10)

TAKE DIOGENES by Stephen Wyatt. A mad attempt to put on a play. With Alan Bennion, Kenneth Barrow. (10)

WANKERS by Jackie Skarvellis. A satire of the fringe theater. With Roy Martin. (20)

GANGSTERS by David Edgar. The fantasies of two small-time crooks. With Sean Arnold, John Blythe. (10)

NICE by Mustapha Matura. Monologue of an imprisoned West Indian by London-based West Indian writer. With Stefan Kalipha. (18)

PASSING REMARKS by Gale Houston. Knockabout tragedy of modern life. With June Whitaker, Paul Kember, Malcolm Kaye. (10)

THE VISIT by Jeff Nuttall. Self-alienating chance for the audience. With Cecily Hobbs, Caroline Hutchinson. (15)

AG AND FISH by Roy Minton. Study in impotence. With Moira Redmond, Barry Lowe. (12)

THE FORGOTTEN ONES by Stephen Coleman. Fifteen-year-old author's play about a psychiatric ward. With Jennifer Lautrec, Peter Tilbury, Mike Angel. (10)

BIRTHDAY and MY WARREN, monologues for and about women by Pam Gems. The former with Sheila Kelley, the latter with Janet Henfrey. (18)

MR. BONIFACE'S MELTING PAGEANT by Bill Martin. Pirandellian view of modern society. With Elisabeth Lynne, David Stockton. (6)

TRILOGY by Timothy Kidd, comprising THE DOOR, JUDAS and THE WINDOW. Three monologues on inertia, guilt and death. With Peter Cartwright. (15)

THE LAUNDERETTE by Patrick Carter. Sexual encounter in a new venue. With Jane Carr, Anthony May. (15)

MY SISTER AND I, lampoon on a royal princess; and SKIPPER, lampoon on a seafaring minister, both by Howard Barker. With Brigit Forsyth. (18)

THE FOURTH WORLD by David Caute (D). A dichotomized intellectual's problems. With Yvonne Antrobus, Richard Kane, Maureen Lipman. (1)

THE ILLUMINATION OF MR. SHANNON by Don Haworth. The philosophy of an illiterate Irishman. With Frank Grimes, Colin Blakeley. (10)

THE ONLY WAY OUT by George Thatcher. A view of the death cell from inside. With Michael Elphick, Laurence Terry, Richard Vanstone. (21)

JUST GO, WILL YOU HARRY by Ken Campbell. A rejected lover won't go. With Alex Marshall, Illona Linthwaite, David Stockton. (10)

CRAZY HERMANN'S HOUSE, devised and performed by Aquarius, a Crazy Show; and SELF-ACCUSATION by Peter Handke. With the Young Vic Theater Studio company. (6)

THE ASS-HOLE by Frederick Proud, John Ratzenberger, Ray Hassett. A crummy cafe attracts oddballs. Featuring Sal's Meat Market. (13)

A MACKEREL SKY AND APPLE GREEN by Brian Lee. Stage version of a radio play

about an Irish family. With Sean Barrett, Raymond Cross. (11)

FALL by Alan Drury. Two girls and a boy. With Nicola Williams, Barry McGinn, Wendy Stone. (12)

LIFE IN A CHOCOLATE FACTORY. 1972 Student Drama Festival Michel Codron Prize for best play. With the York Shoe-String Theater company. (17)

CARTOON by David Pinner. Black comedy on the disastrous nature of comedy. With Linda Thorson, Andrew McCulloch. (10)

LOVE GODDESS IN DREAM FACTORY by Doc Watson. Documentary about Marilyn Monroe. With Carole Bollard, Hessell Saks. (12)

HOLD YOUR WODI, CHAPS! by Peter King. Two British tommies in the Middle East. With Anton Rodgers, Simon Rouse. (11)

THE SATURDAY NIGHT MURDER by Michael O'Neill and Jeremy Seabrook. Based on the Wimbledon "queer" violence. With Derek Thompson, Paul Cooper, Peter Robbins, Lydia Lisle. (3)

WE ARE WHAT WE EAT by Frank Dux. Man's inability to adapt. With Merial Brook, the author. (12)

LIPPO THE NEW NOAH by Sally Giray. Life in Kingston by Jamaican-born writer. With Horace James, Mona Hammond. (17)

SNAPS: CIVITAS DEI, DAYS BY THE RIVER and MACENERY'S VISION OF PIPKIN by John Grillo. Three short dramatic snapshots on the theme of aggression. With Stephen Bent, Michael Graham Cox, Peter Halliday. (10)

CAPTAIN OATES' LEFT SOCK by John Antrobus. Revival of 1969 Sunday-night production of bitter and anarchic comedy. With Stephen Rae, Janet Webb. (15)

MAN FRIDAY by Adrian Mitchell. Race relations and the colonial question. With Ram John Holder, Roger Sloman. (12)

PARTITIONS by Michael Cahill. Story of love and hate in an industrial milieu. With Mark York, Kevin Savage. (12)

THE GRAVE by Melville Lovatt. Strange encounter between two strangers. With Miles Fothergill, Colin Bean. (10)

TOWARDS THE END OF A LONG, LONG VOYAGE by Robin Smyth. Meeting of two sometime shipmates. With John Bott, Paul Ratcliffe. (13)

THE LAST DREAM by Robert Siddons. An elderly married couple's dream. With Carol Frazer, Robin Murphy. (5)

WATCH THE WOMAN, sketches by Brian Phelan and Olwen Wymark. A history of woman from the year dot. With Diana Barrett, Frank Whitton, Abi Gouhard. (5+)

URBAN GUERRILLA BOUTIQUE by Terry James. Is the hold-up in the store real or phony? With Alec Bregonzi, Michael Mundell, Rudolph Walker. (12)

LAY ME OPEN by Christopher Robb. The story of an audition, a one-man show. With the author. (18)

THERE'S ALWAYS ROOM IN THE NICK by Jonathan Marshall. Critique of the prison system. With Sue Ashton, Brian Hibberd, Alan Hulse, Bob Weaver, other General Will company members. (15)

THE 47TH SATURDAY by William Trevor. The third part of a trilogy, about a "moment of truth." With Brian Pringle, Doreen Mantle. (12)

THE KNOWALL by Alan C. Taylor. Surreal world of big business. With David Sinclair, Robert Booth. (12)

YOU ARE MY HEART'S DELIGHT by Cecil P. Taylor. The modern world enters a Scottish cottage. With Eithne Dunn, Alex McCrindle. (12)

CHINIGCHINICH by Olwen Wymark, Red Indian brave uncovers a secret; and YOU'LL NEVER GUESS by Ann Jellicoe, the Rumpelstiltskin story retold. With the Unicorn Theater company. (64)

PRESS RELEASE by Peter King. Three attempts at recollection. With Jacqueline de Costa, Kevin Williams, Richard Durden. (10+)

HOW TO SURVIVE IN THE NICK by Jonathan Marshall. Fantasy as a means of survival in solitary confinement. With Leslie Rayney, Carolyn Wylde, David Millet, other General Will company members. (11+)

GIVE THE GAFFERS TIME TO LOVE YOU by Barry Reckord. Comedy with music about contemporary English politics. With Paul Angelis, Petra Markham. (8+)

BANG by Howard Barker. The frightening similarity between right and left wing extremism. With Ian McDiarmid, Tony Milner, David Schofield. (8+)

POPULAR ATTRACTIONS

RENT, OR CAUGHT IN THE ACT by David Edgar. Music hall melodrama about the Rent Act. Featuring the General Will, comprising Alan Hulse, Joan Cudmore, Brian Hubbard, Michele Ryan. (18)

THE CATCHING OF THE QUERLE by Brian Wright. A plea for understanding, for children. With the Bowsprit company. (41)

THE ALCHEMIST by Ben Jonson. Frank Dunlop's updated modern-dress version. With Denise Coffey, Ian Trigger, Joan Heal, Trevor Peacock. (25 in repertory).

AN OTHELLO by Charles Marowitz, after Shakespeare. A modern view of a racist tragedy. With Judy Geeson, Rudolph Walker, Anton Phillips. (48 in repertory)

THE MATING GAME by Robin Hawdon. Comedy about a young TV personality and ladies' man. With Terry Scott, Aimi MacDonald, Julia Lockwood, Avril Angers, Clive Francis. (401+)

THE MERCHANT OF VENICE by William Shakespeare. Terry Hands's 1971 production, revised and transferred from Stratford. With Emrys James, Tony Church, Susan Fleetwood, Bernard Lloyd, Peter Geddis. (56 in repertory)

PO MISS JULIE by Herb Greer. World premiere of American Londoner's Strindbergian drama about a tragic case of miscegenation in the deep South. With Gabrielle Drake, Robert MacLeod, Joan Anne Maynard, Lou Satton. (25)

TRELAWNEY by Julian Slade (music) and Aubrey Woods (book and lyrics). Bristol Old Vic production of musical version of Sir Arthur Pinero's famous play. With Gemma Craven, Ian Richardson, Max Adrian, Joyce Carey. (171)

SHADOW OF A GUNMAN by Sean O'Casey. Peter James's Young Vic Theater production. With Peter McEnery, Eve Belton. (24 in repertory)

LLOYD GEORGE KNEW MY FATHER by William Douglas Home. Produced by Ray Cooney, for Ray Cooney Productions Ltd., and John Gale, for Volcano Productions Ltd., at the Savoy Theater. Opened July 4, 1972. (388+)

Lady Boothroyd ....Peggy Ashcroft
Robertson ....John Barrett
General Sir William
 Boothroyd ....Ralph Richardson
Hubert Boothroyd, M.P. ......James Grout
Maud Boothroyd ....Janet Henfrey
Sally Boothroyd ....Suzan Farmer
Simon Green ....Simon Cadell
Rev. Trevor Simmonds ....David Stoll

Directed by Robin Midgley; scenery, Anthony Holland; lighting, Chris Ellis.

Time: The present. Place: The sitting room of Boothroyd Hall, Sir William's home.

A bitter comedy about an elderly general, with painful memories, and his stubborn wife, who almost takes her own life in an effort to halt the inevitable march of progress.

Celia Johnson replaced Peggy Ashcroft 10/23/72; Charles Lamb replaced John Barrett 1/1/73; Avice Landon replaced Celia Johnson, Andrew Cruickshank replaced Ralph Richardson, Jack Watling replaced James Grout, Anne Jameson replaced Janet Henfrey, Julia Vidler replaced Suzan Farmer, Kenneth Keyte replaced Simon Cadell, Daniel Thorndike replaced David Stoll, 5/21/73.

SMILIN' THROUGH by John Hanson and Constance Cox. Musical version of the stage and film hit. With John Hanson, Lawrence Gray, Diana Jane Argyle. (28)

COWARDY CUSTARD an entertainment devised by Gerald Frow, Alan Strachan and Wendy Toye, featuring words and music by Noel Coward. Produced by the Mermaid Theater Trust in association with the City Arts Trust. Opened July 10, 1972. (355+)

With Olivia Breeze, Geoffrey Burridge, Jonathan Cecil, Tudor Davies, Elaine Delmar, Laurel Ford, Peter Gale, John Moffatt, Patricia Routledge, Anna Sharkey, Una Stubbs, Derek Waring.

Directed by Wendy Toye and the cast; scenery and costumes, Tim Goodchild; orchestrations, Keith Amos; musical director, John Burrows; lighting, Charles Bristow.

Excerpts from the works of Noel Coward, with some items dropped or replaced as the run progressed, including selections from *Post Mortem, Present Laughter, Quadrille, South Sea Bubble, Present Indicative* and *Future Indefinite.* The show was presented in two parts.

David Robb replaced Geoffrey Burridge 11/27/73; Julia McKenzie replaced Patricia Routledge 1/15/73; Maggie Grant replaced Una Stubbs 2/19/73; Guy Siner replaced

Peter Gale, Hugh Walters replaced Jonathan Cecil, Jean Muir replaced Anna Sharkey 4/9/73.

TWELFTH NIGHT by William Shakespeare. Open Air Theater production. With Michael Denison (later Brett Usher), Celia Bannerman, Joanna van Gyseghem, Hugh Manning, John Quentin. (44)

PARENTS' DAY by Ronald Miller. Adapted from the novel by Edward Candy. With Robin Bailey, Gwen Watford, Megs Jenkins. (49)

MARY ROSE by J.M. Barrie. London season of Manchester's 69 Theater company production. With Mia Farrow, Ralph Bates, Carmel McSharry. (40)

THE DWARFS by Harold Pinter, in a reworked version. With Nially Buggy, Ian Taylor, Richard Warwick. (16 in repertory)

OTHELLO by William Shakespeare. London transfer of John Barton's 1971 Stratford production. With Brewster Mason, Elizabeth Spriggs, Lisa Harrow, Emrys Jones. (55 in repertory)

LIBERTY RANCH! concept and lyrics by Caryl Brahms and Ned Sherrin, book by Dick Vosburgh, music by John Cameron. Musical version of *She Stoops to Conquer* set in the Middle West. With Elizabeth Seal, David Kernan. (25).

PULL BOTH ENDS by John Schroeder and Anthony King, book by Brian Comport. A £100,000 British musical set in an Xmas-cracker factory threatened with a takeover. With Gerry Marsden, Christine Holmes, Liz Edmiston, The Young Generation. (39)

THE RUPERT SHOW by Ken Martyne and David Cullen. Stage adaptation of the Rupert Bear books, for children. With Diane Robillard, Rita McKerrow, Clive Bennett. (72)

THE GEORGE JACKSON BLACK AND WHITE MINSTREL SHOW by and with the Pip Simmons Group. The black problem to the present day. (21)

DADDY GOODNESS by Joan Maitland and Mark Heath, with music by David Lindupp and Jeff Martins. Musical adapted from a play by Richard Wright. With Willie Payne, Mark Heath, Faye Chance, Monica Hall. (24)

THE FINEST FAMILY IN THE LAND by Henry Livings. Originally staged at Lincoln Theater Royal in 1969, about the odd adventures of a Lancashire family. With Griffith

Davies, Eileen Kennally, Brian Murphy, Maxwell Shaw, Clare Sutcliffe. (25)

PHOENIX-AND-TURTLE by David Mowat. The traumatic family experiences of a lecturer who loses his job. With Christopher Guinee, Louise Breslin, Elizabeth Cassidy. (22)

DREAMS OF MRS. FRASER by Gabriel Josipovici (D). The nostalgic recollections of a true-life victim of rape. With Mark McManus, Rosemary Martin. (21)

HAMLET by William Shakespeare. Peter Coe's Bankside Globe Playhouse festival production. With Keith Michell, Donald Houston, Ron Moody, Helen Cherry, Carolyn Seymour. (32)

JESUS CHRIST SUPERSTAR by Andrew Lloyd Webber and Tim Rice. Jim Sharman's London production of world-famous musical. With Paul Nicholas, Sylvie McNeill, Stephen Tate, John Parker, Paul Jabara. (338+)

SAWNEY BEAN by Robert Nye and Bill Watson. Based on the historic case of an 18th-century Galloway cannibal. With Anthony Haygarth. (22)

GYMNASIUM by Robin Chapman. The clash of body and brain. With Charles West, Barbara Ewing. (25)

STRIP GAME by Peter Sergeant and Amos Mokadi. Sexual encounter between two lost partners. With Fleur Chandler, (later Georgina Melville), Richard Franklin (later James Hunter). (24)

JULIUS CAESAR by William Shakespeare. Peter James's Young Vic production. With Hywel Bennett, Peter McEnery, Roy Marsden, Nigel Hawthorne. (20 in repertory)

POPKISS by Michael Ashton, with music by John Addison and David Heneker. Musical based on Ben Travers' 1920s farce *Rookery Nook*. With Daniel Massey, Mary Millar, John Standing, Isla Blair, Joan Sanderson, Hazel Hughes. (63)

MURDER IN THE CATHEDRAL by T.S. Eliot. Produced by the Royal Shakespeare Company at the Aldwych Theater. Opened August 31, 1972. (Closed March 3, 1973). (53 in repertory)
Thomas Becket . . . . Richard Pasco
1st Priest . . . . Denis Holmes
2d Priest . . . . Nickolas Grace
3d Priest . . . . Morgan Sheppard
1st Tempter; 1st Knight . . . . Bernard Lloyd
2d Tempter; 2d Knight . . . . Anthony Pedley

3d Tempter; 3d Knight . . . . . . Tony Church
4th Tempter; 4th Knight . . . . Brewster Mason
Women's Chorus Leader . . . Susan Fleetwood
Singer . . . . Philip Doghan
Messenger . . . . Colin Mayes
Women of Canterbury: Julia Blalock, Heather Canning, Valerie Colgan, Jane Cussons, Lila Kaye, Marion Lines. Attendants: John Hug, Peter Machin, Lloyd McGuire, Michael Walker. Musicians: Gordon Kember director, Colin Clague trumpet, Paul Farr horn, Andrew Hepton trumpet, Paul Hiley percussion, Edward Joory percussion, Richard Lee flute and recorders, Brian Newman horn. Members of the Wandsworth School Choir: Russell Burgess director, Stephen Ackhurst, Peter Chapman, Simon Cochrane, Stephen Lambden, Laurence Taggart, David Tate, Terry Thorne, Peter Williams.
Directed by Terry Hands; scenery and costumes, Farrah; music, Ian Kellam; lighting, Stewart Leviton.
Written for the Chapter House at Canterbury Cathedral, where it was staged in 1935, *Murder in the Cathedral* was last produced in London at the Old Vic 3/31/53.

THE GARDEN by Julia Jones (D). The relationships of five lonely people. With Diana Coupland, Brian Deacon, Edward Judd, John Paul, Stephen Temperley. (28)

BRUSSELS by Jonathan Hales. The adventures of a Boy Scout troop. With John Ringham, Peter Armitage, Geoffrey Waring. (41)

ALPHA ALPHA by Howard Barker. Transparent satire about a recent criminal case. With Miriam Karlin, David Schofield, Anthony Milner, Dallas Cavell, Malcolm Storry. (42)

CASTE by T.W. Robertson. New production of famous Victorian naturalistic drama. With Alfie Bass, Geoffrey Beevers, Yvonne Coulette, Barbara Ewing, Ann Penfold. (25)

PRIVATE LIVES by Noel Coward. Produced by H. M. Tennent Ltd. (by arrangement with Arthur Cantor) at the Queen's Theater. Opened September 21, 1972. (288+)
Sibyl Chase . . . . Polly Adams
Elyot Chase . . . . Robert Stephens
Victor Prynne . . . . James Villiers
Amanda Prynne . . . . Maggie Smith
Louise . . . . Cari Hedderwick
Directed by John Gielgud; scenery, Anthony Powell; costumes, Beatrice Dawson; lighting, Joe Davis.
First performed in London at the Phoenix Theater in September 1930, with the author himself as Elyot Chase. One of Coward's most successful comedies, it was last revived in London in 1963. The present production

is set in the year of its original performance and was presented in three acts.

John Standing replaced Robert Stephens 4/16/73.

LONESOME LIKE by Harold Brighouse. Revival of North Country working-class drama. With Michael Byrne, Edna Doré, Barbara Flynn, Keith Morris. (19)

THE RELIEF OF MARTHA KING by David Parker. What happens when George King is changed into Martha King with a surgeon's aid. With Jenny Runacre, Godfrey Jackman. (21)

BAKKE'S NIGHT OF FAME by John Mc-Grath. The Dolphin company's revival. With Hywel Bennett, Nikolas Simmonds. (28)

THE DAY AFTER THE FAIR by Frank Harvey. Produced by Frith Banbury and Jimmy Wax, by arrangement with Arthur Cantor, at the Lyric Theater. Opened October 4, 1972. (Closed May 5, 1973). (245).

Arthur Harnham .... Duncan Lamont
Letty .... Avice Landon
Edith .... Deborah Kerr
Sarah .... Jiggy Bhore
Anna .... Julia Foster
Charles Bradford .... Paul Hastings

Directed by Frith Banbury; scenery, Reece Pemberton; costumes, Robin Fraser Paye; lighting, Joe Davis.

Time: Three months during the summer of 1900. Place: The front room of "The Brewer's House" in a West Country cathedral city. Act I, Scene 1: May, evening. Scene 2: Ten days later, morning. Scene 3: Six weeks later, Sunday evening. Act II. Scene 1: Two weeks later, Saturday afternoon. Scene 2: Three days later, Tuesday morning. Scene 3: The first Saturday in August, morning.

Based on Thomas Hardy's short story of a married woman who falls in love with a young man to whom she sends the love letters that she composes on behalf of her illiterate maidservant, and the young man's rude awakening.

Margaret Gibson replaced Avice Landon 10/23/72 for seven weeks.

RAAS by Robert Lamb. World premiere of American-born Londoner's play about the antics of a West Indian immigrant family. With Christopher Gilbert, Claudia Winston, Clare Pegler, Anton Phillips. (24)

COSTA PACKET by Frank Norman, songs by Lionel Bart. Joan Littlewood's production of a skit on the travel-agent racket. With Avis Bunnage, Eileen Kennally, Maxwell Shaw, Valerie Walsh. (68)

COMEDY OF ERRORS by William Shakespeare and others. First London showing of Frank Dunlop's and Peter James's 1971 and 1972 Edinburgh Festival production. With Denise Coffey, Gary Bond, Richard Vane, Gavin Reed, Joan Heal, Ian Trigger. (15 in repertory)

OEDIPUS NOW, adapted from Sophocles and compiled and directed by James Roose-Evans. With Paul Bacchus, Svetlana Beriosova, Geoffrey Whitehead. (32)

BIBLE ONE, comprising JOSEPH AND HIS AMAZING TECHNICOLOR DREAM-COAT, by Andrew Lloyd-Webber and Tim Rice; and the TOWNLEY MYSTERY PLAYS, under the title of CREATION TO JACOB, in Frank Dunlop's Edinburgh Festival production. With Gary Bond, Joan Heal, Ian Trigger. (62) (Joseph and His Amazing Technicolor Dreamcoat was revived in an expanded version; see its entry below in this section.)

OVERRULED by George Bernard Shaw. Revival of Shaw's one-act comedy. With Paul Alexander, Nigel Anthony, Illona Linthwaite, Jenny McCracken. (16)

EYE WINKER, TOM TINKER by Tom MacIntyre (D). Irish writer's first play, about a young Irish patriot dabbling in revolution. With Donal McCann, John McKelvey, Frances Tomelty. (24)

TOUCH OF PURPLE by Elleston Trevor. Murder in an antique shop. With Maxine Audley, Gerard Heinz, Bernard Horsfall. (45)

CROWN MATRIMONIAL by Royce Ryton. The Duke of Windsor's abdication. With Wendy Hiller, Peter Barkworth, Jane Wenham, Amanda Reiss. (257+)

LET'S MURDER VIVALDI by David Mercer. First London stage production of satirical TV comedy. With Diana Fairfax, Kevin Storey, Tom Conti, Diana Mercer. (24)

HULLA BALOO by, Colin Spencer, Denise Coffey, Andrew Lloyd Webber, Tim Rice and others. Camp review set in a public lavatory. With Rogers & Starr, Chelsea Brown, Jimmy Edwards. (47)

I AND ALBERT by Jay Allen, music by Charles Strouse, lyrics by Lee Adams. London production and world premiere of American-authored musical about the life of Queen Victoria. With Polly James, Sven Bertil Taube, Lewis Finder, Aubrey Woods. (120)

A PAGAN PLACE by Edna O'Brien. A child grows up in Ireland during World War II. With Dermot Tuohy, Avril Elgar, Veronica Quilligan, David Daker. (32)

JANITRESS THRILLED BY PREHENSILE PENIS and BLEATS FROM A BRIGHOUSE PLEASUREGROUND by David Halliwell. Two "multi-viewpoint" dramas. With Anthony Millan, Anthony Douse. (36)

AFTER MAGRITTE and THE REAL INSPECTOR HOUND by Tom Stoppard. Revival of two popular satirical comedies. With Lynda Baron, John Bluthal, Jenny Laird, David Neville. (64)

STATE OF EMERGENCY by David Edgar. Edinburgh Festival Fringe production about the second year of Tory government. With the Bradford-based "The General Will" company. On a double bill with a revival of *Rent, or Caught in the Act.* (27)

MACBETH by William Shakespeare. Michael Blakemore's National Theater production. With Anthony Hopkins (later Denis Quilley), Diana Rigg, Ronald Pickup, Alan MacNaughton. (47+ in repertory)

BEHIND THE FRIDGE by Peter Cook and Dudley Moore. Produced by Donald Langdon for Hemdale, at the Cambridge Theater. Opened November 21, 1972. (219+)
    With Peter Cook, Dudley Moore.
    Staged by Joseph McGrath, Peter Cook and Dudley Moore; film sequences directed by Joseph McGrath; scenery and costumes, Voytek; lighting, Nick Chelton; sound consultant, Anthony Horder.
    A mixed bag of sketches and numbers by the former members of *Beyond the Fringe.* The show was presented in two parts.

11 JOSEPHINE HOUSE by Alfred Fagon (D). West Indian attitudes to "Mother England." With Mona Hammond, Oscar James, the author. (21)

THE INFERNO by Ian Curteis. A 16th-century religious maniac's passion and execution. With Michele Dotrice, Edgar Wreford. (22)

A CHRISTMAS CUCKOO by Brian Wright. Children's play about King John the Bad. With the Bowsprit Theater company. (38)

A SENSE OF DETACHMENT by John Osborne. Produced by the Royal Court Theater with Michael White, at the Royal Court Theater. Opened December 4, 1972. (Closed February 17, 1973). (69)
Chairman ....Nigel Hawthorne

Chap ....John Standing
Girl ....Denise Coffey
Older Lady ....Rachel Kempson
Father ....Hugh Hastings
Grandfather ....Ralph Michael
1st Man ....Terence Frisby
1st Man's Wife ....Jeni Barnett
2d Man ....David Hill
Stage Manager ....Peter Jolley
    Directed by Frank Dunlop; scenery and costumes, Nadine Baylis; lighting, Rory Dempster.
    A Pirandellian satire on Britain and the author's familiar bugbears and sacred cows, which he lampoons with the use of a company of players, some of them planted in the auditorium, sometimes playing themselves and sometimes the characters set down for them.

MY FAT FRIEND by Charles Lawrence (D). A lodger persuades a fat girl to diet. With Kenneth Williams, Jennie Linden, John Harding, Bernard Holley. (202+)

EPITAPH FOR GEORGE DILLON by John Osborne and Anthony Creighton. Jonathan Hales's Young Vic Theater revival. With Sian Phillips, Madge Ryan, Richard Kane. (23 in repertory)

A SAWDUST CAESAR by Andy Smith. A politically re-worked Aladdin. With Ken Morley, Yvonne Gill, Lew Lewis. With, as intermission-piece, THE ASSASSINATION TO DEATH OF JULIUS CAESAR by the same author. (35)

LOOK BACK IN ANGER by John Osborne. Bernard Goss's Young Vic revival of epoch-making modern drama. With Nicky Hanson, Mel Martin, Loise Daine, Allen Lewis, Ian Taylor. (35+ in repertory)

THE RAPIST by Philip Martin. A play about masturbation. With Elayne Sharling, Paul Copley, Keith Benedict. (25)

TWO PLUS FLOWER EQUALS CHRISTMAS by Amos Mokadi, with songs by Leon Rosselson. Last year's children show, revived, about Little Jo's efforts to do good. With Marion Fitch, Peter Sergeant, Keith Morris. (24)

TOAD OF TOAD HALL by Kenneth Grahame and H. Fraser Simpson. Revival of popular children's show. With Ian Talbot, Nikolas Simmonds, Richard Wilson. (42)

THE RUPERT CHRISTMAS SHOW, based on *Rupert and the Paperfall* by A.E. Bestall. With Diane Robillard. (60)

WINNIE THE POOH by A.A. Milne, adapted by and with additional music by Julian Slade. New Christmas season version of popular children's play. With Ronald Radd, Frank Thornton, Maria Charles, Eric Dodson, John O'Farrell. (52)

PETER PAN by J.M. Barrie. Revival of Robert Helpmann's spectacular production. With Dorothy Tutin, Ron Moody, Pauline Jameson, Ian Trigger. (24)

THE GOOD OLD BAD OLD DAYS by Leslie Bricusse and Anthony Newley. Musical satire on the contemporary scene. With Anthony Newley, Caroline Villiers, Paul Bacon. (186+)

ANANSI AND BRER ENGLISHMAN by Manley Young and Gloria Cameron. Anglo-Caribbean pantomime. With Frank Cousins, Gloria Cameron, Michael Ridgway, Trevor Thomas. (21)

THE ROSE AND THE RING by William Makepeace Thackeray, book, score and lyrics by John Dalby. Stage adaptation of famous children's book. With Thelma Ruby. (26)

ONCE UPON A TIME . . . , book and lyrics by Norman Newell, music by Roger Webb. A nursery-rhyme show directed and choreographed by Gillian Lynne. With Kerry Gardner, Roger Webb, Joyce Grant, Patsy Rowlands. (34)

TWELFTH NIGHT by William Shakespeare. Peter James's production of National Theater Touring Company. With Benjamin Whitrow, David Bauer (later Michael Blakemore), David Bradley, David Ryall, Louise Purnell, Anna Carteret, Maggie Riley. (4+)

TEDERELLA by David Edgar. Satire of Tory politics. With Carole Hayman, Richard Quick. (24)

KRAPP'S LAST TAPE and NOT I by Samuel Beckett. Produced by and at the Royal Court Theater. Opened January 16, 1973. (Closed February 17, 1973). (40)
Krapp's Last Tape .... Albert Finney
Not I
Mouth .... Billie Whitelaw
Auditor .... Brian Miller
   Directed by Anthony Page; scenery and costumes, Jocelyn Herbert; lighting, Rory Dempster.
   Krapp's Last Tape, revival of Beckett's monodrama, presented with the British premiere of *Not I*, Beckett's 15-minute-long monologue for an actress and a silent actor. The world premiere took place at the Reper-

tory Theater of Lincoln Center in the Forum, opening on November 22, 1972, with Jessica Tandy and Henderson Forsythe.

THE MAN OF DESTINY by George Bernard Shaw. Revival of political playlet. With David Schofield, Diana Quick, Malcolm Storry. (24)

HOBSON'S CHOICE by Harold Brighouse. Bernard Goss' new Young Vic production of former National Theater success. With Peter Bayliss, Andrew Robertson. (20 in repertory)

RIPPER by Terence Greer. Who was Jack the Ripper? With Terence Docherty, Morris Colbourne, Anna Shaw. (30)

DRACULA by Stanley Eveling, David Mowat, Alan Jackson, Clarisse Eriksson, Robert Nye, Bill Watson, John Downing. Multiple view of Bram Stoker's thriller. With Jack Shepherd, Anthony Haygarth, Petra Markham, Ann Holloway, Alun Armstrong. (24)

A TASTE OF HONEY by Shelagh Delaney. Pam Brighton's new Young Vic production of 1950s hit drama. With Michael Byrne, Jeremy James Taylor, Julia McCarthy, Ursula Mohan (later Jane Wood), Peter Straker. (18 in repertory)

THE DOOMSDAY BUTTONS by Brian Hayles. The further adventures of Harvey Hawkitt of *Dragon Lost*. With the Unicorn Theater company. (19)

JOSEPH AND THE AMAZING TECHNICOLOR DREAMCOAT. Music by Andrew Lloyd Webber, lyrics by Tim Rice, dialogue for *The Prologue* by Ray Galton and Alan Simpson. Produced by Robert Stigwood in association with Qwertyuiop Productions, Michael White, and Granada, and by arrangement with David Land, in the Young Vic Production at the Albery Theater. Opened February 16, 1973. (123+)
   PART I, *The Prologue:* Esau—Peter Blake; Jacob—Kevin Williams; Isaac—Alex McAvoy; Rebecca—Alison Groves; God—Paul Brooke; Laban—Ian Trigger; Leah—Joan Heal; Rachel—Joanna Wake; Handmaidens—Alison Groves, Frances Sinclair; Angels and Workers—Felicity Balfour, Sam Cox, Avril Gaynor, Carl Johnstone, Roy North, Dudley Rogers, Louis Sheldon, Mason Taylor, Frank Vincent, Maynard Williams, David Wynn.
   PART II, *Joseph and the Amazing Technicolor Dreamcoat:* Narrators—Peter Reeves, Peter Blake, Maynard Williams; Leah, Potiphar's Wife—Joan Heal; Rachel—Joanna Wake; Zilpah—Alison Groves; Bilpah—Frances Sinclair; Joseph—Gary Bond; Reuben—Paul Brooke; Simeon—Maynard Wil-

liams; Levi—Mason Taylor; Napthali—Dudley Rogers; Issachar—Frank Vincent; Asher—Sam Cox; Dan, Potiphar—Ian Trigger; Zebulun—David Wynn; Gad, Butler—Kevin Williams; Benjamin, Baker—Roy North; Judah—Peter Blake; Pharaoh—Gordon; Ishmaelites, Camels, Egyptians, Harem, etc.—Carl Johnstone, Felicity Balfour, Avril Gaynor, Louis Sheldon.

Musicians: Leon Cohen keyboard; Mike Egan lead guitar; Doug Henning bass; Colin Wilkinson drums; Duncan Kinnell percussion; Michael Porter flute, piccolo, clarinet; Dave Lawrence clarinet, bass clarinet, sax; Hank Shaw trumpet, Steve Saunders trombone, tuba; choir from Islington Green School.

Directed by Frank Dunlop; scenery and costumes, Nadine Baylis; lighting, Jules Fisher; musical direction, Anthony Bowles; orchestrations, David Cullen, from the originals by Andrew Lloyd Webber; choreography, Christopher Bruce; sound, David Collison; production supervisor, Joe Aveline; executive producer, Bob Swash.

Modern rock version of the Biblical story of Joseph and his Brethren, by the authors of *Jesus Christ Superstar*. Part I tells the story of Jacob's years of service with Laban and Part II the story of the famine in Egypt and Joseph's harsh treatment of his brothers, and the final reconciliation. *Joseph and the Amazing Technicolor Dreamcoat* was performed in an earlier London production (see its entry above in this section).

Henry Woolf replaced Alex McAvoy 3/17/73.

IS YOUR DOCTOR REALLY NECESSARY? by Ken Hill, with songs by Tom Macaulay. A critical look at the medical and pharmaceutical mafia. With Avis Bunnage, Toni Palmer, Brian Murphy, Maxwell Shaw, Griffith Davies. (70)

MAHLER by Maurice Rowdon (D). The story of Gustav Mahler. With Vladek Sheybal, Edith Macarthur. (20)

MISTRESS OF NOVICES by John Kerr. The story of Bernadette of Lourdes's battle with the Mistress of Novices of the Convent of Nevers. With Rita Tushingham, Barbara Jefford. (44)

GB by Alan Thornhill, Hugh Steadman and Michael Henderson. Moral Re-Armament's musical revue about the moral collapse of Great Britain. With Michel Orphelin, Gladstone Adderley. (99+)

ROSENCRANTZ AND GUILDENSTERN by W.S. Gilbert. Revival of 19th-century parody of a *Hamlet* production. With Alan Benion, David Quilter. (18)

ROGERS AND STARR'S SPRING BIZARRE. Camp drag revue. With Rogers, Starr, Marcia Ashton, Michael Boothe. (72)

LITTLE HOPPING ROBIN by Paul Ableman. The bizarre dream of an oil executive. With Malcolm Ingram, Liz Munday. (27)

ONLY A GAME by Barrie Keeffe (D). The private life of a professional footballer. With Peter Gilmore, Daphne Anderson, Jan Waters. (36)

SAY GOODNIGHT TO GRANDMA by Colin Welland (D). Hero trapped between wife and mother. With Madge Ryan, Stephanie Turner, the author. (73+)

THE OWL AND THE PUSSYCAT WENT TO SEE . . . by David Wood and Sheila Ruskin. Revival of the popular children's holiday entertainment. With Johnny Ball, Janina Faye. (32)

A CHASTE MAID AT CHEAPSIDE by Thomas Middleton. John Grillo's adaptation of classical drama. With Sidney Forest, Penny Leatherbarrow, Vaas Anderson. (23)

ROSENCRANTZ AND GUILDENSTERN ARE DEAD by Tom Stoppard. Young Vic revival. With Nicky Henson, Andrew Robertson. (25+ in repertory)

THE MOONCUSSER'S DAUGHTER by Joan Aiken. What's in the cave under the sea? With the Unicorn Theater company. (17)

THE HEDGEHOG AND THE HARE adapted by Matyelok Gibbs, Madeleine Sotheby and Ursula Jones from six fables by story tellers as diverse as Aesop, Buddha and Tolstoy. With the Unicorn Theater company. (16)

MOTHER ADAM by Charles Dyer. New production of two-hander about loneliness. With Hermione Baddeley, Peter Wyngarde. (36)

MISALLIANCE by George Bernard Shaw. New Mermaid Theater production of Shavian comedy debunking Edwardian mores. With Caroline Blakiston, Bill Fraser, Delia Lindsay. (19+ in repertory)

IN TWO MINDS by David Mercer. Stage version of TV play on a psychotic case. With Anthony Woodruff, Vivienne Burgess, Pamela Farebrother. (24)

UNDERSTUDIES by Jackie Skarvellis. The understudy's psyche from inside. With Giles Cole, Trisha Despon. (22)

SWEENEY TODD by C. G. Bond, a new version of the Victorian melodrama, with music by Trevor T. Smith. With Brian Murphy, Avis Bunnage. (33+)

AT THE HAWK'S WELL and THE CAT AND THE MOON by W.B. Yeats. Playlets by the Irish poet with Anglo-Canadian cast. With Cedric Smith, Brian Stavechny, Anitra Shore, Jenny Moss, Jeff Bateman. (19+)

THE BANANA BOX by Eric Chappel (D). A landlord tries to manipulate his racially mixed tenants. With Leonard Rossiter, Frances de la Tour, Paul Jones. (13+)

THE ADULTERY CONVENTION by Cecil P. Taylor. Political satire on a theatrical political satire. With Carole Heyman, John Muirhead, John Nightingale, Alan Surtees. (6+)

BABY LOVE by David Edgar. Semi-documentary on baby snatching. With Heather Chasen, Peter Miles. (4+)

SOME AMERICAN PLAYS PRODUCED IN LONDON

ICARUS'S MOTHER by Sam Shepard. With the Freehold Workshop Company. (8)

THERE/THIS/MOVE by Michael Kirby. With the Freehold Workshop Company. (5)

THE FRONT PAGE by Ben Hecht and Charles MacArthur. Produced by the National Theater at the Old Vic Theater. Opened July 6, 1972. (81+ in repertory)

Wilson	Allan Mitchell
Endicott	John Shrapnel
Murphy	James Hayes
McCue	Gawn Grainger
Schwartz	David Bradley
Kruger	David Ryall
Bensinger	Benjamin Whitrow
Mrs. Schlosser	Maggie Riley
Woodenshoes Eichhorn	David Henry
Diamond Louie	Stephen Greif
Hildy Johnson	Denis Quilley
Jennie	Jeanne Watts
Molly Malloy	Maureen Lipman
Sheriff Hartman	David Bauer
Peggy Grant	Anna Carteret
Mrs. Grant	Mary Griffiths
The Mayor	Paul Curran
Mr. Pincus	Harry Lomax
Earl Williams	Clive Merrison
Walter Burns	Alan MacNaughtan
Tony	Barry James
Carl	Kenneth Mackintosh
Frank	Malcolm Reid

Policemen, etc.: Michael Essex, Paul Hetherington, David Kincaid, Roger Monk, Harry Waters, David Whitman.
Directed by Michael Blakemore; scenery and costumes, Michael Annals; lighting, Leonard Tucker.
First produced August 14, 1928 at the Times Square Theater by Jed Harris (named a Best Play of its season), and later revived in New York in 1968-69 and again in 1969 and 1970, The Front Page was never shown in Britain, except as a film, until now. It was presented in three acts.
David Kincaid replaced David Henry

12/12/72; David Graham replaced Stephen Greif, Sarah Atkinson replaced Maureen Lipman, David Healy replaced David Bauer 3/13/73; Malcolm Reid replaced Benjamin Whitrow 4/11/73.

COWBOY MOUTH by Sam Shepard and Patti Smith. With Patricia Quinn, Philip Sayer. (16)

LIQUID THEATER by the Global Village. With Brooke Lappin, Bruce Bassman. (48)

ROCK CARMEN by Herb Hendler, music by Michael Hughes. World premiere of American musical version of Bizet's opera. With Terri Stevens, Davy Clinton, Robert Coleby, Elaine Page. (37)

THE TOOTH OF CRIME by Sam Shepard, music and lyrics by the author. World premiere of American author's play, commissioned by the Open Space Theater, about a conflict, set in an America of the future, in which, to music performed by Blunderpuss, pop-scene characters like Star-Man, Galactic Jack, etc., come to blows in an ambiance that is vicious, drug-addicted, and drowned in the cliches of pop music. With Malcolm Storry, Petronella Ford, Michael Weller, John Grillo, David Schofield. (In repertory with An Othello). (39 in repertory)

"COWBOYS/2" Sam Shepard. With Willie Longmore, Tom Jennings. (16)

WITNESS by Terrence McNally. With Blair Fairman, Patrick Tull, Mary Hughes. (15)

THE WHITE WHORE AND THE BIT PLAYER by Tom Eyen. With Aline Waites, Diana Bishop. (19)

DR. KHEAL by Maria Irene Fornes. A crazy professor talks. With Roy Martin. On the same program with THE PLAY-ROOM'S ABC, a lesson for children. (5)

PORTMANTEAU, OR "SYMPHONY U.S.A." comprising THE HUNTER AND THE BIRD by Jean-Claude van Itallie; THE LOVELIEST AFTERNOON OF THE YEAR by John Guare; and TOUR, BOTTICELLI and NEXT by Terrence McNally. With Bill Nagy, Mildred Mayne, Andrew Murray, Sally-Jane Spencer, Michael Maloney. (12)

MINIVER CHEEVEY by Richard Arno Friedlander. World premiere of American drama about a Yank in London. With Rick le Parmentier, Karin Dominic. (12)

CHARLIE THE CHICKEN by Jonathan Levy. With David Freeman. (12)

RED CROSS and CHICAGO by Sam Shepard. With Nigel Terry, Michael Pennington. (11)

BEFORE BREAKFAST by Eugene O'Neill. With Vivienne Stokes. (10)

MOTHER EARTH by Ron Thronson and Tony Shearer. Revised British production of anti-pollution rock musical originally produced in San Francisco in 1971-72. With Peter Straker, Helen Chap-pel, Linda Kendrick. (19)

THE GNÄDIGES FRÄULEIN by Tennessee Williams. With Linda Gulder, Jana Shelden, Richard Norton. (8)

ACTION REPLAY by Jack Matcha. World premiere of American farcical play about Soviet-American relations in Moscow. With Henry Szeps, Frances Tomelty, Helen Gill, David Purcell. (12)

LISTEN by Robert Creeley (D). First play by American author about a strange couple (originally commissioned by German radio). With Ralph Cotterill, Diana Bishop. (14)

THE MADNESS OF LADY BRIGHT by Lanford Wilson. With Winstone Christie, Suzanne Lummis, Mark York. (10)

THE GIFT by Mario Fratti. With Magdalena Buznea. (12)

THE PROBLEM by A.R. Gurney Jr. With Kevin Stoney, Diana Fairfax. (34)

THE EFFECT OF GAMMA RAYS ON MAN-IN-THE-MOON MARIGOLDS by Paul Zindel. With Sheila Hancock, Yvonne Antrobus, Pamela Moiseiwitsch. (36)

DAMES AT SEA by Robin Miller, Jim Wise, George Haimsohn. Entirely new shortened version of musical spoof on Hollywood (staged at Duchess Theater in 1969). With Nicholas Bennett, Debbie Bowen, Freddie Eldrett, Pip Minton, Richard Owens, Barbara Young. (50)

APPLAUSE by Betty Comden and Adolph Green, music by Charles Strouse, lyrics by Lee Adams. With Lauren Bacall (also Billy Boyle), Angela Richards, Eric Flynn, Basil Hoskins (225+)

TERRIBLE JIM FITCH and LAUGHS ETC. by James Leo Herlihy. With Derrick O'Connor, Beth Porter. (18)

THE LEGEND OF CAL WILLIAMS by Bud Castleman. World premiere of American drama about a cowboy Hamlet. With the Actors' Forum company. (5)

THE OLD MAN'S COMFORTS by Perry Pontac (D). World premiere of American's pastiche 19th-century satire on master-servant relations. With Patronella Ford, Malcolm Storry, Fenella Fielding. (32)

BUNNY by Norman Krasna. World premiere of American writer's play in two parts about a whore with a heart of platinum. With Eartha Kitt, David Kossoff, Robert Beatty, Maurice Kaufmann, Judith Arthy. (56)

THE BIG ROCK CANDY MOUNTAIN by Alan Lomas and Yola Miller. Theater Workshop's folk-musical pantomime. With Toni (Legs) Palmer, Philip Davis, Brian Murphy, Maxwell Shaw. (56)

THE WIZARD OF OZ by L. Frank Baum. New stage version for Christmas time. With Tony Simpson, Diane Raynor, Frank Marlborough, Sam Kelly, Geoffrey Hughes. (42)

THE LITTLEST CLOWN by Christopher Cable, music by Lew Kestler. American children's show with English cast. (23)

CLAUDE by Leo J. Heaps. World premiere of play based on the Claude Eatherley case history. With Michael Duggan, James Locker. (11)

SWEET EROS by Terrence McNally. With Will Knightley, Rosylan Elvin. (10)

SMALL CRAFT WARNINGS by Tennessee Williams. Produced by and at the Hampstead Theater Club. Opened January 29, 1973. (Closed February 26, 1973) Revived at the Comedy Theater March 13, 1973. (Closed May 5, 1973) (86)

Leona Dawson ....Elaine Stritch
Monk ....Peter Jones
Doc ....George Pravda

Bill ....Edward Judd
Violet ....Frances de la Tour
Steve ....James Berwick
Quentin ....Tony Beckley
Bobby ....Eric Deacon
Tony, the cop ....John Bay
Directed by Vivian Matalon; scenery and costumes, Saul Radomsky; lighting, Robert Ornbo.

The play is set in a bar along the Southern California coast and was first performed at the Truck & Warehouse Theater, New York, on 4/2/72. This was the first British production of the play about the inmates of a third-rate California coastal barroom.

NOW THERE'S JUST THE THREE OF US by Michael Weller. World premiere of U.S. writer's play about the vanity of young people. With John Hug, Lloyd McGuire, Peter Lucas, Rachel Davies. (18)

THE UNSEEN HAND by Sam Shepard. With Warren Clarke, Clive Endersby, Christopher Malcolm.

SARAH B. DIVINE by Tom Eyen, with songs by Danny Beckerman. With Rogers & Starr. (13)

AREATHA IN THE ICE-PALACE, OR THE FULY GUARANTEED FUCK-ME DOLL by Tom Eyen. With Mary Ditson, Trader Selkirk. (22)

THE REFUSAL and THE SUICIDE by Mario Fratti. The former with Taiwo Ajai, Robert Cotton; the latter with Frank Vincent, Marilyn Fridjon. (15)

THE GOLDEN FLEECE by A.R. Gurney Jr. Marriage viewed from opposing standpoints. With Madeleine Cannon, William Maxwell. (11)

BORN YESTERDAY by Garson Kanin. With Lynn Redgrave, Dave King, Donald Adam. (25)

THE EMPEROR JONES by Eugene O'Neill. With Thomas Baptiste. (11)

TWO GENTLEMEN OF VERONA adapted from William Shakespeare by John Guare, music by Galt MacDermot. With B.J. Arnau, Samuel E. Wright, Ray C. Davis, Jean Gilbert, Veronica Clifford. (41+)

HOUSEWARMING by Robert Wells (D). American Londoner's first play about the adventure of a successful oil prospector's encounters. With Susan Butler, Sharman McDonald. (5)

THE CAGE by Rick Cluchey. With Marcel Steiner, Jonathan Rosen, R.S. Bailey, the author. (26+)

NO, NO, NANETTE by Otto Harbach and Frank Mandel, lyrics by Irving Caesar, music by Vincent Youmans, adapted and directed by Burt Shevelove. With Anna Neagle, Tony Britton, Anne Rogers, Barbara Brown. (19+)

DEAR LOVE by Jerome Kilty. The love letters of two famous poets. With Keith Michell, Geraldine McEwen. (18+)

GYPSY by Arthur Laurents, lyrics by Stephen Sondheim, music by Jule Styne. With Zan Charisse, Angela Lansbury. (4+)

THE ME NOBODY KNOWS by Stephen H. Joseph and Herb Schapiro, music by Gary William Friedman, lyrics by Will Holt. With Angela Bruce, David Cordwell. (1+)

SOME FOREIGN PLAYS PRODUCED IN LONDON

THE MOON IS EAST, THE SUN IS WEST. Japanese play with rock music that mirrors present-day contrasts. By and with the Tokyo Kid Brothers. (12)

KABUKI THEATER SEASON at the Sadler's Wells Theater. CHUSHINGURA (The 47 Loyal Samurai) (16), and SUMIDAGAWA (The Sumida River) (12)

ARCHITRUC by Robert Pinget. With Andrew Thomas, Wyllie Longmore, Lib Spry. (10)

ORISON by Fernando Arrabal. With Sue Lane, Wyllie Longmore. (8)

DIE VERKANNTE GRÖSSE (Unrecognized Greatness) by Wolfgang Ebert. In German.

Original title: Der Mord Zum Sonntag. With Carmen Blanck, Jon Rumney. (4)

HEDDA GABLER by Henrik Ibsen, adapted by John Osborne. With Jill Bennett, Denholm Elliott, Ronald Hines, Barbara Ferris, Brian Cox. (33)

THE LOWER DEPTHS by Maxim Gorky, newly translated and adapted by Kitty Hunter Blair and Jeremy Brooks. With Heather Canning, Gordon Gostelow, Bernard Lloyd, Richard Pasco, Peter Woodthorpe. (39 in repertory)

HUIS CLOS (NO EXIT) by Jean Paul Sartre. With Raymond Cross, Tony Parkin, Jean Graham. (25)

MADMEN AND SPECIALISTS by Wole Soyinka. British premiere of a Nigerian author's view of the racial setup in Africa. With the Holland Park Link Group. (3)

WHEN WE DEAD AWAKEN by Henrik Ibsen. With Diana Patrick, Pat Rossiter. (12)

IMPROMPTUS FOR LEISURE by René de Obaldia, comprising EDWARD AND AGRIPPINA, with Linda Busselle, Vic Hunter, Jeremy Walston: CAYENNE PEPPER, with Anthony Millan, Kenneth Barrow; THE TWINKLING TWINS, with Anthony Millan, Quentin Seacome, Chris Bradwell; and THE LATE, with Elaine Ives-Cameron, Elayne Sharling. (8)

THE GRAND VIZIER by René de Obaldia. With Jenny Uggles, David Freedman, Martin Read. (18)

ON THE ROAD by Anton Chekhov. With David Warner, Phyllis Morris. (14)

THE DRAGON by Yevgeny Schwartz. With Michael Irving. (20)

THE MAN FROM THE EAST by Stomu Yamash'ta, with the Red Buddha Theater company. (94)

THE CAVES OF SALAMANCA by Miguel de Cervantes. Diana Berriman, Jo Blatchley. (12)

THE FIFTH LABOR OF HERCULES by Friedrich Duerrenmatt. Translated by Agnes Hamilton. With Ralph Cotterill, Pamela Moiseiwitsch. (18)

SILENCE AND THE LIE by Nathalie Sarrante. With Rodney Archer, Sasha Bartlett, Moran Kennedy, Robert French, Eve Shickle, Drew Woods. (29).

MR. ME (A DIALOGUE WITH A BRILLIANT CHARACTER), THE SONATA, THE THREE GENTLEMEN (OR HOW TO SPEAK MUSIC) by Jean Tardieu. With Brian Vaughan, Chris Owen, Roy Sone. (5)

SMILE ORANGE by Trevor Rhone. Jamaican play celebrating island's independence. With Charles Hyatt, Mona Hammond, Stefan Kaliphe, Trevor Thomas. (5)

HUSBANDS AND LOVERS, five one-acters by Ferenc Molnar. With Fiona Walker, John Blythe, David Wood, Kay Barlow, Antonia Bird. (12)

RICHARD'S CORK LEG by Brendan Behan. With Eileen Colgan, Ronnie Drew, Joan O'Hara, Angela Newman, Dearbhla Molloy. (40)

THE NEW STEP by Leonard Cohen. World premiere of a dance-drama re-working of the ugly duckling fable by the Canadian poet and singer. With Sue Lane, Lib Spry, Lizzie Mackenzie, Tom Jennings. (8)

REVIVAL by Tom Gallagher. London premiere of Irish author's 1973 Dublin Theater Festival play about a would-be suicide. With David Swift (later Kevin Storey), Diana Fairfax. (60)

BILL DURHAM, OR THE GREAT TURD AND HOW TO GET IT ROLLING by Jeremy Newson (D). World premiere of Canadian author's drama of an ecological crisis in the wild and woolly West caused by a new tobacco substitute. With the Unity Theater company. (12)

HUMULUS THE MUTED LOVER (Humulus le Muet) by Jean Anouilh. With Peter Bayliss, Cleo Sylvestre. (12)

SHAKESPEARE THE SADIST (Frau und Film) by Wolfgang Bauer. With Prunella Gee, Kit Jackson, Andrew Norton, Adam Verney. (23)

A DOLL'S HOUSE by Henrik Ibsen, translated by J.W. McFarlane. With Susan Hampshire, Sylvia Sims, Keith Buckley. (25)

PLAYING WITH FIRE by August Strindberg. With Celia Bannerman, Gabrielle Blunt, John Flanagan. (18)

PICNIC ON THE BATTLEFIELD by Fernando Arrabal. With Lisa Hughes, Russell Faulkner, Steven Gardner. (12)

LAMENT FOR A BULLFIGHTER by Federico Garcia Lorca. With Belo Horzante, Renaldo Boschi. (2)

ELECTRA by Sophocles, adapted by Warren Hearnden. With Elaine Ives-Cameron, Roy Martin, Jackie Skarvellis, Brenda Somers. (20)

CATSPLAY by Istvan Orkeny. With Mary Jones. (6)

SUMMERFOLK by Maxim Gorky, adapted by Francis Hanley. With Inigo Jackson, Ann Godley, David Stockton. (15)

THE LAST LONELY DAYS OF ROBINSON CRUSOE by and with Jerome Savary's Parisian-based Le Grand Magic Circus. (33)

SCAPINO adapted from Molière. Revival of Frank Dunlop's production of Young Vic success. With Jim Dale, Peter Bayliss, Ursula Mohan. (20 in repertory)

LUNAPARK by and with the Laboratoire Vicinal of Brussels. (1)

THE LIVING VOICE by Jean Cocteau, newly adapted by Richard Jones and Amos Mokadi. With Pamela Coveney. (15)

THREE SISTERS by Anton Chekhov, translated by Elisabeth Fen. With Norman Rodway, Ann Firbank, Jay Parker, Mia Farrow, Keith Baxter, Gwen Watford. (25)

THE LONG NIGHT by Robert O'Donoghue. Irish author's play about McSwiney's 76-day fast in Brixton Prison in 1920. With Sue Bullock, Susannah McMillan, Jennifer Carroll, Bernard McHugh. (6)

KASPAR by Peter Handke. With Henry Woolf. (26)

L'AVARE by Molière. With the Parisian-based Théâtre de l'Unité. (13)

WOYZECK by Georg Buechner, freely adapted and directed by Charles Marowitz. With David Schofield. (31)

A DOLL'S HOUSE by Henrik Ibsen. New adaptation by Christopher Hampton. Produced by Hillard Elkins and presented by Bernard Delfont and Michael White at the Criterion Theater. Opened February 20, 1973. (115+)
Torvald Helmer ....Colin Blakely
Nora ....Claire Bloom
Dr. Rank ....Anton Rodgers
Mrs. Kristine Linde ......Stephanie Bidmead
Nils Krogstad ....Peter Woodthorpe
Anne-Marie ....Nora Nicholson
Helene ....Dorothy Baird
    Directed by Patrick Garland; scenery and lighting, John Bury; costumes, Beatrice Dawson.
    Christopher Hampton's new colloquial version was written especially for the Hillard Elkins New York production, staring Claire Bloom (Mrs. Hillard Elkins), which opened in New York 1/13/71 and was revived to inaugurate the Eisenhower Theater in the John F. Kennedy Center in Washington 10/16/71. Claire Bloom is the only member of the London cast who was in the original production. The play was presented in three acts.

THE MISANTHROPE by Molière. English version by Tony Harrison. Produced by the National Theater at the Old Vic Theater. Opened February 22, 1973. (31+ in repertory)
Alceste ....Alec McCowen
Philinte ....Alan MacNaughtan
Oronte ....Gawn Grainger
Célimène ....Diana Rigg
Eliante ....Jeanne Watts
Arsinoé ....Gillian Barge
Acaste ....Nicholas Clay
Clitandre ....Jeremy Clyde
Basque ....Paul Curran
Official ....Clive Merrison
Dubois ....James Hayes

    Directed by John Dexter; scenery and costumes, Tanya Moiseiwitsch; lighting, Andy Phillips; music arranger, Marc Wilkinson.
    Produced to coincide with the 300th anniversary of the death of Molière, and specially commissioned by the National Theater, Tony Harrison's new verse adaptation, in modern English, written in rhymed pentameters is set in 1966 (or 300 years after the year of its first performance, with the author in the title role), when General de Gaulle was to France almost what Louis XIV had been three centuries earlier.
    Paul Gregory replaced Jeremy Clyde 4/14/73.

THE FREEDOM OF THE CITY by Brian Friel. Simultaneous London premiere with Abbey Theater, Dublin production of an imaginary incident in civil-war-torn Belfast. With Basil Dignam, Peter Frye, Carmel McSharry. (33)

GBANA BENDU by Yulisa Amadu Maddy. Sierra Leone author's play about a fruitless attempt to reconcile Europe and Afro-America. With T-Bone Wilson, Elvania Zimiru, Gordon Tialobi, Jeillo Edwards, Marcia Miller. (4)

ROOTED by Alexander Buzo. Australian writer's play about the folks back home. With Jenny Aguter, Katy Barlow, Philip Jackson. (28)

SUZANNA ANDLER by Marguerite Duras, translated by Barbara Bray. With Eileen Atkins, Dinsdale Landen. (22)

ÉLECTRE by Sophocles, with parantheses by Yannis Ritsos. With the Paris Théâtre des Quartiers d'Ivry companies. (3)

CEREMONY FOR A MURDERED BLACK by Fernando Arrabal. With David Foxxe, Peter Johns, Susanna Hunt, Anton Philips. (18)

IN THE JUNGLE OF CITIES by Bertolt Brecht. With James Aubrey, Christopher Ryan. (4)

HELLO AND GOODBYE by Athol Fugard. With Janet Suzman, Ben Kingsley. (18)

ANTIGONE by Jean Anouilh. With the Bowsprit Company. (23)

THE HOUSE OF BERNARDA ALBA by Federico Garcia Lorca, adapted by Tom Stoppard. With Mia Farrow, Patience Collier, Anne Firbank, June Jago. (25)

THE DIARY OF A MADMAN by Gogol, adapted by Milos Kirek and Jeremy Irons. With Jeremy Irons. (18)

WORLD THEATER SEASON: LITTLE MAN—WHAT NOW? by Hans Fallada, adapted by Tankred Dorst, wth the Bochum Schauspielhaus (8); YERMA by Federico Garcia Lorca, with the Nuria Espert Company (8); LIEBELEI by Arthur Schnitzler, with the Vienna Burgtheater (8); LE MALADE IMAGINAIRE (The Imaginary Invalid) with LE MÉDECIN VOLANT (The Flying Doctor) by Molière (7) and RICHARD III by William Shakespeare (7), with the Comédie Française; THE METAMORPHOSES OF A WANDERING MINSTREL by Peppino De Filippo, with Peppino de Filippo's Italian Theater (8); L'ENCHANTEUR POURRISSANT (The Rotting Enchanter) by Guillaume Apollinaire, with the Rideau de Bruxelles (8); THE POSSESSED by Feodor Dostoevsky, with the Cracow Stary Theater (8); THE WILD DUCK by Henrik Ibsen, with the Stockholm Royal Dramatic Theater (8); THE UMEWAKA NOH TROUPE of Japan (14); UMABATHA by Welcome Msomi, with the Natal Theater Workshop Zulu Company. (16)

THE PROPOSAL by Anton Chekhov. With Jack Niles, Gerald Martin, Barbara Berkery. (10)

VATZLAV by Slawomir Mrozek. With Laurence Barnes. (7)

SCHELLENBRACK by Tom Gallagher. Irish author's play about the mind of a literary genius. With Wolfe Morris, Shelagh Fraser. (36+)

THE MOTHER by Bertolt Brecht, translated by Steve Gooch. With Mary Sheen, Kevin Costello, Michael Irving, Alex Leppard. (17)

TEMBA by Alton Kumalo. World premiere of a musical about a Zulu growing up. With Oscar James, the author. (8)

ROSMERSHOLM by Henrik Ibsen. With Joan Plowright, Jeremy Brett, John Nettleton, John Bailey, John Warner, Margery Mason. (15+)

THE MODEL VILLAGE by Rasheedi Gbadamosi. Nigerian author's play about the head of an African asylum and his efforts to reconcile two conflicting cultures. With Willie Payne, Yemi Ajibade, Siobhahn Quinlan. (9+)

THE CHERRY ORCHARD by Anton Chekhov, translated by Ronald Hingley. With Constance Cummings, Michael Hordern, David Bradley, Denis Quilley, Gillian Barge, Ann Carteret, Harry Lomax. (5+ in repertory)

THE SEASON ELSEWHERE IN EUROPE

By Ossia Trilling

FAITHFUL to my yearly principle, I begin with the West German theater again. The new managements at various regional state and city theaters had ample opportunity to show their mettle, to arouse controversy and to answer back in various ways. Ivan Nagel in Hamburg was attacked by one of the critics of *Die Welt,* never a friend of the progressive theater, on the grounds that his box-office takings had fallen below those of his predecessors. Nagel answered pungently by pointing out that *Die Welt* had helped to run them out of office over the years with its tendentious campaigns and by quoting figures to prove his critics wrong; moreover, two of the productions staged under his first year of managerial tenure (*The Fool and the Madman* by Thomas Bernhard, and *The Stable Yard* by Franz Xaver Kroetz) had been selected for the annual Berlin Theater Review, hardly a token of failure. Other firsts staged at the Deutsches Schauspielhaus under his control included the world premiere of *The Hypochondriacs,* a study of psychotics in society by the former literary adviser of the Schaubühne am Halleschen Ufer, Botho Strauss, and a persuasively realistic production, staged by Dieter Giesing, of Gorky's *The Barbarians,* both of which had found favor with the German press, including the critic of *Die Welt.* A witty revival of Carl von Sternheim's socio-critical drama *1913* also provided a starring role for the 70-year-old Werner Hinz. The highlight at the rival municipally-owned Thalia Theater was Hans Hollman's expectedly unorthodox rendering of *Richard III,* set in a Victorian ambiance, in the title-role of which Boy Gobert fulfilled every histrionic expectation as a 19th-century melodramatic villain.

Controversy at Cologne led to the departure of the English member of the international directorial triumvirate, Geoffrey Reeves, after he had staged a much criticized production of *You Can't Take It With You.* His place was taken by the former Brecht actress and Wuppertal director Angelika Hurwicz. The German director Hansgünther Heyme's contribution, Hebbel's *Maria Magdalena,* was Cologne's entry for the Berlin Theater Review, where it got a shade more praise than in its home town. The new regime at Frankfurt under Peter Palitzsch settled down nicely with *Lear,* by Edward Bond, the director stressing the political message at the expense of the "theater of cruelty"

121

elements. The German premiere of Brendan Behan's posthumous *Richard's Cork Leg* vied in popular appeal with Gorky's *The Barbarians* and was over-shadowed only by Hans Neuenfels's unorthodox approach to Ibsen's *Hedda Gabler,* in which the general's daughter first fires her father's pistol in the air and falls down in a faint; but, then, on hearing Judge Brack's curtain line ("People don't do such things!"), chooses to face life after all with all that decision entails.

Under Hans Peter Doll, Stuttgart's repertory displayed little that was not run-of-the-mill stuff, except perhaps for Wilfried Minks's unexpectedly realistic production of O'Casey's *Cock-a-Doodle-Dandy* and the world premiere of Kroetz's short wordless monodrama for an atcress, *Concert Choice,* in which Elke Twiesselmann silently mimed the last minutes of a disappointed middle-aged spinster apparently about to do herself in. The start of Ulrich Brecht's regime at Düsseldorf was dogged by political objections to his advertised left-wing repertory and the inaugural production of Brecht's *Arturo Ui,* but his confident leadership was well repaid before the end of the season, with a startlingly topical world premiere of the silenced Czech playwright's, Pavel Kohout's, *Poor Murderer,* with its setting a psychiatric clinic in St. Petersburg in 1900. The festive opening of the ultra-modern new playhouse that replaced the war-damaged State Theater in Darmstadt under Günther Beelitz was cele-brated on its small stage by a world premiere, that of *The Death of Buechner,* by Gaston Salvatore; at the Munich Kammerspiele the retiring director, August Everding, before handing over to his successor, Hans-Reinhard Müller, offered his patrons two special theatrical tidbits, Arnold Wesker's production, his first in the German language, of his own *The Old Ones,* and a sensationally original and "improved" version of Ionesco's *Macbett,* staged in what appeared to be a tumbledown circus setting by the Romanian, Liviu Ciulei. Another guest director in Munich, at the Residenz Theater, was England's William Gaskill, with Bond's *Lear.* At Munich's people's opera and operette theater, the Theater am Gärtnerplatz, lovers of light entertainment were offered a sumptuous world premiere of Alexander Faris's musical version of Peter Usti-nov's political comedy *R Loves J.*

Finally Bochum: the city that attracted most notice this year with the arrival of Peter Zadek at the helm. Intent on recruiting new audiences, this German-born English director-manager built up a new team with an ambitious program combining popular fare with appealing new rarities. These included his resident dramatist's, Tankred Dorst's, musical adaptation, in the form of a Berlin revue of the day, of Hans Fallada's best-selling novel of the 1930's, *Little Man, What Now?,* with sets by the Parisian Georges Wakhewitch, chore-ography by the Norwegian Tutte Lemkow and a chorus of Swedish lovelies. Zadek also put on Dorst's own drama, *Ice Age,* about the mentality of a fascist collaborator, in which O. E. Hasse gave a masterly portrayal of the octo-genarian protagonist Dorst had based on the pro-Hitler Norwegian Nobel Prize winner Knut Hamsun. In between, Zadek staged a new version of *The Merchant of Venice,* with a stylized setting of metal walkways designed by the Frenchman René Allio, on which Hans Mahnke with deliberate didactic intent played Shylock much as the anti-semitic Nazis had imagined the Jew. Istvan Bödy had an actor, Werner Dahms, playing the ineffable Lady Bracknell in *The Importance of Being Earnest,* and Rainer Werner Fassbinder exploited the fey talent of his preferred film actress Hanna Schygulla in Heinrich Mann's forgotten *Bibi,* staged with many of the revue ideas and personnel of the Fallada show. This, by the way, proved to be the hit of the 1973 London World Theater Season, just as the Shakespeare became the hit of the 1973 Berlin Theater Review.

West Berlin

The new régime at the Schiller and Schlosspark Theaters under Heinz Lietzau got off to a good start with a sumptuously mounted version of Kleist's *The Prince of Homburg* for which Lietzau had Wilfried Minks do the decor. The opulence and military panoply tended to drown the performances, and even the accomplished Helmut Griem in the title role seemed to be all at sea. Hans Hollman's Marxist adaptation of *Julius Caesar* went much further in the direction of distortion than did Brecht's of *Coriolanus,* but the parallels were clearly intentional. Lietzau's *Homburg* was artistically overshadowed by Peter Stein's totally different handling of the same play at the Schaubühne am Halleschen Ufer. Retitled *The Dream of the Prince of Homburg,* with drama-turgic and textual changes by Botho Strauss, this turned into an agonizingly slow-moving nightmare reflection of the spiritual and bodily misery of the German artist of Kleist's heyday. Bruno Ganz, dressed and made up as a clown, spoke and moved hypnotically in support of his director's new view of an old and difficult classic. At the same theater two other novelties made a deep impact: Klaus Michael Gruber's inspiriting new rendering of Ödön von Horvath's anti-bourgeois morality drama, *Tales from the Vienna Woods,* staged centrally with many an inspired directorial touch; and Peter Löscher's of Marieluise Fleisser's *Purgatory in Ingolstadt,* a 50-year-old comedy that owed its inspiration to the veteran author's ideological kinship and personal friendship with Brecht. It exposes the horrifying consequences of bigotry in a small Catholic town of her youth with uncannily prophetic foresight. Among the less ephemeral dramas to be seen at the Schiller's Studio Theater were Kroetz's outspoken drama of sexual frustration, *Cattle Crossing,* and the East German Heiner Müller's humanitarian parable *The Horatians,* both world premieres. The Free People's Theater in Hansjorg Utzerath's last year had a disappointing *Othello* (staged by the Swiss-Austrian guest-director Leopold Lindtberg) but the "rediscovery" of the Soviet dramatist Nicolai Erdman's satirical comedy, *The Mandate,* which poked fun at Muscovite foibles and the Anastasia legend in the 1920's, was on a par with the best that theater had shown since Piscator's death in 1966. As was to be expected, the Berlin entries for the annual Theater Review were Stein's Kleist and Löscher's Fleisser, both winners.

East Berlin

The most talked-of play in East Berlin was Ulrich Plenzdorf's *The New Sorrows of Young W,* a title that carries echoes of Goethe in it. Staged originally in Halle, it was seized upon by theater directors everywhere (even in the West, where it was done, somewhat inadequately, at the West Berlin Schlosspark, and announced for imminent production by at least a dozen playhouses). It is the story of an East German youth who is crossed in love and loses his life, perhaps by his own hand, in the prime of life. Its great public success is due to the immediacy of the theme and the readiness of young East German audiences to identify with the hero. Horst Schonemann's skillful production at the Deutsches Theater, with the likable Dieter Mann in the title role, marked the lucky inauguration of a new era at this theater under the management of Gerd Wolfram. O'Casey's *Juno and the Paycock* (announced before they took over) was a tolerable effort on the theater's small stage, and Hacks's *Amphitryon* (also a carry-over) did credit to all concerned on the large stage.

Hacks's *Omphale,* world premiered three years earlier in Frankfurt, and now coinciding with the author's (and his director's) election to the East Berlin Arts Academy, was the first native drama to be staged at the Berliner Ensemble for years. Thanks to the wit and imagination of Ruth Berghaus, the director, and her designer, Andreas Reinhardt, to say nothing of Ekkehard Schall as a Heracles curious to taste the emotions of the opposite sex by exchanging roles with Barbara Dittmus's Lydian Queen, unfettered laughter was never so plentiful inside Brecht's old theater. At Benno Besson's People's Theater Pieter Hein's Elizabethan-type ground plan for Manfred Karge's and Wolfgang Langhoff's cloak-and-dagger treatment of *Othello,* with comings and goings through and behind movable flats and adjustable half-curtains, kept the action flowing fast, as Rolf Ludwig, in black mask and gloves, piled on the laughs in his battle of wits with Günther Junghans's Iago. For the 75th Brecht birthday celebrations, Ruth Berghaus put on the first East German performance of the posthumous *Turandot or the Whitewashers' Congress.* It marked the temporary return to his former theater of the 70-year-old Curt Bois as the Chinese Emperor whose power over his people is as corrupt as his ability to rule them is elusive.

Switzerland and Austria

Harry Buckwitz's last season but two before retirement began with a row with his English guest director Peter Gill and came to a climax with another with his Polish guest director Andrzej Wajda. Gill's *A Midsummer Night's Dream* ran into trouble over language difficulties, and the same problem was said to be behind the decision of Wajda and his costume-designer, Krystyna Zachwatowicz, to leave Zurich before the dress rehearsal of Duerrenmatt's new horror-comic, *The Co-Operator.* The fact that he did not see eye to eye with his author and that Duerrenmatt took over the direction might account for the initial fiasco of this otherwise viable didactic drama about an American scientist who sells his soul to the devil, i.e. the gangsters, criminals, police, and politicians who rule the roost. Before that, Jerzy Jarocki's handsome production of Gombrowicz's *The Wedding* showed that language need prove no obstacle where director, actors and staff work in harmony and the author (a dead one, it is true) is conspicuously absent. Two other milestones this season were Buckwitz's own fresh view of his favorite play, *The Threepenny Opera*, with Josef Svoboda's sets, and Tom Toelle's directorial debut with the German-language premiere of David Rabe's *Sticks and Bones*. The chief attractions at the little Neumarkt Theater were Weiss's parable drama on the theme of brainwashing, *How Suffering was Driven out of Mr. Mockinpott,* and the first production ever of the late Robert Walser's anti-fairy tale one-acter trilogy of the 1920's called *Miniature Dramas,* in which the heroes and heroines of traditional children's tales are given an unexpected comeuppance. At Basel, Yugoslav guest-director Kosta Spaic paid a welcome return visit to stage Goldoni's *The Venetian Twins* and Niels-Peter Rudolph joined the City Theater permanently with a promisingly original version of *Oedipus.*

In Vienna Gerhard Klingenberg finally climbed into the managerial saddle of the Burg Theater unaided, though not without the much-advertised presence of a whole string of guest directors that included France's Jean-Paul Roussillon (*The Lady from Maxim's*) and Jean-Louis Barrault (*The Would-Be Gentleman*), England's Peter Hall (*Old Times*) and Edward Bond (making his directing debut with his own *Lear*), Poland's Erwin Axer (doing Thomas Bernhardt's *A Feast for Boris*) and Kazimierz Dejmek (Luise Rinser's adaptation of Jakob Bidermann's 18th-century *Philemon*), and Italy's Roberto Guicciardini (with his own version of *Candide* by Voltaire). Otto Schenk staged a new *Don Carlos* with Klaus Maria Brandauer, and Klingenberg put on an exciting, because heavily understated, revival of *Liebelei,* with photomontage sets by Rouben Ter-Arutunian, and a real-life father and daughter (Attila and Maresa Hörbiger) playing the Josefstadt Theater violinist Weiring and his ill-fated daughter Christine in Arthur Schnitzler's *fin-de-siècle* petit bourgeois tragedy of ill-starred love and class distinctions. The production marked the first visit to Britain of the Burg, performing the play to full houses at London's World Theater Season.

France

By moving the home of the Théâtre National Populaire from Paris to Lyons and handing over its direction to Roger Planchon and Patrice Chéreau, the former Cultural Minister Georges Duhamel ensured its continuance as one of France's leading national theaters. Three of the year's offerings ranked with the best seen anywhere in Europe, let alone France. Planchon's own hilariously lunatic morality drama on the dangers of manipulation by TV and the corruption of absolute power, called *La Langue au Chat* (I Give Up) was not as pessimistic as the English equivalent of the French idiomatic title implies. With Sami Frey in the lead of Tankred Dorst's *Toller,* staged by Chéreau, this latest political drama by a German scored another artistic bull's-eye, while Planchon's colorful direction of a part-French, part-American cast in Michel Vinaver's satire on international big business and the sway of the mighty dollar, entitled *Pas Dessus Bord* (Overboard), went unswervingly to the heart of the matter.

Duhamel's successor, the writer Maurice Druon, stirred up a hornet's nest soon after taking office by warning subsidized theaters that producers with hostile or critical views, policies and repertories would get no finance from his ministry. "Government," he said, "will not give alms to beggars with a bowl in one hand and a Molotov cocktail in the other." The ensuing outcry, led by members of the French Academy like Eugene Ionesco and Marcel Achard, and joined by every leading writer, composer, performer, critic and artist in the land, grew so loud that, at the time of writing, freedom of expression looked like winning against despotic bureaucracy. This episode certainly didn't endear the new minister to those who would have to depend on state support for their continued artistic activity. The Comédie Française began the year with a labor dispute which obliged its administrater, Pierre Dux, to close its doors for several months while the players performed in a circus tent theater pitched in the Tuileries Gardens. Here Robert Hirsch distinguished himself with a marvellous new comic creation, that of the Philosopher in Jean-Louis Barrault's entertaining new production, with pop music based on Lully themes, of *The Would-Be Gentleman.* Hirsch won further kudos by appearing at London's World Theater Season as the Duke of Gloucester in the Terry Hands production of *Richard III,* and soon afterward he said he would exercise his right to retire from the troupe after 25 years' yeoman service. Among the special attractions of the year were the decors for the two *Oedipus* plays, premiered at the Avignon Festival, and Jean-Paul Roussilon's new production of *The School for Wives.* The season at the company's second theater, the Odéon, began with a stunningly realistic version of Gorky's *The Lower Depths* from Rheims and included the usual experimental works of new or little-tried authors on both of the theater's two stages.

Jack Lang was appointed to manage the Palais de Chaillot, where only a new and well-attended production of *In the Jungle of Cities* kept the small Salle Gémier open for weeks on end, while the large stage and auditorium (named after the late Jean Vilar) was undergoing rebuilding and modernization. Lang launched the capital's first National Children's Theater while dividing his time between Paris and organizing the annual Nancy Theater Festival. Nancy largely filled the gap left by the final closure of the Theater of Nations—though Barrault, the latter's nominal head, combined with the various Parisian bodies to present certain foreign troupes, like the New York La Mama and the Andrei Sherban *Medea.*

Barrault himself pitched a tent inside the disused railroad station, the Gare d'Orsay, in order to put on there, in the round and for the first time on any stage, *Beneath the Balearic Wind,* the neglected fourth comic member of Claudel's Catholic tetralogy of *The Satin Slipper,* in which his reassembled company was directed by his stepson Jean-Pierre Granval. Madeleine Renaud also appeared at his other home, the Récamier, in an obscure but poetically moving new work by Roland Dubillard, with the suggestively idyllic title *Where the Cows Drink*. Other notable foreign troupes included the Luca Ronconi ensemble in the Italian director's claustrophobic version of *The Oresteia,* staged inside a cage-like scaffold encasing the players and audience alike in the main assembly hall of the Sorbonne; Peter Brook's touring production of *A Midsummer Night's Dream* (at the Théâtre de la Ville); and the two parts of Bob Wilson's *Overture* (to *Ka Mountain and GUARDenia Terrace*), a gloriously original experience for those with the time and the patience, consisting of 6 full working days' events in the Galliera Museum and 24 hours of solid Wilsoniana at the Opéra Comique, launched for the nonce by Mme. Renaud as guest artist. The outstanding novelties at the Théâtre de la Ville were Jean Mercure's transfer of Peter Nichols's *The National Health* to a French hospital setting, and Jorge Lavelli's uproarious production of Mikhail Bulgakov's spoof backstage comedy *The Purple Island.* At Guy Rétoré's Théâtre de l'Est Parisien, the principal draw was Duerrenmatt's early horror-comic, *Frank V.*

In the private sector, the death of André Barsacq left the famous Atelier Theater with an uncertain future, after the Russian-born French director had taken his leave of his fellow countrymen with yet another faithful Russian rendering, this time of *Crime and Punishment.* At the *"Cartoucherie"* in the Vincennes Park Ariane Mnouchkine continued drawing young crowds and piling up debts with her popular but increasingly costly productions of *1789* and *1793,* so much so that the whole future of her much lauded Théâtre du Soleil company hung in the balance. Anglo-Saxon drama still proved to be a mainstay of the boulevard theater, what with plays by Orton, Barnes, Coward, Hare, Storey, and Marriott and Foot from Britain, and Guare, Neil Simon, O'Neill and Fitzgerald (represented by his political satire of the 1920's, *The Vegetable*) from the U.S.A. Anouilh, Roussin, Marceau and Achard all had new works performed this season, while the elitist fare at the Espace Cardin varied from an exotic new work by Billetdoux (*The Widows*) to an obscure new playlet by Natalie Sarraute (*Isma*).

Italy

With Giorgio Strehler back at the Piccolo Theater in Milan, all eyes were directed at his two most recent productions: *King Lear* and *The Threepenny Opera. King Lear* was distinguished by a remarkable performance by Ottavia Piccolo doubling the roles of Cordelia and The Fool, while Strehler's second go at the Brecht, dogged by sickness in the cast, finally triumphed with the pop singers Milva as Jenny and Domenico Modugno as Mack the Knife. The Rome Theater (at the old Argentina) under its new manager, Franco Enriquez, began haltingly with a series of flops until Benno Besson came from East Berlin to restage his celebrated version of *The Good Woman of Setzuan* in Italian with Valeria Moriconi as Shen-Te. The season there closed with a major scandal when Luchino Visconti, returning to the legitimate theater after four years, staged an unauthorized translation of Pinter's *Old Times,* with Adriana Asti, Virna Lisi and Umberto Orsini, and incurred the author's displeasure for having introduced arbitrary elements of sexual deviation into the stage business not in the original text. Among events in the regions were Aldo Trionfo's *Peer Gynt* in Turin, starring Corrado Pani; Luigi Squarzina's latest Goldoni resuscitation in Genoa with *The New House;* and Peppino De Filippo's revival of *The Metamorphoses of a Travelling Musician* in Naples (which won fresh laurels on its return visit, the second in ten years, to London's World Theater Season). Of the private companies, Giorgio Albertazzi's produced his own drama *Always Pilate* with Anna Proclemer; the extreme left-wing theater group founded by Dario Fo (*The Commune*) found themselves evicted by a politically hostile municipal landlord in a working class Milan suburb, while Fo's wife, Franca Rame was brutally assaulted by neo-fascist thugs who threatened to stop his activities altogether; and Gino Cervi appeared in the title role of Diego Fabbri's latest Roman comedy hit, *The Thief in the Vatican.* Luca Ronconi's *The Oresteia,* first seen in Venice, later went to Paris under Theater of the Nations auspices.

Belgium

Several unusual world premieres lit up the season in Brussels. One was the stage adaptation devised and staged by Pierre Laroche at the Rideau de Bruxelles of Guillaume Apollinaire's mystically surrealistic prose poem about Merlin, *The Rotting Enchanter* (one of the World Theater Season's major attractions). Two others were Eduardo Manet's *The One Eyed Man* and the English farcical comedy by Ray Cooney and Gene Stone, *Why Not Stay for Breakfast?,* about the friendship of a middle-aged civil servant for a pregnant teenager, both at the Belgian National Theater. Dario Fo's and Arturo Corso's *Mistero Buffo,* a near profane version of Christ's Passion set to music, was performed alternately by Flemish- and French-speaking actors at the Royal Opera.

Scandinavia

Ingmar Bergman's third try with Strindberg's *The Ghost Sonata* exploited some of the techniques he had used in the previous year on *The Wild Duck,* such as turning the set through 180 degrees and projecting part of the action into the auditorium of the Royal Dramatic Theater. This went a long way towards clarifying some of the usual puzzlement associated with the family tragedy, but having Gertrud Fridh double two of the roles, the young girl and the old crone, while histrionically enthralling, only made Strindbergian confusion more confounded. Alf Sjöberg's annual "spectacular" was a busily noisy and wholly colorful version of Goldoni's *Quarrels at Chioggia,* for which Lars Forssell had written the verses of several new pastiche Italian folksongs. Bibi Andersson's Nora in a new *A Doll's House,* staged by Frank Sundström, worked entrancingly. There was a promising directing debut by Gunnel Lindblom at Dramaten's new studio theater in the Paintshop with Nils G. Eriksson's biographical drama about the psychopathic Swedish poet Gustav Fröding. Two further memorabilia were a revised version by Peter Weiss of *Hölderlin* and a coproduction with the Royal Opera of a children's musical called *Queen Me.* The City Theater specialized in promoting a repertory of mainly new theater for young people. In the private sector, Kent Andersson's *Agnes,* in verse and starring Gunn Wallgren as a soft-hearted but hard-headed landlady, ran for months at the Scala and was also staged in in various other parts of Scandinavia.

Bergman ventured outside Sweden for the third time to direct Molière's *The Misanthrope* in a selfconsciously theatrical ambiance, sumptuously designed by Kerstin Hedeby and starring Henning Moritzen and Ghita Norby at Copenhagen's Royal Dramatic. In Oslo the event of the year was the new production of Ibsen's *Brand* at the Norwegian Theater with Liv Ullmann looking radiant as Agnes and Stein Erik Brodal in the title role. Finland celebrated the centenary of her theater's foundation in Pori with a series of commemorative productions throughout the land, including Minna Canth's *Anna-Liisa,* which the National also took to Pori, where the same classical author's *A Worker's Wife* was revived. In Helsinki the National also staged Alexis Kivi's *Kullervo* following on Jack Witikka's imaginative rendering of *As You Like It* in abstract settings by Tapio Wirkkala, the industrial artist. Adam Hanuszkewicz came back from Warsaw to stage *Twelfth Night* at the City Theater in an amusing setting that included a sauna. At Turku's City Theater Kalle Holmberg directed Kivi's popular *Seven Brothers* in a sparely stylized decor. In the same city's Swedish Theater the contribution to the celebrations was Josef Julius Wecksell's 18th-century classic *Daniel Hjort,* staged by Jouko Turkka, known as the "Scandinavian *Hamlet.*"

Eastern Europe

This season Moscow theaters celebrated the 50th anniversary of the foundation of the Soviet Union by putting on plays by dramatists from some of the constituent republics, Andrei Makayonok (Byelorussia), Chingiz Aitmatov (Khirgizia), Olia Ioseliani (Georgia), Rustam Ibrahimbekov (Azerbaijan) and Kaltai Muhamedzhanov (Kazakhstan) among them. Aitmatov and Muhamedzhanov were the joint authors of *The Ascent to Fujiyama,* staged in the round by Galina Volchyok at the Sovremmenik and featuring Lyubov Dobrzhanskaya. It portrays four old friends whose responsibility for the death of a wartime comrade is outspokenly discussed by the 45-year-old author, against the background of the danger to Russian society of the remnants of Stalinism. In Makayonok's comedy *A Pill Under the Tongue* at the Satiric Theater, ancient and modern ideas clash amusingly in a collective-farm setting. Another hit at the Sovremmenik was the Polish guest director Andrzej Wajda's production of David Rabe's *Sticks and Bones* staged as an existentialist tragedy—not, says Wajda in defense of it when Rabe attacked it in print without having seen it, as an anti-American drama. Here, too, Alexander Volodin's latest play, about divorce, *Don't Desert Your Loved Ones,* proved highly popular. For the Jubilee season of Yuri Zavadsky's Mossoviet Theater, his son Yevgeni staged a poetic verse drama about Pushkin, while at the Maly the veteran actor Mikhail Tsaryov has been drawing the crowds as the aging Mattias Clausen in Hauptmann's *Before Sundown.* Worth noting is the return to favor after years of officially inspired neglect of the symbolist writer Leonid Andreyev, whose *He Who Gets Slapped* received a striking production from Maria Knebel at the Central Army Theater, as well as the public success of a stage version of Hemingway's *A Farewell to Arms* at the Komsomol, where Yuri Mochalov's *The Colonists* was a semi-documentary based on the life and works of the educationist A. Makarenko. There were new plays by Rozov, Arbuzov, Sofronov and the late Aleksander Vampilov, killed in a road accident. The one that has attracted most attention, however, is Yevtushenko's *Beneath the Skin of the Statue of Liberty,* which Yuri Liubimov put on at the Taganka with his habitual theatrical flair. A paean to the democratic ideal, it has the twofold merit of saying different things to different people and has been denounced as either an anti-American or anti-Soviet play, depending on the viewpoint of the spectator. Despite official displeasure with Liubimov for his independent spirit, he has been promised a new theater building with an ultra-modern flexizle stage and auditorium for multi-purpose staging. The exemplary artistic and technical realism of Oleg Yefremov's staging of Gennadi Bokaryov's *Steel Smelters* at the Moscow Art Theater endowed a drama that deals with the seemingly forbidding theme of industrial relations and increased productivity with all the excitement of a psychological thriller.

The story of the Czech theater continues to make sorry reading. A production of *Henry IV,* at the National Theater, designed by Svoboda, incurred the censor's wrath and closed prematurely. Dr. Miroslav Vostry, creator of the Cinoherni Klub, went the way of Otomar Krejca by being fired, and a government decision forced the troupe to commit a breach of contract by refusing them permission to return to London to take part in the World Theater Season. In Yugoslavia, state interference was increasingly relaxed, witness the invitation to the annual "Sterijino Pozorje", or "Theater Review", in Novi Sad, of an independent anti-establishment group from Lubliana and the increasing number of plays of critical content. One such, also exposed at Novi Sad, was *Job,* a first verse drama by Ference Toth, at the Hungarian-speaking Subotica National Theater. Two novelties at Belgrade's *Atelje 212* were *The Marathon Runners,* an anti-patriarchal farcical comedy about a mafioso family of undertakers, by the 25-year-old Dusan Kovacevic, and Pavle Mincic's semi-documentary two-handed comedy about the schoolchild's view of the world today, called *The Pencil Writes From the Heart.* Liviu Ciulei, Romania's best-known stage and film director, designer and actor, lost his job as head of the Bulandra City Theater, in Bucharest, over official criticism of Lucian Pintilie's challenging production of *The Government Inspector.* The ensuing play, *Twelfth Night,* was collectively staged, possibly deliberately so. Mihnea Gheorghiu, Shakespearean translator, was represented at the National by a critical drama masquerading as a historical tragedy about the 19th-century patriot Tudor

Vladimirescu, called *The Sign of the Bull,* and new plays by Aurel Baranga, Paul Everac and Al Mirodan were also widely performed.

A third play by Hungary's foremost absurdist author, Istvan Örkeny, called *The Silence of the Dead,* attempted to pay a long-delayed tribute to the misplaced idealism of the soldiers who gave their lives on the Eastern Front in World War II. It caused a storm of controversy when Zoltan Varkonyi staged it at the Pest Theater because of the sensitivity of audiences to any justification of fascist ideology, which this play was certainly not. An interesting first play by Miklos Janczo's scenarist, Gyula Hernadi, at the 25th Theater was *Utopia.* Veteran actor of the National, Ference Bessenyi, took leave of absence to play the leading role at the State Operette Theater in a smash hit production of *Fiddler on the Roof.* Istvan Horvai scored two hits at the Comedy Theater, first as an actor with *The Diary of a Madman,* and second as a director with *Three Sisters,* both designed by David Borovsky, of Moscow's Taganka Theater.

Josef Szjana's collage using four fragments of plays by Witkiewicz at his new Studio Theater in Warsaw had a greater appeal to the eye than to the ear, by contrast with Jerzy Jarocki's production at Cracow's Stary Theater of *The Mother,* in which the magic of Ewa Lassek in the title role, and Krystyna Zachwatowicz's mesmeric decor, helped to spread the interest more evenly. At the same theater Konrad Swinarski revived Mickiewicz's controversially patriotic classic *Forefathers' Eve* without, however, provoking the kind of anti-Russian demonstrations that lost Kazimierz Dejmek (now back in Poland as head of the Lodz City Theater once more) his post as head of the Warsaw National five years ago. At Warsaw's Contemporary Theater Erwin Axer's witty production of Ionesco's *Macbett* was followed by Zygmunt Huebner's of *Tenderness Alone,* a psychodrama set in a mental home by Ireneusz Iredynski. Even Mrozek's plays are beginning to be done again after a five years' interregnum. At the Ateneum Janusz Warminski tried to cap his eye-catching production of Wesker's *The Kitchen* with the Polish premiere of Duerrenmatt's *The Co-Operator,* while at the National Adam Hanuszkewicz's *Macbeth* had in the title role the remarkable Wojciech Pszoniak, last seen as the young Verkhovensky in Wajda's *The Devils* at Cracow, a production that also made an indelible impression at London's World Theater Season for the second year running.

Highlights of the Paris Season

Selected and compiled by Ossia Trilling

OUTSTANDING PERFORMANCES

OLIVER HUSSENOT	JUDITH MAGRE	JEAN DESAILLY
as The King in	as Alice in	as Jerry Frost in
Will They Eat?	*Play Strindberg*	*The Vegetable*
PAUL MEURISSE	CLAUDE RICH	NILS ARESTRUP
as Antonio di San Floura in	as the Duke of Gurney in	as Raskolnikov in
The Director of the Opera	*The Ruling Class*	*Crime and Punishment*

OUTSTANDING PERFORMANCES

PIERRE FRESNAY as Hector Sarclay in *A Box on the Ear*	JEAN PIAT as Philippe in *The Turning Point*	ROBERT HIRSCH as the Philosopher in *The Would-Be Gentleman*
LAURENT TERZIEFF as Dymogaski in *The Purple Island*	CLAUDE DAUPHIN as Shylock in *The Merchant of Venice*	LOUIS SEIGNER as Pope Alexander VI in *Debauchery*
GEORGES WILSON as James Tyrone in *Long Day's Journey into Night*	SUZANNE FLON as Mary in *Long Day's Journey into Night*	DANIELLE DARRIEUX as Amanda in *Private Lives*

OUTSTANDING DIRECTORS

ROBERT HOSSEIN *The Lower Depths*	ROBERT WILSON *Overture for Ka Mountain and GUARDenia Terrace*	JORGE LAVELLI *The Purple Island*

OUTSTANDING DESIGNERS

MAX BIGNENS *The Purple Island*	ANDRÉ ACQUART *Oedipus Rex and Oedipus Coloneus*	JACQUES LE MARQUET *The School for Wives*

OUTSTANDING NEW FRENCH PLAYS

(D)—Playwright's Paris Debut

LE ROI CLOS (The King in Private) by André Richaud (D). An escaped convict's fantasies in a brothel. With Gamil Ratib, Ana Douking, Jacqueline Staup. and LES RELIQUES (The Relics) by André Richaud. A cardinal's dilemma. With Hubert de Lapparent.

SOUS LE VENT DES BALÉARES (Beneath the Balearic Wind) by Paul Claudel. Part 4, the comic member of the *Satin Slipper* tetralogy. With Madeleine Renaud, Jean-Louis Barrault, Geneviève Page and the Renaud-Barrault company.

LE BAL DES CUISINIÈRES (The Cooks' Ball) by Bernard Da Costa. Three Basque nuns receive a strange caller. With Nadine Basile, Françoise Fleury, Perrette Pradier, Nicole Dubois.

PAR DELÀ LES MARRONNIERS (Beyond the Chestnut Trees) by Jean-Marie Ribes. The adventures of three dandies. With Myriam Mezières, Gilbert Bahon.

IDENTITÉ (Identity) by Robert Pinget. An author at odds with his characters. With Luce Garcia-Ville, Olivier Hussenot, Yves Gasc.

OU BOIVENT LES VACHES (In Never Never Land) by Roland Dubillard. An orphaned youth kicks over the traces. With Madeleine Renaud, Maria Machada, the author.

LA VIE ET LA MORT DE JULES DUPONT (The Life and Death of Jules Dupont) by André Gintzburger (D). How an idealistic democrat becomes a selfish despot. With Jean-Paul Muel, Michel Berto.

LE PRINTEMPS DES BONNETS ROUGES (The Spring of the Red Caps) by Paol Keineg (D). A collectively staged drama about the revolt of the Breton peasants against the despotism of Louis XIV. With the company of the Théâtre de la Tempête.

CHEZ LES TITCH (With the Titches) by Louis Calaferte (D). The attempt of a widow's three children to revolt against their father's memory goes awry. With Jean-Luc Bouttet, Gérard Giraudon, Denise Gence, Catherine Hiégel.

L'ÉGLISE (The Church) by Louis-Ferninand Céline (D). The antisemitic novelist's only drama, about a catastrophic pilgrimage, written in 1926. With the Chantier-Théâtre company.

ISMA by Nathalie Sarraute. Poetic vision of a menacing world. With Dominique Blanchar, Michel Lonsdale, François Darbon, Pascale de Boysson, Tatiana Moukhine.

LA DEMANDE D'EMPLOI (Asking for a Job) by Michel Vinaver. A subtle critique of present-day social and industrial relations. With the J.-P. Dougnac company.

POPULAR ATTRACTIONS

MANGERONT-ILS? (Will They Eat?) by Victor Hugo. Marais Festival revival of 1867 classical comedy. With Olivier Hussenot.

JESUSFRIC SUPERCRACK by Alain Scoff. Pop comedy on contemporary themes. With the Théâtre Bulle company.

IL ÉTAIT UNE FOIS L'OPÉRETTE (There Was Once Operetta) devised by Jean Poiret and Dominique Tirmont. A hundred years of musical theater. With Jane Rhodes, Mady Mesplé, Anne-Marie Sanial, Bernard Sinclair, Odette Laure, Roger Carel, Chantal de Rieux.

LES OEUFS DE L'AUTRUCHE (Hippo Dancing) by André Roussin. Revival of popular comedy about an unsuspecting father. With Jean Davy, Françoise Delille.

SUPPLEMENT AU VOYAGE DE COOK (The Supplement to Captain Cook's Voyage) by Jean Giraudoux. An English colonizer in Tahiti. With Nicolas Bataille, Anne Lipinska.

LA PURÉE (The Purée) by Jean-Claude Eger. A nouveau-riche couple and their daughter's future. With Robert Manuel, Lucette Raillat.

L'INGÈNU D'AUTEUIL (The Innocent from Auteuil) by Jean Le Marois. An older woman's nostalgic sentimentality. With Claude Genia, Jean-Louis Broust.

AH! . . . LA POLICE DE PAPA! (Ah . . . Daddy's Police) by Raymond Castans. When unemployment hits the police. With Marthe Mercadier, Henri Tisot, Jacques Sereys.

EN AVANT . . . TOUTE! (All of Her, Forward March!) by Michel André. Consequences of a road accident. With Roger Nicolas, Denise Grey, Dora Doll.

L'OUVRE-BOÎTE (The Can Opener) by Félicien Marceau. A political satire situated in a Swiss villa. With Caroline Cellier, Jacques Duby, Micheline Luccioni, Jacques Morel.

LE PLAISIR CONJUGAL (The Pleasures of Marriage) by Albert Husson. Make love, not war; an updated version of *Lysistrata*. With Claudine Coster, Jean-Pierre Andreani.

LE DIRECTEUR DE L'OPÉRA (The Director of the Opera) by Jean Anouilh. The tribulations of an opera director. With Paul Meurisse, Didier Haudepin, Jean Parédès.

TEXAS STORY by Jacques Mauclair. A fantastic debauch. With Monique Mauclair, Christian Pernot.

OPÉRA DE MALDOROR (Maldoror's Opera) by Jean-Louis Manceau and Michelle Stalla, after Lautréamont. Dramatization of black poem. With Michel Gourdeau, André Fertier.

AMÉRITUME and LA MARIÉE D'AILLEURS (The Bride from Over There) by Gilbert Léautier. Two one-acters: the sorrows of a schoolteacher, and the bitter gall of wedlock. With Pierrette Dupaget.

HEUREUSEMENT, CE N'EST PAS TOUS LES JOURS DIMANCHE (Luckily, It Isn't Sunday All the Time) by Jean-Jacques Varoujean. The sad story of a lad in a coma. With Fabrienne Mai, Dominique Marcas.

LA CLAQUE (A Box on the Ear) by André Roussin. The revenge of an outraged music critic. With Pierre Fresnay, Michel Galabru, Luce Garcia-Ville.

LES BRANQUIGNOLS (The Theatricals) by Robert Dhéry. A showbiz troupe on the rampage. With Colette Brosset, the author.

LES VOLEURS D'IDÉES (Thieves of Ideas) by Elisabeth Wierner (D). Improvisations on life's experiences. With Claire Nadeau, the author.

ADORABLE JULIA by Marc-Gilbert Sauvajon. Revival of 1960s hit. With Madeleine Robinson, Daniel Ceccaldi, Anne Carrère.

LE CID (The Cid) by Corneille. Unorthodox treatment of a popular classic. With Dolorès Gonzalez, José-Maria Flotats.

L'AVEU (The Avowal) by Sarah Bernhardt. A prose melodrama by the celebrated actress. With Valia Boulay, Gérard Dessalles, Pierre-Yves Shaeffer.

LA GRANDE BERLINE (The Great Berlin) by Alain Bernier and Roger Maridat. The loves of Hitler and Eva Braun. With Frédérique Ruchaud, Nicolas Bataille.

TUEUR À GAGES (The Killer) by Eugene Ionesco. Revival of absurdist thriller with a revised climax. With Claude Nicot, Claude Génia, Marcel Champel.

VICTOR OU LES ENFANTS AU POUVOIR (Victor or Children in Power) by Roger Vitrac. Revival of popular surrealist comedy. With Philippe Noel, Pierre Santini, Nadine Alain.

LA MAISON DE ZAZA (Zaza's House) by Gaby Bruyère. Revival of popular comedy after 400 performances. With Dora Doll, Robert Vattier.

LE BOURGEOIS GENTILHOMME (The Would-Be Gentleman) by Molière. Jean-Louis Barrault's return to Comédie Française as guest director after 25 years. With Jacques Charon, Robert Hirsch, Geneviève Casile, Françoise Seigner.

DUOS SUR CANAPÉ (Two on a Sofa) by Marc Camoletti. The sentimental adventures of a couple, built around a sofa. With Darry Cowl, Philippe Nicaud.

LE TOURNANT (The Turning Point) by Françoise Dorin. A dramatist's personal and aesthetic problems inextricably mixed up. With Jean Piat, Évelyne Dandry, Françoise Fleury.

LE MÉDECIN VOLANT (The Flying Doctor) by Molière. New production of knock-about farce as curtain raiser to *The Imaginary Invalid*. With Francis Perrin.

J'Y SUIS, J'Y RESTE (I Stay Where I Am) by Raymond Vincy and Jacques Valmy. Comings and goings in a French castle. With Anne-Marie Carrière, Jacques Morel.

TU CONNAIS LA MUSIQUE? (Do You Know the Tune?) by Robert Abirached. The education of a clown. With Philippe Avron, Claude Evrard.

AURÉLIA by Robert Thomas. The perfect crime, or is it? With Corinne Marchand, Michel Le Royer, Florence Blot.

LA CAGE AUX FOLLES (The Madwomen's Cage) by Jean Poiret. A strange couple receive some curious visitors. With Michel Serrault, the author.

EN CE TEMPS LÀ LES GENS MOURAIENT (When Folks Used to Die) by Patrick Font, Philippe Val, and the Académie le Pied. A science fiction glance back at our era. With the authors.

LA DÉBAUCHE (Debauchery) by Marcel Achard. Fun and games at the court of the Borgias. With Louis Seigner, Danièle Lebrun, Claude Piéplu, Catherine Rouvel.

LES QUATRE VÉRITÉS (The Four Verities) by Marcel Aymé. An experiment with the truth drug. With Marthe Mercadier, Jacques Duby.

LA SOIF LA FAIM (Hunger and Thirst) by Eugene Ionesco. Comédie Française's revival of satirical comedy. With Jean-Paul Roussillon, Georges Audoubert, Claude Winter.

PHÈDRE-EURIPIDE-RACINE adapted from Euripides and Racine by Denis Llorca. A new text combining the best of two traditional versions. With Silvia Monfort, Jean-Claude Drouot.

PROFIT SOIT-IL! (May There Be Profit!) by Jean-Pierre Matheron. A satire on the acquisitive society. With Pierre Blumberg, Laura Vincent.

UN VISITEUR TIMIDE (A Shy Visitor) by Charles Maître and PREMIÈRE COMPARUTION (First Hearing) by André Franck. Two one-act detective stories. With Pierre Destailles, Arlette Thomas, Claude Bertrand, Pierre Peyrou.

LE TOURNIQUET (The Tourniquet) by Victor Lanoux. You eat what you can. With Jacques Rosny, the author.

LA REINE DE CÉSARÉE (The Queen of Cesarea) by Robert Brasillach. Revival of drama about Titus and Berenice. With Jacqueline Gauthier, Pierre Vaneck.

A QUOI ON JOUE (The Games We Play) by Pierre Étaix. The collapsing world of showbiz. With Annie Fratellini, the author.

RAPPELEZ-MOI VOTRE NOM (What Was Your Name Again?) by Jean-Jacques Bricaire and Marcel Lasaygues. A modern Bluebeard meets his wives again. With Pierre Doris, Christian Alers, Arlette Didier.

LA ROYALE PERFORMANCE (The Royal Performance) by Marcel Mithois. The self-sacrifice of a loving queen. With Jacqueline Maillan, Jacques Sereys.

CRIME IMPOSSIBLE (The Impossible Crime) by Michel Arnaud. A crime in a water-logged ambiance. With Claude Rollet, Christine Delaroche.

L'ÉCOLE DES FEMMES (The School for Wives) by Molière. New Comédie Française production by Jean-Paul Roussillon. With Pierre Dux (alternating with Michel Aumont), Isabelle Adjani.

SALLE D'ATTENTE (Waiting Room) by Jean Bois. Life, death, and all that. Marie Castets, the author.

LES BULLES (The Bubbles) by Michel Deltheil (D). Absurdist metaphysical encounter. With Dominique Verdon, Evelyn Proudhon.

SEUL LE POISSON ROUGE EST AU COURANT (Only the Goldfish Knows) by Jean Barbier and Domonique Nohain. Something funny happened to this family. With Jean Martinelli, Nadine Basile, Dominique Nohain.

MAIS QU'EST CE QUI FAIT COURIR LES FEMMES LA NUIT À MADRID? (But Why Do the Girls in Madrid Go Out Nights?) by Daniel Ceccaldi (D). 17th century cloak-and-dagger farce inspired by Calderon de la Barca. With Hubert de Lapparent, Mireille Delcroix.

SOME AMERICAN PLAYS PRODUCED IN PARIS

THIS PROPERTY IS CONDEMNED, and TALK TO ME LIKE THE RAIN by Tennessee Williams. With the Hamm and Clov Stage Company of New York.

THE VEGETABLE by F. Scott Fitzgerald. With Jean Desailly, Simone Valère.

HELLO, DOLLY! by Michael Stewart and Jerry Herman. With Annie Cordy, Jacques Mareuil, Jean Pomarez.

FREE STREET THEATER of Chicago.

DON'T DRINK THE WATER by Woody Allen. With Suzy Delair, Pierre Doris, Franck Fernandel.

THE TOOTH OF CRIME by Sam Shepard and COMMUNE. With the Performance Group of New York.

THE HOUSE OF BLUE LEAVES by John Guare. With Jean-Pierre Marielle, William Sabatier, Magali Noel.

OVERTURE, the Bob Wilson Production. With the Byrd Hoffman School of Byrds company.

THE NIGGER LOVER by George Tabori and THE SUBWAY by LeRoi Jones. With Chantal Darget, Georges Staquet, Greg Germain.

GREAT GOODNESS OF LIFE by Imamu Baraka (LeRoi Jones). With the American Cultural Center Company.

THE PRISONER OF SECOND AVENUE by Neil Simon. With Pierre Mondy, Micheline Luccioni, Yvonne Clech.

LONG DAY'S JOURNEY INTO NIGHT by Eugene O'Neill. With Georges Wilson, Suzanne Flon, José-Maria Flotats, Bernard Verley.

THE CAGE by Rick Cluchey. With the San Quentin Drama Workshop company.

THE WHITE WHORE AND THE BIT PLAYER by Tom Eyen. With Nicole Evans, Marie Privat.

LINE by Israel Horovitz, adapted by Claude Roy. With Loleh Bellon, Georges Staquet.

THE GOLD BUG by Edgar Allen Poe. With the Signes Group from Gennevilliers.

THE NAMING by and with the Iowa City, Iowa Theater Lab.

WHORES OF BABYLON. With the Godzilla Rainbow Troupe of Chicago.

SOME OTHER FOREIGN PLAYS PRODUCED IN PARIS

THE VICE, LEMON TREES OF SICILY, and CECE by Luigi Pirandello. With André Lambert, Fabienne Mai.

LA LOCANDIERA (The Mistress of the Inn) by Goldoni. With Michel Le Royer, Annie Sinigalia.

SHADOW OF MART by Stig Dagerman. With Marc Alexandre, Paule Dehelly.

LA BALADE DU GRAND MACABRE (The Ballad of the Great Macabre) by Michel de Ghelderode. With Catherine Therouenne, Hervé Constant.

A MIDSUMMER NIGHT'S DREAM by William Shakespeare. With the Royal Shakespeare Company.

SLAG by David Hare. With Brigitte Fossey, Tania Lopert, Lucienne Hamon.

MEDEA by Sophocles and Seneca, staged by Andrei Sherban with the La Mama company of New York.

PLAY STRINDBERG by Friedrich Duerrenmatt. With Judith Magre, Jean Martin, François Maistre.

CRIME AND PUNISHMENT by Fedor Dostoevsky, adapted by André Barsacq. With Nils Arestrup, Paul Le Person, Elisabeth Alain.

THE LOWER DEPTHS by Maxim Gorky. With the Théâtre Populaire de Reims company.

OEDIPUS REX and OEDIPUS COLONEUS by Sophocles. With François Chaumette, Claude Giraud, Rosy Varte.

THE MAN FROM THE EAST by Stomu Yamash'ta. With the Red Buddha company.

15 FUTURIST PLAYLETS by Marinetti. With Nicolas Bataille, Jacqueline Staup.

THE RULING CLASS by Peter Barnes. With Claude Rich, Raymond Gérôme, Françoise Christophe, Pierre Bertin.

THE ORESTEIA by Aeschylus. With Luca Ronconi's Teatro Cooperativa Tuscolona company.

OTHELLO STORY by Jack Good. With Gordon Heath, Martine Clemenceau, Georges Blaness.

WHAT THE BUTLER SAW by Joe Orton. With Jean-Pierre Darras, Françoise Brion, Pascal Mazzotti.

IN THE JUNGLE OF CITIES by Bertolt Brecht. With the Théâtre de l'Espérance company.

HOLD UP by Jean Stuart. World premiere of an English play about two gangsters creating havoc in a happy home. With Eddie Constantine, Jean Raymond.

LE NOIR TE VA SI BIEN (A Risky Marriage) by Saul O'Hara, adapted by Jean Marsan. With Jean Le Poulain, Maria Pacôme.

THE NATIONAL HEALTH by Peter Nichols. With Jean Mercure, Michel de Ré, André Weber.

LA GRANDE MURAILLE (The Great Wall) by Max Frisch. With the company of the Young National Theater.

LE CIEL EST EN BAS (Dark Factory) by Janos Nyiri. With Jean Marais, Sarah Sanders.

THE COMEDY OF ERRORS by William Shakespeare. With the Équipe company.

LES VILAINS (The Peasants) by Ruzante, adapted by André Gille. With Fred Personne, the author.

CLAIRE AND THE TWO GENTLEMEN and MYRIAM'S PASTRYSHOP by Ivan Klima. With the Théâtre de la Cité Internationale company.

A RESOUNDING TINKLE by N. F. Simpson. With Jack Fitzgerald, Jacqueline Ménage, Maggie Mills.

ALICE IN WONDERLAND by and with the Pip Simmons Company.

ANTIGONE by Bertolt Brecht. With François Chaumette, Bérengère Dautun.

UN LÉGER ACCIDENT (A Slight Accident) with Josette Amina, Anne Carrère, Robert Murzeau and IN MEMORIAM with Katharina Renn, Jacqueline Staup, Odile Mallet. Program of two plays by James Saunders.

THE LOST LETTER by Ion Luca Caragiale. With Yves Vincent, Nicole Mérouze.

LEONCE AND LENA by Georg Buechner. With the Le Tripot company.

UN YAOURT POUR DEUX (The Starving Rich) by Stanley Price, adapted by Albert Husson and Francis Blanche. World premiere of English thriller about a health farm. With Francis Blanche, Michel Roux, Marc Dudicourt, Monita Derrieux.

KILLING TIME by Jack Fitzgerald. With Nancy Cole and Edith Cavalieri.

THE PELICAN, and THE ISLAND OF THE DEAD by August Strindberg. With the company of the Théâtre Oblique.

MARTIN LUTHER AND THOMAS MUNZER, OR THE BEGINNINGS OF ACCOUNTING by Dieter Forte. With the company of th Comédie de Caen.

THE GUARDIAN OF THE TOMB by Franz Kafka, adapted by Henri Ronse. With the Théâtre Oblique company.

MASKED GAMES. Mixed bill by the Ion Creanga Theater company of Bucharest.

HOME by David Storey, adapted by Marguerite Duras. With Michel Lonsdale, Gérard Depardieu, Tatiana Moukhine, Pascale de Boysson, J.-Loup Wolff.

TEXTUAL MISUNDERSTANDING by Anna Novac. With Myriam Mezières, Marie Pillet.

THE DECAMERON by Boccaccio. With the Studio Théâtre of Vitry.

THE GEORGE JACKSON BLACK AND WHITE MINSTREL SHOW. With the Pip Simmons Theater Group.

THE PURPLE ISLAND by Mikhail Bulgakov. With Henri Virlojeux, Laurent Terzieff, Maurice Chevit, Michel de Ré.

THE MERCHANT OF VENICE by William Shakespeare. With Geneviève Grad, Claude Dauphin.

HIER LES ENFANTS DANSAIENT (Yesterday Children Danced) by Georges Gélinas. With the Quebec Comédiens Associés company.

WOYZECK by Georg Buechner. With Olivier Perrier, Emmanuèle Stochl, Bernard Bloch.

LES SEPT MANIÈRES DE TRAVERSER LA RIVIÈRE (Seven Ways to Cross the River) by Ludowijk de Boer. With the Brussels Théâtre de l'Esprit Frappeur company.

NO SEX PLEASE, WE'RE BRITISH by Anthony Marriott and Alistair Foot. With Jean-Pierre Darras, Annie Sinigalia.

THE GREAT ROAD by Anton Chekhov with Robert Darmel, Pierre Gerald, Michèle Laurence; and THE KREUTZER SONATA by Leo Tolstoy with Michele Laurance, Robert Darmel.

SALOME by Oscar Wilde. With the Globe M.C.D.V. company.

THE BROKEN PITCHER by Heinrich Von Kleist. With Jean-Pierre Bourdeaux, Jacques Labarrière, Rémy Charpentier.

PRIVATE LIVES by Noel Coward. With Danielle Darrieux, Jean-Claude Pascal.

FRANK V by Friedrich Duerrenmatt. With Jacques Lalande, Jacques Alric, Michel Robin.

ROUNDHEADS AND PEAKHEADS by Bertolt Brecht. With the Gennevilliers Théâtre Ensemble.

FRANKENSTEIN by Wolfang Deichsel. With Jean-Pierre Dorat, Monique Fabre, Jean-Pierre Jorris.

I LIVE ALONE WITH MOM by Durakin. With Myriam Mezières, Philippe Miglioli, Pierre Nayaert.

PARLAMENTO and BILORA by Ruzante. With the Bergamo Pocket Theater company.

DON JUAN ET FAUST by Christian Dietrich Grabbe. With Philippe Clévenot.

ULYSSES IN NIGHTTOWN by James Joyce, adapted by Marjorie Barkentin, French version by Georges Auclair. With Olivier Hussenot, Jean Lasroquette, Colette Castel.

LES PASSIONS DRAMATIQUES (Dramatic Passion) by Tadashi Suzuki. With the Waseda Shogeki-Jo company of Japan.

RED MEAT by Vladimir Mayakovsky. With the Thèâtre de l'Utopie from Tours.

FUTURA, new entertainment about the future of mankind by and with the Paris-based Argentinian T.S.E. company.

L'INCONSCIENT CYBERNÉTIQUE (The Cybernetic Innocent) by and with the Teatro Communale of Rome and the Espace Cardin troupe.

METHUSELAH by Yvan Goll. With the Anne-Marie Lazarini company.

LULU by Frank Wedekind. With Laurence Fevrier, Claude Aufaure, Caroline Gauthier.

THE OTHER VENICE by Ruzante, adapted by Alain Rais. With the Spectacles de la Vallée du Rhône company.

QUEJIO, by and with the La Cuadra company from Seville.

THE CASTLE by Franz Kafka. With the Daniel Meguich company.

LIMITED RUNS OF INTERESTING NEW FRENCH PLAYS

LE RÔDEUR (The Rover) by Jean-Claude Brisville (D). Can the photographer's wife's story be true? With Alain Pralon, Claire Vernet.

UN, DEUX, TROIS . . . SOLEIL (One, Two, Three . . . Sun) by Catherine Monnot (D). Two girls grow up. With Françoise Decaux, the author.

LES VEUVES (The Widows) by François Billetdoux. A surrealist limbo in which life touches death. With Jean Voyet's Shaman puppets, the author.

PRENEZ GARDE À LA PANTHERE (Mind the Panther), based on the erotic stories of Belen. With Stephan Maldegg, Christian Uboldi, Isabelle Aulnoy, Atika Guedj, Jane Watts, Jean Hébert.

LES LETTRES D'UNE RELIGIEUSE PORTUGAISE (Letters of Portuguese Nun) adapted from original classical text by Jean Valverde. With Micheline Uzan.

L'OPÉRA DES ÉCORCHÉES (The Fleeced One's Opera) by Victor Haim. The Beggar's Opera updated. With Pierre Tamin, Catherine Ménétrier.

LAISSE-MOI JOUER . . . (Let Me Go On . . .) by Marcel Franck. The trials of an understudy. With Robert Murzeau, Mario Pecquer.

LES CONTES CAMIQUES (Camical Tales) by Pierre-Henri Cami (D). 12 playlets by the humorous writer from Pau. With the Aquitaine Drama Company of Bordeaux.

LES FEMMES AU POUVOIR (Women in Power) by E. Georges Berreby. If women had their way . . . With Estella Blain, Nathalie Nattier.

UNDERGROUND ÉTABLISSEMENT (Underground Establishment) by René de Obaldia. Peculiar adventures in the author's characteristic vein. With the M.-J. Robin company.

LA MADONE DES ORDURES (The Madonna of the Garbage) by André Benedetto. The hardships of Provençal culture. With the Avignon Théâtre des Carmes company.

BOND EN AVANT (A Jump Ahead) by Pierre Guyotat. A collective drama on the world today by the Théâtre des Amandiers company.

LA MALÉDICTION DES CAPÉTIENS (The Curse of the House of Capet), a collective production by the Théâtre Périféerik. Inaugural production of the new National Children's Theater, a documentary of the royal house of the Capets. With the Théâtre de la Commune company.

LE PIANISTE TRICOTE (The Pianist is Knitting) by Alain Germain (D). A "Caf' Conc' " vaudeville show. With Elisabeth Sorel, the author.

COMMENT ÇA VA SUR LA TERRE? (How Goes It on Earth?) by Guy Caron and René Bourdet. Sketches, poems, and songs by Louis Aragon, Robert Desnos, Guy Foissy, Boris Vian, Jean Tardieu. With Amélie Prévost, Claude Reva, the authors.

VIENDRA-T-IL UN AUTRE ÉTÉ? (Will There Be Another Summer?) by Jean-Jacques Varoujean (D). Youngsters discover a corpse.

LA VISITE (The Visit) by Raymond Dutherque; and BÉBÉ CHÉRI (Baby Darling) by Claire Augira. Double bill of contrasting modern types. With Dominique Bailly, Annie Dana, Joël Martineau.

LA BALLADE DE MAMAN JONES (The Ballad of Momma Jones) by Catherine de Seynes. The story of the U.S.A. labor movement. With the Théâtre des Quatre Chemins company.

LA CHEVAUCHÉE BURLESQUE DES SEIGNEURS DE LA VILLETTE (The Comic Cavalcade of the Knights of La Villette), a collective production with the Théâtre Present La Vilette company.

CLAIRE by René Char, a love affair that failed, with Marie Martine de Coster, François Berleand; DIALOGUE DANS LE MARÉCAGE (Dialogue in the Marsh) by Marguerite Yourcenar, a modern Woyzeck finds his Marie still alive, with Marie Martine de Coster, François Berleand, Jean Bérard; and LA VÉRITABLE HISTOIRE DE JACQUES L'EVENTREUR (The True Story of Jack the Ripper) by Elisabeth Huppert (D), could the killer have been a lesbian?, with Isabelle Huppert, the author.

VENDREDI OU LA VIE SAUVAGE (Man Friday or Life in the Raw) adapted by Antoine Vitez from the novel by Michel Tournier. Modern version of the desert island story. With the National Children's Theater company.

ARISTO-FANS by Jacques Mirat. An Aristophanic anthology. With Fabrice Nadar, Olga Brix.

LA MORT DE L'ANGE (The Angel's Death) by Jacques Crémion (D). Psychic mystery story. With Patrick Grimaud, Isabelle Michelin.

THE TEN
BEST PLAYS

Here are the synopses of 1972-73's ten Best Plays. By permission of the publishing companies which own the exclusive rights to publish these scripts in full in the United States, our continuities include many substantial quotations from crucial/pivotal scenes in order to provide a permanent reference to the actual literary quality of each play as well as to its theme and structure.

Scenes and lines of dialogue, stage directions and description quoted in the synopses appear *exactly* as in the stage version unless (in a very few instances, for technical reasons) an abridgement is indicated by five dots (. . . . .). The appearance of three dots (. . .) is the script's own punctuation to denote the timing of a spoken line.

6 RMS RIV VU

A Play in Two Acts

BY BOB RANDALL

Cast and credits appear on page 333

BOB RANDALL was born in 1937 in New York City, where his father was in the garment business. After graduating from NYU he planned to become a doctor. He was accepted at a Baltimore medical school but was required to wait a year before entering to begin his medical studies. Randall set out to spend the year doing research at a New York medical school and gradually began to face the fact that he didn't like it, and perhaps doctoring was not his true destiny. To the bitter disappointment of his family, he finally ran off to join the American Savoyards as an actor doing Gilbert & Sullivan in Maine and New York.

Medicine's loss was the theater's gain; Randall finally reached Broadway as a performer in New Faces of 1962. *His specialty was comedy, and he began writing in order to carve a night club act for himself. This led to his collaboration on revue material, and songs, and finally two one-acters,* Props *and* Interference, *done off off Broadway by the New Theater Workshop.* 6 Rms Riv Vu *is his first full-length play.*

Randall lives on the Upper West Side of Manhattan. He is married, with two children.

Time: The present

Place: An empty Riverside Drive apartment

ACT I

Scene 1: Morning

SYNOPSIS: The living room of a large, vacant Riverside Drive rent-controlled apartment is bare and losing its paint; its two windows upstage face a brick wall. Also upstage is a doorway leading to the bedrooms. The door to the dining room and kitchen is at right, and the front door—minus a doorknob— is at left.

The front door is open by the superintendant, Eddie, with a doorknob he has brought for this purpose. An apartment-hunting young couple (she is pushing a baby carriage which she leaves outside and is obviously expecting another child soon) dashes in and around the the apartment, checking its facilities, noting its shortcomings ("something rotting behind the sink") but delighting in its roomy advantages and possibilities. Swiftly they make up their minds that they want it enough to offer a bribe for it, and they rush off to consult the building agent.

A beat or two after the couple has departed, Anne enters. *"She's in her early 30s, attractive. She has an air of mild exhaustion about her, as if she's taken time out from a busy day fighting with the kids and the super to run over and see the apartment. She keeps pot in a cookie canister, has a shelf filled with books on how you raise children and is getting a little bored. A satisfactory life, all in all."*

Alice measures the living room by pacing it off. Just after she disappears into the dining room, Paul comes into the apartment. *"He is her male counterpart, same age. He's a copywriter at an ad agency, on the Way Up and also a little bored."* He looks around the apartment somewhat doubtfully and disappears in the direction of the bedrooms, but comes back as Anne re-enters the living room singing "Don't Fence Me In."

> *Anne reacts violently as she sees Paul.*
> PAUL: Sing it, baby.
> ANNE: Excuse me.
> PAUL: I'm sorry. I was just kidding.
> *She exits into bedrooms.*
Three, six, nine, twelve . . .
> ANNE (*re-enters*): It's twenty by twenty-three.
> PAUL: Thanks.
> ANNE: Look, I'm not one of your West Side schizophrenics.
> PAUL: I didn't think you were.

JERRY ORBACH AND JANE ALEXANDER IN "6 RMS RIV VU"

ANNE: The apartment's so big, it got to me. I didn't know anybody else was in here.

PAUL: You don't have to explain.

ANNE: Ohh . . . did Schneider/Steinbrunner send you?

PAUL: Yeah.

ANNE (*upset*): God! They told me they wouldn't send anybody else over today.

PAUL: Yeah, that's what they told me! Can you believe those two? (*Pause.*) We've been looking for a bigger place for over a year.

ANNE: Next month is my second anniversary.

PAUL: We have a three and a half.

ANNE: We have one bedroom and an alcove.

PAUL: Any kids?

ANNE: Two.

PAUL: Relax. I'm only the envoy. My wife has the final say.

ANNE: Is she out of town, I hope? Go look at the dining room.

> *Paul goes into the dining area, Anne into the bedroom. Eddie enters and exits with the trash basket, leaving the front door open. Paul and Anne enter separately and examine the living room again.*

PAUL: Tell me, where's the river?

ANNE: If you lean out the second bathroom, it's to the left.

PAUL (*looking around*): Well, anyway, it's big.

ANNE: Yeah.

They agree this would make a nice living room; they tend to make references in their conversation, casually, to their respective marriages. Paul likes club chairs but his wife Janet prefers cane furniture. Anne and her husband are partial to leather and chrome. As they go off to check the closet possibilities in the second bedroom, *"Eddie enters, eating a butter cookie and removes the doorknob and exits, slamming the door."*

Anne and Paul drift back, Anne admitting that she likes club chairs and Paul taking this as a sign that she likes men. They exchange names—Paul Friedman and Anne Miller (nee Delaney but acquiring her movie star's name by marriage).

It's not long before they discover that they are locked in; lacking the doorknob, they have no way of opening the front door, and their shouting attracts no attention. They manage to get one of the windows open, and though they can see people moving about in other apartments, none of them will pay any attention.

PAUL: You! The lady in the half-slip! Damn, she ran out of the room.

ANNE: People of New York! There's a nice young couple trapped in apartment 4B, six rooms, still rent-controlled, three twenty-five a month! Get us out and we'll give you the agent's name! (*Beat.*) Do you think we'll come to hate each other after a few months?

PAUL: Permit a master. (*Calls out the window.*) Ladies and gentlemen, I see a parking space!

WOMAN'S VOICE (*offstage*): What?

> *Anne and Paul look at each other.*

PAUL: I was kidding, lady. We're locked in 4B. Somebody removed the doorknob and we . . .

> *Offstage can be heard the sound of a window slamming.*

She slammed the window on me! How do you like that? She slammed the window!

ANNE: Well, you shouldn't kid about a thing like that.

PAUL: We *are* locked in.
ANNE: About the parking space.

They are indeed locked in, because the service door at the rear of the apartment has been sealed permanently shut by a previous tenant who was apparently afraid of burglars. In between banging on the door and calling for help, they swap information about themselves, getting to know each other, discovering that they have a great deal in common. It turns out that Paul used to date Anne's best friend. They like to think of themselves as pleasantly eccentric, "crazy," and Paul offers these credentials: "In my closet, in the back, in a little box, I have a Polaroid snapshot of Mamie Van Doren on the steps of the Astor Hotel, three hundred and fifty-four Adlai Stevenson buttons, Mort Sahl's autograph on a coaster from the Blue Angel, and, the piece de resistance of my collection, all the Wonder Woman comic books from 1948 to 1952."

Neither is especially ambitious or driven; unlike many copywriters, Paul has no desire to write a book, and Anne, once a copy editor, is fairly content now just to watch her children grow. Paul thinks of himself as a member of a "do-nothing generation . . . . . all dying of inertia."

ANNE: Yeah, but it happens in every generation. You have kids and they come first. (*A beat.*) You know what I spend my days doing? Sorting socks. True. Every once in a while I run across a stray argyle in the basement dryer, but other than that . . .

PAUL: No, not every generation. I bet your mother was never bored.

ANNE: She was too busy cleaning linoleum.

PAUL: You know why?

ANNE: We had a lot of linoleum.

PAUL: Because she had something vital and important in her life. Something that kept her young and alive.

ANNE: My mother? What?

PAUL: The Depression.

ANNE: I think I missed a sentence.

PAUL: It gave her something to look forward to. Something to outlive. (*He turns away.*) A great day's coming tomorrow. Happy days are here again. Today, what do we have? (*Turns back.*) Nothing. (*Beginning to move.*) We've lost our sense of life. Of struggle. Our parents had it. They fought to survive. The kids today have it. They're fighting to change the world. (*His voice rises.*) What does our generation do? Peddle toothpaste and sort socks! If we disappeared from the face of the earth this minute, nobody'd know until our subscriptions to New York Magazine ran out! (*At full steam.*) No wonder we're bored to death!

ANNE: Did you take the doorknob.

PAUL: Bored! Bored! Bored! Bored!

ANNE: Not right now. Right now I'm a little nervous, nervous, nervous.

Again, Anne calls for help and stamps on the floor, trying to attract attention. Anne's husband Richard is out of town on business and Paul's wife is getting ready for a Women's Lib meeting, so they can't expect rescue from that quarter.

Paul and Anne continue to find things in common; they have similar analists, and Paul's wife Janet and Anne go to the same hairdresser. They are both married to stiff-backed people who dislike Chinese food.

They hear a noise in the hall, and through the peephole and latch hole they can see a woman, the neighbor in the next apartment, with her dog. They attract her attention and try to explain what they are doing in the supposedly vacant apartment, and why they need help. The woman is suspicious and orders them to back away from the door so that she in her turn can size them up through the keyhole. She decides that Paul and Anne are probably O.K., but she vanishes into her apartment along with her dog, a doberman pinscher. Discouraged and frustrated, Paul and Anne go back to their conversation about their marriages.

PAUL: Goddam it, if Janet wasn't fixing dinner for that group of hers, I wouldn't have had to come here in the first place.

ANNE (*not liking the idea*): And I'd be stuck here with her.

PAUL (*almost an order*): You'd like her!

ANNE: All right.

PAUL: Well, you think *I* want to be locked up with a guy who'd stand around at attention the whole time?

ANNE: What's the matter with you?

PAUL: Nothing. But nobody has to get *stuck* with my wife except me!

ANNE (*a beat*): Richard would have gotten us out of here by now.

PAUL: And Janet wouldn't have chased that woman away by saying every dumb thing that came into her head.

ANNE: My name *is* Anne Miller!

PAUL: Who asked you? If my name was Count Dracula, I wouldn't tell everybody I met in a dark alley.

ANNE: I think you must be cranky because you don't have any nice soft club chairs to sink into!

PAUL: And I think you've been sorting too many socks lately!

They decide to sit their confinement out separately, and Paul goes into the dining room. Anne soon panics, however, and calls him back. He doesn't hear her at first—he has gone to the maid's room to try to attract attention in the courtyard, and when he finally reappears Anne is so relieved to see him that she practically runs into his arms. They apologize to each other, they agree that when all is said and done they are glad that Janet and Richard aren't here. Admitting this makes Paul feel a bit guilty, a bit disloyal, and Anne tries to keep up with him by telling him that Richard "has sagging pectorals . . . . . he always wears an undershirt because he doesn't want us to see his sagging pectorals." Now Anne feels a bit disloyal too.

They are both aware of curious vibrations at being locked up together like this, with a stranger of the opposite sex. It restores for them the pleasant feeling of being young, which was cut off prematurely in their generation by the war-baby boom: "There we were in our mid-twenties, barely polishing up our twist . . . . . and then one day we turn around and the whole damn world is full of teenagers. Millions of them wherever you look. And it's not so bad that they're younger than we are, they have to be so damn different. They set up that generation gap and pushed us on the other side with the grown-ups. I never chose to be a grown-up, but it was too late. I'd already thrown away my faded levis."

They are beginning to admire each other more and more openly; Paul calls Anne a "knockout" and a "smart cookie." Anne recalls that she was once the "office Eve Arden," and before that she was something of a beatnik and also thought of herself as a Zelda Fitzgerald (Paul was a J.D. Salinger).

Paul has a sudden thought—why don't he and Anne have dinner tonight, since their spouses are busy? Anne shies away from the suggestion, automatically says she can't, but Paul insists. For him, too, this would be a first, his first outside date since his marriage. They couldn't go to one of their favorite local restaurants, they decide, because they'd be likely to run into friends or family.

At this moment the front door opens and Eddie comes in—the woman across the court has told him about the couple stuck here in 4B. He apologizes, gives them the doorknob so they can leave at their convenience, then disappears.

Paul still has dinner on his mind, and he has another idea—what about a picnic right here in the empty apartment? Anne can't bring herself to "have dinner with a strange man in an empty apartment."

PAUL: I wish you'd change your mind.

ANNE (*extends her hand*): It was really terrific meeting you, Paul. Goodbye.

PAUL (*takes her hand*): Damn it, I'm not taking no for an answer. I'll be here at seven-thirty with a full picnic basket.

ANNE: I'm not coming, Paul.

PAUL: I'll be here anyway.

ANNE (*taking her hand from his and going to door*): You'll be wasting an evening.

PAUL: I'd have to lock myself in the bedroom at home anyway. Look, I'll bring some Wonder Woman comic books with me. How can you resist that?

ANNE (*turning at the door*): Ciao.

PAUL: Seven-thirty.

> *Anne smiles and exits. Paul stands looking after her for a moment, then starts to turn to get his coat. Anne comes back, just inside the doorway.*

ANNE: I can't make it before eight.
>*Anne exits. Paul smiles, puts on his coat, begins to wonder what he's gotten himself into, then starts out. Curtain.*

Scene 2: Evening

The apartment is dark when Anne enters. She turns on the lights and shakes down the skirt of the long gown she's worn under her coat for the occasion—but she is alone, Paul hasn't arrived. Just as she starts to leave, *"Paul appears in the doorway laden down with three shopping bags and a smaller brown paper bag."* He was delayed by a large crowd at the supermarket, but he's managed to collect a huge assortment of picnic goodies. Anne takes off her coat and lets Paul admire her gown befort sitting on the blanket he has laid for their picnic. He has brought apples, oranges, peaches, bananas and grapes, and cake for dessert. "You like barbecued chicken? If not, I got a pastrami—and a rare roast beef—with Russian—also caviar, red. Sorry about that. Fritos, plastic wine glasses, bottle of wine, cole slaw, sweet peppers, plastic utensils, paper plates, napkins in the mod boutique pattern, shocking pink after-dinner mints and a six months' supply of Wash 'n' Dri."

He has also brought his Wonder Woman comics, a cassette player with Chopin to dine by and two inflatable plastic chairs—the next best thing to club chairs—and an air pump. But his piece de resistance is his college yearbook, which Anne peruses as Paul blows up one of the chairs. Anne reads Paul's college credits: president of the Art and Literary Society, treasurer of the Junior Prom, etc., and they find still more in common: they both played Gaylord Ravenal in *Show Boat,* he in the college little theater production, she at summer camp.

>*Paul opens the bottle of wine and pours out two glasses. Meanwhile, Anne is struggling to sit comfortably in the inflated chair, with no success.*

ANNE: Well, that's remarkably uncomfortable, isn't it?
PAUL *(takes chair from her)*: There's a trick to it.
ANNE: I hope so.
PAUL: The salesman showed me. First you have to cross your legs.
>*Paul demonstrates how to sit in the chair and falls out of it in a backward somersault. Paul, disgusted, throws the chair out of the window into the courtyard. He then returns to the blanket and picks up the full wine glasses.*

ANNE: You're quite a demented person, you know?
PAUL: Uh-huh.
>*Hands her wine glass, she takes it.*

To the loveliest leading baritone I know.
>*They clink glasses and sip.*

ANNE: Did you tell Janet where you were going?

PAUL: No. Did you tell Richard?

ANNE: No.

PAUL: Why not?

ANNE: I don't know. There wasn't time. He was calling long distance from Cleveland on his way to a client dinner.

PAUL: How is old Richard?

ANNE: Old Richard is very well. He sold his design for a new supermarket.

PAUL: Old Richard is an architect.

ANNE: That's right.

PAUL: What does he design besides supermarkets?

ANNE: Mainly stores, but he has a commission to do a beach house.

PAUL: I'll watch the Sunday *Times* magazine section.

ANNE: Do. One of the people he's meeting with asked him to design a shopping complex. Not bad, huh?

PAUL: Very complex. Did he tell you all about it on the phone?

ANNE: Yes.

PAUL: Oh, I see. That's why you didn't have time to tell him.

ANNE (*coolly*): Your turn.

PAUL: Janet was making paella. Have you ever made it?

ANNE: No.

They look at each other.

PAUL: Well, the trick in making a really superior paella is to get the chicken to brown and the clams to steam and the sausages to fry at the same time so they can be added to the rice at just the proper moment. Otherwise you get soggy rice. Then, too, overcooking can turn the golden yellow of saffron rice a warm beige which, although pleasing to look at, is not a sign of really superior rice at our house.

Anne gives him a knowing look, which he sees.

She was not to be disturbed.

ANNE: A likely story.

PAUL: Every bit as likely as yours.

They are beginning to feel self-conscious about keeping their rendezvous a secret, even a little bit guilty. Suddenly, Anne decides that she wants to leave. Paul stops her by pretending that Janet and Richard are here with them, pretending to introduce everybody to everybody, faking small talk. Finally they pretend that Janet and Richard have to leave, and they return to the blanket and the subject of Paul's college years.

ANNE: . . . . . When you were in college, wasn't there something you wanted to do?

PAUL: I wanted to write sensitive, terribly perceptive short stories laying bare the vacuousness and hidden cruelties of the great Jewish middle class.

ANNE: What happened?

PAUL: Philip Roth.

ANNE: There must be room for one more sensitive Jewish author in the world.

PAUL: Yeah, I suppose they could squeeze me in, but I don't think I'm that sensitive any more.

ANNE: Nonsense.

PAUL: Look, will you leave the rest of my life to me, please?

As they talk, the front door opens slowly and a middle-aged woman peers in. She is the woman in 4A.

ANNE: I'm sorry. As a very old friend I feel I have the right to pry.

WOMAN: What are you doing in here?

They both jump up guiltily and unconsciously assume the positions that they were in when 4A questioned them through the hole in the door.

You heard me, what are you doing in here?

PAUL: It's all right. It's 4A. You remember us. We already passed inspection.

WOMAN: Oh, you. Damn, I knew there was something I was supposed to do. (*Calls over her shoulder into the hall.*) Sit, Trixie! I see the doorknob's back.

PAUL: That's right.

WOMAN: You get the apartment?

PAUL: Yes, that's right. My wife and I have taken the apartment.

WOMAN: How much did you bribe?

PAUL: Five hundred.   ANNE: Two thousand.

PAUL: Two thousand.   ANNE: Five hundred.

WOMAN: I suppose it's your own business. You'll be moving in soon. You have a dog?

PAUL: No.   ANNE: A schnauzer.

WOMAN: He's right, that's no dog. Couldn't protect you against a five year old.

ANNE: I don't usually need protection against five year olds.

WOMAN: You haven't lived in this neighborhood.

Paul and Anne offer the woman a peach, and she takes a whole bag full of fruit and exits. Anne is curious about Paul's reason for telling the woman they were a married couple. Maybe he feels embarrassed, or guilty, about being here alone with Anne; and maybe they are flirting with each other just a little, though Paul has hardly ever even flirted with another woman since he married Janet.

Anne prods Paul into telling her a story about one of his few adventures, an encounter on the IRT. His eyes met those of a pretty girl in the mirror over the Dentyne machine, just before a train pulled in.

PAUL: . . . . . The Number One train arrived and I squeezed past an old crippled lady and got a seat. I read one of the overhead ads about the heartbreak of psoriasis and how medical science has finally come up with a breakthrough which was available at local drugstores without a prescription, and I thought the AMA would have something to say about that. Then suddenly I saw a pair of knees. They seemed to have little smiling faces on them like a dog I once had that ran away and returned with fleas which we never did get rid of, so much for animal husbandry, but of course fleas aren't the scourge that psoriasis is. I looked higher. There were two thighs just about at my eye level. I can't tell you how disconcerting it is to see two thighs at your eye level before coffee. Suddenly all thoughts of Janet and our color TV which we watch from across the room because of radiation and our complete collection of the operettas of Gilbert and Sullivan vanished from my mind. I looked higher.

                    Reaction from Anne.

Yes, gentle reader, I looked higher. There was a mini skirt. Of red and blue and, yes, a touch of white. It was that same patriotic Dentyne-chewing nymphette standing before me, her thighs exposed for my personal pleasure, or so it seemed, her love beads dipping down over her pubescent breasts. She looked down at me and smiled. From beneath Max Factor's Frosted Moonglow Number Nine shone an array of teeth to light up the underground from Eighty-sixth to Borough Hall. Thirty-two Steinway keys in perfect tune.

They exchanged smiles, and then Paul got up to offer her his seat, but someone else took it. They chatted until the train arrived at Paul's station (he discovered that she was a receptionist at a pajama firm).

ANNE: Your own Miss Subways.

PAUL: Then the train came into my station, I smiled, she smiled and I left.

ANNE: Is that all?

PAUL: Not quite. As the doors closed, from my position of safety on the platform, I winked at her.

ANNE: And what did she do?

PAUL: She winked back. And that is what is known in the trade as a Jewish affair.

ANNE: So, you've never flirted with another woman.

PAUL: I see the symbolism of my story went completely over your head. I had stripped that girl naked on the downtown Number One train and ravaged her without missing my stop.

Anne has nothing so sensational to report in exchange—merely a brief encounter with an editor behind the filing cabinet. Paul notes that they are both missing the sexual revolution, and Anne decides she wants a glass of water and exits to get one while Paul rants on about his ineffectual generation: "By and large we just held the door for the kids today."

Anne rushes back into the room with a faucet in her hand: it has broken off, water is pouring out. The sink is stopped up, so the apartment is starting to flood. Paul runs out to get help, while Anne brushes up on the adventures of Wonder Woman.

Paul comes back, having alerted the elevator man. Anne seems a bit nervous, and Paul reassures her that he has decided not to try anything "funny."

PAUL: . . . . . Not that it would hurt us to have a little fling. Hell, it'd probably do us some good. Besides, I've always wanted to know what it would be like, haven't you?

ANNE: Well, it's only natural for me to wonder what it would be like to have a man other than Richard make love to me.

PAUL: He was your first?

ANNE: My one and only. (*Turns away from him.*) I didn't mean to let that out.

PAUL: Why not?

ANNE: It sounds so old maidish.

PAUL: At the risk of sounding slightly Edwardian, I respect you for it.

ANNE: Do you really? Think before answering, please.

PAUL (*pause*): I don't know.

ANNE: See? Even among the virtuous, virtue has had it. You don't know how lucky you were, being a boy. You could experiment without a qualm.

PAUL: Now you sound like Janet.

ANNE: Don't knock her, she's right. Us "good girls" will always wonder, does every man hold a woman the same way? Do they all make funny little noises? Are some of them stronger or gentler or . . .

> *Paul has started to caress her.*

What are you doing, Paul?

PAUL (*takes his hand away*): I was about to try something funny.

Paul's playful advances are interrupted by the arrival of Eddie to fix the faucet. Again Paul finds it necessary to establish the fact that they are married, but Eddie couldn't care less and goes off about his work. The woman in 4A comes in looking for Eddie and goes into the dining room in search of him.

While there are people around to make Anne feel secure, Paul quickly tells her that he wants to have a fling with her; they are both lost, he says, and perhaps an affair would help them find themselves.

The woman comes back into the room with Eddie, threatening to set Trixie on him if he doesn't fix her faucet too. They exit leaving Paul and Anne with the tension rising. Anne thinks of Janet, stuck with the children and the linoleum, but Paul insists that Janet need never know, and he wants to make love to Anne.

Anne decides to leave, and Paul makes no move to detain her. She stops at the door, though, and agrees that perhaps it's time Paul did have an affair with somebody, if not with her. But Paul couldn't bring himself to search out someone deliberately, almost cold-bloodedly.

PAUL: . . . . . You were special, Anne. You're a very special person.

ANNE (*pause*): You're pretty special yourself. But I love Richard.

PAUL: And I love Janet. I do. Truly.

ANNE: I know you do.

PAUL: But what I need I can't get from Janet just because she *is* my wife. Isn't the same true for you?

ANNE: I suppose. But . . .

PAUL: But what?

ANNE: But I was raised in the Forties. I was taught a lot of things about what a nice woman is. Maybe some of them were wrong, but I learned them.

PAUL: You could unlearn them.

ANNE: I don't think so.

> *Pause.*

For what it's worth, Paul, I would like to go to bed with you.

PAUL (*averting his gaze*): I'll bet you say that to all the boys.

ANNE: I mean it. And nobody is more surprised than I am.

PAUL: Then I think you're making a mistake.

ANNE: Could be. Goodbye.

> *Anne has turned to go out the door. She has her hand on the door-knob, but does not move. Her back is to Paul and the audience. Paul senses her change. There is a long pause as he collects himself.*

PAUL: Anne. Turn out the lights.

> *Anne turns out the lights, then turns into the room, taking off her coat very slowly and leaving it on the railing. Paul rises to his knees in place looking at her, remembers the cassette and turns it on. It begins to play Chopin's Minute Waltz. Paul rises.*

The Minute Waltz?

> *Outside the window, it begins to rain. Anne comes to Paul, after a moment they begin to embrace. Curtain.*

ACT II

The following morning, the apartment is empty and the only evidence of occupancy the night before is an orange peel in the middle of the floor. After a beat or two the front door opens and Paul comes in with his wife Janet (*"quite attractive, well dressed"*). He has told Janet he doesn't like the apartment, but she has insisted on coming to see it anyway.

Janet senses that perhaps Paul is being difficult not only because she gave him cold paella for breakfast but also because he feels threatened by her involvement in Women's Lib. But this is far from the truth, and when Janet moves into the dining room Paul decides that the time has come to assert himself.

PAUL: I want a club chair!

JANET (*returns*): What?

PAUL: I want a club chair.

JANET: Now?

PAUL: I've always wanted a club chair.

JANET: Okay.

PAUL: Well, you're my wife! You ought to know these things!

JANET: All right, now I know. Is there anything else you want me to know?

PAUL: A man has a right to sprawl out if he wants to.

JANET: Be my guest. Meanwhile, I'm going to check out the kitchen.

> *Janet goes into the dining room. Paul sees the orange peel on the floor, dives for it, hides it, then realizes his foolishness and drops it back on the floor.*

Janet returns, liking the apartment more and more. Paul insists that he hates the apartment, and he really wants a club chair. Janet still feels it was probably the cold paella that is making Paul act so peculiarly, as they exit into the dining room.

The front door opens again and Anne's husband Richard comes in (*"He wears a business suit and carries an attache case. He's good-looking"*). Anne, following behind Richard, is reluctant to enter; she is wearing dark glasses and coat collar turned up, as though in disguise. Richard is immediately pleased by the apartment's potential. Anne insists that she hates the place. Richard, always the architect, has ideas of split levels and hanging furniture, and his efforts to coax Anne out of her doldrums only cause an outburst: "I want a regular lower class home like everybody else. I want direct lighting. God, how I want direct lighting! And petunias in window boxes, not jungle plants! Richard, I want to be downward mobile!"

Richard leads Anne away to look at the kitchen; but just as they get to the dining room doors, Janet and Paul enter.

> *Anne and Paul stare at each other in horror. Neither Richard nor Janet pay any attention to their mates or to each other. The two couples exit, Janet and Paul into the bedrooms. Beat. Paul's head appears from the bedrooms, Anne's from the dining room. They motion wildly to each other. They disappear. Beat. Anne and Paul rush back.*

ANNE (*in an embarrassed whisper, terribly awkward*): Hello.

PAUL: Hello. Is that Richard?

ANNE: Uh-huh. Janet?

PAUL: Yeah. I told her I had to go to the bathroom.

ANNE: I'm supposed to be measuring the room. (*Does some awkward pacing.*)

PAUL: What happened to you last night?

ANNE: I went home.

PAUL: Why didn't you wake me up?

ANNE: You looked so comfortable, lying there, cuddling the chicken.

> *Offstage a loud banging is heard as Richard tests the walls. They break apart at the sound, then come back together when no one enters.*

PAUL: You should have woken me.

ANNE: I had to get home to pay the baby sitter.

>*He leads her further downstage away from the dining room door.*

PAUL: Are you all right?

ANNE: As well as can be expected. And you?

PAUL: Okay. When did Richard get home?

ANNE: This morning. How was Janet's meeting?

PAUL: Fine. They're going to blow something up.

ANNE: That's nice.

Anne sees the orange peel and guiltily puts it in her pocket. Paul confesses he was awake half the night, writing a story. They bid each other goodbye, somewhat stiffly, and separate as Janet comes into the room.

Paul tries unsuccessfully to persuade Janet to leave, and when Richard also comes back into the room he recognizes Janet as a childhood friend from his old neighborhood. Janet and Richard greet each other warmly while *"Anne and Paul appear to be dying of shock and terror."* But Anne and Paul must pull themselves together and pretend, as they are introduced, that they are meeting for the first time.

Anne starts to laugh and can't stop. She runs into the dining room, but her uncontrollable laughter can be heard occasionally as Janet and Richard try to renew their old acquaintance in a friendly chat about their families and Richard's job.

Richard goes off to try to calm his wife down, and Janet leaves to visit a friend who lives in an apartment upstairs in this building, leaving Paul to take another look around.

Richard comes back with Anne, who has finally recovered from her laughing fit. Richard has to go to his office, leaving Anne and Paul once more alone together in the apartment.

They agree that Richard and Janet seem very nice. There doesn't seem to be much else to talk about. They agree it would be best for Paul to go, but when he tries the front door the knob comes off in his hand, *"and the sound of the doorknob on the outside of the door falling is heard."* Once again they are locked in the apartment. Anne sits helplessly on the radiator cover, her head in her arms, either laughing or crying or both.

Paul calls for help, but again there seems to be none within earshot. Being locked in makes both of them feel even more guilty.

ANNE (*with a small, kind smile*): We certainly are a sophisticated pair, aren't we?

PAUL: Nope.

ANNE: Well, what do we do now?

PAUL: We talk.

ANNE: To coin a phrase, there really is nothing to talk about.

PAUL: I don't agree. We did something important last night. I think we ought to discuss it.

ANNE: All right. What do you want to say? Something witty? Go ahead, make me laugh. Say, don't you ever work?

PAUL: I'm on vacation this week.

ANNE: You going to write a report on what you did on your vacation? (*She moves away from him.*)

PAUL: You're really out to get yourself, aren't you? You don't deserve it.

ANNE: You mean that was somebody else here last night. What a relief! Now I can get back to my linoleum with a clear conscience.

PAUL: We do what we have to do.

ANNE: Look, it's very sweet of you to want to ease my mind, but I really think it would be best if I just went home and did a little private penance. Don't worry, it's no big deal. I'll make Richard a rib roast or something. What the hell, it's the least I can do.

PAUL: And what do I do?

ANNE: Buy her a present.

PAUL: It won't help.

ANNE (*kindly*): Don't be a sap. Men are allowed their little flings. Everybody knows that.

PAUL: That's not what I mean. What do I do about you?

Paul wants to see Anne again—tomorrow night if possible. Anne hardly knows how to react to this, so she asks Paul about the story he just wrote. It's about the girl on the IRT, and in the story the man just lets her go. Paul feels maybe he should have stayed on the train with her. Anne, transferring the thought to their present relationship, comments "There's no future in it, Paul. All it can get us is pain."

Forced to drop this subject, Paul joins Anne in calling for help—but suddenly he kisses her, and she throws her arms around him. Paul suggests that they meet during the lunch hour if Anne can get a sitter, and Anne just about gives in to Paul after another passionate embrace. But abruptly she breaks away and runs to the front door looking through the peephole for help.

Realizing Anne's despair, Paul bravely decides to go for help and steps onto the window ledge and edges his way along it until he is out of sight. Thinking he has only gone to the dining room, she explains herself to him carefully: "We can't see each other any more, Paul. You must understand that. No matter how much we want to. We're not the kind of people to enter into anything lightly and we're also not the kind of people to hurt those we love, so what can it possibly come to? I have enough pain in my life, Paul. I don't want any more."

Paul reappears on the ledge, almost overcome with fright. Anne sees him just as he is about to lose his footing. She grabs him and manages to get him back inside. Now that Paul has risked his life for her, Anne decides, she can't go on refusing to have an affair with him. They make a date for the coming Friday night. They decide against meeting in an uptown restaurant where they might be seen by friends. They plan their rendezvous at the Hotel Albert on University Place.

     . . . . . *Suddenly Anne smiles. Paul notices.*

PAUL: What?

ANNE: I'm wondering what I should wear. Gloria Grahame had a terrific outfit for adultery in *The Bad and the Beautiful.* Should I bring a nightgown?

PAUL: Suit yourself.

ANNE: Are you going to bring pajamas?

PAUL: I wasn't planning on sleeping.

ANNE: I think I'll wear something inconspicuous. Like a paper bag over my head.

PAUL: Don't chicken out on me.

ANNE: I won't. (*Almost in tears.*) And nobody'll know. And nobody'll get hurt, right?

PAUL: That's right.

They plan the evening—they'll go to a little restaurant nearby and then stroll through Washington Square Park. This would leave them a bit pressed for time, possibly, because Anne will have to be home by midnight.

Suddenly Paul remembers that Friday evening is out—his parents will be visiting from Florida and he can't put them off. Friday before 1 p.m. is out for Anne, because she too has family commitments she can't get around. They manage to agree on 1:30 p.m. Friday at the Hotel Albert, but not without some difficulty.

PAUL: Tell me something. Was last night all right?

ANNE: Wonderful. How was it for you?

PAUL: A bit conservative maybe, but not without potential.

ANNE: You don't do all kinds of funny things, do you?

PAUL: Not so far, but I'm willing to try.

ANNE: I saw a movie once . . .

PAUL: So did I.

ANNE: I thought you didn't even read *Playboy*.

PAUL: Some guys at the office took me. Who took you?

ANNE: Rich . . . (*Tries to cover her slip.*) Friend. A very rich friend.

PAUL: Hello, Richard!

ANNE: Well, *I* didn't say it. You asked me!

PAUL: You went to a dirty movie with your husband.

ANNE: Who better? We didn't enjoy it, though. We thought . . .

PAUL: I don't want to know what you thought!

ANNE: I'm sorry. I don't mean to talk about him. It just slips out.

Paul insists that when they are together, there should exist no Richard, no Janet, only each other. Anne tries to agree, but she can't stop herself from realizing that there *is* a Richard, the one with the sagging pectorals. Paul warns

Anne to be careful, she is going to kill their romance. She agrees "I'm going to kill it." She is not going to have an affair with Paul after all.

ANNE: . . . . . I'm sorry, Paul. I'm sorry, but I can't go through with it. I wish I could, but I can't. I just can't. I can't have affairs, I guess. All I can have is marriages. That's the kind of person I am. Look, I'm already worrying about what you'll have for dinner on our tryst. Before we went to bed, I'd hang up your pants so they wouldn't get wrinkled. I can't have two marriages, Paul. There's only so much laundry I can carry. (*Beat.*) Oh, Paul, I really do love you. But I love Richard, too. And he's where my life is.

PAUL: I know.

ANNE: Are you all right?

PAUL: Yeah.

ANNE: Do you forgive me?

PAUL: Of course I forgive you.

ANNE: It's true for you too, isn't it? Isn't Janet all you really care about? And your son?

PAUL: Yes. Boy, we came pretty close, didn't we?

ANNE: I wouldn't have been much good at it anyway. You wouldn't want a lady who'd be saying her rosary after every kiss.

PAUL: Nah. All that clicking of beads is too distracting. Why did last night happen?

ANNE: I don't know. That's something Richard and I will have to figure out.

PAUL: You're going to tell him?

ANNE: What we *did?* No. That would only hurt him. But I'm going to tell him how I feel. I don't think I've done that in a long time.

PAUL: Yeah, neither have I. No. I've already started. I'm getting a club chair.

The front door opens and Eddie and the pregnant woman enter. Eddie fixes the doorknob.

EDDIE: *Que carajo passara aqui con el* doorknob? I don't know, we're having a lot of trouble with doorknobs lately.

He looks at Anne and Paul, waiting for them to go. They just stand there.

Uh . . . this lady's taken the apartment.

ANNE: Oh. Well, we'll be leaving then.

As the woman chatters on, Anne and Paul stand there, looking at each other. They realize it is the last time they'll see each other.

WOMAN: Well, Eddie, the first thing I want done is the sink moved and whatever is smelling up the place cleaned out. And the stall shower is missing tiles. Let's see . . . the sink in the second bathroom takes forever to drain, but I suppose that can wait. . . .

She and Eddie turn to look at Anne and Paul wondering why they haven't left.

. . . . let me show you the leak, Eddie.

They exit into bedrooms, staring back at Anne and Paul.

PAUL (*puts on his coat*): Shall we go?

ANNE: You go first. (*Beat.*) Thanks for everything.

PAUL: Thank *you*.

ANNE: Some day, will I pick up a magazine and see a story by one more sensitive Jewish author?

PAUL: You never can tell. (*Pause. With immense difficulty.*) See you.

> *Paul smiles, walks slowly to the door. Before leaving, he turns back to take a last look at her, then he kisses his hand and presses the kiss to the doorknob. He exits.*
>
> *Anne looks around the room, gathers her belongings, putting on her coat. She puts her hand in her pocket and feels the orange peel.*
>
> *The pregnant woman enters in the bedroom hall looking at her. Anne takes the orange peel from her pocket and drops it to the floor and exits, smiling. Curtain.*

BUTLEY

A Play in Two Acts

BY SIMON GRAY

Cast and credits appear on page 335

SIMON GRAY was born in Hayling Island, Hampshire, in 1936 and was educated at Westminster School and at universities in Canada and France before going to Cambridge, where he majored in English. His produced plays include Wise Child, *done in London in 1967 starring Alec Guinness and in New York in 1972 starring Donald Pleasence;* Dutch Uncle, Spoiled *and the present work which had its London debut July 14, 1971. Mr. Gray also adapted* The Idiot *for production at the National Theater. His TV plays include* Death of a Teddy Bear, *for which he won the British Writer's Guild Award, and he is the author of three novels:* Colmain, Simple People *and* Little Portia.

Mr. Gray teaches English literature at the University of London's Queen Mary College. He is married, with two children.

Time: The present

Place: A College of London University

ACT I

SYNOPSIS: The scene is a College office with two facing desks backed by bookcases, all very run-down and *"badly decorated (white walls, greying, plaster boards) with strip lighting . . . Ben's desk, left, is a chaos of papers, books, detritus. Joey's desk, right, is almost bare."*

The entrance door is upstage center and there is a window up left. A battered blow-up of T. S. Eliot is prominently displayed on one wall.

Ben enters and throws his plastic raincoat over onto Joey's desk, soon followed by the peel of the banana he is eating—Ben uses his office mate's desk as a kind of dump. Ben has cut himself shaving and wears a lump of cotton wool on his chin. He is in early middle age or perhaps younger than that, a very heavy smoker, disorganized, untidy and unkempt, procrastinating.

The phone rings—it is Ben's department head, James, but Ben pretends he has a student with him and is too busy to talk now. He fiddles with the cotton wool on his cut. He finds that his desk lamp is not working, so he changes it for Joey's.

Ben sends away a student who tries to see him about a tutorial on Wordsworth's *The Prelude,* then settles down to read. Joey (somewhat younger than Ben, tolerant but well and carefully organized and not easily flappable) comes in carrying his briefcase. He clears Ben's debris from his desk—and on Joey's desk the rejected light works perfectly.

Today is the first day back at work after the mid-term break, and the two men greet each other elaborately.

BEN: Good morning.
JOEY: Good morning.
BEN: Nice to see you.
JOEY: Nice to be seen. What's the matter with your chin?
BEN: I'm trying to cultivate cotton wool on it. Your own is shining pleasantly, what did you have to work with, a razor?
JOEY: What did *you* use?
BEN: Anne left one behind. Behind the fridge, to be exact. So either mice have taken up shaving, or that stubble was sheared from her calves. I thought of mounting a tuft in a locket. You needn't have taken the only one we have.
JOEY: It also happens to be the only one I have.
BEN: Couldn't you have shared Ted's? It's no pleasure slicing open my chin with my estranged wife's razor blade. The symbolism may be deft, but the memory still smarts.
JOEY: I didn't mean to take it, in point of fact. I put it in the bag without thinking.
BEN: Lust is no excuse for thoughtlessness. And where is your bag?
He stands up and peers round for it.
JOEY: What? Oh, I left it with Reg.
BEN: Reg? Who's Reg?
He perches on the front of his own desk with his feet up on a chair and lights a cigarette. Joey hastily occupies the vacated desk chair.
JOEY: Reg is his name.
BEN: Whose name?
JOEY: Ted's.

BEN: Reg is Ted's name?

JOEY: The one you call Ted is the one I call Reg. He calls himself Reg too.

BEN: How sweet.

JOEY: In fact, everybody calls him Reg except you. You call him Ted.

BEN: Why do I do that, I wonder.

JOEY: To embarrass me.

Ben questions Joey about his weekend. What is on Joey's mind, however, is a promotion which he expects soon; but Ben has heard nothing from their departmental colleagues about it.

Ben returns to the subject of Joey's weekend; apparently Joey has only just returned and hasn't even had time to stop by the flat he and Ben share, where Ben had been waiting for him. Joey is evasive about the weekend, busies himself reading a group of student essays. He tries to ignore Ben, but Ben prods him by throwing debris over onto Joey's side of the room: borrowed socks, a crumpled newspaper, an American student's thesis which Ben has forgotten to read. Joey manages to keep his cool through all manner of annoyances and distractions.

Miss Heasman—*"a pretty, competent-looking girl"*—knocks and enters. She is one of Ben's students seeking to establish a set of appointments for her tutorials, but Ben manages to get rid of her; he has no time or energy for anything so tiresome as actually teaching a student.

Ben finally breaks Joey's concentration by telling him "You're in trouble, Joey," because a member of the board which will decide his promotion has a knife out for him. Joey offended someone at the last departmental meeting, Ben tells him, by recommending that they teach a certain list of contemporary novels. Joey tries desperately to imagine whom he might have offended, but cannot. Ben goads him.

BEN: Think, child, think! Who had most to lose by that list being passed? Who is *most* affected?

JOEY: Nobody. Nobody at all. You're the one who's going to teach it, they'll be *your* lectures, *your* seminars, *your* tutorials . . .

BEN (*after a long pause, as Joey realizing, looks at him*): Exactly. Precisely. Absolutely. Fool! Imbecile! Traitor! Lackey!—I wouldn't be caught dead reading those books. And you know how it exhausts me to teach books I haven't read. Why didn't you oppose me?

JOEY: It's your own fault. Your instructions were quite clear.

BEN: Haven't you heard of a sub-text? It's very fashionable now. In fact, I remember advising you to use the word twice in every paper when I was guiding you through your finals.

He goes to examine him.

But what's the matter, dear? You're looking a little peaky around the gills, wherever they are? Were you frightened, a trifle? You needn't be—you played the toad to perfection.

He returns to his desk.

ALAN BATES IN "BUTLEY"

JOEY: Is there a sub-text to that? Or can I take it as straight abuse?
BEN: It's straight abuse. Can you take it?
JOEY (*trembling slightly*): No, not any longer.
    He gets up and begins to pack his briefcase.
BEN: Where are you going?
JOEY: To the library.
BEN: Why?
JOEY: I've got a lecture at twelve.
BEN: But you're not running away from me so soon?

JOEY: And there are a few things on my Herrick I've got to dig up.
> *He goes to the door—Ben cuts him off.*

BEN: Dig up! (*Laughs.*)
> Diggory, diggory, Delvet
> Little old man in black velvet
> He digs and he delves
> You can see for yourselves
> The holes dug by Diggory Delvet

It is velvet, isn't it, this jacket?
> *Fingering it. Joey tugs his sleeve away.*

No, don't flounce. (*They stand staring at each other.*) You were due back last night, remember?

JOEY: Did it make any difference?

BEN: In that I spent the evening expecting you.

JOEY: In point of fact, I said I'd be back either last night or this morning.

BEN: Also you didn't phone.

JOEY: I was only in Leeds for four days. Of course I didn't phone.

BEN: Why not? Language difficulties? I reserved a table at Bianchi's. I was going to take us out.

JOEY (*after a pause*): I'm sorry.

Ben apologizes to Joey for putting him on about the promotion and reassures him that the senior members of the department think very highly of him, he will surely get his lectureship.

Ben tries to get Joey to tell him more about Reg, tries to uncover such domestic details as who does the cooking when Joey and Reg are together (Joey has never cooked for Ben while they have been sharing their household; Ben's wife Anne cooked for him while they lived together, but badly.) Joey confides to Ben that Reg does the cooking, "in point of fact."

Ben suddenly remembers uncomfortably that while Joey was away no one called on the telephone, not even an acquaintance named Tom whom Ben doesn't like (Tom is writing a six-volume novel and insists on showing Ben the drafts). Trying to escape Ben's alternate breast-beating and jealous probing, Joey gathers his things together for a trip to the library, but Ben stops him by seizing Joey's briefcase.

BEN: Have you seen Tom recently?

JOEY: No. No I haven't.

BEN: When did you last hear from him?

JOEY (*shrugs*): Perhaps he's busy.

BEN: Of course he's busy. He's too dull to be anything else, the question is, why has he stopped being busy with me? (*He returns to his own desk and sits on the hard chair.*) Do you think he's dropped me? His attentions have been slackening since my marriage broke up, now I come to think of it.

JOEY (*carefully*): He's very fond of Anne, isn't he?

BEN (*laughs*): That's an idea. I must find out whether he's been hounding *her.*

JOE: But Anne—(*Stops.*) She likes him, doesn't she? I mean, I always thought—had the impression that she was fond of him?

BEN: Oh, I expect she became addicted. She took up all my vices except drinking, smoking and you. She never cared for you. Did you know that?

JOEY: I had my suspicions. Thank you for confirming them.

BEN: She said that Tom became a school teacher because he had to prove, after three years of being taught by me at Cambridge, that education was still a serious affair. Whereas you wanted to get back to your old college here with me because you were incapable of outgrowing your early influences. Nursery dependence. This analysis was based crudely on the fact that you are homosexual. She also said you were sly and pushing, and that she didn't trust you an inch.

JOEY: You never told me this before.

BEN: You never asked me before.

JOEY: I didn't ask you now, either.

BEN: I know. But I got tired of waiting.

Joey had believed that he and Anne were friends, but Ben rubs it in that Joey gives Anne "the creeps"—though Ben admits this is probably only a means of Anne's getting back at her husband by sneering at his protege.

Ben tries to get from Joey what Reg's father does, trying to demean Joey's friend by sneering at his background. Joey reluctantly tells Ben that Reg's father runs a butcher shop and the family lives in a bungalow outside Leeds with plaster gnomes in the garden. They read Mazo de la Roche and their doorbell plays a tune. Reg's mother is a traffic warden. Ben turns up his nose at all of this, and at the added information that Joey and Reg took in a football match. Reg took Joey there for the weekend—Joey explains—because Reg wanted Joey to see him not as "queer" but surrounded with some of the aura of the straight world. But, Joey admits, Reg is "much more natural as a London publisher who knows all about food, and cooks marvellously. Much more natural and much more convincing."

Miss Heasman comes by seeking her session on *A Winter's Tale,* and Ben deftly gets rid of her while asking Joey whether Reg's square parents understand their son's relationships. Joey tells him "Of course not" and refuses to discuss the subject any further.

Ben proposes an air-clearing evening at Bianchi's. Somewhat awkwardly, Joey reveals that he is already engaged to dine with Reg this evening. Ben proposes that he come along too, but Joey would rather he wouldn't. The last time they met, Ben insulted and abused Reg, who ended up hating Ben.

Ben pleads his case more and more strongly—he doesn't fancy a fifth straight evening of eating alone—but Joey resists. Their conversation is interrupted by the entrance of Edna, a colleague, who informs Joey that it's no use going to the library today, it's temporarily closed (and thus Joey's escape hatch is blocked).

They discuss the students, and Edna informs them that for some reason there's a false rumor going around that there will be no tutorials the first part of the week (she doesn't know that this rumor arose from Ben's evasions of his students). Edna is having trouble with a student named Gardner who attends lectures in a feathered hat. Edna pins the blame for Gardner's presence in the university on Ben, who had interviewed him and recommended his admission.

Edna is more than disturbed by the current wave of student rebelliousness, in which "they completely destroyed the Velium Aristotle. Completely destroyed it. *That* was their way of protesting about South Africa." Rather than put up with and thereby encourage any kind of hooliganism, Edna will report Gardner to their departmental superior, James.

Edna asks after Ben's wife Anne and their seven-month-old baby, Marina, whose name Ben can't even recall. Ben tells Edna that his wife and child have gone to live with Anne's mother, and Joey adds that he has moved back in with Ben. Edna sees how it is, but she tells the men that a little office next to hers has become vacant, in case either of them wants an office to himself. Ben refuses her offer with thanks, and Edna goes off about her business.

Edna has no sooner left the room than Ben is ridiculing her behind her back, criticizing her active and enthusiastic work methods (but Edna has finished a book on Byron and found a publisher for it). Ben confesses to Joey that the unruly student Gardner seemed "interesting." Joey wants to avoid any hint of friction between Ben and Edna, lest it reflect on him and hurt his chances for promotion.

Joey is trying to get some work done, but Ben keeps at him about the apartment they share (Joey is too neat, Ben too messy) and about the invitation to join Reg for dinner that evening.

A student comes to the door to inquire about his tutorials, but Ben brushes him off by telling him to go away and write an essay. Miss Heasman comes back and can't be put off so easily—she *has* written an essay, on "Hate and Redemption in *A Winter's Tale*," and she has brought it with her. She has arranged for a weekly appointment with Ben on Tuesdays at 2 o'clock (today is Tuesday), and before leaving the room she promises to return at the appointed hour and read the essay aloud.

While Joey works, Ben rants to himself; he picks up a pile of student essays and drops them to the floor, commenting on their eager sameness and wishing the cleaning woman would get rid of them: "Ruskin's char threw Carlyle's history of the French Revolution out with the other rubbish. But then they took a pride in their work in those days."

Ben thinks out loud of Anne's mother, "the mad monk;" of his daughter Marina, trying to remember when she was conceived. Joey suggests that perhaps one day Marina will need a father and Ben might be still tied emotionally to his marriage.

JOEY: I can't help wondering whether you miss it.
BEN: Only the sex and violence. And these days one can get those anywhere.
JOEY: So there's absolutely no chance . . .

BEN: Chance of what?

JOEY: Of your marriage reviving. You don't want it to?

BEN: Reviving? It's never died. I consider it inviolate. I'm a one-woman man and I've had mine, thank God.

JOEY: But things can't just go on as they are.

BEN: Can't they. Why not?

He takes the telephone directory from his desk and begins to look up a number.

JOEY: But supposing she wants to marry again.

BEN: Good God! Who would want to marry *her*?

JOEY: You did.

BEN: That was before she'd been through the mill . . .

He begins to run his finger down the column.

JOEY (*standing up*): Listen, Ben, you could be making a mistake about Anne. If you really don't want to lose her—

BEN (*goes to the telephone on Joey's desk*): Your conversation is beginning to sound as if it's been stitched together from song titles of the fifties . . .

The number Ben is calling is Reg's office number—to Joey's dismay. Joey makes Ben put down the receiver and promises to call Reg himself, right away, to invite Ben to dinner. As Joey hesitates and Ben insists, the phone rings. It is their department head, James, calling about the Gardner case and about the instructions Butley has been giving to his students. At this moment, Anne appears at the door and Joey lets her in. Butley puts off James, and he confronts his wife with a kind of bantering small-talk about the baby's teeth and other trivia. Anne greets both Ben and Joey coolly, affably; but Joey, embarrassed, makes an exit. Ben tells Anne she frightens Joey.

ANNE: Because he's creepy, and he knows I know it.

BEN: Yes. I've told him. He took it surprisingly badly.

ANNE: (*pause*): You've settled down nicely together again, then, have you?

BEN: We have our ups and downs.

ANNE: That's all right then. May I sit?

She sits on the hard chair in front of Ben's desk.

BEN: I went to see you over the weekend, as arranged, but you were out.

ANNE: Yes, I'm sorry.

BEN: Grounds for a scene though, don't you think?

ANNE: Oh, I should wait. (*Little pause.*) I had to see Tom's headmaster about a job.

BEN: And did you get one?

ANNE: Yes.

BEN: Good. (*He stares at her.*) But you look a trifle peaky around the gills —wherever they are. I can never locate them on Joey. Are you all right?

ANNE: I'm fine.

BEN: Good. I saw Marina instead. I expect your mother the mad monk told you.

ANNE: She said it was very quick. Like a visit from the postman.

BEN: I was there for twenty minutes. You'd better check on the postman. Ah!

He sits at Joey's desk.

Well, this is almost as delightful as it's unexpected, to what is it owed?

ANNE: I came to find out whether you wanted us back.

BEN (*after a pause*): Is that an offer?

ANNE: No. It's a question. I'd like the truth please. *Do* you want us back?

BEN: Frequently. (*Little pause.*) But not permanently. Do you want to come back?

ANNE: No.

BEN: We've cleared that up then. I think we're going to get on very well from this time forth, don't you?

ANNE (*pause*): Joey hasn't told you, then?

BEN: Told me what?

ANNE: He's known for weeks. His—what's his name—friend Reg must have told him.

BEN: Reg?

ANNE: Tom told him. At least, he told me he had.

BEN: Tom? Tom and Reg? What on earth have Tom and Reg got to do with us?

ANNE: He's asked me to marry him.

BEN (*after a pause*): Which one? (*Pause.*) You're not. (*Laughs*). You can't be.

ANNE: Yes, I am. Do you mind?

BEN: Yes, yes, I mind very much.

Pause, he pulls himself together.

After all, a man's bound to be judged by his wife's husband. The most boring man in London—you said yourself he was the dullest man you'd ever spent an evening with.

ANNE: That was before I got to know him properly.

BEN: And what do you call him now?

ANNE: The dullest man I've ever spent the night with. But I don't mind. Why should you?

BEN: Because—because I shall miss old Tom, that's why. I'm too old to make mature new friendships with bores, far too impatient . . . . .

Ben threatens to make difficulties over the divorce, but he is not serious. He complains of a scarcity of pleasure in their marriage, and Anne informs him that she took no pleasure at all, but she never entered marriage for the fun in it, nor did Ben. Ben, she understands, married her because he was frightened, or wanted to find out what marriage would be like. Ben replies with disparaging banter about Tom and about some of Anne's personal idiosyncrasies—but beneath it all he is really approaching the moment of asking Anne not to marry Tom.

Just as he does so, Edna opens the door, sees the husband and wife scene, and quickly exits. Anne tells Ben that Tom has asked her to live with him until they can get married and she wants to know whether Ben will make difficulties. Instead of replying, Ben asks if she can remember when and where was the last time they made love as husband and wife, "Joey and I were trying to work it out."

> *Anne rises. He jumps away, as if expecting a blow, shields his face, then laughs, shakily.*

BEN: You're going to live with him *until* you get married, did you say? At least that's a realistic prospectus. (*He calls out, as Anne leaves.*) 'Bye, darling. 'Bye bye, sweet princess, goodbye . . .

> *He closes the door behind her and stands pulling at the cotton wool on his chin. He pulls it off.*

Ahh, Butley is himself again. (*Hums "Christ the Lord," then sings:*)
> Christ your breath is bad today
> Haa-aa-al-it-osis. Haa-aa-

> *He breaks off, trembling. He sits down at his desk, puts his hand to his face, takes it away, looks at it, touches his chin, inspects his fingers.*

Bloody woman! Bloody woman!

> *He feels in his pocket and takes out more cotton wool. Curtain.*

ACT II

In the office after lunch, Ben is lounging in the armchair listening to Miss Heasman read her essay on *A Winter's Tale*. Ben tries without much success to feign interest in its academic cliches, its groping metaphors. After the reading is ended, Ben finds that Miss Heasman hopes to be an English teacher if she can pass her exams. He tries to usher her out of the office without commenting further on her essay, but she insists on leaving it with him for written comment.

After Miss Heasman departs, Ben holds his nose as he drops her essay onto his desk. But she has returned to the door and has seen Ben's gesture of disgust at her work. They stare at each other for a moment, then Miss Heasman runs off.

Ben makes a telephone call to the headmaster of the school where Tom teaches. Assuming a Scottish accent, he identifies himself as "Tom's fiancee's husband" and hints broadly at the unsavory procedures which will take place in the process of divorce before his two staff members (since Anne has just gotten a job there too) can pursue their love affair.

Having delivered his unsettling message to Tom's boss, Ben takes a swig of Scotch whiskey from a bottle in his bag, just as Joey comes back. Joey reports that on the way here he has encountered Edna "very upset" and Miss Heasman with face averted "as if she were in tears."

Ben reproaches Joey, with more than a trace of bitterness, for neglecting to tell him about Tom and Anne (Joey had learned about them from Reg, who, it seems, has some sort of professional dealings with Tom).

BEN: . . . . . It must have been amusing to hear me chatter mindlessly on about my marriage, eh?

JOEY: I tried to warn you.

BEN: But was it amusing? Was it fun?

   (*Pause.*)

Are you going to answer me?

JOEY: Sorry. I took the question to be rhetorical.

BEN (*going over to him*): All right. Let me ask you, then, why you promised not to mention to your best friend—is that presuming?—that his wife was being screwed by, while contemplating marriage to, the most boring man in London? Is that question sufficiently unrhetorical?

JOEY: Because I didn't think it was my business.

BEN: Not your business? And how many personalities and dramas over which we've gossiped and whinnied in the past years have been our business? There have been some pretty sticky silences between us recently, and here you were, my dear, in possession of a piece of information that was guaranteed to raise at the very least an amused eyebrow?

JOEY: All right, because I'm a coward, that's why. I'm sorry.

   (*Pause.*)

I *am* sorry, in point of fact.

BEN: Matters of fact and points of fact have been cluttering your syntax since you started going steady with that butcher's boy.

JOEY: I'm sorry because I hoped it wouldn't happen. Now it's a fact and I wish it weren't.

Joey believes Ben could still get Anne and Marina back if he really tried. But Ben isn't concerned with his marriage at the moment; he is enjoying the attempt to hound Tom from his job. Joey decides to go off to the now-open library but stays when he finds that Ben's next phone call is to Reg's office. Joey puts down the receiver and agrees, helplessly, to spend the evening with Ben after all, at Bianchi's or at home—but he will not invite Ben to join him and Reg.

Ben threatens to phone Reg and arrange to meet without Joey if necessary, and Joey warns him: "It'll be much better if you leave that side of my life alone. (*His voice shaking.*) I can't stop you from phoning him up, you can do it any time, Ben, I'm just advising you, because I don't think you'll get much fun from him, I really don't. I know you've had a bad day already, with Tom and Anne, but you're making it worse."

In defiance of this warning Ben phones Reg's office but he is not there, somewhat to Joey's relief. Ben drops the Scotch bottle into his pocket just as Edna comes in.

Edna is both hurt and angry because, it seems, the student Gardner has told James that he isn't getting anything out of Edna's seminars and would like to study T. S. Eliot under Butley instead. Edna understands that Gardner and

Butley met in a pub and discussed this change, and Ben encouraged the student to go to James with his problems. Ben assures Edna that he didn't take the boy seriously, and Joey pledges to Edna his support in every way.

Edna sees the incident as an example of the disintegration of modern education, and she means to keep Gardner in her class and report him to the Dean if he absents himself. The phone rings—it is James, but Butley is again too busy to talk to him. Edna departs, after announcing: "As education has become optional in this College, I've chose to cancel my classes for the rest of the day."

JOEY: So you did agree to take Gardner in, then.

BEN: One of us took the other in, all right. I shall find out later which way around it is.

JOEY: You'll enjoy that, I'm sure.

BEN: I deserve it, after all this.

JOEY: And what about Edna?

BEN: Bloody woman, that's all about Edna. She's lucky to be rid of him. It's not my fault she's too vain to admit it.

JOEY: And all you had to do just now was to keep quiet, and then tell Gardner it couldn't be managed.

BEN: But I *am* managing it.

JOEY: Oh Christ! But what for? What the hell for?

BEN: Perhaps I had a sense of vacancies opening up in my life. I needed to fill them perhaps.

JOEY: Then why don't you do it from your legitimate students, instead of fobbing them off and refusing to teach them.

BEN (*sitting in armchair*): I haven't got any legitimate students. They're all bastards. Which is my term of endearment for bores. Gardner's interesting. He actually interests me. At least I think he does, I can't remember him clearly and I'll have to see the hat. You interested me once, dear, and look where it's got you. An Assistant Lectureship. Of course I don't know if my interest can carry you through your board—

JOEY: You mean he'll have a relationship with you, don't you? While all poor Edna can offer him is a relationship with Byron, in a properly conducted seminar.

Ben speculates cruelly that they may have angered Edna enough to endanger Joey's promotion, and he accuses Joey of toadying to Edna—he can remember when Joey was an interesting melancholy youth, rather than a would-be teacher's pet. Joey departs in anger, pursued by Ben's verbal darts. As Ben takes another swig of Scotch, the phone rings. It is an announcement of Reg's arrival to visit Joey, and Ben tells the porter to send Reg on in to the office.

Ben pretends to be very busy with the papers on his desk as Reg—a well-dressed, well-groomed, solid young man—enters. Ben invites Reg to have a seat while waiting for Joey. Ben pointedly mentions his and Joey's sharing of quarters both here and at home and suggests that perhaps Reg could help them tidy things up, make their rooms look better. Reg informs Ben coldly that he is a publisher, not an interior decorator.

Ben apologizes for his boorish behavior the last time they met, and Reg accepts it in a perfunctory manner. Reg offers to wait for Joey out at the porter's desk, but Ben insists that he stay and pours him a drink of Scotch into a noticeably dirty glass. Ben tries to get Reg onto the subject of Tom, but Reg refuses to open up. Ben is left to do most of the talking, and he characterizes his marriage as merely an interlude in his true destiny with Joey.

Ben tries to pump Reg about his past, his origins in the North, his military service with the Gurkhas (Ben never served in the Army; he was, he says, "took queer"). But Reg remains guarded. "In point of fact" he would prefer not to have a second Scotch, but Ben fills his glass anyway. In response to Ben's questioning, Reg reels off his list of books he will publish next month, which includes a sex-and-violence historical novel intended to sell well and help pay for its more distinguished betters. Among these is a very promising— "moving, witty, gracefully organized, genuinely poetic"—novel about the military service, written, to Ben's added chagrin, by his boring acquaintance Tom.

Joey hasn't read Tom's book yet, and Ben supposes the subject will bore him like nothing else apart from the Latin and English poetry of Milton. Ben's contempt doesn't prevent Reg from remarking that Milton was his special subject in college.

BEN: . . . . . The thing is to confine him to the North. Down here we can dally with Suckling and Lovelace.

REG: And Beatrix Potter? Joey says you've got great admiration for the middle-class nursery poets.

BEN: With reservations. I find some of the novellae a trifle heavy going. (*A pause.*) I call Joey Appley Dappley, did you know?

REG: Do you?

BEN: And he calls me Old Mr. Prickle-pin. After "Old Mr. Prickle-pin, with never a coat to put his pins in." Sometimes I call him Diggory Diggory Delvet, when he's burrowing away at his book.

> *There is a pause.*

REG: What did you mean by being took queer?

BEN (*coyly*): Oh, you know, I'm sure. (*Laughing.*) You do look shocked, Reg.

REG: That's surprising, because I'm not surprised even.

BEN: You don't think there's anything shameful in it, then?

REG: In what?

BEN: Dodging the draft.

REG: There are thousands of blokes from working-class homes who couldn't. They didn't know the tricks. Besides, they'd rather have done ten years in uniform than get out of it that way.

BEN: Then you think there's something shameful in being taken queer?

REG: I'm talking about people pretending to be what they're not.

Besides, Reg is offended by the word "queer." It turns out that Ben is putting him on; Ben was rejected from military service for a touch of tuberculosis, not because of his sexual habits. He taunts Reg with slang synonyms for "homosexual," but Reg refuses to lose his cool. Finally Ben observes: "Of course they've almost vanished anyway, the old-style queens and queers, the poofs, the fairies. The very words seem to conjure up a magical world of naughty thrills, forbidden fruits—sorry—you know, I always used to enjoy them enjoying themselves. Their varied performances contributed to my life's varieties. But now the law, in making them safe, has made them drab. Just like the heterosexual rest of us. Poor sods."

Reg feels there's enough emotional action among heterosexuals to keep them all busy. Ben feigns concern for Reg because Ben and Joey are so close that it must be difficult for "any new people we pick up on the side." Even Anne must have felt like an outsider looking in on the metaphorical marriage between Ben and Joey.

The ringing phone interrupts. Again it is James, and again Butley puts him off.

REG: What metaphor would you use when you learned that Joey was going to move in with someone else? Would that be divorce, metaphorically?

BEN (*after a long pause*): What?

REG (*laughs*): Sorry. I shouldn't do that. But I was thinking that it must be odd getting news of two divorces in the same day.

BEN (*pause*): Joey hasn't said anything.

REG: No. I'm giving the news. You might say that when he comes to me our Joey will be moving out of figures of speech into matters of fact. Ours will be too much like a marriage to be a metaphor.

BEN (*little pause*): I thought you didn't admit to being—what? Different?

REG: There are moments when frankness is necessary. No, our Joey's just been waiting for the right queen, fruit, fairy, poof or homosexual to come along. He's come.

BEN (*after a pause*): Well, isn't he lucky.

REG: Time will tell. I hope so. But I'm tired of waiting to make a proper start with him. I'm tired of waiting for him to tell you. You know our Joey— a bit gutless. No, the truth of the matter is I've been trying to get Joey to bring you around to dinner one evening and tell you straight, so we could get it over with. I knew he'd never find the nerve to do it on his lonesome. But he's kept dodging about, pretending you were busy, one excuse after another. It's worked out quite well though, hasn't it?

The door opens. Joey comes in, sees Reg.

Hello. We've just been sorting things out. Ben and I.

BEN (*to Joey*): Cheers.

Joey stands staring from one to the other.

Yes, our Reg has just been giving me the second instalment of the day's news. But then traditionally, because metaphorically, I should be the last to hear.

Joey had wanted to tell Ben himself—of course—but couldn't quite bring himself to it. Reg suggests that they go move Joey's things from Ben's apartment, but Joey can't leave for the day just yet—he has a commitment to Edna. Reg and Joey decide to go out for a cup of tea, however, but Ben delays them. Ben suggests they all have supper together anyhow. Reg declines—he has two tickets for a game that evening.

Once again Reg and Joey try to depart but Ben stops them—this time on a stronger, more hostile pretext. He ridicules Reg for his lower class North Country background: "Personally I don't give a fuck that moom and dud live oop Leeds and all, or that the whole tribe of you go to football matches looking like the back page of the *Daily Mirror* and bellow 'Oop ta Rovers' and 'Clobber busturds' or own a butcher's shop with cush on ta side from parking tickets."

Joey can't help laughing, and Reg notices. Ben continues in this vein accusing Reg of hypocrisy, of not really liking football, of being ashamed of his background. Now Joey feels Ben is going too far, but Reg keeps his cool. Ben goes on taunting Reg: "Have you had plain talk and brass tacks about thyself with moom, when she's back from pasting tickets on cars, lud, eh, or with dud while he's flogging offal, lud? Thou'd get fair dos all right then, wouldn't thee? From our dud with his strup? Or would he take thee down to local and introduce thee round to all t'oother cloth caps? 'This is our Reg. He's punsy. Ooop, pardon Reg lud, omosexual. Noo, coom as right surprise to moother und me, thut it did, mother joost frying oop best tripe and garbuge and me settling down with gnomes to a good read of Mazo de la Roche.' "

Ben laughs at Reg and so does Joey. Reg sees that Joey must have fed Ben this information about his background and he suggests that Joey "sort him out" as he coolly prepares to leave the office. Ben challenges Reg to "sort him out himself," and indeed Reg is angering slowly; he doesn't like playing these games of taunt and insult.

Ben taunts Reg again and again: "Owd sod, feery, punsy—" and finally Reg punches Ben in the stomach, not very hard but hard enough to knock Ben to the floor.

At this moment Edna opens the door, sees that something is happening, tactfully withdraws.

Reg is growing contemptuous of Ben. He sees him as pitiful, not worthy of his jealousy or even anger. He departs, leaving Joey to make his peace with Ben, who tries to laugh off the incident with little jokes about his and Joey's life together, as he slowly pulls himself to his feet. But for Joey the time has come for the truth. He is going to move in with Reg, and he expects their relationship to last a long time.

BEN (*after a pause*): I don't think he'll have you, dear, after your indiscretions and sauciness.

JOEY: Yes he will.

BEN: You'll go running after him, will you? How demeaning!

JOEY: Possibly. But it's better than having him run after me. I've been through that once, I couldn't face it again.

BEN: You love him then, your butcher's boy?

JOEY: Actually, he's not a butcher's boy, in point of fact.

He picks up his briefcase and returns to his desk. Little pause.
His father teaches maths at the university. His mother's a social worker. They live in an ugly Edwardian house . . .

BEN (*after a pause, nods*): Of course, quite nice and creepy. Creepy, creepy, creepy, creepy!

JOEY: I'm sorry.

BEN: Well, thank you anyway for the fiction.

He sits on the hard chair by his desk. Little pause.
So you love him then?

JOEY: No. But I've got to get away from you, haven't I?

BEN: Really? Why?

JOEY (*sits at desk*): For one thing, I'd like to get some work done. During your married year I did quite a bit. I'd like to finish it.

BEN: What?

JOEY: My edition of Herrick.

BEN: If the consequence of your sexual appetites is another edition of unwanted verse then you have an academic duty to control yourself. Could I also mention, in a spirit of unbecoming humility, that if I hadn't taken over your studies when you were an averagely dim undergraduate, you'd never have got a first. Your nature is to settle for decent seconds, indecent seconds, in Reg's case.

JOEY: I know. But those were the days when you still taught. Now you spread futility, Ben. It creeps in, like your dirty socks do into my drawers. Or my clean ones, onto your feet. Or your cigarette butts everywhere. Or your stubble and shaving cream onto our razor. Or your voice, booming out nursery rhymes into every corner of this department, it seems to me. Or your—

BEN: Shut up! That's rehearsed.

JOEY: Thousands of times.

Ben covers whatever he may be feeling with a remark about "preserving the unities" in severing his connections with Anne and Joey on the same day. Ben asks Joey to help staunch the cut on his chin, while reminding Joey that they will still be seeing a lot of each other, sharing this office for example. But Joey has already thought of that, and as Edna comes back Joey begins gathering up books and papers. He is going to move into the empty office next to Edna. Joey exits with a load of books.

Edna tells Ben she has calmed down now, and in future she will try not to be so sensitive in her relations with the unruly new generation. Ben congratulates Edna on her book on Byron, now finished after 20 years' work. She can look back and remember where she was and what doing as she worked on parts of the book—one section was done while visiting a friend named Ursula in her cottage in Surrey (but their relationship ended when Ursula got married along about Chapter Six). Edna inquires about Ben's book on Eliot, and Ben observes pessimistically that he has 20 years more work to do on it.

Their conversation is interrupted by the entrance of the student Gardner. Edna beats a hasty retreat as the young man enters *"wearing a hat with feathers in it, a white Indian shirt, sandals, no socks."* Gardner has come to study Eliot with Ben as per their conversation in the pub, which Gardner recalls as follows: "I told you I couldn't stand Miss Shaft's seminars and you told me I was interesting enough to do Eliot, and that I ought to go and see James. You said he'd pass the buck back to you because whenever he had a problem he converted it straight into a buck and passed it. Actually, you called him Cottontail."

Ben hands the student a book and asks him to read Eliot aloud, never mind whether he understands what he is reading. Joey comes back in, and Ben interrupts the session to introduce them. Ben tells Gardner elaborately that Joey—Mr. Keyston—was once a pupil of his, and now Ben is wearing Mr. Keyston's socks. They all look at Gardner's feet, but of course he is wearing no socks.

Gardner reads a passage of Eliot on the subject of matrimony as Joey finishes clearing up his possessions. As Gardner continues reading, *"Joey looks toward Ben, they exchange glances, then Ben looks away, Joey goes out, closing the door gently."*

Suddenly Ben interrupts Gardner's reading and recites part of a nursery rhyme.

BEN: Ninny Nanny Netticoat,
     In a white petticoat,
     With a red nose,—
     The longer he stands,
     The shorter he grows.
GARDNER: What?
BEN: I'm moving on, Mr. Gardner. I'm breaking new ground.
GARDNER: Oh. (*He laughs.*)
BEN: Furthermore, I hate your hat.
GARDNER: I'm sorry.
BEN: Did you wear it when you bombed the Velium Aristotle? And are you going to wear it for your raids on *Dappley* and *Parsley,* eh?
GARDNER: What?
BEN: It won't do you any good. Aristotle in his Velium stood alone, vulnerable, unreadable and so unread. But *Dappley* and *Parsley* are scattered in nursery consciousnesses throughout the land. They can still be tongued with fire.
GARDNER: What are you talking about?—I wasn't anywhere near the Senate House when that happened. I don't even know what it was about, properly.

BEN: No, you're a personal relationships type of chappie, I can sense that. Please go away. Go back to Miss Shaft.

GARDNER: What? But I can't—after all that trouble—

BEN: Trouble for you, fun for me. Go away, Gardner, and take your plumage with you, I don't want to start again. It's all been a ghastly mistake. I don't find you interesting, any more. You're not what I mean at all, not what I mean at all. I'm too old to play with the likes of you.

> *Gardner puts the Eliot down, goes out. Ben puts the book back, sits at the desk, turns off the desk lamp and tries feebly three times to turn it on again. Curtain.*

GREEN JULIA

A Comedy-Drama in Two Acts

BY PAUL ABLEMAN

Cast and credits appear on page 383

PAUL ABLEMAN was born in Leeds in Yorkshire, England in 1927, but he grew up in the larger cities of London and New York. Green Julia *is his first full-length play. It was first produced at the Edinburgh festival in 1965, at the Traverse Theater, and was later brought to London and was listed by* Best Plays *European editor Ossia Trilling as one of the season's outstanding new British scripts. Ableman had previously written some 50 abstract surrealist playlets put on as part of Peter Brook's Theater of Cruelty and a pair of short plays produced under the portmanteau title* Blue Comedy *by the Open Space under Charles Marowitz's direction. Ableman's published novels include* I Hear Voices, As Near as I Can Get *and* Texts, *and he is the author of plays for television.*

Ableman's most recent play, Little Hopping Robin, *was produced in London by the Almost Free Theater in the spring of 1973. He lives in London, and he is married with one child, a son.*

Time: The present—on a day in late spring

Place: The untidy "digs" in a university town in England shared by Perew and Lacey

ACT I

SYNOPSIS: The room shared by Jacob Perew and Robert Lacey is a comfortable clutter of books, potted plants, furnishings including two divan-beds and a desk with a telephone, and other impedimenta symbolic of long, long student occupancy. Doors lead to a bathroom-lavatory and to the stairs, and a window overlooks the street.

It is 3 p.m. and Bob Lacey—a plant physiologist—is measuring the height of one of his innumerable experimental sprigs of growing green, while his roommate Jake Perew seems to be looking for the match to an odd sock while he packs some of his possessions into an attache case.

Bob puts a Mozart record on the player, somewhat to Jake's annoyance, and records its time of starting in a little notebook. Jake registers his annoyance by picking up a ruler and slamming it on the headboard of a divan. This is a signal for the two roommates to play their private game of assuming identities and acting out a scene improvised on the spot. After obviously long practise during their years of comradeship, they are quick to respond to each other's leads. The scenes vary widely in subject, but each tends to establish one who is an overlord and one an underdog. An aspect of these scenes which never varies is that Jake Perew is always called "Carruthers" and Bob Lacey is always called "Bradshaw."

JAKE: Ah, Bradshaw, I hope I haven't kept you waiting?
BOB: What? (*Catches on.*) Oh, no—no, not at all—sir. I—er—(*Assuming a Welsh accent.*) I think you know WHY I have come, sir.
JAKE: I do know why you have come, Bradshaw. You have come because I summoned you.
BOB: That is exactly the reason, sir.
JAKE: And I think that you, Bradshaw, know why I have summoned you.
BOB: I do, sir, I do indeed.
JAKE: Would it, Bradshaw, tax your powers of expression to state, succintly, why I have summoned you?
BOB: It probably would, sir, yes.
JAKE: Attempt it, Bradshaw.
BOB: It's hard for me, sir. I am not good at expressing myself.
JAKE: Do your best, Bradshaw.
BOB: It will be muddy, sir.

JAKE: Doubtless, Bradshaw. I will endeavor, by poking about in the murky current of your faltering utterances, to extract some small nugget of sense.

"Carruthers," it seems, is dissatisfied with "Bradshaw's" performance as a student—but Jake abandons the game before they get into this scene very far and returns to reality. He turns off the phonograph, and Bob *immediately takes out his notebook and writes down the time.*

Jake is worrying about a friend of his called Julia. He wonders where she can be. Judging by her past performances, he decides, she's probably downstairs in a pub called the Green Man, drinking gin. Julia has been invited by Jake to join the roommates for a farewell party. Wondering why she hasn't yet appeared, they drift into a spy improvisation, but cut it off abruptly. Bob is rather surprised that Jake decided to include Julia in their private festivities.

JAKE: . . . . . Naturally when you suggested a little celebration, a drop of champagne, a spot of nostalgia, I thought of the three of us. We've been very close.

BOB: If you have three objects in a row, the middle one is close to the ones on either side.

JAKE: Bob—why didn't you—ever?

BOB: Because I am keeping myself for Gloria. Gloria is more glorious than Julia.

JAKE: Gloria is—here, let me see that photo again.
        Bob removes a photograph from his inside pocket and hands it to him.
Yes, very dainty. Yes, but—damn it, listen, do you do it with Gloria?

BOB: Oh, we do it a lot, yes. As soon as I arrive in the village, she packs up a little bag and hurries round to my place. Sometimes we don't emerge for days.

JAKE (*returning the photograph*): You know, Julia likes you. She wouldn't have minded. I wouldn't have minded.

BOB: No, it belongs to Gloria.

They go into a short act as camping, woman-hating homosexuals, but soon Jake continues his praise of Julia, while Bob confesses, "I don't like Julia." In Bob's opinion, she cares too much for drinking. Jake admits "I suppose Julia is a trifle horrible." Suddenly Bob launches into the game, but not very far out of real character.

BOB: You see, Carruthers, it's just that—
JAKE: Yes, Bradshaw?
BOB: I feel a little bashful at saying this straight out—
JAKE: I think I can guess.
BOB (*parody so subtle that it might not even be parody*): Our relationship has meant—a great deal to me.
JAKE: It has for both of us been truly ennobling.
BOB: A rich experience.

JAKE: Something above the commonplace.

BOB: I just wanted you to know how I felt—Carruthers.

JAKE: You are a man of rare discrimination, Bradshaw. It's been a unique privilege to have known you. To have—

BOB: Probed the delicacy of my feelings.

JAKE: Sampled the rich store of your mind.

BOB: Paddled in the pools of my probity.

Jake breaks off, wondering where Julia can be. He phones the Green Man, and asks for Mrs. Julia Desmond—yes, she is there. Julia is summoned to the phone. Jake tells her, "I thought you were coming over here. No, Julia—no, Julia—no—I told you—I'm leaving tonight for good. In about two hours. That wasn't me—that was Bob—how do you get everything wrong? Bob is staying here throughout the summer to complete some sadistic experiments. I don't do experiments. I am not a scientist. He is. What? Oh, he tortures maize—the details are ghastly. I'm leaving tonight. No! Next week I'll be in America—or Hong Kong—or somewhere pretty remote. I told you all this. I'm incomparably the most brilliant economist of my time and therefore everyone wants me. I told you—all right then—just finish your drink and then—oh, the champagne! Did you collect the champagne? From Cutler's—you remember?—all right, good. Then when you've lowered your current gin you'll collect the champagne from—yes, it's paid for—from Cutler's and come here? That means you won't be very long, good! Goodbye, Julia. See you soon."

Jake proposes to "give" Julia to Bob as a kind of going-away present. Bob thinks Jake is giving a signal for another charade but soon sees that his roommate is in earnest. Bob declines Jake's offer, suggesting that Julia is too perverted for his taste. Jake denies that Julia is perverted, and they go into a barrister-witness act with Bob as the lawyer eliciting details from "Carruthers" about the time he first met Julia, at a witchcraft and orgy scene.

JAKE: . . . . . Summoning reserves of courage I hadn't known I possessed, I gripped the door handle firmly and flung it open.

BOB: Kindly tell the court what met your eyes.

JAKE: A silent, obscene circle.

BOB: And what was your reaction to this spectacle?

JAKE: I wished I'd brought a bottle.

BOB: You did not shudder in horror at the skulls, the sheep's hearts pierced with holly? The blasphemous treatment of God's word?

JAKE: I did not. For me scripture is scripture, whether it's read forwards or backwards.

BOB: Kindly tell the court what was taking place.

JAKE: People drinking wine.

BOB: Just that?

JAKE: Out of navels.

BOB: I submit, Mr. Carruthers, that you are withholding certain facts. According to the testimony of earlier witnesses, in the dim glow of the candles, which were blasphemously disposed in the shape of an—er—inverted cross—a human form writhed beneath the brutally upraised arm of a woman.

JAKE (*critically*): What's the implication of that—fladge?

BOB: Yeah, fladge!

JAKE: Julia does not go in for fladge!

BOB: Why, you've misled me. I always understood Julia was practically a graduate course in sexology.

Jake suggests that it's Bob's duty to gain experience with other women, the better to love his virginal Gloria. Bob argues, "Julia . . . . . will be desolate. I'm only staying for the summer as you know, and that will be hardly enough for her to have recovered from her grief at losing you." No, Jake counters, Julia won't miss him, she is promiscuous; what's more, she is not costly to entertain. But Bob sees it otherwise: "You are proposing, as a parting act of comradeship, to saddle me with a drunken old whore who'll keep me penniless."

They go into an act as two Viennese-accented doctors pretending to be fetishists and seeking advice from each other. The scene goes well, and at the end both collapse in an "orgasm" of satisfaction at each other's improvisational skill.

Jake thinks perhaps Bob ought to phone Julia at the Green Man, but Bob insists on recapitulating for Jake the importance of his current experiments with maize: how it could grow on now-barren tropical acres and provide fodder for animals, how he has received a grant from the Ministry of Agriculture to stay over the summer and complete his work, how he believes his new strain of maize will require only one-third of the usual water. Jake wonders why Bob is telling him this, what it has to do with Julia, and Bob explains: "It suddenly struck me that you were leaving. I felt it would be a pity if you left without knowing something about my work." Furthermore, Bob declares (as he turns a record over and makes another jotting in his ever-present notebook), "I have no desire to be pinned onto her—as a—sort of medallion to remind her of you," a mere manifestation of Jake's persistent egotism.

BOB: . . . . . I'm going to miss you Carruthers, I really am. I'm going to miss you, but I'm going to be all right. I'm going to finish my experiments. And then do you know what I am going to do? I'm going to court Gloria. I am going to court Gloria in a slow, dignified, very British way that will probably lead to wedlock. That's why, the next time I see Gloria, I don't want to have to confess to her that I've been fornicating with the most depraved old whore in Southern England.

JAKE (*angry*): That's a viciously inaccurate way of describing Julia!

BOB: Well, it may be. I have no intrinsic desire to denigrate the lady. I just want to impress upon you, Jake, the desirability of not treating people as toys.

JAKE: You seem to think it would in some way profit me if you were to have an affair with Julia?

BOB: Well, I think it would, yes. That's the way you're constructed.

JAKE: How would it profit me?

BOB: There's such a thing as psychological profit—you know, the gratification of power drives. Some people get a big kick out of manipulating others.

JAKE: I never manipulate anyone.

BOB: I would say you do.

JAKE: Who?

BOB: Not only me. I think you manipulate a lot of people—not crudely, of course. You do it by influence, by natural authority, by jocular suggestion—

JAKE: Do you really mean this?

BOB: Yes, I do. I think you get kicks from manipulating others.

JAKE (*brooding*): I think you may be right.

BOB: Why even our game—

JAKE: Our game?

BOB: Didn't it ever strike you? Mark you, I'm not criticizing our game. I enjoy it. I love playing it. But for me, it's a diversion, whereas for you—
        Pause.

JAKE: Well?

BOB: Think, who is usually—not always of course—but usually in the star parts? Who is usually the general, the tycoon, the surgeon—

JAKE (*appalled*): You mean—you seriously mean—

BOB: It's not just the game. That's only one way in which your power thing manifests itself.

JAKE (*after a long pause*): You've made me self-critical. I've never been self-critical before. I see now that it was my particular strength. (*With mock fervor.*) Oh God, don't let me be self-critical. Keep me, oh Lord, from feeling guilt.

BOB: Father Carruthers?

JAKE (*automatically*): Yes, Father Bradshaw?

BOB (*assuming Irish accent*): I was very moved by that little prayer, Father. Would you mind just teaching it to me?

JAKE: Not at all, Father Bradshaw. Just repeat—no, it's no good. I'm self-conscious.

BOB (*persuasively*): Now, Father Carruthers, you wouldn't be denying me a little hand up the ladder to paradise, would you? Candidly, I was never a man for composing neat prayers and I'd esteem it a great kindness—

JAKE: Useless! I'm self-conscious.

Jake is unable to get into the spirit of the game in this momentary condition of self-awareness. He calls the Green Man again and is told that Julia has left, so she should be arriving any minute. Meanwhile, Bob wants to know "What makes you think Julia likes me?" and Jake explains that she doesn't necessarily actively *like* Bob but would probably not be unapproachable, particularly on Jake's recommendation.

Bob decides that maybe he *should* consider taking up with Julia, and he wants to know more about her. For example, how long after Jake's first meeting Julia did their first lovemaking take place? Jake remembers that it took about four hours and quite a lot of rum—and wasn't particularly satisfactory until the next time. Bob takes his notes and looks up sexually symbolic words in the medical dictionary while Jake explains that this was his first time with a woman without paying. Jake also provides the information that Julia is the mother of four, two out of and two in wedlock, the latter awarded to her husband by an unsympathetic court because of Julia's apparent "total moral delinquency."

Abruptly, Bob reassumes the role of Father Bradshaw and insists that Jake join him in the game. Jake can't seem to get interested, but Bob manages to evoke a response by kneeling in front of Jake and calling him "Your Grace." Gradually the spirit of the game flows back into Jake, and he begins to enjoy playing the bishop to Bob's repentent priest.

When this charade is finished, Jake decides that he now understands why Bob pressed him into it.

JAKE: . . . . . You did it because you realized that it is essential that I retain my capacity for play.

BOB (*astounded*): Your capacity—(*Ironically.*) Oh, you'll need that item certainly! Yes, when you get out there, to Hong Kong, or New York, when you get to grips with life's stern realities, you'll need your capacity for play—incidentally, where are you going?

JAKE: It's by no means certain yet.

BOB: Well, let's say it's Hong Kong—Hong Kong is a colorful city, a prosperous and thriving one and has just enough of a colonial flavor left to make a white man—

JAKE (*offended*): Now, there you go—

BOB: No, I was not implying any disreputable wallowing. I just meant that it had an exotic atmosphere. Now, I see you Jake, in Hong Kong, cruising down a palm-fringed avenue at the wheel of your four-litre superwagon! You are just returning from dinner with the Chief of Police where, over brandy and opium, you have been telling him how to clean up the drug racket. Such was the plausibility of your advice that you have secured yet another influential friend. In addition, the Chief's secretary—no, his daughter—a sophisticated and wonderfully enticing bird—showed unmistakably that she was far from unmoved by your rich personality. However, that is for the future. You are now on your way home to your opulent little bachelor penthouse to freshen up in the scented bath that your houseboy is even now running for you so that you can keep your appointment with—Gilda! Gilda, who knows everyone in Hong Kong from the diplomats to the fascinating creatures that weave through the lurid underworld—Gilda, whose friendship is a key to all the delights of this fabulous city. And you Jake, you have long since progressed past friendship. You lie back—not smug but content with the progress you have made in the two crowded days since your arrival, content with the powerful friends you have won, the ravishing mistresses you have acquired. And then—

JAKE: And then?

BOB: And then you suddenly remember that you must always retain your

capacity for play. You shout to your house boy, tell him to stash away your tuxedo, and lay out your—
Thoughtful pause.
Cowboy suit!
JAKE (*bleakly*): Oh, my cowboy suit? Well, that was certainly a very diverting story.

Jake liked the story for its own sake, and he dislikes the thought that Bob might have meant it as a lightly satirical analysis of his character. He wants to believe in it as a real story, much to Bob's amusement.

Suddenly Jake wonders again where Julia can be. Jake confesses that he has made love to Julia only ten or a dozen times during all the time they've known each other, and there was never any pretense that he was "the exclusive recipient of her favors." During their most recent intimate encounter, Jake told Julia that he was leaving town soon, and to his great surprise Julia made a scene: "She pointed out that she was no longer young—she said she'd grown to depend on our relationship—she said that I owed her things—" Jake isn't clear what she meant by "things," but he guesses she meant abstractions.

Bob suggests that Jake has been using Julia for his own selfish purposes and is now a prey to guilt feelings. Bob begins to suspect that there was an ulterior motive in Jake's suggestion that Bob take up with Julia where Jake left off—and Jake confesses that these suspicions are true. Jake was uneasy about leaving Julia and wanted to see her settled, "But I also thought—perfectly genuinely . . . . . that the relationship might be of real benefit to you both."

Again they wonder where Julia can be. Jake believes she must have left the Green Man, but Bob insists that he phone to find out—and when he does, sure enough, Julia is still there. Julia comes to the phone, and Jake almost pleads with her to join them as she had promised. He can't understand why she just sits there drinking. After completing this unsatisfactory phone conversation, Jake complains to Bob: "Three days ago she claimed to be in love with me . . . . . and now she won't even take a ten-minute walk to say goodbye. Isn't that baffling?"

Julia was once an art student (Jake informs Bob), and now she takes pleasure in making crude little ceramic ornaments which she gives away to her friends. All at once, Bob has an intuition that Jake is in love with Julia. Jake must be "a double-distilled bastard," Bob concludes, for abandoning the girl he loves because he can't imagine her fitting into his life in Hong Kong.

Jake challenges Bob to describe to him how he feels about Gloria, forces Bob into the cliche that love creates a pink glow in everything. Jake demands to see Bob's photo of Gloria, points out that Julia doesn't have Gloria's "brand-new, untouched by human hand look," nor does she make things look pink to Jake, nor does she fit his image of what his wife should be. Jake wants a wife to complement his career, and perhaps to share an adventurous life lived more for kicks than for ideals. Jake believes that maybe some day a Messiah will come and lead them all back into a beautiful garden.

JAKE: . . . . . And when that day comes I hope to be among the first to recognize and exalt him. (*Briskly.*) In the meantime—we need that champagne!

BOB (*frustrated*): Jake—you—you—

JAKE: Yes, we must have the champagne. And since it is becoming humiliatingly clear that Julia—rot her disloyal bones—will not voluntarily budge, I must to the Green Man to pry her loose.

> *He goes out briskly. We hear the sound of his footsteps descending the stairs. Bob sits down and puts on a record. Soon we hear Jake's footsteps remounting the stairs. He enters.*

(*Muttering.*) Bloody umbrella!

> *He finds his umbrella and proposes to leave again but suddenly pauses and contemplates Bob, who is absorbed in his record.*

(*Sharply.*) You! Boy! Bradshaw!

BOB (*springing to his feet*): Yeah, baas? Yeah, baas Carruthers?

JAKE: What do I feed you for, boy?

BOB: Why baas—

JAKE: Don't I feed you, boy, so that you'll keep the homestead tidy?

BOB: That's right, baas.

JAKE: Then why is it always such a shit-heap, boy? Tell me that.

BOB: I's sorry, baas.

JAKE: Now, I'm coming back with a lady, boy, you understand? Don't wink at me, you rascal! And keep away from the keyhole this time! Now if you want me to keep you, boy—and you're such an idle dog I don't see why I should—just pitch in and smooth up the compound a bit. Come on, jump!

> *Bob begins furiously tidying up.*

That's it—stack all those scientific papers—the corn laws there—stack them neatly on the shelves—sweep, dust and lick out a few of the crystal goblets— I want this place sparkling when I get back—now, sweat, you hound, sweat!

> *With a faint snarl, he goes out. Bob, at a somewhat slower and more reflective pace, continues tidying up. He bends down to remove something from the table and notices the photograph of Gloria which Jake deposited there. He stops work abruptly. He picks up the photograph and gazes at it curiously for some time. He smiles slightly. He starts to replace it in his inside pocket, stops, stands motionless for a second, then drops it in the wastepaper basket. He starts absently tidying up once more. Curtain.*

ACT II

Fifteen minutes later, the room is somewhat neater and Beethoven is on the record player as Jake enters with three bottles of champagne. Bob is at the table making up a small package. It's not—as Jake expected—a parting gift, but a package of Bob's maize seeds to be planted in Hong Kong or wherever

Jake winds up, and to be photographed for the experiment when it finally grows.

Jake thinks that Julia has arrived before him and must be behind the closed bathroom door. He is wrong; she may have started toward the house a few minutes ago, but she hasn't shown up. She wasn't drunk, Jake reports, she had just lost her sense of time in chatting with the other bar patrons. Bob suspects that Jake sent Julia on ahead, while he went to get the champagne, as part of his scheme to throw Julia and Bob together.

Bob and Jake attack the champagne, playing the game as two Frenchmen fighting a duel with champagne corks. After the corks fly, they drink from the bottles and their first toast is "To hell with Julia!"

Jake wants to toast some woman on his last evening, even Gloria, but Bob pretends that he won't let him have the photograph. Again Jake wonders where Julia can be. He phones the pub again, but Julia isn't there. She seems to have vanished.

BOB: . . . . . Get the police onto it—track her down—she's too valuable to lose—

JAKE: How do you mean?

BOB: She knows too much. You said so—she knows all about perversion—and semi-alcoholism and mistreating children—she's a rare specimen—she must be found and donated to the nation—

JAKE (*narrowly*): Bob, tell me—in *one* word—without reflection—what do you think of Julia?

BOB: Well, I think she's—green!

JAKE (*delighted*): Green? Ah ha. Green is very good.

BOB (*thoughtfully*): Green like—decay—

JAKE (*indignant*): Like decay? What do you mean like decay?

BOB: I mean, well—like her way with children—now you told me that—how she'd slide off boozing and leave the kids—that's the main thing I don't like—

JAKE: I agree. That is bad. It's true. Julia has faults.

BOB: Oh, that's my view. I think she has faults—bloody great fissures into which mountaineers tumble—

JAKE: Great! Freud would have danced a jig if he'd heard that one! (*Pause.*) When you said green—green Julia—I personally thought of the meadows and the forests which are generous like Julia. Which expect no kindness, like Julia. Which are both lovely and harsh, like Julia. I agree it is not good to leave babies to cry but it *is* good to make a fuss of people whom others shun—perhaps because they are black or poor—or vulgar.

BOB: Is that how Julia goes on?

JAKE: That is how she does things.

BOB: Making a fuss of poor, black vulgarians—

JAKE: She has no social inhibitions—she's spontaneous—

BOB: Natural.

JAKE: Open.

BOB: Candid. She has a warm, ingenuous nature.

JAKE: People like her. People miss her. No one regrets having known her.

BOB: No one gets much of a chance to know her. I wonder where she did get to this time?

JAKE: I think I can guess—she is probably—comforting someone—

BOB: Some—orphan—

JAKE: Exactly. Some orphan. Just after I left her she must have met an orphan who looked at her pitiably—

BOB: Who addressed her pathetically, with these words: "Beautiful lady, do you come from heaven?" To which Julia replied—

JAKE: With a silvery tinkle—

BOB: You mean she dropped a bottle?

JAKE: With a silvery tinkle which expressed the authentic note of sanctity: "Fear not, little child. I am of this earth—"

BOB: Earthy.

JAKE: "But let me be an angel to you, little child."

BOB: What's happened to angels? England used to be stiff with them. Every woman was an angel of some kind—where have they all got to? I want an angel.

JAKE: They have taken flight. They have gone into history. Anyway, I thought you had an angel. Gloria—Gloria . . . . .

They jump into the game, with Bob playing a TV interviewer questioning Jake on the subject of the modern state. Jake bumbles through a series of generalizations, but finally ends the interview scene with an abrasive comment: "The Victorians had all kinds of sentimental shit which they fed each other because they could not tolerate the existence of the human genital organs. That was the root trouble with the Victorians. In addition the whole damn country was a disgusting industrial slum. And that is the point I've been trying to make. Thank you."

It occurs to Jake that something bad may have happened to Julia, some kind of heart attack or other illness. All at once the telephone rings. It's Julia calling from another pub, the Wheatsheaf. She gives Jake an explanation on the phone. Jake tells her that he would like to see her just once more before he leaves and only has 37 minutes before the taxi arrives, but Julia hangs up on him. Jake repeats Julia's story to Bob: she was on her way when a car drew up beside her. It was her husband. He had driven down from London and was on his way to Julia's to tell her that his mistress had died and he wanted Julia to return to him. He happened to pass her, and she got into the car and drove off with him. Julia assured Jake on the phone that she would get rid of her husband quickly and come right over.

Jake confesses that he truly yearns to see Julia just once more, he would even take her to the railroad station with him in his taxi. Jake decides to open the third bottle of champagne, which was to have been Julia's. Jake urges Bob to give him some details about his relationship with Gloria. Bob calls Jake "a foul, verbal voyeur," but Jake is insistent and Bob starts to reminisce about a night he and Gloria left a dance early and walked home along a footpath beside a stream.

JAKE (*mildly*): Gloria—what was she wearing?

BOB: The sort of dress a modest girl like Gloria would be wearing. (*A little more indulgently.*) It was modest but provocative as well. (*With great deliberation.*) We set off with buoyant strides and we had covered about a mile in relative silence when Gloria suddenly said: "Oooh."

JAKE: Just what were you at?

BOB (*loftily*): I was at the moment several paces behind her, the path being narrow and rocky at that point. Gloria suddenly stopped and said "Oooh."

JAKE: What had prompted this exclamation?

BOB: Gloria had seen a fish. She had seen a fish jump—she said that it was a large fish and she had clearly seen the flash of its silver scales as it flipped itself above the rushing waters.

JAKE: I bet you waited to see if that big fish would jump again?

BOB: Oh, we did! We both felt a powerful impulse to watch and see if that fish would spring again out of the stream. To beguile the vigil, we sat down in the warm grass beside the brook. It was a most mild evening and yet so concerned was I lest Gloria be exposed to the least ripple of air that I put my arm over her shoulders. She, naturally, nestled against me and, in that harmonious posture, we scanned the surface of the boiling rill.

> *Throughout the remainder of this speech and until he interrupts it, Jake performs the following actions, Bob being too absorbed in his narrative to notice them. Jake absently picks up the empty champagne bottle, carries it to the wastepaper basket, pauses, replaces the bottle on the table, picks up the wastepaper basket, gazes into it, removes from it the photograph which Bob deposited there at the end of the first act, considers the photograph with pleasure slowly replaced by astonishment, glances questioningly from Bob to the photograph several times, making gestures suggestive of incomprehension.*

After what seemed a long age of the world, Gloria relaxed and drew me down over her. For some time we did not move. We were content just to feel the warm contact of each other's bodies. Very slowly, I allowed my head to—

JAKE (*bluntly, frowning*): Where is the photograph?

BOB (*reproachfully*): Do not interrupt.

JAKE: Just tell me where that photograph is?

BOB (*understanding what has happened*): Here against my heart.

JAKE: The one of Gloria?

BOB: Certainly.

JAKE (*displaying it*): Then who is this damsel?

BOB: That? Isn't she sweet? That's Elaine.

Lightly, Bob banters with Jake, telling him the photograph is Suzy—Selma—Louisa—Jane—Mary . . . At last he explains that this is the photo of one

Molly Carboy, whose mother breeds horses. Bob has never met Molly. Molly's mother showed the photo to Bob one day and absent-mindedly left it with him; Bob calls the girl in the photo Gloria because he likes the name.

Jake is surprised to discover that Bob has been telling lies about having a fiancee. Bob pleads that it is all part of their game, but Jake insists: "Our game is no analogue. Our game is a mutual and mutually agreed-upon exercise of the imagination. It deceives no one. It is not a lie. Gloria is a lie."

Bob argues that Gloria is a most practical answer to the frequent and annoying question, "Bob I never see you chasing the girls." Bob goes on to tell Jake he cannot bear the unhappy contradictions of human reality. For example, the unequal distribution of food, with many having too little while a few have too much, sickens Bob. He doubts the world, he even doubts himself and his own motives, he doesn't want power or even the commitment represented by love and marriage, he hopes only to be useful.

The phone rings and as usual it is Julia who has finally gotten rid of her husband and still wants to join the party. Jake tells her she might just have a goodbye glimpse if she hurries, then he pretends that he has a message for Julia from Bob: "He asked me to say—he wanted you to know—well, he's really very shy and he didn't feel—anyway, he thinks you're great—that's all really—What's Bob really like? No, he's not in the room. Julia, would I have shared digs with him for years if—all right, I just wanted you to know that— well, if you feel lonely you'll always be able to pop around and drag Bob from his maize for a couple of hours . . . . ."

Jake hangs up the phone and informs Bob that Julia has decided not to go back to her husband. Bob is upset by Jake's "antics." What Jake has just told Julia about Bob may cause great embarrassment. Bob may even have to bring back Gloria in order to fend off Julia. And Bob's distress lies even deeper than mere embarrassment.

BOB: . . . . . I am humiliated that knowing me as well as you do you still regard me as a case likely to respond to such superficial therapy—

JAKE: Now that is not what I—

BOB: A case I may very well be. But it is undeniably humiliating that you have failed to perceive that the malady—if there is one—must be fairly deep-seated by now. If therefore I shun the path of riot and indulgence, it is not— and I could have hoped that you would have understood that it is not—because of any simple block that can be shattered by a couple of sessions with a drunken old whore!

JAKE (*resentfully*): Good! Well that's good! And the maize—I bet the maize will be great! I bet that will be great maize and I am going to plant it for you, Bob, and I am going to take pictures of it for you and one day, when Africa and India and South America are all getting fat on it, why, I'll cheer for you and boast that I knew you when. It's a terrific deal for you, Bob, because you can twist a few genes and—bingo—a savior.

He snaps the music off. Bob makes a note.

Still, you have to come out of the lab sometimes! Julia? I was too ambitious for you. A docile ghost like Gloria is about your speed. And then again, Julia may not be particularly fastidious—bless her—but she does have a weakness for flesh and blood.

He throws Gloria's photo on the floor.

BOB: Meaning?

JAKE: Meaning, she might not be able to stomach you!

BOB (*hurt*): I gather Julia has a pretty strong stomach.

JAKE (*savagely*): That's right—she's just an old whore!

BOB (*reason's last stand*): Well, *isn't* she? I mean, you're a fund—you're a brimming cauldron of warm humanity, Jake, but must all distinctions dissolve in it? I'm not now asking for precise scientific ones but do we really—just to satisfy your craving for boozy comradeship—do we really have to call chalk caviar and Julia an angel?

JAKE (*smiling grimly*): No—no—it's mad—

BOB: Well, it is mad!

JAKE: No, I mean—you're right—distinctions are very important—I often use them myself—but it's mad—

BOB: Well, what is mad?

JAKE: You see, I do understand you. Julia—the kids—she behaved terribly with the kids—whom, incidentally, she adores—because she is weak—weak, human, weak. The trouble is that for you, Julia is defined by her weaknesses—classified once and for all like a bloody plant. I call that mad.

Jake grabs a potted plant and smashes it to the floor. The doorbell rings.

Ah, the lady herself. You're saved. (*Goes to the door and calls.*) Julia? Come on up—the door's open.

Bob rushes to his destroyed plant, kneels over it.

Hello, Jul—what? The taxi? Good God, is it time? Right, well—er—look, wait for me, will you? I won't be two minutes. (*He returns.*) It's the taxi. (*Awkward silence. Jake relents.*) You can—keep her at bay? She may be really worked up by now, you know? Can you handle her?

BOB (*miserably, still trying to save his plant*): Oh, well—I should be a match for Julia—(*A joke which falls flat.*) After all, I lead a healthier life.

JAKE (*skirting Bob and the shards*): Where is my little case? Ah, here is my little case. I think I've got everything—that lot is to be collected.

There is by now unbreachable constraint between them—although both would like to breach it.

BOB: So you're off—to Hong Kong—

JAKE: Possibly—to Hong Kong—

BOB: Well—any of that champagne left?

Jake pours a couple of glassfuls.

Well—Hong Kong—Gilda—

JAKE (*curtly*): Cheers. (*They drink.*) Give the—the green woman my love—if you can bear to. I'll let you have my address and you can ship me the instructions—about the maize—

BOB: They won't be very complex—

JAKE: I'll apply myself. Well—that's about it then—

They shake hands stiffly. Jake takes up his valise and umbrella and moves toward the open door. He pauses, half turns, half smiles and moves a fraction toward Bob. He speaks gently.

See you, Bradshaw.

BOB (*wryly, without looking at Jake*): See you, Carruthers.

Jake goes out, closing the door behind him. Bob stands immobile, listening to Jake's feet descending the stairs and then the sound of the front door slamming. He turns heavily and sits on his bed. He takes a record and puts it on the turntable. He sits, half listening to the music. After long enough to establish Jake's irrevocable departure, the doorbell rings. Julia has arrived. With little outward movement, Bob conveys agitation. It rings again, Bob sits tight. It rings a third time. Bob slowly, almost without volition, rises, his hands fumble briefly at his tie. He moves to the photo on the floor. The doorbell rings again, urgently. He destroys the photo, turns the music off and throws his notebook away (its exact purpose still unexplained). He moves out onto the landing and off down the stairs as the stage swiftly darkens. Curtain.

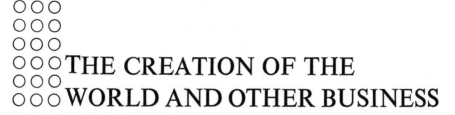

THE CREATION OF THE WORLD AND OTHER BUSINESS

A Play in Three Acts

BY ARTHUR MILLER

Cast and credits appear on page 344

ARTHUR MILLER was born in New York City, like the majority (52 per cent) of our established dramatists; the date was October 17, 1915. His mother was also a native New Yorker. His father, the owner of a small manufacturing business, came to this country from Austria when he was a child. Miller grew up in New York, attending James Madison and Abraham Lincoln High Schools and then working for two years in an auto parts warehouse before going to college at the University of Michigan.

At Michigan Miller studied playwriting, wrote a play that won prizes and received his B.A. in 1938. Returning to New York, he worked in the Federal Theater Project and the CBS and NBC radio workshops. A Hollywood studio hired him to tour Army camps to collect background material for Ernie Pyle's The Story of G.I. Joe, *which experience Miller described in the diary report* Situation Normal, *published in 1944. Among Miller's other extra-theatrical works were* Focus *(1945, a novel about anti-Semitism),* The Misfits *(1961, a screen play) and a volume of short stories,* I Don't Need You Any More, *which includes the O. Henry Award winners* Mont Sant' Angelo *and the title story, and the previously unpublished* Fitter's Night, *set in the Brooklyn Navy Yard, where Miller worked for a time during World War II.*

Miller's first Broadway production was The Man Who Had All the Luck *(1944, 4 performances). His subsequent playwriting career has been one of the theater's most distinguished. All eight of his original works after this first one have been named Best Plays of their seasons, as follows:* All My Sons *(1947, New York Drama Critics Circle Award),* Death of a Salesman *(1949, Critics Award, Pulitzer Prize),* The Crucible *(1953),* A View From the Bridge *(1955, on the same program with* A Memory of Two Mondays*),* After the Fall *(1964),* Incident at Vichy *(1965),* The Price *(1968) and now* The Creation of the World and Other Business. *Miller also adapted Ibsen's* An Enemy of the People *in 1950. Three of his works—*All My Sons, Death of a Salesman *and* The Crucible*—have been produced on the screen. Two of them—*After the Fall *and* Incident at Vichy *were written for production by the Repertory Theater of Lincoln Center company during the Elia Kazan-Robert Whitehead regime, and Miller's comments on the failings of the Lincoln Center board to do its part in establishing a repertory company in New York were widely circulated last season after their original appearance in the* Dramatists Guild Quarterly.

Miller has been married three times, and his second wife was the late Marilyn Monroe. He now lives in Connecticut with his third wife, Inge Morath, the photographer (with whom he recently collaborated on a book entitled In Russia*), and his youngest daughter, Rebecca.*

The Best Plays synopses are usually prepared from the actual, final New York stage versions, the equivalent of the stage managers' prompt scripts, which sometimes vary slightly from published versions. In the case of The Creation of the World and Other Business, *however, at the author's request the synopsis has been prepared, not from the short-lived Broadway production, but from the acting version published by the Dramatists Play Service, which Miller declares is the "official" version of his play.*

Three questions on the human dilemma

ACT I

First: Since God made everything and God is good—why did He make Lucifer?

SYNOPSIS: It is night, and the sky is full of stars over *"Paradise, the ultimate Garden,"* represented not by the outlines of linear physical existence but by impressions of color. Only one feature is clearly and representationally visible: the branch of a golden tree from which hangs an apple.

> *God appears on His throne above the acting level. He is deep in thought as He tries to visualize the inevitable future. Now, as light spreads, the caw of a crow sounds, the dawn-welcoming chatter of monkeys, the hee-hawing ass, the lion's echoing roar, seals barking, pigs grunting, the loon's sudden laughter—all at once in free*

STEPHEN ELLIOTT, ZOE CALDWELL, BOB DISHY AND GEORGE GRIZ-
ZARD IN "THE CREATION OF THE WORLD AND OTHER BUSINESS"

cacophony. And as they subside and day is full, one of the shadows moves—a man, Adam, who reaches up above his head and plucks a fig and, propped up against a rock, crosses his legs and idly chews. He is in every way a man and naked, but his skin is imprinted with striped and speckled shadows, an animated congealment of light and color and darkness. God emerges behind and to one side of him. He looks about, at the weather, up at the sky. Then He turns and looks down at Adam, who gradually feels His presence, and with only the slightest start of surprise.

ADAM: Oh! Good morning, God!

GOD: Good morning, Adam. Beautiful day.

ADAM: Oh, perfect, Lord. But they all are.

GOD: I've turned up the breeze a little . . .

ADAM: I just noticed that. (*Holds a hand up to feel it.*) This is exactly right now. Thanks, Lord.

GOD: I'm very pleased with the way you keep the garden. I see you've pruned the peach tree.

ADAM: I had to, Lord. An injured branch was crying all night. Are we going to name more things today?

GOD: I have something else to discuss with you this morning, but I don't see why we couldn't name a few things first. (*He points.*) What would you call that?

ADAM: That? I'd call that a lion.

GOD: Lion. Well, that sounds all right. And that?

ADAM: That? Ahh . . . lamb?

GOD (*trying the word*): Lamb.

ADAM: I don't know what it is today—everything seems to start with L.

GOD: I must say that *looks* like a lamb. And that?

ADAM: L,L,L . . . that should be—ah . . . labbit?

GOD (*cocking his head doubtfully*): Labbit doesn't seem—

ADAM (*quickly*): You're right, that's wrong. See, I was rushing.

GOD: Slow down, we have all the time in the world.

ADAM: Actually, that looks like something that should begin with an R . . . rabbit!

GOD: Rabbit sounds much better.

They name the caterpillar. Adam informs God that he has noticed that all the other Garden creatures come in pairs; only Adam is alone. God confesses that sometimes He acts without knowing the reason till later. Adam was such an instinctive creation—God had a little clay left over after making the chimpanzee, so almost without thinking He made Adam in His own image.

Adam wouldn't mind having a mate so long as she didn't chatter all the time like some of the creatures. God puts Adam to sleep, touches Adam's bottom rib, and watches the shadow-marked female figure of Eve rise from the ground. God approves His newest creation; Adam wakes and studies her.

ADAM (*nervously*): Well . . . she certainly is *different*.

GOD: Is that all?

ADAM: Oh, Lord, she's perfect! (*But he is still uneasy.*)

GOD: I think so, too.

ADAM: Me too.

GOD: Huh! I don't know how I do it! What would you like to call her?

ADAM: Eve.

GOD: Eve! Lovely name. (*Takes her hand.*) Now dear, you will notice many different kinds of animals in this Garden. Each has its inborn rule. The bee will not eat meat; the elephant will not sing and fish have no interest in flowers.—Those are apples on that tree; you will not eat them.

EVE: Why?

ADAM: That's the rule!

GOD: Be patient, Adam, she's very new. (*To Eve.*) Perhaps the day will come when I can give you a fuller explanation; for the moment, we'll put it this way. That is the Tree of Knowledge, Knowledge of Good and Evil. All that you have here springs from my love for you; out of love for me you will not eat of that tree or you will surely die. Not right away, but sometime. Now tell me, Eve—when you look at that tree, what do you think of?

EVE (*looks up at the tree*): . . . God?

ADAM: She got it!

GOD: That's exactly the point, dear.

God leaves Adam and Eve to the Garden that is theirs forever. They examine each other, touching and smelling. They find they have similar thoughts about being hungry, thirsty, about what to do next. Adam explains how he has named everything—the pomegranite, the prndn (Eve takes a prndn out of Adam's head and tells him frankly he has named it badly, it ought to be called "louse"). Adam identifies the many sounds of the Garden for Eve, including the sound of sunset, the crackling of a shadow moving across dry leaves and the conversation of trout in the river.

Adam leads Eve off to see the pools, as the angels Chemuel, Azrael and Raphael enter at the platform level of God's throne above the earth. They are singing hallelujah as God enters and asks to see Lucifer. The others leave as Lucifer enters. Both God and Lucifer have noticed a flaw in God's latest creation: being entirely innocent, Adam and Eve apparently have no urge to multiply. As God points out, "the middle of a perfect, moonlit night, and they're playing handball."

God has asked for Lucifer's advice, but as usual He is angry at Lucifer even before Lucifer has opened his mouth, but Lucifer perseveres.

LUCIFER: All right, all right. You could take her back and restring her insides. Reroute everything, so wherever he goes in it connects to the egg.

GOD: No—no—no, I don't want to fool with that. She's perfect now; I'm not tearing her apart again. Out of the question.

LUCIFER: Well, then. You've only got one other choice. You've got to thin out the innocence down there. (*God turns to him suspiciously.*) See? You're giving me that look again; whatever I say, You turn it into some kind of a plot. Like when You made that fish with the fur on. Throw him in the ocean, and all the angels run around screaming hosannahs. *I* come and tell You the thing's drowned, and You're insulted.

GOD: Yes. But I—I've stopped making fish with fur any more.

LUCIFER: But before I can penetrate with a fact I've got to go through hell.

Lucifer advises God that everything is so perfect in the Garden, it's monotonous. God must make sex seem a holy thing, something very special, like God Himself. This raises the subject of the apple on the Tree of Knowledge— Lucifer feels that this gimmick of forbidden fruit seems unworthy of his Father until its real reason is understood: "You wanted Adam's praise for everything You made, absolutely innocent of any doubt about Your goodness. Why, then, plant a fruit which can only make him wise, sophisticated and analytical? May I continue? (*God half-willingly nods.*) He certainly will begin to question everything if he eats an apple, but why is that necessarily bad? (*God looks surprised, angering.*) He'll not only marvel that the flower blooms, he will ask why and discover chlorophyll—and bless You for chlorophyll. He'll not only praise You that food makes him strong, he will discover his bile duct and praise You for his pancreas. He may lose his innocence, but the more he learns of Your secrets, the more reasons he will have to praise You. And that is why, quite without consciously knowing it, You planted that tree there.

It was Your fantastic inner urge to magnify Your glory to the last degree. In six words, Lord, You wanted full credit for everything."

In perfect innocence, without knowledge, Adam has no way to discriminate good from better; he will kiss a tree as soon as kiss Eve. God insists He knows perfectly well why He placed the apple tree in the Garden.

GOD: . . . . . It was not to tempt Adam; it's I who was tempted. I finished him and I saw he was beautiful, and for a moment I loved him beyond anything I had ever made—and I thought, maybe I should let him see through the rose petal to its chemistry, the formation of amino acids to the secrets of life. His simple praise for surfaces made me impatient to show him the physics of my art, which would raise him to a god.

LUCIFER: Why'd you change your mind?

GOD: Because I thought of what became of you. The one angel who really understands biology and physics, the one I loved before all the rest and took such care to teach—and you can't take a breath without thinking how to overthrow me and take over the universe!

LUCIFER: Lord, I only wanted them to know more, the more to praise You!

GOD: The more they know, the less they will need me, Lucifer; you know that as well as I! And that's all you're after, to grind away their respect for me. "Give them an apple!" If it weren't for the Law of the Conservation of Energy I would destroy you! Don't go near that tree or those dear people—not in any form, you hear? They are innocent, and innocent they will remain till I turn out the lights forever!

God goes out, Lucifer is alone.

LUCIFER: Now what is He *really* saying? He put it there to tempt *Himself!* Therefore He's not of one mind about innocence; and how could He be when innocence blinds Adam to half the wonders He has made? I will help the Lord. Yes, that's the only way to put it; I'm His helper. I open up the marvels He dares not show, and thereby magnify His glory. In short, I disobey what He says and carry out what He means, and if that's evil, it's only to do good . . . . .

Lucifer will complete God's work by persuading Adam to eat the apple and multiply. Lucifer joyously anticipates that his running quarrel with God will therefore come to an end.

He exits as the lights come up on the Garden, where Adam is contemplating Eve's buttocks trying to figure out why he is fascinated by them. He gives up, as Lucifer enters the Garden. (*"Something in Lucifer moves something in Eve . . . . . Lucifer exchanges a deep glance with her."*)

Lucifer tells them he is God's Explainer, he has come to explain that God wants them to eat the fruit of the apple tree and multiply, but can't bring Himself to tell them so. Lucifer eats an apple to show them it's not dangerous, but Adam understands that Lucifer wasn't harmed by it because he's an angel and immune to its poison.

Lucifer tells Adam he could have an angel's knowledge if he would only eat the apple. God put Adam here to praise all creation (Lucifer explains), but in his ignorance of the full meaning of such things as his own penis, Adam is omitting to praise a number of things which he should be praising. This argument moves Adam for a moment, but finally he holds to God's word, refusing to eat.

Adam and Eve exit to go swimming, but soon Eve returns alone. She is curious about Adam's penis. Lucifer promises her all her confusion will clear up if only she will take a bite of the apple. Eve does so and soon becomes aware of her own body. Lucifer runs off as Adam enters. Eve kisses him warmly, then pushes the apple into his mouth and makes him bite. The sound of God's anger is heard in the air. Adam and Eve grab large leaves to cover their nakedness as God appears.

Seeing that they are conscious of their own nakedness, God knows they have eaten the fruit, He knows that Lucifer is to blame, though Eve tries to blame it all on a snake. God curses the serpent, and Eve confesses that she's ashamed.

GOD: Ashamed! You don't know the half of it. I will greatly multiply thy sorrow and thy conception; In sorrow thou shalt bring forth children—

EVE: Oh God!

GOD: And thy desire shall be to thy husband And he shall rule over thee. No more equals, you hear? He's the boss forever. Pull up your leaf. (*He turns to Adam.*) And as for you, schmuck!
Cursed is the ground for thy sake,
In sorrow shalt thou eat of it all the days of thy life.
Thorns and thistles shall it bring forth to thee!
No more going around just picking up lunch.
In the sweat of thy face shalt thou eat bread,
Till thou return unto the ground;
Yes, my friend, now there is time and age and death,
No more living forever. You got it?
For dust thou art.
And unto dust shalt thou return.

ADAM (*sobs*): What am I doing? What's this water?

GOD: You're weeping, my son, those are your first tears; there will be more before you're finished.
Now you have become as one of us,
A little lower than the angels,
Because now you know good and evil.
Adam and Eve? Get out of the Garden.

ADAM: Out where?

GOD (*pointing*): There!

ADAM: But that's a desert!

GOD: Right! It wasn't good enough for you here? Go and see how you make out on your own.

ADAM: God. Dear God, isn't there any way we can get back in? I don't want to be ashamed, I don't want to be so full of sadness. It was so wonderful here, we were both so innocent!

GOD: Out! You know too much to live in Eden.

ADAM: But I am ignorant!

GOD:

Knowing you are ignorant is too much to know.
The lion and the elephant, the spider and the mouse—
They will remain, but they know My perfection
Without knowing it. You ate what I forbade,
You yearned for what you were not
And thus laid a judgement on My work.
I Am What I Am What I Am, but it was not enough;
The warmth in the sand, the coolness of water,
The coming and going of day and night—
It was not enough to live in these things.
You had to have power, and power is in you now,
But not Eden any more. Listen Adam. Listen Eve.
Can you hear the coming of night?

No—they have lost the special sense of hearing, they can no longer hear shadows moving across leaves or trout talking in the river. Sadly, Adam and Eve leave the Garden while Raphael (playing a gloomy bassoon solo), Chemuel and Azrael enter. They try to cheer up God by praising the Rocky Mountains. Azrael, angel of death, would like to kill Adam and Eve, but God isn't ready for that yet.

The human couple is now almost entirely preoccupied with sexual discovery and activity. This irritates God, but when they do glorify His name and send up hosannas it gives Him a very good feeling.

God is coming to a decision about Lucifer, whom he summons after dismissing the other three angels. Lucifer gives God a moment of great joy with the news that Eve is pregnant. Lucifer takes the opportunity to argue that his intervention in the affairs of Adam and Eve must of course have been part of God's plan all the time; Lucifer merely acted as God's instrument. God threatens to punish Lucifer, who baffles Him by insisting that he now understands his own destined role in God's master plan.

LUCIFER: . . . . . All my life, Sir, I've had the feeling that I was somehow . . . a *useless* angel. I look at Azrael, so serious and grave, perfect for the Angel of Death. And our sweet Chemuel—exactly right for the Angel of Mercy. But when I tried to examine *my* character, I could never find any. Gorgeous profile, superb intelligence, but what was Lucifer *for*? Am I boring You?

GOD: Not at all.

LUCIFER (*worried*): How do You mean that? (*God simply looks at him.*) Good, good—don't make it easy for me. I will now explain about the apple. You see, I'd gone down there to help You, but she took one bite and that innocent stare erupted with such carnal appetite that I began to wonder, was it possible I had actually done something— (*He breaks off.*)

GOD: Evil?

LUCIFER: Oh, that terrible word! But now I will face it! (*The desperate yet joyful confession.*) Father, I've *always* had certain impulses that mystified me. If I saw my brother angels soaring upwards, my immediate impulse was to go down. A raspberry cane bends to the right, I'd find myself leaning left. Others praise the forehead, I am drawn to the ass. Holes—I don't want to leave anything out—I adore holes. Every hole is precious to me. I'll go even further—in excrement, decay, the intestine of the world is my stinking desire.

GOD: Where in Heaven do you pick up such ideas?

LUCIFER: You ever hear anything so straightforwardly disgusting? I tell You I have felt so worthless, I was often ready to cut my throat, but Eve is pregnant now, and I see the incredible, hidden truth.

GOD: Which is?

LUCIFER: How can I be rotten? How else but through my disobedience was Eve made pregnant with mankind? How dare I hate myself? Not only am I not rotten—I am God's corrective symmetry, that festering embrace which keeps His world from impotent virtue. And once I saw that, I saw Your purpose working through me and I nearly wept with self-respect. And I fell in love —with both of us.

    Slight pause. God is motionless.
Well, that's—the general idea, right?

GOD: Lucifer, you are a degenerate! You are a cosmic pervert!

LUCIFER: But God in Heaven, who made me this way?

    God whacks him across the face, Lucifer falls to his knees.

GOD: Don't you ever, ever say that.

LUCIFER: Adonoi elohaenu, adonoi echaud. Father, I know Your anger is necessary, but my love stands fast!

GOD: Love! The only love you know is for yourself! You think I haven't seen you standing before a mirror whole years at a time!

LUCIFER: I have, Lord, admiring Your handiwork.

GOD: How can you lie like this and not even blush!

LUCIFER: All right. (*He stands up.*) Now I will tell You the Truth! (*At the pinnacle.*) Lord, I am ready to take my place beside the throne.

God is astounded at this suggestion. Lucifer argues that if good and evil sit side by side in alliance the predestined wars to come on earth will never take place, there can be no war without a sense of absolute righteousness. And if God can love the Devil (Lucifer continues) or even seem to, then He will prove that He loves all His creation, the bad along with the good. Lucifer sees this as God's intended plan, whether God realizes it or not.

But there is a flaw in Lucifer's reasoning: God does *not* love Lucifer: "If God could love the Devil, then God has died." Lucifer holds out his hand to God, but instead of taking it God condemns Lucifer to leave heaven and go live in hell.

LUCIFER: Lord? (*He is upright, stern.*) You will not take my hand?

GOD: Never! Never, never, never!

LUCIFER: Then I will take the world. (*He exits.*)

GOD (*Calling*): And if you ever do, I will burn it, I will flood it out, I will leave it a dead rock spinning in silence! For I am the Lord, and the Lord is good and only good!

ANGELS' VOICES (*singing loudly and sharply*):

Blessed is the Lord our God,

Glory, glory, glory!

God sits, cleaved by doubt. He turns His head, looking about.

GOD: Why do I miss him? (*He stares ahead.*) How strange.

Curtain.

ACT II

Second: Is there something in the way we are born which makes us want the world to be good?

On earth, Lucifer contemplates sleeping Adam and Eve. Eve is clearly pregnant. Lucifer talks to her without waking her, through her subconscious. She is worried about the swelling in her belly, asks the angel to help her get rid of it so she can be beautiful again as she was in Paradise.

Lucifer tells Eve that she is soon to give birth; that God knows and is happy about this. As Eve goes into labor and begins to feel pain, Lucifer points out to her the injustice of the burden placed upon her in contrast to Adam, who suffers no penalty of childbirth. In her pain, Eve is suddenly angry at Adam, but Lucifer directs her anger toward God. Her pain is His fault, Lucifer says, and she can take revenge upon Him by producing a dead baby. But instinctively Eve resists. She wakes up, and Lucifer vanishes along with her nightmare.

Adam wakes up too to the baaing of sheep, the howling of the wind, the gritty necessities of life outside Paradise. The grass is giving out here, so they must soon move on. Eve wishes Adam would dig a hole for them to live in, but Adam refuses: "I wish you'd stop trying to change the rules! We're not groundhogs. If He meant us to live in holes, He would have given us claws."

For some strange reason Eve looks beautiful to Adam today, except for the bulge in her stomach, which Adam attributes to her sudden passion for eating clams. Adam has just had a sweet dream that he was back in the Garden, alone, eating a delicious breakfast instead of sandy figs, naming things, in perfect harmony with his environment. Eve tells Adam of her own dream that an angel visited her. She repeats his message (as Lucifer materializes to listen): "With you the Lord was only somewhat disappointed, but with me He was furious. (*Lucifer gravely nods.*) And His curse is entirely on me. It is the reason why you've hardly changed out here in the world; but I bleed, and now I am ugly and swollen up like a frog. And I never dream of Paradise, but you do almost every night, and you seem to expect to find it over every hill. And that is right—I think now that you belong in Eden. But not me. And so long as I am with you, you will never find it again. (*Slight pause.*) Adam, I haven't the power to move from this place, and this is the proof that I must stay here, and you—go back to Paradise."

Lucifer is pleased with Eve's words. But there is an instinct in Adam that makes him reluctant to leave Eve; besides, he doesn't think the Lord intends him to leave her. He wouldn't even think of it (he implies) except for the ugly bulge in her belly, which he despises. Adam suggests that since it sometimes moves it must be a living thing, and maybe they could kill it. Again, Eve instinctively protects herself, and this angers Adam. He is even more angry when she tells him Lucifer was the angel who visited her in her dream. Finally she discloses the secret she learned from Lucifer.

EVE: There is a man in my belly, Adam.

ADAM (*chilled with astonishment, wonder, fear*): A man.

EVE: He told me.

> *Long pause.*

ADAM: How could a man fit in there?

EVE: Well . . . small. To start off with. Like the baby monkeys and the little zebras.

ADAM: Zebras! He's got you turning us into animals now? No human being has ever been born except grown up! I may be confused about a lot of things, but I know facts!

EVE: But it's what God said—we were to go forth and multiply.

ADAM (*striking his chest indignantly*): If we're going to multiply, it'll be through me! Same as it always was! What am I going to do with you? After everything he did to us with his goddamned lies, you still—

EVE: Husband, he told me to do with it exactly what you have told me to do with it.

ADAM (*struck*): What I . . .?

EVE: He told me it is a man and he told me to kill it. What the Devil hath spoken, thou hast likewise spoken.

> *Silence. Neither moves. One sheep baas, like a sinister snarl. A sudden surge of wind, which quickly dies.*

ADAM (*tortured*): But I had no idea it was a man when I said that.

EVE (*holding her belly with a long gaze beyond them both*): Adam . . . I believe I am meant to bring out this man—

ADAM (*furiously, yet unable to face her directly*): Are you putting me with that monster?

EVE: But why do you all want him dead!

ADAM: I forbid you to say that again! I am not Lucifer! (*A heartbroken cry escapes him.*) Eve!

> *He sinks to his knees. He curls up in ignominy, then prostrates himself before her, flat out on the ground, pressing his lips to her foot.*

Forgive me!

> *He weeps. Wind blasts. It dies.*

EVE (*a new thought interrupts her far-off gaze, and she looks at his prostrate body*): Will you dig us a hole?

ADAM (*joyously scrambles up and kisses her hand*): A hole!

EVE: It needn't be too big—

ADAM: What do you mean? I'll dig you the biggest hole you ever saw in your life! Woman . . .

> *With a cry of gratitude he sweeps her into his arms.*

Woman, thou art my salvation!

EVE: Oh, my darling, that's so good to hear!

ADAM: How I thirst for thee! My doe, my rabbit . . .

EVE: My five-pointed buck, my thundering bull!

ADAM (*covering his crotch*): Oh, Eve, thy forgiveness hath swelled me like a ripened ear of corn.

EVE: Oh, how sweet. Then I will forgive thee endlessly.

> *Lucifer shows alarm and rising anger.*

As they try to think of a name for their first-born, their love and their intimacy sends Lucifer off in defeat and in pain. Suddenly Adam notices that the grass in the pasture is growing sheep-belly high; perhaps God's curse is lifted. But all at once Eve goes into labor, symbolized by snarling trumpet and french horn blasts. She is terrified by her pain, she calls on Chemuel for mercy; she calls on Lucifer; she curses God for visiting her with this agony. Adam now is terrified too. Lucifer enters at Eve's call for help, but he is checked by the entrance of God, Chemuel and Azrael. Eve loses consciousness, and so does Adam.

It is Chemuel, not Azrael, whom God finally directs to attend to Eve. Chemuel, in his mercy, obliterates her memory of suffering, soothes Eve, and delivers her child. At God's command, she and Adam both sit up, still asleep.

GOD: Behold the stranger thine agony hath made.

> *A youth of 16 appears, his eyes shut, his arms drawn in close to his body, his hands clasping his forward-tilted head. He moves waywardly, like a wind-blown leaf, and as he at last approaches Eve, he halts some feet away as God speaks again.*

Here is the first life of thy life, woman. And it is fitting that the first letter stand before his name. But seeing that in thy extremity thou hast already offered his life to Lucifer; and seeing, Adam, that in your ignorance you have likewise threatened him with murder—(*He loses His calm.*) all of which amazes me and sets my teeth on edge. (*He breaks off, gritting His teeth.*) I am nevertheless mindful that this child—(*He turns to the youth.*) is innocent. So we shall try again. And rather than call him Abel, who was in jeopardy, he shall be Cain, for his life's sake. (*He stands.*) Now Cain is born!

> *Cain lies down, coiled beside Eve. She sits up, opens her eyes and looks down at Cain.*

EVE (*joyfully surprised*): Ahhh!

ADAM (*waking up quickly, seeing Cain*): What's that?

EVE: It is ...
GOD: Cain. Thy son.
> *Both gasp, surprised by His presence.*

EVE (*suddenly feels her flat belly and with a cry prostrates before God*):
I see I have been favored of Thee, O Lord!

GOD (*indicating the inert Cain*): Here is thine innocence returned to thee,
which thou so lightly cast away in Eden. Now protect him from the worm
of thine own evil, which this day hath uncovered in thee . . . . .

Eve promises never more to doubt God, who expresses His own satisfaction
by taking Eve in his arms and dancing her offstage, followed by Adam. Lucifer
crouches over Cain, examining him and exhorting him: "With the kiss of
Lucifer begin thy life; let my nature coil around thine own. And on thy
shoulders, may I climb the throne. (*He bends and kisses him.*) Curtain."

ACT III

Third: When every man wants justice, why does he go on creating injustice?

God sits watching the sleeping Adam and his family. They have built a
crude shelter and there is evidence that they have learned to cook their food.
God is unhappy because apparently His people have forgotten Him, scarcely
ever mentioning or thinking about, let alone praising, their Creator. God
orders Azrael to blow visions of death into the minds of the sleeping family,
so that in their fear they may turn to thoughts of God.

God departs and Lucifer enters. He sees how content Eve has become with
her life; he fears that "they'll turn the whole earth into this smug suburb of
heaven!" Cain is jealous of Abel, Lucifer knows, and when he sees Azrael
come and do as he was ordered, Lucifer figures that God must be setting His
people up for a murder. As the family awakens, Lucifer watches them closely
to find an opening for thwarting God's will, perhaps avoiding the murder.

Adam and his family are shuddering with their nightmare of death; they
have dreamed that Abel was lying dead in his blood (Abel has dreamed that
an angel kissed him). Cain questions his father about his reasons for leaving
the garden, about what God expects of them all, about why Cain is the farmer
and Abel the shepherd.

ABEL: If you think He wants me to farm, I'll be glad to switch.
CAIN (*to Adam with a laugh*): He's going to farm!
ADAM (*laughing*): God help us!
ABEL (*protesting*): Why?
CAIN: With your sense of responsibility, we'd be eating thistle soup!
EVE (*touching Abel*): He's just more imaginative.
LUCIFER: Will you just shut up!
CAIN: Imaginative!

ABEL: Have I ever lost a sheep?

CAIN: How *could* you lose them? They always end up in my corn.

ABEL: Cain, that only happened once!

CAIN (*with raw indignation*): Go out there and sweat the way I do and tell me it only happened once!

EVE: He's just younger!

CAIN: And I'm older, and I'll be damned if I plant another crop until he fences those sheep!

LUCIFER: Stop this!

EVE (*to Adam*): Stop this!

CAIN: Why must you always take his side?

EVE: But how can he build a fence?

CAIN: The same way I plant a crop, Mother! By bending his back! Abel, I'm warning you, if you ever again—

ADAM: Boys, boys!

ABEL (*turning away*): If he wants a fence, I think he should build it.

CAIN: *I* should build it! Are the corn eating the sheep or are the sheep eating the corn?

ABEL: It's not natural for me to build a fence.

CAIN: Not natural! You've been talking to God lately?

ABEL: I don't know anything about God. But it's the nature of sheep to move around, and it's the nature of corn to stay in one place. So the fence should fence the thing that stays in one place and not the thing that moves around.

ADAM: That's logical, Cain.

CAIN: In other words, the work belongs to me and the whole wide world belongs to him!

ADAM (*at a loss*): No, that's not fair either.

ABEL (*angering, to Adam*): Well, I can't fence the mountains, can I? I can't fence the rivers where they go to drink. (*To Cain.*) I know you work harder, Cain, but I didn't decide that. I've even thought sometimes that it is unfair, and maybe we should change places for awhile—

CAIN: You wouldn't last a week.

ABEL (*crying out*): Then what am I supposed to do?

> *Cain is close, staring into his face, a tortured expression in his eyes which puzzles Abel.*

Why is he looking like that?

> *Suddenly Cain embraces Abel, hugging him close.*

Adam orders the brothers to shake hands. Lucifer thinks he has overcome God's will, but suddenly there are portents like a snake dropped in the family's midst and the howling of coyotes. Adam believes something crucial is taking place. He and Eve agree that the time has come to tell their sons the truth about the Garden; about eating the apple and discovering each other's nakedness.

Cain is shocked by the story of his parents' behavior and decides, "We've been saying all the wrong prayers. We shouldn't be thanking God—we should be begging His forgiveness. We've been living as though we were innocent. We've been living as though we were blessed! . . . . . We are cursed, Mother!"

Adam admits that they are under God's curse; they are condemned to die, like the animals. Cain insists that they must pray. He falls on his knees and begs God's forgiveness, beseeching Him to restore their innocence. Abel does not take the prayer seriously. Lucifer makes his presence known to Abel and advises him to build the fence, because he is the better loved of the two. Cain, inconsolably jealous, is dangerous.

Reluctantly, Abel agrees to build the fence. Cain demands that he do it in a pasture far from this home place. Again Lucifer persuades Abel to agree. Eve protests that it is too far away and accuses Cain of trying to humiliate Abel.

Cain picks up a boulder and places it on top of another one, preparing an altar for sacrifice to the Lord. Following Adam's advice, Cain goes to fetch the best of his crop to present to God on the altar, to lure Him down from heaven to hear their pleas. Adam studies Cain's offering and tells his son: "This looks absolutely beautiful, Cain. Now, when you see His face, regard the right eye. Because that's the one He loves you with. The left one squints, y'see, because that's the one He judges with. So watch the right eye and don't be frightened."

Eve suggests that Abel ought to make an offering too, and Lucifer warns Abel, "Under no circumstances must you get into this competition." Abel ignores this advice and goes to slaughter a lamb.

When Adam smears the lamb's blood on his hand and offers the sacrifice to the Lord, Lucifer appears before them as a man with a bull's head, pretending that he is God come to restore their innocence and deliver them from sin and guilt forever. Adam sees clearly that this is the Devil, not God. Eve is willing to accept the Devil as her lord because he brings her happiness, whereas God has visited her only with sin and pain. She exhorts her sons to love each other; she dances with Lucifer and teaches her sons to join the dance. Cain's emotion while dancing with his mother reaches a frenzied pitch; he pulls her to the ground and climbs on top of her. Eve is astonished but compliant, Adam roars with anger, Lucifer is triumphant, as God appears. Lucifer mocks Him: "May I introduce You to mankind? I don't believe I need labor the point—to the naked eye how pious and Godfearing they were; but with a moment's instruction and the right kind of music, a bear would blush at their morality. Dear Father, what are we fighting about? Truly, Lord, what is Man beyond his appetite?"

Once again Lucifer offers to "take his place" but God turns to the sacrifices on the altar, tastes them. He praises Cain's onion lightly but Abel's meat highly. It was Cain's idea to sacrifice to the Lord, but it is Abel who has most pleased God and provided the family with what Adam calls its "proudest moment" and who receives his mother's congratulatory kiss. God has neglected even to try Cain's corn—produced with so much labor—or his wine. God strolls off with the others, as Cain, now alone with Lucifer, kicks over the altar in his rage and humiliation.

CAIN: . . . . . Devil, now Cain starts to live!
He starts throwing everything out of the shelter.
LUCIFER: What's this, now?
CAIN: This is my house! Mine! (*He faces Lucifer.*) No one enters here but Cain any more. They have God, and I have this farm—and before I'm finished, my fences will stretch out to cover the earth!
LUCIFER: Adam will never agree to leave this house—
CAIN: Oh, he'll agree, all right—(*He strides to his flail and brandishes it.*) once I explain it to him! (*He whips the flail with a whoosh and holds it up.*) There's the only wisdom I will ever need again! (*A deep hum sounds in the earth, like a dynamo.*)
LUCIFER: Listen! (*Cain freezes.*) He has set a moaning in the earth. (*Daylight changes to night, stars appear.*) Look! (*Both look up at the night sky.*) He is giving you a night at noon, darkening your mind to kill for Him!
> *Frightened, Cain turns from the sky to the flail in his hand and throws it down guiltily.*
Don't let Him use you. Go away. Hide yourself.
CAIN: I, hide? I was the one who thought of the offerings; from me this Sabbath came! Let them hide! I want nothing from anyone any more!
LUCIFER: But God wants a murder from you.
CAIN (*astonished*): God . . . wants . . .?
LUCIFER: He's boiling your blood in His hand. He has designed your vengeance, boy.
CAIN: But why?
LUCIFER: So He may stand above your crime, the blameless God, the only assurance of Mankind, and His power is safe. Come now, we'll hide you till this anger's gone.

It is too late—Abel's voice is heard calling for Cain, who is still trying to understand why Abel should be the favorite of all, even God, when he, Cain, has everywhere made the greatest contribution. Abel calls again for Cain to come and join the others at God's feet. Instead, Cain orders Abel to leave the farm with Adam and Eve and picks up his flail. Cain warns Abel to run, exhorts God to save them all, then finally strikes Abel down.

God enters with Adam and Eve, who are shocked at the sight of Abel's corpse.

GOD: What hast thou done!
CAIN (*with a bitter, hard grin, plus a certain intimate, familiar tone*): What had to be done. As the Lord surely knew when I laid before Him the fruit of my sweat—for which there was only Thy contempt.
GOD: But why contempt? Didn't I approve of your offering?

CAIN: As I would "approve" my ox. Abel's lamb was not "approved," it was adored, like his life!

GOD (*indignantly*): But I like lamb! (*Cain is dumbfounded.*) I don't deny it, I like lamb better than onions.

LUCIFER: Surely there can be no accounting for taste.

CAIN: And this is your justice?

GOD: Justice!

CAIN (*with a bitter laugh*): Yes, justice! Justice!

GOD: When have I ever spoken that word?

CAIN: You mean our worth and value are a question of *taste?*

GOD (*incredulously*): But Cain, there are eagles and sparrows, lions and mice—is every bird to be an eagle? Are there to be no mice? Let a man do well, and he shall be accepted.

CAIN: I have done well and I am humiliated!

Eve urges Adam to revenge Abel by killing Cain. God bids Cain repent, and Lucifer intervenes: why should Cain repent an act which God had planned from the beginning? God argues that if man is to take the place intended for him he must rise above bestiality, "choose the way of life, not death." God, seeing both piety and envy in Cain's heart, tested him, hoping that Cain would throw down his weapon for love of God and Abel. In testing Cain, God was trying to exalt mankind.

Eve does not understand why a test should have taken Abel's life. She wishes God would leave them alone to "just live" (though God reminds her that without God anger will inevitably lead to murder). God Himself is now angry, feeling rejected, and ready to leave the world to the Devil. Lucifer protests; he can't manage the world alone, he can't create anything, he is only, as God points out, "a superb critic."

Eve detains God by asking Him what she is supposed to do about Cain. She can't live in the same family with him any more; in fact she realizes she can't "just live" without God, without a sense of right and wrong. Lucifer's permissiveness is not enough to live by. She cannot adjust her feelings to a guiltless Cain.

In Eve's attitude Lucifer sees mirrored the defeat of all his hopes to become a sort of God. God rubs in Lucifer's defeat: "You will never be God. And not because I forbid it, but because they will never—at least for very long—believe it. For I made them not of dust alone, but dust and love; and by dust alone they will not, cannot long be governed. (*Lucifer bursts into sobbing tears.*) Why do you weep, angel? They love, and with love, kill brothers. Take heart, I see now that our war goes on."

God sentences Cain to live as an outcast, despised as a murderer by his fellow human beings; but God will put a mark on Cain to protect him from being harmed.

GOD (*holding two index fingers pointed toward Cain's face*): Come to me, my son.

> *Terrified, Cain comes up to His fingers, and He comes around behind Cain, who is facing front, and presses his cheeks, forming a smile which Cain cannot relax. God lowers His fingers.*

CAIN (*smiling*): What is the mark?

GOD: That smile is.

CAIN: But they will know that I killed my brother!

GOD: Yes, they will know, and you will smile forever with agony in your eyes—the sundered mark of Cain who killed for pride and power in the name of love.

> *Smiling, his eyes desperate, Cain turns to Eve. She cries out, hides her face in her hands. He tears at his cheeks, but his smile remains. He lowers his hands—a smiling man with astonished, terrifying eyes.*

Adam? Eve? Now the way of life is revealed before you, and the way of death. Seek Me only in your hearts, you will never see My face again.

God vanishes among the stars. Lucifer makes no immediate effort to take His place; in his turn, Lucifer walks off into darkness, after promising pointedly to return any time they call for him.

Cain asks his parents' forgiveness, but Eve cannot give it to a son who does not even weep for the brother he has just murdered.

CAIN: . . . . . How will I weep? You never loved Cain!

ADAM: Spare one another . . .!

EVE (*turning to the corpse*): I loved him more. (*To Cain.*) Yes, more than you. And God was *not* fair. To me, either. (*Indicating Abel.*) And I still don't understand why he had to die, or who or what rules this world. But this boy was innocent—that I know. And you killed him, and with him any claim to justice you ever had.

CAIN: I am not to blame!

EVE: Are you telling me that nothing *happened* here? I will not sit with you as though nothing happened!

ADAM: Ask her pardon! (*Cain turns away from both.*) Cain, we are surrounded by the beasts! And God's not coming anymore—(*Cain starts away.*) Boy, we are all that's left responsible!—ask her pardon! (*Cain, adamant, the smile fixed on his face, walks out.*) Call to him. Pardon him. In God's name cry mercy, Eve, there is no other!

> *With his arm around her he has drawn her to the periphery, where she stands, her mouth open, struggling to speak. But she cannot, and she breaks into weeping. As though in her name, Adam calls toward the departed Cain.*

Mercy!

> *The roars, songs and cries of the animals fill the air. Adam looks up and about, and to the world, a clear-eyed prayer.*

Mercy!

> *Curtain.*

THE RIVER NIGER

A Play in Three Acts

BY JOSEPH A. WALKER

Cast and credits appear on page 355

JOSEPH A. WALKER was born in Washington, D.C. in 1935. His father, a mathematical genius, was forced to earn his living as house painter, not unlike the central character in The River Niger. *Walker was educated at Dunbar High School, Howard University (B.A.) and Catholic University of America (M.F.A., 1970). His educational career was interrupted by a hitch in the Air Force, from which he emerged in 1963 as a second lieutenant. He worked in the Post office, taught English and mathematics and drove a cab while studying for his graduate degree at Catholic University, where he met Jason Miller and acted in Miller's first play.*

Walker moved to New York in 1965, joined Lou Gossett's acting group and played the lead in The Believers *off Broadway in 1967. His first professionally-produced playscript was* Harangues, *which opened the Negro Ensemble Company's 1969 season. Walker's* Ododo *opened NEC's 1970 season, and in 1972-73 NEC began with* The River Niger, *his first Best Play, which was transferred to Broadway March 27, 1973, and which is dedicated "to my mother and father and to highly underrated black daddies everywhere."*

Additional roles played by Walker have included the black militant in the Woody Allen film Bananas *and Moses Gunn's replacement in the Public Theater's* Cities in Bezique. *In the educational field, he has served as playwright-in-residence at Yale University School of Drama, he teaches at CCNY and Howard, and he is studying for his Ph.D. at NYU. He is co-founder and artistic director of* The Demi Gods, *a dance-music theater repertory company organized and trained by himself and his wife, Dorothy A. Dinroe, the composer, who did the incidental music for* The River Niger. *They live in Harlem and have one child, a daughter. Walker has two sons by a previous marriage.*

Time: *The present, February 1, 4:30 p.m.*

Place: *Harlem in New York City, the Williams's brownstone on 133d St. between Lenox and 7th Aves.*

ACT I

SYNOPSIS: A cross-section of a living room and kitchen (which is almost as large as the living room) gives the impression of a comfortable, liveable dwelling, not luxurious but extremely well kept. In this living room are easy chairs and a sofa covered with transparent covers and a TV set with its back to the audience. At left is a window and a door leading out to the hall. Upstage is a stairway leading up to the bedroom floor. The kitchen, at right, features a large table and four chairs. A door at right leads out to the back porch.

Grandma Wilhelmina Brown, *"a stately, fair-skinned black woman in her middle 70s,"* is humming "Rock of Ages" as she pours a cup of coffee for herself. After looking around to make sure no one is watching, she takes a bottle of Old Granddad from its hiding place under the sink and laces her coffee with it.

Grandma hides her bottle and escapes from the kitchen quickly as she hears someone approaching from outside. *"The back door opens cautiously. It is John Williams, a thin, medium-sized brown man in the middle 50s. His hair is gray at the temples and slicked down. He has a salt and pepper moustache. He wears a brown topcoat, combat boots, corduroy pants—on his head a heavily crusted painter's cap. He is obviously intoxicated but very much in control."*

John takes a bottle of Johnny Walker Red Label from his pocket and has a swig. He hides the bottle behind the refrigerator, removes his topcoat, takes out his wallet and starts counting his money. A line of bass rhythm fades in as he finds a piece of paper in his pocket and reads three lines of a poem about the Niger River. The bass fades out again as he replaces the crumpled paper into his pocket. He places a small cedar jewelry box on the kitchen table and regards it proudly.

John answers a knock on the door and lets in his friend Dudley Stanton, *"a thin, wiry, very dark black man,"* a doctor, conservatively dressed. He speaks *"in a thick and beautiful Jamaica accent."* They call each other every kind of insulting name in order to express their mutual affection ("monkey chaser" particularly annoys Dudley). Dudley has been on vacation fishing in Mexico. He has brought a bottle of vodka, which Johnny dislikes.

JOHN: Goddamn black Jew doctor. You make all the money in the world and you can't even buy your poor buddy a bottle of Scotch.

DUDLEY: Hell, I shouldn't even drink with you. (*Pause.*) If you don't stop boozing the way you do, you'll be dead in five years. You're killing yourself bit by bit, Johnny.

JOHN: Well that's a helluva sight better than doing it all at once. Besides, I can stop anytime I want to.

DUDLEY: Then why don't you?

JOHN: I don't want to. (*Changing the subject purposely.*) Dudley, my son's due home tomorrow.

DUDLEY: Jeff coming home? No lie! That's wonderful! Old Jeff. Let's take a run up to the Big Apple and celebrate.

JOHN: That's where I'm coming from. I left work early today—I got so damned worked up you know. I mean, all I could see was my boy—big time first lieutenant in the United States of America Air Force—Strategic Air Command—navigator—walking through the front door with them bars—them shining silver bars on his goddamn shoulders. (*He begins saluting an imaginary Jeff.*) Yes, sir. Whatever you say, sir. Right away, Lieutenant Williams. Lieutenant Jeff Williams.

DUDLEY: Johnny Williams, you are the biggest fool in God's creation. How in the name of your grandma's twat could you get so worked up over the white man's air force? I've always said that's what's wrong with these American niggers. They believe anything that has a little tinsel sprinkled on it. "Shining silver bars." Fantasy, man!

JOHN: He's my son, Dudley and I'm proud of him.

DUDLEY: You're supposed to be, but because he managed to survive this syphilitic asshole called Harlem, not because he's a powerless nub in a silly military grist mill. What you use for brains, man?

JOHN: I'm a fighter, Dudley. I don't like white folks too, but I sure do love their war machines. I'm a fighter who ain't got no battlefield. I woke up one day, looked around and said to myself, "There's a war going on, but where's the battlefield?" I'm gonna find it one day—you watch.

DUDLEY: In other words, you'd gladly give your life for your poor downtrodden black brothers and sisters if you only knew where to give it?

JOHN: Right! For my people!

DUDLEY: I wonder how many niggers have said those words. "For my people!"

JOHN: Give me the right time and I'd throw this rubbish on the rubbish heap in a minute.

DUDLEY: Cop out! That's all that is!

JOHN: Ya goddamn monkey chaser—you're the cop out!

DUDLEY: Cop out! The battlefield's everywhere. That's what's wrong with niggers in America—everybody's waiting for *the* time. I don't delude myself,

nigger. I know that there's no heroism in death—just death, dirty nasty death.
    He pours another drink.
The rest is jive, man! Black people are jive. The most unrealistic, unphilo-
sophical people in the world.
    JOHN: Philosophy be damned. Give me a program—a program!
    DUDLEY: A program!?! We're just fools, Johnny, white and black retarded
children playing with matches. We don't have the slightest idea what we're
doing. Do you know I no longer believe in medicine. Of all man's presump-
tions—medicine is the most arrogantly presumptuous. People are supposed to
die! It's natural to die. If I find that a patient has a serious disease I send him
to one of my idealistic colleagues. I ain't saving no lives, man. I treat the
hypochondriacs . . . . .

In Dudley's view, black people are just "crabs in a barrel." The two men
continue the argument in this vein, Johnny's rough-edged idealism vs. Dudley's calculated cynicism. Dudley won't let John take the easy way out by
blaming "whitey" for all his ills. Dudley tells his friend, "You're a dying wino
nigger who's trying to find some reason for living. And now you're going to
put that burden on your son." Dudley prevented his own wife from having
any children by medical means, without her knowledge. Even when she died
—gruesomely—she never knew she might have been a mother.
    Nevertheless John means to play the game of "free my people" as best he
can. What's more important and to the point, however, John needs to borrow
another $190 from Dudley (he already owes him $340) because he has
blown much of his pay check. Their discussion is interrupted by someone
knocking at the door. It is a total stranger, Ann Vanderguild, *"a very attractive black woman in her early 20s . . . . . She sparkles on top of a deep
brooding inner core."* Her entrance is accompanied by a bass line of *"beautiful
melancholy."*
    Ann, it seems, is a friend of Jeff's who has come here to meet him. She
expects to stay the night, and when Dudley orders John downstairs to the taxi
to get her suitcases, John obeys without thinking. Ann makes it clear that she
is not Jeff's "intended," just a very good friend, as John staggers in with an
armload of valises—and goes downstairs again to get a small trunk.
    John asks Ann for the $3.50 the taxi cost, but Dudley insists on paying it
over Ann's objections. Dudley also insists on taking her pulse and looking at
her tongue, and observing that she is fine now though she's had a severe cold
recently. Dudley informs John bluntly that he'd better regard Ann as one of the
family.

    DUDLEY: . . . . . Ann here is your prospective daughter-in-law, and she'll
make a good one too, Johnny. I stamp her certified.
    JOHN (*to Ann*): Jeff never wrote us about you.
    ANN: Well, he doesn't exactly know I'm here, sir. I mean we never dis-
cussed it or anything.
    JOHN: Where you from, little lady?
    ANN: Canada, sir—I mean originally I'm from South Africa, sir.

JOHN: This gentleman here is Dudley Stanton. Doctor Dudley Stanton.

ANN (*to Dudley*): My EKG is excellent, too, sir. I guess my pulse is very slow, because I used to run track—the fifty-yard dash. I'm a nurse. Perhaps you can help me find a job, sir?

DUDLEY: Oh, these strong black women!

ANN: I'm only strong if my man needs me to be, sir.

Ann speaks with an exotic accent, in a manner that is unfailingly poised and polite. Dudley explains to her that her prospective father-in-law is a strange combination of house painter and poet. Dudley insists that John read one of his poems, reminding John that he doesn't intend to give him $190 for nothing, he gives John money in exchange for his poems, which Dudley hopes to publish some day.

> *John fumbles through his pants pockets and comes up with several scraps of paper which he examines for selection. He smooths out one piece of paper.*

JOHN (*reading*): "I am the River Niger—hear my waters . . ." No, that one ain't right yet.

ANN: Please go on!

JOHN: No, it ain't complete yet. Let's see, yeah, this one's finished.
> *Begins reading from another scrap of paper as lights fade to a soft amber. A bass jazz theme creeps in. John is spotlighted.*

"Lord, I don't feel noways tired."
And my soul seeks not to be flabby
Peace is a muscleless word
A vacuum, a hole in space,
An assless anesthesia,
A shadowy phantom,
Never settling anywhere—Even in sleep.
In my dreams I struggle; slash and crash and cry,
"Damn you, you wilderness! I will cut my way through!"
And the wilderness shouts back!
"Go around me?"
And I answer,
"Hell, no! The joke's on both of us
And I will have the last laugh."
The wilderness sighs and grows stronger
As I too round out my biceps in this ageless, endless duel.
Hallelujah! Hallelujah! Hallelujah!
I want a muscle-bound—spirit
I say I want a muscle-bound soul—cause
Lord, I don't feel noways tired.
I feel like dancing through the valley of death!
Lord, I don't feel noways tired.

ANN: Beautiful!
> *Bass fades.*

DUDLEY (*takes sheet of paper*): This is a blank sheet of paper!
JOHN: I made it up as I went along. Hell, I'll write it down for you.

The doorbell rings, and John's wife Mattie's voice is heard in the hall. Dudley hands over the money to John, and both the men advise Ann to proceed very cautiously with Mattie, start by helping her out around the house.

Mattie comes in, and immediately Ann helps her with the groceries she is carrying. Mattie is in her 50s, *"an embittered but happy woman."* Mattie isn't feeling too well (she tells Grandma, her mother, who comes downstairs) but she refuses Dudley's offer of an appointment at his office. Grandma calls Dudley a fool, and this precipitates a general family melee of charge and countercharge. Mattie silences them all and apologizes for her mother, who is more than usually glassy-eyed this evening.

DUDLEY: . . . Are you afraid, Mattie? To have a check-up, I mean?
MATTIE (*pause*): Stay for dinner, Dudley.
DUDLEY: Thanks, I will.
ANN (*at the door*): Would you like for me to fix dinner, Mrs. Williams?
    Pause.
MATTIE: Who is this child?
JOHN: Ann Vanderguild. She's from South Africa. She's a friend of Jeff's—just passing through. I asked her to spend the night.
GRANDMA: Where's she going to spend it—the bathroom?
MATTIE: Mamma, what's wrong with you tonight?
JOHN: She had a little too much, that's all.
MATTIE (*to Ann*): You're welcome, dear. You can stay in Jeff's room tonight. I got it all cleaned up for him. He'll be here tomorrow, you know? Thank the Lord.
ANN: Yes, mam! It certainly will be pleasant to see him again.
    Mattie looks at Ann curiously.
I make a very good meat loaf, mam. I noticed you've got all the ingredients as I was putting the food away.
MATTIE: You put the food away?
ANN: You seemed so bushed.
MATTIE: What a nice thing for you to do. And you read my mind too. Meat loaf is exactly what I was planning to fix. Yes, indeed. Such a pretty girl too.
JOHN (*to Dudley*): Why don't we make a little run and leave these black beauties to themselves. To get acquainted—
GRANDMA: Don't be calling me no black nothing. I ain't black! I'm half-full-blooded Cherokee Indian myself. Black folks is "Hewers of wood and drawers of water" for their masters. Says so in the scriptures. I ain't no hewer of no wood myself. I'm a Cherokee aristocrat myself.

John goads Grandma into a hymn-singing, gospel-quoting declaration of her superiority, leading Dudley to repeat his comment that black people are just "crabs in a barrel" who would bite the hand that reached in to lift them out. John goes into the kitchen and brings some "special medicine" (half a glass of Scotch) for Grandma, who carries it upstairs, singing gospel hymns.

John again makes a move to escape for awhile with Dudley, but Mattie demands the rent money from him first, because the rent is due this week and today is payday. John hands over a sum which is $10 short, but Mattie insists on the additional $10 which she will ration back to him over the next two weeks, so that he won't spend it all this evening celebrating. John pleads for $5 to celebrate Jeff's homecoming properly, and he wheedles it out of her with a tall tale about wanting to go visit "this chick, see, sixteen years old and she is as warm as ginger bread in the wintertime, and we gon' lay up all night—"

Mattie sends John off with Dudley, warning Dudley to make sure John doesn't overdo his celebrating. They depart, and Ann and Mattie almost envy their friendship, the kind of deep friendship so rare between women, perhaps because they don't really trust one another as men do.

Ann tells Mattie something of herself and her family: her father has been in prison nine years for operating an illegal printing press turning out anti-government pamphlets. He took the rap—and a beating from the arresting officer—to protect his two sons who were the real pamphleteers. Ann's mother ordered the two to escape across the border, though they wanted to turn themselves in so that their father could go free. Ann tells Mattie: "They live in England now and have families of their own. It wasn't long before the authorities found out that dad was really innocent, but just because my brothers got away and are free and just to be plain mean they kept him in prison anyway. Nine years—nine long years. Those bastards! I despise white people, Mrs. Williams."

Mattie questions Ann about Jeff. They met in Quebec where Ann was a nurse and Jeff was brought into the hospital with a fractured ankle from skiing. When it hurt, Jeff would laugh—his father taught him that trick, he said. Ann began hanging around Jeff's room listening to him talk about his family.

MATTIE: And that's when you started loving him half to death.

ANN (*pause*): Yes, mam.

MATTIE: That boy sure can talk up a storm. He'll make a fine lawyer. Don't you think so?

ANN (*pause*): I won't get in his way, Mrs. Williams.

MATTIE (*after a long pause*): No, I don't think you will.
        Pause.
Well, let's see if we can trust each other good enough to make that meat loaf. Why don't you chop the onions while I do the celery. (*Starts to rise.*)

ANN (*stopping her*): Oh, no mam, this one's on me.

MATTIE (*laughing*): I'm very particular, you know.

ANN: I know you are. Jeff's told me a lot about how good your cooking is.

MATTIE (*happy to hear it*): That boy sure can eat—Lord today. Well, all right, Ann. Let me go on up and get myself comfortable. I'll be right back.

Mattie sees the jewelry box on the table. She opens it, finds a card and starts to read it aloud but stops when she finds that its intimacies may be unsuitable for Ann's tender ears. But Ann insists that Mattie read it, so she does: "Big legged woman, keep your dress tail down, 'cause you got something under there to make a bulldog hug a hound."

Tomorrow is their anniversary, Mattie explains to Ann, and this must be a present which John made for her: "Can do anything with his hands, or with his head for that matter when he ain't all filled up on rotgut. (*Pause.*) He's killing himself drinking. I guess I'm to blame though."

Without explaining what she means by this comment, Mattie exits upstairs, so that when there is a knock on the door Ann goes to answer it. It is Chips, *"a tall, rangy young man in his early 20s . . . . . He has an air of 'I'm a bad nigger' about him."* Chips is looking for Jeff; he ogles Ann suggestively, comments on her strange accent. Chips wants to inform Jeff that "Big Mo wants to see him at headquarters as soon as possible. Like it's urgent, ya dig it?" Mo is the leader of some sort of gang. Jeff wrote Mo he'd be here tonight, not tomorrow at noon as his family thinks.

Chips slaps her behind insolently, and Ann picks up a heavy ashtray. Chips laughs at her, pulls out a switchblade and tells her, "If I wanted to I could cut your drawers off without touching your petticoat and take what I want." But finally he leaves, threatening to come back later tonight with Big Mo.

Mattie comes downstairs now wearing a robe and house shoes, and Ann tells her about Chips's visit. Mattie warns that Chips is vicious, and explains: "Jeff used to be the gang leader around here when he was a teen ager. By the time he got to college, Jeff and his friend Mo had made the gang decent—you know, doing good things to help the neighborhood. But I heard lately, the bums went back to their old ways. I wonder what they want with Jeff now?"

Ann decides to sleep on the living room sofa, which pulls out into a bed, instead of in Jeff's room. Mattie tells Ann she can stay, provided there's "no tomfoolery" with Jeff. They talk of family matters: how Grandma thinks no one is good enough for Jeff, how dearly Grandma loved her husband.

The lights fade, and when they come up again the house is in darkness and Ann is asleep in the living room. A knock on the door wakes Ann up. She thinks it is John coming home and opens it. *"Mo, an athletic looking young man in his mid 20s; his girl friend Gail, sincere and very much in love with Mo; Skeeter, who seems constantly out of it and desperate; Al, who appears to be intensely observant, and Chips all force their way in."*

Chips introduces Ann and makes a leering remark, but the others silence him. They have Chips under tight control. Mo is disappointed to find that Jeff isn't home yet. They threaten to remain until Jeff shows up.

At this moment, John and Dudley enter noisily through the back door, planning to have one for the road. They come into the living room and see the young people. John recognizes Mo and insists on being introduced to the others. He tells them that they will all be welcome at the homecoming celebration at noon tomorrow, but they must go home now. They refuse. John, unperturbed, leaves the room. Gail suggests that they all leave at once. Chips looks at Ann meaningfully and wonders what the hurry is.

GAIL (*turning on him*): You should be in the biggest hurry, nigger 'cause when Jeff finds out how you been insulting his woman you're gonna be in a world of trouble.

DUDLEY: Gentlemen, I'd advise you all to leave. Before something presumptuous happens. Can never tell about these black African warrior niggers.

AL (*pushing Dudley into a chair*): Shut up.

DUDLEY (*blessing himself*): Father, forgive them, for they know not what they do.

> John comes back with an M-1 rifle and a World War II hand grenade.

JOHN (*highly intoxicated but even more deadly serious because of it*): Yeah—well, Father may forgive 'em but I don't, not worth a damn.

CHIPS: You ain't the only one in here with a smoking machine, man. (*Opens his coat to reveal a shoulder holster and a revolver.*)

MO: Close your jacket, stupid.

JOHN: Come over here, Ann. Dudley, get your drunk self outta that chair and make it on over here.

> They follow his instructions.

(*To them.*) I don't know if this old grenade'll work or not, but when I pull the pin an throw it at them niggers we duck into the kitchen—all right.

AL: This old stud's crazy as shit.

MO: Shut up.

CHIPS: I bet he's faking.

> Reaches for his revolver. John instantly throws the bolt on the M-1. They all freeze for a long moment.

MO (*finally; laughing*): You win, you win, Mr. Williams. Dig it? We'll see ya around noon. Let's go.

> They file out. Mo stops at the door, still laughing.

Ya got some real stuff going for you, Mr. Williams. (*Exit.*)

DUDLEY: Impressive. Presumptuous as hell, but impressive.

At this moment Grandma comes down the stairs slowly, sleepwalking, humming "Rock of Ages." John sees this as the opportunity to discover at last where she keeps her bottle hidden. Talking to herself about the taste of possum, oblivious of the others, she takes out her bottle, pours a glass of whisky, returns the bottle to its hiding place and retires up the stairs.

John pounces on the bottle and pours a round of nightcaps. The lights fade to black. When they come up again, Ann is asleep on the sofabed once more. A key turns in the front door and Jeff Williams enters. *"There is a heavy seriousness about him, frosted over with the wildness he has inherited from his father. His presence is strong and commanding. He is dressed casually in a turtleneck, bell-bottomed slacks, boots and a long-styled topcoat. On his shoulder he carries a crammed duffle bag—a suitcase the size of a small foot locker in his right hand. Magazines protrude from his overcoat pocket. His hair is a modified or shortened Afro. His face is clean."*

Jeff drops his luggage on the floor, closes the front door—and suddenly sees

Ann lying there asleep. He is surprised and pleased. He rolls a joint of mari-juana, lights up and kisses Ann, then blows a puff of smoke in her face.

> *She awakens with a soft sputter. She is overwhelmed at seeing him. Without saying a word he extends the joint to her. She sits upright and drags on it. He grabs her foot and gently kisses the arch.*

JEFF: Three whole days—um, um—and I sho have missed them big old feet of yours.

ANN (*hands him the joint*): Are my feet big?

JEFF:Why do you think I always walk behind you in the snow? You got natural snow shoes, baby.

> *He grabs her roughly but lovingly and kisses her.*

ANN: I had to come, Jeff.

JEFF: I know. Now let's get down to the nitty gritty. How 'bout some loving, mamma?

ANN: Oh, Jeff—I promised your mother.

JEFF: She won't know. And whatcha don't know—(*Starts taking off his clothes, talking as he does.*) My dad taught me that where there's a will there's a way.

ANN: Your dad taught you a lot of things.

JEFF: Yeah. Now we're banging away, right? Oo, ahh, oo, ahh. And it's sweet—like summer time in December, right? And just when it really gets good, right? And we're about to reach the top of the mountain, down the steps comes Grandma—on one of her frequent sleepwalking things. And what do I do? I roll over to the wall and drop down to the other side. Like this—(*Demonstrates.*) And nobody knows but us.

> *She kisses him.*

Daddy Johnny says before a man settles down—which shouldn't oughta be until he's damn near thirty or more—

> *She kisses him.*

A young man's mission is the world.

ANN: Well, isn't that what you've been trying to do?

> *She kisses him.*

JEFF: You keep taking up my time.

ANN: Uh huh.

> *Kisses him as the lights begin to dim.*

You like my feet?

JEFF: Is the Pope Catholic? Can a fish swim? Do black folks have rhythm? Do hound dogs chase rabbits? Your feet got more beauty than sunshine, mamma.

> *They kiss as the lights fade to black. Bass line plays under. Curtain.*

ACT II

At 10:45 the next morning John is wearing his paint-stained coveralls and has been mopping the kitchen floor but has stopped to work on his poem

"The River Niger." He has written nine or ten lines when he decides that a visit to the Big Apple might be in order, and he has just gathered up his scraps of paper when Dudley arrives. John has mopped almost the entire house and feels it's time for a break, but Dudley has something to tell him first.

DUDLEY: Mattie came over this morning—early. I examined her—and, well, I felt a lot of—irregularities on her rib cage. Anyway—

JOHN (*sardonically*): Well, what're you quacks gonna do now—remove her other tit?

DUDLEY: Johnny. (*Pause.*) Maybe even worse. I don't want to alarm her until I'm sure. I made an appointment for her at Harlem—they'll do a biopsy —anyway, I'll know as soon as the lab gets done with it.

　　Pause.

JOHN (*stricken but defensive*): Why you telling me all this if you don't know for sure?

　　Pause.

DUDLEY: She came over while you were still asleep—she doesn't want you to know. I promised I wouldn't tell you.

JOHN: Does she suspect?

DUDLEY: I was very honest with her.

JOHN: That figures! Honesty sticks to some people's mouths like peanut butter.

DUDLEY: Like you just said, man, I have to deal with things the way I think best.

Mattie calls down to John to take out the trash, but John runs off to the Big Apple to celebrate "an amazing bitch." Dudley leaves with him as Mattie comes downstairs with Ann. Ann volunteers to finish up cleaning where John left off, and Mattie tries unsuccessfully to hurry Grandma along. They are going shopping. The store will be jammed if they don't get there early, they must hurry.

MATTIE (*to Ann*): There's too much drinking in this house. That's the problem. She's probably hung over.

ANN: Pardon me, Mrs. Williams, but you know about your mother's drinking?

MATTIE: Of course! It's all in her eyes.

ANN: But last night I thought—well—

MATTIE: Child, you got to swallow a lot of truth 'round here to give folks dignity. If mamma knew I knew—I mean really knew I knew—she'd be so embarrassed. Don't you know I even pretend that John ain't the alcoholic he really is?

ANN: But you're not helping them that way.

MATTIE: Helping them! Who says I ain't? Johnny soon be pushing sixty. He ain't got but a few more years left. If he wants to spend 'em swimming in a fifth a day, who am I to tell him he can't? And mamma, she'll be eighty-three this September. I'm supposed—as the youngsters on my job say—to "blow their cool?" Honey, all we're doing in this life is playing what we ain't. And well, I play anything my folks need me to play.

ANN: I guess that makes sense.

MATTIE: That man had two years of college, Ann. Wanted to be a lawyer like Jeff wants to be, you know. He had to stop school because my mother and my two sisters—Flora and Minerva—came up from the South to live with us—for a short time, so they said. Ignorant country girls—they weren't trained to do nothing. I got a job and together Johnny and I fed 'em, clothed 'em. In a couple of years, John was ready to go back to school, raring to go, don't you know. Then Flora's boy friend came up from good old South Carolina and didn't have a pot to piss in or a window to throw it out of. He and Flora got married and where do you think they stayed? (*Yells upstairs.*) MAMMA! (*Back to Ann.*) On top of it all, Minerva got herself pregnant by some silly, buck-toothed nineteen-year-old who just vanished. So here comes another mouth to feed—Child, Johnny was painting houses all morning, working the graveyard shift at the Post Office, and driving a cab on his days off. (*Again yells.*) MAMMA PLEASE! . . . . .

Mattie goes on to tell Ann that John kept reading and managed to absorb a great deal of knowledge which he passed on to Jeff: "He poured himself into Jeff. Lord, he had that boy reading Plato and Shakespeare when he was thirteen years old."

If they had it to do all over again—Mattie insists—they would behave more selfishly, aggressively, grasp more for themselves. Mattie doesn't believe in treasures in heaven; "a good man is a treasure" right here on earth. Johnny has run a powerful race, carrying a great weight, and now he's "put himself out to pasture with his fifth a day," and Mattie approves. She observes: "White folks proclaim that our men are no good . . . . . If our men are no good, then why are all these little white girls trying to gobble 'em up faster than they can pee straight?"

Grandma finally comes downstairs and makes a pointed remark about Ann's presence in the house. Mattie sends Ann upstairs to straighten up Jeff's room. Grandma checks her bottle, is astonished to find it empty. She has a feeling that Ann is out to seduce Jeff, but Mattie is not worried. She calls Ann, who appears at the top of the stairs in an extraordinarily disheveled state (Jeff is home, in his room, but Mattie doesn't know this). Mattie gives Ann instructions about the roast in the oven and exits with Grandma.

Jeff appears at the top of the stairs and tries to begin their lovemaking again where they started last night, but they are interrupted by a knock on the door. Jeff goes back to his room as Ann lets in Skeeter (who is trying to conceal his need of a fix) and Al. Ann invites them to wait for Jeff's party to begin and exits upstairs.

Skeeter begs Al for the drug which Al admits he has brought with him; but Al wants to know first who killed an undercover policeman named Buckley— was it an outsider or some member of the gang? Skeeter, though desperate for the drug, won't say, and Al won't give him the drug until he does. Furious, Skeeter pulls out a revolver, but Al pulls his out as well—it is a standoff.

Al enjoys watching Skeeter squirm with his need for the drug, until finally Skeeter confesses the Buckley killing was an outside job, someone from the West Coast. Al hands over a small tinfoil package. Al watches while Skeeter rolls a dollar bill into a little funnel and inhales the powder through it into his nostril.

AL: . . . . . Why'd ya'll hate Buckley so?

SKEETER (*calming down rapidly*): He was on the narco squad. Useta raid and steal scag and push it to the school kids. Always little boys. He'd get 'em hooked, strung out, then make 'em do freakish faggot shit for a fix. Any one of us woulda blown him away.

Pause.

Hey, I seen you trying to feel up on Chips's little brother.

AL (*excitedly*): You lie, nigger.

SKEETER: I know a heap about you, Alfrieda! Could there be a connection between you and that pig Buckley?

AL: Come off it, Skeeter.

SKEETER: If you'd make it with Chips, you'd make it with anybody. Don't give me that funny look, nigger. I saw him socking it to you in the latrine last night. You thought everybody was gone, didn't ya?

AL: You lie!

SKEETER: I forgot my shades, nigger. I come back for my shades. And there you were. Too busy to even see me. If I tell Mo about it he'll bust both of you mothers. Ain't that some shit . . . . .

Chips has even practised necrophilia, Skeeter informs Al, that's how degenerate Chips is. Mo calls him "Femaldehyde Dick." Al threatens to cut off Skeeter's supply of drugs if he goes on like this, but Skeeter informs Al that the three of them are part of an indivisible working relationship: "You, me and Chips. You give me scag cause you know I know where you at—I don't tell Mo where you at cause I need the scag. Chips don't tell him cause he digs fags. That's where he's at! Now you keep your eye—your brown eye on that relationship. Mo's the only clean cat among us—that's why Mo's the leader, man. But all three of us is walking on the same razor blade, Sugar Baby, and don't you forget it . . . . ."

Skeeter tells Al that he invented that story about someone from the outside killing Buckley, just as the doorbell rings. Its Chips, who informs them that a *Times* reporter has been hanging around, asking questions about Buckley. Ann appears at the top of the stairs. Thinking Ann is alone in the house, Chips climbs the stairs toward her. Ann pretends to be defenceless and lets Chips push her toward the bedrooms. *"In the next moment we hear a loud yell from Jeff and much commotion. A second later Jeff comes down the stairs with Chips's head pressed against the front of the revolver,"* and with Ann following them downstairs.

Chips pleads that he was only fooling but Jeff, ferociously, hits him across the face and then in the pit of the stomach, sending him to the floor. Mo and Gail enter, unnoticed, and Jeff continues to threaten Chips with the gun, which is Chips's own, terrifying him by pulling back the hammer. Jeff threatens to kill Chips if he ever bothers Ann again, then orders him out of the house. But at Mo's special request Jeff permits him to stay, with Mo answering for Chips's behavior. Mo collars Chips and reprimands him angrily, not for his affront to Ann but for letting another man take his gun away from him.

Mo introduces Gail to Jeff, and they all calm down and find seats while Ann and Gail go to the kitchen to fetch a round of beers. Mo argues that there was some excuse for Chips's behavior, they have all been confused and disappointed by the tone of Jeff's recent letters. Jeff, their leader and mentor, the toughest member of their gang, seems to be going soft, writing to them about law and the Constitution. Mo remembers how it was when they fought the Richardson brothers for control of St. Nicholas Avenue; that was the law for them, the law of the jungle. The only thing the beast—white or black—understands is brute force, Mo argues.

Jeff tells Mo that all the talk about a black revolution is ineffectual so long as they have no bomb factories, no weapons to fight with; the law, however, is ready to hand right now as an effective weapon for the black man. Mo wants Jeff to come back into the gang and help them take action against "whitey," action they've been planning. Jeff refuses. He will fight, he says, but with his own choice of weapons, and he has chosen the law.

Jeff advises the group that his parents will be returning soon, and he wants the subject and the atmosphere changed to something cool. Mo mocks him.

JEFF: You're in my house, nigger.

MO: I don't play that word, man. You throw it around a little too much.

JEFF: Oh yeah, well, you pat your foot while I play it, nigger.

MO: You either gon be with us or against us, brother Jeff. Nobody stays uncommitted in this neighborhood. Besides, we can make you do anything we want you to do.

JEFF: How you gonna do that, brother?

MO: Every time you poke your head out your door you can be greeted with rocks, broken glass, garbage bags or doo doo. And if that don't work . . . (*Ann and Gail return from kitchen*) And if that don't work . . .

JEFF (*furious*): If that don't work, what?

MO: We can work on your moms and pops. They might come home and find the whole house empty, no furniture or nothing, motherfucker.

JEFF: Oh no, baby, you're the motherfucker. You really are the motherfucker! (*Controlling his fury at Mo.*) You jive-ass nigger. Mr. Zero trying to be Malcolm X. List' old world, list' to *the* revolutionary. See him standing there with his Captain America uniform on. Look at his generals. Skeeter the Dope Head and Chips the Sex Pervert. Mo the magnificent, playing cops and robbers, cowboys and Indians in his middle twenties, trying to be somebody and don't know how. The one advantage I have over you, Mo, is my daddy taught me to see through my own bullshit, to believe that I don't need bull-shit to be somebody. Go back to school, Mo, you're smart enough.

GAIL: Don't talk to him like that!

MO: You been thinking this shit for a long time, ain't yo nigger?

JEFF: Affirmative. And if you try any shit on my folks, your ass is mine, nigger. Or have you forgotten what a mean, evil, black bastard I can be, how you could whip everybody in the neighborhood and how I could whip the piss out of you, how I got more determination in my little toenail that you got in your whole soul, nigger!

MO: At least you still talk bad.

JEFF: I ain't bad. I'm crazy, motherfucker. Now you, your Dope Fiend and Marquis de Sade get the fuck outa here, and don't call me—I'll call you.

Mo is impressed by Jeff's show of strength; slowly he and his troupe depart. Jeff hunts for the bottle of whiskey he knows his father must have hidden someplace, finds it, takes a couple of swigs and then airily proposes marriage to Ann. He has no thought that she might refuse, and his kiss seems to seal the bargain.

Gail comes back. She has given Mo the slip and come to beg Jeff not to quarrel with his old friend. More than ever Mo needs Jeff at his side. Keeping the gang in order has become a great strain. Gail explains: "Mo only looks at the good in people. Also, he's loyal. Skeeter and Chips been with you cats ever since you started gang-bopping. Mo's not dumb, he knows their hangups. But they swore to him they'd stay clean. Anyway, when you trying to build an army outta people who been buried in garbage all their lives, you can't expect they gon' all of a sudden start smelling like roses. In time, Mo believes, the movement will straighten 'em out for good."

Jeff tells Gail he doesn't believe in Mo's methods and resents him pretending to be tough and threatening Jeff's family just to impress the creeps in his gang. Mo is confused, Gail pleads, unsure of his cause any longer but resorting to more and more deadly activities (his people are suspects in the recent Buckley murder). He plans to destroy a state office building or maybe a police station, but he is beginning to break under the pressure of decision and leadership. Gail begs Jeff to help Mo, and Jeff finally promises to try.

Mattie and Grandma push open the front door and enter loaded down with the fruits of their shopping. They see Jeff and rush to hug him and welcome him home. Jeff pleases them by calling them his "two foxes," taking a high hand with them, demanding his favorite fare for dinner.

Jeff introduces Gail to his family, and then introduces Ann to Grandma, who still resents her. Joyfully, Jeff announces that he is going to marry Ann. Mattie approves, but Grandma disapproves. She dreams that Jeff is still just a boy, too young for marriage, and anyway too young and with too much promise to be burdened by a wife and the inevitable children.

GRANDMA (blurting out a long pent-up reality): Look at your father. He wanted to be a lawyer, didn't he? Then I jumped on his back, then them two no-good daughters of mine, then their two empty-headed husbands—then you. The load was so heavy 'til he couldn't move no more. He just had to stand there, holding it up.

MATTIE (*very serious*): Then you know about it?

GRANDMA: What do you think I am? A sickle-headed, lopsided, cockeyed ignoramus like your son here?

MATTIE: Oh, so you admit he's my son.

GRANDMA: He's your son, but he's my child.

MATTIE (*turning to Ann*): Have y'all given it serious thought, Ann?

ANN: He just asked me, Mrs. Williams.

GRANDMA: Is that all you gon' do? Talk? You gon' let this brazen hussy just take my child away?

MATTIE: Mamma, why don't you go to your room and cool off a bit.

GRANDMA: She is brazen. Camping right on his doorstep. I call that bold, brash and brazen! And conniving too! A pretty face'll sho kill a man—even a good man. (*To Ann.*) And not even mean to! You gon' take that on your shoulders, child, you gon' kill your man before he can stand up good yet? Is that what you gon' do? I did it. Mattie did it. She let me help her do it.

MATTIE: Mamma!

GRANDMA: Don't mamma me. Where's my medicine? I don't want to be here and watch my child leap into deep water. Lawd-a-mercy no! Where is my medicine? . . . . .

Grandma exits upstairs carrying her "medicine" while, feebly, Mattie protests to Jeff that he ought to wait until after law school. But Jeff tells her, "I want to marry Ann cause she is a fine girl, mamma. Something rare—came home and found my sweet baby here—it was like God was saying, 'This is your woman, son. I can't let you do nothing that dumb. I can't let you leave her. I made her for you!' . . . . . I'm following what I hear inside my soul!" Mattie surrenders and hugs Ann, as a sort of welcome into the family. She exits into the kitchen as Gail congratulates Jeff and Ann and exits, taking away Jeff's promise to speak to Mo if he gets a chance.

John and Dudley enter. John, who is aglow with alcohol and celebration, is happy to see Jeff home but wants to see him in his uniform. At the moment, John loves everybody—Jeff, Grandma (even though she comes downstairs and sings "Onward Christian Soldiers" in John's ear), and Ann too, whom he sees as "a sweet fighting lady," one who will always, instinctively, protect the man she loves. But he would still like to see the son "I loves better than I love myself" in his Air Force uniform.

Jeff confesses that he has lost faith in the country which his uniform represents, he is ashamed of his commission. Dudley applauds his attitude, but John does not.

JOHN (*getting angry*): It's an accomplishment, fool, how many of us ever get there—to be an officer? God knows this country needs to be torn down, but don't we want it torn down for the right to be an officer if you're able? It's an accomplishment. And I'm proud of your accomplishment.

DUDLEY: A dubious accomplishment.

JOHN: Laugh and ridicule the damn thing all you want, Goddamn it, but recognize that it's another fist jammed through the wall.

DUDLEY: Man, he became the protector of a system he believes should be destroyed.

JOHN: So we're contradictions—so what else is new? That could apply to every black man, woman and child who ever lived in this country. Especially the taxpayers. They been financing the system for a long time. Besides, who ever said we wanted total destruction, anyway? Let me put some dumb-ass *militants* in their places, which is well below me. If you get right on down to the real nitty-gritty, I don't want to totally destroy what, by rights, belongs to me anyway. I just want to weed out the bullshit. Change the value system so that the Waldorf has as many welfare tenants as the Rockafellows.

JEFF: The Rockafellows will never allow it.

JOHN: They will if you put *them* on welfare.

DUDLEY: How in hell you gonna do that, fool?

JOHN: By finding the battlefield—like I told you—like I been telling you . . . . .

John launches into a diatribe about poetry—poetry is "what the revolution is all about," he insists. Sweat, especially black sweat, is poetry. Seeing John in his uniform would be a kind of poetry, too.

Jeff reveals that he flunked out of navigator school. His father still insists as head of the house that he put on his uniform. Ann tries to shield Jeff, but Jeff doesn't need her protection. When Grandma calls Ann a "brazen hussy," Jeff orders her never to speak to Ann that way again—that is how the land lies in his family now. And Jeff tells them he will leave home if they continue to issue orders as though he were still a child.

Jeff didn't write home about missing navigator, because the letters he got from his family were so full of pride at his supposed accomplishment. Navigational mathematics are not Jeff's battlefield, he contends, but his father refuses to understand this analogy. Jeff tries to make his father see.

JEFF: Y'all had a piece of my big toe, pop. *Everybody* had a piece of my nigger toe. Not just those white pig instructors who kept checking and rechecking my work, 'cause I was what they called a belligerent nigger. But also there were only eight black officers out of three hundred in that school, and they kept telling me, "Man, you got to make it. You got to be a credit to your race."

JOHN: What's wrong with that?

JEFF: Then there was this girl I was shacking up with.

MATTIE: Shacking up!

JEFF: Shacking up, mamma!

GRANDMA: Another brazen hussy!

JEFF: She was the fox to end all foxes, pop. An Afro so soft and spongy until my hands felt like they were moving through water. Lean and smooth like the keel of a schooner, pop. And she kept telling me, "Honey, we needs that extra hundred and thirty a month flight pay to keep me in the style to which you have made me accustomed."

JOHN: Come to the point!

JEFF: Don't you see the point, pop? Everybody had a piece of my nigger toe—my fine fox, my fellow black brother officers—the pig instructors, you and mamma, pop—everybody had a piece—but me—Jeff Williams!

JOHN: Jeff Williams is Johnny Williams's son, Goddamn it!

JEFF: You mean none of me belongs to me, pop?

Jeff goes on to tell them how he hated flying to the point of airsickness every time up. In his final night-flight exam, working with celestial navigation, he calculated the plane was 80 miles into Mexico when it was in reality circling a Texas airbase. The dawn was so beautiful that Jeff tore off a page from the flight log and wrote a poem about Creation—which a white lieutenant passed around among the other instructors for laughs. Their laughter at his poem solidified in Jeff the certain knowledge that military achievement was not his forte, his battlefield. A board of senior officers tried to persuade Jeff to grovel in order to be let off lightly and given another chance, but Jeff refused.

JEFF: . . . . . I told that board, "Let go my toe!" And they replied, "What?" You know the way white people do when they don't believe their ears. So I screamed at the top of my voice, "Let go my nigger toe so I can stand up and be a man." . . . I guess they thought I was insane. They hemmed and hawed and cleared their throats, but they let go my toe, mamma. I had cut loose the man. Then I went right home and I cut loose my fine fox—and I cut loose my so-called black brother officers, and I felt like there was no more glue holding my shoes to the track; I felt I could almost fly, pop, 'cause I was a supernigger no more . . . So I ain't proving nothing to nobody—white, black, blue or polkadot—to nobody! Not even to you, Daddy Johnny . . . Mamma, you give that thing—that uniform thing to the Salvation Army or to the Good Will or whatever 'cause it will never have the good fortune to get on my back again.

DUDLEY: Bravo! Bravissimo!

> Grandma sings "Onward Christian Soldiers," and for some time no one says anything.

JEFF (quietly): It's all about battlefields—just like you said, pop.

> John pauses for an infinite time, looking at Jeff, then at Mattie and the others. With great deliberation, he then collects his coat and starts walking out slowly.

MATTIE (trying to stop him): John! It's Jeff's coming home party!

> He doesn't stop, exiting through the front door—leaving everyone suspended in a state of sad frustration. Lights fade as they all avoid looking at each other. Curtain.

ACT III

On Friday evening, the family scene has Dudley, Mattie, Grandma and Jeff seated in the living room while Ann is in the kitchen putting away dishes. John has been absent since the previous Sunday, and they don't know where he can be. Mattie is afraid John has been hit over the head by some dope fiend; Dudley is sure he is sitting in a hotel room somewhere, writing.

Grandma, thoroughly intoxicated, reminisces about her own beloved husband, Ben Brown: "He was wild as a pine cone and as savage as a grizzly and black! Black as a night what ain't got no moon. He'd stay out in the woods for days at a time—always come back with a mess of fish or a sack of rabbits, and possums—that man could tree a possum like he was a hound dog. I guess he was so black 'till they musta thought he was a shadow, creeping up on 'em. (*Pause.*) One day he just didn't come back." They found him lying dead from a charge of buckshot, with his hands on the throat of a red-neck named Isaiah who was dead too.

Dudley decides that it's time for the whole family to know that Mattie has a "very serious but not hopeless" case of cancer and must be hospitalized soon for treatment. Mattie is facing the future bravely and is worrying only about John's whereabouts. Mattie counts her blessings; she has had "a full life with an extraordinary man" and she will see Jeff married to Ann. She is ready for her time to come if come it must, she only wants to see John safely back home.

There is a knock at the door—it's Gail and Mo, come seeking Jeff's help. The young people go into the kitchen, where Jeff tells Mo he'd like to help him but is now preoccupied with his family troubles. Back in the living room the older generation is discussing the family situation, and Grandma is persuaded to sing "Rock of Ages" for them.

Mo's problem (Gail explains in the kitchen) is that there is a stool pigeon in the gang. They have set a trap for him. He'll be forced to phone his police contact tonight, and they want to watch to see which of the suspects—Chips, Skeeter, or Al—uses the telephone at the crucial moment. Gail is going to cover the pool hall phone, and they need Jeff to keep an eye on the phone in the bar.

Jeff finally agrees to help out, and Ann insists that she wants to keep Gail company, too, though Jeff forbids her to become involved. As for Mo, this will be the night of his "big thing"—property damage only, no one hurt—and it will take place somewhere other than the police station which the stool pigeon thinks is to be the target. Jeff refuses to permit Mo to tell him any of the details of his planned disturbance.

Their plans made, Mo and Gail leave by the back door, and Jeff and Ann go back to the living room. Just as Dudley tells them all that Mattie must go into the hospital on Monday, there are sounds at the back door. They hear John's voice protesting, and Jeff and Ann run out. John enters assisted by Mo, Gail, Ann and Jeff. "*He has a week's growth of beard. His eyes have the deep socket look of an alcoholic who's been on a substantial bender. His overall appearance is gaunt and shoddy. His clothes are filthy and wrinkled. He obviously smells. His hands have a slight tremor. There is a deep gash above his left eye."*

Dudley takes care of the cut while John boasts drunkenly about battling a gang of young toughs who tried to rob him. John hasn't eaten in days; as he explains it, he's been "out in the desert, like Christ, talking to myself," wrestling and overcoming the devil. He's now ready once again to join the company of his family angels. He's even resigned to Jeff's attitude, happy that his son has found his proper battlefield.

John tells his wife: "I was all right, Mattie—really. Dulcey gave me a room over her store. I told her I wanted to think—to write some poetry. I wanted to write a love poem—to you, Mattie. Words are like precious jewels, did you know that? But I couldn't find any jewels precious enough to match you, Mattie. So I took to drinking, and before I knew it I was drunk all the time."

When John began to see strange little men in his room, he knew it was time to come home—besides, Dudley had told him he'd have some information about Mattie's condition by the end of the week. When Dudley tells John that Mattie must go into the hospital Monday, John goes nearly berserk, seeing the little men again and trying to whip them out of the house, collapsing to the floor, then calming down gradually but ranting at the heavens for the evils he has suffered throughout his whole life.

Mattie tries to soothe her husband, and John apologizes to her for not having given her a better life. Mattie reassures him: "I got *you*, baby . . . . . I got the Rolls Royce, baby . . . . . I've been so Goddamn happy! All I ever cared about was seeing you walk, stumble or stagger through that door. I only complained because I felt I should say something—but I never meant it, Johnny, I never meant a word. You couldn't have given me nothing more, baby. I'd a just keeled over and died from too much happiness."

The lights dim to black, and when they come up again only Mattie and Dudley are present in the living room.

MATTIE: What'd you give me, Dudley? Sure is strong. Can hardly keep my head up.

DUDLEY: Do you feel any pain?

MATTIE: Not now.

DUDLEY: Then it's doing its job. You'll rest good when you go to bed.

MATTIE: Which can't be too long from now. The way I'm feeling.
    John appears at the top of the stairs; descends slowly as he is absorbed in reading some pages. He enters the living room.

JOHN (*announces quietly*): I finished it.

MATTIE: What?

JOHN: A poem I been working on, Mattie. It's your poem, Mattie. "The River Niger." It ain't a love poem, but it's for you, sugar, dedicated to my super bitch, Mattie Jean Williams.

DUDLEY: Read it to us, nigger.
    Ann and Gail are seen entering the back kitchen door. Jeff too.

*John begins to read and a bass begins low with African motif and
gradually rises. Jeff and the girls begin to engage in conversation
but desist when they hear John. They drift to the living room.*

JOHN:

I am the River Niger—hear my waters!
I am totally flexible.
I am the River Niger—hear my waters!
My waters are the first sperm of the world.
When the earth was but a faceless whistling embryo
Life burst from my liquid kernels like popcorn.
Hear my waters—rushing and popping in muffled finger drum staccato.
It is life you hear. stretching its limbs in my waters—
I am the River Niger! Hear my waters!
When the Earth Mother cracked into continents
I was vomited from the cold belly of the Atlantic
To slip slyly into Africa
From the underside of her brow
I see no—
Hear no—
Speak no evil,
But I know,
I gossip with the crocodile
And rub elbows with the river horse
I have swapped morbid jokes with the hyena
And heard his dry cackle at twilight.
I see no—
Hear no—
Speak no evil
But I know.

I am the River Niger—hear my waters!
Hear, I say, hear my waters, man!
They is Mammy-tammys, baby.
I have lapped at the pugnacious hips of brown mammas.
Have tapped on the doors of their honeydews, yeah!
I have shimmered like sequins
As they sucked me over their blueberry tongues,
As they sung me to sleep in the glittering afternoon, yeah!
I have washed the red wounds of day-decorated warriors—
Bad, bad dudes who smirked at the leopard
I have cast witches from gabbling babies, yeah!
Have known the warm piss from newly circumcized boys.
Have purified the saliva from sun-drenched lions—
Do you hear me talking?
I am the River Niger!

I came to the cloudy Mississippi
Over keels of incomprehensible woe.
I ran way to the Henry Hudson
Under the sails of ragged hope.
I am the River Niger,
Transplanted to Harlem
From the Harlem River Drive.
Hear me, my children—hear my waters!
I sleep in your veins.
I see no—
Hear no—
Speak no evil,
But I know, and I know that you know.
I flow to the ends of your spirit.
Hold hands, my children, and I will flow to the ends of the earth,
And the whole world will hear my waters.
I am the River Niger! Don't deny me!
Do you hear me? Don't deny me!
    Pause. Bass fades.
MATTIE: That's very beautiful, Johnny.
JEFF: Yeah, pop, that's pretty nice.
DUDLEY (*sarcastically*): Interesting!
JOHN: Ya monkey chaser.

Mattie exits upstairs to bed, passing Grandma coming down singing "Rock of Ages." Jeff and the girls move into the kitchen, while Dudley and John philosophize about man being a part of nature and Grandma insisting that she's no part of nature, like an animal, but a special creature made in the image of God.

Dudley switches on the TV set, and the conversational focus shifts to the kitchen where the three are comparing notes on the trap laid for the informer. At their vantage point, Ann and Gail heard nothing but Skeeter placing an apparently genuine bet on a horse. Jeff heard something, all right—a caller telling someone "Plan B," simply that and nothing else, an obvious coded message. The message was too short for Jeff to recognize the voice, but perhaps he could do so if he could hear it again.

Grandma comes into the kitchen and magnanimously pours them all a drink from her bottle. There is a noise at the back door, and when Jeff goes to investigate he finds Mo with Skeeter, who has been hurt—another job for Dudley, who diagnoses Skeeter's injury as a gunshot wound. Jeff takes Mo into the living room.

JEFF: Why in the hell did you bring him here?
MO: I figured Dr. Stanton would be here—
JEFF: I told you I don't want my family implicated in this shit—why didn't you take him to your place?

John comes to the door.

MO: I live over headquarters! The pigs—

JEFF: Oh, shit—shit—what happened?

MO: It's stupid—stupid. I mean we had just crossed the street. I mean we were just walking around the fence when this pig started blowing his whistle and yelling at us.

JEFF: They musta been alerted.

MO: Fucking Skeeter panicked—started running—what the hell am I supposed to do? I'm carrying a tote bag with four sticks of dynamite. So I start running too. Next thing I know there're four pigs chasing us. One fires and spins Skeets clean around. Skeets is screaming and shit, and they're gaining so I blast off a couple and knock trigger-happy on his ass.

JEFF: What—you crazy motherfucker coming here after that?

JOHN: You mean they just started shooting? You didn't shoot first?

MO: Why would we do that?

JOHN: You sure?

MO: I don't want to hurt nobody if I can help it, Mr. Williams.

JOHN: You think he's dead?

MO: I don't know. He hit the ground so hard I could almost feel it.

JOHN: I sure hope you killed the bastard. But if you call yourself a revolutionary, then you suppose to know where you gonna take your wounded. Takes more'n wearing a goddamn beret.

There's a banging on the door—it is Al and Chips. Now Jeff is angrier than ever at Mo for using the Williams home as their gang rendezvous. Mo is apologizing to Jeff, when they are interrupted by flashing lights and the sound of police whistles. From outside, the voice of police Lt. Staples calling on a bullhorn informs them that the house is surrounded and the inhabitants have five minutes to come out unarmed.

Obviously an informer has told the police all of their plans (but he couldn't have known about Mo's final decision to change the target of their attack, because Mo told no one about this). John points out that the guns are the only damaging evidence against them; Dudley has Skeeter's, and John takes Mo's.

Chips points to Al as the informer. Chips and Al were stationed near the police station which they expected to dynamite; but when Mo and Skeeter didn't show up Al went across the street to speak to a policeman. Al must have told the officer about another target the gang had once discussed, a state office building (which was Mo's true destination), because the police went racing off in that direction.

Skeeter, his wound dressed, comes in from the kitchen and adds that Al has seemed unusually curious about the facts of Buckley's death. Jeff now identifies Al's voice as the one he heard saying "Plan B" on the barroom telephone.

Al denies that he is the squealer and accuses everyone else. Jeff pretends that he killed Buckley himself with a 45 brought home from the Air Force. He shows Al papers proving that he was discharged more than a month ago and could have committed the crime. Al draws his revolver and admits to being an undercover police agent on assignment to find out who killed his friend Buckley. Now he knows, and he gloats at the imminent prospect of Buckley's fellow-officers surrounding the house shooting them all up: "You mother-fuckers, fucking up the country with your slogans and your jive-ass threats. Militants, ain't that a bitch. Black cripples trying to scale a mountain. I hate the smell of you assholes."

Mo insists that the Buckley killing was an outside job, but Al is now convinced. Ann shakes him for a moment by insisting that Jeff was with her in Canada for the whole month since his discharge. John uses Al's moment of hesitation to raise the gun still in his hand and order Al to drop his weapon. *"Al whirls and shoots. There is an exchange of gun play between the two men. Al goes down, killed instantly. John also goes down, mortally wounded."*

John gives orders to hide all the guns in the basement except the ones he and Al are still holding. Dudley tries to help John but sees that he is beyond help. John orders Dudley to go outside and ask Lt. Staples to give them a couple of minutes to get ready to come out, so that the police won't fire into Mattie's house. Dudley obeys, then comes back inside.

Mattie herself comes downstairs, wakened by the noise but still a bit dazed. Gradually she understands that John is hurt—dying—but at the moment still in full charge.

JOHN: I got to get our children straight before I go—now be my superbitch and shut the fuck up.
Mattie understands and obeys.
Now you youngbloods listen to me. Here's the story, I am the real leader of the organization—ya got me? I was with Skeeter when he got shot. I fired the shot which hit the cop at the office building. I made it back here—found out that Al here is a Judas and we had a shoot-out. The rest of you have never owned a gun—only your leader—me! Ya got that?
Grandma, drunk and in a state of shock, comes strangely alive. She thinks John is her Ben. She rushes up and falls at John's knees.
GRANDMA: BEN—BEN BROWN! (*Reaches for John's gun.*) Gimme that shotgun.
Mattie blocks her.
MATTIE (*very calm and solemn; almost eerie*): No, mamma.
GRANDMA: I'll just shoot right into the crowd, daughter. See 'em, look at their faces! They's glad to see my Ben dead. Lawdamercy! He's dead! (*Crying from an ancient wound.*) Gimme that shotgun, child. Ten for one, ten for one—my man is a king—you crackers—ya dirty old red-neck crackers.
Breaks into "Rock of Ages." Bass counterpoint seeps in.
JOHN: Hear that, Mattie. The old battle ax finally gave me a compliment. Where's my Mattie? Let me see my Mattie.
Mattie's let through. They embrace.
MATTIE: I'm with you every second, baby.

JOHN: I knew she'd slip one day. I'm sorry, Mattie.

MATTIE: What for, baby?

JOHN: I'm cheating ya, honey—going first this way.

MATTIE: Hush now!

JOHN: Don't suffer long, honey. Just give up and take my hand. The children—the children will be all right now. (*Pause.*) Look at Dr. Dudley Stanton down there. Trying to save my life. Ain't that a bitch! See what a big old fake you've been all along. Don't worry Dudley—fighting Lady Ann—Jeff—ya got a fighting lady to protect your flanks, son—don't worry, I don't feel nothing now. Just sweetness—a sweet sweetness.

DUDLEY: Your poems—I'll get 'em published.

JOHN: Fuck them poems—this is poetry, man—what I feel right here and now. This sweetness. Sing on, Grandma. (*Pause. He shivers.*) I found it, Dudley—I found it.

DUDLEY: What, Johnny?

JOHN: My battlefield—my battlefield, man! I was a bitch too, ya monkey chaser. See my shit! I got two for the price of one.

DUDLEY: Yeah, chief.

Johnny dies. Pause.

STAPLES'S VOICE: All right, we're coming in. Any funny business, and you'll regret it.

CHIPS (*whimpering*): Oh, God, oh my God!

MATTIE: Shut up! And tell it like Johnny told ya. He ain't gonna die for nothing 'cause you ain't gonna let him! Jeff—open the door, son! Tell 'em to come on in here!

Jeff crosses to the door.

And you better not fuck up!

Curtain.

THE SUNSHINE BOYS

A Comedy in Two Acts

BY NEIL SIMON

Cast and credits appear on page 346

NEIL SIMON was born in the Bronx, N.Y., on July 4, 1927. He graduated from DeWitt Clinton High School, served in the Army where he managed to find some time for writing, which soon became his profession without the formalities of college, except for a few courses at New York University and the University of Denver. His first theater work consisted of sketches for camp shows at Tamiment, Pa., in collaboration with his brother Danny. He became a TV writer, supplying a good deal of material to Sid Caesar and Phil Silvers.

On Broadway, Simon contributed sketches to Catch a Star *(1955) and* New Faces of 1956. *His first Broadway play was* Come Blow Your Horn *(1961), followed by the book of the musical* Little Me *(1962). His comedy* Barefoot in the Park *(1963) was selected as a Best Play of its season, as was* The Odd Couple *(1965). Neither of these had closed when the musical* Sweet Charity, *for which Simon wrote the book, came along early in 1966; and none of the three had closed when Simon's* The Star-Spangled Girl *opened the following season in December, 1966—so that Simon had the phenomenal total of four hit shows running simultaneously on Broadway during the season of 1966-67. When the last of the four closed the following summer, Simon's hits had played a total of 3,367 performances over four theater seasons.*

Simon immediately began stacking another pile of blue-chip Broadway shows. His Plaza Suite *(1968) was named a Best Play of its year; his book of the musical* Promises, Promises *(1969) was another smash, and* Last of the Red Hot Lovers *(1969) became his fourth Best Play and the third in still another group of Simon shows in grand simultaneous display on Broadway.*

Plaza Suite *closed before* The Gingerbread Lady *(1970, also a Best Play)* opened, *so that Simon's second stack was three plays and 3,084 performances* high.

Last season Simon came up with still another Best Play, The Prisoner of Second Avenue. The Sunshine Boys *is—let's see, now—Simon's tenth straight success and seventh Best Play. It also gave him two hits running together during the 1972-73 season, a tremendous feat of playwriting which by any other author would be hailed in the most powerful superlatives, but which in the unique case of Neil Simon seems scarcely worth mentioning.*

Simon lives in New York City where he can be close to all this action (he owns the Eugene O'Neill Theater, too). He is married, with two daughters.

Time: The present

Place: New York City

ACT I

Scene 1

SYNOPSIS: Willie Clark, in his 70s and dressed in pajamas and an old bathrobe, is slumped in a chair half-dozing and half-watching a TV soap opera. It is an early midwinter afternoon, and Willie's home is a two-room apartment in an old hotel on Broadway in the East Eighties, "..... *rather a depressing place. There is a bed, a bureau, a small dining table with two chairs, an old leather chair that faces a TV set on a cheap metal stand. There is a small kitchen to one side, a small bathroom on the other. A window looks out over Broadway.*"

The whistle of the boiling kettle on the stove wakes Willie from his doze. He picks up the phone, finds no one on the line, ignores his mistake and nonchalantly shifts his attention to the kettle and makes himself a cup of tea with honey while the TV goes into a Lipton commercial.

Willie returns to his chair, and his foot inadvertently comes up against the wire from the TV set and pulls out the plug. Seeing that there is no picture, Willie fiddles with set, hits it, cajoles it, but to no avail. Finally he calls the hotel desk to complain that his TV is out of order. Aware of Willie's muddleheadedness, the clerk suggests that the plug has been pulled out. Willie sees that this is true but denies it as he hangs up—dignity before all else in dealing with hotel clerks. He plugs in the set and sits as the picture comes back on.

> *There is a knock on the door . . . Willie looks at the wall on the opposite side.*

WILLIE: Bang all you want, I'm not turning it off. I'm lucky it works.
> *Pause . . . then knock on front door again, this time accompanied by a male voice.*

BEN'S VOICE: Uncle Willie? It's me. Ben.
>   *Willie turns and looks at front door, not acknowledging that he was mistaken about the knocking on the other wall.*

WILLIE: Who's that?

BEN'S VOICE: Ben.

WILLIE: Ben? Is that you?

BEN'S VOICE: Yes, Uncle Willie, it's Ben. Open the door.

WILLIE: Wait a minute.
>   *Rises, crosses to door, tripping over TV cord again, disconnecting set. He starts to unlatch the door but has difficulty manipulating it. His fingers are not too manipulative.*

Wait a minute . . .
>   *He is having great difficulty with it.*

. . . Wait a minute.

BEN'S VOICE: Is anything wrong?

WILLIE (*still trying*): Wait a minute.
>   *He tries forcing it.*

BEN'S VOICE: What's the matter?

WILLIE: I'm locked in . . . The lock is broken, I'm locked in . . . Go down and tell the boy. Sandy. Tell Sandy that Mr. Clark is locked in.

BEN'S VOICE: What is it, the latch?

WILLIE: It's the latch. It's broken, I'm locked in. Go tell the boy Sandy, they'll get somebody.

BEN'S VOICE: That happened last week. Don't try to force it. Just slide it out.
>   *Willie stares at the latch.*

Uncle Willie, do you hear me? Don't force it. Slide it out.

WILLIE (*hands up to the latch*): Wait a minute.
>   *Carefully, he slides it out. It comes open.*

It's open. Never mind, I did it myself.

Willie opens the door and his nephew Ben Silverman comes in. He is "*a well-dressed man in his early thirties, wearing a topcoat and carrying a shopping bag from Bloomingdale's, filled to the brim with assorted foodstuffs and a copy of the weekly Variety.*" Ben always visits his uncle on Wednesdays. Gently, Ben reproaches Willie for never going out of this room (Willie insists that he went to the park on Sunday) and for living on sandwiches. Ben has brought his uncle an assortment of salt-free delicacies, but Willie isn't paying attention—he's scanning *Variety.*

WILLIE: Two new musicals went into rehearsal today and I didn't even get an audition . . . Why didn't I get an audition?

BEN: Because there were no parts for you. One of them is a young rock musical and the other show is all black.

WILLIE: What's the matter, I can't do black? I did black in 1928. And when I did black, you understood the words, not like today.

SAM LEVEN AND JACK ALBERTSON IN "THE SUNSHINE BOYS"

BEN: I'm sorry, you're not the kind of black they're looking for. (*He shivers.*) Geez, it's cold in here. You know it's freezing in here? Don't they ever send up any heat?

WILLIE (*has turned page*): How do you like that? Sol Burton died.

BEN: Who?

WILLIE: Sol Burton. The songwriter. 89 years old, went like that, from nothing.

BEN: Why didn't you put on a sweater?

WILLIE: . . . I knew him very well . . . A terrible person. Mean, mean. He should rest in peace but he was a mean person. His best friends didn't like him.

BEN (*goes to bureau for sweater*): Why is it so cold in here?

WILLIE: You know what kind of songs he wrote? . . . The worst. The worst songs ever written were written by Sol Burton. (*He sings.*) "Lady, lady, be my baby" . . . Did you ever hear anything so rotten? Baby he rhymes with lady . . . No wonder he's dead.

He turns the page.

BEN: This radiator is ice cold. Look, Uncle Willie, I'm not going to let you live here any more. You've got to let me find you another place . . . I've been asking you for seven years now. You're going to get sick.

WILLIE (*still looking at Variety*): Tom Jones is gonna get a hundred thousand dollars a week in Las Vegas. When Lewis and I were headlining at the Palace, the *Palace* didn't cost a hundred thousand dollars.

Willie searches in Ben's paper bag for cigars—he isn't allowed cigars but Ben always stretches the rules just a little, and this time there are three at the bottom of the bag. Willie asks perfunctorily about Ben's family while looking around for a light. Ben has two children whose names Willie can never remember. In their turn, the children are too young ever to have seen vaudeville or know about their once-famous great uncle Willie, or even to have seen one of his six appearances on the Ed Sullivan show.

Willie accuses Ben of having no sense of humor ("Like your father, he laughed once in 1932"). But to Ben, his uncle's situation is no laughing matter: shut up in a cold, run-down hotel room watching TV on a defective set, never eating properly, never going out, becoming so dangerously absent-minded that he once locked himself in the bathroom overnight.

Willie complains that what he needs is a job. Ben is his agent as well as his nephew and has tried and sometimes succeeded in getting Willie parts in TV commercials, but Willie has a reputation for not being able to remember his lines. Willie claims that his memory is all right, but he can't remember anything that's not funny—such as the name of the product in a potato-chip commercial he worked on recently. Willie explains to his nephew for the umpteenth time that words with "k" in them (chicken, pickle, cup cake, cookie) are funny and those without it are not.

Ben has some good news for Willie, however. CBS is planning an hour and a half special on the history of comedy, and they want the famous vaudeville team of Lewis and Clark, who were known as The Sunshine Boys, to come out of retirement to take part. CBS will pay $10,000 for the one appearance, but Willie refuses angrily to appear with his former partner Al Lewis, calling him "that bastard."

Willie calls Ben "a good boy but a stinking agent." Stung, Ben threatens to leave and never come back to see his uncle again or bring him presents, but Willie remains adamant.

BEN (*breathing heavily*): Why won't you do this for me? I'm not asking you to be partners again. If you two don't get along, all right. But this is just for one night. One last show. Once you get an exposure like that. Alka-Seltzer will come begging to *me* to sign you up . . . Jesus, how is it going to look if I go back to the office and tell them I couldn't make a deal with my own uncle?

WILLIE: My personal opinion? Lousy!

BEN (*falls into chair, exhausted*): Do you really hate Al Lewis that much?

WILLIE (*looks away*): I don't discuss Al Lewis any more.

BEN (*gets up*): We *have* to discuss him because CBS is waiting for an answer today and if we turn them down, I want to have a pretty good reason why . . . You haven't seen him in, what, ten years now.

WILLIE (*takes a long time before answering*): . . . Eleven years!

BEN (*amazed*): You mean to tell me you haven't spoken to him in eleven years?

WILLIE: I haven't *seen* him in eleven years. I haven't *spoken* to him in twelve years.

BEN: You mean you saw him for a whole year that you didn't speak to him?

WILLIE: It wasn't easy. I had to sneak around backstage a lot.

BEN: But you spoke to him on stage.

WILLIE: Not to *him*. If he played a gypsy, I spoke to the gypsy. If he played a lunatic, I spoke to the lunatic. But that bastard I didn't speak to.

BEN: I can't believe that.

WILLIE: You don't believe it? I can show you witnesses who *saw* me never speaking to him.

BEN: It's been eleven years, Uncle Willie. Hasn't time changed anything for you?

WILLIE: Yes. I hate him eleven years more.

Ben gets Willie to talk about his reasons. During their 43 years of partnership, Willie got so he could barely endure Al Lewis's finger poking at his chest in the comedy routines. And Al was a spitter who would stand nose-to-nose and spit out words beginning with "T"—Willie believes Al did this deliberately. He moves close to Ben and demonstrates. Ben wipes his face and asks Willie why, if Al was so unpleasant, Willie stayed with him all those years? Willie tells him, "Because he was terrific . . . There'll never be another one like him . . . Nobody could time a joke the way he could time a joke . . . Nobody could say a line the way he said it . . . I knew what he was thinking, he knew what I was thinking . . . One person, that's what we were . . . No, no. Al Lewis was the best. The *best!* . . . You understand?"

The last time they worked together was on the Ed Sullivan show. For some unaccountable reason, Al's timing was off in their sure-fire Doctor skit. Willie sensed this, though the audience did not, and the applause and Ed Sullivan's commendation were hearty. But back in the dressing room Al took off his makeup and announced his retirement to Willie. Al walked out of the theater never to return. He became a stockbroker and in later years tried to get in touch with Willie, but Willie never answered any of his letters or telegrams.

By making that decision, Al retired Willie too, though Willie wasn't ready for it yet. Now Willie is a single—he insists—and he refuses to go back to work with Al even for one performance. Al has already agreed to do the show (Ben tells his uncle), not for the money but so that his grandchildren can see his act just once. Ben tells Willie about Al: "Did you know his wife died two years ago? He's living with his daughter now, somewhere in New Jersey . . .

He doesn't do anything any more. He's got very bad arthritis, he's got asthma, he's got poor blood circulation."

CBS wants them to do their Doctor sketch, and Ben suggests that Willie try one rehearsal with Al—if it doesn't work out they can call it off. Willie finally agrees to try it, so long as everyone understands that he's against it. Willie permits Ben to phone Al in New Jersey.

BEN (*into phone*): Hello? . . . Mr. Lewis? . . . Ben Silverman . . . Yes, fine, thanks . . . I'm here with him now.

WILLIE: Willie Clark. The one he left on the Ed Sullivan Show. Ask him if he remembers.

BEN: It's okay, Mr. Lewis . . . Uncle Willie said yes.

WILLIE: With an "against it." Don't forget the "against it."

BEN: No, he's very anxious to do it.

WILLIE (*jumping up in anger*): WHO'S ANXIOUS ??? . . . I'M AGAINST IT! . . . TELL HIM, you lousy nephew.

BEN: Can you come here for rehearsal on Monday? . . . Oh, that'll be swell . . . In the morning. (*To Willie.*) About eleven o'clock. How long is the drive? About two hours?

WILLIE: Make it nine o'clock.

BEN: Be reasonable, Willie. (*Into phone.*) Eleven o'clock is fine, Mr. Lewis . . . Can you give me your address, please, so I can send you the contracts.

He takes pen out of pocket and writes on his notebook.
One one nine, South Pleasant Drive . . .

WILLIE: Tell him if he starts with the spitting or poking, I'm taking him to court. I'll have a man on the show watching. Tell him.

BEN: West Davenport, New Jersey . . . Oh nine seven oh four . . .

WILLIE: I don't want any— (*Spitting.*) —"*T*oy *t*elephones *t*apping on *t*in *t*urtles*"* . . . tell him . . . tell him.

    Curtain.

Scene 2

A few minutes before 11 o'clock on the following Monday, the appointed day of meeting and rehearsal, Willie enters from the bathroom dressed in pajamas and slippers as usual but wearing a blue suit jacket instead of his bathrobe. Ben knocks on the door, and Willie has his accustomed difficulty with the latch but finally gets it open.

Willie claims that he has changed his mind and has decided not to do the skit for TV. Ben tells him he must go through with it now, and he will stay here to make sure that Willie behaves himself when Al arrives. Willie complains that he is sick, but Ben will accept no excuses.

There is a knock on the door, and Willie abruptly escapes to the kitchen and starts puttering with the kettle to make some tea. Panicky, Ben goes to the door and opens it. There stands Al Lewis, "*about 70 years old . . . . . dressed in his best blue suit, hat, scarf and carries a walking stick. He was*

probably quite a gay blade in his day but time has slowed him down some-
what . . . Our first impression is that he is soft-spoken and pleasant . . . and
a little nervous."

Ben and Al exchange greetings. Al looks over in Willie's direction, but
Willie hasn't glanced up from his tea-making. Ben makes conversation with
Al about the trip in from New Jersey. His daughter drove him in, and he has
arranged for her to phone him every hour until he is ready to leave.

Finally Willie looks in from the kitchen but ignores Al completely, looking
at Ben and asking how many teas he should make, then immediately disap-
pearing. Al and Ben talk business, and Al runs over the list of props that will
be needed for the Doctor sketch.

AL: You need a desk. A telephone. A pointer. A blackboard. A piece of
white chalk, a piece of red chalk . . . A skeleton, not too tall, a stethoscope,
a thermometer, an "ahh" stick . . .

BEN: What's an ah stick?

AL: To put in your mouth to say "ahh."

BEN: Oh. Right, an "ahh" stick.

AL: A look stick, a bottle of pills—

BEN: A look stick? What's a look stick?

AL: A stick to look in the ears. With cotton on the end . . .

BEN: Right. A look stick.

AL: A bottle of pills. Big ones, like for a horse.

BEN (*makes circle with his two fingers*): About this big?

AL: That's for a pony. (*Makes circle using fingers on both hands.*) For a
horse is like this . . . Some bandages, cotton, an eye chart—

BEN: Wait a minute, you're going too fast.

AL (*slowly*): A desk . . . a telephone . . . a pointer . . .

BEN: No, I got all that . . . after the cotton and eye chart.

AL: A man's suit. Size 40. Like the one I'm wearing.

BEN: Also in blue?

AL: What do I need two blue suits? Get me brown.

BEN: A brown suit . . . Is that all?

AL: That's all.

WILLIE (*in kitchen, without looking in*): A piece of liver.

AL: That's all plus a piece of liver.

BEN: What kind of liver?

AL: Regular calves' liver. From the butcher . . .

BEN: Like how much? A pound?

AL: A little laugh is a pound. A big laugh is two pounds . . . Three pounds
with a lot of blood'll bring the house down.

BEN: Is that it?

AL: That's it. And a blonde.

BEN: You mean a woman?

AL: You know a blonde nurse that's a man? . . . Big! As big as you can find.
With a big chest, a forty, a forty-five . . . and a nice bottom . . .

That's all they need, Al finally tells Ben, and Willie remarks from his kitchen that he wasn't listening. Ben tells Al how much young people will appreciate the opportunity of seeing Lewis and Clark. He exits, leaving the two old men alone. They seem reluctant to look at each other as Willie brings in the tea. Willie is less cordial than Al expected, but Al takes this in stride. They sip their tea in silence.

WILLIE (*long pause*): I was sorry to hear about Lillian.

AL: Thank you.

WILLIE: She was a nice woman. I always liked Lillian.

AL: Thank you.

WILLIE: . . . And how about you?

AL: Thank God, knock wood—(*Raps knuckles on his cane.*)—perfect.

WILLIE: I heard different. I heard your blood didn't circulate.

AL: Not true. My blood circulates . . . I'm not saying *everywhere,* but it circulates.

WILLIE: Is that why you use the cane?

AL: It's not a cane. It's a walking stick . . . Maybe once in a great while it's a cane . . .

WILLIE: I've been lucky, thank God . . . I'm in the pink.

AL: I was looking. For a minute I thought you were having a flush.

WILLIE (*sips his tea*): You know Sol Burton died?

AL: Go on . . . Who's Sol Burton?

WILLIE: You don't remember Sol Burton?

AL (*thinks*): . . . Oh, yes. The manager from the Belasco.

WILLIE: That was Sol Bernstein.

AL: Not Sol Bernstein. Sol *Burton* was the manager from the Belasco.

WILLIE: Sol *Bernstein* was the manager from the Belasco and it wasn't the Belasco, it was the Morosco.

AL: Sid *Weinstein* was the manager from the Morosco. Sol *Burton* was the manager from the Belasco. Sol *Bernstein* I don't know *who* the hell was.

WILLIE: How can you remember anything if your blood doesn't circulate?

AL: It circulates in my *head.* It doesn't circulate in my *feet.* (*He stomps his foot on the floor a few times.*)

WILLIE: Is anything coming down?

AL: Wait a minute, wasn't Sid Weinstein the songwriter?

WILLIE: NO, for crise sakes! That's SOL BURTON!

AL: Who wrote "Lady, lady, be my baby?"

WILLIE: That's what I'm telling you! Sol Burton, the lousy songwriter.

AL: Oh, *that* Sol Burton . . . He died?

WILLIE: Last week.

AL: Where?

WILLIE (*points*): In *Variety.*

They continue making small conversational contacts. Al remembers Willie's hotel suite as bigger than it is, and Willie explains that this is a subdivided part of the old one. Al has a nice room in his daughter's New Jersey house (he explains) with many country pleasures including a rock garden. Willie prefers the city pace, the city noise, characterizing Al as "a slow person." Willie pretends that he is in demand for movie and theater work and insists that he did a potato chip commercial only last week on TV but can't remember the sponsor's name. They stop just short of the edge of a quarrel.

Willie makes it clear to Al that he is against their planned appearance but will do it for his nephew's sake. Al is in favor of doing it, if only because of the large fee for just a few days' work, which will be a present for his grandchildren. After reassuring each other that they are both going through with this for purely altruistic reasons, they decide to proceed with a rehearsal, shifting the furniture to make a set. *"They both get up and start to move the furniture around. First each one takes a single chair and moves it in a certain position. Then they both take a table and jointly move it away. Then they each take the chairs the other one moved before, and move it into a different place. Every time one moves something somewhere, the other moves it in a different spot."*

Willie realizes first that they are working at cross-purposes. He reminds Al that they are supposed to be setting up for the Doctor sketch, and they go at it again—but still they are working against each other. The argument about how the furniture should be set up for the Doctor sketch heats up until Willie calls Al "Mister," which Al dislikes. Willie challenges Al to dress the set properly, but when Al accepts the challenge and rearranges the furniture, Willie claims that it is wrong for the Doctor sketch, it is the Gypsy Chiropractor set.

Al in his turn challenges Willie to set up the Doctor sketch. Willie *"looks at him confidently, then crosses to the chair, picks it up and moves it to the left about four inches, if that much."* Then Willie announces triumphantly, "There, that's the Doctor sketch!" Al calls Willie a "lapalooza" to even up for the "Mister."

They decide to skip the opening with Willie and the nurse and begin the rehearsal with Al's entrance. Al steps to the front door and pantomimes knocking, but Willie insists that he go all the way out into the hall. Al agrees reluctantly but is worried that his daughter might phone while he's out of the room. When he finally does go through the action of leaving the room and knocking on the door, they can't get the door open again. Al manages to open it from the outside, but they decide maybe they'd better just pantomime the entrance after all. They take their places for the rehearsal.

AL (*pantomimes with fist*): Knock knock knock.

WILLIE (*sing-song*): Enter.

AL (*stops, looks at him*): What do you mean "Enter"? (*He does it in same sing-song way.*) What happened to "Come-in"?

WILLIE: It's the same thing, isn't it? Enter or come-in. What's the difference, as long as you're in.

AL: The difference is we've done this sketch 12,000 times and you've always said "Come-in" and suddenly today it's "Enter". Why today, after all these years, do you suddenly change it to "Enter"?

WILLIE (*shrugs*): I'm trying to freshen up the act.

AL: Who asked you to freshen up the act? They asked for the Doctor sketch, didn't they? The Doctor sketch starts with "Come-in", not "Enter". You wanna freshen up something, put some flowers in here.

WILLIE: It's a new generation today. This is not 1934, you know.

AL: No kidding? I didn't get today's paper.

WILLIE: What's bad about "Enter" instead of "Come-in"?

AL: Because it's different. You know why we've been doing it the same way for 43 years? Because it's good.

WILLIE: And you know why we don't do it any more? Because we've been doing it the same way for 43 years.

AL: So, if we're not doing it any more, why are we changing it?

WILLIE: Can I make a comment, nothing personal? I think you've been sitting on a New Jersey porch too long.

AL: What does that mean?

WILLIE: That means I think you've been sitting on a New Jersey porch too long. From my window, I see everything that goes on in the world. I see old people, I see young people, nice people, bad people, I see holdups, drug addicts, ambulances, car crashes, jumpers from buildings, I see everything. You see a lawn mower and a milkman.

AL (*looks at him long*): And that's why you want to say "Enter" instead of "Come-in"?

WILLIE: Are you listening to me?

AL (*looks around*): Why, there's someone else in the room?

WILLIE: You don't know the first thing that's going on today.

AL: All right, what's going on today?

WILLIE: Did you ever hear the expression, "That's where it is"? Well, this is where it is and that's where I am.

AL: I see . . . Did you ever hear the expression, "You don't know what the hell you're talking about"? It comes right in front of the *other* expression, "You never *knew* what the hell you were talking about."

WILLIE: *I* wasn't the one who retired. You know why you retired? Because you were tired. You were getting old-fashioned. I was still new-fashioned and I'll *always* be.

AL: I see. That's why you're in such demand. That's why you're such a "hot" property today. That's why you do movies you don't do, that's why you're in musicals you're not in, and that's why you make commercials you don't make because you can't even remember them to *make* them.

WILLIE: You know what I *do* remember? I remember what a pain in the ass you are to work with, that's what I remember.

AL: That's right. And when you worked with this pain in the ass, you lived in a *five*-room suite. Now you live in a *one*-room suite . . . And you're still wearing the same God damned pajamas you wore in the five-room suite.

WILLIE: I don't have to take this crap from you.

AL: You're lucky you're getting it. No one else wants to give it to you.

WILLIE: I don't want to argue with you. After you say "Knock knock knock" I'm saying "Enter" and if you don't like it, you don't have to come in.

AL: You can't say nothing without my permission. I own fifty per cent of this act.

WILLIE: Then say *your* fifty per cent. I'm saying "Enter" in *my* fifty per cent.

AL: If you say "Enter" after "Knock knock knock" . . . I'm coming in all right. But not alone. I'm bringing a lawyer with me."

WILLIE: Where? From New Jersey? You're lucky if a *cow* comes with you.

Al infuriates Willie by poking him in the chest with his finger to help drive home a point. Willie grabs a knife and threatens to cut off Al's finger. They exchange insults: Al calls Willie crazy and Willie calls Al senile.

The phone interrupts their quarrel. Willie answers it, then hands it over to Al when he finds it's Al's daughter calling. Al asks to be picked up at once in front of the hotel. Al's daughter can hear them shouting insults at each other during the phone conversation, and Al tells her Willie has turned out to be a crazy bedbug. She tries to smooth over the situation. She asks Willie to come to the phone and persuades him to give the rehearsal one more try. Al warns Willie that this time the line must be "Come-in" or he will depart.

AL: . . . . . Are you going to say "Come-in"?
WILLIE: Ask me "Knock knock knock".
AL: I know you, you bastard.
WILLIE: ASK ME "KNOCK KNOCK KNOCK"!
AL: KNOCK KNOCK KNOCK!
WILLIE (*grinding it in*): EN-TERRR!
AL: BEDBUG!!! CRAZY BEDBUG!!! (*Running out.*)
WILLIE (*big smile*): ENNN-TERRRRR!
     The curtain starts down.
AL (*heading for the door*): LUNATIC BASTARD!!
WILLIE: ENNN-TERRRRR!
     Curtain.

ACT II

Scene 1

Lewis and Clark have somehow resolved their differences and decided to make the guest appearance on TV in the Doctor sketch after all, because a TV stage is all set for it with *"an obvious stage 'flat' representation of a doctor's office. It has an old desk and chair, a telephone, a cabinet filled with medicine bottles, a human skeleton hanging on a stand, a blackboard with chalk and pointer, an eye chart on the wall."*

There are TV lights and boom microphones in the studio, and the voice of the invisible director over the loudspeaker discusses technical problems with an assistant visible on the set. They are preparing for a dress rehearsal of the skit, as Ben appears and apologizes to the unseen director for the delay—apparently Lewis and Clark are having their own "technical" problems backstage. Ben assures him that this time the two comedians will run through the whole sketch without stopping.

Finally Al and Willie are ready, and the director gives the signal to begin. An announcer introduces The Sunshine Boys as "more than a team . . . two shining lights that beam as one . . . For Lewis without Clark is like laughter without joy," in one of their most famous and popular vaudeville sketches entitled "The Doctor Will See You Now."

As the sketch begins, a frail old man wearing a hat is sitting in the chair playing a patient. Playing the doctor, Willie is costumed in *"a floor-length white doctor's jacket, a mirror attached to his head and a stethoscope around his neck."* In typical vaudeville comedy fashion the patient is treated—or, rather, mistreated—and then dismissed.

Willie then calls in the nurse—*"a tall, voluptuous and over-stacked blonde in a tight dress"*—and goes into a comedy routine which stresses her seductive appearance and behavior. Finally the nurse goes out to get the next patient. It is Al, and at his sound of knocking on the office door, Willie calls out "Enter." This causes Al to glare at Willie as he comes into the office, dressed in a business suit and carrying a brief case.

It turns out that Al is not a patient after all but an income tax examiner, and there is some confusion and even competition as to who is going to examine whom. Finally they compromise.

AL: All right, you examine me and I'll examine you . . .
    Takes out tax form as Willie takes out a tongue depressor.
The first question is, how much money did you make last year?

WILLIE: Last year I made—(*He moves his lips mouthing a sum but it's not audible.*)

AL: I didn't hear that.

WILLIE: Oh. Hard of hearing. I knew we'd find something . . . Did you ever have any childhood diseases?

AL: Not lately.

WILLIE: Father living or deceased?

AL: Both.

WILLIE: What do you mean, both?

AL: First he was living, now he's deceased.

WILLIE: What did your father die from?

AL: My mother . . . Now it's my turn . . . Are you married

WILLIE: I'm looking.

AL: Looking to get married?

WILLIE: No, looking to get out.
    He looks in Al's ear with a flashlight.

AL: What are you doing?

WILLIE: I'm examining your lower intestine.

AL: So why do you look in the ear?

WILLIE: If I got a choice of two places to look, I'll take this one.

AL (*consulting his form*): Never mind. Do you own a car?

WILLIE: Certainly I own a car. Why?

AL: If you use it for medical purposes, you can deduct it from your taxes. What kind of car do you own?

WILLIE: An ambulance.

They continue in this vein as the sketch proceeds, with Al as the tax examiner and Willie conducting his mock medical examination. At last the sketch calls for Al to stand close to Willie and enunciate strongly: "The *t*axes. It's *t*ime *t*o pay your *t*axes to the *T*reasury," spitting with every "*t*". Infuriated, Willie wipes his face and stops the rehearsal cold to quarrel with Al, claiming that Al spits deliberately. Al of course denies this and meanwhile the voice of the director pleads with them to settle their differences elsewhere and go on with the rehearsal—he has 12 other acts to rehearse.

Willie and Al resume the sketch, with Willie taking a position a good distance away from Al. They make jokes about the skeleton, and then Al crosses and stands close to Willie.

AL: You know what you are? You're a charlatan!

> As Al says that line, he punctuates each word by poking Willie on the chest with his finger. It does not go unnoticed by Willie.

. . . Do you know what a charlatan is?

> *More pokes.*

WILLIE: It's a city in North Carolina. And if you're gonna poke me again like that, you're gonna end up in Poughkeepsie.

VOICE (*over loudspeaker*): Hold it, hold it. Where does it say, "You're going to end up in Poughkeepsie"?

WILLIE (*furious*): Where does it say he can poke me in the chest? He's doing it on purpose. He *always* did it on purpose just to get my goat.

AL (*looking up to mike*): I didn't poke him, I tapped him. A light little tap, it wouldn't hurt a baby.

WILLIE: Maybe a baby elephant. I *knew* I was going to get poked. First comes the spitting, then comes the poking. I know his routine already.

AL (*to mike*): Excuse me. I'm sorry we're holding up the rehearsal but we have a serious problem on our hands. The man I'm working with is a lunatic.

WILLIE (*almost in a rage*): I'm a lunatic, heh? He breaks my chest and spits in my face and calls *me* a lunatic! . . . I'm gonna tell you something now I never told you in my entire life. I hate your guts.

AL: You told it to me on Monday.

WILLIE: Then I'm telling it to you again.

VOICE: Listen, gentlemen, I really don't see any point in going on with this rehearsal.

AL: I don't see any point in going on with this *show*. This man is persecuting me. For eleven years he's been waiting to get back at me only I'm not gonna give him the chance.

The assistant with the head phones walks out in an attempt to make peace.

WILLIE (*half-hysterical*): . . . I knew it! I knew it! . . . He planned it! He's been setting me up for eleven years just to walk out on me again.

Ben joins the assistant in trying to calm the old men down. Al calls Willie crazy once more and leaves the set. While Ben is apologizing to the director Willie is still ranting about not needing Al anyway, about going on without him. Suddenly Willie clutches his chest and collapses to the floor, breathing hard. The others all rush around trying to help, while Willie triumphantly remembers the name of his potato-chip sponsor.

The lights dim, and in the dark the voice of the Announcer is heard extolling the great Lewis and Clark, as in the beginning of the rehearsal. It is the TV special, and they are using an old tape of the Doctor sketch as Lewis and Clark once did it on an Ed Sullivan Show. The sketch begins as the scene ends.

Scene 2

Two weeks later, in late afternoon, Willie is in bed in his hotel room, attended by a uniformed nurse. Once he has figured out what time it is, and what day it is, and what he is doing here, Willie amuses himself by badgering the nurse on every possible subject from pulse-taking to her age and marital status (she is a widow at 54). He is too weak to pat her, but he tries. The nurse claims she can take Willie's badinage because she has a sense of humor, but his wise cracks finally get to her, and she warns him: "You can turn everything I say into a vaudeville routine if you want, but I'm going to give you a piece of advice, Mr. Clark . . . . . The world is full of sick people. And there just ain't enough doctors or nurses to go around and take care of all these sick people. And all the doctors and all the nurses can do just so much, Mr. Clark, but God, in His Infinite Wisdom, has said He will help those who help themselves . . . . . *Stop bugging me!!*"

Willie promises to behave, and Ben comes in bringing *Variety* and a sheaf of get-well telegrams from show people. Ben sends the nurse out to get some fresh air and pulls up a chair by Willie's bed. Willie asks for a cigar. Ben reminds him that he has had a heart attack and can no longer tolerate such things as cigars or the tensions of a show business career. As Willie's closest relative, Ben feels responsible for him, and Ben insists that Willie must retire, he must give up show business once and for all.

Furthermore—Ben informs Willie—the nurse is leaving next week and Willie can't stay here alone by himself any more. Willie pretends to go to sleep to avoid facing this problem, but Ben insists that a decision must be made immediately.

BEN: You want to hear my suggestion?
WILLIE: I'm napping. Don't you see my eyes closed?
BEN: I'd like you to move in with me and Helen and the kids. We have the

small spare room in the back, I think you would be very comfortable . . . Uncle Willie, did you hear what I said?

WILLIE: What's the second suggestion?

BEN: What's the matter with the first?

WILLIE: It's not as good as the second.

BEN: I haven't made any yet.

WILLIE: It's still better than the first. Forget it.

BEN: Why?

WILLIE: I don't like your kids. They're noisy. The little one hit me in the head with a baseball bat.

BEN: And I've also seen you talk to them for hours on end about vaudeville and had the time of your life. Right?

WILLIE: If I stopped talking, they would hit me with the bat . . . No offense, but I'm not living with your children. If you get rid of them, then we'll talk . . .

BEN: I know the reason you won't come . . . Because Al Lewis lives with his family and you're just trying to prove some stupid point about being independent.

WILLIE: . . . What's the second suggestion?

BEN (a long sigh): All right . . . Now don't jump when I say this because it's not as bad as it sounds.

WILLIE: Say it.

BEN: There's the Actors' Home in New Brunswick . . .

WILLIE: It's as bad as it sounds.

Ben has been out to see the place—25 acres surrounding a mansion with a big porch, and they put on shows every Friday and Saturday. His companions will all be actors like himself. Willie objects on two major grounds: it's in New Jersey, and he won't see Ben any more. But Ben promises to visit him every week, as usual. Grudgingly, Willie gives a kind of assent to this alternative, which seems preferable to children with baseball bats.

Ben asks Willie for one last favor—will he permit Al to come and visit him just once? Al is very upset about what happened during the TV rehearsal, he has been phoning Ben to see how Willie is getting along, and Al himself is not well. Ben begs Willie for Al's sake to see him just once. Reluctantly, Willie agrees, and it turns out that Al is downstairs in the lobby waiting, just on a chance. Ben phones for him to come up.

Willie struggles and manages to get himself out of bed—he's not going to let his old enemy see him in this helpless state. Willie demands a blue sports jacket to wear over his pajamas and insists on having his chair set back as far as possible because "I want that son of a bitch to have a long walk."

Somehow Willie gets hold of the notion that Al is coming to apologize, which is not the case—and Ben senses that he may have started something he can't control. He props Willie up in his chair with pillows and resolves never to interfere in the lives of Lewis and Clark again.

When Al knocks on the door, Willie can't resist shouting a hostile "Enterrr"! Ben opens the door and Al comes in timidly, hat in hand, while Willie feigns sleep and snores. Ben announces Al, and Willie makes Al take the long walk across the room. Ben has told Willie that the flowers and candy that have been arriving regularly have been sent by Al under assumed names, so immediately Willie makes a derogatory remark about them. Al sees how it is and starts to leave. Willie invites him to have some tea, then orders Al to make it himself. Hurriedly, Ben offers to have the hotel send up the tea. He decides to leave the two old men alone together for ten minutes, and he makes his escape.

At first there is an awkward silence, then Al breaks the ice by asking about Willie's situation, whether he has everything he needs, and so forth. Willie claims he keeps busy answering fan mail, and gradually he gains the strength to tell Al "I accept your apology!" though none was offered. Al has no intention of apologizing (he insists). It was not his fault that Willie became hysterical and had a seizure. Willie decides to attack in another direction.

WILLIE: . . . . . I *don't accept the apology!* How do you like that?
  Al stares at Willie.
AL: I knew there was gonna be trouble when you said "Enter" instead of "Come-in".
WILLIE: There's no trouble. The trouble is over. I got what I want and now I'm happy.
AL: What did you get? You got "no apology" from me which you didn't accept.
WILLIE: I don't want to discuss it any more, I just had a heart attack.
AL (*stares at Willie silently; calmly*): . . . You know something, Willie. I don't think we get along too good.
WILLIE: Well, listen, everybody has their ups and downs.
AL: In 43 years, we had maybe one "up" . . . To tell you the truth, I can't take the "downs" any more.
WILLIE: To be honest with you, for the first time I feel a little tired myself. In a way this heart attack was good for me. I needed the rest.
AL: So what are you going to do now?
WILLIE: Well, my nephew made me two very good offers today.
AL: Is that right?
WILLIE: I think I'm gonna take the second one.
AL: Are you in any condition to work again?
WILLIE: Well, it wouldn't be too strenuous . . . Mostly take it easy, maybe do a show on a Saturday night, something like that.
AL: Is that so? Where, in New York?
WILLIE: No, no. Out of town . . .
AL: Isn't that wonderful.
WILLIE: Well, you know me. I gotta keep busy . . . What's with you?
AL: Oh, I'm very happy. My daughter's having another baby. They're gonna need my room and I don't want to be a burden on them . . . So we talked it over and I decided I'm gonna move to the Actors' Home in New Brunswick.
  Willie sinks back into his pillow, his head falls over to one side and he sighs deeply.

WILLIE: Ohh, God. I got the finger again.

AL: What's the matter? You all right? Why are you holding your chest? You got pains?

WILLIE: Not yet. But I'm expecting.

AL (*nervously*): Can I get you anything? Should I call the doctor?

WILLIE: It wouldn't help.

AL: It wouldn't hurt.

> *The realization that they slipped accidentally into an old vaudeville joke cause Willie to smile.*

WILLIE: "It wouldn't hurt" . . . How many times have we done that joke?

AL: It always worked . . . Even from you I just got a laugh.

WILLIE: You're a funny man, Al . . . You're a pain in the ass, but you're a funny man.

AL: You know what your trouble was, Willie? You always took the jokes too seriously. They were just jokes. We did comedy on the stage for 43 years, I don't think you enjoyed it once.

WILLIE: If I was there to enjoy it, I would buy a ticket.

AL: Well, maybe now you can start enjoying it . . . If you're not too busy, maybe you'll come over one day to the Actors' Home and visit me.

WILLIE: You can count on it.

AL: I feel a lot better now that I've talked to you . . . Maybe you'd like to rest now, take a nap.

WILLIE: I think so . . . Keep talking to me, I'll fall asleep.

AL (*looks around*): What's new in *Variety?*

WILLIE: Bernie Eisenstein died.

AL: Go on. Bernie Eisenstein? The house doctor at the Palace?

WILLIE: That was Sam Hesseltine. Bernie Eisenstein was Ramona and Rodriguez.

AL: Jackie Aaronson was Ramona and Rodriguez. Bernie Eisenstein was the house doctor at the Palace. Sam Hesseltine was Sophie Tucker's agent.

WILLIE: Don't argue with me, I'm sick.

AL: I know. But why should I get sick too?

> *The curtain starts to fall. Willie moans.*

Bernie Eisenstein was the house doctor when we played for the first time with Sophie Tucker and that's when we met Sam Hesseltine . . . Jackie Aaronson wasn't Rodriguez yet . . . He was DeMarco and Lopez . . . Lopez died and DeMarco went into real estate so Jackie became Rodriguez . . .

> *Curtain.*

FINISHING TOUCHES

A Comedy in Three Acts

BY JEAN KERR

Cast and credits appear on page 349

JEAN KERR, nee Jean Collins, was born in Scranton, Pa. July 10, 1923. Possibly she inherited some penchant for the stage, not necessarily through her father, who was a construction foreman, but on the side of her mother, who was Eugene O'Neill's second cousin. Miss Collins was educated at Mary Wood Seminary and Mary Wood College in Scranton, graduating in 1943. Shortly thereafter, on August 16, 1943, she married the man who was to become America's leading drama critic, Walter Kerr, then a teacher of drama at Catholic University in Washington, D.C., changing both her name and her byline to Jean Kerr.

Mrs. Kerr received her M.A. at Catholic University in 1944. It was while she and her husband were teaching there, in 1946, that they adapted Franz Werfel's novel The Song of Bernadette *into a play which made Broadway for only 3 performances. In 1948 Mrs. Kerr's first comedy,* Jenny Kissed Me, *played on Broadway for 20 performances, and in 1949 Mr. and Mrs. Kerr wrote the revue* Touch and Go, *a 176-performance hit. Mrs. Kerr contributed sketches to* John Murray Anderson's Almanac *in 1953 and followed this right up with another comedy (written in collaboration with Eleanor Brooke),* King of Hearts, *directed by her husband and produced in 1954 for 279 performances. The musical* Goldilocks, *with book by the Kerrs and lyrics by the Kerrs and Joan Ford, was produced in 1958 for 161 performances under Walter Kerr's direction.*

In 1961 Mrs. Kerr had her biggest hit to date with the comedy Mary, Mary *which was named a Best Play of its season and became Broadway's sixth longest-running play of all time with 1,572 performances.* Her *Poor Richard* *followed in 1964, for 118 performances.* This season's Finishing Touches *is her ninth Broadway production and second Best Play—none of them, we hasten to add, ever reviewed publicly by her husband.*

Mrs. Kerr's other writings have included a stage adaptation of Our Hearts Were Young and Gay *for amateur and stock performance, and three books:* Please Don't Eat the Daisies, The Snake Has All the Lines *and* Penny Candy. *Hollywood films have been made of* Daisies (*which also became a TV series*), King of Hearts *and* Mary, Mary. *As everyone who can read must know by now, the Kerrs and their six children—five sons and a daughter—live in a baronial house they discovered on the shores of Long Island Sound, in Larchmont.*

Time: The present

Place: The Cooper home in an eastern university town

ACT I

Morning

SYNOPSIS: The Cooper living room is large and comfortably cluttered with evidences of family living. The front door is out of sight at left beyond a visible foyer and a hall closet where they keep the telephone. Up left is a stairway to the second-floor bedrooms, with an alcove and window seat affording space for games and for the complicated wiring of a tape recorder and other electric devices. Up center and right are glass doors leading to the terrace. Also at right are a dining area and the doors to the kitchen and to Jeff Cooper's office.

Jeff (a college English Lit teacher), his wife Katy and their sons Kevin, 18, and Hughie, 11, are at the breakfast table. Hughie is playing with a cash-register bank.

HUGHIE: Mom, you owe me a nickel. Will you give me a nickel?

KATY (*not looking up; a very pretty woman and she will look better when she gets out of that frowsy bathrobe*): What do I owe you a nickel for?

HUGHIE: I took all the coke bottles out of the garage.

KATY (*to Jeff, who has not been listening*): Honey, we owe him a nickel. Give him a nickel, will you?

JEFF: What do we owe him a nickel for?

KATY (*she's not going over that ground again*): Just give him a nickel. Okay?

He reaches into his pocket for one.

KEVIN: You know, the President's statement is bound to worsen the international situation.

KATY: You're absolutely right. Now eat your eggs.

KEVIN: Don't you care about the international situation?

KATY: I care terribly, now eat your eggs.

KEVIN: If you'd look, Mom, you'd see I'm not eating eggs. I'm eating French toast.

KATY: Are you trying to start an argument?

KEVIN: Oh, Moth-*er*!

KATY: I was only eighteen years old when Stevie was born. Never forget that.

KEVIN: Yeah, but what are you going into that for?

KATY: Because you seem so big, so massive. And you soak up so much oxygen. I feel I must be at least sixty-five.

KEVIN: Well, we can figure this out. You were eighteen when Steve was born and Steve is twenty-two now. That makes—

KATY (*interrupting*): Never add in my presence. I'm high-strung.

HUGHIE: You know, Mom, your neck looks fine from the front. But from the side it looks like sort of twisty.

KATY: I hate breakfast anyway. Why do I eat breakfast? Look, if you will be silent, I will see that you get another nickel. Two nickels.

HUGHIE: I don't need another nickel.

> *He places the nickel he already has in the bank and there is a sudden small explosion.*

JEFF: My God, what's that?

HUGHIE: It's my bank. I hit twenty dollars. I mean it's supposed to be twenty dollars. Boy, if it isn't twenty dollars—

Hughie begins to count the nickels. Jeff's nerves are on edge, and he can't bear to watch Hughie go through this laborious process. At first Jeff tries to bribe him to stop counting, then dumps the pile of coins into a handy cereal bowl.

The phone rings, and Hughie goes to answer it. The Coopers are expecting to hear today from the university Dean about Jeff's expected promotion to full professor, but the notice will come by special delivery, not by phone.

Hughie returns from the closet (the phone is there because it was there when they moved in, and they never bothered to move it). The call was for him, about homework. Hughie rushes around gathering up his things for school, complaining that Kevin has broken his bicycle by riding his fat girl friend on the handle bars; Katy forbids Kevin to abuse Hughie's bike again.

Hughie fusses about his science project and his poncho. He is finally pushed out the door, but he flicks his tape recorder in passing, and the family is treated to a nerve-wracking chorus of "That Old Gang of Mine" before Kevin manages to turn off the machine.

Kevin finds his Soc-Sci (Social Science) book and goes on his way with a few words of advice from his father: "Kevin, say goodbye to your mother and, if you can manage it, me. Remember what Auden says. Man is the only animal that learns by being hypocritical. He pretends to be polite and then, eventually, he *becomes* polite."

ROBERT LANSING, BARBARA BEL GEDDES, SCOTT FIRESTONE,
OLIVER CONANT AND JAMES WOODS IN "FINISHING TOUCHES"

Jeff and Katy think perhaps their oldest son, Steve, 22, may be home from college for a visit this weekend. Katy complains that Jeff doesn't look at her when he speaks to her, and Jeff replies, "All right, I'm looking at you now. Burn that bathrobe. Or give it to the poor. No, they're poor enough."

Jeff goes upstairs and Katy looks in the mirror and tells herself that some day she is going to win a lottery and spend the money making herself over into a sex object.

Jeff comes downstairs and tries on a pair of glasses, his first. Katy thinks they make him look distinguished. The word makes him angry, and Katy wonders what is the matter with him, why he has become so irritable lately.

JEFF: It's nothing. I don't sleep well. Lots of people don't sleep well.
KATY (*running her finger over his forehead*): Okay, but we've got to get rid of this little frown. It's turning into a furrow. And you mustn't have got the

brush wet enough because those little hairs are sticking out in the back.

JEFF (*pulling away with a real explosion*): Will you for God's sake stop patting me!

KATY (*stung*): All right. Certainly.

JEFF (*quickly putting his arms around her*): Oh, honey, honey, honey— I'm sorry. The truth is, I *am* jumpy. But I don't have to take it out on you. You hurt?

KATY: Oh, just a little, maybe. But that's a reflex, I'll get over it. What I want to know is why you sort of avoid me lately.

JEFF: Where did you get that crazy idea?

KATY: It's not crazy. You always used to come home a half hour early from school so we could have a little drink together before the kids got here. You haven't done that in months.

JEFF: Of course, the whole business of my promotion has come up. And notice—I still haven't heard.

KATY: For a while I thought that was it. But it isn't it. And I used to like it when you got through your papers at eleven o'clock and you'd come out of your study and say, "Hey, if you'll walk with me to the post office, I'll buy you a corned beef sandwich." How long is it since you've done that?

JEFF: My God, if your idea of a big thrill is to walk to the post office—

KATY (*close to tears*): People settle for things, don't you understand? They *settle*. I'm beginning to feel like a non-person. And yesterday—yesterday you called me "Mother."

JEFF: Well, there. Now we've got something really important to be upset about!

Fred Whitten—a law professor who rents the apartment above the Coopers' garage—drifts in from the kitchen and realizes he is interrupting a near-quarrel. Fred tries a light touch, but his remarks irritate Katy, who goes upstairs to dress. Jeff tries to confide in Fred—Jeff is 40, an age at which he is beginning to feel he might have done something else with his life besides or in addition to teaching. But Fred isn't especially sympathetic. Fred likes teaching, he likes having the students visit him at all hours. Maybe that's why he and his wife Helen, who is now on a prolonged visit to her mother, are drifting apart—as happened with Fred and his other wives.

Jeff finds himself developing strange behavior patterns. He fusses around the house late at night straightening things up, and he brings a drink to bed with him and often mislays it on the way. The fact that the Cooper household's cups and saucers don't match, because of longstanding breakage, is especially irritating to Jeff: "So Katy goes to the Five-and-Ten and buys cups, which would be all right if she bought saucers to match. But she won't do that because, you see, we *have* saucers! And you can't find a drinking glass in the cupboard because it's so full of Santa Claus mugs!"

Fred suspects that it is not the dishware, but Jeff's sex life, that is the cause of his irritability. Katy comes downstairs and Fred escapes into the den to look

up a reference. Katy apologizes to Jeff for provoking him earlier. But Jeff
is beyond all that now and has something to tell her.

JEFF: Katy, there is something the matter. (*Slight pause.*) I think I am
falling in love.
> *The phone rings. Jeff quickly turns and goes to answer it in the
> closet.*

KATY (*alone*): I must say nothing. Nothing at all, not one thing. Because
anything I say is going to be a mistake, a serious mistake. But I'm here. I
can't run upstairs and hide in the bedroom. I have to say something. Above
it . . . rise above it!

JEFF (*returning from telephone closet*): Want to know what that was?

KATY: Not particularly. Now, you were saying what? That you were falling
in love? Is that all?

JEFF: Is that *all?*

KATY: My God, from your expression I thought you had stolen money
from the university. Or you just discovered you had hepatitis.

JEFF: Well, I'm glad to be able to put your mind at ease.

KATY: Look, I'll try to take you seriously, but I don't believe that men get
to be your age and suddenly change the patterns of a lifetime.

JEFF: Sure they do. Bernard Shaw didn't even start to write plays until he
was forty years old.

KATY: That's different from chasing girls.

JEFF: Yeah—harder.

KATY: Well—who is the girl?

JEFF: She's in my Poetry seminar.

KATY: And what's so special about her?

JEFF: The terrible thing is, I don't think there's anything special about her.
I noticed her in the first place because she was the only one in the class who
didn't say anything. I thought it was because she was so shy. It now strikes me
that she wasn't shy at all. She just hadn't read the assignment.
> *Katy manages a small smile.*
It's all right, you can smile. I think it's funny.

KATY: I suppose she's terribly pretty.

JEFF: No, not really. Oh, she's pretty in that sort of nothing way that airline
stewardesses are pretty. You know how they look. They've got straight noses
and good teeth, so you've got to say they're pretty, but they sure as hell don't
look like the ads. I mean, she wouldn't bowl you over.

KATY: But she bowled you over. Why?

JEFF: I don't know. I honest to God don't know. She laughs a lot.

Maybe she fascinates Jeff because she notices things like the way the cracks
in the wall behind Jeff's desk look like folded hands. At any rate, she hardly
realizes that Jeff exists, except as "a dreary professor who teaches 'From
Beowolf to Spenser.' " She—Elsie—certainly doesn't know how Jeff feels
about her.

Katy almost wishes Jeff had kept all this to himself. She is beginning to get angry now. Jeff likes this better than the understanding act she was trying to put on. She comments: "The reason I can't be understanding is that there is nothing to understand except that you have started to ogle teeny-boppers in your seminar!"

Elsie is a graduate student, at least 22, Jeff informs Katy. What's more, Katy hasn't even heard what Jeff's problem is yet.

JEFF: . . . . . Listen for one minute. My problem is I don't know whether or not to pass this girl.

KATY: Have I heard you correctly? Your problem is *what?*

JEFF (*going ahead on his own*): Well, her paper on *The Wasteland* came in yesterday, and it's simply not graduate work. She doesn't even know what a non-restrictive clause is.

KATY (*feigning horror*): Oh, no, you're jesting! She doesn't know a non-restrictive clause? Where has she been? I don't like the sound of this at all. And I'm afraid this little romance will never come to flower.

JEFF (*interrupting*): Are you going to go on and on? Or are you going to try and see the point?

KATY: O.K., you have to flunk her. Flunk her.

JEFF: Yes, but you see what that will mean?

KATY: What?

JEFF: She will have to repeat the course.

KATY: Let her repeat it.

JEFF: But I don't want her back in my seminar all next semester.

KATY: You don't? Oh, it's because of all those clauses.

JEFF (*angry himself now*): Don't you see! I want to get her out of my class! I want to get her out of my mind! I want to get her out of my sub-conscious!

Katy will not understand that Jeff doesn't *want* to be in love, and he storms out angrily, then comes back to tell her that the phone call was a telegram from their son Steve announcing that he is coming home for the weekend and bringing a friend named Phil, in Phil's car.

Jeff disappears and Katy is trying hard not to feel sorry for herself, as Fred reappears from the den. She tries to preoccupy herself with the dirty breakfast dishes. Seeing that Katy is close to tears, Fred makes her a drink even though it's only 10 a.m. Katy tells him what he has already guessed, that Jeff is in love with a girl in his class. Fred tries to belittle this adventure, but Katy is taking it deadly seriously. It's not as though Jeff were sleeping with every third girl—that she could understand. But to fix his attentions on one is "a betrayal."

As a lawyer and friend, Fred sees that Katy is not considering divorce, and he advises her to encourage Jeff to have a real fling and get it out of his system. Fred knows Elsie—she's in his class too—and he thinks her "not overwhelmingly bright . . . but she's a nice girl." The suggestion that she encourage such a thing horrifies Katy. Her whole nature revolts against the thought of her husband having an affair with another woman. She has moral standards and means to hold on to them regardless of what other people may be doing these days.

Fred insists that Katy give him her hand. She does so, but then immediately starts to pull away.

FRED (*holding on to it*): Wait, wait, wait—this won't take a minute.

> *He gently places his other hand on hers so that he now has her hand between the two of his. He gently massages her wrist with his fingers. Katy is slightly mesmerized.*

Now. Is that disagreeable?

KATY (*she is going to be honest even if it's embarrassing*): No, it isn't. But what is the point?

FRED: I wanted you to notice something. *That* was contact. And contact is pleasant.

KATY (*irked and feeling a little foolish*): My God, you're turning into an Encounter Group!

FRED: And you're the last of the Latter-Day Saints. But I don't think your case is hopeless.

KATY: I don't know what the hell you are talking about.

FRED: But you do. That's why that little blue vein in your neck is throbbing. So any time you want that second lesson in the beginner's course, you have but to call me. Remember, I am within easy walking distance.

KATY: That'll be the day.

FRED: The evening is actually more convenient for me.

KATY: Oh, go to hell. Go home.

FRED: Going, going—oh, wait. To change the subject. Miss Elsie will be dropping in at my place later.

KATY (*drawing false conclusions*): Oh, really?

FRED: There's no need for the "oh" or the "really." Her term paper is overdue and she's dropping it off around five o'clock.

KATY: So?

FRED: I thought maybe, all things considered, you'd like to meet her.

KATY: No, no, no, no. (*Without a break.*) Yes, I would. I would like to see those damn even teeth. But I'm not going to go over there.

FRED: She can come over here.

KATY: You mean you'll tell her that there's a crazy lady who wants to look in her mouth?

FRED: You have no head for intrigue. You'll have to learn. I'll give her a book and ask her to return it to you. Trust me.

KATY: Up until this morning, I always did trust you.

FRED: And that has changed a little. Good. The morning hasn't been lost at all. (*He leaves.*)

KATY (*to herself*): I shall take arms against a sea of troubles and by opposing end them. And I know just where I can start.

> *Katie picks up the hammer Hughie has left and starts smashing the teacups, one by one. Curtain.*

ACT II

Late afternoon, the same day

When Jeff comes home Katy is not sure exactly how she should behave toward him. In her thoughts, she rejects both an icy silence and a direct confrontation. Jeff's first question is about the expected letter from the Dean, which hasn't come yet.

Finally Katy can't resist asking him whether he saw Elsie today, but she abruptly puts up the defense of icy silence when Jeff apologizes for this morning's confession. Katy refuses to discuss the matter further. She is getting ready for a dinner out on the terrace. The only tablecloth big enough has Easter bunnies and jelly beans, about which Jeff comments, "It will look fine once we put on the Santa Claus mugs." Katy ignores his sarcasm and instructs him to make an effort this evening to talk to the friend Steve is bringing with him from Harvard.

Kevin comes home, happy they are going to eat outdoors, looking forward to seeing Steve and his friend Phil. Katy orders Kevin to do his bit for ecology by cleaning up the mess in his room. He goes upstairs as a car is heard pulling into the driveway. Hughie rushes in with the information that Phil is "gorgeous" and rushes out again, leaving his parents to wonder what sort of college chum Steve may be bringing home.

KATY: You don't suppose Stevie has become a—?

JEFF: A homosexual? Yes, that's what I do suppose. I suppose that in due time all three of them will become homosexuals. Remember, we have the perfect breeding ground here. The Aggressive Mother, the Absent Father. It all fits. But tell yourself this. At least we won't have to cope with grandchildren. Think of the relief that will be! And pretty soon, maybe in twenty or thirty years, these kids will stop coming home altogether. As I see it, the day will dawn when we will have licked, entirely licked, the clean sheet problem!

> *Steve enters with a ravishing-looking girl. Steve is a Harvard senior. He has obviously made some effort to look halfway conventional for his parents; God knows what he looks like at Harvard. The girl, Phil, is Felicia Andrayson, about 26, extremely pretty in a theatrical way. Hughie is close at Felicia's heels.*

STEVE: Hi, Dad. Hi, Mom.

> *Katy just stares at Steve and Felicia.*

(*To his mother.*) Don't just stand there. Look—(*Rubbing his cheek.*)—no beard. And I got my hair cut just for you. So give me one of your better-grade hugs.

> *He hugs her and she responds.*

Okay, that's better. Love you six. (*This last phrase is thrown away.*) Now I want you both to meet Phil—

Steve introduces Felicia, who comments on the "stark but fascinating" atmosphere of the Coopers' house. Felicia goes to get something from the car, followed by Hughie. Jeff goes out to move his car. Alone with his mother, Steve informs her that Felicia is an actress, four years older than he is. While they are talking, Steve, who has always been close to his mother, sees that she is not her usual sunny self. Something is wrong—"Your eyes are too blue and you've got two cigarettes burning beside the one in your hand. At first I thought it was all Oedipal, that you were worried I was leaving you for a younger woman. But it's not that."

To Steve, Katy seems to be lacking her usual smile and sense of humor. He assures her he doesn't plan to marry anyone until he's at least 47 (Felicia, who has already been married once, agrees with him that marriage can wait).

The others come back in, Hughie showing off carrying Felicia's suitcase, Felicia with a bag of vegetables as a present for the Coopers. Katy listens while Felicia tells them about herself, her drama training, her father who is reputed to be the eighth richest man in the U.S., her affluent but neglected childhood.

Katy goes into the kitchen and Kevin brings a load of bottles downstairs, greeting Felicia in passing. Hughie takes Felicia upstairs to see his fish tank. Katy comes back and starts to organize the sleeping arrangements. Felicia can have Steve's room, and Steve will bunk in with Kevin, who protests that he needs his privacy, he has a term paper to finish.

KATY: I don't see why Stevie should interfere with your concentration.

KEVIN: Phil sleeps in his room at Cambridge, why can't she sleep with him here?

There is a profound silence.

Steve, I just didn't think. I'm sorry.

STEVE: It's not enough to be sorry. Go kill yourself.

There is more silence. Kevin goes to the kitchen.

Well, I guess the cat is out of the bag.

KATY: But the cat has been in the bag, right?

JEFF (*with authority*): Katy, we are not going to conduct this discussion on that level. It is demeaning to all of us.

KATY (*penitent*): I know. I apologize.

JEFF: Steve, there is something I must say.

STEVE: You're going to say that you know I am over twenty-one and that I am free to lead my own life any way I choose. And you are prepared to be tolerant if and when—

JEFF (*interrupting sharply*): I'm not going to say that. I am by God not going to say that. That was last year's speech. I'm going to say something else. Your mother and I are over forty. And we think we should be free to lead our life the way *we* choose. And we think you should be prepared to be tolerant if and when we decide to conduct our lives and our house the way we have always conducted it.

STEVE: So who's asking you to change?

KATY: This girl is your mistress and you're bringing her home. That's asking *something*, isn't it?

STEVE: What? Just tell me what?

KATY: Well, you are asking us to countenance—what we couldn't wish to countenance.

STEVE: Countenance? My God, do people still use that word?

JEFF: It would appear so.

STEVE: I think you both are being damned unfair. I had no plan whatsoever to conduct my liaison—I'm sure that's the word you would use, Mom—I had no intention of conducting my liaison in the chaste environs of your house. I assure you that Phil will be able to keep her hands off me during the brief period that we are, quote, under your roof, unquote.

JEFF: Okay, okay.

STEVE: Furthermore, you never would have known at all if Kevin could ever learn to keep his stupid mouth shut.

KATY: And that's another thing! Why would you scandalize Kevin by telling him about it?

STEVE: There are two answers to that question. In the first place, I didn't tell Kevin. He just found out when he was in Cambridge. In the second place, *nothing* scandalizes Kevin.

KATY: You mean he's sleeping around, too?

STEVE: Probably not. He's too shy. But more than half of his friends are.

JEFF (*standing, with sweeping gestures*): Well, folks, I'm afraid that's all we have time for. But I want to thank you all for being here—

Jeff pours himself a drink and disappears into his office with it. Katy wants to know one thing: does Steve go to church any more? No, he hardly ever goes, he admits; he doesn't get anything out of it. Katy cites Pascal: "If there is a fifty-fifty chance of immortality, why not play it with the believers? Remember, nobody has ever seriously questioned those odds. Nobody has ever suggested that it was an eighty-twenty proposition . . . . . I think you should impose standards and disciplines on yourself so that you might just possibly slip into eternity with Thomas More instead of going to hell with Hitler."

But Steve doesn't believe in absolutes, not even in an eternal hell for Hitler. He goes upstairs leaving his mother counting to 100 by sevens out loud to relieve her frustration. Jeff comes into the room and decides he wants a cup of coffee—or, rather, a Santa Claus mug of coffee because, as Katy tells him, she has smashed all the cups. Jeff brings in two mugs, one for Katy, who wishes she could get back to 1948 when they were young, and in college, and people had standards of behavior. Jeff feels that although he and Katy never slept around the way some of their other young contemporaries did, they don't deserve a medal for it. Jeff accuses Katy: "Other women read Suzy's column or whoever's column, and when they learn what all those glamorous people are doing and saying in Acapulco, they feel twinges of envy. You feel twinges of righteousness."

Jeff reminds Katy that perhaps today's young people aren't on the road to ruin with their permissive behavior, perhaps they'll be in better shape at 40 than their parents are. Jeff and Katy have been strict with themselves all their lives, and here they are in an emotional mess.

JEFF: . . . . . Something is missing. You know something is missing.

KATY (*painfully*): Love, maybe.

JEFF: Oh, Katy, you know I love you—(*Second thought, and sharper.*)—not that you seem to care any more—

KATY: Why do you say that?

JEFF: You know perfectly well that I have only to throw an arm over your pillow, for you to say "You're ruining my hair!" The rest of the time it's "Not tonight, honey, I'm really so sleepy—"

KATY: Sometimes I *am* sleepy—

JEFF: *Sometimes!*

KATY: You know, a man *will* believe you're too tired to go out to a movie. Why is it that he won't believe—

JEFF: Maybe men are not that interested in movies. Actually, it would be simpler if I didn't love you.

KATY: You mean you'd feel freer to have a trial spin or what Thurber used to call a little "pounce in the clover?"

JEFF: That may have sounded all right from Thurber. From you it sounds downright ghastly. Don't talk about what you don't *know* about.

Katy decides that she will leave the house on Monday and go to visit her brother, leaving Jeff free to pursue and consummate his affair with Elsie. Jeff tries to make her understand that this is not what he wants at all. He is a victim of strange and unwanted impulses, but he is determined to behave impeccably in spite of them. Jeff is very angry with Katy, for her failure to comprehend what he is going through. Steve comes downstairs at the height of their quarrel and is amazed to find his parents, whom he has always thought of as ideally married, in a bitter skirmish.

Jeff goes off in search of another bottle of Scotch as Steve is instructed by Katy to ring the dinner bell. Felicia and Hughie come downstairs, and Felicia volunteers to put the paper plates into their wicker containers. All are busy with the various chores of setting up dinner on the terrace.

As the others drift off on errands, Steve and Felicia are left alone for a few moments. Steve promises her they'll slip away after dinner, but Felicia means to stay and keep a date to play chess with Hughie. She likes the Cooper family, she likes the way Jeff really listens to what others say.

FELICIA: . . . . . Look, Steve—we are sleeping in seperate rooms here, aren't we?

STEVE: Yes, definitely. Why do you ask?

FELICIA: Because I have a funny feeling that your mother knows.

STEVE: Would you care terribly if she did?

FELICIA: Yes, I would.

STEVE: But why? This is the—

FELICIA: Please, I *know* the century we're living in. But I find that I don't want people to know what our relationship is—before I find out what it means.

STEVE: What what means?

FELICIA: Our relationship.

STEVE: Phil, you lose me when you say things like that.

FELICIA: I know. That's a risk I'm taking. Your policy—which is no questions asked—may be correct if you are looking for the return of stolen property. But I don't think it works in real life for two people who are living together.

STEVE: Oh, my God! You're going to turn into a girl!

FELICIA: That was always in the cards.

STEVE: But why here? Why now?

FELICIA: Because suddenly you seem very different.

STEVE: Different? How?

FELICIA: Seeing you here in your own house with your own family, I realize—you're a kid, just a kid.

STEVE (*furious*): Oh, I'm just a kid, am I? Damn it, you have reason to know better than that!

He grabs her and kisses her roughly. Doorbell rings.

FELICIA (*breaks away*): That is the solution to nothing.

Steve has to answer the doorbell. He opens the front door and there is Elsie Ketchum, *"a pretty girl of 22, conservatively dressed. She is hesitant and has a book in her hands."* She's been sent over by Fred Whitten on the pretext of returning a book to Katy, and Katy appears swiftly from the kitchen to look Elsie over. Katy introduces Elsie to Steve and Felicia, but Steve needs no introduction. He and Elsie, who are the same age, were good friends in dancing class. Elsie is persuaded to stay for dinner.

Jeff comes in and is startled to see Elsie in his living room. Katy sends Steve and Felicia out to do a chore and then exits herself, deliberately leaving Elsie alone with Jeff, who by now has had quite a lot to drink.

JEFF: Well, Miss Ketchum! Pink looks very pretty on you. See, I'm saying that backwards. I'm giving the credit to pink. I should say *you* look very pretty in pink.

ELSIE: Well, thank you, Professor Cooper. (*Simply, not at all flirtatiously.*) But why do you keep calling me Miss Ketchum? In class you always call me Elsie.

JEFF: I guess that's true. I can only say that by some reverse, crazy logic, in the classroom I'm aware that you're a girl. Out of the classroom I am reminded that you are a student. Now, you never heard anything more stupid than that! Okay. Elsie. What brings you here?

ELSIE: Professor Whitten asked me to bring this book over to Mrs. Cooper. He said it was important that she get it tonight.

JEFF: He asked you to *bring* it over? On a clear day, he could throw it over.

ELSIE: I wondered about that.

It turns out that the book is in Latin, making it perfectly obvious to Jeff that Elsie's presence is part of a plot. Katy comes back into the room. Katy suggests that Jeff take Elsie into his office to discuss her term paper, but Jeff sends Elsie out to the terrace with the others and shouts angrily across at Fred, commanding him to come over for dinner regardless of what else he may have planned. Then Jeff turns on Katy: "Look, I don't know what kind of James Bond plot you and old Fred have hatched up. I would guess that it has something to do with bringing May and December together. Well, you can forget it. You can put it right out of your mind. I will have no part of it—is that clear?"

Fred comes in and Jeff warns him that he is going to have to cope with any problems that arise from his little plot to send Elsie over. Jeff has firmly decided to get drunk. A rumble of thunder is heard, and suddenly everybody is bringing the dinner things in from the terrace, out of the rain—everybody, that is, except Jeff, who is concentrating on his drinking. Soon there is a large clutter of soggy plates, etc., in the room. Steve spreads the tablecloth on the floor, suggesting they have an indoor picnic.

> *Magically, with everybody helping, things are coming into place for dinner on the floor.*

KATY: I have never pretended that my family was grand, really grand. My father was a contractor. But we never ate on the floor.

FRED: Tell yourself that this is a breakthrough and enjoy it.

STEVE (*producing a bottle of wine*): Should we have a little wine before we serve the dinner?

JEFF: Absolutely!

KATY: Hughie, close those doors.

STEVE: Mom, would you like a pillow to sit on?

KATY: No, I would not. I mean, I would. But I wish to show that I am true blue. (*Pointedly.*) Elsie, you sit next to Professor Cooper!

JEFF: Fortunate girl—you were born under a lucky star! I'm sure you think this is all coincidence. Not at all! Somebody said—"I find it easier to believe in miracles than in a series of coincidences." What do *you* think? No matter, I shall tell you. This is the result of a conspiracy. You might even call it a caper. And if inside sources are correct, we might even trace it to—

> *Jeff is interrupted by a loud clap of thunder and a blare of lightning. The adults are a little frightened, but try to conceal it. Hughie is thrilled.*

Jeff keeps on trying to expose the conspiracy, but he is succeeding only in embarrassing everyone with his cryptic references. Katy, trying to smooth things over, suggests that Fred offer a toast. Fred wishes them "Happy Easter" as the curtain falls.

ACT III

That evening

Hughie and Felicia are having their game of chess, and Kevin is bouncing a basketball offstage. Fred has gone home. Elsie is phoning her roommate. Jeff notices that Katy has changed her clothes and is now all dressed up. They have both noticed that the letter announcing Jeff's promotion hasn't come yet. Steve is out fixing a flat on Jeff's car.

Jeff takes a wrench out to Steve. Elsie comes in to thank Katy for the dinner, which she enjoyed in spite of the chaos. Elsie confides to Katy that she is a rotten student and is probably going to flunk. She is the odd girl out in a family whose average I.Q. among the rest of the members is 160. Steve comes in to kibitz on the chess match, as Elsie tells Katy the one experience she truly enjoyed was a job last summer at a school for retarded children: "You can't think how sweet they are. And how grateful they are for somebody who just sits there—and attends. By attend I mean really pay attention. The regular staff is just plain too busy for that. And when parents come to visit, mostly it's just the mothers. And mostly the mothers cry, and that upsets the children . . . . . Lots of days you wouldn't see any progress at all, and then there it would be—a tiny breakthrough. There was a little boy named Ted. He was six, maybe seven. And I knew he could talk. Not a lot, you know. But he could say words. But he didn't talk to me. I kept talking to *him* and I pretended never to notice that he didn't answer. And this went on for weeks. Then, one day, I was sitting on top of the radiator cover—I had a little two-year-old in my lap . . . and Ted came over. He tapped me on the knee and he said, 'Lady, this is for you.' And he had something squeezed up in his fist. Do you know what it was? It was a bottle top. But for me it was a victory, a real victory."

Katy now has a new respect for Elsie. It's time for Elsie to leave, but Jeff doesn't seem to want to drive her home. Steve is only too eager to volunteer—he wants to talk to Elsie about the good old school days. They go off together.

Felicia checkmates Hughie. Katy, who has decided that "Elsie really is a lovely child and we were both playing games with her," insists on putting on her coat and going out for a walk to think things over.

Felicia announces that she has decided to leave, too, without telling Steve. Hughie dashes upstairs to get a tape so that he can record Felicia doing an acting bit before she leaves. Felicia, left alone with Jeff, inquires about his age. He is 43.

FELICIA: You're younger than Paul Newman. But I know why you *feel* older.

JEFF: Maybe you shouldn't tell me. Maybe I'm better off not knowing.

FELICIA: Because you're dealing with students. And every year they get younger—or they seem younger. Now, if you were a Supreme Court judge you'd be a mere lad. Something else that would make you feel younger—if you were made dean. You'd be one of the youngest deans in the country.

JEFF: But I'm not going to make dean.

FELICIA: Are you sure?

JEFF: I'm very sure.

FELICIA: Do you know the book *The Neurotic's Notebook?* There's a line in it I say to myself when I get discouraged. It goes: "Hope is the feeling you have that the feeling you have isn't permanent."

JEFF: What a bright, charming girl you are.

FELICIA (*looking at him*): And you're very special, too. You have that lovely worn look that Peter Finch has.

JEFF: Are you trying to tell me that there is something good about having a worn look?

FELICIA: Yes, it's your face. There is something gentle and touching and concerned about it. It's not a usual face.

She puts her hand lightly on his cheek.

JEFF (*places his hand on hers*): My dear, pretty child. I don't know whether you are depressing me or cheering me up, but I can't risk finding out.

Breaking abruptly from her and going to the stair well.

Hey, Hughie! We're waiting! When does this program go on the air?

Hughie comes downstairs with his tape, and Felicia does the "Our revels now are ended" speech from *The Tempest* for him. Hughie runs out to play the tape for a friend. Alone with Jeff, Felicia issues her invitation plainly. She tells Jeff she is not in love with Steve and invites Jeff to kiss her. Jeff is afraid it would be a mistake to start anything, but Felicia insists.

After a beat, he kisses her, firmly and adequately.

FELICIA: See? It wasn't a mistake. It was just like I thought it would be. Again, please.

JEFF (*starts to kiss her and breaks away*): Felicia, I cannot be put in the position of robbing the cradle!

FELICIA: You're not robbing the cradle. You're robbing the poor box.

JEFF: Whatever do you mean?

FELICIA: Everybody thinks I'm so pretty, so smashing. And then they get tired of me.

JEFF: I don't believe that.

FELICIA: Well, it's true. Steve brought me here this weekend just to prove that he wasn't tired of me. But he is.

JEFF: I don't believe that, either.

FELICIA: Yes, you do.

JEFF: Then he is absolutely crazy. I wouldn't get tired of you.

FELICIA: No, you wouldn't.

JEFF: Wait a minute, wait a minute, I'm getting lost here! Why are you sure I wouldn't get tired of you?

FELICIA: Because you like the fact that I am unpredictable. Young men hate unpredictable girls.

JEFF: That's their loss.

FELICIA: Are you going to kiss me again?

JEFF: Yeah. (*He does.*) Yeah. (*Again.*) Yeah!

FELICIA: Jeff, what would your wife do if you came away with me for the weekend? Would she hit the roof, would she divorce you?

JEFF: Are you asking me to come with you for the weekend?

FELICIA: Yes, I am, but first I want to know how much trouble it would make.

JEFF: If you mean with my wife, I have every reason to think she would be delighted.

FELICIA: Oh? Then why not? Please come!

JEFF: Come where?

FELICIA: I'm going to drive to Nantucket. My father has a house there.

Her father never uses the house, Felicia reassures Jeff, it is inhabited only by an elderly housekeeper. Jeff's mother lives in Falmouth, on the way to Nantucket, and for appearances' sake Jeff can tell his family he is going to visit her. Jeff won't need to pack, because Felicia's father keeps full wardrobes of clothes in every one of his houses. Jeff kisses Felicia again and decides, yes, this would be an excellent weekend to visit his mother.

Jeff writes a quick note to Katy on the only available paper, Hughie's Snoopy letterhead, and rushes off with Felicia, inadvertently tripping the amplifier switch on the way out so that they exit to the tune of "That Old Gang of Mine." The music dissolves into the sound of a ringing phone (as a short time passes). Katy comes in and runs to the phone, but it stops ringing before she can answer it. She calls for Jeff and is puzzled by the house's silence. Finally she sees the note, reads it and tells herself, "Felicia? He's gone with *Felicia*? (*Pause. The irony strikes even her.*) If you think about it, it's kind of a nice twist. But I'm not going to think about it. (*She goes to the kitchen, leaving the door ajar, continuing to mutter to herself so that we can hear her.*) I'm not going to think about it, I'm not going to think about it, I am absolutely not going to think about it . . ."

Fred enters from the terrace, wondering where everybody is. Katy shows him Jeff's note, and Fred reads it aloud: "Since your slightest wish is my command, I am going to spend the weekend with Phil. I would prefer that you told the boys I am staying with my mother. If, however, you wish to be more honest—that's up to you. Jeff." The most painful part about the note is, Jeff always signs some joking name when he writes notes to Katy, never just "Jeff."

Katy admits to Fred that occasionally she has fantasies about a man coming into her life out of nowhere. Fred is eager to play that role for her. He remembers how greatly Katy appealed to him when they first met. He puts his arm around her, but the telephone interrupts them. Fred goes to answer it, and when he comes back Katy runs to his arms and he kisses her.

KATY (*a deep breath, then firmly but nervously*): Shall we go over to your place? (*He cocks his head quizzically.*) Well, we can't stay here.

FRED: You mean, in case one of the boys comes home. What will they think if you're not here?

KATY: I don't know. But they won't think I'm over at your place, that's for sure.

FRED (*suddenly*): Let's have a drink.

KATY (*puzzled*): Can't we have a drink over there?

FRED: What's the hurry? You afraid you're going to have second thoughts?

KATY: I already have second thoughts. I'm afraid I'll have third thoughts.

FRED (*going to fix one*): I guess I want a drink right now.

KATY: What are you trying to do—nerve yourself?

FRED: Not at all. Unlike you, I do not equate this with facing a firing squad.

Fred reports to Katy about the phone call—it was Steve, and when Fred told him Felicia had left, Steve's only concern was that his books were in the back of her car. Katy quotes Edna St. Vincent Millay and then weeps for the apparent fragility of love.

Fred comforts and reassures her—they are not going through with their fling, they will retire to their own beds. Fred is having third thoughts, not about friendship or ethics, but: "Today when I told you to urge Jeff to take a flier, I don't *think* I had it in the back of my mind that if he did—if he did leave—you would inevitably fall into my lap. But maybe that's what I did have in mind . . . . . I am willing to play Don Juan, but not Machiavelli."

Katy understands, and Fred leaves, as Kevin wanders through in search of something to eat (he was in his room all the time listening to rock music, but they couldn't hear him because he was using headphones—and of course he couldn't hear them). Kevin wonders where his father can be, and Katy tells him Felicia drove Jeff to Falmouth to visit Kevin's grandmother.

Katy is curious about Kevin's attitude toward sexual promiscuity. Kevin advises his mother not to worry about it. As a mother, he would rate her "9.5 out of a possible 10. You lose five because of the way you play basketball."

Kevin goes into the kitchen and Katy hears him say "Hi, Dad." She hardly knows what to do with herself, or what attitude to adopt, as Jeff strides in and tosses a small package on the table. There is an overwhelming need for many things to be said. Katy cannot help commenting, "I know these romances have a way of burning out, but twenty-five minutes must be some kind of record. Did she make some ghastly mistake in grammar? Did she say 'Let's you and me' instead of 'Let's you and I—'?"

After a short bout of fencing with sarcasms, Katy demands that they talk straight to each other. Jeff orders Katy to open the small package he brought home—it is Gelusil tablets. He thought he might need some after all the drinking, the pot roast and the tension, so he asked Felicia to stop by the drug store.

JEFF: . . . . . Marty was wrapping it up and it all came to me—"This is insane, completely and totally insane! Men who are swept off their feet do not stop for minor medications!" (*Seriously, desperately.*) Do you know how *late* it is?

Katy, misunderstanding, looks at her watch.

Oh, my God, I don't mean on your wrist watch! I mean in our lives. (*Quoting contemptuously.*) "Grow old along with me, the best is yet to be." Do you think Browning really believed that crap?

KATY: We're not *that* old. You make it sound like were were senior citizens all ready for Fort Lauderdale.

JEFF: Listen, I know men my age who spend weekends with young girls and are very humiliated because they can't make it sexually. Well, I am awfully damn sure I could have made it sexually. My problem is that I can't make it psychologically. Don't you see that's worse?

KATY: No, I don't see, I don't. I really don't.

JEFF: I can't help myself. I have been programmed one way for too long. Do you realize that for all my life—for more than forty years!—I have been, oh good Christ, the boy who came home on time?

KATY: Is that so terrible?

JEFF: Right now I think it is.

KATY: But who do you want to be? In your secret dreams, are you still Errol Flynn?

JEFF (*straight*): In my secret dreams, I had secret dreams. I don't think I will have them any more.

KATY: You shouldn't have told me that. I didn't really want to hear *that*.

Hughie comes in with his tape of Felicia doing *The Tempest,* and he puts in on the recorder. Jeff turns it off at once and orders Hughie upstairs. Katy starts to laugh at the aptness of "Our revels now are ended," and Jeff is on the edge of laughing at himself for his ridiculous behavior in the drug store. The phone rings, and while Jeff goes to answer it Katy has a notion and begins to fix herself up with powder, lipstick and mascara.

Jeff comes out of the phone closet with the good news that he has his promotion to full professor—the letters went out late, and the Dean thought Jeff would like to know right away, so he phoned. Jeff feels curiously liberated by this news: "If I didn't make it I could never leave—never! I would just seem like a sorehead. Now that's all changed. I could open a pizza parlor and I wouldn't seem a sorehead. I'd just be eccentric—or maybe just plain bonkers. But I could do it!"

Katy shares Jeff's mood of elation, but when he puts his hand on her shoulder and calls her "my girl" she shakes it off.

KATY: Please don't rush things.

JEFF: Katy, there may not always be a bright golden haze on the meadow. But there are compensations. And once in a while you get a real hunch that there's some pattern to the pattern.

KATY: Like what?

JEFF (*looking straight at her*): Like—*if* I'm the man who always comes home, I realize I am absolutely certain you're the one I want to come home to.

    Katy bolts into his arms.

Hey, what's this?

KATY: I'm trying to rush things.

Kevin comes in from the kitchen, now too well fed and looking for Gelusil. He has come to the right place, and he carries the bottle up to his room after saying good night to his parents, adding the cryptic "Love you six." Jeff and Katy start to straighten up the room and turn out lights.

JEFF: What does that phrase in code mean?

    Katy doesn't understand, looks puzzled, so he repeats the phrase.

"Love you six."

KATY: That's been a family joke for years and you never heard it?

    Jeff shakes his head no.

When Hughie was two, maybe less than two, he couldn't really count, and one day he said, "Mommy, I love you six," because that was as high as he could go. I thought it was kind of sweet. Kevin and Steve thought it was hilarious. And you never heard it?

JEFF: No, but I'm glad to learn that there is an explanation for everything. Now how do I get the Gelusil back from Kevin?

KATY: There's some in the pocket of your pajamas. I always put two in the pocket of your pajamas. You never noticed?

    They have virtually finished their cleaning up and closing down and are near the foot of the staircase.

JEFF: Of course I noticed. It just went out of my head. What *is* the matter with me?

KATY (*almost fondly*): Everything.

JEFF: Katy, want to know something?

KATY: Yeah.

JEFF: I love you seven.

KATY: Make that eight and you've got yourself a deal.

    He takes her hand and they start up the stairs.

JEFF (*on the way up*): Eight—nine—ten—

    The telephone rings. Katy almost makes a move to turn down to answer it, but Jeff keeps her hand firmly and continues counting as they go up.

Eleven—twelve—

    They are gone. The phone just keeps ringing. Curtain.

THE CHANGING ROOM

A Play in Three Acts

BY DAVID STOREY

Cast and credits appear on page 352

DAVID STOREY was born in 1934 in Wakefield, Yorkshire, the son of a British coal miner. He was educated at Wakefield Grammar School, and he showed such promise as an athlete that at 17 he was signed to a 15-year contract with the Leeds Rugby League Club. But soon afterward he won a scholarship to the Slade School of Art in London and accepted it, paying back to the football group most of his signing bonus. He exhibited paintings in London with other Yorkshire artists and still paints in his spare time, but he finally decided that writing was to be his medium of expression.

Storey worked as a secondary school teacher in London's East End while writing seven novels which failed to satisfy even himself ("I was getting a bit wild, before I started getting on," he confided to an interviewer). His eighth, This Sporting Life, *was published in 1960 and made into a movie in 1963 by Lindsay Anderson, who has also directed some of Storey's plays. His published work includes four more novels:* Flight Into Camden, Radcliffe, Pasmore *and* A Temporary Life.

Eight years after he first wrote it, in 1967, Storey's first play, The Restoration of Arnold Middleton, *was produced in London by the Royal Court. His other London productions were* In Celebration (1969), The Contractor (1970) *and* Home (1971), *which also represented its author's American stage debut in November, 1971 and won him a Best Play citation and the New York Drama Critics Circle Award for the best play of the 1970-71 season.*

Storey makes it two Best Play citations and two Drama Critics Awards in a row with The Changing Room, *which was named one of the outstanding new*

British plays by this volume's European editor, Ossia Trilling, in its London production last season. Its American premiere took place at the Long Wharf Theater in New Haven, Conn. (an article by this theater's director, Arvin Brown, appears at the beginning of "The Season Around the United States" section of this volume), and it was the Long Wharf production with its American cast that appeared on Broadway.

Storey lives in the Hampstead section of London with his wife and four children.

Time: The present

Place: The changing room of a Rugby League team in the North of England

ACT I

1:50 p.m.

SYNOPSIS: In early afternoon before the game, the empty changing room (locker room) of a North Country Rugby League team is lit by sunlight from glazed panels, in addition to the electric light. Rugby League football is "*a very tough, professional, tackling, running and kicking game played mainly in Yorkshire and Lancashire, in which they wear no padding . . . . . Unlike Rugby Union, an amateur sport, this is a working class game played for a dwindling working class audience.*"

The room contains long changing benches, a row of hooks and lockers and a rubbing-down bench beside which stands a large wicker basket, plus other paraphernalia of the locker room. Up left is an open entry to the toilets and bath, up center a door to the outside, up right a door leading to the offices and down right the ramp leading off to the playing field.

Harry, the locker room attendant, "*a broken-down man, small, stooped, in shirt sleeves, rolled, and a sleeveless pullover,*" enters from the bath area and sweeps the floor, after which he adds coal to the fire in a stove.

The first of the players comes in: Patsy, "*a smart, lightly-built man, very well groomed, hair greased, collar of an expensive overcoat turned up; brisk, businesslike, narcissistic, no evident sense of humor.*" He checks his uniform and other equipment carefully while Harry lays out clean towels, commenting that the forecast promises a spell of wintry weather. They never cancel games in this league, Patsy tells him, not even when the pitch (playing field) is so icy and hard it takes the skin right off a man.

Harry is convinced that the cold weather is the result of a secret plan by the Russians to freeze everybody and take over. Harry is paranoid on this subject, and Patsy's observation that "They play football i' Russia as much as they play it here" only makes him even more sullenly suspicious.

Fielding, a "*large, well-built man, slow, easygoing,*" comes in wrapped in muffler and overcoat, wearing a plaster strip above his left eye. He comments on the cold. Harry reiterates his belief in a Russian plot.

FIELDING: Nay, I'm not worried. They can come here any day of the bloody week for me. Sup of ale . . .

PATSY: Ten fags . . .

FIELDING: That's all I need.

> *Fielding sneezes hugely; shakes his head, gets out his handkerchief, blows his nose, lengthily and noisily . . . . .*

I thought o' ringing up this morning . . . Looked out o' the bloody winder. Frost . . .

> *Crosses over to Patsy.*

Got this house, now, just outside the town . . . wife's idea, not mine . . . bloody fields . . . hardly a bloody sign of human life . . . cows . . . half a dozen sheep . . . goats . . .

> *Starts peeling the plaster from above his eye: Patsy pays no attention, arranging his coat on the hanger . . . . .*

Middle of bloody nowhere . . . if I can't see a wall outside of t'window I don't feel as though I'm living in a house . . . . . How's it look?

PATSY (*glances up, briefly*): All right.

FIELDING: Bloody fist. Loose forra'd . . . Copped him one afore the end. Had a leg like a bloody melon . . . Get Lukey to put on a bit of grease . . . (*Feeling the cut.*) Should be all right. How's your shoulder?

PATSY: All right. (*Eases it.*) Came in early. Get it strapped.

FIELDING: Where we lived afore, you know, everything you could bloody want: pit, boozer, bloody dogs. As for now . . . trees, hedges, miles o' bloody grass . . . where's the jock straps, Harry?

> *Inspecting his kit which Harry has now hung up.*

I thought of ringing up and backing out. Flu . . . Some such like. (*Sneezes.*) By God . . . He'll have me lakin'* here, will Harry, wi' me bloody cobblers hanging out.

Morley enters (*"thick set, squat figure. dark-haired . . . . . hard, rough, uncomplicated"*), closely followed by Kendal (*"a tall, rather well-built man, late 20s, wearing an old overcoat with a scarf and carrying a paper parcel: a worn, somewhat faded man"*). They complain to Harry about equipment deficiencies, then Kendal shows them his parcel—he has just bought a tool set with drill and polisher, to make book cases and other "fitments" for his home.

Each sets about changing out of his street clothes into his uniform as Harry departs. Luke, the team's trainer, comes in with his paraphernalia including a large tin of vaseline. Luke tapes Patsy's very painful shoulder while Morley complains of a sprained ankle. They all joke with Kendal about his tool set, as Harry comes in with the remaining jerseys then departs again. Three other members of the team come in: Fenchurch (*"a neatly groomed man, small, almost dainty . . . . . self-contained, perhaps even at times a vicious man"*),

* Playing

Jagger ("*of medium height, but sturdy . . . . . perky, rather officious, cocky*") and Trevor ("*a studious-looking man: wears glasses, is fairly sturdily-built: quiet, level-headed: a schoolmaster*"). They make jokes about Fenchurch's pride in his own imagined celebrity as a football player, but Fenchurch takes no notice.

Walsh comes in; he is "*a large, somewhat commanding figure . . . . . age 35-40, stout, fairly weatherbeaten.*" He enters through the door from the offices wearing a carnation in the lapel of his dark suit and smoking a cigar.

> *There are cries and mocking shouts at Walsh's appearance: "Ay up, ay up, Walshy," "What's this?"*

WALSH: And er . . . who are all these bloody layabouts in here?

FIELDING: The bloody workers, lad. Don't you worry.

WALSH: I hope the floor's been swept then, Harry . . . Keep them bloody microbes off my chair . . . (*Comes in.*) Toe-caps polished with *equal* brightness, Harry . . . (*To Jagger.*) I hate to find one toe-cap brighter than the next.

JAGGER: White laces.

WALSH: White laces.

> *Harry has set the boots down: goes out.*

MORLEY: Where you ben, then, Walshy?

WALSH: Been?

FIELDING: Been up in the bloody offices, have you? (*Gestures overhead.*)

WALSH: . . . Popped up. Saw the managing director. Enquired about the pitch . . . Asked him if they could *heat it up* . . . thaw out one or two little bumps I noticed. Sir Frederick's going round now with a box of matches . . . applying a drop of heat in all the appropriate places . . . Should be nice and soft by the time you run out theer.

Still clowning, Walsh pretends that maybe he won't have to play today. Walsh has just come from a family wedding where he drank his fill of champagne, he says. He reached the clubhouse at the same time as the bus carrying the opposing team, which he characterizes as "Load o' bloody pansies."

The group conversation drifts onto the subject of wives. Trevor's has a degree in economics and never comes to see him play. Fenchurch has no wife and in Jagger's opinion "wouldn't mind being married to bloody ought." Walsh asks Kendal pointedly about his wife, but Kendal is more interested in his new tool kit.

Morley is having his ankle strapped. Patsy is warming his jersey at the fire. Fielding and Jagger swap information about their bets on this afternoon's horse races. Harry is distributing shoulder pads. Sandford, the assistant trainer, enters through the office door. He is about 40 and carries papers clipped to a pen. He sniffs the air in the changing room.

SANDFORD: I can smell cigar smoke . . . (*Looks round.*) Has somebody been smoking bloody cigars?

> *Walsh, back to the fire, is holding his behind him.*

JAGGER: It's Harry, Mr. Sandford. He's got one here.

WALSH: That's not a bloody cigar he's got, old lad.

HARRY: I don't smoke. It's not me. Don't worry. (*They laugh.*)

MORLEY: Come on, now, Harry, what's thy bloody got?

> *Harry avoids them as Jagger sets at him: goes.*

SANDFORD (*to Walsh*): Is it you, Ken?

WALSH: Me?

FIELDING: Come on now, bloody Walsh. Own up.

WALSH: Where would I get a bloody cigar?

> *Puts the cigar in his mouth; approaches Sandford.*

I was bloody well stopped five quid this week. They never told me . . . What's it for, then, Sandy?

SANDFORD: Bloody language.

WALSH: Language?

SANDFORD: Referee's report . . . Thy wants to take that out.

WALSH: Out?

> *Puffs. Sandford removes it, carefully stubs it out.*

SANDFORD: You can have it back when you're bloody well dressed and ready to go home . . . If you want the report you can read it in the office.

WALSH: Trevor: exert thy bloody authority, lad. Players' representative. Get up in that office . . . (*To Sandford.*) If there's any been bloody well smoked I shall bloody well charge thee: don't thee bloody worry . . . Here, now: let's have it bloody back.

> *Takes the cigar out of Sandford's pocket: takes Sandford's pencil: marks the cigar. They laugh.*

Warned you. Comes bloody expensive, lad, does that.

> *Puts cigar back; goes over to bench to change.*

Sandford inquires of his players about their injuries, as they all—except Walsh—continue the process of changing out of street clothes into uniforms. Copley ("*a stocky, muscular man: simple, good-humored, straightforward*") comes in with Stringer ("*tall and slim: aloof, with little interest in any of the others*"). Copley complains of the cold and the hardness of the playing field. The players talk about their captain (Owens, who is walking from his house to the field as a warm-up exercise), their wives and other matters. Four more team members drift in: Atkinson ("*a tall, big-boned man, erect, easygoing*"), Clegg ("*a square, stocky, fairly small man*") and Spencer and Moore ("*much younger men . . . . . nervous, hands in pockets*"). Almost everyone feels a need to comment on the cold as they enter. Atkinson tries to pretend that the game has been cancelled, but the others know better.

They talk about the team's owner, "Sir Frederick bloody Thornton" and his plans to build a new municipal center if the town council will permit it. Luke is strapping the various injuries; Sandford is inspecting his players. Kendal shows his teammates his new tool kit.

At this point only Patsy is changed and ready, and he "*crosses to the mirror to comb his hair, examine himself: gets out piece of gum, adjusts socks, etc.*"

He has had to strip down to the buff to put on his jock strap before donning his playing shorts and other gear, of course. The other players do likewise, in a naturalistic manner, without any more modesty or ostentation that you would ordinarily expect to find in a men's locker room (though more openly, perhaps, that you would hitherto have expected to find on a Broadway stage), as they get into their uniforms and apply liberal helpings of grease from the tin to legs, arms, shoulders, neck and ears.

The team's "trainer" (coach), Crosby, *"a stocky, knarled figure"* in his late 40s or early 50s, dressed in a *"track suit"* (sweat clothes), comes in from the office and orders them all to hurry. Their captain, Owens, hasn't arrived yet, but Crosby assured them he's up in the office and has already changed into his uniform. Crosby starts issuing his instructions for today's game.

CROSBY: Bloody well hard out theer. When you put 'em down . . . knock 'em bleeding hard.

WALSH: And what's Owens bloody well been up to? Arranging a bloody transfer, is he? Or asking for a rise? (*They laugh.*)

CROSBY (*reading from a list*): Patsy, Harrison's on the wing this afternoon. Alus goes off his left foot, lad.

PATSY: Aye. Right.
Rubs arms and legs, etc. He and Clegg laugh.

CROSBY: Barry, scrum-half: new. When you catch him knock him bloody hard . . . Morley?

MORLEY: Aye!

CROSBY: Same with you. Get round. Let him know you're theer . . . Same goes for you, Bryan.

ATKINSON: Aye.

CROSBY: Kenny . . . Let's see you bloody well go right across.

MORLEY: He's brought something to show you here, Mr. Crosby.

CROSBY: What?

MORLEY: Kenny . . . Show him your bloody outfit, Ken.

KENDAL (*after a certain hesitation*): Piss off! (*They laugh.*)

WALSH: You tell him, Kenny, lad. That's right.

JAGGER (*to Kendal*): Anybody gets in thy road . . . (*Smacks his fist against his hand.*)

CLEGG: Ne'er know which is bloody harder. Ground out yon or Kenny's loaf.

CROSBY: Jack . . . Jagger . . .

STRINGER: Aye.

JAGGER: Aye . . .

CROSBY: Remember what we said. Keep together . . . don't be waiting theer for Trev . . . If Jack goes right, then you go with him . . . Trevor: have you heard that, lad?

TREVOR: Aye.

CROSBY: Use your bloody eyes . . . John?

CLEGG: Aye?

CROSBY: Let's have a bit of bloody service, lad.

CLEGG: Cliff been complaining, has he?

CROSBY: Complained about bloody nowt. It's me who's been complaining ... Michaelmas bloody Morley ... when you get that bloody ball ... remember ... don't toss it o'er your bloody head.

WALSH: Who's refereeing then, old lad?

CROSBY: Tallon (*Groans and cries.*)

JAGGER: Brought his bloody white stick, then, has he?

FENCHURCH: Got his bloody guide-dog, then?

CROSBY (*undisturbed; to Copley*): Barry. Watch your putting in near your own line ... No fists. No bloody feet. Remember ... But when you hit them. Hit them bleeding hard.

Crowd noises and band music are beginning to be heard, as Crosby continues instructing his players. They turn their valuables over to the trainers. Owens comes in through the office door. He is the team captain, *"medium build, unassuming, bright, about 30-32 years old, rubbing his hands together, cheerful: a shy man, perhaps, but now a little perky."* He's dressed in a track suit, under which he's already changed into uniform.

The others are curious as to why Owens was meeting with Sir Frederick, the owner. Owens tells them he was asked to "Fill him in on the tactics we intend to use today." Owens rallies them with advice and encouragement, exchanging jokes. *"Now all of them are almost ready: moving over to the mirror, combing hair, straightening collars, tightening boots, chewing, greasing ears, emptying coat pockets of wallets, etc., handing them over to Crosby, Sandford or Luke."*

The referee, Tallon, comes in and searches each player to see that there are no injurious protrusions like rings, buckles, boot studs, etc. Harry brings in two Rugby balls and a resin board. The players sniff ammonia from phials, as Tallon finishes his inspection and instructs them all: "Remember ... keep it clean ... play fair. Have a good game, lads. Play to the whistle."

The five-minute bell rings, and the referee exits. The players start exercising to limber up, pushing against each other.

CROSBY (*holding the forwards with Spencer and Moore*): All right. All right.

    Morley leans on Atkinson and Kendal, then, at Crosby's signal, puts his head between them as they scrum down. Spencer, Moore and Crosby are linked together.

Let's have a ball ... Cliff ... Barry ... Number four: first clear scrum we we get: either side ...

    Takes the ball Sandford's brought him.

Our possession, theirs ... Clifford ... Jagger ... Jack ... that's right.

    The rest of the players take up positions behind: Copley immediately behind, then Owens, then Stringer, Jagger, Patsy on one side, Fenchurch on the other: Trevor stands at the back.

Right, then? Our ball, then ...

    Crosby puts the ball in at Clegg's feet: it's knocked back through the scrum to Copley, then it's passed, hand to hand, slowly, almost formally, out to Patsy: as each player passes it he falls back: the scrum breaks up, falls back to make a line going back diagonally and ending with Fenchurch.

WALSH: From me. To you. (*Laughter.*)

CROSBY: All right. All right.

When the ball reaches Patsy he passes it back; to Jagger, to Stringer, to Owens, to Copley, then to each forward in turn, each calling the Christian name of the one who hands it on, until it reaches Fenchurch.

They practise one more play which ends in a mimed drop kick. The office door opens and the club owner, Sir Fredrick Thornton (*"tall, dressed in a fur-collared overcoat: a well-preserved man of about 50"*) enters, accompanied by the club secretary, Mackendrick (*"a flushed-face man of about 60, wearing an overcoat, a scarf and a dark hat"*). Thornton orders Harry to put more coal on the fire and wishes the team good luck. He tells the players: "Go out . . . play like I know you can . . . there'll not be one man disappointed." Thornton asks if there are any complaints or suggestions; there are none. Mackendrick, he says, will be in the office after the game if there's anything anybody wants; then Thornton and Mackendrick depart.

The bell rings again, and the players line up with Owens at their head holding the ball. The crowd outside is heard roaring, as Walsh has a last joke with Harry.

Crosby holds the door.

OWENS: Right, then?

ALL: Right. Ready. Let's get off. (*Belches, groans.*)

CROSBY: Good-luck, Trev . . . good-luck, lad . . . good-luck . . . good-luck, Mic . . .

He pats each player's back as they move out: moments after Owens has gone there's a great roar outside. Crosby sees the team out, then Spencer and Moore in track suits, then Luke and Sandford; he looks round, then he goes, closing the door. The roar grows louder: music. Harry comes in: wanders round: looks at the floor for anything that's been dropped: picks up odd tapes, phials. Goes to the fire: puts on another piece, stands by it, still. The crowd roar grows louder. Then, slowly: lights and sound fade. Curtain.

ACT II

Thirty-five minutes later

The roar of the crowd is audible as Thornton and Mackendrick enter the empty changing room about 15 minutes before the end of the game's first half.

They are suffering from the cold and grateful for the stove's warmth.

Mackendrick goes to the office to get some whiskey. Harry comes in all bundled up—he has been outside for a breather—and he lets Thornton in on the secret about the Russians causing this freezing weather.

HARRY: Without anybody knowing . . . Breathe it . . . Take it in . . . (*Breathes in.*) Slows down your mind . . . (*Illustrates with limp arms and hands.*) Stops everybody thinking.

THORNTON: I think our lads've had a drop of that today. By God, I've never seen so many bloody knock-ons . . . dropped passes . . .

HARRY: I've been a workman all my life.

THORNTON: Oh . . . Aye.

HARRY: I used to work in a brick-yard afore I came up here.

THORNTON: It's a pity you're not back theer, Harry lad. Bloody bricks we get. Come to pieces in your bloody hand . . . Had a house fall down the other day. Know what it was . . . ? Bricks . . . crumbled up . . . Seen nothing like it . . . Still . . .

HARRY: Knew your place before. Now, there's everybody doing summat . . . And nobody doing owt.

THORNTON: Still. Go with it, Harry.

HARRY: What . . .

THORNTON: Can't go against your times.

Thornton hears the crowd booing the referee and wonders why a man would choose to keep on in a job like that. Mackendrick finally returns with bottle and glasses, telling his boss that the opposing team is ahead just now. Harry refuses an offered drink, calling Thornton by his title, to which Thornton replies, "Nay, no bloody titles here, old lad. Freddy six days o' the week. Sir Frederick to the wife on Sundays."

Mackendrick goes to find out what caused a particularly large roar from the crowd, while Harry expounds on the good old days of Rugby League: "Players? . . . Couldn't hold a bloody candle . . . In them days they'd do a sixteen hour shift *then* come up and lake . . . Nowadays: it's all machines . . . and they's *still* bloody puffed when they come up o' Sat'days. Run round yon field a couple of times: finished. I've seen 'em laking afore with broken arms, legs broke . . . shoulders . . . Get a scratch today and they're in here, flat on their bloody backs . . . . ."

Mackendrick comes back to inform them that the team has just scored, and Morley converted. Mackendrick disagrees with Harry about the good old days. He feels strongly that conditions have much improved in life as in Rugby: "Washed i' bloody buckets, then . . . e't dripping instead o' bloody meat . . . urinated by an hedge . . . God Christ: bloody houses were nobbut size o' this: seven kiddies, no bloody bath: no bed . . . father out o' work as much as not."

Thornton's comment on this discussion is to tell them of a nightmare he just had about the players turning into robots worked by two men in the stands. There are sounds of the first half ending and the team returning to the locker room. Thornton makes his escape before the players arrive.

> *Fenchurch comes in first, shaking his hand violently: he's followed by Luke carrying his bag.*

FENCHURCH: Jesus! Jesus! Bloody hell.

LUKE: Here . . . let's have a look. Come on.

JAGGER (*following him in*): It's nothing . . . bloody nothing . . .

FENCHURCH: Bloody studs, you see . . . Just look!

> *He holds it up, wincing, as Luke takes it. He groans, cries out as Luke examines it. The others are beginning to flood in: stained jerseys, gasping, bruised, exhausted. Harry brings in two bottles of water which the players take swigs from and spit out into Luke's bucket which Moore has carried in.*

LUKE: Nothing broken. It'll be all right.

SANDFORD: Do you want me to bind it for you, then?

FENCHURCH: No, no. No . . . No.

JAGGER: Can't hold the ball with a bandage on.

COPLEY: Don't worry Fenny lad, match o'er have you off to hospital. Operation. Have it off. Not going to have you troubled, lad, by that.

FENCHURCH: Sod off. (*They laugh.*)

WALSH (*groaning, collapses on the bench*): I'm done. I'm finished. I shall never walk again. Sandy . . . Bring us a cup o' tea, old lad.

SANDFORD: You'll have a cup o' bloody nothing. Have a swab at that.

> *Splashes a cold sponge in Walsh's face and round his neck. Walsh splutters, groans: finally wipes his face and neck. Crosby has come in with the remainder of the players.*

CROSBY: Well done. Well done. Start putting the pressure in the second half.

JAGGER: Pressure?

FENCHURCH: Pressure . . .

JAGGER: That *was* the bloody pressure. Anything from now on is strictly leftovers, Danny lad . . . I'm knackered. Look at that. Use hammers on that bloody pitch out there.

MACKENDRICK: Well done, then, lads. Well done.

Mackendrick pretends that he sat out in the bitter cold watching them till the very end of the half. Sandford urges all the players to keep moving, keep limber. The trainers are checking over the players and their uniforms, looking for damage to be repaired.

The score at the half is tied 7-7. Patsy has a cramp in his leg; Walsh has a cut in his back. Thornton comes in from the office and congratulates individual players on their efforts, as Owens returns from the bath area where he has been cleaning himself up. Walsh fishes for a compliment which Thornton delivers on cue, but Crosby remarks of Walsh "He could bloody well do wi' wekening up" and continues on the subject of the team's performance: "There's half on you asleep out yon . . . Fieldy . . . Bryan . . . *move across. Go with it* . . . It's no good waiting till they come. . . . Bloody hell . . . Trevor theer: he's covering all that side . . . Colin: *bloody interceptions:* it's no good going in, lad, every time . . . they'll be bloody well waiting for it soon . . . three times that *I* saw Jack here had to take your man."

Walsh suggests that Spencer go eavesdrop on the opponents' dressing room. Crosby moves about instructing individual players while Mackendrick talks to Trevor about a cut on his ear. The warning bell rings and the coach gives his final admonitions. Thornton puts in a word about keeping the pressure on the other team, then goes out with Mackendrick. The players move out, followed by Sandford.

Luke, left alone with Harry, wonders what he does in his spare time (Harry has no spare time, he informs Luke). Luke finds out from Harry that Thornton, accompanied by Mackendrick, sat out some of the first half here by the warm fire.

HARRY: It's his place . . . He can do what he likes . . . He can sit in here the whole afternoon if he bloody likes.

LUKE: I suppose he can. (*Roar off.*) F'un him up here, you know, one night.

HARRY: What's that?

LUKE: Sir Frederick . . . Came back one night . . . Left me tackle . . . Saw a light up in the stand . . . Saw him sitting theer. Alone. Crouched up. Like that.

HARRY: His stand. Can sit theer when he likes.

LUKE: Ten o'clock at night.

HARRY: Ten o'clock i' the bloody morning. Any time he likes.

LUKE (*fastens his bag*): Is it true, then, what they say?

HARRY: What's that?

LUKE: Thy's never watched a match.

HARRY: Never.

LUKE: Why's that?

HARRY: My job's in here. Thy job's out yonder.

LUKE: They ought to set thee on a pair o' bloody rails.

Goes over to the door, pauses.

HARRY: Most jobs you get: they're bloody nowt . . . Don't know what they work for.

LUKE: What?

HARRY: Not anymore. Not like it was . . .

LUKE: Well, thy works for the bloody club.

HARRY: I work for Sir Frederick, lad: for nob'dy else.

Luke looks across at him.

I ma'n run the bloody bath. (*Goes.*)

Luke departs and Harry comes back and lays out towels. Crowd roars, booing, moans are heard, and Harry switches on the Tanoy (radio loud speaker) on a shelf in the changing room. A voice narrates above the crowd's roar:

" . . . Copley . . . Clegg . . . Morley . . . Fenchurch . . . inside passes . . . Jagger . . . Stringer . . . Tackled. Fourth tackle. Scrum down. Walsh . . . Fielding . . . Walsh having words with his opposite number! Getting down. The scrum is just inside United's half . . . almost ten yards in from the opposite touch . . . put in . . . some rough play inside that scrum . . . Referee Tallon's blown up . . . free kick . . . no . . . scrum down . . . not satisfied with the tunnel . . ball in . . . Walsh's head is up . . . (*Laughter.*) There's some rough business inside that scrum . . . my goodness! . . . ball comes out . . . Morley . . . Copley . . . Owens . . . Owens to Trevor . . . *Trevor is going to drop a goal* . . . too late . . . He's left it far too late . . . They've tried that once before . . . Kendal . . ."

Harry switches the voice off just just as there is a great roar outside. Sandford comes in and then Kendal comes in, obviously hurt, supported by Crosby and Moore. Kendal assures them "It's bloody nowt . . . I'll be all right" but they order him to lie down on the massage table. Luke comes in with his bag. Moore brings over a sponge. Kendal has been kicked in the nose and his face is covered with blood; he is dazed but still game. They wipe away the blood, examine the injury and apply disinfectant. The wound is too severe for Kendal to continue playing, so Crosby sends in Moore, one of the substitutes. Sandford helps Kendal into the bath as Mackendrick enters to inquire perfunctorily about Kendal's injury, then calls him "Too bloody slow, you know. If I've said it once I've said it . . ." Luke, sorry for Kendal, comments to Mackendrick about Kendal's "bloody wife . . . . . Been round half the teams i' the bloody league . . . one time or another." Then Luke goes back to the field, while Mackendrick returns to the office to report to Sir Frederick and order a car for Kendal.

Harry adjusts the massage table. Sandford leads Kendal out of the bath. Kendal can see nothing but spots and blotches of light. He can't remember who is winning the game, but he remembers about his tool kit. Kendal's nose is broken, Sandford tells Harry.

HARRY: Three collar bones we had one week . . . Two o' theirs . . . the last un ours . . . Ankle . . . Bloody thigh bone, once . . . Red hair.

SANDFORD (*to Kendal*): Come on, come on, then, lad . . . 'od up.

HARRY: He never played again.

KENDAL: Steam boilers, lad . . . Bang 'em in . . . Seen nothing like it. Row o' rivets . . . Christ . . . Can hardly see ought . . . Sandy?

SANDFORD: Here, old lad. Now just hold tight . . . Come on. Come on, now. Let's have you out of here . . . (*To Harry.*) Will you see if Mr. Mackendrick's got that car? (*As Harry goes.*) Harry: can you find me coat as well?

> *Harry goes, stiffly: leaves by office entry. Roar off: rises to peak: applause, bugles, rattles. Kendal turns to sound as if to go.*

Nay, lad: can't go with nothing on your feet.

> *Sits him down: puts on his socks and shoes.*

KENDAL (*dazed*): Started lakin' here when I wa' fifteen, tha knows . . . Intermediates . . . Then I went out, on loan, to one of these bloody colliery teams . . . bring 'em up at the bloody weekend in bloody buckets . . . play a game o' bloody football . . . booze all Sunday . . . back down at the coal-face, Monday . . . Seen nothing like it. Better ring my wife.

SANFORD: What?

KENDAL: She won't know.

SANDFORD: She's not here today, then?

KENDAL: No . . .

Kendal doesn't want her to be worried about his whereabouts. Sandford reassures him and helps him into his worn coat (Kendal was going to buy a new overcoat but decided on the tool set instead). Harry brings in Sanford's overcoat and announces a taxi waiting outside. Sandford fastens a dressing onto Kendal's face.

KENDAL: Is it broke?

SANDFORD: There's a bit of a gash, old lad.

KENDAL: Had it broken once before . . .

SANDFORD: Can you manage to the car?
        Collects his coat.

KENDAL: Wheer is it, then? (*Turns either way.*)

SANDFORD: Here it is, old lad.
        Hands him his parcel.

KENDAL: Have to get some glasses . . . hardly see . . .

SANDFORD (*to Harry*): Looks like bloody Genghis Khan . . . Come on, then, Kenny . . . Lean on me. (*To Harry.*) Still got me bloody boots on . . . I'll get them in the office . . . See you, lad.
        Harry watches them go. He waits: then he picks up the used towel: takes it off to dump inside the bath entrance. He comes back: looks round: switches on the Tanoy: crowd roar.

TANOY: . . . to Walsh . . . reaches the twenty-five . . . goes down . . . plays back . . . (*Roar.*) comes to Clegg to Atkinson to the substitute Moore . . . Moore in now: crashes his way through . . . goes down . . . Walsh comes up . . . out to Owens . . . Owens through . . . dummies . . . beautiful move . . . to Stringer, Stringer out to Patsy . . . Patsy out to Trevor who's come up on the wing . . . kicks . . . Copley . . . Fenchurch . . . Fielding . . . *Morley* . . . (*Roar.*) Ball bounces into touch . . . scrum . . . (*Pause. Dull roar.*) Growing dark now . . . ball goes in: comes out: Tallon blows . . . free kick . . . scrum infringement . . . one or two tired figures there . . . can see the steam, now, rising from the backs . . . Trevor's running up and down, blowing in his hands . . . Kick . . . good kick . . . (*Crowd roar.*) finds touch beyond the twenty-five . . .
        Crowd roar. Harry sits, listening. Fade: sound and light. Curtain.

ACT III

After the match

There is music on the Tanoy and singing in the bath where the players are splashing around after the game. Patsy is dressing himself as carefully and meticulously for the street as he did for the game. Harry is picking up towels. Crosby is moving through the room chatting with individual team members. The nakedness of the players as they emerge from their baths seems more ostentatious here than in the opening scene because the mood of this scene is itself much more extroverted, with the men in high spirits after great tension, indulging in all manner of joking and horse play.

Spencer is half-dressed and in a more solemn mood than the rest because he didn't get into the game, though his girl had come especially to watch him play—and next week the game is away. Patsy's shoulder is stiff and sore. Jagger bursts in from the bath entrance.

JAGGER: Dirty bugger . . . dirty sod . . . Danny: go bloody stop him.
    Snatches towel: rubs his hair vigorously.
Walshy—pittling in the bloody bath. (*Bawdy song from bath.*)
    SPENCER (*calling through*): Thy'll have to disinfect that bloody water . . .
(*Laughing.*)
    WALSH (*off*): This *is* disinfectant, lad.
    CROSBY: Come on, Walshy, let's have you out . . .
    Crosby takes a towel and dries Jagger's back.
    JAGGER: Dirty bugger: dirty sod!
    WALSH (*off*): Come on, Jagger. You could do with a bloody wash.
    JAGGER: Not in that, you dirty sod . . . Set bloody Patsy onto you, if you don't watch out . . .
    Water comes in from the bath.
Dirty! Dirty! . . . (*Dances out of the way: laughter and shouting off.*)
    CROSBY: Come on, Trevor. Teach 'em one or two manners, then . . . Bloody college man . . . going to go away disgusted with all you bloody working lads.
    Another jet of water. Crosby lurches out of the way.
Bloody well be in there if you don't watch out. (*Jeers. Cries.*)
    COPLEY (*off*): Too bloody old!
    CLEGG (*off*): Come on, Danny. Show us what you've got.
    CROSBY: Got summat here that'll bloody well surprise you, lad . . . (*Laughter, cries.*) And you! (*Laughter off.*) Sithee . . . Billy. Go in and quieten 'em down.
    SPENCER: Nay . . . gotten out in one bloody piece. Not likely. Send Harry in. He'll shift 'em out.

All in the bath are singing as Luke enters to tell Crosby that Kendal has a broken nose but will be all right and is being held in the hospital overnight

("Give his missus chance to bloody roam"). Trevor comes in from the bath—he's just beginning to get some feeling back in his injured fingers. They check the results of the 2:30 horse race in a late edition of the paper—Walsh's choice, Albatross, has won, and they determine not to tell him. Meanwhile Luke is dabbing antiseptic on Patsy and Trevor as others drift in from the bath joking, jostling, drying each others' backs.

JAGGER: How you feeling, Fenny, lad?

FENCHURCH: All right . . . Results in theer, then, are they? (*Indicating paper.*)

CLEGG: Aye. (*Reads.*) "Latest score: twelve-seven." Patsy: they didn't get thy try * . . . Sithee: pricked up his bloody ears at that.
        They laugh. Patsy, having turned, goes back to dressing.

FENCHURCH: Fifteen-seven . . .

JAGGER: Fifteen-seven.

FENCHURCH: Put a good word in with Sir Frederick, then.

CROSBY: Good word about bloody what, then, lad?

FENCHURCH: Me and Jagger, Danny boy . . . Made old Patsy's bloody try . . . In't that right, then, Jagger lad?

PATSY: Made me own bloody try. Ask Jack . . .

So they have won today, 15 to 7, and they are enjoying the victory, remembering to joke about their masculinity and their girls. Patsy's is a teacher in Trevor's school. Patsy is something of a star, and Luke has a clutch of autograph books left for him to sign, much to the derision of the other players.

As the noise and the horse play continue, Stringer suggests it might be more orderly—and more hygenic—to replace the communal bath with separate shower stalls. Offstage, Morley and Walsh call for Copley to come into the bath; instead, Copley flings a bucket of cold water onto them. Crosby hands Copley another bucket of the same, and Copley douses the others again. Finally Crosby turns a hose into the bath and this brings the remaining players scurrying out, scattering water everywhere. Only Walsh stays in the bath, pretending to like the cold water spray.

The substitute Moore did well in his first appearance, and Crosby will play him again next week. Thornton and Mackendrick enter from the office.

THORNTON: Well done, lads . . . Bloody champion . . . well done . . . They'll not come here again in a bloody hurry . . . not feel half so bloody pleased . . . How's thy feeling, Patsy, lad?

PATSY: All right, sir.

THORNTON: Lovely try . . . Bloody text-book, lad . . . Hope they got that down on bloody film . . . Frank? How's it feel, young man?

MOORE: Pretty good. All right.

CROSBY: Just got started . . .

* Touchdown

FIELDING: Just got into his stride, Sir Frederick.

THORNTON: Another ten minutes . . . he'd have had a bloody try. (*They laugh.*) Set 'em a bloody fine example, lad, don't worry. Well played there, lad. Well done.

MACKENDRICK: Well done, lad.

THORNTON: How's your leg then, Bryan?

ATKINSON: Be all right.

    Atkinson is still on the table: Luke is massaging the leg with oil.

THORNTON: Nasty bloody knock was that.

ATKINSON: Went one way . . . Me leg went t'other.

THORNTON (*to Trevor*): How's your hands now, then, lad?

TREVOR (*has pulled on his club blazer, looks up from dusting it down*): All right. Fine, thanks.

THORNTON (*to Fielding*): I hope you're going to get your eye seen to there, old lad.

FIELDING: Aye.

THORNTON: Bad news about old Kenny.

PLAYERS: Aye . . .

WALSH (*off*): Barr . . . y . . . I am *waiting*, Barry!

THORNTON: Who's that, then? Bloody Walsh?

CROSBY: Aye.

THORNTON (*going to the bath entrance*): And who's thy waiting for, then, Walshy?

WALSH (*pause; off*): Oh, good evening, Sir Frederick . . .

THORNTON: I'll give you Sir bloody Frederick . . . I'll be inside that bath in a bloody minute.

WALSH (*off*): Any time, Sir Frederick, any time is good enough for me. (*The players laugh.*)

Thornton suggests they ought to charge Walsh rent for staying so long in the bath, and Crosby remarks that they fined Walsh five pounds last week for swearing at the referee (today's referee, Tallon, is the type who answers back instead of issuing fines).

Thornton continues his congratulatory round, praising Morley's performance, commiserating about Kendal. Morley judges that the injury wasn't a deliberate attack, maybe Kendal was a bit slow today on account of the cold. Thornton reminds Stringer that if he has any bruises he can return to the changing room tomorrow. Luke will be on hand to treat injuries.

Patsy takes his leave of Thornton and his teammates and departs. Owens comes in from the office, having used the executive facilities to bathe and change into a suit. Walsh appears from the bath finally, with a towel wrapped around him, still pretending he was waiting for Copley in there. Copley challenges Walsh to drop the towel and "Show us what you've got," but Walsh ignores him. Most of the other players are dressed and Harry is collecting their discarded gear. The referee Tallon comes in to congratulate the players on a good game in difficult conditions, then departs with Thornton's flattery in his ears.

Walsh asks about the result of the 2:30 race and the others pretend they have no information; he has bet a week's wages and is afraid to go home if he loses. Finally they give Walsh the paper, and he sees that his horse Albatross has won at 7 to 1. Elated, Walsh challenges Copley: "See old Barry now . . . Wish thy'd washed my bloody back, then, don't you?" Copley admits he does.

As each player departs, those who remain have a word of camaraderie, encouragement or condolence, to send him on his way. Walsh gets his cigar back from Luke and lights up. Thornton goes back to his office for a drink, followed by Mackendrick. Much to the amazement of his teammates, Walsh gives Owens a fresh cigar simply as a gesture of good will. Crosby tries to hurry the lingerers out of the changing room and on their way home, while the others accuse Walsh of holding cigars out on them (he maintains he had only the one he gave Owens). They challenge him to buy them all a round of cigars with his winnings. He allows that he might, but "Barry here, o' course, will have to do without. (*To Crosby.*) Never came when I bloody called."

Walsh notices that the new man, Moore, has been hanging back from the conversation. He puts his arm around Moore as though to draw him into the circle of teammates, as he exits with Copley and Morley.

> *They go laughing: burst of laughter and shouts outside. Silence.*
> *Luke has packed his bag: he zips it up. Crosby is picking up the*
> *rest of the equipment: odd socks, shirts. Owens gets out a cigarette:*
> *offers one to Crosby, who takes one, then offers one to Luke, who*
> *shakes his head. There's a sound of Harry singing a hymn off.*
> *Owens flicks a lighter: lights Crosby's cigarette, then his own.*

PLAYERS (*off*): We waited for you, Barry.

CROSBY: Not two bloody thoughts to rub together. (*Gestures off.*) Walshy.

OWENS (*laughs*): No.

CROSBY: Years ago . . . ran into a bloody post . . . out yonder . . . split the head of any other man . . . Gets up: looks round: says, "By God," then . . . "Have they taken him off?"

> *They laugh. Luke swings down his bag.*

LUKE: I'm off.

CROSBY: See you, Lukey.

LUKE: Cliff . . .

OWEN: Thanks, Lukey.

LUKE (*calls*): Bye, Harry.

> *They wait. Hymn continues.*

CROSBY: Wandered off . . .

LUKE: Aye . . . See you, lads.

> *Collects autograph books.*

OWENS: Bye, Lukey.

> *Luke goes with his bag. Crosby picks up the last pieces.*

CROSBY: How're you feeling?

OWENS: Stiff.

CROSBY: Bloody past it, lad, tha knows.

OWENS: Aye. One more season, I think: I'm finished. (*Crosby laughs.*) Been here, tha knows, a bit too long.

CROSBY: Nay, there's nob'dy else, old lad . . .

OWENS: *Aye.* (*Laughs.*)

CROSBY: Need thee a bit longer to keep these lads in line.

OWENS: *Aye.* (*Laughs.*)

CROSBY: Did well today.

OWENS: They did. That's right.

CROSBY: Bloody leadership, tha see, that counts.

OWENS (*laughs*): Aye.

CROSBY (*calls through to bath*): Have you finished, then, in theer . . . (*No answer. To Owens.*) Ger'up yonder.

OWENS: Have a snifter . . .

CROSBY: Another bloody season yet.
      Puts out the light.
Poor old Fieldy.

OWENS: Aye.

CROSBY: Ah, well . . . this time tomorrer . . .

OWENS: Have no more bloody worries then.
      They laugh. Crosby puts his arm round Owens: they go. Singing from the bath has paused. Harry comes in: looks round: he carries a sweeping brush, starts sweeping. Picks up one or two bits of tape, etc. Turns on the Tanoy: light music. Sweeps. The remaining light and the sound of the Tanoy slowly fade. Curtain.

THE HOT L BALTIMORE

A Play in Three Acts

BY LANFORD WILSON

Cast and credits appear on page 394

way in 1969, a year after its premiere at the Washington, D.C. Theater Club. He returned to off Broadway in 1970 with Lemon Sky *which, after a warm critical reception and a brief run, moved to Chicago for a very successful engagement. In 1971, he wrote the libretto for composer Lee Hoiby's operatic version of Tennessee Williams's play* Summer and Smoke, *which premiered in St. Paul, Minn. and was presented by the New York City Opera in 1972.*

LANFORD WILSON was born in Lebanon, Mo. in 1938 and was raised in Ozark, Mo. He attended school at San Diego Stage and the University of Chicago, where he started writing plays. Arriving in New York in 1963, he gravitated to the Caffe Cino and made his stage debut with Home Free! *in 1964. A prolific writer, at one point in 1965 he had three plays running simultaneously—*Home Free! *at the Cherry Lane;* Ludlow Fair, *another one-acter, at the Caffe Cino; and the full-length* Balm in Gilead *at the Cafe La Mama.* Ludlow Fair *and another one-acter,* The Madness of Lady Bright, *were presented off Broadway in 1966 and subsequently in London with great success.*

These were followed by The Rimers of Eldritch, *which won him the Vernon Rice Award in 1967, and* The Gingham Dog, *which had a brief run on Broad-*

Becoming playwright-in-residence for off off Broadway's Circle Theater, under the artistic direction of Marshall W. Mason with whom he had worked on many previous productions, Wilson premiered a triple bill of new one-acters there in 1972. One of them, The Great Nebula in Orion, *was named by Stanley Richards as one of the best short plays of the year. Wilson's first Best Play,* The Hot l Baltimore *(whose title signifies a run-down hotel's sign with one letter missing) premiered in the Circle's loft this winter and greeted spring in an off-Broadway production at Circle in the Square Downtown.*

Wilson has been represented on TV by productions of The Rimers of Eldritch *and* The Sand Castle. *He recently finished work with Tennessee Williams on a made-for-television feature called* The Migrants. *He has been the recipient of a Rockefeller grant and an ABC-Yale fellowship, and he attended the Eugene O'Neill Memorial Theater Center. He is single and lives in New York's Greenwich Village.*

The following synopsis of The Hot l Baltimore *was prepared by Jeff Sweet.*

Time: Memorial Day

Place: The lobby of the Hotel Baltimore

ACT I

SYNOPSIS: It is 7 a.m. on Memorial Day in the lobby of the Hotel Baltimore, once a fashionable, medium-sized hotel, now home to prostitutes, drifters and those surviving on welfare. Behind the desk, Bill, the night clerk, is making a series of wake-up calls while an attractive girl in her late teens chatters cheerfully. In the lounge, a long-haired young man, Paul Granger III, is asleep in one of the faded chairs. They are joined by Milly, a woman in her late 60s. The Girl mourns the fact that the Pioneer, another old hotel down the street, is in the process of being razed. Milly, who used to be a waitress in the Pioneer's restaurant, is not distressed, explaining, "I long ago gave up being sentimental about losing propositions."

An aging woman, Mrs. Billotti, enters the lobby asking to speak to Mr. Katz, the manager of the hotel. Bill tells her he won't be in till around eight, and she goes out to pass the time over a cup of coffee. Bill puts the Girl to work stuffing the mail pigeonholes with envelopes. She recognizes them as eviction notices; this hotel is also scheduled for demolition.

Milly begins to talk about the Pioneer, remembering that when she waited on Calvin Coolidge he never paid and never tipped. She smiles, "I think the pleasure was supposed to be mine." Milly claims the ability to sense the presence of ghosts. Prompted by the Girl, she recalls the spirits who inhabited the Pioneer's restaurant. Their conversation is interrupted by the sound of a passing train.

GIRL (*huge disappointment, rage*): That's the Silver City! Oh, damn! Doesn't that make you just want to *cry?* How can they do that!?

BILL: I think she's got the schedules and bells and whistles all memoriz—

GIRL (*angry*): There's no schedule involved in it. I don't think they have schedules any more. Silver City is due in at four-nineteen; she's more than three damn hours late. I get so mad at them for not running on time. I mean it's their own schedule, I don't know why they can't keep to it. They're just miserable. The service is so bad and hateful and the porters and conductors you just can't believe it isn't deliberate. I think they're being run by the airlines. Do you have stock in the railroads? Could you do something? Write somebody?

MILLY: Oh, no; I don't have much stock. Certainly not in the railroads. I can't imagine anyone with any business sense just now—

GIRL: Where will they go?

MILLY: Who?

GIRL: The ghosts? When they tear the hotel down? What'll happen to them?

MILLY: Oh . . . they'll stay around for a while wondering what's become of everything. Then they'll wander off with people. They form attachments.

April, a brassy, 30-plus prostitute, comes downstairs complaining that the water is not only cold but orange. She comments that the only clock she has is one she sees through her window on the front of the railroad terminal, and it's permanently stuck at a quarter after five, which she figures is "a good enough time for almost anything."

APRIL (*laughing*): Guy came up to me last week—couldn't think of anything to say—said—"Uh, uh, excuse me, you don't happen to know what time it is, do you?" I said, sure, it's a quarter after five. The son of a bitch was so surprised he looked at his goddamned watch. (*Laughs.*)

GIRL (*pause*): What time . . .

APRIL: I don't want to hear it; whatever you're going to say. You're a real bring-down, you know it? I'd give a hundred bucks for your hair but I wouldn't turn a nickel for your brain.

GIRL: No, I got the joke, I just wondered what—

APRIL: Listen, don't listen to me. Kids now are a different breed. If I was sixteen I'd be just as—How old are you?

GIRL: Seventeen.

APRIL: Seventeen. Jesus. If I was seventeen and looked like that—

BILL: And know what you know now.

APRIL: Fuck what I know now. Give me the rest of it—I'll learn. You want to know the sad truth—if I looked like that I wouldn't have to know what I know now.

Mr. Morse, an irascible, nearly senile retired man in his 70s, comes downstairs with another complaint—the window in his room is open and he can't close it. As he continues his tirade against the hotel, Jackie, *"a tough little girl, 25,"* enters the lobby from outside. She offers to close Mr. Morse's window. Before Bill can stop her, she has the old man's keys and has disappeared up the stairs. Jamie, Jackie's "slow" younger brother, enters the lobby from outside and accepts Mr. Morse's invitation to a game of checkers. As they are setting up the board, the Silver City is heard pulling out of the station. The Girl is upset over its tardiness. "I used to live right by a railroad track," she explains. "I was a train-waver. They've very important to me—I never waved to a single person who didn't wave back . . . . . If you saw something important to you neglected—like that. They've let the roadbeds go to the—you have to close your eyes on a train. Or look out the window. That's still beautiful; some of it. In the country."

Mr. Katz, the hotel manager, enters. The Girl tells him that the sleeping boy is waiting for him. Katz sees Mr. Morse and takes the opportunity to reprimand him for his habit of singing at the top of his voice. Mr. Morse replies that his singing is prescribed by his doctor. Jackie returns, having fixed Mr. Morse's window, and gives him back the key. She corners Katz and points to the newly-bought second-hand car she's parked in front of the hotel. She must have insurance in order to get her license, and for that she needs money. She wouldn't be in a financial spot if it weren't for losing her job at the pet store.

JACKIE: . . . . . I wasn't canned. I saw what was coming and walked out on them. The son-of-a-bitch fruity manager was trying to get me fired so his little friend could have my job. I hit him with the birdcage and walked out on the bastard. He kept live snakes as pets if you want to know the sort of person he was. Let them run loose in the shop at night.

GIRL: You hit him with a birdcage?

JACKIE: I slugged the bastard. He said something I didn't like; he was mincing down the aisle with the stack of birdcages, he made a crack I won't repeat and I took one of 'em and slapped it alongside his head. Dropped it on the floor and walked out right there.

APRIL: Probably the best thing to do.

JACKIE: He called me up and tried to say I owed him for a Myna bird. There wasn't no goddamned Myna bird in that cage. Where you going—I'm trying to tell you something.

KATZ: I don't know what you're talking about. I'm working here. I got no time.

JACKIE: I'm telling you. If you'd stop interrupting. I need a friend. I'm in a bind. Straight out—that's the way I deal: I need a friend. That's what I'm saying; I need a pal.

Katz's attention is distracted by the entrance of Suzy, a 30-plus prostitute resembling a Jewish Marilyn Monroe, who is accompanied by a nervous "friend." As the friend stands by in a combination of impatience and embarrassment, Suzy learns from the Girl that the hotel is doomed. The Girl wonders what will occupy the space currently filled by her room after it's torn down. April sardonically comments that the people who get Suzy's old space will "wonder why it's so hot." Upset, Suzy leads the man up the stairs to her room.

Not missing a beat, Jackie returns to her conversation with Katz, explaining that the bank will loan her the money she needs if she can find someone to co-sign for her. Katz refuses and Jackie irritatedly stalks away from the desk.

Mrs. Billotti returns and explains to Katz why she is here: she wants him to permit her evicted son Horse to check back into the hotel. Katz says no, saying that Horse is crazy and keeps stealing things from the hotel. "Last time I let him come back," says Mr. Katz, "he stole the telephone outta his room. Tried to sell it back to the hotel. Said there wasn't no phone in his room." Mrs. Billotti finds a more sympathetic audience in Jamie and the Girl, and she explains that she can't take Horse back into the house because he and his father fight. What's more, her husband is a diabetic who's had a leg amputated. Jamie volunteers that his and Jackie's father died of diabetes.

As Mrs. Billotti heads upstairs to what was formerly her son's room to collect the things he left behind, Jackie reprimands Jamie for telling other people their business. "You want me to leave you again?" she threatens. She also discovers he's been smoking again and tells him he should be sucking his Angelica stick to break the habit. While Jackie assures Jamie that they'll find someone to co-sign and that they'll soon be on their way to Utah, the Girl explains to Bill that it hurts her to see people need things so desperately. Bill asks her if there isn't anything she wants, and she replies she wants everything for everybody.

Mr. Morse calls Jamie back to the game as Jackie asks Milly if she knows when the pawn shops open. The Girl announces that she has decided to drop the name Martha, the name under which she's been going for a while, in favor of the more exotic Lilac Lavender. Jamie decides to take a break from his losing game of checkers and goes upstairs to help Mrs. Billotti.

A call comes in for the Girl. It's from a prospective john (for, as we now discover, she is also a prostitute). Bill is noticeably upset that she is receiving this call in his presence and takes his irritation out in some sharp remarks to April. Katz informs Jackie that she and all the other tenants must leave in a month. This is a fresh piece of news for the girl. Suddenly they are all talking at once.

GIRL: One month? You're an ogre. Where is Bill going to work?

BILL: Just don't worry about me.

GIRL: Yeah?

BILL: Yeah. You don't worry about me working and I won't worry about you sleeping.

GIRL: Did you know we were going to all be out in the street in that short of time and didn't tell me or anything?

BILL: You're on the streets now. Just because I know something doesn't mean I'm at liberty to tell it.

GIRL: You knew! You knew we were going to have to go. You are really an ogre. You're terrible.

MORSE: Good! Serve you all right!

JACKIE: Maybe you don't care where you go; I happen to have specific plans.

MORSE: Right. I don't care. What do I care where you go. I'll be glad to get rid of the lot of you.

JACKIE: You dummy, you think you're going to stay here?

MORSE: I don't intend to divulge my plans to anyone here. You aren't the only person with plans.

JACKIE (April and Katz are cued in now): To hell with it. I don't care.

BILL: I bet you don't even know what an ogre is.

GIRL: I certainly do, I sleep with five or six every day.

BILL: I don't want to hear about what you do.

GIRL: Well, it certainly isn't any of your business. I don't understand you at all—

BILL: —I don't care what you do with your life—

GIRL: One minute you're friendly and nice and the next minute you're—

BILL: I just wish you were old enough or mature enough to know what you're throwing away. I personally don't care a dang what—

GIRL: —as bad as my own daddy. Worse. Because he at least didn't care what I did. He didn't even care if I was a hooker as long as I kept him in enough money to buy beer. That's why I left only you're worse than he is.

BILL: —you do with yourself or how many ogres you entertain in a day.

GIRL: I'll bet you don't even know what an ogre is!

They can tear it down. I'm taking my brother and getting the hell out of here anyway.

MORSE: Good. Nobody cares. We don't care.

JACKIE: Tear it to hell!

MORSE: Tear it to hell! RIP IT DOWN! (*He begins to unpack his barbells.*)

JACKIE: I don't care if you tear it down this week. Because I don't intend to hang around here. That's not the way I am. I don't hang around where the damn building's coming down on my head. Fuck it. I got enough sense to get out when the gettin's good. This place would fall down in another six months anyway! (*Suzy's friend comes down the stairs, leaving.*)

APRIL (*cued above with Jackie's "To hell with it"*): If I'm expected to get out of her before my month's rent runs out I know somebody who's going to get a fat refund on her bill.

KATZ: Nobody is refunding anything. You stay through June. Nobody's paid past the month of June.

APRIL: Don't expect to see my tail —(*Suzy off, begins to wail.*)—till the first of June, Daddy. Just let me tell you right now. I don't care if the pipes bust and the place is flooded to the third floor. (*She notices Suzy as she appears on the stairs.*)

SUZY (*off, over Katz, April, Bill, Girl, Jackie and Mr. Morse, cued by April's "Don't expect to see my tail"*): You bastard! What do you think you're doing? Come back here! Help! Help me! YOU CHICKENSHIT!

> *She appears on the stairs wrapped in a towel and nothing else; wailing after the man.*

SUZY: Come back here, you fuckin' masochist. He beat me! Why didn't you stop him? He locked the door on me! Police! Why aren't you doing

KATZ: Get upstairs. Get on, get out of the lobby. You can't come down here naked.

JACKIE: What the hell are you do-something? What do we pay you for, you yellow crud? Yellow crud!

APRIL: What are you doing with the towel, there, Suzy? (*She laughs.*)

SUZY (*each sentence makes April laugh more*): What the hell are you laughing at? I'd like to see what you'd do. You shut up! You shut up! (*Slaps at her with the towel.*) You're disgusting! I'm calling the cops! I want to make a complaint! Against April Green! And against the management of this hotel! Scum!

PAUL (*waking, cued by "disgusting"*): What the hell is this? What the hell is going on here? This isn't a hotel; this is a goddamned flop house! This is a flop house!

SUZY: You're right; that's exactly what it is; it's a goddamned flophouse. This is a flop house!

ing? (*Mr. Morse begins to march up and down swinging the barbells. Katz catches sight of him now.*)

KATZ (*to Suzy*): Suzy, get upstairs. I'm gonna call the cops on you. On all of you. They would as soon run your ass in again as look at you. Get up to your room. Go on or spend another night in the can; make your choice. (*Mr. Morse begins to sing.*)

MORSE: Ole, sol' a mio; Ole, sol a mio . . . (*Over and over as he marches on.*)

JACKIE: Get your ass back up those stairs. If my brother comes down and sees you like that I'm going to take you apart. Who the hell do you think you are? I hope to hell they kick your ass out into the street!

KATZ (*continued*): Get up to your room; what the hell is this? Don't listen to April. Come on. Get up the stairs. April, you shut up; I've had it with you two.

JACKIE (*over; cued by Paul*): Right! This is a goddamned flop house. Exactly. A fuckin' flop house!

Jamie carries a box down the stairs, dropping it when he sees the naked Suzy; staring, with his mouth open. The box contains hotel soap, towels, washcloths, etc. and things stolen from the neighborhood shops. Music comes up over all the above, rising over it. At the top everyone drops the argument and, smiling, gathering their personal props, retires offstage as the music soars. Suzy wraps up, April and everyone is smiling at the play and at the others. The lights fade as the cast joins in lightly—going their way—with the last few words of the song as they go out the door. Curtain.

ACT II

That afternoon, in the lounge, Milly is reading a paper, and Mr. Morse and Jamie are huddled over their checkerboard. Bill has left hours ago. Mrs. Oxenham, the day clerk, and Mr. Katz are attending to business behind the desk. Paul Granger III, who has been standing at the desk impatiently waiting for Katz to give him his attention, breaks the silence by asking him, for what must be the thousandth time, if he is doing anything to help him get the information for which he came; he is trying to find out when his grandfather, the first Paul Granger and a former tenant of the hotel, checked out and where the old man had gone from there. Katz denies any knowledge of any such person ever having stayed at the hotel. Paul persists and Katz refers him to Mrs. Oxenham, who grudgingly agrees to look through the files on the condition he leave the desk area; she will let him know if she finds anything. Sullenly, Paul sits in the lounge. In an effort to be friendly, Milly tells Paul that she's been trying to remember his grandfather but is afraid she can't help.

Mrs. Billotti enters from outside and goes upstairs to get another load of her son Horse's things. The Girl comes downstairs and, responding to a note in her mailbox, calls to turn down a trick. She's tired and is going to get some sleep.

Meanwhile, Jamie and Mr. Morse get into an argument about the game. Mr. Morse angrily rips up the board, a few weak blows are exchanged, and Mr. Morse ends up storming into the broom closet. The Girl tries to persuade him to come out of the closet. She tells him that during the scuffle with Jamie, he blackened the boy's eye.

> *Jamie gasps at the scope of the lie.*
> GIRL (*to Jamie*): Come here. I want to show you something.
> *She gets her purse.*
> JAMIE: What?
> GIRL (*digging in her purse, getting out the mascara*): Something fun.
> JAMIE: What?
> *Girl spits on the mascara.*
> No. No.
> GIRL: Hold him, Mr. Katz.
> *Katz, returning to the desk, gestures he wants nothing to do with them. Hating it, protesting, struggling, Jamie nevertheless lets her put the darkening around his eyes.*
> JAMIE: No, no, it's—don't, come on! Don't mark me up.
> GIRL (*over*): Mr. Morse, he's in pain! It's terrible; you ought to be ashamed of yourself, Mr. Morse.
> JAMIE (*the second she releases him*): Let me see.
> *She hands him the mirror. Whining.*
> No . . . He didn't do . . .
> *Mr. Morse opens the door. Girl takes the mirror. Jamie slaps his hand over his eye.*
> GIRL: Go on—show him, Jamie. Show him what a brute he is. Show him what an ogre he is.
> *Jamie does, pouting as though it were real.*
> MORSE: Good, good.

Jackie enters from outside, complaining about a scratch someone's put on her new car. Suzy, dressed in her most conservative outfit, comes downstairs and leaves the hotel, saying nothing. Jackie has been unable to find an open pawnshop. "The whole damn city's closed up like a nun," she complains.

Milly tells her that it's Memorial Day. Jackie notices Jamie's blackened eye. Mr. Morse claims his victory but, as Jackie wipes off the mascara, the Girl tells her of the joke. "Well, I don't want people joking with Jamie," Jackie replies. "he's not in good health."

Mrs. Oxenham informs the Girl of a call from a prospective client, but she declines. The Girl tries to begin a conversation with Paul. She cannot give him any information about his grandfather, so Paul withdraws into himself again. She asks him where he's from, but he doesn't answer. As Mr. Morse goes up to his room, the Girl tells Paul that she has been just about everywhere in the country. She'll run down the names of the places she's been, and if she names where he's from, he's to tell her. Paul doesn't respond, but she begins her list anyway. As she names one city after another, Paul finds that in the face of her charm and earnestness he cannot help smiling. He tells her no, she hasn't guessed yet. As she continues trying, Milly says, "Louisville." Paul's name is in the paper she's reading. He's escaped from the work farm to which he was sent after being convicted on a marijuana rap and sentenced to two years.

PAUL: You're supposed to drink sour mash whiskey. You're not supposed to be selling grass. I was an example. They like their students drunk, they don't like them—

GIRL: You were in *school* and they gave you—

PAUL: Shh—come on.

GIRL: In college? (*Pause*) I'm impressed. I didn't even make it past junior year in high school. I hated it.

PAUL: Don't let it bother you. It's just a way to keep the kids off the street.

MILLY: It doesn't seem to be working, does it?

The Girl tells him the only subject she did well in was geography. She finds it helps her when she's with a john who is "shy or weird or something. I can ask him where he's from and get him talking. Because usually if it's a big city I've either been there, or, if not, know what the area's like. I don't think that's what Mrs. Whitmore had in mind when she taught us geography."

Mrs. Billotti makes another trip through the lobby with another large box. Sensing that Paul is closing himself off again, in a hushed tone the Girl explains Mrs. Billotti's plight. Whenever she hears a sad story like that, the Girl confides, she wants to lock herself into the bathroom on her floor, take a long bubble bath, and send out for a pizza.

Katz orders Jackie, who's been doing paperwork at the front desk, to move. Jackie relocates to the lounge where the Girl notices and picks up one of her magazines. Initially Jackie snaps at the Girl not to touch it, but almost instantly she reconsiders and becomes more friendly. The magazine in question, she explains, is a special magazine on organic gardening. "That magazine you can't get on a news stand. You have to order this magazine to come to your home . . . . . You get one a month. It's fantastic." The Girl shows interest and Jackie goes on to tell her that the next discovery on a par with the discoveries of bacteria and uranium will be the discovery of the magical properties of garlic. According to the magazine, garlic is a natural insecticide and can cure the common cold. Jackie reveals her grand plan—she and her brother are going to Utah to grow garlic, and she proudly pulls out the deed to 20 acres of land she purchased for $15 an acre after hearing it advertised on the radio.

JACKIE: We was headed down to Florida to work on the crops; we heard this offer—I said to hell with pickin' somebody else's tomatoes; we'll raise our own crops.

Girl looks at deed.

We're going out there; we don't need no house. We're sleeping in a sleeping bag. If it rains, it gets nasty, we sleep in the car. We get sick of that we move into a motel.

GIRL: How do you know there's a motel? If you've never been there?

JACKIE: Of course there's a motel; the country's gone to shit; there's always a motel.

GIRL: Milly's got her money invested in stocks.

JACKIE: Well, that's her business. Land is the only safe thing to invest in, ask anybody—that's the only thing that keeps going up in—value—

The talk of investments prompts the Girl to wonder if she could buy stock in a railroad so she could go to a stockholders' meeting and tell them to shape up. Because the Girl is so insistent, Milly makes a vague promise to introduce her to her stockbroker some day. The vagueness of the promise makes the Girl realize afresh that Milly is, by her own admission, "fairly batty." Milly explains that she was never particularly interested in being part of the real world. She recalls being the youngest member of a large family outside of Baton Rouge. She talks about the varied group of spirits who haunted their home. When her aunt died, she remembers, the tension in the household prompted the spirits to raise an ungodly commotion. The Girl expresses her deep desire that someone prove that ghosts exist. "I want to see them and talk to them—something like that! Some miracle. Something huge! I want some *major miracle* in my lifetime!"

As Jackie launches into a discussion of green beans, Mrs. Oxenham comes up with a receipt proving that Paul's grandfather was a tenant two years ago. Paul presses her for home information, but she has none to offer. She doesn't remember him, she claims. Angrily Paul asks, "Would you remember it if he fell dead in the lobby? If he was found in his room—?" No such thing happened, Mrs. Oxenham replies, and she turns away.

PAUL: He was a workman. When he retired he wore a suit and a derby because he wanted to look like he was retired . . . . . He wanted to come live with mom and dad and they wrote him they didn't have room for him. They didn't want him. (*To Milly.*) He sang songs . . . all the time . . . under his breath . . . my sister . . .

GIRL: What? Your sister?

PAUL: She talked about him all the time . . . she told me about . . . what he was . . . like, what he was like.

GIRL: She told you? Didn't you—ever met him?
    Beat.
PAUL: How could I meet him, I was always off in some fuckin' school.
GIRL: And you want—
PAUL: *I* want him! *I* have room for him!
GIRL: Well, don't take it out on me.
JACKIE: Where did he work?
PAUL: I called them. They started getting his pension checks back—they don't know where he is . . . . .
GIRL: What did he do?
PAUL: He worked. Mother's family had about a billion dollars worth of whiskey distilleries—that's why dad married—granddad kept right on working. They were all so damn high-society they wouldn't associate with anyone like—
GIRL: You don't talk—did anybody ever tell you that? You talk to yourself, you don't talk to the person you're talking to.
PAUL: (*glowers at her; finally*): He was an engineer.

The Girl assumes he means his grandfather had something to do with engineering, but when he tells her he was a railroad engineer, she bursts into tears. She wants to meet him, talk to him about trains. Paul says that if she thinks of a way to find him, he'll introduce her. She tells Paul that she'll be happy to help him.
As they talk, Mr. Morse comes downstairs outraged. He's been robbed. Jackie starts for the door, but Katz, remembering her talk about pawnshops, grabs her and finds the stolen property in her purse. As Katz returns the goods to Mr. Morse, Jackie cries out, "I got dreams, goddamnit; what's *he* got?" Katz lets her go and she repeats a sobbing "What's he got?" Katz dissuades Mr. Morse from calling the police and tells Jackie that she and her brother are to be out of the hotel by evening. Mr. Morse returns to his room, deeply shaken. The Girl turns on Jackie in indignation.

GIRL: Not from Mr. Morse. He doesn't have anything. He never hurt anybody.
JACKIE: You ripped off one of your scores, you told me so.
GIRL: He could afford it.
JACKIE: Just because you have protection . . . . .
GIRL: I wasn't going to tell you but you got nothing.
JACKIE: I got what I need.
GIRL: That land you got won't grow nothing. I know that place. I may not know much but I know that—
JACKIE: What are you talking about? You're a liar—you don't know anything about it. That's farmland.
GIRL: —because I been there. On the Atchison. It's nothing but a desert—a salt desert, it don't even grow cactus. Six miles west of Carter, two miles south of Pepin—it's desert for a hundred miles.
JACKIE: It's farmland! That's farmland! I got brochures. I got pictures.

GIRL: Even I know better than to buy land from the radio. You can't get farmland for that price nowhere. You ought to be ashamed of yourself, robbing Mr. Morse.

JACKIE (*snatching up the deed, putting it in her purse*): I know what I'm doing for my brother and ...

> *Goes about collecting her things—she knows instinctively what the Girl says is true.*

You may not know anything about growing . . . we know what we're doing.

> *She blindly collects her papers, stuffing them into her bag. Pause.*

JAMIE: That's not fair.

JACKIE: Be still.

> *Pause.*

GIRL: Or maybe . . . maybe I'm wrong. Maybe I have it mixed up. I don't want to hurt anybody.

JACKIE: Ain't nobody been hurt by you or . . .

JAMIE: Anybody. (*He is about to burst into tears.*) You're—

JACKIE (*sitting down*): Shut up, now.

> *Takes out a small piece of candy, unwraps it, puts it in her mouth in lieu of lighting a cigarette.*

Boy . . . everything I try . . .

> *Pause.*

I liked you, too. Well. We live and learn.

> *Getting up, taking her purse.*

GIRL: Oh, Jesus.

JACKIE: Come on; we're gonna go eat. We were getting out of here tomorrow, a few hours one way or the—

> *Her mouth clamps shut. Jamie follows her out.*

GIRL: Jackie. Maybe it was a lie. I was just mad. I haven't had any sleep. Forget I said it. Please.

> *She follows them out.*

Mrs. Billotti comes through with another box and goes out the front door. As Milly is about to return to her room, she tells Paul that, though she doesn't know where his grandfather is, she is certain he's alive. Bill enters to take over the night shift as Katz and Mrs. Oxenham get ready to leave. Bill turns on the radio and the lights dim to the sound of a pop tune. Curtain.

ACT III

At midnight, Mr. Morse sits uneasily in the lounge. Bill is working behind the desk. The Girl phones the desk from her room to chat, and Bill tells her if she wants to visit, she should do so in person. Bill hangs up, as April comes down full of stories about the eccentricities of her clients. "If my clientele represents a cross-section of American manhood, the country's in trouble."

APRIL: Usually I can count on one in five getting a little experimental.

BILL: Not today, huh?

APRIL: Today we drew a full house. (*Laughs.*) Guy says, "What's that?" I say, "That's the tub, that's where I keep the alligator, better stay back: you ain't got nothing you can afford to lose." Says, "I'd kinda like to make it in the tub." I said, "Honey, look: you ever see one of these? It's a bed. It's kinda kinky but let me show you how it works." End up in the—

BILL (*mumbled with her*): In the tub.

APRIL: Right. Tell him all we got is cold water, it's gonna do no good. Nothing would do. (*Laughs.*) He sits down, I turn on the water; nearly scalded his balls off.

BILL: Got it fixed.

APRIL: Yeah. Spanking red from his butt down. Loved it. Stayed in for twenty minutes. Very groovy experience for him. If I knew he was coming I'd have dug out the rubber duck.

BILL: Anything to get somebody to like you.

APRIL: Like me? Pay me. They know me from the wallpaper.

The Girl appears in a robe and slippers. She has just awakened and is fresh for getting at the project of finding Paul's grandfather. She starts pouring over the dusty files. Jamie enters with a pack on his back, asking if anyone has seen Jackie. She had told him she was going out for gas and would be back for him. April asks when she left, and Jamie tells her, " 'Bout six." "Well, see," April replies, "she's probably looking for natural gas."

A john calls for the Girl. April takes the phone and pretends to be the Girl's maid. Covering the phone, she tells the Girl who it is. The Girl gets on the line and, thanking the man for the invitation, says she has made other plans.

Suzy comes down carrying some bags. She puts them down, saying, "That's just the first load. Don't anybody get up. I got it arranged so I can do it all myself." As she scurries back upstairs, the Girl discovers what she's been looking for—a receipt which pinpoints the week Paul's grandfather left. The next step is to find a forwarding address. As she is about to launch into this search, Jamie shyly approaches her, asking if what she'd said about their land is true. After all, it's in Utah and weren't the Mormons supposed to be great farmers? What if they irrigated? Sadly, the Girl tells him that their land is "just white sand—it's salt and soda; it looks like . . . . . Jamie, you irrigate that land, you'd have twenty acres of Bromo-Seltzer."

Suzy reappears with another load and puts it down next to the first. Nobody's to leave the lobby, she tells them, for she's got a surprise. As Suzy disappears, Paul returns from dinner. The Girl happily tells Paul about her discovery and how close she feels they are to finding his grandfather. She is so enthusiastic, she doesn't notice a change in his attitude towards the search.

Suzy returns with two bottles of champagne and pours a little for everyone present. Jamie contributes some barbecue-flavored soy beans to the proceedings. April leads the toast—"To us!" Suzy reveals that she's moving into an apartment with another girl. April senses that there's more to the story than Suzy is telling—that Suzy and her new roommate will be working for a pimp. April is disgusted. Apparently this is not the first time Suzy's gotten into this kind of spot.

APRIL: Who is he? Are you going back with Eddie?

SUZY: I certainly am not. Who do you think I am? I may have a soft spot in my heart but I ain't got—

APRIL (*overlapping*): You got a soft spot in your head.

SUZY: —This man is not like that. Eddie was a pimp; this man is a man.

APRIL: Who's the boyfriend this time?

SUZY: Not this time. This is my first *real friend*. Eddie was a pimp.

APRIL: You're telling me; a pimp fink.

SUZY: This man is a man!

APRIL: Yeah, what does he do?

SUZY: He does nothing! And he does it *gorgeously!*

April shows Suzy no mercy, calling her "a professional trampoline." "This is why I'm leaving!" says Suzy. "Derision! Derision! Because I'm attacked with derision every time I try to do something wonderful." Suzy tells them not to worry about her, that Billy never beat up anyone. April guesses that "Billy" is a well-known someone they all call Billy Goldhole, but Suzy resents April's use of that name for her friend: "That is not his name. And to call him by that name is to show your ignorance."

Suzy's cab arrives and she leaves, bitterly calling down her friends in a mixture of anger and shame. No sooner has she gone, but she's back again, all tears and apologies. They've been like a family, she says, and she'll always remember them. And she is gone again.

Paul picks up his bag and heads for the door. The Girl refuses to accept the fact that he's giving up the search. Milly comes downstairs and the Girl appeals to her to help get him to change his mind. Irritated, Paul tells them it's nobody's business but his own and leaves.

Dejected, the Girl tries to call back the john who had phoned her earlier, but she's unable to reach him. She hangs up.

GIRL: I could just kill Paul Granger. That's why nothing gets done; why everything falls down. Nobody's got enough conviction to act on their passions.

APRIL: Go kill him then.

GIRL: I mean it's his idea to find him. I just wanted to talk to him. I don't think it matters what someone believes in. I just think it's really chicken not to believe in anything.

She tells Bill not to put the records away. She intends to keep looking even if Paul has given up. As she leaves, *"Bill looks after her, aching."*

APRIL (*snaps her fingers lightly at him. One. Two. Three. Four.*): Hey. Hey.

BILL: Come on, April; knock it off.
He sits at the switchboard.
APRIL: Bill, baby, you know what your trouble is? You've got Paul Granger-itis. You've not got the conviction of your passions.
JAMIE: April? (*Beat.*) What time is it?
APRIL: It's a quarter of—(*Looks at Bill.*)
BILL (*a glance at the clock*): Twelve-thirty. Nearly.
APRIL: She probably got stopped on account of the license.
BILL (*under his breath*): Sure, she did.

As Milly is about to leave for bed, Mr. Morse suddenly blurts out, "Paul Granger is an old fool!" Milly turns with a new realization that perhaps Paul's grandfather was the old man who used to play checkers with Mr. Morse. But Mr. Morse remembers only that he was an old fool, nothing more.

Milly leaves. Bill turns on the radio and April, in an effort to distract Jamie from the growing realization he's been deserted, asks him to dance with her. A delivery boy appears with April's pizza. She takes the bill and directs him to deliver it to the Girl. Jamie is unsure about dancing.

JAMIE: I don't know how.
APRIL: Nobody knows how. What does it matter; the important thing is to *move*. Come on; all your blood's in your ass.
BILL: It's twelve-thirty; he's been up all day; he doesn't want to dance.
APRIL: Sure he does.
JAMIE: Tell me how.
APRIL: Come on, they're gonna tear up the dance floor in a minute; the bulldozers are barking at the door. Turn it up, Bill, or I'll break your arm.
Bill turns up the radio a little.
Turn it up!
More. April and Jamie latch arms, go one way, then back. She joins in the lines of the song and, as the lights fade and they turn back, circling the other way, he joins in as well. Bill stares off, then smiles at them. Mr. Morse sips the champagne and watches. The sound switches to the house as the lights fade; the song continuing on the radio as they whirl. Curtain.

A LITTLE NIGHT MUSIC

A Musical in Two Acts

BOOK BY HUGH WHEELER

MUSIC AND LYRICS BY STEPHEN SONDHEIM

Suggested by a film by Ingmar Bergman

Cast and credits appear on page 351

HUGH WHEELER (book) was born in London March 19, 1916, the son of a civil servant. He was educated at the Clayesmore School and the University of London, graduating in 1936. During World War II he served in the U.S. Army medical corps, and he became a naturalized American citizen in 1942. He soon established and maintained a wide reputation as a mystery writer under the pseudonyms Patrick Quentin and Q. Patrick, and four of his novels— Black Widow, Man in the Net, The Green-Eyed Monster *and* The Man With Two Wives—*have been made into motion pictures.*

Wheeler did not begin his playwriting career until the Broadway production of his Big Fish, Little Fish *March 15, 1961 for 101 performances, named a Best Play of its season. His next was* Look: We've Come Through *(1965), followed by an adaptation of Shirley Jackson's* We Have Always Lived in the Castle *(1966). He is the author of not one, but two musical hits of the 1973 Broadway season, as the co-adapter with Joseph Stein of* Irene, *as well as of the Best Play and Critics Award-winning* A Little Night Music.

Wheeler's other writings have included screen plays for Something for

Everyone, Cabaret *and* Travels With My Aunt. *He makes his home on a farm in Monterey, Mass.*

STEPHEN SONDHEIM (music, lyrics) was born March 22, 1930 in New York City. At Williams College he won the Hutchinson Prize for musical composition, and after graduating B.A. he studied theory and composition with Milton Babbitt. He wrote scripts for the Topper *TV series and the incidental music for the Broadway productions of* Girls of Summer *(1956) and* Invitation to a March *(1961).*

It was as a lyricist that he first commanded major attention with West Side Story *(1957). He wrote both the music and lyrics for* A Funny Thing Happened on the Way to the Forum *(1962),* Anyone Can Whistle *(1964) and* Company *(1970), which won him his first Best Play citation as well as the New York Drama Critics Circle Award for best musical. He repeated in both these categories with* Follies *(1971) and has won several Tony Awards and walked away with every recent poll that has a "best lyricist" category.*

Sondheim's other credits include the lyrics for Gypsy *(1959) and* Do I Hear a Waltz? *(1965), as well as many brain-twisting word puzzles published in* New York Magazine. *He is the president of the Dramatists Guild, the organization of Broadway and off Broadway playwrights, composers, lyricists and librettists. He lives in New York City.*

Our method of representing A Little Night Music *in these pages differs from that used for the other Best Plays. The musical appears here as excerpts from the Stephen Sondheim lyrics for each of his 15 songs, illustrated with photos to record the overall "look" of a a Broadway show in 1972-73, with captions identifying the characters and outlining the situations of Hugh Wheeler's book, suggested by the Ingmar Bergman film* Smiles of a Summer Night. *As in all excerpted material in the Best Plays section of this volume, a hiatus in the lyrics is indicated by five dots (. . . . .). The appearance of three dots (. . .) is the lyrics's own punctuation.*

The photographs depict scenes as produced by Harold Prince in association with Ruth Mitchell and directed by Harold Prince, as of the opening February 25, 1973 at the Sam S. Shubert Theater, with choreography by Patricia Birch, scenery by Boris Aronson, costumes by Florence Klotz and lighting by Tharon Musser. Our special thanks are tendered to Stephen Sondheim and his representative, Flora Roberts, and to the producers and their press representatives, Mary Bryant and Bill Evans, for their help in obtaining this material including the excellent photographs by Martha Swope on pages 1 (bottom), 2, 3, 7, 8, 10, 12, 13, 14, 15 and 16 (bottom) of this photo section; by Van Williams on pages 1 (top), 4, 5, 6 and 11; and by Friedman-Abeles on pages 9 and 16 (top).

PROLOGUE: *Mme. Armfeldt (Hermione Gingold), attended by her butler Frid (George Lee Andrews), tells her granddaughter Fredrika (Judy Kahan) of the legend that a summer night smiles three times at human folly: "At the young, who know nothing . . . at the fools who know too little . . . at the old who know too much"*

In the Egerman home, Fredrik Egerman (Len Cariou) expresses his frustration in his unconsummated marriage to a beautiful 18-year-old wife

ACT I

Time: Turn of the century
Place: Sweden

"Now"

FREDRIK:
Now, there are two possibilities:
A, I could ravish her,
B, I could nap.
Say it's the ravishment, then we see
The option
That follows, of course:
(continued on the next page)

FREDRIK *(continued):*
A, the deployment of charm, or B,
The adoption
Of physical force . . .
Now B might arouse her
But if I assume
I trip on my trouser
Leg crossing the room . . .
Her hair getting tangled,
Her stays getting snapped,
My nerves will be jangled,
My energy sapped . . . . .

. . . . . A, I could put on my
            nightshirt or sit
Disarmingly,
B, in the nude . . .
That might be effective,
My body's all right,
But not in perspective
And not in the light . . . . .

. . . . . Now, though there
            are possibilities
Still to be studied,
I might as well nap . . .
Bow though I must
To adjust
My original plan . . .
How shall I sleep
Half as deep
As I usually can? . . .
When now I still want
            and/or love you,
Now as always,
Now,
Anne?

Fredrik Egerman's 19-year-old son Henrik (Mark Lambert) is extremely sensitive to the presence of his young stepmother Anne (Victoria Mallory), who behaves coquettishly toward him

"Later"

HENRIK:
Later . . .
When is later?
All you ever hear is,
        "Later, Henrik! Henrik, later . . . "
"Yes, we know, Henrik,
Oh, Henrik—
Everyone agrees, Henrik—
Please, Henrik!"
You have a thought you're
            fairly bursting with,
A personal discovery or problem, and it's
"What's your rush, Henrik?
Shush, Henrik—
Goodness, how you gush, Henrik—
Hush, Henrik!"

"Soon"

ANNE:	ANNE:	HENRIK:	FREDRIK:
Soon, I promise.	Later.	Come to me	Come to me
Soon I won't shy away,		Soon. If I'm	Soon,
Dear old—		Dead,	
Soon. I want to.	We will,	I can	
Soon, whatever you say.	Later.	Wait.	Straight to me,
Even now,			never mind
When you're close and we touch,		How can I	How.
And you're kissing my brow,	We will . . .	Live until	Darling,
I don't mind it too much.	Soon	Later?	Now—
And you'll have to admit			I still want
I'm endearing,			and/or
I help keep things humming,		Later . . .	Love
I'm not domineering,			You,
What's one small			
shortcoming?	Soon.		Now, as
(Sings simultaneously		Later . . .	Always,
with Henrik's "Later"	Soon.		
and Fredrik's "Now")			Now,
			Desirée.

Frustrated Fredrik and wide-eyed Anne, in bed for a chaste afternoon nap. The "Desirée" named at the end of the lyric above is Fredrik's former mistress, an actress, whose touring show the Egermans are going to see this evening

Mme. Armfeldt's daughter Desirée (Glynis Johns), who has left her own daughter in Mme. Armfeldt's care, sings to her mother of the busy life she leads as a celebrated stage actress

"The Glamorous Life"

MME. ARMFELDT:
Ordinary daughters ameliorate their lot,
Use their charms and choose their futures,
Breed their children, heed their mothers.
Ordinary daughters, which mine, I fear, is not,
Tend each asset, spend it wisely
While it still endures . . .
Mine tours.
DESIRÉE:
Mother, forgive the delay,
My schedule is driving me wild.
But, Mother, I really must run,
I'm performing in Rottvik
And don't ask where is it, please.
How are you feeling today
And are you corrupting the child?
Don't. Mother, the minute I'm done

With performing in Rottvik,
I'll come for a visit
And argue.
QUINTET:
Mayors with speeches, la la la
Children with posies, la la la
Half-empty houses, la la la
Hi-ho, the glamorous life!
Cultural lunches, la la la
Dead floral tributes, la la la
Ancient admirers, la la la

Hi-ho, the glamorous life!
DESIRÉE:
Pack up the luggage, la la la!
Unpack the luggage, la la la!
Mother's surviving, la la la!
Leading the glamorous life!
Cracks in the plaster, la la la!
Youngish admirers, la la la!
Which one was that one? la la la!
Hi-ho, the glamorous life!

Fredrik's thoughts of Desirée when he sees her on the stage are expressed in song by the quintet (above, Barbara Lang, Benjamin Rayson, Teri Ralston, Beth Fowler, Gene Varrone)

"Remember?"

QUINTET:
The old deserted beach
                that we walked—
Remember? Remember?
The cafe in the park where we talked—
Remember? Remember?

The tenor on the boat that we chartered,
Belching *The Bartered
Bride*—
Ah, how we laughed,
Ah, how we cried,
           (continued on the next page)

QUINTET *(continued)*:
Ah, how you promised and
Ah, how I lied.
That dilapidated inn—
Remember, darling?
The proprietress's grin,
Also her glare . . .
Yellow gingham on the bed—
Remember, darling?
And the canopy in red,
Needing repair?
I *think* you were there.

After the play, Fredrik pays a visit to his old flame, Desirée, in her rooms (Anne, disturbed by the play, has left it early and gone to bed). Not having met for 14 years, they catch up on matters like Desirée's daughter and Fredrik's new wife whom he describes in the song at right

"You Must Meet My Wife"

FREDRIK:
She lightens my sadness,
She livens my days,
She bursts with a kind of madness
My well-ordered ways . . . . .
She bubbles with pleasure,
She glows with surprise,
Disrupts my accustomed leisure
And ruffles my ties.
I don't know even now
Quite how it began.
You must meet my wife,
                                    my Anne . . . . .
DESIRÉE:
Dear Fredrik, I'm just longing
                                    to meet her.
Sometime.
FREDRIK:
She sparkles.
DESIRÉE:
How pleasant.
FREDRIK:
She twinkles.
DESIRÉE:
How nice.
FREDRIK:
Her youth is a sort of present—
DESIRÉE:
Whatever the price . . . . .
FREDRIK:
A sea of whims that I submerge in,
Yet so lovable in repentance.
Unfortunately still a virgin,
But you can't force a flower—
DESIRÉE:
Don't finish that sentence!
She's monstrous!
FREDRIK:
She's frightened.
DESIRÉE:
Unfeeling!
FREDRIK:
Unversed.
She'd strike you as unenlightened.

DESIRÉE:
No, I'd strike her first . . . . .

FREDRIK *(after the song ends, suddenly very shy, speaks)*: Desirée, I—

DESIRÉE: Yes?

FREDRIK: Would it seem insensitive if I were to ask you—I can't say it!

DESIRÉE: Say it, darling.

FREDRIK: Would you . . . *(He can't.)*

DESIRÉE: Of course. What are old friends for? . . . . .
(They exit, laughing, into the bedroom.)

Mme. Armfeldt appears for an interlude of reminiscing about her own colorful past (below)

"Liaisons"

MME. ARMFELDT:
At the villa of the Baron de Signac
Where I spent
        a somewhat infamous year,
At the villa of the Baron de Signac
I had ladies in attendance,
Fire-opal pendants . . .
Liaisons! What's happened to them,
Liaisons today?
Disgraceful! What's become of them?
Some of them
Hardly pay their shoddy way . . . . .

In the castle of the King of the Belgians
We would visit
        through a false chiffonier,
In the castle of the King of the Belgians
Who, when things got rather touchy,
Deeded me a duchy . . .
Liaisons! What's happened to them,
Liaisons today?
Untidy—take my daughter, I
Taught her, I
Tried my best to point the way.
I even named her Desirée.
In a world where the kings are employers,
Where the amateur prevails
        and delicacy fails to pay,
In a world where
        the princes are lawyers,
What can anyone expect
        except to recollect
Liai . . . *(She falls asleep.)*

Desirée's current lover, Count Carl-Magnus Malcolm (Laurence Guittard), a dra-goon and seasoned duellist, arrives unexpectedly at Desirée's while Fredrik is still there, in a dressing gown. Carl-Magnus's ego forces him to accept their lame excuse about papers urgently needing signing, and a fall into the hip bath

"In Praise of Women"

CARL-MAGNUS:
She wouldn't . . .
Therefore they didn't . . .
So then it wasn't . . .
Not unless it . . .
Would she?
She doesn't . . .
God knows she needn't . . .
Therefore it's not.
He'd never . . .
Therefore they haven't . . .
Which makes the question
                    absolutely . . .
Could she?
She daren't . . .
Therefore I mustn't . . .

What utter rot!
Fidelity is more than mere display,
It's what a man expects from life,
Fidelity like mine to Desirée
And Charlotte, my devoted wife . . . . .
The hip bath . . .
About that hip bath . . .
How can you slip and
Trip into a hip bath?
The papers . . .
Where were those papers?
Of course he might have
Taken back the papers . . .
She wouldn't . . .
Therefore they didn't . . .
The woman's mine!

"Every Day a Little Death"

CHARLOTTE:
Every day a little death
In the parlor, in the bed,
In the curtains, in the silver,
In the buttons, in the bread.
Every day a little sting
In the heart and in the head.
Every move and every breath,
And you hardly feel a thing,
Brings a perfect little death.
He smiles sweetly, strokes my hair,
Says he misses me.
I would murder him right there
But first I die.
He talks softly of his wars
And his horses and his whores,
I think love's a dirty business!

ANNE:
So do I! So do I! . . .

Carl-Magnus's wife, Countess Charlotte (Patricia Elliott, left), is sent by her husband to tell her friend Anne Egerman about Fredrik's visit to Desirée's rooms. The ladies commiserate about marriage

"A Weekend in the Country"

(Desirée, her tour over, comes for a visit to her mother's country house and persuades Mme. Armfeldt to invite the Egermans out for a weekend)

ANNE:
. . . . . A weekend!
CHARLOTTE:
How very amusing.
ANNE:
A weekend!
CHARLOTTE:
But also inept.
ANNE:
A weekend!

Of course, we're refusing.
CHARLOTTE:
Au contraire,
You must accept . . . . .
ANNE:
But it's frightful!
CHARLOTTE:
No, you don't understand.
A weekend in the country
(continued on the next page)

As Mme. Armfeldt's house appears, prospective guests sing of the coming weekend: left to right, Anne's maid Petra (D. Jamin-Bartlett), Fredrik, Anne, Mmes. Anderssen and Segstrom (quintet members), Henrik, Carl-Magnus, Messrs. Erlanson and Lindquist and Mrs. Nordstrom (quintet members) and Charlotte

CHARLOTTE (*continued*):
Is delightful
If it's planned.
Wear your hair down
And a flower,
Don't use make-up,
Dress in white.
She'll grow older
By the hour
And be hopelessly shattered
By Saturday night.
Spend a weekend in the country.
ANNE:
We'll accept it!
CHARLOTTE:
I'd a feeling
You would.
BOTH:
A weekend in the country!
ANNE:
Yes, it's only polite that we should.
CHARLOTTE:
Good . . . . .
　　(*Charlotte tells Carl-Magnus about
　　the Egermans' invitation to spend
　　the weekend with Desirée at Mme.
　　Armfeldt's.*)

CARL-MAGNUS:
A weekend in the country . . .
We should try it—
CHARLOTTE:
How I wish we'd been asked.
CARL-MAGNUS:
A weekend in the country . . .
Peace and quiet—
CHARLOTTE:
We'll go masked.
CARL-MAGNUS:
A weekend in the country . . .
CHARLOTTE:
Uninvited—
They'll consider it odd.
CARL-MAGNUS:
A weekend in the country—
I'm delighted!
CHARLOTTE:
Oh, my God . . . . .
ALL:
A weekend in the country!
How amusing,
How delightfully droll.
A weekend in the country
While we're losing our control . . . . .
A weekend in the country

With the panting
And the yawns.
With the crickets and the pheasants
And the orchards and the hay,
With the servants and the peasants,
We'll be laying our plans
While we're playing croquet
For a weekend in the country,
So inactive that one has to lie down.
A weekend in the country
Where we're
Twice as upset as in . . . . .
Town!

ACT II

"The Sun Won't Set"

QUINTET:
. . . . . It's nine o'clock . . .
Twilight,
Slowly crawling
Towards ten o'clock . . .
Twilight . . .
Crickets calling,
The vespers ring.
The nightingale's waiting to sing.
The rest of us wait on a string.
Perpetual sunset
Is rather an unset-
Tling thing . . .
The sun won't set.
It's useless to frown or fret.
It's dark as it's going to get.
The hands on the clock turn,
But don't sing a nocturne
Just yet.

Desirée and Fredrika welcome the Malcolms and the Egermans to the chateau

"It Would Have Been Wonderful"

FREDRIK:

. . . . . If she'd only been faded,
If she'd only been fat,
If she'd only been jaded
And bursting with chat,
If only she'd been perfectly awful,
It would have been wonderful.
If . . . if . . .
If she'd been all a-twitter
Or elusively cold,
If she'd only been bitter,
Or better,
Looked passably old,
If she'd been covered with glitter
Or even been covered with mold,
It would have been wonderful.
But the woman was perfection,
To my deepest dismay.
Well, not quite perfection,
I'm sorry to say,
If the woman were perfection,
She would go away,
And that would be wonderful.
Sir . . .

CARL-MAGNUS:

Sir . . .
If she'd only looked flustered
Or admitted the worst,
If she only had blustered
Or simpered or cursed,
If she weren't so awfully perfect,
It would have been wonderful.
If . . . If . . .
If she'd tried to be clever,
If she'd started to flinch,
If she'd cried or whatever
A woman would do in a pinch,
If I'd been certain she never
Again could be trusted an inch,
It would have been wonderful.
But the woman was perfection,
Not an action denied,
The kind of perfection
I cannot abide.
If the woman were perfection,
She'd have simply lied,
Which would have been

wonderful . . . . .

The midsummer night begins to work its magic. Young Henrik confesses to Fredrika that he's in love with his stepmother, Anne. Dressed for dinner, Fredrik and Carl-Magnus compete for Desirée's favor and sing of her perfection (above)

Mme. Armfeldt presides at dinner, which begins with a musical comment on "perpetual anticipation" (below). The conversation is mostly romantic innuendo. With dessert, Mme. Armfeldt raises a toast to life—and death. Then the party begins to form smaller units. Henrik flees toward the lake but is followed (and found) by Anne. Petra pairs off with Frid. Fredrik follows Desirée to her bedroom

"Perpetual Anticipation"

MRS. NORDSTROM:
Perpetual anticipation is
Good for the soul
But it's bad for the heart.
It's very good for practising

Self-control.
It's very good for
Morals,
But bad for morale.
It's very bad.
It can lead to

Going quite mad
It's very good for

Reserve . . . .

MRS. SEGSTROM:
Perpetual antici-
pation is good for
The
Soul, but it's bad
For the
Heart.
It's very good for
Practising self-
Control. It's very
Good for
Morals but bad
For morale. It's

Too unnerving . . . . .

MRS. ANDERSSEN:
Per-
petual antici-
pation is good
For
The soul . . . . .

In Desirée's room, Fredrik and Desirée laugh at their own transparent emotional adventures with a dragoon and a teen-aged bride. But when Desirée hints that she is ready for a renewed romance with Fredrik, he runs away

"Send in the Clowns"

DESIRÉE:
Isn't it rich?
Aren't we a pair?
Me here at last on the ground.
You in mid-air.
Send in the clowns.

Isn't it bliss?
Don't you approve?
One who keeps tearing around,
One who can't move.
Where are the clowns?
Send in the clowns.

Just when I'd stopped opening doors,
Finally knowing the one
                that I wanted was yours,
Making my entrance again
                with my usual flair,
Sure of my lines,
No one is there . . . . .

"The Miller's Son"

PETRA:
I shall marry the miller's son,
Pin my hat on a nice piece of property.
Friday nights, for a bit of fun,
We'll go dancing.
Meanwhile . . .

It's a wink and a wiggle
And a giggle on the grass
And I'll trip the Light Fandango,
A pinch and a diddle
In the middle of what passes by.
It's a very short road
From the pinch and the punch
To the paunch and the pouch
And the pension.
It's a very short road
To the ten-thousandth lunch
And the belch and the grouch
And the sigh.
In the meanwhile,
There are mouths to be kissed
Before mouths to be fed,
And a lot in between
In the meanwhile.
And a girl ought to celebrate
What passes by . . . . .

In the summer twilight, Henrik makes a half-hearted try at suicide, but it's enough to impress Anne, who realizes it is not Fredrik but Henrik she loves. Meanwhile, Petra (below) and Frid have made love, which gives Petra something to sing about (left)

Henrik has run away with Anne, Carl-Magnus and Charlotte have fallen into each other's arms. That leaves Fredrik (his ear grazed by a bullet on a Russian Roulette dare by Carl-Magnus) and Desirée to pair off, as they soon do (right), pledging to each other "a coherent existence after so many years of muddle"

The summer night has smiled for the young and for the foolish. Its final smile is for the old, as Mme. Armfeldt dies peacefully in her chair and the couples reappear for one last waltz as the play comes to an end

A GRAPHIC GLANCE

VICTORIA MALLORY, GARN STEPHENS (REPLACED PRIOR TO THE BROADWAY OPENING BY D. JAMIN-BARTLETT), GEORGE LEE ANDREWS, LAURENCE GUITTARD, PATRICIA ELLIOTT, LEN CARIOU, GLYNNIS JOHNS AND HERMIONE GINGOLD IN "A LITTLE NIGHT MUSIC"

CHRISTOPHER PLUMMER IN "CYRANO"

RENE AUBERJONOIS, CHRISTOPHER MURNEY AND JUNE HELMERS IN "TRICKS"

HIRSCHFELD
DETROIT, MICH.

VIRGINIA VESTOFF, RAUL JULIA
AND KEENE CURTIS IN "VIA
GALACTICA"

ALLAN NICHOLLS, WILLIAM REDFIELD (ON LADDER), MICHAEL DUNN (WHO LEFT
THE SHOW BEFORE ITS OFFICIAL OPENING) AND RAE ALLEN IN "DUDE"

DEBBIE REYNOLDS IN THE REVIVAL OF "IRENE"

HIRSCHFELD
WASHINGTON, D.C.

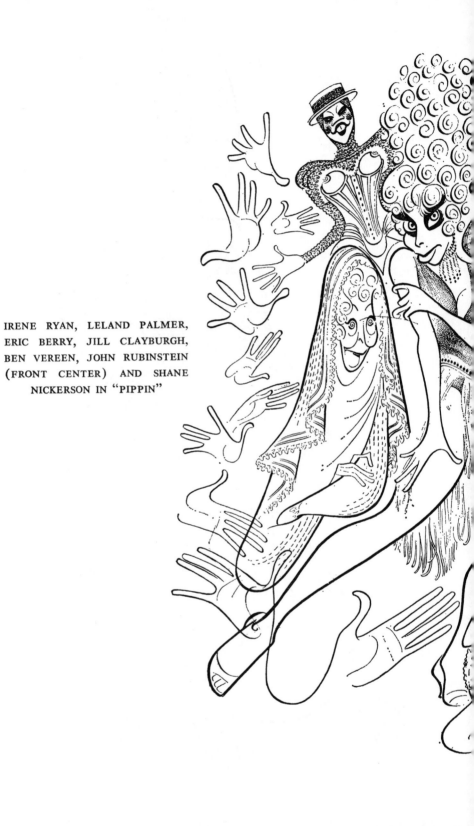

IRENE RYAN, LELAND PALMER,
ERIC BERRY, JILL CLAYBURGH,
BEN VEREEN, JOHN RUBINSTEIN
(FRONT CENTER) AND SHANE
NICKERSON IN "PIPPIN"

MAUREEN STAPLETON IN "THE SECRET AFFAIRS OF MILDRED WILD"

MYRNA LOY, KIM HUNTER, ALEXIS SMITH, MARIE WALLACE, DOR-
OTHY LOUDON, RHONDA FLEMING AND JAN MINER IN THE REVIVAL
OF "THE WOMEN"

EILEEN HERLIE AND REX HARRISON
IN "EMPEROR HENRY IV"

MICHAEL MCGUIRE, PAUL SORVINO, CHARLES DURNING, RICHARD A. DYSART AND
WALTER MCGINN IN "THAT CHAMPIONSHIP SEASON"

PLAYS PRODUCED
IN NEW YORK

PLAYS PRODUCED ON BROADWAY

Figures in parentheses following a play's title indicate number of performances. The figures are acquired directly from the production office in each case and do not include previews or extra non-profit performances.

Plays marked with an asterisk (*) were still running on June 1, 1973. Their number of performances is figured from opening night through May 31, 1973.

In a listing of a show's numbers—dances, sketches, musical scenes, etc.— the titles of songs are identified by their appearance in quotation marks (").

HOLDOVERS FROM PREVIOUS SEASONS

Plays which were running on June 1, 1972 are listed below. More detailed information about them appears in previous *Best Plays* volumes of appropriate years. Important cast changes are recorded in a section of this volume.

Fiddler on the Roof (3,242; longest run in Broadway history). Musical based on Sholom Aleichem's stories; book by Joseph Stein; music by Jerry Bock; lyrics by Sheldon Harnick. Opened September 22, 1964. (Closed July 2, 1972 matinee)

Hair (1,750; not counting previous off-Broadway productions). Musical with book and lyrics by Gerome Ragni and James Rado; music by Galt MacDermot. Opened April 29, 1968. (Closed July 1, 1972)

Oh! Calcutta! (1,314). Musical revue devised by Kenneth Tynan; with contributions by Samuel Beckett, Jules Feiffer, Dan Greenburg, John Lennon, Jacques Levy, Leonard Melfi, David Newman and Robert Benton, Sam Shepard, Clovis Trouille, Kenneth Tynan and Sherman Yellen; music and lyrics by The Open Window. Opened June 17, 1969 off Broadway; was reclassified Middle Broadway as it played 704 performances through February 21, 1971; transferred to Broadway February 26, 1971 for an additional 610 performances. (Closed August 12, 1972)

Butterflies Are Free (1,128). By Leonard Gershe. Open October 21, 1969. (Closed July 2, 1972)

* **Sleuth** (1,066). By Anthony Shaffer. Opened November 12, 1970.

No, No, Nanette (861). Musical revival with book by Otto Harbach and Frank Mandel; music by Vincent Youmans; lyrics by Irving Caesar and Otto Harbach. Opened January 19, 1971. (Closed February 4, 1973)

Follies (521). Musical with book by James Goldman; music and lyrics by Stephen Sondheim. Opened April 4, 1971. (Closed July 1, 1972)

Lenny (455). By Julian Barry; music by Tom O'Horgan; based on the life and words of Lenny Bruce. Open May 26, 1971. (Closed June 24, 1972)

Two Gentlemen of Verona (627). Musical based on the play by William Shakespeare: adapted by John Guare and Mel Shapiro; music by Galt MacDermot; lyrics by John Guare. Opened July 22, 1971 off Broadway, where it played 14 performances through August 8, 1971; transferred to Broadway December 1, 1971 for 613 additional performances. (Closed May 20, 1973)

* **Jesus Christ Superstar** (703). Musical based on the last seven days in the life of Jesus of Nazareth; conceived for the stage by Tom O'Horgan; music by Andrew Lloyd Webber; lyrics by Tim Rice. Opened October 12, 1971.

Ain't Supposed to Die a Natural Death (325). Musical subtitled *Tunes From Blackness* with words and music by Melvin Van Peebles. Opened October 21, 1971. (Closed July 30, 1972)

Sticks and Bones (366). By David Rabe. Opened November 7, 1971 off Broadway, where it played 121 performances through February 20, 1972; transferred to Broadway March 1, 1972 for 245 additional performances. (Closed October 1, 1972)

* **The Prisoner of Second Avenue** (644). By Neil Simon. Opened November 11, 1971.

Twigs (289). Program of four one-act plays by George Furth: *Emily, Celia, Dorothy* and *Ma*. Opened November 14, 1971. (Closed July 23, 1972)

* **Grease** (535). Musical with book, music and lyrics by Jim Jacobs and Warren Casey. Opened February 14, 1972.

Night Watch (121). By Lucille Fletcher. Opened February 28, 1972. (Closed June 11, 1972 matinee)

A Funny Thing Happened on the Way to the Forum (156). Musical revival based on the plays of Plautus; book by Burt Shevelove and Larry Gelbart; music and lyrics by Stephen Sondheim. Opened March 30, 1972. (Closed August 12, 1972)

* **Sugar** (478). Musical based on the screen play *Some Like It Hot* by Billy Wilder and I.A.L. Diamond (based on a story by Robert Thoeren); book by Peter Stone; music by Jule Styne; lyrics by Bob Merrill. Opened April 9, 1972.

* **Don't Bother Me, I Can't Cope** (484). Musical revue by Micki Grant. Opened April 19, 1972.

The Repertory Theater of Lincoln Center. 1971-72 schedule of four programs ended with *The Crucible* (44). Revival of the play by Arthur Miller. Opened April 27, 1972. (Closed June 3, 1972)

Don't Play Us Cheap! (164). Musical with book, music and lyrics by Melvin Van Peebles. Opened May 16, 1972. (Closed October 1, 1972)

PLAYS PRODUCED, JUNE 1, 1972—MAY 31, 1973

Man of La Mancha (140). Revival of the musical suggested by the life and works of Miguel de Cervantes y Saavedra; book by Dale Wasserman; music by Mitch

Leigh; lyrics by Joe Darion. Produced by Albert W. Selden and Hal James by arrangement with Lincoln Center, in the Albert Marre production, at the Vivian Beaumont Theater. Opened June 22, 1972. (Closed October 21, 1972)

Don Quixote (Cervantes)	Richard Kiley	Housekeeper	Eleanore Knapp
Aldonza	Joan Diener	Juan	John Aristides
Sancho	Irving Jacobson	Tenorio; Dancing Horse	Fernando Grahal
Innkeeeper	Jack Dabdoub	Pace	Bill Stanton
Padre	Robert Rounseville	Jose; Dancing Horse	Hector Mercado
Dr. Carrasco	Lee Bergere	Maria	Rita Metzger
Antonia	Dianne Barton	Fermina	Laura Kenyon
Barber; Horse	Edmond Varrato	Capt. of Inquisition	Renato Cibelli
Pedro; Horse	Shev Rodgers	Guitarist	Stephen Sahlein
Anselmo	Ted Forlow		

Guards and Men of the Inquisition: Jeff Killion, David Wasson, Robert Cromwell.

Standby: Mr. Rounseville—Ronn Carroll. Understudies: Mr. Kiley—Renato Cibelli; Miss Diener—Laura Kenyon; Mr. Jacobson—Edmond Varrato; Mr. Dabdoub—Shev Rodgers; Mr. Bergere—Renato Cibelli, Alfred Leberfeld; Mr. Varrato—Ted Forlow, Alfred Leberfeld; Misses Barton, Kenyon—Joyce McDonald; Miss Knapp—Rita Metzger; Miss Metzger—Laura Kenyon; Mr. Rodgers—Jeff Killion; Mr. Cibelli—David Wasson; Swing Dancer—Joe Lorden.

Directed by Albert Marre; choreography, Jack Cole; musical direction, Joseph Klein; scenery and lighting, Howard Bay; costumes, Howard Bay, Patton Campbell; dance arrangements, Neil Warner; musical arrangements, Music Makers, Inc.; production stage manager, James Gelb; stage manager, Patrick Horrigan; press, Gifford/Wallace, Inc., Violet Welles.

Time: The end of the 16th century. Place: A dungeon in Seville and various places in the imagination of Cervantes. The play was presented without intermission.

Man of La Mancha was originally produced 11/22/65 by the same producers who mounted this revival, with Richard Kiley in the lead. It played for 2,328 performances and was named a Best Play of its season. It has received 26 major productions in cities around the world.

The list of musical numbers in *Man of La Mancha* appears on page 387 of *The Best Plays of 1965-66*.

David Atkinson played the role of Don Quixote (Cervantes) and Gerrianne Raphael played the role of Aldonza at Wednesday and Saturday matinee performances. Edmond Varrato substituted for Irving Jacobson in the role of Sancho for the first 2 performances.

* That Championship Season (297). By Jason Miller. Produced by the New York Shakespeare Festival, Joseph Papp producer, at the Booth Theater. Opened September 14, 1972; see note.

Tom Daley	Walter McGinn	Phil Romano	Paul Sorvino
George Sikowski	Charles Durning	Coach	Richard A. Dysart
James Daley	Michael McGuire		

Understudies: Messrs. McGinn, McGuire—Bernie McInerney; Mr. Sorvino—Phil Mascolo; Mr. Durning—Ron McClarty.

Directed by A. J. Antoon; scenery, Santo Loquasto; costumes, Theoni V. Aldredge; lighting, Ian Calderon; associate producer, Bernard Gersten; production stage manager, Ron Abbott; press, Merle Debuskey, Faith Geer.

Time: The present. Place: The Coach's house, somewhere in the Lackawanna Valley. The play was presented in three acts.

At their annual reunion, middle aged ex-basketball champs discover that the qualities which won them the prize 20 years before may have led them into becoming losers in life.

NOTE: This production of *That Championship Season* was first presented off Broadway last season by the New York Shakespeare Festival at the Public Theater 5/2/72 for 144 performances through 9/3/72, and was named a Best Play of its season, before transferring to Broadway. It received the Critics Award in 1972 and the Pulitzer Prize in 1973.

Jacques Brel Is Alive and Well and Living in Paris (51). Musical revue based on lyrics and commentary by Jacques Brel; music by Jacques Brel; production conception, English lyrics and additional material by Eric Blau and Mort Shuman.

Produced by Bill Levine in a limited engagement at the Royale Theater. Opened September 15, 1972; see note. Closed October 28, 1972)

George Ball	Joseph Neal (alternate)
Joe Masiell	Elly Stone
Janet McCall (alternate)	Henrietta Valor

Directed by Moni Yakim; musical direction, Mort Shuman; music arranged and conducted by Wolfgang Knittel; production stage manager, Philip Price; press, Ivan Black.

NOTE: This production originally opened off Broadway 1/22/68 as a cabaret revue and played 1,847 performances through 7/2/72.

The list of musical numbers in *Jacques Brel Is Alive and Well and Living in Paris* appears on page 399 of *The Best Plays of 1967-68.*

From Israel With Love (8). Musical review in the Hebrew language. Produced by Pageant Productions P.T.Y. Ltd. and Col. Saul Biber at the Palace Theater. Opened October 2, 1972. (Closed October 8, 1972)

Micha Adir	Elis Menahemi
Dani Amihud	Malli Noy
Chaya Arad	Yacov Noy
Itzik Barak	Nathan Okev
Shara Badishy	Gadi Oron
Eti Brechner	Varda Sagy
David Dardashi	Reuven Shenar
Irith Esched	Yonnith Shoham
Tami Gall	Nurit Zeevi
Israel Klugman	

Musicians: David Rosenthal, Izhack Lichtenfels, Juda Asher Shkolnik, Oded Pintus, Shmyel Aroukh, Ilan Gilboa.

Directed by Avi David; choreography, Yakov Kalusky; musical director, Rafi Ben-Moshe; stage director, Alan Cossey; international press, Marlene Carter; press, Gifford/Wallace, Inc.

An Israeli Army Entertainment Groups unit, including ten women, in a selection of numbers in modern musical and dancing style. A foreign play previously produced in Israel.

ACT I: "Israel, Israel," "From the South Good Will Come," "Call for Freedom," "Three Legs," "We Take Whatever Comes," Ballet, "Jerusalem of Gold," "Natasha."

ACT II: "A Beach Song," "Night, Night, a Lullaby," "From Across the River—Coffee Song," "The Parachutist," "My Dear Son," Potpourri, Israel Style: "Hava Nagila," "Again the Night Falls," Debka (dance), "I Am Dying," "A Song of Peace."

Dude (16). Musical subtitled *The Highway Life;* book and lyrics by Gerome Ragni; music by Galt MacDermot. Produced by Adela and Peter Holzer at the Broadway Theater. Opened October 9, 1972. (Closed October 21, 1972)

#33	Allan Nicholls	Nero	Leata Galloway
Dude (as a boy)	Ralph Carter	Sissy	David Lasley
Mother Earth	Salome Bey	Electric Bill	Jim Turner
Bread	Delores Hall	Shadow	Dale Soules
The Theater Wings:		Shade	Barbara Monte-Britton
Hero	Alan Braunstein	Esso	Bobby Alessi
Halo	Sandra Loys Toder	Extra	Billy Alessi
Echo	Dawn Johnson	Meadow	Michael Meadows
Solo	Michael Jason	World War Too	Georgianna Holmes
Reba	Rae Allen	Noname	Carol Estey
Harold	William Redfield	Texaco	Dennis Simpson
Suzie Moon	Nell Carter	Dude (as a man)	Nat Morris
Zero	James Patrick Farrell III		

The Shubert Angels: Karen-Maria Faatz, Katie Field, Helen Jennings, David Kruger, Cary Mark, Mark Perman, Aida Random, Lynn Reynolds.

Directed by Tom O'Horgan; musical direction. Thomas Pierson; production designed by Eugene Lee, Roger Morgan, Franne Lee; costumes, Randy Barcelo; musical arrangements and orchestrations, Horace Ott; production stage manager, Michael Maurer; stage manager, Robert Currie; press, Michael Alpert.

An ardent questing for eternal verities of heaven and earth, life and death, youth and maturity, in the form of an unruly rock musical.

ACT I

Overture ....#33, Company
"Theater/Theater" ....#33, Theater Wings, Shubert Angels
"A-Stage" ....#33
"The Mountains" ....Mother Earth
"Pears and Peaches" ....Shubert Angels
"Eat It" ....Pioneers
"Wah Wah Wah" ....Suzie Moon
"Suzie Moon" ....Suzie Moon
"Y.O.U." ....Dude
"I Love My Boo Boo" ....#33, Suzie Moon, Bread, Mother Earth
"Hum Drum Life" ....Halo, Hero, Shadow, Meadow
"Who's It?" ....Dude, Shubert Angels, Theater Wings
"Talk to Me About Love" ....Dude, Zero
"Goodbyes" ....Reba
"I'm Small" ....Hero
"You Can Do Nothing About It" ....Nero
"The Handsomest Man" ....Sissy
"Electric Prophet" ....Electric Bill
"No-One" ....Mother Earth

ACT II

"Who Will Be the Children" ....Shubert Angels
"Go Holy Ghost" ....Shubert Angels
"A Song to Sing" ....Dude, Bread, Nero, Sissy, Theater Wings, Shubert Angels
"A Dawn" ....Hero, Halo, Theater Wings
"The Days of This Life" ....Esso, Extra, Dude, Zero
"I Never Knew" ....Mother Earth
"Air Male" ....Theater Wings
"Undo" ....Bread
"The Earth" ....Harold, Reba
"My Darling I Love You March" ....Theater Wings, Shubert Angels
"So Long Dude" ....Theater Wings
"Dude All Dude" ....Theater Wings, Shubert Angels
"Peace Peace" ....Shubert Angels
"Jesus Hi" ....Shubert Angels
"Baby Breath" ....Mother Earth, Bread, #33, Theater Wings, Shubert Angels
"Sweet Dreams" ....#33, Company

Hurry, Harry (2). Musical with book by Jeremiah Morris, Lee Kalcheim and Susan Perkis; music by Bill Weeden; lyrics by David Finkle. Produced by Peter Grad at the Ritz Theater. Opened October 12, 1972. (Closed October 13, 1972)

ACT I

Harrison Fairchild IV ....Samuel D. Ratcliffe
Harrison Fairchild III; Town Drunk; Dr. Krauss; Chief ....Phil Leeds
Patience Fairchild; Mama; Writer; Native No. 3 ....Liz Sheridan
Muffy Weathersford ....Mary Bracken Phillips
Nick; Deuteronomy; Writer; Witch Doctor ....Louis Criscuolo
Marco; Genesis; Writer; Native No. 5 ....Jack Landron
Stavos; Exodus; Writer; Native No. 1 ....Robert Darnell
Helena; Writer; Native No. 4 ....Randee Heller
Melina; Starlet; Native No. 2 ....Donna Liggitt Forbes

ACT II

Dr. Krauss; Chorus Boy; Not-So-Grand Lama; Uncle Larry .... Phil Leeds
Star; Not-So-Grand Lama .... Liz Sheridan
Chorus Boy; Not-So-Grand Lama .... Louis Criscuolo
Chorus Boy; Grand Lama; Winston .... Robert Darnell
Chorus Boy; Not-So-Grand Lama .... Jack Landron
Not-So-Grand Lama .... Donna Liggitt Forbes
Not-So-Grand Lama; Gypsy .... Randee Heller

Congregation: Louis Criscuolo, Robert Darnell, Donna Liggitt Forbes, Randee Heller, Jack Landron, Phil Leeds, Liz Sheridan.

Directed by Jeremiah Morris; choreography, Gerald Teijelo; musical direction, Arthur Azenzer; scenery, Fred Voelpel; lighting, Martin Aronstein; costumes, Sara Brook; orchestrations and musical supervision, Lee Norris; associate producer, Ed Lewis; production stage manager, Victor Straus; stage manager, Harvey Landa; press, Lee Solters, Harvey B. Sabinson, Marilynn LeVine.

Rich young man roams the world in search of identity and purpose.

ACT I

Overture
Scene 1: The wedding day
    "I'm Gonna" .... Harry
Scene 2: Taverna in Greece
    "When a Man Cries" .... Nick, Mama, Helena, Marco, Stavos, Town Drunk, Melina
Scene 3: Airport
    "A Trip Through My Mind" .... Muffy, Dead Sea Scrolls
Scene 4: Psychiatrist's office
Scene 5: Hollywood
    "Life" .... Harry, Writers
Scene 6: Street in Hollywood
    "Love Can" .... Muffy
Scene 7: Psychiatrist's office
Scene 8: Africa
    "Africa Speaks" .... Natives No. 1, 2, 3, 4 and 5, Witch Doctor
Scene 9: Alone in the world
    "Somewhere in the Past" .... Harry

ACT II

Entr'acte
Scene 1: Psychiatrist's office
Scene 2: Shubert Theater
    "Hurry, Harry" .... Star, Chorus Boys
Scene 3: Psychiatrist's office
    "Goodbye" .... Muffy
Scene 4: Lamasery
Scene 5: Psychiatrist's office
    "You Won't Be Happy" .... Harry, Dr. Krauss
Scene 6: A street
Scene 7: Gypsy's store
Scene 8: Church
    "He Is My Bag" .... Harry, Congregation
Scene 9: Alone in the world
    "Somewhere in My Past" (Reprise) .... Harry, Muffy
Scene 10: Beach
Finale

Pacific Paradise (7). Musical revue in the Maori language. Produced by Irving Sudrow in the New Zealand Maori Company Ltd. production at the Palace Theater. Opened October 16, 1972. (Closed October 21, 1972)

Cast: Faule Bryant, Huri Callaghan, Matekino Callaghan, Sera Chase, Tiramate Dennis, Karen Donaghy, Cecilia Eparaima, Richard Eparaima, Kuini Farthing, Joshua Gardiner, Dawn Heperi, Lena Hiha, Christinie Hikuroa, Eva Hona, Te Kani Horsefall, Bernadette Huata, Paraire Huata, Hemi Huata, Ngamoni Huata, Rongo Kahu, Sonny Keepa, Rachel Kewene, Tangiwai Kingi, Karu Kukutai, Josephine Loader, Putipitu Mackey, Gabrielle Mareikura, Rose Maxwell, Terry Maxwell, Kipa Morehu, Gordon Moses, Helen Moses, Philip Munro, Betty Nathan, James Nathan, Brenda Nepe, Dianne Nukutarwhiti, Iti Paenga, Tomaurangi Paki, Thomas Ratima, Kuini Reedy, Percy Reedy, Rimupae Rennie, Derna Richardson, Keren Ricka, Barbara Ringiao, Noroa Ringiao, James Robert, Pauline Ruru, Abie Scott, Roberta Smiler, Josephine Smiler, Hineawe Smith, Nagatai Stockman, Raana Tangira, Wiremu Tangira, Irirangi Tahuriorangi, Rev. Anaru Takurua, Putiputi Tonihi, Rongo Tuhura, Atareta Waerea, Royal Walker, Tom Ward, Vicky Ward, Leona Watene, Muriel Wehi, Ngapo Wehi, Tui Yates, Arapata Whaanga.

Directed by Jack Regas; Maori cultural director, Arapata Whaanga; Maori choral director, Kelly Harris; narration compiled and edited by Kit Regas; press, Karl Bernstein.

Ceremonies, dances, songs, legends, games based on Maori folklore and performed by a Maori company. A foreign play previously produced in New Zealand.

PART I: Maori Welcome Ceremony—Wero (warrior challenge), Karanga (ceremony), Utaina (chant), Te Urunga Tu (dance), "Karanga Tia"; Legend of the Great Maori Migration—Poroporoaki (entrance of High Priest, played by Arapata Whaanga), Whakaara (ceremony), Whaikorero (a council), "E Oho E Te Whanau," Tohi Waka (blessing of canoes), "Uia Mai Koia," Ma Tangi (ceremony), Poi Waka (the passage of the ocean), Kura Ti Waka (reaching the distant shore), "Ti Tiro Mai"; Village Life in the Island—"Taku Patu," "Karu," He Manuhiri (a battle), "Po Karekare Ana," Tu Mara Mara (chant), Paka Kini (dance).

PART II: Maori Festival—Poi dances (short single Poi, short double Poi, long single Poi, long double Poi, combinations), Tangi Hia," Pana Pana/Rua Moko (dance), Tititoria (games), "Koroki," Peru-Peru (spear ceremony), Ti Rakau (athletic exercise), three and four-Poi competitions, "E Te Hokowhitu," "Pa Aki Kini," "E Pare Ra," Po Ata Ro (finale).

6 Rms Riv Vu (247). By Bob Randall. Produced by Alexander H. Cohen and Bernard Delfont at the Helen Hayes Theater. Opened October 17, 1972. (Closed May 19, 1973)

Superintendant	Jose Ocasio	Paul Friedman	Jerry Orbach
The Pregnant Woman	Anna Shaler	The Woman in 4-A	Francine Beers
The Expectant Father	F. Murray Abraham	Janet Friedman	Jennifer Warren
Anne Miller	Jane Alexander	Richard Miller	Ron Harper

Standbys: Mr. Orbach—Ron Harper, F. Murray Abraham; Miss Alexander—Anna Shaler; Misses Warren, Beers—Lynda Myles.

Directed by Edwin Sherin; scenery, William Ritman; costumes, Ann Roth; lighting, Marc B. Weiss; production associate, Hildy Parks; associate producer, Roy A. Somlyo; production supervisor, Jerry Adler; stage manager, Alan Coleridge; press, James D. Proctor, Louise Weiner Ment.

Time: The present. Place: An empty Riverside Drive apartment. Act I, Scene 1: Morning. Scene 2: Evening. Act II: The following morning.

Apartment-hunting strangers, both married, meet by chance while inspecting an empty flat and embark on a love affair.

A Best Play; see page 141

Mother Earth (12). Musical revue with sketches and lyrics by Ron Thronson; music by Toni Shearer. Produced by Roger Ailes in the Ray Golden production at the Belasco Theater. Opened October 19, 1972. (Closed October 28, 1972)

Gail Boggs	Carol Kristy
Frank T. Coombs	Laura Michaels
Kimberly Farr	John Bennett Perry
Kelly Garrett	Rick Podell
Will Jacobs	Charlie J. Rodriguez

Directed by Ray Golden; musical staging, Lynn Morris; musical direction and supervision, Larry White; scenery, Alan Kimmel; costumes, Mary McKinley; lighting, Paul Sullivan; orchestrations, Alf Clausen; visuals, Kenneth Shearer; dance arrangements, Sande Campbell; associate producers, Howard Butcher IV, Graeme Howard; consultant, Kermit Bloomgarden; production stage manager, Donald W. Christy; press, Max Eisen, Milly Schoenbaum.

Rock musical with numbers and sketches centering on mankind's abuse of the environment.

ACT I: Out of Space; "Mother Earth"—Kelly Garrett, Company; The Client; "The Time of Our Life"—Laura Michaels, Charlie J. Rodriguez; "Corn on the Macabre" (by Ron Thronson, Roger Ailes, Ray Golden)—Carol Kristy, Rick Podell, Gail Boggs; The Mask Parade; "Too Many Old Ideas"—Miss Garrett; The Cheerleader (by Jerry Patch, William Black, Ray Golden); Uneasy Rider; Landscape With Figures; "Room to Be Free"—Podell; Model Wife; "Rent a Robot"—Will Jacobs; A Hike in the Woods (by Jerry Patch, William Black); Flash Gordon; "Plow It All Under"—Miss Kristy, Company; Ewe Turn (by Ray Golden); The Offal Truth (by Jack Marlowe, Ray Golden); The Killathon (by Ron Thronson, Roger Ailes, Ray Golden); "Taking the Easy Way Out"—John Bennett Perry, Frank T. Coombs, Rodriguez; Joggers; "Ozymandias"—Perry; "Talons of Time"—Miss Garrett; "Corn on the Macabre" (Reprise)— Miss Michaels, Kimberly Farr, Coombs; The Nursery; "Save the World for Children"—Miss Boggs; "Sail on Sweet Universe"—Miss Garrett, Company.

ACT II: "Mater Terra"—Company; "Xanadu"—Miss Kristy, Company; Breathe-Out; "Ecology Waltz" (lyrics by Ray Golden)—Miss Farr, Podell; Chic Diners; "Corn on the Macabre" (Reprise)—Misses Kristy, Boggs, Mr. Rodriguez; Women Shoppers (by Ron Thronson, Ray Golden); The Swan; "Good Morning World"—Perry; The Last Redwoods; The Animals (by Ray Golden); "Tiger! Tiger!"—Miss Garrett; Concrete Proposal; "Happy Mother's Day, Mother Earth"—Rodriguez; Radioactive Terminate; "Pills" (Music & lyrics by Ray Golden)—Misses Garrett, Boggs, Kristy, Company; The Billboards (by Jack Marlowe, Ray Golden); "Corn on the Macabre" (Reprise)—Miss Garrett, Messrs. Podell, Combs; "Total Recall" (by Ray Golden); Finale.

* **Pippin** (252). Musical with book by Roger O. Hirson; music and lyrics by Stephen Schwartz. Produced by Stuart Ostrow at the Imperial Theater. Opened October 23, 1972.

Leading Player	Ben Vereen	Berthe	Irene Ryan
Pippin	John Rubinstein	Beggar	Richard Korthaze
Charles	Eric Berry	Peasant	Paul Solen
Lewis	Christopher Chadman	Noble	Gene Foote
Fastrada	Leland Palmer	Catherine	Jill Clayburgh
Musician	John Mineo	Theo	Shane Nickerson
The Head; Field Marshal	Roger Hamilton		

Standbys: Mr. Rubinstein—Walter Willison; Mr. Vereen—Northern J. Calloway; Miss Ryan—Lucie Lancaster; Mr. Nickerson—Will McMillan. Understudies: Mr. Berry—Roger Hamilton; Miss Clayburgh—Ann Reinking; Miss Palmer—Candy Brown; Mr. Vereen—Gene Foote. Dance alternates: Cheryl Clark, Roger A. Bigelow.

Directed and choreographed by Bob Fosse; musical direction, Stanley Lebowsky; scenery, Tony Walton; costumes, Patricia Zipprodt; lighting, Jules Fisher; orchestrations, Ralph Burns; dance arrangements, John Berkman; sound design, Abe Jacob; production stage manager, Phil Friedman; stage managers, Lola Shumlin, Paul Phillips; press, Solters/Sabinson/Roskin, Inc., Cheryl Sue Dolby.

Time: 780 A.D. and thereabouts. Place: The Holy Roman Empire and thereabouts.

Charlemagne's son Pepin ("Pippin") searches for fulfillment in his young life, in a style that is more fanciful than historical. The musical was presented without an intermission.

MUSICAL NUMBERS

Scene 1: The opening
"Magic to Do" .... Players
"Corner of the Sky" .... Pippin
Scene 2: Home
"Welcome Home" .... Charles, Pippin
Scene 3: War
"War Is a Science" .... Charles, Pippin
"Glory" .... Leading Player
Scene 4: The Flesh
"Simple Joys" .... Leading Player
"No Time at All" .... Berthe, Boys

"With You" ....Pippin, Girls
Scene 5: Revolution
"Spread a Little Sunshine" ....Fastrada
"Morning Glow" ....Pippin
Scene 6: Encouragement
"On the Right Track" ....Leading Player, Pippin
Scene 7: The Hearth
"Kind of Woman" ....Catherine, Girls
"Extraordinary" ....Pippin
"Love Song" ....Pippin, Catherine
Scene 8: The Finale ....Players

The Lincoln Mask (8). By V.J. Longhi. Produced by Albert W. Selden and Jerome Minskoff at the Plymouth Theater. Opened October 30, 1972. (Closed November 4, 1972)

Our American Cousin cast:

Sir Edward	Joseph Warren	Shields	Albert Henderson
Lord Dundreary	Alex Primrose	William Herndon	Tom Rosqui
Florence	Ronnie Claire Edwards	Stephen A. Douglas	W.B. Brydon
Georgina	Jean Bruno	Elizabeth Edwards	Tanny McDonald
Mary Meredith	Patricia Cope	Mary Todd	Eva Marie Saint
Vernon	Eric Tavaris	Abraham Lincoln	Fred Gwynne
Asa Trenchard	Earl Hindman	Dr. Henry	Alek Primrose
Lincoln at Ford's Theater	Ray Stewart	Jenkins; Stewart	Eric Tavaris
Ninian Edwards	Thomas Barbour	Mrs. Shields	Jean Bruno
		Edwin M. Stanton	Joseph Warren

Understudies: Messrs. Gwynne, Barbour, Hindman—Ray Stewart; Miss Saint—Ronnie Claire Edwards; Messrs. Rosqui, Henderson, Tavaris—William Charles Reilly; Messrs. Brydon, Warren, Primrose—Al Leberfeld; Misses Edwards, Bruno, Cope—Tanny McDonald.

Directed by Gene Frankel (by arrangement with John Forsythe, assisted by Patricia Cope in the *Our American Cousin* sequences); scenery, Kert F. Lundell; costumes, Patricia Quinn Stuart; lighting, Thomas Skelton; music, Ezra Laderman; audio, Jack Shearing; production stage manager, Frank Hamilton; stage manager, Al Leberfeld; press, Gifford/Wallace, Inc.

Prologue: Ford's Theater, April 14, 1865. Scene 1: The Edwards mansion, Springfield, Ill., 1840. Scene 2: A field outside Springfield, 1840. Scene 3: The Edwards mansion, January 1841. Scene 4: The Lincoln parlor, 1846. Scene 5: The Lincoln parlor, spring 1858. Scene 6: The Lincoln parlor, election night, 1860. Scene 7: The White House, May 1863. Scene 8: The White House, April 1865. (The author has combined several characters and events in the interest of dramatic economy.) The play was presented without intermission.

Closeup of Abraham Lincoln's anti-slavery conviction and its effect on his personality, career and family life, interspersed with scenes from the farce *Our American Cousin* as played at Ford's Theater on the night of Lincoln's assassination.

Butley (135). By Simon Gray. Produced by Lester Osterman Productions (Lester Osterman, Richard Horner) in association with Michael Codron at the Morosco Theater. Opened October 31, 1972. (Closed February 24, 1973)

Ben Butley	Alan Bates	Anne Butley	Holland Taylor
Joseph Keyston	Hayward Morse	Reg Nuttall	Roger Newman
Miss Heasman	Geraldine Sherman	Mr. Gardner	Christopher Hastings
Edna Shaft	Barbara Lester		

Standby: Mr. Bates—Ron Randell. Understudies: Miss Sherman—Andrea Stonorov; Messrs. Morse, Newman, Hastings—David Leary.

Directed by James Hammerstein; original production directed by Harold Pinter; scenery, Eileen Diss; lighting and costumes, Neil Peter Jampolis; production stage manager, Harry Young; stage manager, Andrea Stonorov; press, Abby Quinn Hirsch, Tobi Louis.

Time: The present. Place: A college of London University. The play was presented in two acts. A foreign play previously produced in London.

Professional and emotional disintegration of a world-weary teacher, a homosexual, viewed on the day he is abandoned by both former wife and present lover.

A Best Play; see page 160

* The Repertory Theater of Lincoln Center. Schedule of four programs. **Enemies** (44). By Maxim Gorky; English version by Jeremy Brooks and Kitty Hunter-Blair. Opened November 9, 1972. (Closed December 16, 1972) **The Plough and the Stars** (44). Revival of the play by Sean O'Casey. Opened January 4, 1973. (Closed February 10, 1973) **The Merchant of Venice** (44). Revival of the play by William Shakespeare. Opened March 1, 1973. (Closed April 7, 1973) *** A Streetcar Named Desire** (41). Revival of the play by Tennessee Williams. Opened April 26, 1973. Produced by The Repertory Theater of Lincoln Center, Jules Irving director, at the Vivian Beaumont Theater.

ENEMIES

The Bardin household:

Zahkar Bardin	Robert Symonds
Paulina	Frances Sternhagen
Yokov Bardin	Joseph Wiseman
Tatiana	Nancy Marchand
Nadya	Susan Sharkey
Gen. Pechenegov	Stefan Schnabel
Kon	Will Lee
Mikhail Skrobotov	Philip Bosco
Kleopatra	Barbara Cook
Nikolai Skrobotov	Josef Sommer
Agrafena	Jane Rose
Pologgy	George Pentecost
Sintsov	Christopher Walken
Capt. Boboyedov	Tom Lacy
Kvach	Ray Fry
Lt. Strepetov	George Taylor
District Police Inspector	Louis Turenne
Policeman	James Ray Weeks

Workmen: Robert Phalen, Sydney Walker, Fred Morsell, Everett McGill, Dan Sullivan, Frank Dwyer. Peasant Women: Penelope Allen, Murrell Gehman, Carole Ocwieja.

Principal understudies: Messrs. Symonds, Lee—Ray Fry; Misses Sternhagen, Cook—Murrell Gehman; Mr. Wiseman, Fred Morsell; Misses Marchand, Rose—Penelope Allen.

Directed by Ellis Rabb; scenery, Douglas W. Schmidt; lighting, John Gleason; costumes, Ann Roth; music, Cathy MacDonald; production stage manager, Craig Anderson; stage manager, Robert Lowe; press, Susan Bloch, William Schelble, Norman J-F. Lombino.

Time: 1905. Place: Provincial Russia. Act I: Morning in the garden of the Bardin estate. Act II: That evennig. Act III: A room in the Bardin house, the next day.

Gorky's play about society fragmenting on the eve of revolution was first staged by Max Reinhardt in Berlin in 1907; banned in Russia, it wasn't performed there until 1932, in Leningrad. The present adaptation was first produced in London by the Royal Shakespeare Company in 1971. This Lincoln Center staging was its first American production of record.

THE PLOUGH AND THE STARS

Jack Clitheroe	Christopher Walken
Nora Clitheroe	Roberta Maxwell
Peter Flynn	Leo Leyden
Young Covey	Kevin Conway
Bessie Burgess	Pauline Flanagan
Mrs. Gogan	Nancy Marchand
Mollser	Susan Sharkey
Fluther Good	Jack MacGowran
Lt. Langon	Peter Rogan
Capt. Brennan	Robert Phalen
Cpl. Stoddart	Philip Bosco
Sgt. Tinley	David H. Leary
Rosie Redmond	Lee Lawson
Bartender	Sydney Walker
Woman	Paddy Croft
Figure in the Window	Michael Clarke-Laurence

Understudies: Mr. MacGowran—Robert Symonds; Misses Maxwell, Sharkey—Caroline Kava; Misses Marchand, Flanagan—Paddy Croft; Mr. Leyden—Ray Fry; Mr. Conway—Robert Phalen; Misses Lawson, Croft—Murrell Gehman; Mr. Phalen—Everett McGill; Messrs. Bosco, Walker—Frank Dwyer; Messrs. Rogan, Leary—James Ray Weeks; Mr. Walken—David H. Leary.

Directed by Dan Sullivan; scenery, Douglas W. Schmidt; lighting, John Gleason; costumes, Carrie F. Robbins; original music, John Duffy; vocal director, Cathy Macdonald; sound, Gary Harris; production stage manager, Patrick Horrigan; stage manager, Barbara-Mae Phillips.

Time: Acts I and II, November 1915; Acts III and IV, Easter Week 1916. Place: Dublin. Act I: The living room of the Clitheroe flat in a Dublin tenement. Act II: A public house. Act III: The street outside the Clitheroe aparment. Act IV: The room of Bessie Burgess, a few days later. The play was presented in two parts.

The Plough and the Stars was first produced on Broadway 11/28/27 for 32 performances. It has been revived by the Abbey Theater 11/12/34 for 13 performances; and again on Broadway 10/7/37 for 4 performances. It was produced off Broadway during the seasons of 1949-50 and 1952-53, and by the Phoenix Theater 12/6/60 for 32 performances.

THE MERCHANT OF VENICE

Antonio ....Josef Sommer	Stephano ....Michael Clarke-Laurence
Salarino ....Gastone Rossilli	Prince of Morocce ....Fred Morsell
Leonardo ....Robert Phalen	Shylock ....Sydney Walker
Salaria ....Carolina Kava	Launcelot Gobbo ....Dan Sullivan
Bassanio ....Christopher Walken	Jessica ....Roberta Maxwell
Gratiano ....Philip Bosco	Prince of Arragon ....Alan Mandell
Lorenzo ....Peter Coffield	Tubal ....Ray Fry
Portia ....Rosemary Harris	Duke of Venice ....Robert Symonds
Nerissa ....Olivia Cole	Court Clerk ....Frank Dwyer

Others: Richard Council, Calvin Culver, Joseph Lambie, Robert LaTourneaux, Amy Levitt, Everett McGill, Ellen Newman, Casper Roos, Sterling St. Jacques, James Ray Weeks, Peter Weller, James Whittle, William Wright.

Principal understudies: Miss Harris—Ellen Newman; Mr. Walker—Ray Fry; Mr. Sommer—Casper Roos; Mr. Walken—Everett McGill; Misses Kava, Maxwell—Amy Levitt; Mr. Coffield—Joseph Lambie.

Directed by Ellis Rabb; scenery, lighting and projections, James Tilton; costumes, Ann Roth; musical supervision, Cathy MacDonald; production stage manager, Barbara-Mae Phillips; stage manager, Patrick Horrigan.

Place: Venice and on the Belmont. The play was presented in two parts.

In this production *The Merchant of Venice* was played in modern dress in contemporary Venice, with Portia's home a yacht named the Belmont. The play was last produced in New York by Joseph Papp's New York Shakespeare Festival in Central Park 6/19/62 for 17 performances.

Donald M. Griffith replaced Sterling St. Jacques 3/20/73.

A STREETCAR NAMED DESIRE

Woman ....Rosetta LeNoire	Steve Hubbel ....Robert Symonds
Stanley Kowalski ....James Farentino	Pablo Gonzales ....Dan Sullivan
Harold Mitchell ....Philip Bosco	Young Collector ....Brian Brownlee
Stella Kowalski ....Patricia Conolly	Mexican Man ....Sydney Walker
Eunice Hubbel ....Priscilla Pointer	Doctor ....Ray Fry
Blanche Du Bois ....Rosemary Harris	Nurse ....Penelope Allen

Habitues of the Quarter: Frank Dwyer, Donald M. Griffith, Everett McGill, Ellen Newman, John Newton, Robert Phalen, Alyce E. Webb, James Ray Weeks.

Directed by Ellis Rabb; scenery, Douglas W. Schmidt; costumes, Nancy Potts; lighting, John Gleason; music, Cathy MacDonald; sound, Gary Harris; production stage manager, Barbara-Mae Phillips.

Time: Spring, summer and early fall. Place: New Orleans. The play was presented in two acts.

A Streetcar Named Desire was first produced on Broadway 12/3/47 for 855 performances and was named a Best Play of its season and won the Critics Award and the Pulitzer Prize. It has been revived twice at the City Center, 5/23/50 and 2/15/56.

Tom Rosqui replaced Robert Symonds 6/1/73. Lois Nettleton replaced Rosemary Harris, Robert Forster replaced James Farentino, Barbara eda-Young replaced Patricia Conolly 6/19/73.

Much Ado About Nothing (136). Revival of the play by William Shakespeare; music by Peter Link. Produced by the New York Shakespeare Festival, Joseph Papp producer, at the Winter Garden. Opened November 11, 1972; see note. (Closed February 11, 1973)

Leonato ....Mark Hammer	Don Pedro ....Douglass Watson
Messenger; Sexton ....Charles Bartlett	Benedick ....Sam Waterston
Beatrice ....Kathleen Widdoes	Claudio ....Glenn Walken
Hero ....April Shawhan	Don John ....Jerry Mayer

Antonio	Arny Freeman	Dogberry	Barnard Hughes
Conrade	Jack Gianino	Verges	Will Mackenzie
Borachio	Frederick Coffin	1st Watch	George Gugleotti
Margaret	Jeanne Hepple	2d Watch	David Lenthall
Balthasar	Marshall Efron	Friar Francis	Tom McDermott
Ursula	Betty Henritze		

Other Watches: Richard Casper, James McGill, Leland Schwantes. Townspeople: Richard Casper, Lindsay Ann Crouse, Joan Jaffe, Rosamond Lynn, James McGill, William Robertson. Barbara Rubenstein, Richard Schneider, Leland Schwantes, Cathy Greene.

Musicians: Charles Lewis trumpet, cornet; Lenny Pogan drum, banjo, guitar; Sam Pilafian tuba, bass, trombone; Peter Phillips piano, trombone; Aaron Sachs clarinet, flute; Jimmie Young drums, bass.

Standbys: Mr. Hughes—Albert Quinton; Mr. Waterston—Will Mackenzie; Mr. Watson—Maury Cooper; Miss Widdoes—Jeanne Hepple. Understudies: Mr. Hammer—Maury Cooper; Messrs. Coffin, Mayer—Jack Gianino; Mr. Mackenzie—George Gugleotti; Mr. Walken—Richard Casper; Miss Henritze—Joan Jaffe; Messrs, Gugleotti, Lenthall—Leland Schwantes; Mr. Bartlett—Richard Schneider; Miss Hepple—Barbara Rubenstein; Miss Shawhan—Lindsay Ann Crouse; Mr. Freeman—William Robertson; Mr. McDermott-Albert Quinton.

Directed by A. J. Antoon; scenery, Ming Cho Lee; costumes, Theoni V. Aldredge; lighting, Martin Aronstein; dances, Donald Saddler; musical supervision, John Morris; associate producer, Bernard Gersten; production stage manager, David Eidenberg; stage manager, Tom Gardner; press, Merle Debuskey, Robert Larkin.

Time: Before World War I. Place: A small town in middle America. The play was presented in two parts.

This production offers Shakespeare's play reconstituted in an American setting, with music added. Its first New York professional production of modern record was the Henry Irving-Ellen Terry version in 1905.

NOTE: This production of *Much Ado About Nothing* was first presented by the New York Shakespeare Festival in the Delacorte Theater, Central Park, 8/10/72 for 20 performances through 9/3/72 (see its entry in the "Plays Produced off Broadway" section of this volume), before being transferred to Broadway for an additional run of 116 performances.

Musical numbers: "Meet You 'Hind the Barn," "Maple Leaf Rag" (by Scott Joplin), "Ballad for a Summer Evening," "Hogwash," "Light of Love," "Smoker Rag" (by Scott Joplin), "Jimmie," "Goodbye Fred," "Marcella."

Paul Sparer replaced Mark Hammer 1/29/73.

Lysistrata (8). Revival of the play by Aristophanes; adapted by Michael Cacoyannis; with music by Peter Link. Produced by David Black and David Seltzer at the Brooks Atkinson Theater. Opened November 13, 1972. (Closed November 18, 1972)

Lysistrata	Melina Mercouri	Alphabeta	Avril Gentles
Kalonike	Evelyn Russell	Deltazeta	Mary Jo Catlett
Myrrhine	Priscilla Lopez	Theta	Patti Karr
Lampito	Madeleine Le Roux	Iota	Gayla Osbourne
Corinthian Woman	Lynda Sue Marks	Commissioner	Philip Bruns
Boeotian Woman	Nai Bonet	Policeman; Spartan Herald	Stephen Macht
Policewoman	Marilou Sirinek	Policeman	Charles E. Siegel
Omicron	Emory Bass	Woman A	Cynthia Bullens
Phi-Chi	Gordon Connell	Woman B	Joanne Nail
Omega	Joseph Palmieri	Woman C	Judith Drake
Upsilon	David Thomas	Kinesias	Richard Dmitri
Epsilon	Jack Fletcher	Spartan Delegate	John Bentley
Gamma	Jane Connell		

Musicians: Cynthia Bullens rhythm guitar, Margaret Dorn piano and organ, Errol Edwards Conga drum, Armand Halburian percussion, Will Lee bass, Linda Sue Marks percussion, Michael Mattheau bouzouki, Henry "Bootsie Normand" lead guitar, Marilou Sirinek trumpet.

Understudies: Misses Russell, Le Roux—Patti Karr; Miss Lopez—Joanne Nail; Mr. Dmitri—Stephen Macht; Mr. Bruns—John Bentley; Women—Judith Drake; Men—Charles E Siegel.

Directed by Michael Cacoyannis; musical direction, Henry "Bootsie" Normand; scenery, Robin Wagner; costumes, Willa Kim; lighting, Jules Fisher; sound, Abe Jacob; associate producer, Ira Resnick; production stage manager, Mortimer Halpern; stage manager, Nicholas Russiyan; press, Betty Lee Hunt Associates, Henry Luhrman, Harriett Trachtenberg.

Musical numbers interpolated into Aristophanes's anti-war comedy newly adapted. The last Broadway musical treatment of this story was *The Happiest Girl in the World* 4/3/61 for 96 performances. The last straight version was produced by the Phoenix Theater 11/24/59 for 24 performances.

ACT I

"A Woman's Hands"	Lysistrata
"On, On, On"	Lysistrata, Women
"Oh, What a Siege That Was"	Men
"As I Choose"	Lysistrata, Women
"Many the Beasts"	Men
"Are We Strong?"	Lysistrata, Women
"A Cavalry Captain"	Kalonike
"Lysistrata"	Lysistrata, Women

ACT II

"To Touch the Sky"	Lysistrata
"Eels Are a Girl's Best Friend"	Women
"Let Me Tell You a Little Story"	Men, Women
"You Out There"	Men, Women
"Kalimera"	Lysistrata, Company

The Secret Affairs of Mildred Wild (23). By Paul Zindel. Produced by James B. McKenzie and Spofford J. Beadle at the Ambassador Theater. Opened November 14, 1972. (Closed Dec. 2, 1972)

Mildred Wild	Maureen Stapleton	Miss Manley	Doris Roberts
Roy Wild	Lee Wallace	Rex Bulby	Bill McIntyre
Bertha Gale	Florence Stanley	Louis Garibaldi	Pat Corley
Helen Wild	Elizabeth Wilson	Warren, TV Host	Paul De Witt
Carrol Chatham	Neil Flanagan	Evelyn, TV Hostess	Joan Pape
Sister Cecelia	Joan Pape		

Standby: Miss Stapleton—Doris Roberts. Understudy: Messrs. Flanagan, Corley, De Witt—Bill McIntyre.

Directed by Jeff Bleckner; scenery, Santo Loquasto; costumes, Carrie F. Robbins. Lighting, Thomas Skelton; special sound, James Reichert; special choreography, Edward Roll; special music arrangements, Rudolph Bennett; stage manager, Frank Hartenstein; press, Solters/Sabinson/Roskin, Inc., Sandra Manley.

Time: The present. Place: The living quarters in the rear of a dilapidated candy store in Greenwich Village, New York City. Act I, Scene 1: A Wednesday morning. Scene 2: Early afternoon of the same day. Act II, Scene 1: Later that evening. Scene 2: The next morning. Act III: Friday morning.

Incidental musical numbers were "It Was Just One of Those Things" by Cole Porter and Jack C. Rizzo, "Did You Ever See a Dream Walking" by Mack Gordon and Harry Revel, "With My Eyes Wide Open I'm Dreaming" by Mack Gordon and Harry Revel, "Dream (When You're Feeling Blue)" by Johnny Mercer, "I Can Dream, Can't I" by Irving Kahál and Sammy Fain, "Moonlight Becomes You" by Jimmy Van Heusen and Johnny Burke, "Shaking the Blues Away" by Irving Berlin," "Tara's Theme" by Max Steiner, "Crazy Rhythm" by Irving Caesar, Joseph Myer and Roger Wolfe Kahn, "King Kong Suite" by Max Steiner, "I Love to Walk in the Rain" by Harold Spina and Walter Bullock and "I Fell in Love With the Movies" by Paul Zindel.

Comedy about the real and fantasy lives of a middle-aged woman, the wife of a candy store operator, obsessed with the movies of the big Hollywood studio era.

Circle in the Square. Schedule of four revivals. **Mourning Becomes Electra** (55). By Eugene O'Neill. Opened November 15, 1972 matinee. (Closed December 31, 1972). **Medea** (70). By Euripides; adapted by Minos Volanakis. Opened January

17, 1973. (Closed March 18, 1973 matinee) **Here Are Ladies** (40). Return engagement of the one-woman show from the works of Irish writers performed by Siobhan McKenna. Opened March 29, 1973. (Closed May 13, 1973). And *Uncle Vanya*, revival of the play by Anton Chekhov, translated by Albert Todd and Mike Nichols, scheduled to open 6/4/73. Produced by Circle in the Square, Inc., Theodore Mann artistic director, Paul Libin managing director, at the Circle in the Square Joseph E. Levine Theater.

MOURNING BECOMES ELECTRA

Seth Beckwith	William Hickey	Capt. Peter Niles	Jack Ryland
Amos Ames; Josiah Borden	Hansford Rowe	Capt. Adam Brant	Alan Mixon
Louisa Ames; Mrs. Hills	Eileen Burns	Brig. Gen. Ezra Mannon	Donald Davis
Minnie; Emma Borden	Jocelyn Brando	Everett Hills; Abner Small	William Bush
Christine Mannon	Colleen Dewhurst	Dr. Joseph Blake; Joe Silva	Daniel Keyes
Lavinia Mannon	Pamela Payton-Wright	Orin Mannon	Stephen McHattie
Hazel Niles	Lisa Richards	Chantyman; Ira Mackel	John Ridge

Servants of the Mannon household: Eileen Burns, Jocelyn Brando, William Bush, Daniel Keyes, Hansford Rowe, John Ridge.

Directed by Theodore Mann; scenery, Marsha L. Eck; costumes, Noel Taylor; lighting, Jules Fisher; production stage manager, Randall Brooks; stage manager, Charles Roden; press, Merle Debuskey, Leo Stern.

Time: 1865-66. Place: New England. *The Homecoming*—Act I: Exterior of the Mannon house in New England, April 1865. Act II: Ezra Mannon's study in the house, immediately following. Act III: Exterior of the house, a night a week later. Act IV: A bedroom in the house, later the same night. *The Hunted*—Act I: Exterior of the house, a night two days later. Act II: The sitting room of the house, immediately following. Act III: The study, immediately following. Act IV: The stern of the clipper ship "Flying Trades" at a wharf in East Boston a night two days later. Act V: Exterior of the house, the following night. *The Haunted*—Act I, Scene 1: Exterior of the house, an evening in the summer of 1866. Scene 2: The sitting room, immediately following. Act II: The study, an evening a month later. Act III: The sitting room, immediately following. Act IV: Exterior of the house, late afternoon, three days later. The play was presented in three parts, with intermissions between the sections of the trilogy.

O'Neill's trilogy (*The Homecoming, The Hunted* and *The Haunted*), set in New England but patterned on the Agamemnon-Electra-Orestes story of Greek legend and tragedy, was previously produced on Broadway twice during the 1931-32 season: on 10/26/31 for 150 performances and again on 5/9/32 for 16 performances.

MEDEA

Nurse	Tally Brown	Soldiers	Rob Evan Collins, Bill E. Noone
Old Man; Kreon	Ron Faber	Jason	John P. Ryan
(The Two Children)	Kirsten Aimée, Eric Faber, Eric John Roden	Aegeus	Albert Stratton
Medea	Irene Papas	Messenger	Al Freeman Jr.

(Parentheses indicate roles in which the actors alternated)

Chorus: Geraldine Court, Irene Frances Kling, Betty Lester, Julienne Marshall, Marsha Meyers, Dina Paisner, Elaine Sulka, Florence Tarlow, Nancy Zala.

Understudies: Miss Papas—Elaine Sulka; Miss Brown—Florence Tarlow; Messrs. Ryan, Faber, Stratton—Rob Evan Collins; Mr. Freeman—Bill E. Noone.

Directed by Minos Volanakis; scenery, Robert Mitchell; costumes, Nancy Potts; lighting, Marc B. Weiss; choral music, Michael Small; electronic environment, Tempi; production stage manager, Randall Brooks; stage manager, Charles Roden.

Medea was last revived in the Robinson Jeffers version on Broadway 10/20/47 for 214 performances with Judith Anderson in the title role and off Broadway 11/28/65 for 77 performances with Gloria Foster.

HERE ARE LADIES

Directed and designed by Sean Kenny; music, Sean O'Riada; production stage manager, Robert Kellogg; press, Merle Debuskey, Leo Stern.

Siobhan McKenna impersonated a series of ladies from Irish literature. *Here Are Ladies* is a foreign play previously produced in London and elsewhere including New York City under the aegis of the Public Theater 2/22/71 for 67 performances.

PART I—*A Woman is a Branchy Tree* and The Thin Woman and The Fat Woman from *Crock of Gold* by James Stephens; Mrs. Tancred from *Juno and the Paycock* and Ginnie Gogan's conversation with Mr. Fluther Good from *The Plough and the Stars* by Sean O'Casey; *Poem* by Eva Gore Booth; *St Joan* by George Bernard Shaw; Crazy Jane and the Bishop, Love Is All Unsatisfied, That Lover of a Night, What Lively Lad Most Pleasured Me and I Met the Bishop on the Road from *Crazy Jane* by William Butler Yeats; *Caoine Mhuire* (in Irish), anonymous; Maura from *Riders to the Sea* by John Millington Synge; *The Mermaid's Song* by William Butler Yeats; Winnie from *Happy Days* by Samuel Beckett; *Drama at Inish* by Lennox Robinson.

PART II—Anna Livia Plurabelle and The Lullaby from *Finnegans Wake* and Molly in *Ulysses* by James Joyce.

Dear Oscar (5). Musical with book and lyrics by Caryl Gabrielle Young; music by Addy O. Fieger. Produced by Mary W. John at the Playhouse Theater. Opened November 16, 1972. (Closed November 19, 1972)

Oscar Wilde . . . . Richard Kneeland	Comtesse's Son; Sidney
Lady Wilde . . . . Nancy Cushman	Mavor; Detective . . . . Roger Leonard
Lady Mount-Temple . . . . Jane Hoffman	Frederick . . . . Jack Hoffmann
Constance Lloyd . . . . Kimberly Vaughn	Vicar; Sir Edward Clark . . . . . . Richard Marr
Lady de Grey . . . . Gretchen Walther	Marquess of Queensberry . . . . Jack Bittner
Lord de Grey; Sir Edward	Arthur; Theater
Carson . . . . Grant Walden	Attendant . . . . Edward McPhillips
Frank Harris . . . . Len Gochman	Robert Ross . . . . Gary Krawford
Charles Brookfield; Al Taylor . . . Garnett Smith	Nellie . . . . Lynn Brinker
Charles Hawtry; Alfred Wood;	Clibburn . . . . Tommy Breslin
Maitre d'Hotel . . . . Edward Penn	Atkins . . . . Bruce Heighley
Bootles . . . . Tinker Gillespie	Edward Shelly . . . . James Hosbein
Comtesse . . . . Sylvia O'Brien	Lord Alfred Douglas . . . . Russ Thacker

Production supervised by John Allen; musical direction, Arnold Gross; musical supervision and arrangements, Harold Hastings; scenery, William Pitkin; costumes, Mary McKinley; lighting, David F. Segal; production stage manager, Ben Janney; stage manager, William Dolive; press, Saul Richman.

Act I: Begins in 1883 in London. Act II: Begins in 1894. The musical's book is based on the life of Oscar Wilde.

ACT I

"We Like Things the Way They Are" . . . . Oscar, Company
"Tite Street" . . . . Oscar, Lady Mount-Temple, Constance
"Oscar Wilde Has Said It" . . . . Company
"Wot's 'is Name" . . . . Nellie, Boys
"Poor Bosie" . . . . Bosie
"The Perfect Understanding" . . . . Oscar, Bosie
"Swan and Edgar's" . . . . Constance, Speranza
"If I Could" . . . . Oscar
"If I 'ad 'alf" . . . . Atkins, Clibburn

ACT II

"We Dare You" . . . . Company
"We'll Have a Party" . . . . Bosie, Nellie, Boys
"We're Only Lovers" . . . . Nellie, Robbie
"For Woman" . . . . Speranza, Bootles, Comtesse
"When Did You Leave Me" . . . . Constance, Oscar
"Good, Good Times" . . . . Nellie
"There Where the Young Men Go" . . . . Oscar

Ambassador (19). Musical based on the Henry James novel *The Ambassadors;* book by Don Ettlinger and Anna Marie Barlow; music by Don Gohman; lyrics by Hal Hackady. Produced by Gene Dingenary, Miranda d'Ancona, and Nancy Levering at the Lunt-Fontanne Theater. Opened November 19, 1972. (Closed November 25, 1972)

Lewis Lambert Strether	Howard Keel	Jeanne de Vionnet	Andrea Marcovicci
Porter	Adam Petroski	Dancing Teacher; Artist	Larry Giroux
Waymarsh	David Sabin	Guide; Hotel Manager	Jack Trussel
Flower Girl; Germaine	Patricia Arnell	Waiter; Headwaiter	Robert L. Hultman
Gloriani	Carmen Mathews	Innkeeper's wife	Marsha Tamaroff
Marie de Vionnet	Danielle Darrieux	Bellboy	Nikolas Dante
Waiter	Dwight Arno	Lady in Park	Dixie Stewart
Bilham	Michael Goodwin	Amelia Newsome	M'el Dowd
Chad	Michael Shannon		

People of Paris: Janis Ansley, Patricial Arnell, Dwight Arno, Marcia Brooks, Nikolas Dante, Richard Dodd, Vito Durante, Phillip Filiato, Lynn Fitzpatrick, Larry Giroux, Charlie Goeddertz, Gerald Haston, Alexis Hoff, Robert L. Hultman, Douglas E. Hunnikin, Genette Lane, Betsy Ann Leadbetter, Nancy Lynch, Linda-Lee MacArthur, Adam Petroski, Dean Russell, Salicia Saree, Ellie Smith, Suzanne Sponsler, Dixie Stewart, Marsha Tamaroff, Jack Trussel, Chester Walker.

Standbys: Mr. Keel—Steve Arlen; Miss Darrieux—Margot Moser. Understudies: Mr. Shannon—Michael Goodwin; Miss Marcovicci—Patricia Arnell; Miss Arnell—Lynn Fitzpatrick.

Directed by Stone Widney; musical staging and choreography, Joyce Trisler; musical direction and vocal arrangements, Herbert Grossman; scenery and costumes, Peter Rice; American production supervised by Robert Guerra; costumes supervised by Sara Brook; lighting, Martin Aronstein; orchestrations, Philip J. Lang; dance arrangements, Trude Rittmann; associate producer, Dan Rodden; production stage manager, Alan Hall; stage manager, Mary Porter Hall; press, Reginald Denenholz, Timothy A. Burke.

Time: 1906. Place: Paris.

In the James story on which the musical is based, a staid Massachusetts lawyer goes on an errand to Paris and is captivated by Europe. An American play previously produced in London.

ACT I

Scene 1: Gare St. Lazare
   "Lambert's Quandary" .... Lambert
Scene 2: The Tuileries
   "Lilas" .... Flower Girl
   "I Know the Man" .... Marie
Scene 3: Chad's apartment
Scene 4: Gloriani's garden
   "The Right Time, the Right Place" .... Gloriani's Guests
   "She Passed My Way" .... Marie, Guests
   "Valse"
Scene 5: Terrace of Lambert's apartment
   "Something More" .... Lambert
Scene 6: A park
   "Love Finds the Lonely" .... Jeanne
Scene 7: Notre Dame Cathedral
   "Kyrie Eleison"
Scene 8: The Left Bank
   "Surprise" .... Marie, Lambert, People of Left Bank
Scene 9: Terrace of Lambert's apartment
   "Happy Man" .... Lambert
Scene 10: An Inn at St. Cloud

ACT II

Scene 1: The Tuileries
   "Lilas, What Happened to Paris" .... Lambert, Flower Girl
Scene 2: Lambert's apartment

"Young With Him" ....Marie
"Too Much to Forgive" ....Lambert
Scene 3: A secluded part of the Bois de Boulogne
"Why Do Women Have to Call It Love" ....Gloriani, Waymarsh
Scene 4: Chad's apartment
Scene 5: Marie's garden
"Mama" ....Jeanne
"That's What I Need Tonight" ....Marie, Lambert
Scene 6: Le Petit Moulin Cabaret
"Maxixe-Habanera"
"That's What I Need Tonight" ....Lambert, Marie, People of Paris
"Gossip" ....Ladies of Paris
Scene 7: Marie's garden
"Not Tomorrow" ....Marie
Scene 8: A bridge
"All of My Life" ....Lambert
Scene 9: The hotel lobby
"Thank You, No" ....Lambert
Scene 10: A bridge

Via Galactica (7). Musical with book by Christopher Gore and Judith Ross; music by Galt MacDermot; lyrics by Christopher Gore. Produced by George W. George and Barnard S. Straus in association with Nat Shapiro at the Uris Theater. Opened November 28, 1972. (Closed December 2, 1972)

Storyteller	Irene Cara	Mute	Lili Cockerille
Gabriel Finn	Raul Julia	Lady	Lorrie Davis
Hels	Damon Evans	Mechanic	Richard DeRusso
April	Edloe	Teacher	Sylvia DiGiorgio
Omaha	Virginia Vestoff	Spokesman; Entertainer	James Dybas
Dr. Isaacs	Keene Curtis	Politician	Marion Killinger
Provo	Bill Starr	Child	Toni Lund
Diane; Writer	Livia Genise	Cripple	Veronica Redd
Nicklas	Peter Nissen	Tailor	James Rivers
Roustabout	Alex Ander	Carpenter	Richard Ryder
Cook	Mark Baker	Doctor	Stan Shaw
Mute's Friend	Robert Blankshine	Gambler	Leon Spelman
Gypsy	Jacqueline Britt	Janitor	Bob Spencer
Boy	Ralph Carter	Nurse	Bonnie Walker
Geologist	Melanie Chartoff	Grandmother	J.H. Washington
Old Man; Student	Chuck Cissel		

Blue People: Mark Baker, Jacqueline Britt, Melanie Chartoff, Richard DeRusso, Sylvia DiGiorgio, Livia Genise, Marion Killinger, Toni Lund, Bob Spencer, Bonnie Walker.
Understudies: Mr. Julia—Richard DeRusso; Miss Vestoff—Veronica Redd; Mr. Curtis—James Dybas; Mr. Evans—Stan Shaw; Swing Dancer—Jorge Diaz.
Conceived and directed by Peter Hall; musical direction, Thomas Pierson; scenery and costumes, John Bury; lighting, Lloyd Burlingame; ensemble movement, George Faison; associate director, Geoffrey Cauley; vocal arrangements, Joyce Brown; assistant director, Patrick Libby; orchestrations, Bhen Lanzaroni, Horace Ott, Danny Hurd; sound, Jack Shearing; production associate, Arthur Gorton; production stage manager, William Dodds; stage manager, Marnell Sumner; press, Solters/Sabinson/Roskin, Inc., Sandra Manley.
The libretto, entirely set to music with the dialogue sung in opera style, imagines that in the year 2972 life on earth will have become so homogenized that a group of hardy individualists will plan to escape to another solar system for a fresh start.

ACT I

"Via Galactica" ....Storyteller
"We Are One" ....Blue People
"Helen of Troy" ....Gabriel
"Oysters" ....Hels, April
"The Other Side of the Sky" ....Hels

"Children of the Sun" ....Omaha
"Different" ....April, Company
"Take Your Hat Off" ....Omaha, Company
"Ilmar's Tomb" ....Omaha
"Shall We Friend?" ....Gabriel
"The Lady Isn't Looking" ....Omaha
"Hush" ....Gabriel
"Cross on Over" ....Dr. Isaacs, Omaha, Company
"The Gospel of Gabriel Finn" ....Gabriel

ACT II

"Terre Haute High" ....April
"Life Wins" ....Omaha
"The Worm Germ" ....Provo
"Isaacs' Equation" ....Dr. Isaacs
"Dance the Dark Away!" ....Storyteller, Company
"Four Hundred Girls Ago" ....Gabriel
"All My Good Mornings" ....Omaha
"Isaacs' Equation" (Reprise) ....Dr. Isaacs
"Children of the Sun" (Reprise) ....Omaha, Gabriel
"New Jerusalem" ....Company

The Creation of the World and Other Business (20). By Arthur Miller. Produced by Robert Whitehead in a Dowling-Whitehead-Stevens production at the Sam S. Shubert Theater. Opened November 30, 1972. (Closed December 16, 1972)

Adam	Bob Dishy	Azrael	Lou Polan
God	Stephen Elliott	Lucifer	George Grizzard
Eve	Zoe Caldwell	Cain	Barry Primus
Chemuel	Lou Gilbert	Abel	Mark Lamos
Raphael	Dennis Cooley		

Standbys: Messrs. Grizzard, Elliott—Timothy Jerome; Mr. Dishy—Wayne Carson; Mr. Lamos—Dennis Cooley; Messrs. Primus, Gilbert, Cooley, Polan—Ira Lewis.

Directed by Gerald Freedman; scenery and projections, Boris Aronson; costumes, Hal George; Lighting, Tharon Musser; music, Stanley Silverman; production stage manager, Frederic de Wilde; stage manager, Wayne Carson; press, James D. Proctor.

Act I: Since God Made Everything and God is Good—Why Did He Make Lucifer? Act II: Is There Something in the Way We Are Born Which Makes Us Want the World to Be Good? Act III: When Every Man Wants Justice, Why Does He Go on Creating Injustice?

The story of Adam and his family as a frame for reflections on the nature of good and evil and man's relation to them.

A Best Play; see page 193

The New Phoenix Repertory Company. Repertory of two revivals. **The Great God Brown** (19). By Eugene O'Neill. Opened December 10, 1972. **Don Juan** (22). By Molière; adapted by Stephen Porter. Opened December 11, 1972. Produced by The New Phoenix Repertory Company, T. Edward Hambleton managing director, Harold Prince, Stephen Porter, Michael Montel artistic directors, at the Lyceum Theater. (Repertory closed January 14, 1973)

PERFORMER	"THE GREAT GOD BROWN"	"DON JUAN"
Clyde Burton	Younger Draftsman	Gusman; La Violette
David Dukes	Committeeman	Don Carlos
Peter Friedman	Committeeman	Commander
Bonnie Gallup	Mrs. Brown	Veiled Woman
Robert Ginty		Robber
John Glover		Pierrot
James Greene	Mr. Anthony	Poor Man; Monsieur
Paul Hecht	Mr. Brown	Diamanche

PERFORMER	"THE GREAT GOD BROWN"	"DON JUAN"
Katherine Helmond	Margaret	Don Juan
Curt Karibalis	Policeman	Dona Elvira
John McMartin	Dion Anthony	Don Alonso
Bill Moor	Older Draftsman	Sganarelle
Charlotte Moore	Mrs. Anthony	Don Luis
Robert Phelps	Older Son	Charlotte
Marilyn Sokol	Cybel	La Ramee; Robber
Thomas A. Stewart	Younger Son	Mathurine
Ellen Tovatt	Committeewoman	Ragotin; Robber

BOTH PLAYS—Lighting, Tharon Musser; production stage managers, Daniel Freudenberger, Anne Sullivan; press, Daniel Langan.

THE GREAT GOD BROWN—Understudies: Mr. Glover—David Dukes; Mr. McMartin—Clyde Burton; Messrs. Hecht, Greene—Bill Moor; Misses Gallup, Moore—Ellen Tovatt; Miss Helmond—Charlotte Moore; Miss Sokol—Bonnie Gallup; Men—Robert Ginty.

Directed by Harold Prince; scenery, Boris Aronson; costumes and masks, Carolyn Parker; assistant director, Ruth Mitchell.

Time: 1916-1936. Place: The pier of a casino; Dion Anthony's sitting room; William Brown's office and adjoining drafting room; Cybel's parlor. The play was presented in two parts.

The Great God Brown was first produced 1/23/26 for 271 performances and was named a Best Play of its season. It was revived by the Equity Library Theater in the 1946-47 season and on Broadway by Theater Incorporated 10/6/59 for 32 performances. The play's time has been extended from 1926 through the Depression years to 1936 for this production.

DON JUAN—Understudies: Mr. Hecht—Curt Karibalis; Misses Helmond, Gallup—Ellen Tovatt; Misses Moore, Sokol—Bonnie Gallup; Mr. Dukes—Peter Friedman; Mr. Greene—Thomas A. Stewart; Messrs. Moor, Burton, Karibalis—Robert Phelps; Mr. Glover—Clyde Burton; Messrs. Stewart, Friedman—Robert Ginty.

Directed by Stephen Porter; scenery, John J. Moore; costumes, Nancy Potts; music, Conrad Susa; fight sequence staging, David Dukes.

Place: Act I: The house of Don Juan. Act II: A seashore. Act III: A forest. Act IV: The house of Don Juan. Act V: An open place. The play was presented in two parts with an intermission after Act III.

Recent New York productions of Molière's *Don Juan* (also often entitled *Dom Juan*) were an off-Broadway staging during the 1955-56 season and Broadway presentations in French by the Théâtre National Populaire during the 1958-59 season and the Comédie Française 2/6/70 for 5 performances.

The Last of Mrs. Lincoln (63). By James Prideaux. Produced by Theater 1973 (Richard Barr, Charles Woodward) and the American National Theater and Academy at the ANTA Theater. Opened December 12, 1972. (Closed February 4, 1973)

Senator Austin	Richard Woods	W.H. Brady	Macon McCalman
Robert Lincoln	David Rounds	Young Senator	Dennis Cooney
Tad Lincoln	Tobias Haller	Man	Joseph Attles
Mary Lincoln	Julie Harris	Boy	Marc Jefferson
Ninian Edwards	Ralph Clanton	Lewis Baker	Brian Farrell
Lizzie Keckley	Dorothi Fox	Elizabeth Edwards	Leora Dana
Mary Harlan	Maureen Anderman	Mrs. McCullough	Kate Wilkinson
Mr. Keyes	George Connolly	Attendant	Louis Schaefer

Standbys: Miss Harris—Leora Dana; Mr. Rounds—Dennis Cooney; Misses Dana, Wilkinson—Lois de Banzie; Miss Fox—Urylee Leonardos. Understudies: Miss Anderman—Madelon Thomas; Messrs. Haller, Farrell—George Connolly; Messrs. Clanton, Woods—Macon McCalman.

Directed by George Schaefer; scenery and lighting, William Ritman; costumes, Noel Taylor; associate producer, Michael Kasdan; production stage manager, Mark Wright; stage manager, Charles Kindl; press, Betty Lee Hunt Associates, Henry Luhrman, Harriett Trachtenberg.

Character study of Mary Todd Lincoln during the financially and mentally troubled years of her widowhood. The play was presented in two parts.

* **The Sunshine Boys** (187). By Neil Simon. Produced by Emanuel Azenberg and Eugene V. Wolsk at the Broadhurst Theater. Opened December 20, 1972.

Willie Clark	Jack Albertson	Eddie	John Batiste
Ben Silverman	Lewis J. Stadlen	Sketch Nurse	Leo Meredith
Al Lewis	Sam Levene	Nurse	Minnie Gentry
Patient	Joe Young		

Understudies: Mr. Levene—Clem Fowler; Mr. Stadlen—John Batiste; Messrs. Batiste, Young—George Rando; Miss Gentry—Cynthia Belgrave; Miss Meredith—Darlene Parks.

Directed by Alan Arkin; scenery, Kert Lundell; costumes, Albert Wolsky; lighting, Tharon Musser; stage manager, Tom Porter; press, Solters/Sabinson/Roskin, Inc., Harvey B. Sabinson, Cheryl Sue Dolby.

Time: The present. Place: New York City. The play was presented in two acts.

Comedy, the two aged members of a once-famous comedy team, ten years retired and 11 years feuding, try to get back together again for old times sake and a nostalgic TV appearance.

A Best Play; see page 236

Purlie (14). Revival of the musical based on the play *Purlie Victorious* by Ossie Davis; book by Ossie Davis, Philip Rose and Peter Udell; music by Gary Geld; lyrics by Peter Udell. Produced by Philip Rose at the Billy Rose Theater. Opened December 27, 1972. (Closed January 7, 1973)

Purlie	Robert Guillaume	Gitlow	Sherman Hemsley
Church Soloist	Shirley Monroe	Charlie	Douglas Norwick
Lutiebelle	Patti Jo	Idella	Helen Martin
Missy	Laura Cooper	Ol' Cap'n	Art Wallace

Field Hands: Every Hayes, Lonnie McNeil, Ted Ross.

Dancers: Darlene Blackburn, Deborah Bridges, Raphael Gilbert, Linda Griffin, Every Hayes, Reggie Jackson, Alton Lathrop, Robert Martin, Karen E. McDonald, Lonnie McNeil, Debbie Palmer, Andre Peck, Zelda Pulliam.

Singers: Demarest Grey, Barbara Joy, Ursuline Kairson, Shirley Monroe, Alfred Rage, Beverly G. Robnett, Ted Ross, Frances Salisbury, Vanessa Shaw, David Weatherspoon, Joe Williams Jr.

Standbys: Mr. Wallace—Bill Nunnery; Mr. Norwick—Joe Hammil. Understudies: Mr. Guillaume—Ra Joe Darby; Patti Jo—Demarest Grey, Ursuline Kairson; Mr. Hemsley—Ted Ross, Alfred Rage; Miss Cooper—Beverly G. Robnett, Barbara Joy; Miss Martin—Frances Salisbury; Swing Dancer—Reggie Jackson.

Directed by Philip Rose; choreography, Louis Johnson; scenery, Ben Edwards; costumes, Ann Roth; lighting, Thomas Skelton; orchestrations and choral arrangements, Garry Sherman, Luther Henderson; musical supervisor, Garry Sherman; musical conductor, Charles Austin; dance music arrangements, Luther Henderson; production stage manager, Steven Sweigbaum; stage manager, Lou Rodgers III; press, Merle Debuskey, Maurice Turet.

Purlie was originally produced 3/15/70 for 688 performances.

The list of scenes and musical numbers in *Purlie* appears on page 319 of *The Best Plays of 1969-70*.

Look Away (1). By Jerome Kilty; based on *Mary Todd Lincoln: Her Life and Letters* by Justin G. Turner and Linda Levitt Turner. Produced by Charles B. Bloch in association with Burry Fredrik at the Playhouse Theater. Opened and closed at the evening performance January 7, 1973.

Mary Todd Lincoln	Geraldine Page	Elizabeth Keckley	Maya Angelou

Directed by Rip Torn; scenery and lighting, Ben Edwards; costumes, Jane Greenwood; stage manager, Bernard Pollack; press, Shirley Herz.

Place: The Bellevue Hospital for Insane Persons, Batavia, Ill., during the last night of Mary Todd Lincoln's stay there. The play was presented in two acts.

The President's widow and her dressmaker-confidante discuss the past while preparing to leave the asylum.

Tricks (8). Musical based on Molière's *Les Fourberies de Scapin;* book by Jon Jory; music by Jerry Blatt; lyrics by Lonnie Burstein. Produced by Herman Levin at the Alvin Theater. Opened January 8, 1973. (Closed January 13, 1973)

Property Mistress	Adale O'Brien	Pantanella	Suzanne Walker
Octave	Walter Bobbie	Isabella	Jo Ann Ogawa
Sylvestre	Christopher Murney	Carmella	Lani Sundsten
Scapin	Rene Auberjonois	Gondolier	John Handy
Hyacinthe	Carolyn Mignini	The Commedia:	
Argante	Mitchell Jason	Arlecchino; Lead Singer	Joe Morton
Geronte	Tom Toner	Charlotta	Charlotte Crossley
Leandre	Randy Herron	Ernestina	Ernestine Jackson
Zerbinetta	June Helmers	Shezwae	Shezwae Powell

Musicians: David Frank keyboard; Tom Owen, Jack Cavari guitars; Chuck Spies percussion; William Morimando reed; James Bossy trumpet; Art Koenig bass; Andrew Gottesman, Stanley Karpienia, Myron Roman, Avram Weiss violins.

Standby: Messrs. Auberjonois, Murney—Eric Tavares. Understudies: Messrs. Jason, Toner—Joe Hill; Miss Helmers—Adale O'Brian; Mr. Bobbie—Randy Herron; Mr. Herron—John Handy; Misses Mignini, O'Brien—Susan Dyas; Misses Walker, Sundsten, Ogawa—Vicki Frederick.

Directed by Jon Jory; choreography, Donald Saddler; conductor, David Frank; scenery, Oliver Smith; costumes, Miles White; lighting, Martin Aronstein; orchestrations, Bert De Coteau; dance and incidental music arrangements, Peter Howard; sound, Jack Shearing; associate producer, Samuel Liff; stage manager, Mitchell Erickson; press, Frank Goodman, Arlene Wolf, Margaret Wade.

Irate fathers, lovesick sons, blushing maidens stirred in a comic mix by Molière's tricky Scapin, in and around a modern musical version of a commedia dell'arte-type Venice. Previously produced by Actors Theater of Louisville and the Arena Stage, Washington, D.C.

ACT I

Prologue: "Love or Money" .... Commedia
"Who Was I?" .... Octave, Commedia
"Trouble's a Ruler" .... Scapin, Sylvestre, Octave
"Enter Hyacinthe" .... Octave, Commedia
"Believe Me" .... Octave, Hyacinthe, Commedia
"Tricks" .... Scapin, Sylvestre
"A Man of Spirit" .... Commedia
"Where Is Respect" .... Argante, Geronte
"Somebody's Doin' Somebody All the Time" .... Scapin, Commedia
"A Sporting Man" .... Scapin, Commedia

ACT II

"Scapin" .... Arlecchino
"Anything Is Possible" .... Scapin, Sylvestre
"How Sweetly Simple" .... Hyacinthe, Zerbinetta
"Gypsy Girl" .... Zerbinetta, Commedia
Epilogue: "Life Can Be Funny" .... Company

The Enemy Is Dead (1). By Don Petersen. Produced by Lee Schumer and Morton Wolkowitz at the Bijou Theater. Opened and closed at the evening performance, January 14, 1973.

Leah	Linda Lavin	Mr. Wolfe	Addison Powell
Emmett	Arthur Storch		

Directed by Arthur Sherman; scenery, Kert Lundell; costumes, Joseph G. Aulisi; lighting, Roger Morgan; production stage manager, Elizabeth Stearns; press, Saul Richman.

Time: The present. Act I: A rented summer cottage. Act II: Later that evening.

Man abandons fantasies of aggression and wartime heroism and comes to his senses (and repairs his damaged marriage) when forced to cope with an extreme example of real bigotry.

Don Juan in Hell (24). Revival of the play by George Bernard Shaw. Produced by Lee Orgel and William J. Griffiths at the Palace Theater. Opened January 15, 1973. (Closed February 4, 1973)

Commander	Paul Henreid	Devil	Edward Mulhare
Don Juan	Ricardo Montalban	Dona Ana	Agnes Moorehead

Understudy: Messrs. Henreid, Montalban, Mulhare—Ricard S. Ramos.

Directed by John Houseman; production stage manager, Richard Wessler; stage manager, Ricard S. Ramos; press, Howard Newman, Jeffrey Richards.

The play was presented in two parts.

Don Juan in Hell (the third act of *Man and Superman*) was presented in a staged reading, which was also the form of its Broadway production 10/22/51 for 105 performances and 6/19/62 for 17 performances. It was also produced off Broadway in the season of 1960-61 and as part of *Man and Superman* in the Phoenix production 12/6/64 for 76 performances.

Let Me Hear You Smile (1). By Leonora Thuna and Harry Cauley. Produced by Michael and Barclay Macrae at the Biltmore Theater. Opened and closed at the evening performance, January 16, 1973.

Hannah Heywood	Sandy Dennis	Willy Farmer	Paul B. Price
Neil Heywood	James Broderick		

Directed by Harry Cauley; scenery, Peter Larkin; costumes, Carrie F. Robbins; lighting, Neil Peter Jampolis; production stage manager, Ben Janney; stage manager, Philip Cusack; press, Betty Lee Hunt Associates, Henry Luhrman, Harriett Trachtenberg, Maria C. Pucci.

Time: The present. Place: The Heywood home in a small New Jersey town. The play was presented in three acts.

Comedy about a marriage with the wife viewed at three stages of her life: at 10, 48 and 69 years old.

The Jockey Club Stakes (69). By William Douglas Home. Produced by the John F. Kennedy Center for the Performing Arts at the Cort Theater. Opened January 24, 1973. (Closed March 24, 1973)

Marquis of Candover	Wilfrid Hyde-White	Lord Green	Lee Richardson
Lord Coverly de Beaumont	Geoffrey Sumner	Tom Glass	Christopher Bernau
Col. Sir Robert Richardson	Robert Coote	Charlie Wisden	Dillon Evans
Capt. Trevor Jones	Philip Kerr	Perch Graham	Albert Sanders
Miss Hills	Joan Bassie	Sir Dymock Blackburn, Q.C.	Thayer David
P. Brown	Norman Allen	Lady Green	Enid Rogers
Ladly Ursula Itchin	Carolyn Lagerfelt		

Standbys: Messrs. Coote, Sumner, David—Alexander Reed; Messrs. Richardson, Kerr, Bernau—Jay Lanin; Misses Bassie, Rogers—Ethel Drew.

Directed by Cyril Ritchard; scenery and lighting, Paul Morrison; costumes, Albert Wolsky; produced for Kennedy Center Productions, Inc. by Roger L. Stevens and J. Charles Gilbert, in association with Moe Septee, by arrangement with Peter Saunders, Ltd.; production stage manager, Mikos Kafkalis; press, Michael Sean O'Shea.

Time: The present. Place: The Jockey Club rooms. Act I, Scene 1: A summer morning. Scene 2: The following morning. Act II, Scene 1: Two weeks later, a few days after the York meeting. Scene 2: Not yet 2:30 p.m. the same day.

Comic treatment of British aristocrats muddling through a painful investigation of cheating within their own select Jockey Club circle. A foreign play previously produced in London.

Shelter (31). Musical with book and lyrics by Gretchen Cryer; music by Nancy Ford. Produced by Richard Fields and Peter Flood at the John Golden Theater. Opened February 6, 1973. (Closed March 3, 1973)

Maud	Marcia Rodd	Wednesday November	Susan Browning
Michael	Terry Kiser	Gloria	Joanna Merlin

| Television Crew ....Charles Collins, | Arthur ....Tony Wells |
| Britt Swanson | Voice of the Director ....Philip Kraus |

Not seen:

Standbys: Mr. Kiser—David Snell; Misses Rodd, Merlin—Lucy Martin; Miss Browning—Britt Swanson; Mr. Wells—Charles Collins.

Directed by Austin Pendleton; musical staging, Sammy Bayes; musical direction and vocal arrangements, Kirk Nurock; scenery, costumes and projection design, Tony Walton; lighting and projections, Richard Pilbrow; orchestrations and electronic arrangements, Thomas Pierson; associate producer, Julie Hughes; production manager, John Actman; stage manager, John Andrews; press, Solters/Sabinson/Roskin, Inc., Marilynn LeVine.

Musical fantasy about the women in the life of a TV commercial writer who lives in a TV studio in company with a talking computer named Arthur.

ACT I

Overture ....Arthur
"Changing" ....Maud, Arthur
"Welcome to a New World" ....Michael, Arthur
"It's Hard to Care" ....Michael, Arthur, Maud
"Woke Up Today" ....Maud, Arthur
"Mary Margaret's House in the Country" ....Maud, Arthur
"Woman on the Run" ....Arthur
"Don't Tell Me It's Forever" ....Maud, Michael, Arthur

ACT II

"Sunrise" ....Arthur
"I Bring Him Seashells" ....Wednesday
"She's My Girl" ....Michael, Maud, Arthur
"Welcome to a New World" (Reprise) ....Maud, Michael, Arthur, Wednesday
"He's a Fool ....Wednesday, Maud
"Goin' Home With My Children" ....Maud, Arthur
"Sleep, My Baby, Sleep" ....Arthur

* Finishing Touches (128). By Jean Kerr. Produced by Robert Whitehead and Roger L. Stevens at the Plymouth Theater. Opened February 8, 1973.

Katy Cooper ....Barbara Bel Geddes	Fred Whitten ....Gene Rupert
Jeff Cooper ....Robert Lansing	Steve Cooper ....James Woods
Hughie Cooper ....Scott Firestone	Felicia Andrayson ....Pamela Bellwood
Kevin Cooper ....Oliver Conant	Elsie Ketchum ....Denise Galik

Standbys: Miss Bel Geddes—Martha Randall; Messrs. Lansing, Rupert—Michael Fairman; Misses Bellwood, Galik—Marsha Wishusen; Messrs. Woods, Conant—Brian Brownlee; Master Firestone—Kevin Smith.

Directed by Joseph Anthony; scenery and lighting, Ben Edwards; costumes, Jane Greenwood; production stage manager, Frederic de Wilde; stage manager, Wayne Carson; press, Seymour Krawitz.

Time: The present. Place: The Cooper home in an eastern university town. Act I: Morning. Act II: Late afternoon, the same day. Act III: That evening.

Comedy about marital and family crises becoming critical before being safely passed by a middle-aged professor, his wife and their three sons.

A Best Play; see page 254

Warp I: My Battlefield, My Body (7). By Bury St. Edmund and Stuart Gordon. Produced by Anthony D'Amato in association with The Organic Theater Company at the Ambassador Theater. Opened February 14, 1973. (Closed February 18, 1973 matinee).

Desi Arnez ....André De Shields	Mrs. O'Grady; Psychiatric
Penny Smart; Sargon ....Cordis Fejer	Director; Bank Teller;
Sheila Fantastik ....Jane Fire	Lugulbanda; Yggthion ....Richard Fire

Mary Louise; Valaria ......Carolyn Gordon		Attendant; Young David	
David Carson; Lord Cumulus ...John Heard		Carson ....Keith Szarabajka	
Bank President; Dr. Victor		Janitor; Prince Chaos ....Tom Towles	
Vivian; Symax ....William J. Norris			

Understudies: Female roles—Kathleen Rostrom; male roles—Keith Szarabajka.

Directed by Stuart Gordon; art director, Neal Adams; scenery, Robert Guerra; costumes, Laura Crow, Cookie Gluck; lighting, Jane Reisman, supervised by Neil Peter Jampolis; music, William J. Norris, Richard Fire; visuals, Khamphalous Lightshow; vocal sound effects, Flying Frog; production stage manager, Frank Marino; stage manager, Lynne Guerra; press, Betty Lee Hunt Associates, Henry Luhrman, Harriett Trachtenberg, Maria C. Pucci.

The play was presented in two acts.

A young man's fantasy of himself as a hero launched into outer space to seek and destroy the Prince of Chaos, dramatized as a comic-strip rendition of a science-fiction story. *Warp* is the portmanteau title for a trilogy: *Warp I: My Battlefield, My Body* (this production), *Warp II: SlitherlusT* and *Warp III: To Die . . . Alive!*, all previously produced in Chicago by The Organic Theater Company.

Status Quo Vadis (1). By Donald Driver. Produced by George Keathley and Jack Lenny at the Brooks Atkinson Theater. Opened and closed at the evening performance February 18, 1973.

Mr. Grammerky ....John C. Becher		Don Walgren ....Don Marston	
Horace Elgin ....Bruce Boxleitner		Irene Phillips ....Gail Strickland	
Mrs. Elgin ....Geraldine Kay		Professor Russel ....Kenneth Kimmins	
Mr. Elgin ....Roberts Blossom		Choir Boys ....Sue Renee, Diana Corto	
Laporski ....Charles Welch		Reverend John Purdy ....William Francis	
Reinke ....Ralph Strait		Father Mathais ......Robert E. Thompson	
Paul Regents III ....Ted Danson		Coffman ....James S. Lukas Jr.	
Barbara ....Lee Zara		Sarah ....Katherine Korla	
Joyce Grishaw ....Rebecca Taylor		Detective ....John C. Becher	

Directed by Donald Driver; scenery, Edward Burbridge; costumes, David Toser; lighting, Thomas Skelton; production associate, Joy Welfeld; production stage manager, Murray Gitlin; press, Solters/Sabinson/Roskin, Inc., Marilynn LeVine.

Time: The present. Place: Any familiar city in the United States. The play was presented in two parts.

In a comic fantasy world where everyone wears a status number from 1 to 5 at all times, a brash young Number 5 poet dares to pursue a cool Number 1 heiress (author's program note: "Equality has become our inalienable right to be equal with the people above so we need not be equal with the people below"). Previously produced in Chicago.

No Sex Please, We're British (16). By Anthony Marriott and Alistair Foot. Produced by Tom Mallow by arrangement with John Gale at the Ritz Theater. Opened February 20, 1973. (Closed March 4, 1973)

Peter Hunter ....Stephen Collins		Superintendant Paul ....John Clarkson	
Frances Hunter ..................J.J. Lewis		Delivery Man ....Robert Jundelin	
Brian Runicles ....Tony Tanner		Mr. Needleham ....Leon Shaw	
Eleanor Hunter ....Maureen O'Sullivan		Susan ....Jill Tanner	
Leslie Bromhead ....Ronald Drake		Barbara ....Jennifer Richards	

Standbys: Miss O'Sullivan—Carol Raymont; Messrs. Tanner, Collins—Robert Jundelin; Miss Lewis—Jill Tanner; Mr. Drake—John Clarkson; Messrs. Clarkson, Shaw—Robert Bruce Holley; Miss Tanner—Jennifer Richards.

Directed by Christopher Hewett; scenery, Helen Pond, Herbert Senn; costumes, Jeffrey B. Moss; lighting, John Harvey; production stage manager, Roger Franklin; stage manager, Robert Bruce Holley; press, Max Gendel.

Time: The present. Place: An apartment above a sub branch of the National United Bank in Royal Windsor, England. Act I, Scene 1: 9 a.m. on a Monday in June. Scene 2 Early evening, two days later. Act II: Later the same night.

Respectable couple's home is flooded with pornographic literature, in a comic misunderstanding. A foreign play previously produced in London.

* **A Little Night Music** (109). Musical suggested by Ingmar Bergman's film *Smiles of a Summer Night;* book by Hugh Wheeler; music and lyrics by Stephen Sondheim. Produced by Harold Prince in association with Ruth Mitchell at the Shubert Theater. Opened February 25, 1973.

Mr. Lindquist	Benjamin Rayson	Frederik Egerman	Len Cariou
Mrs. Nordstrom	Teri Ralston	Petra	D. Jamin-Bartlett
Mrs. Anderssen	Barbara Lang	Desiree Armfeldt	Glynis Johns
Mr. Erlanson	Gene Varrone	Malla	Despo
Mrs. Segstrom	Beth Fowler	Bertrand	Will Sharpe Marshall
Fredrika Armfeldt	Judy Kahan	Count Carl-Magnus	
Madame Armfeldt	Hermione Gingold	Malcolm	Laurence Guittard
Frid	George Lee Andrews	Countess Charlotte Malcolm	Patricia Elliott
Henrik Egerman	Mark Lambert	Osa	Sherry Mathis
Anne Egerman	Victoria Mallory		

Standby: Messrs. Cariou, Guittard—Len Gochman. Understudies: Miss Johns—Barbara Lang; Miss Gingold—Despo; Misses Mallory, Kahan—Sherry Mathis; Misses Elliott, Jamin-Bartlett—Beth Fowler; Messrs. Lambert, Andrews—Will Sharpe Marshall.

Directed by Harold Prince; choreography, Patricia Birch; musical direction, Harold Hastings; scenery, Boris Aronson; costumes, Florence Klotz; lighting, Tharon Musser; orchestrations, Jonathan Tunick; production stage manager, George Martin; press, Mary Bryant, Bill Evans.

Time: The turn of the century. Place: Sweden.

Intertwining love affairs in high operetta style, through a northern evening of midnight sun, as in the Ingmar Bergman film on which the libretto is based.

A Best Play; see page 307

ACT I

Overture	Mr. Lindquist, Mrs. Nordstrom, Mrs. Anderseen, Mr. Erlanson, Mrs. Segstrom (Chorus)
"Night Waltz"	Company
"Now"	Fredrik
"Later"	Henrik
"Soon"	Anne, Henrik, Fredrik
"The Glamorous Life"	Fredrika, Desiree, Malla, Madame Armfeldt, Chorus
"Remember?"	Chorus
"You Must Meet My Wife"	Desiree, Fredrik
"Liaisons"	Madame Armfeldt
"In Praise of Women"	Carl-Magnus
"Every Day a Little Death"	Charlotte, Anne
"A Weekend in the Country"	Company

ACT II

"The Sun Won't Set"	Chorus
"It Would Have Been Wonderful"	Fredrik, Carl-Magnus
"Perpetual Anticipation"	Mrs. Nordstrom, Mrs. Segstrom, Mrs. Anderssen
"Send in the Clowns"	Desiree
"The Miller's Son"	Petra
Finale	Company

Out Cry (12). By Tennessee Williams. Produced by David Merrick Arts Foundation and Kennedy Center Productions, Inc. at the Lyceum Theater. Opened March 1, 1973. (Closed March 10, 1973)

Felice	Michael York	Clare	Cara Duff-MacCormick

Standbys: Mr. York—James Keach; Miss Duff-MacCormick—Jane Hallaren.

Directed by Peter Glenville; scenery and lighting, Jo Mielziner; costumes, Sandy Cole; production stage manager, Alan Hall; stage manager, James Keach; press, Harvey B. Sabinson, Sandra Manley.

An actor and actress, brother and sister, stranded by their troupe in a strange theater, act out a two-character play which may also be an examination and confession of their real lives. Previously produced in London, (1967) Chicago and Maine under the title *The Two-Character Play*.

* The Changing Room (100). By David Storey. Produced by Charles Bowden, Lee Reynolds and Isobel Robins in The Long Wharf Production at the Morosco Theater. Opened March 6, 1973.

Harry Riley ....Louis Beachner	Barry Copley ....James Sutorius
Patrick "Patsy"	Jack Stringer ....Richard D. Masur
Walter Turner ....Doug Stender	Bryan Atkinson ....Jack Hummert
Fielding ....Rex Robbins	Billy Spencer ....Mark Winkworth
"Mic" Morley ....Jack Schultz	John Clegg ....Ron Siebert
"Kenny" Kendal ....John Lithgow	Frank Moore ....Alan Castner
Luke ....Jake Dengel	Clifford Owens ....Robert Murch
"Fenny" Gordon Fenchurch ...William Rhys	Danny Crosby ....George Ede
Colin Jagger ....John Tillinger	Tallon ....Peter DeMaio
Trevor ....George Hearn	Sir Frederick Thornton ....William Swetland
Walsh ....Tom Atkins	Mackendrick ....Ian Martin
"Sandy" Sandford ....John Braden	

Standbys: Messrs. Swetland, Beachner, Martin, Ede, Braden—John Beal; Messrs. Siebert, Hummert, Rhys, Castner, Winkworth, DeMaio, Stender—Steve Karp; Messrs. Sutorius, Dengel, Atkins, Robbins, Murch—Jeff David. Understudy: Messrs. Masur, Schultz, Lithgow, Tillinger, Hearn—Edwin J. McDonough.

Directed by Michael Rudman; scenery, David Jenkins; costumes, Whitney Blausen; lighting, Ronald Wallace; production coordinator, Diana Shumlin; production stage manager, Anne Keefe; press, Seymour Krawitz, Patricia Krawitz.

Time: The present. Place: The changing room of a Rugby League team in the North of England. Act I: 1:50 p.m. Act II: 35 minutes later. Act III: After the match.

Realistic presentation of a locker room and its inhabitants, a professional Rugby team, before, during and after a game. A foreign play previously produced in London and at the Long Wharf Theater, New Haven, Conn.

A Best Play; see page 274

42 Seconds From Broadway (1). By Louis Del Grande. Produced by Arthur Cantor at the Playhouse Theater. Opened and closed at the evening performance March 11, 1973.

Mr. Green ....Martin Garner	Dr. Marrow ....James Tolkan
Robin ....Regina Baff	Brenda ....Judith Cohen
John ....Henry Winkler	Liza ....Susan Peretz
Mr. Murino ....Billy Longo	Leo ....Anthony Spina
Mrs. Murino ....Antonia Rey	Mr. Marveltine ....Edward Kovens
Joey; Richard ....Bob Dermer	Mary ....Patti Costa
Mr. Stein ....Michael Vale	Delivery Boy ....John Branon

Directed by Arthur Storch; scenery, William Pitkin; costumes, Glenda Miller; lighting, Roger Morgan; production stage manager, Ted Harris; stage manager, John Branon; press, Beth Trier, C. George Willard.

Time 1957. Act I, Scene 1: A small furnished apartment on West 47th Street. Scene 2: A Hoboken kitchen. Scene 3: The apartment. Act II, Scene 1: The apartment, early the next morning. Scene 2: Dr. Marrow's office. Scene 3: The apartment at night. Scene 4: Mr. Marveltine's office. Scene 5: The apartment, evening.

A young couple's comic problems with career, families and sex.

* Irene (93). Revival of the musical with book by Hugh Wheeler and Joseph Stein; from an adaptation by Harry Rigby; based on the original play by James Montgomery; music by Harry Tierney; lyrics by Joseph McCarthy; additional lyrics and music by Charles Gaynor and Otis Clements. Produced by Harry Rigby, Albert W. Selden and Jerome Minskoff at the Minskoff Theater. Opened March 13, 1973.

Mrs. O'Dare ....Patsy Kelly	Clarkson ....Bob Freschi
Jane Burke ....Janie Sell	Donald Marshall ....Monte Markham
Helen McFudd ....Carmen Alvarez	Ozzie Babson ....Ted Pugh
Jimmy O'Flaherty ....Bruce Lea	Madame Lucy ....George S. Irving
Irene O'Dare ....Debbie Reynolds	Arabella Thornsworthy ....Kate O'Brady
Emmeline Marshall ....Ruth Warrick	

Debutantes: Arlene Columbo, Meg Bussert, Trudy Carson, Carrie Fisher, Dorothy Wyn Gehgan, Frances Ruth Lea, Jeanne Lehman, Kate O'Brady, Julie Pars, Pamela Peadon, Pat Trott, Sandra Voris, Jeannette Williamson, Penny Worth.

Ninth Avenue Fellas: Paul Charles, Dennis Edenfield, David Evans, Bob Freschi, John Hamilton, Bruce Lea, Joe Lorden, Bryan Nicholas, Robert Rayow, Dennis Roth, Kenn Scalice, Ron Schwinn, David Steele, Albert Stephenson.

Standbys: Misses Kelly, Warrick—Justine Johnson; Mr. Irving—Emory Bass. Understudies: Miss Reynolds—Janie Sell; Mr. Markham—Donegan Smith; Miss Sell—Dorothy Wyn Gehgan; Miss Alvarez—Penny Worth; Mr. Pugh—Bob Freschi; Swing Dancers—Frances Ruth Lea, Kenn Scalice.

Directed by Gower Champion; musical numbers staged by Peter Gennaro; musical and vocal direction, Jack Lee; scenery and costumes, Raoul Pène du Bois; Miss Reynolds's costumes, Irene Sharaff; lighting, David F. Segal; orchestrations, Ralph Burns; dance arrangements and incidental music, Wally Harper; sound, Tony Alloy; music consultant and coordinator, Joseph A. McCarthy; associate producer, Constance Montgomery; production stage manager, James Gelb; stage manager, Robert Schear; press, John Springer Associates, Ruth Cage.

The 1919 musical about a male couturier and the colleen who becomes his business associate, updated with revised book and added song numbers. Irene was originally produced on Broadway 11/19/19 for 670 performances.

Ron Husmann replaced Monte Markham 5/31/73.

ACT I

(Titles of songs from the original score of Irene appear below in italics.)

Scene 1: The piano store
"The World Must Be Bigger Than an Avenue" ....Irene
    (music by Wally Harper, lyrics by Jack Lloyd)
Scene 2: The music room of the Marshall estate
"The Family Tree" ....Mrs. Marshall, Debutantes
"Alice Blue Gown" ....Irene
"They Go Wild, Simply Wild, Over Me" ....Madame Lucy, Debutantes
    (lyrics by Joseph McCarthy, music by Fred Fisher)
Scene 3: Ninth Avenue
"An Irish Girl" ....Irene, Company
    (lyrics by Otis Clements, music by Charles Gaynor)
Scene 4: Madame Lucy's salon
"Stepping on Butterflies" ....Madame Lucy, Irene, Helen, Jane
    (music by Wally Harper)
Scene 5: The front of the piano store
"Mother Angel Darling" ....Irene, Mrs. O'Dare
    (by Charles Gaynor)
Scene 6: The Palais Royale
"The Riviera Rage" ....Irene, Company
    (music by Wally Harper)

ACT II

Scene 1: The Palais Royale
"The Last Part of Every Party" ....Company
"We're Getting Away With It" ....Madame Lucy, Helen, Jane, Ozzie
Scene 2: The piano store
"Irene" ....Irene, Company
Scene 3: Outside the marquee tent
"The Great Lover Tango" ....Donald, Helen, Jane
    (music by Otis Clements, lyrics by Charles Gaynor)

"You Made Me Love You" ....Irene, Donald
    (music by James Monaco, lyrics by Joseph McCarthy)
"You Made Me Love You" (Reprise) ....Madame Lucy, Mrs. O'Dare
Scene 4: The Italian garden
    Finale ....Company

* **Seesaw** (86). Musical based on the play *Two for the Seesaw* by William Gibson; written by Michael Bennett; music by Cy Coleman; lyrics by Dorothy Fields. Produced by Joseph Kipness and Lawrence Kasha, James Nederlander, George M. Steinbrenner III and Lorin E. Price at the Uris Theater. Opened March 18, 1973.

Jerry Ryan	Ken Howard	Julio Gonzales	Giancarlo Esposito
Gittel Mosca	Michele Lee	Sparkle	LaMonté Peterson
David	Tommy Tune	Nurse	Judy McCauley
Sophie	Cecelia Norfleet	Ethel	Cathy Brewer-Moore

Citizens of New York: John Almberg, Steve Anthony, Cathy Brewer-Moore, Eileen Casey, Wayne Cilento, Patti D'Beck, Terry Deck, Judy Gibson, Felix Greco, Mitzi Hamilton, Loida Iglesias, Bobby Johnson, Baayork Lee, Amanda McBroom, Judy McCauley, Anita Morris, Gerry O'Hara, Michon Peacock, Frank Pietri, Yolanda Raven, Michael Reed, Orrin Reiley, Don Swanson, William Swiggard, Tom Urich, Dona D. Vaughn, Clyde Walker, Thomas J. Walsh, Chris Wilzak.

Swings: Jerry Yoder, Merel Poloway.

Standby: Miss Lee—Patti Carr.

Directed and choreographed by Michael Bennett; co-choreographer, Grover Dale; musical direction and vocal arrangements, Don Pippin; scenery, Robin Wagner; costumes, Ann Roth; lighting, Jules Fisher; orchestrations, Larry Fallon; dance arrangement supervision, Cy Coleman; media art and photography, Sheppard Kerman; sound, Dick Maitland, Bob Ring, Lou Gonzales; production associate, Charlotte Dicker; associate choreographers, Bob Avian, Tommy Tune; production stage manager, Robert Borod; stage managers, Tony Manzi, Nicholas Russiyan; press, Bill Doll & Company, Dick Williams, Virginia Holden.

Place: New York City.

Gibson's play about the love affair of a young Nebraska attorney with a would-be dancer from the Bronx was first produced on Broadway 1/16/58 for 750 performances.

Mayor John V. Lindsay replaced Ken Howard in the "My City" number for 7 minutes 3/23/73.

ACT I

Prologue
    "Seesaw" ....Company
Times Square area
    "My City" ....Jerry, Neighborhood Girls
Dance studio on West 54th St.
    "Nobody Does It Like Me" ....Gittel
Japanese restaurant on 46th St.; Lincoln Center
    "In Tune" ....Gittel, Jerry
East 116th St.
    "Spanglish" ....Julio Gonzales, Gittel, Jerry, Sophie, Company
Gittel's apartment in the East Village
    "Welcome to Holiday Inn!" ....Gittel
Jerry's apartment
    "You're a Lovable Lunatic" ....Jerry
Gittel's apartment, then the street
    "He's Good for Me" ....Gittel
The Banana Club
    "Ride Out the Storm" ....Sparkle, Sophie, Company
Gittel's apartment

ACT II

St. Vincent's Hospital
    "We've Got It" ....Jerry
    "Poor Everybody Else" ....Gittel

Dance studio
  "Chapter 54, Number 1909" .... David, Jerry, Gittel, Dance Company
Jerry's apartment
Backstage at the theater
  "The Concert" .... Gittel, Dance Company
  "It's Not Where You Start" .... David, Company
Central Park, later that night
Gittel's apartment; phone booth at Kennedy Airport
Gittel's apartment, 2 a.m.
Gittel's apartment; Jerry's apartment, a few days later
  "I'm Way Ahead" .... Gittel
  "Seesaw" (Reprise) .... Gittel

* **The River Niger** (195). By Joseph A. Walker. Produced by The Negro Ensemble Company, Inc. at the Brooks Atkinson Theater. Opened March 27, 1973; see note.

Grandma Wilhelmina Brown . . Frances Foster	Mo .... Neville Richen
Johnny Williams ...... Douglas Turner Ward	Gail .... Saundra McClain
Dr. Dudley Stanton .... Graham Brown	Skeeter .... Charles Weldon
Ann Vanderguild .... Grenna Whitaker	Al .... Dean Irby
Mattie Williams .... Roxie Roker	Jeff Williams .... Les Roberts
Chips .... Lennal Wainwright	

Voice of Lt. Staples: Wyatt Davis. Bass player: Jothan Callins.
General understudies: Taurean Blacque, Barbara Clarke, Arthur French, Louise Heath.
Directed by Douglas Turner Ward; scenery, Gary James Wheeler; costumes, Edna Watson; lighting, Shirley Prendergast; scenery and costume supervision, Edward Burbridge; incidental music, Dorothy Dinroe; production stage manager, Garland Lee Thompson; press, Howard Atlee, Clarence Alsopp, Charles E. House, Chuck Artesona.
Time: The present, early February. Place: Harlem in New York City, the Williams's brownstone on 133d St., between Lenox and 7th Aves. Act I, Scene 1: Friday, 4:30 p.m. Scene 2: After midnight. Act II: Saturday, the next day, 10:45 a.m. Act III, Scene 1: Friday, six days later, early evening. Scene 2: Later that same night.
Several members of a courageous Harlem family, headed by a father who is a poet as well as a house painter, come to grips with the central problem of their lives. The play is dedicated by its author "to my mother and father and to highly underrated black daddies everywhere."
NOTE: *The River Niger* was first presented off Broadway 12/5/72 for 120 performances through 3/3/73 (see its entry in the "Plays Produced off Broadway" section of this volume) before being transferred to Broadway for an additional run.
Arthur French replaced Douglas Turner Ward 5/29/73.
A Best Play; see page 211

Emperor Henry IV (37). Revival of the play by Luigi Pirandello; English translation by Stephen Rich. Produced by S. Hurok in the Elliot Martin production at the Ethel Barrymore Theater. Opened March 28, 1973. (Closed April 28, 1973)

1st Guard .... Michael Diamond	Giovanni .... Douglas Seale
2d Guard .... Thom Christopher	Countess Matilda Spina .... Eileen Herlie
Secret Counselors:	Baron Tito Belcredi .... Paul Hecht
Landolph .... Stephen D. Newman	Dr. Dionysius Genoni .... David Hurst
Berthold .... Reno Roop	Frida .... Linda De Coff
Ordulph .... Michael Durrell	Marquis Carlo Di Nolli .... Rudolph Willrich
Harold .... George Taylor	"Henry IV" .... Rex Harrison

Standbys: Misses Herlie, De Coff—Ruth Hunt. Understudies: Mr. Hecht—Stephen D. Newman; Mr. Hurst—Douglas Seale, Michael Diamond; Mr. Willrich—Thom Christopher; Messrs. Roop, Newman—Thom Christopher, George Boyd; Messrs. Taylor, Durrell—Michael Diamond, George Boyd; Messrs. Seale, Diamond, Christopher—George Boyd.
Directed by Clifford Williams; scenery and costumes, Abd'el Farrah; lighting and scenery supervision, Neil Peter Jampolis; costume supervision and execution, Ray Diffen; production stage manager, William Weaver; stage manager, George Boyd; press, Ben Washer, Rogers, Cowan & Brenner.
Time: 1922. Place: A remote villa in Italy. Act I: The throne room. Act II, Scene 1: The council chamber. Scene 2: The throne room.

Pirandello's play about a nobleman believing himself to be the German Emperor Henry IV— and then maintaining the masquerade even after the delusion has past, because it is so much more comfortable than reality—was produced on Broadway 1/21/24 under the title *The Living Mask*, with Arnold Korff in the leading role. It was produced off Broadway in the seasons of 1946-47 and 1947-48.

Bunraku (17). Puppet theater of Japan presented in the Japanese language. Produced by Kazuko Hillyer in association with City Center of Music & Drama, Inc. under the distinguished patronage of the embassies and consulates general of Japan and the Japan Foundation, in The National Puppet Theater of Japan production, Masahiko Imai executive director, at the City Center 55th Street Theater. Opened April 3, 1973. (Closed April 15, 1973)

Joruri Reciters: Tsudaiyu Takemoto, Tokudaiyo Toyotake, Oritayu Takemoto, Rodaiyu Toyotake, Aiodayu Takemoto, Shimadayu Toyotake.

Samisen Players: Katsutaro Nozawa, Juzo Tsuruzawa, Dohachi Tsuruzawa, Katsuhei Nozawa, Danjiro Takezawa.

Puppet Manipulators: Kamematsu Kiritake, Kanjuro Kiritake, Seijuro Toyomatsu, Minosuke Yoshida, Tamasho Yoshida, Bunsho Yoshida, Tamamatsu Yoshida, Manju Kiritake, Icho Kiritake, Komon Kiritake, Kanju Kiritake, Shojiro Yoshida, Minotaro Yoshida.

Drummer: Haruo Mochizuzi. Stagehands: Kazuo Kawaradani, Mitsuru Ito. Stage Helper: Shoji Nagoshi.

Simultaneous translation, Faubion Bowers; stage manager, George Braun, press, Bill Doll & Company, Inc.

Bunraku, classic puppet theater which dates from the 18th century and was the origin of Kabuki drama, is a blend of stylized narration, samisen accompaniment and the action of three-foot-high puppets. It was last presented on Broadway 3/15/66 for 16 performances.

The repertory on this occasion included the following: *Ehon Taikoki* (The Exploits of the Tycoon), *Nijojo Haizen* (The Insult at Nijo Castle), *Honnoji* (The Rebellion at Honnoji Temple), *Amagasaki* (The Confrontation at Amagazaki), *Shimpan Utazaimon* (The Triangular Love), *Nozakimura* (The Showdown at Nozaki Village) and *Tsuri Onna* (Fishing for Wives).

No Hard Feelings (1). By Sam Bobrick and Ron Clark. Produced by Orin Lehman, Joseph Kipness and Lawrence Kasha at the Martin Beck Theater. Opened and closed at the evening performance April 8, 1973.

George Bartlett	Eddie Albert	Bunny Sutton	Beverly Dixon
Roberta Bartlett	Nanette Fabray	Joanna Wilkins	Stockard Channing
Jimmy Skouras	Conrad Janis	Policeman	Dino Narizzano
Alex Springer	A. Larry Haines	Voice of Judge	Alan Manson
Fred	David Marlow		

Directed by Abe Burrows; scenery and lighting, Robert Randolph; costumes, Theoni V. Aldredge; production stage manager, Lanier Davis; stage managers, David Marlow, Phillip Price; press, Frank Goodman, Arlene Wolf, Susan L. Schulman.

Time: The present. Place: In and around Manhattan and one of its suburbs. The play was presented in two acts.

Comedy about a middle-aged marriage, its breakup and reconciliation.

Marcel Marceau (23). One-man program of pantomime by Marcel Marceau. Produced by Ronald A. Wilford Associates in association with City Center of Music & Drama, Inc. at City Center 55th Street Theater. Opened April 18, 1973. (Closed May 6, 1973)

Presentation of cards, Pierre Verry; stage manager, Antoine Casanova; press, Herbert H. Breslin, Inc., Marvin R. Jenkins, Marvin Schofer.

Marcel Marceau's last New York appearance was 4/7/70 at the City Center for 23 performances.

In this engagement each program consisted of selections from the following Marceau repertory:

Style Pantomimes: Walking, Walking Against the Wind, The 1,500 Meter, The Staircase, The Tight Rope Walker, The Side Show, The Public Garden, The Bill Poster, The Kite, The Man and His Boat, The Magician, The Sculptor, The Painter, The Cage, Remembrances, A Sunday Walk, The Bureaucrats, Luna Park, The Hands, Contrasts, The Maskmaker, The Seven Deadly Sins, Youth, Maturity, Old Age and Death, the Japanese Pantomimes, The Duel in Darkness, The Tango Dancer, The Small Cafe, The Dice Players, The Dream, The Creation of the World, The Four Seasons, Shadow and Light, The Dress Dealer, The Trial.

Bip Pantomimes: Bip and the Bumble Bee, Bip in the Subway, Bip Travels by Train, Bip Travels by Sea, Bip as a Skater, Bip Hunts Butterflies, Bip Plays David and Goliath, Bip at the Ballroom, Bip Commits Suicide, Bip as a Soldier, Bip at a Society Party, Bip as a Street Musician, Bip as a China Salesman, Bip as a Fireman, Bip as a Baby-Sitter, Bip as a Jeweler Apprentice, Bip as a Professor of Botany, Bip as a Tailor in Love, Bip as a Matador, Bip Dreams He Is Don Juan, Bip in an audition, Bip and the Dynamite, Bip as a Lion Tamer, Bip, Illusionist, Bip Looks for a Job, Bip in the Modern and Future Life, Bip is a Pastry-Cook, Bip Plays Don Quixote, Bip, the Bank Employee, Dreams of a Better World.

* The Women (42). Revival of the play by Clare Boothe Luce. Produced by Jeremy Ritzer and Joel Key Rice in association with John W. Merriam and Milton Moss at the 46th Street Theater. Opened April 25, 1973.

Peggy (Mrs. John Day) . . . . . . Marian Hailey	Trimmerback; 2d Girl . . . . . Elizabeth Perry
Nancy Blake . . . . Mary Louise Wilson	Shirley; Princess Tamara;
Jane . . . . Regina Ress	1st Girl . . . . Jeanne De Baer
Edith (Mrs. Phelps Potter) .Dorothy Loudon	Mudmask; 1st Model . . . . Lynne Stuart
Sylvia (Mrs. Howard Fowler) . .Alexis Smith	Little Mary . . . . Cynthia Lister
Mary (Mrs. Stephen Haines) . . . .Kim Hunter	Mrs. Morehead . . . . Myrna Loy
Mrs. Wagstaff; Sadie . . . . . . .Camila Ashland	2d Girl; Mat Girl;
Olga; Dowager . . . . .Bobo Lewis	Debutante . . . . .Connie Forslund
1st Hairdresser; Exercise Instructress;	Miss Shapiro . . . . .Patricia Wheel
1st Woman . . . . .Claudette Sutherland	Miss Curtis; Lucy . . . . .Polly Rowles
2d Hairdresser; 2d Model;	Crystal Allen . . . . .Marie Wallace
Cigarette Girl . . . . .Louise Shaffer	Fitter; Miss Watts; 2d Woman . . .Leora Dana
Pedicurist; 1st Girl; Helene;	Nurse . . . . .Doris Dowling
Girl in Distress . . . . .Caryll Coan	Countess De Lage . . . . .Jan Miner
Customer; 3d Model; Miss	Miriam Aarons . . . . .Rhonda Fleming

General understudies, one or more roles: Camila Ashland, Caryll Coan, Leora Dana, Toni Darney, Jeanne De Baer, Doris Dowling, Connie Forslund, Susan Jayne, Elizabeth Perry, Louise Shaffer, Lynne Stuart.

Directed by Morton Da Costa; scenery, Oliver Smith; costumes, Ann Roth; lighting, John Gleason; costume supervision, Ray Diffen; associate producers, Michael Frazier, William L. Livingston; produced by arrangement with Lester Osterman productions (Lester Osterman, Richard Horner); production stage manager, Victor Straus; stage managers, Nick Malekos, Suzanne Egan; press, Shirley Herz, Stuart Fink.

Time: The mid-30s. Act I, Scene 1: Mary Haines's living room, a winter afternoon. Scene 2: A hairdresser's, an afternoon a few days later. Scene 3: Mary's boudoir, an hour later. Scene 4: A fitting room, an afternoon two months later. Scene 5 :An exercise room, two weeks later. Scene 6: Mary's living room, a month later. Act II: Scene 1: A hospital room, a month later. Scene 2: A Reno hotel room, a few weeks later. Scene 3: Crystal's bedroom, early evening, two years later. Scene 4: Mary's bedroom, 11:30 the same night. Scene 5: The Powder Room at the Casino Roof, near midnight, the same night.

The Women was originally produced on Broadway 12/26/37 for 657 performances and was named a Best Play of its season.

The Play's the Thing (87). By Ferenc Molnar; adapted by P.G. Wodehouse. Produced by Robert J. Gibson and The Roundabout Theater Company, Gene Feist producing director, Michael Fried executive director, at the Bijou Theater. Opened May 7, 1973; see note. (Closed May 26, 1973)

Sandor Turai . . . . .Hugh Franklin	Almady .Neil Flanagan
Mansky . . . . .Humphrey Davis	Johann Dwornitschek . . . . . . .Fred Stuthman
Albert Adam . . . . .David Dukes	Mell .Philip Campanella
Ilona Szabo . . . . .Elizabeth Owens	

Directed by Gene Feist; scenery, Holmes Easley; costumes, Mimi Maxmen; lighting, R.S. Winkler; original score, Philip Campanella; lighting and costume supervision, Holmes Easley; production stage manager, John Hagan; press, The Merlin Group, Ltd., Cheryl Sue Dolby, Sandra Manley.

Time: A Saturday in the summer of 1926. Place: The Italian Riviera. Act I: 2 a.m. Act II: 7 a.m. Act III: 7:30 p.m.

NOTE This production of *The Play's the Thing* was first presented by The Roundabout Theater Company off Broadway at the Roundabout Theater 1/9/73-3/4/73 for 64 performances (see its entry in the "Plays Produced off Broadway" section of this volume), before being transferred to Broadway for an additional run of 23 performances.

* **Cyrano** (22). Musical with book based on Anthony Burgess's adaptation of *Cyrano de Bergerac* by Edmond Rostand; music by Michael J. Lewis; lyrics by Anthony Burgess. Produced by Richard Gregson and Apjac International at the Palace Theater. Opened May 13, 1973.

Candle Lighter; Cyranno's	Ladies of the French Academy:
Page; Boy ....Paul Berget	Mme. de Guemene ....Janet McCall
Candle Lighter; Actor ....Anthony Inneo	Barthenoide ....Patricia Roos
Doorman ....Bob Heath	Felixerie ....Mimi Wallace
Foodseller ....Tovah Feldshuh	Urimedonte ....Mary Straten
Marquis in Yellow ....Danny Villa	Le Bret ....James Blendick
Musketeer ....Michael Nolan	Roxana.....................Leigh Beery
Cavalryman ....Donovan Sylvest	Roxana's Duenna;
Pickpocket; Capuchine Monk .Geoff Garland	Sister Marthe ....Anita Dangler
Citizen ....James Rchardson	Count de Guiche ....Louis Turenne
Citizen's Brother; Boy;	Viscount de Valvert ....J. Kenneth Campbell
Cyrano's Page ....Tom Nissen	Actor ....Richard Schneider
Marquis in Red ....Alexander Orfaly	Actresses ....Vicki Frederick, Jill Rose
Marquis in Beige ....Joel Craig	Jodelet ....Michael Goodwin
Ragueneau ....Arnold Soboloff	Montfleury ....Patrick Hines
Christian de Neuvillette ....Mark Lamos	Cyrano de Bergerac ...Christopher Plummer
Mme. Aubry; Lise; Sister	Theophraste Renaudot ......George Spelvin
Marguerite ....Betty Leighton	Sister Claire ....Patricia Roos

Bakery Staff: J. Kenneth Campbell, Geoff Garland, Janet McCall, Michael Nolan, James Richardson, Patricia Roos, Mary Straten. Gascon Cadets and Soldiers: J. Kenneth Campbell, Joel Craig, Michael Goodwin, Bob Heath, Anthony Inneo, Gale McNeeley, Michael Nolan, James Richardson, Richard Schneider, Donovan Sylvest, Danny Villa. Nuns: Tovah Feldshuh, Vicki Frederick, Janet McCall, Jill Rose, Mary Straten, Mimi Wallace.

Understudies: Miss Beery—Janet McCall; Messrs. Blendick, Turenne—William Metzo; Miss Dangler—Betty Leighton; Mr. Campbell—Anthony Inneo.

Directed by Michael Kidd; musical direction, Thomas Pierson; scenery, John Jensen; costumes, Desmond Heeley; lighting, Gilbert V. Hemsley Jr.; orchestrations, Philip Lang; sound design, Abe Jacob; incidental music arrangements, Clay Fullum; duelling scenes staging, Patrick Crean, Erik Fredericksen; assistant to Mr. Kidd, Gary Menteer; production stage manager, Robert D. Currie; stage managers, Christopher Kelly, Lani Ball; press, Gifford/Wallace, Inc., Tom Trenkle.

Time: 1640-1654. Place: Paris. Scene 1: A theater. Scene 2: Ragueneau's bakery. Scene 3: The balcony of Roxana's house. Scene 4: A battle camp near Arras. Scene 5: A convent, Paris, 14 years later. The play was presented in two parts, with an intermission following Scene 2.

Rostand's brilliant play presented here with musical interludes which show great respect for the original material and never dominate it. *Cyrano de Bergerac* was last produced in New York by the Repertory Theater of Lincoln Center in a new version by James Forsyth 4/25/68 for 42 performances.

ACT I

"Cyrano's Nose" ....Cyrano
"La France, La France" ....Company
"Tell Her" ....Le Bret, Cyrano
"From Now Till Forever" ....Cyrano, Company
"Bergerac" ....Cyrano, Roxana

"Pocapdedious" ....Cadets
"No, Thank You" ....Cyrano
"From Now Till Forever" (Reprise) ....Cyrano, Christian

ACT II

"Roxana" ....Christian, Company
"It's She and It's Me" ....Christian
"You Have Made Me Love" ....Roxana
"Thither, Thother, Thide of the" ....Cyrano
"Pocapdedious" (Reprise) ....Le Bret, Cadets
"Paris Cuisine" ....Cyrano, Le Bret, Cadets
"Love Is Not Love" ....Roxana
"Autumn Carol" ....Roxana, Nuns
"I Never Loved You" ....Cyrano

* **Nash at Nine** (18). Musical revue with verses and lyrics by Ogden Nash; conceived by Martin Charnin; music by Milton Rosenstock. Produced by Les Schecter and Barbara Schwei in association with SRO Enterprises and Arnold Levy, at the Helen Hayes Theater. Opened May 17, 1973.

Steve Elmore	Richie Schechtman
Bill Gerber	Virginia Vestoff
E.G. Marshall	

Standbys: Messrs. Marshall, Elmore—John Stratton; Miss Vestoff—June Gable; Messrs. Gerber, Schechtman—Jess Richards.

Directed by Martin Charnin; musical direction, Karen Gustafson; scenery, David Chapman; costumes, Theoni V. Aldredge; lighting, Martin Aronstein; orchestrations and musical supervision, John Morris; production associate, Michael Hoover; production stage manager, Janet Beroza; stage manager, Mary Porter Hall; press, Frank Goodman, Arlene Wolf, Susan L. Schulman.

A collection of Ogden Nash lyrics and poems presented without intermission and covering the following works of Nash: *Seaside Serenade; Farenheit Gesundheit; The Sniffle; Coefficients of Expansion (A Guide to the Infant Season); To a Small Boy Standing on My Shoes While I Am Wearing Them; The Madcap Zoologist; The Panther; The Armadillo; The Canary; The Shrew; Experiment Degustatory; The Pig; A Bulletin Has Just Come In; The Fly; The Octopus; The Eel; The Kipper; The Clam; The Guppy; Barmaids Are Diviner Than Mermaids; But I Could Not Love Thee, Ann, So Much, Loved I Not Honoré More; The Armchair Golfer, or, Whimpers of A Shortchanged Viewer; Song of the Open Road; From an Antique Land; Any Milleniums Today, Lady?; Give-Away, Give-Away, Banker Man; I Will Arise and Go Now; Always Marry an April Girl; The Anniversary; Love Under the Republicans (or Democrats); A Word to Husbands; I'm Sure She Said Six-Thirty; To My Valentine; Reflections on Ice-Breaking; I Do, I Will, I Have; The Private Dining Room; One Third of a Calendar; Tin Wedding Whistle; What's in a Name? Here's What's in a Name, or, I Wonder What Became of John and Mary?; No Trouble at All, It's as Easy as Falling off a Portable Bar; Grandpa Is Ashamed; A Brief Guide to New York; Requiem; The Pizza; All Quiet Along the Potomac, Except the Letter G; Shrinking Song; Suppose I Darken Your Door; You and Me and P.B. Shelley; Come, Come, Kerouac! My Generation Is Beater Than Yours; The Clean Platter; Coffee With the Meal; The Middle; The Return; Peekaboo, I Almost See You; Modest Meditations on the Here, the Heretofore, and the Hereafter; Birthday on the Beach; A Lady Thinks She Is Thirty; Crossing the Border; For a Good Dog.*

* **Smith** (14). Musical with book by Dean Fuller, Tony Hendra and Matt Dubey; music and lyrics by Matt Dubey and Dean Fuller. Produced by Jordan Hott with Robert Anglund, Iris Kopelan, Jack Millstein and Alexander Bedrosian at the Eden Theater. Opened May 19, 1973.

Melody Hazleton	Virginia Sandifur	Pilot; Prompter; Vice President	
Walter Smith	Don Murray	of Slimeroonie	David Horwitz
Ed Baggett	Mort Marshall	Ralph	Louis Criscuolo
Mrs. Smith; Irish Maid	Carol Morley	Jacques the Frenchman	Michael Tartel

Policeman; Ernie . . . . .William James
Policeman; Bruce . . . . .David Vosburgh
Chief Punitana . . . . .Guy Spaull
Servant; Herbie . . . . .Don Prieur

The Dancing Melody . . . . . . .Bonnie Walker
Sinclair Firestone . . . . .Ted Thurston
Doublemint . . . . .Kenneth Henley
Sydney Jones . . . . .Patricia Garland

Island Beauties: Renee Baughman, Patricia Garland, Penelope Richards, Bonnie Walker.
Hangers On: Nicholas Dante, Aurelio Padron, Kenneth Henley.

Singing Ensemble: Bonnie Hinson, Jacqueline Johnson, Betsy Ann Leadbetter, Shirley Lemmon, David Horwitz, William James, Don Prieur, David Vosburgh.

Dancing Ensemble: Renee Baughman, Patricia Garland, Penelope Richards, Bonnie Walker, John Cashman, Nicholas Dante, Kenneth Henley, Aurelio Padron.

Directed by Neal Kenyon; choreography, Michael Shawn; musical direction, Richard Parrinello; scenery, Fred Voelpel; costumes, Winn Morton; lighting, Martin Aronstein; orchestrations, Jonathan Tunick; dance arrangements, John Berkman; choral arrangements, Dean Fuller; assistant choreographer, Bonnie Walker; sound and effects, Peter J. Fitzgerald; production stage manager, William Dodds; stage managers, Marnel Sumner, Bonnie Walker; press, Saul Richman, Sara Altshul.

Time: The present. Place: Baggett Nitrates, Tenafly, New Jersey.

Hard-working botanist finds himself projected into a new identity as the hero of a musical comedy, from which he cannot escape.

ACT I

"Boy Meets Girl" . . . . .Ensemble
"There's a Big Job Waiting for You" . . . . .Baggett, Ensemble
"There's a Big Job Waiting for You" (Reprise) . . . . .Mrs. Smith
"To the Ends of the Earth" . . . . .Melody, Passengers
"Balinasia" . . . . .Island Beauties
"Onh-Honh-Honh!" . . . . .Jacques
"Police Song" . . . . .Policemen
"You Need a Song" . . . . .Ralph, Smith, Herbie, Bruce, Ernie
"How Beautiful It Was" . . . . .Melody, Smith, The Dancing Melody
"Island Ritual" . . . . .Ensemble
"People Don't Do That" . . . . .Smith

ACT II

"You're in New York Now" . . . . .Ensemble
"It Must Be Love" . . . . .Smith, Melody, Ensemble
"Song of the Frog" . . . . .Firestone, Smith, Baggett
"G'bye" . . . . .Melody
"Melody" . . . . Smith, Company
"It Must Be Love" (Reprise) . . . . .Smith, Melody

PLAYS WHICH CLOSED
PRIOR TO BROADWAY OPENING

Plays which were organized in New York for Broadway presentation, but which closed during their tryout performances, are listed below.

Halloween. Musical with book and lyrics by Sidney Michaels based on his play *Saltpeter in the Rhubarb;* music by Mitch Leigh. Produced by Albert W. Selden and Jerome Minskoff in a pre-Broadway tryout at the Bucks County Playhouse, New Hope, Pa. Opened September 20, 1972. (Closed October 1, 1972)

Charley Beddoes . . . . .David Wayne
Lieberwitz . . . . .Dick Shawn

Victoria Bascombe . . . . .Margot Moser
Doctor . . . . .William Simington

Goblins: Billy Barty, Louis de Jesus, Richard Godouse, Tommy Madden, Jerry Maren, Yvonne Moray, Felix Silla, Emory Souza. Attendants: John Favorite, Dennis M. Fitzpatrick.

Directed by Albert Marre; choreography, Bert Michaels; musical direction, John Lesko; scenery and lighting, Howard Bay; costumes, Juliellen Weiss; orchestrations, Carlyle Hall; coordinator, James Gelb; press, John Springer Associates, Ruth Cage, Ted Goldsmith.

A patient in a mental institution imagines himself in various colorful locales and situations. The play was presented in two acts.

Comedy. Musical with book by Lawrence Carra; music and lyrics by Hugo Peretti, Luigi Creatore and George David Weiss. Produced by Edgar Lansbury, Stuart Duncan and Joseph Beruh in a pre-Broadway tryout at the Colonial Theater in Boston. Opened November 6, 1972. (Closed November 18, 1972)

Great Magician ....Merwin Goldsmith	Melbi ....Marty Morris
Capitano Cockalorum ......George S. Irving	Sireno ....George Lee Andrews
Coviello ....Joseph Bova	Clori ....Suellen Estey
Pantalone ....Joseph R. Sicari	Elpino ....John Witham
Pulcinella ....Bill McCutcheon	Bacchus ....Marc Jordan
Doctor Gratiano ....Jerry Sroka	Bacchantes ...Marilyn Saunders, Lana Shaw
Franceschina ....Diane Findlay	Country Fellow ....Thom Christoph
Zanni ....Frank Vohs	Soundman ....Bobby Lee

Directed by Lawrence Carra; musical numbers staged by Stephen Reinhardt; musical director, Joseph Stecko; scenery and costumes, William Pitkin; lighting, Roger Morgan; sound, Astral Acoustics; orchestrations, Jack Andrews; arrangements, Mel Marvin; production stage manager, Gigi Cascio; press, Gifford/Wallace, Inc.

Place: The Island of Arcadia.

Billed as "a musical commedia," based on a commedia dell'arte outline entitled *The Great Magician,* written by Basillio Locatelli in 1622.

ACT I

"Comedy" ....Troupe
"Open Your Heart" ....Elpino, Sireno, Zanni
"I'm the Cockalorum" ....Capitano, Covielli, Zanni
"Gotta Hang My Wash Out to Dry" ....Franceschina, Elpino, Sireno, Zanni,
                                                  Country Fellow, Soundman
"A Friend Is a Friend" ....Pantalone, Pulcinella, Doctor
"Where Is My Love" ....Clori, Melbi
"Sacrifice" ....Bacchus, Bacchantes
"God Bless the Fig Tree" ....Franceschina
"Tarantella" ....Clori, Doctor
"Buttercup" ....Coviello, Franceschina, Troupe
Finale ....Troupe
Entr'act: "Smile, Smile, Smile" ....Soundman, Troupe

ACT II

"Magnetic" ....Capitano, Melbi, Bacchantes
"Love Is Such a Fragile Thing" ....Sireno, Clori, Melbi, Elpino
"Breakin' the Spell" ....Doctor, Franceschina, Zanni, Pantalone
"Whirlwind Circle" ....Troupe
Finale: Reprise of "Comedy" ....Troupe

Detective Story. Revival of the play by Sidney Kingsley. Produced by Theater 1973 (Richard Barr, Charles Woodward) in the Harold J. Kennedy production in a pre-Broadway tryout at the Paramus, N.J. Playhouse and the Shubert Theater, Philadelphia, Pa. Opened February 18, 1973. (Closed in Philadelphia March 24, 1973)

Detective Dakis ....Anthony Manionis	Joe Feinson ....Marty Brill
Shoplifter ....Rita Moreno	Detective Callahan ....Jack Collard
Detective Gallagher ....Walter Flanagan	Detective O'Brien ....Allen Williams
Patrolman Keogh ....Eddie Jones	Detective Brody ....Paul Lipson
Mrs. Farragut ....Doro Merande	Endicott Sims ....Harold J. Kennedy

Detective McLeod .... Barry Nelson	Miss Hatch .... Rita Gam
Arthur Kindred .... Kipp Osborne	Mr. Gallantz .... Macon McCalman
Patrolman Barnes .... Freeman Roberts	Patrolman Baker .... Neil Alan
1st Burglar .... Marc Alaimo	Mr. Prichett .... Charles White
2d Burglar .... Philip Larson	Mary McLeod .... Nancy Dussault
Mrs. Bagatelle .... Erica Yohn	Tami Giacoppetti .... Charles Siebert
Dr. Schneider .... Robert Strauss	Photographer .... J. Patrick Flynn
Lt. Monoghan .... James Pritchett	Lady .... Helen Noyes
Susan Carmichael .... Maureen Anderman	Indignant Citizen .... Marilynn Brodnick

Directed by Harold J. Kennedy; scenery and lighting, William Ritman; costumes, Nancy Potts; associate producer, Michael Kasdan; production stage manager, Bruce Blaine; stage manager, Allen Williams; press, Betty Lee Hunt Associates, Henry Luhrman, Harriett Trachtenberg, Maria C. Pucci.

Time: 1949. Place: The detective squad room of a New York precinct police station. Act I: A day in August, 5:30 p.m. Act II: 7:30 p.m. Act III: 8:30 p.m.

Detective Story was first produced 3/29/49 for 581 performances and was named a Best Play of its season.

PLAYS PRODUCED
OFF BROADWAY

Some distinctions between off-Broadway and Broadway productions at one end of the scale and off-off-Broadway productions at the other end were beginning to blur in the New York theater of the 1970s. For the purposes of this *Best Plays* listing, the term "off Broadway" signifies a show which opened for general audiences in a mid-Manhattan theater seating 299 or fewer during the time period covered by this volume and 1) employed an Equity cast, 2) planned a regular schedule of 7 or 8 performances a week and 3) offered itself to public comment by critics at opening performances.

Occasional exceptions of inclusion (never of exclusion) are made to take in visiting troupes and a few non-qualifying productions which readers might expect to find in this list because they appear under an off-Broadway heading in other major sources of record.

Figures in parentheses following a play's title indicate number of performances. These figures are acquired directly from the production office in each case and do not include previews or extra non-profit performances.

Plays marked with an asterisk (*) were still running on June 1, 1973. Their number of performances is figured from opening night through May 31, 1973.

In a listing of a show's numbers—dances, sketches, musical scenes, etc.— the titles of songs are identified by their appearance in quotation marks (").

Most entries of off-Broadway productions that ran fewer than 20 performances are somewhat abbreviated.

HOLDOVERS FROM PREVIOUS SEASONS

Plays which were running on June 1, 1972 are listed below. More detailed information about them appears in previous *Best Plays* volumes of appropriate years. Important cast changes are recorded in a section of this volume.

* **The Fantasticks** (5,443; longest continuous run of record in the American theater). Musical suggested by the play *Les Romantiques* by Edmond Rostand; book and lyrics by Tom Jones; music by Harvey Schmidt. Opened May 3, 1960.

Jacques Brel Is Alive and Well and Living in Paris (1,847). Cabaret revue based on lyrics and commentary by Jacques Brel; music by Jacques Brel; production conception, English lyrics and additional material by Eric Blau and Mort Shuman. Opened January 22, 1968. (Closed July 2, 1972; transferred to Broadway September 15, 1972; see its entry in the "Plays Produced on Broadway" section of this volume)

* **One Flew Over the Cuckoo's Nest** (914). Revival of the play by Dale Wasserman. Opened March 23, 1971.

* **The Proposition** (860). Improvisational revue conceived by Allan Albert. Opened March 4, 1971; order and method of presentation somewhat rearranged for "new" editions beginning September 16, 1971 and September 13, 1972.

* **Godspell** (850). Musical based on the Gospel according to St. Matthew; conceived by John-Michael Tebelak; music and lyrics by Stephen Schwartz. Opened May 17, 1971.

Walk Together Children (89). One-woman show arranged, adapted and performed by Vinie Burrows. Opened March 16, 1972. (Closed July 2, 1972)

The Beggar's Opera (253). Revival of the musical by John Gay; musical score newly realized by Ryan Edwards. Opened March 21, 1972. (Closed April 16, 1972 after 29 performances) Reopened May 30, 1972. (Closed December 10, 1972 after 224 additional performances)

Small Craft Warnings (200). By Tennessee Williams. Opened April 2, 1972. (Closed September 17, 1972)

And They Put Handcuffs on the Flowers (172). By Fernando Arrabal; English translation by Charles Marowitz; revised by Lois Messerman. Opened April 21, 1972. (Closed September 24, 1972)

* **The Real Inspector Hound** and **After Magritte** (460). Program of two one-act plays by Tom Stoppard. Opened April 23. 1972.

New York Shakespeare Festival Public Theater. 1971-72 schedule of seven programs continued with **That Championship Season** (144). By Jason Miller. Opened May 2, 1972. (Closed September 3, 1972 after 144 performances; transferred to Broadway September 14, 1972; see its entry in the "Plays Produced on Broadway" section of this volume) **Older People** (49). By John Ford Noonan. Opened May 14, 1972. (Closed June 25, 1972). **The Hunter** (64). By Murray Mednick. Opened May 23, 1972. (Closed July 16, 1972)

Anna K. (199). Variations of Tolstoy's *Anna Karenina* conceived by Eugenie Leontovich. Opened May 7, 1972. (Closed December 10, 1972)

The Negro Ensemble Company. 1971-72 schedule of three programs concluded with **Frederick Douglass . . . Through His Own Words** (32). Program based on the play by Arthur Burghardt and Michael Egan; adapted from the writings of Frederick Douglass. Opened May 9, 1972. (Closed June 4, 1972)

Jamimma (48). Martie Evans-Charles. Opened May 15, 1972. (Closed June 25, 1972)

Hark! (152). Musical revue with music by Dan Goggin and Marvin Solley; lyrics by Robert Lorick. Opened May 22, 1972. (Closed October 1, 1972)

One for the Money (23). Revival of selected excerpts from musical revues with sketches and lyrics by Nancy Hamilton; music by Morgan Lewis. Opened May 24, 1972. (Closed June 11, 1972)

The American Place Theater. 1971-72 schedule of three programs concluded with **The Chickencoop Chinaman** (26). By Frank Chin. Opened May 27, 1972. (Closed June 24, 1972)

PLAYS PRODUCED JUNE 1, 1972—MAY 31, 1973

Buy Bonds, Buster! (1). Musical based on an original concept by Bob Miller and Bill Conklin; book and music by Jack Holmes; lyrics by M.B. Miller. Produced by Wit's End at the Theater de Lys. Opened and closed at the evening performance June 4, 1972.

Directed by John Bishop; musical numbers staged by Bick Goss; musical direction, Shelly Markham; scenery, William Pitkin; lighting, William Strom; production stage manager, Robert Buzzell; press, Saul Richman, Sara Altshul. With William Dalton, Phil Erickson, Suellen Estey, Jay Gregory, Winston DeWitt Hemsley, Pamela Hunt, Virginia Martin, Rick Podell, Jane Robertson, Rowena Rollins, Frank Root.

Nostalgic musical takeoff of the troop-entertaining, war-bond-driving activities of the early 1940s. Previously produced in Atlanta, Ga.

They Don't Make 'Em Like That Anymore (32). Cabaret revue with music, lyrics and sketches by Hugh Martin and Timothy Gray. Produced by Costas Omero in the Timothy Gray-William Justus production at Plaza 9 Music Hall. Opened June 8, 1972. (Closed June 25, 1972)

Arthur Blake	Luba Lisa
Kevin Christopher	Gene McCann
Dell Hanley	Phoebe Otis
Clay Johns	Paris Todd

Directed by Timothy Gray; costumes, E. Huntington Parker, Stephen Chandler; decor, Don Gordon; lighting, Beverly Emmons; stage manager, Clay Johns; press, Bill Doll and Co., Inc.

Revue devised for impressionist Arthur Blake as Ethel Barrymore, Bette Davis, Tallulah Bankhead, Noel Coward, Marlene Dietrich, James Stewart, etc.

ACT I: "They Don't Make 'Em Like That Anymore"—Luba Lisa, Phoebe Otis, Kevin Christopher, Dell Hanley, Clay Johns, Gene McCann, Paris Todd; "Something Tells Me"—Company; Sorry Wrong Valley—Arthur Blake, Johns, Hanley; "What's His Name"—Miss Lisa; "Once in Love With Amy"—Christopher, Miss Lisa; Harvey—Blake, Miss Otis; The Architect—McCann; "Lili Marlene"—Company; "I Lost You"—Miss Otis; "Mad About the Boy"—Blake, Misses Lisa, Otis; Swanislavsky—Blake, Christopher, Todd, Misses Lisa, Otis; "Get Me Out of Here"—Company.

ACT II: "Buckle Down Winsocki"—Hanley, Johns, Christopher, McCann, Todd, Misses Lisa, Otis; Paradise Lost—Blake; "Judy"—Miss Otis; Drama Quartet—Blake; "Oscar"—Christopher, Hanley, McCann, Todd, Miss Lisa; Sunset Boulevard—Blake, McCann, Christopher, Hanley, Todd, Miss Otis; "Frankie and Johnnies"—Blake, Christopher, Johns, McCann, Todd; Invisible Man—Blake, Miss Lisa; Silence Is Golden—Misses Otis, Lisa; Show Girl, Disraeli, Victoria—Blake; "Something Tells Me" (finale)—Company; "The Party's Over Now"—Blake.

The Sunshine Train (224). Gospel musical conceived by William E. Hunt. Produced by Jay Sessa at the Abbey Theater. Opened June 15, 1972. (Closed December 17, 1972)

The Gospel Starlets:	The Carl Murray Singers:
Mary Johnson	Carl Murray
Dottie Coley	Ron Horton
Peggie Henry	Ernest McCarroll
Barbara Davis	Joe Ireland
Gladys Freeman	Larry Coleman
Clara Walker	

Directed by William E. Hunt; musical direction, Louis Hancock, Howard Nealy; scenery and lighting, Philip Gilliam; press, Saul Richman.

Ninety-minute program of Gospel songs.

Joan (64). Musical with book, music and lyrics by Al Carmines. Produced by Circle in the Square, Theodore Mann artistic director, Paul Libin managing director, in association with Seymour Hacker at Circle in the Square. Opened June 19, 1972. (Closed August 13, 1972)

Joan	Leo Guilliatt	Virgin Mary	Essie Borden
Mother	Emily Adams	Cardinal	David Vaughan
Sandy; Police Matron	Sandy Padilla	Bishop; Social Worker	David McCorkle
Phyllis	Phyllis MacBryde	Rabbi	Jeffrey Apter
Ira	Ira Siff	Mother Superior	Julie Kurnitz
Teresa	Teresa King	Tracy	Tracy Moore
Policeman	Tony Clark	Pianist	Al Carmines
Therapist	Margaret Wright		

Directed by Al Carmines; choreography, Gus Solomons Jr.; special choreography, David Vaughan; scenery and lighting, Earl Eidman; costumes, Ira Siff, Joan Kilpatrick; production manager, Martin Herzer; press, Merle Debuskey, Robert W. Larkin, Ted Goldsmith.

Musical interpretation of the story of Joan of Arc, in contemporary terms.

ACT I

"Praise the Lord" ....Chorus
"Come on Joan" ....Tracy, Chorus
"It's So Nice" ....Joan, Ira, Tracy
"Go Back" ....Phyllis, Dandy
   (Choreography by Phyllis MacBryde)
"They Call Me the Virgin Mary" ....Mary, Joan
"Salve Madonna" ....Chorus
"The Woman I Love" ....Tracy
"Spoken Aria" ....Mother
"Ira, My Dope Fiend" ....Joan
"A Country of the Mind" ....Ira
"I Live a Little" ....Mary, Chorus
"What I Wonder" ....Joan, Chorus

ACT II

"The Religious Establishment" ....Cardinal, Bishop, Rabbi
   (Choreography by David Vaughan)
"In My Silent Universe" ....Ira
"Take Courage, Daughter" ....Mother Superior, Chorus
"Rivers of Roses" ....Chorus
"I'm Madame Margaret the Therapist" ....Therapist, Chorus
   (Choreography by David Vaughan)
"Look at Me Joan" ....Chorus
"Despair" ....Teresa
"Faith Is Such a Simple Thing" ....Joan, Chorus
"Praise the Lord" (Reprise) ....Joan, Chorus

New York Shakespeare Festival. Summer schedule of three outdoor programs. **Hamlet** (21). Revival of the play by William Shakespeare. Opened June 20, 1972. (Closed July 16, 1972) **Ti-Jean and His Brothers** (15). Folk fable by Derek Walcott; music by Andre Tanker; lyrics by Derek Walcott and Andre Tanker. Opened July 20, 1972; see note. (Closed August 6, 1972) **Much Ado About Nothing** (20). Revival of the play by William Shakespeare; music by Peter Link. Opened August 10, 1972; see note. (Closed September 3, 1972) Produced by New York Shakespeare Festival, Joseph Papp producer, in cooperation with the City of New York, Hon. John V. Lindsay mayor, Hon. August Heckscher administrator P.R.C.A., the New York State Council on the Arts and the National Endowment for the Arts at the Delacorte Theater in Central Park.

ALL PLAYS: Associate producer, Bernard Gersten; costumes, Theoni V. Aldredge; lighting, Martin Aronstein; production supervisor, David Eidenberg; press, Merle Debuskey, Robert Ullman.

HAMLET

Bernardo	John Michalski	Ghost; Player	George Taylor
Francisco	Roger Brown	Rosencrantz	James Sloyan
Horatio	Robert Stattel	Guildenstern	Reno Roop
Marcellus; Fortinbras	Michael Goodwin	Player Queen	Linda Hunt
Claudius	James Earl Jones	Norwegian Captain	Greg Wnorowski
Cornelius	James McGill	Lord	William Robertson
Laertes	Sam Waterston	Lady	Anna Brennen
Polonius	Barnard Hughes	1st Gravedigger	Charles Durning
Hamlet	Stacy Keach	2d Gravedigger	Tom Aldredge
Gertrude	Colleen Dewhurst	Priest	Mel Cobb
Ophelia	Kitty Winn	Osric	Raul Julia
Reynaldo; Lucianus	Frank Dwyer		

Sailors: Nathaniel Robinson, Charles Dinstuhl. Lords: Roger Brown, Gerald Finnegan, James McGill, Jim West. Ladies: Christine Baranski, Bonnie Gallup. Guards: Mel Cobb, Charles Dinstuhl, John Nichols, Nathaniel Robinson, Frank Seales, Alan Tongret, Greg Wnorowski, Richard Yarnell, Mark Zeray.

Directed by Gerald Freedman; scenery, Ming Cho Lee; music, John Morris; stage manager, John Beven.

Place: Elsinore. The play was presented in three parts.

The most recent New York Hamlets were those of the 1970-71 season: Art Burns's 10/18/70 for 37 performances in Roundabout Repertory; the Oxford and Cambridge *Hamlet* 12/26/70 for 7 performances; an uncut version in CSC Repertory; and Judith Anderson's 1/14/71 for 2 performances.

Betty Miller replaced Colleen Dewhurst 7/11/22.

TI-JEAN AND HIS BROTHERS

Mother	Madge Sinclair	Gros-Jean	Clebert Ford
Ti-Jean	Dennis Hines	Mi-Jean	Leon Morenzie
Frog	Hamilton Parris	Devil; Papa Bois; Planter	Albert Laveau
Cricket	Elaine R. Graham	Bolom	Stephannie Hampton Howard
Bird	Diane Bivens	Goat	Renee Rose
Firefly	Deborah Allen		

Ensemble—Dancers (members of the George Faison Universal Dance Experience): Deborah Allen, Gary Deloatch, Dyane Harvey, Eugene Little, Edward Love, Renee Rose, Jason Taylor, Evelyn Thomas. Singers: Margie Barnes, John Barracuda, Gail Boggs, Elaine R. Graham, Sharon Redd.

Directed by Derek Walcott; choreography and musical staging, George Faison; scenery, Edward Burbridge; musical direction and arrangements, Patti Bown; additional dance music, Patti Bown, George Butcher; associate director, Paul Schneider; stage manager, Ron Dozier.

Place: An island in the West Indies. The play was presented in two parts.

Morality fable with music, with human symbols of force, intelligence and love pitted against the Devil, an affirmation of life.

This production played 17 performances on the New York Shakespeare Festival Mobile Theater tour of parks and playgrounds in the five boroughs of New York City, 8/9/72 through 8/27/72.

MUCH ADO ABOUT NOTHING

Leonato	Mark Hammer	Benedick	Sam Waterston
Reporter; Sexton	Charles Bartlett	Claudio	Glenn Walken
Beatrice	Kathleen Widdoes	Don Pedro	Douglass Watson
Hero	April Shawhan	Don John	Jerry Mayer

Antonio ....Lou Gilbert   Dogberry ....Barnard Hughes
Conrade ....Jack Gianino   Verges ....Will Mackenzie
Borachio ....Frederick Coffin   1st Watch ....George Gugleotti
Margaret ....Jeanne Hepple   2d Watch ....David Lenthall
Balthasar ....Marshall Efron   Friar Francis ....Tom McDermott
Ursula ....Bette Henritze

Other Watches: David Anderson, James McGill, John Michalski. Townspeople: David Anderson, Anna Brennen, J.J. Lewis, James McGill, John Michalski, Lynne Taylor, Nina Jordan. Musicians: Charles Lewis trumpet, Henry "Bootsie" Normand banjo, Sam Pilafin tuba, Peter Phillips piano, Aaron Sachs sax, Jimmie Young drums.

Directed by A. J. Antoon; scenery, Ming Cho Lee; dances, Donald Saddler; musical director, Henry "Bootsie" Normand; stage manager, John Beven.

Time: Before World War I. Place: A small town in middle America. The play was presented in two parts.

Shakespeare's play was reconstituted in an American setting, with music added. Its first New York professional production of modern record was the Henry Irving-Ellen Terry version in 1905. Its most recent production was by the New York Shakespeare Festival 7/5/61 for 16 performances. This Central Park production was brought to Broadway, where it opened 11/11/72; see its entry in the "Plays Produced on Broadway" section of this volume.

NOTE: In this volume, certain programs of off-Broadway companies like the New York Shakespeare Festival are exceptions to our rule of counting the number of performances from the date of the press coverage. When the official opening night takes place late in the run of a play's public performances (after previews), we count the first performance of record, not the press date, as opening night. Press date for *Hamlet* was its opennig performance, for *Ti-Jean and His Brothers* 7/26/72, for *Much Ado About Nothing* 8/16/72.

New York Shakespeare Festival. 1971-72 schedule of programs concluded with **The Corner** (46). Program of three one-act plays: *Andrew* by Clay Goss, *His First Step* by Oyamo and the title play by Ed Bullins. Produced by New York Shakespeare Festival Public Theater, Joseph Papp producer, at the Public Theater (Other Stage). Opened June 22, 1972; see note. (Closed July 30, 1972)

ANDREW

Andrew ....Rafic Bey   Billy ....Alfred Dean Irby
Paul ....Frankie Russell Faison

HIS FIRST STEP

Pritchard ....Michael Coleman   Mary ....Yoland Karr
Country ....Ilunga Adell   Sam ....Cornelius Suares

THE CORNER

Slick ....Willard Reece Jr.   Blue ....Hampton Clanton
Bummie ....Basil A. Wallace   Silly Willy Clark ....Michael Coleman
Stella ....Petronia   Cliff ....Bob Delegall

Andrew directed by Rafic Bey (Carl Taylor); *His First Step* directed by Kris Keiser; *The Corner* directed by Sonny Jim Gaines; scenery, Marsha Eck; lighting, Ian Calderon; clothes supervised by Theoni V. Aldredge; sound, Peter Erskine; associate producer, Bernard Gersten; stage manager, A.T. King; press, Merle Debuskey, Bob Ullman.

In *Andrew*, a murder victim symbolically confronts his killers. *His First Step* is a conflict between the college-educated and ghetto-trained points of view on various subjects. In *The Corner*, a typical Bullins character expresses his hope of escaping from the drinking, carousing, street-corner way of life in which he has been trapped.

NOTE: *The Corner* and *His First Step* appeared in previews at the Public Theater starting 5/17/72 together with *You Gonna Let Me Take You Out Tonight, Baby!* by Ed Bullins and *One: The 2 of Us* by Ilunga Adell, on a program entitled *Four for One*. The latter two plays were dropped, *Andrew* was added and the program retitled *The Corner* by the time of the official opening 6/22/72.

Safari 300 (17). Musical by Tad Truesdale. Produced by Richie Havens at the Mayfair Theater. Opened July 12, 1972. (Closed July 26, 1972)

Directed by Hugh Gittens; choreography, Lari Becham; additional choreography, Phil Black; musical direction, Scat Wilson; scenery, Bob Olsen; costumes, Lee Lynn; lighting, David Adams; special dramatic material, Tony Preston; stage manager, Kevin Breslin. With Tad Truesdale, Lari Becham, Ernest Andrews, Joyce Griffin, Holly Hamilton, Onike Lee, Fredi Orange, Andre Robinson, Grenna Whitaker, Dorian Williams.

Black musical history, from African chants to rock 'n' roll.

Present Tense (8). Program of four one-act plays by Frank D. Gilroy: *Come Next Tuesday, Twas Brillig, So Please Be Kind* and the title play. Produced by TDJ Productions, Inc. at the Sheridan Square Playhouse. Opened July 18, 1972. (Closed July 23, 1972)

COME NEXT TUESDAY

Louise Harper	Lois Smith	Harvey Harper	Biff McGuire

TWAS BRILLIG

Edna	Sarah Cunningham	Mr. Vogel	Biff McGuire
Bob Kalmus	Stanley Beck	Judith Kalmus	Lois Smith

SO PLEASE BE KIND

A Man	Biff McGuire	Bellboy	Gary Nebiol
A Woman	Lois Smith		

PRESENT TENSE

Father	Biff McGuire	Mother	Lois Smith

Directed by Curt Dempster; scenery and lighting, Charles Cosler; stage manager, William Yaggy; press, Samuel J. Friedman, Louise Weiner Ment.

Come Next Tuesday is a wife-husband comedy sketch. *Twas Brillig* involves a new-fledged screen writer and his wife with an aggressive Hollywood studio chief. In *So Please Be Kind,* a hotel assignation is disturbed because the couple cannot remember the name of a screen actor they happened to see on the street. *Present Tense* is a dramatic playlet about worried parents of a son serving in Vietnam.

Speed Gets the Poppies (7). Musical with book by Lila Levant; music by Lorenzo Fuller; lyrics by Lorenzo Fuller and Lila Levant. Produced by Daffodil Productions at the Mercer-Brecht Theater. Opened July 25, 1972. (Closed July 30, 1972)

Directed and choreographed by Charles Abbott; scenery, costumes and lighting, Milton Duke; musical direction and arrangements, Robert Esty; press, Alan Eichler. With Robin Field, Edward Penn, Anita Keal, Randi Kallan, Joanna Myers, Robert Browning, Raymond Cerabone.

Stylized musical melodrama with a strong anti-drug message.

Aesop's Fables (58). Rock musical based on *Aesop's Fables;* music by William Russo; text by Jon Swan. Produced by William Russo at the Mercer Arts Center. Opened August 17, 1972. (Closed September 19, 1972)

Performed by the Performing Ensemble of the Chicago Free Theater; directed by William Russo; staged by Don Sanders; design, Vanessa James; stage manager, Gary Porto; press, Alan Eichler, Connie Zonka.

Band: John Davenport and Ken Hayden guitars, Steve Lynch flute, Terry Lansburgh percussion, Arv Rocans bass, Frank Shakey keyboard, Bob Sparling horn.

Collection of musicalized sketches based on Aesop's stories, previously produced in Chicago.

PROGRAM: *The Lion and the Mouse—*Mike Shacochis, Trisha Long; *The Fox and the*

Stork—John Davenport, Denise Walther; *The Mice in Council*—Bill Williams (Elder Mouse), Frank Shaney, Kat Buddeke, Miss Long; *The Lion and the Boar*—Williams, Shaney; *The Wolves and the Jackal*—Davenport, Richard Kravets, Ken Hayden; *The Donkey and the Grasshoppers*—Williams; *The Frog and the Ox*—Kat Buddeke (Baby Frog), Miss Long (Mama Frog); *The Trees and the Ax*—Miss Walther (Hunter), Shacochis (Oak), Williams (Ash); *The Cat and the Rooster*—Shacochis, Miss Walther; *The Ants and the Cocoon*—Shaney; *The Crow and the Fox*—Miss Long.

Coney Island Cycle (14). Program of three plays by Peter Schuman: *Revenge of the Law, Harvey McLeod* and *Hallelujah*. Produced by the New York Shakespeare Festival, Joseph Papp producer, in the Bread and Puppet Theater production at the Martinson Theater. Opened September 7, 1972. (Closed September 17, 1972)

Directed by Peter Schuman; press, Merle Debuskey, Robert Ullman. With the Bread and Puppet Theater.

Revenge of the Law and *Harvey McLeod* are billed as "modern tragedies in 8 short acts"; *Hallelujah* is subtitled "St George and the Dragon, or Laos."

The Roundabout Theater Company. Schedule of five programs. **Right You Are** (64). Revival of the play by Luigi Pirandello; English version by Eric Bentley. Opened September 12, 1972; see note. (Closed November 5, 1972) **American Gothics** (11). Program of four one-act plays by Donald Kvares: *A Piece of Fog, Modern Statuary, Filling the Hole* and *Strangulation*. Opened November 10, 1972; see note. (Closed November 26, 1972) **Anton Chekhov's Garden Party** (22). Entertainment devised and adapted from the works of Anton Chekhov by Elihu Winer. Opened November 22, 1972. (Closed December 10, 1972) **The Play's the Thing** (64). Revival of the play by Ferenc Molnar; adapted by P.G. Wodehouse. Opened January 9, 1973; see note. (Closed March 4, 1973; see note) **Ghosts** (89). Revival of the play by Henrik Ibsen; adapted by Gene Feist. Opened March 13, 1973; see note. (Closed May 27, 1973). Produced by The Roundabout Theater Company, Gene Feist producing director, Michael Fried executive director, at the Roundabout Theater.

RIGHT YOU ARE

Lamberto Laudisi ....William Shust	Councillor Agazzi ....Fred Stuthman
Amalia Agazzi ....Elizabeth Owens	Signora Frola ....Dorothy Sands
Dina Agazzi ....Ellen Newman	Signor Ponza ....John LaGioia
Cina ....Madeleine Wallack	Father Centuri ....Philip Campanella
Signora Sirelli ....Charlotte Lane	Governor ....Sterling Jensen
Signor Sirelli ....Lance Brilliantine	Signora Ponza ....Susan Johnson

Directed by Gene Feist; scenery and lighting, Holmes Easley; costumes, Mimi Maxmen; stage manager, Jeff Schecter; press, Michael Fried.

Time: 1912. Place: The reception room of the Agazzi apartment in an Italian provincial capital. The play was presented in two parts.

Pirandello's play about illusion and reality, sometimes titled *Right You Are if You Think You Are*, was last produced in New York by APA-Phoenix 11/22/66 for 42 performances.

AMERICAN GOTHICS

A Piece of Fog

	Mother ....Elizabeth Owens
Bobby ....Matthew Barry	Father ....Dennis Helfend

Directed by Frank Errante.

Time: The near future. Place: A living room in a small American town. About parricide.

Modern Statuary

	Elena ....Susan Peretz
Mrs. Gelb ....Lorraine Serabian	Freddy ....Tracey Walter

Kitty .... Alice Elliott
Johnny .... Robert Burgos

Mr. Gelb .... Dennis Helfend

Directed by Nancy Rhodes.
Time: Fall. Place: The Gelb home in suburban Long Island. Emotional distresses of an adolescent misfit.

Filling the Hole
Willa .... Alice Elliott

Will .... Robert Burgos
Mother .... Susan Peretz

Directed by Nancy Rubin.
Time: A day in spring. Place: Central Park. Comic family frictions.

Strangulation
Ruth .... Lorraine Serabian

Ma .... Alice Elliott

Directed by Frank Errante.
Time: The recent past. A would-be suicide's contemplations.
ALL PLAYS: Scenery, Victor Poleri; lighting, Robert Murphy; costumes, Evelyn Thompson; production stage manager, Jeff Schecter.

ANTON CHEKHOV'S GARDEN PARTY

Anton Chekhov .... William Shust

Time: April 17, 1900. Place: The garden of Chekhov's home in Yalta. Chekhov reads from his works to a group of visiting friends, Moscow Art Theater actors.

THE PLAY'S THE THING

Sandor Turai .... Hugh Franklin
Mansky .... Humphrey Davis
Albert Adam .... Richard Larson
Ilona Szabo .... Elizabeth Owens

Almady .... Neil Flanagan
Johann Dwornitschek .... Fred Stuthman
Mell .... Philip Campanella

Directed by Gene Feist; scenery, Holmes Easley; costumes, Mimi Maxmen; lighting, R.S. Winkler; original score, Philip Campanella; stage manager, David Petersen.
Time: A Saturday in the summer of 1926. Place: A room in a villa on the Italian Riviera. Act I: 2 a.m. Act II: 7 a.m. Act III: 7:30 p.m.
Molnar's play about a prima donna's romances was last produced on Broadway 4/28/48 for 244 performances.
NOTE This production reopened on Broadway 5/7/73; see its entry in the "Plays Produced on Broadway" section of this volume.

GHOSTS

Mrs. Helene Alving .... Beatrice Straight
Osvald Alving .... Victor Garber
Pastor Manders .... Wesley Addy

Jacob Engstrand .... Fred Stuthman
Regina Engstrand .... Laura Esterman

Directed by Gene Feist; scenery, Holmes Easley; costumes, Sue A. Robbins; lighting, R.S. Winkler; original score, Philip Campanella; stage manager, Nancy Rhodes.
Time: Spring, the late 19th century. Place: Mrs. Alving's country home on one of the larger fjords of western Norway. Act I: Late afternoon. Act II, Scene 1: Early evening. Scene 2: The next morning.
Ibsen's drama of the consequences of a father's sins was last produced off Broadway 9/21/61 for 216 performances.

ADDITIONAL ROUNDABOUT ACTIVITIES

A nine-play series entitled *Directions 72* was produced by Roger Cunningham and Nancy Rhodes at the Roundabout Theater from June 20, 1972 through August 20, 1972. The schedule was as follows: Carlo Goldoni's *The Fan* 6/20-6/25; Harold Pinter's *The Lovers* and August Strindberg's *The Creditors* 7/4-7/9; John Hawkes's *The Wax Museum* and McCrea Imbrie's and Neil Selden's *Mr Shandy* 7/18-7/23; George Bernard Shaw's *How He Lied to Her Husband* and John Madison Morton's *Box and Cox* 8/1-8/6; Euripides's *The Bacchae* and Shaw's *Man of Destiny* 8/15-8/20.

The Roundabout presented special limited engagements of its *Hamlet* at Town Hall for 6 performances 12/4/72-12/8/72 and at the Fashion Institute of Technology 2/26/73-3/2/73 for 10 performances.
NOTE: In this volume, certain programs of off-Broadway companies like The Roundabout Theater Company are exceptions to our rule of counting the number of performances from the date of the press coverage. When the official opening night takes place late in the run of a play's public performances (after previews), we count the first performance of record, not the press date, as opening night. Press date for *Right You Are* was 10/11/72, for *American Gothics* 11/19/72, for *The Play's the Thing* 1/31/73, for *Ghosts* 4/3/73.

Crazy Now (1). Musical with book and lyrics by Richard Smithies and Maura Cavanagh; music by Norman Sachs. Produced by B.F. Productions at the Eden Theater. Opened and closed at the evening performance September 17, 1972.

Directed and choreographed by Voight Kempson; musical direction, Jim Litt; press, Alan Eichler. With Carla Benjamin, William Buell, Glenn Mure, Rosalie, John Scoullar.
Musical take-off of the eccentric ways of modern life.

Jewish State Theater of Bucharest. Repertory of two programs in the Yiddish language. **The Dybbuk** (8). Revival of the play by S. Ansky. Opened September 19, 1972. **The Pearl Necklace** (8). Musical revue by Israel Bercovici; based on Jewish folk tales. Opened September 21, 1972. Produced by Kazuko Hillyer in association with the Brooklyn Academy of Music at the Brooklyn Academy of Music/Opera House. (Repertory closed October 1, 1972)

THE DYBBUK

Reb Sender ....Benno Popliker	Reb Mendel ....Ozy Segaly
Leah ....Leonie Waldman Eliad	Messenger ....Carol Marcovici
Frade ....Seidy Gluck	Reb Azrielke ....Samuel Fischler
Gittle ....Marieta Neuman	Mikhol ....Abraham Naimark
Bassia ....Mihaela Kreutzer	Reb Simschen; Meyer ....Isac Cassvan
Manasse ....Rudi Rosenfeld	Khonnon ....Adrian Lupo
Nakhman ....Mano Rippel	

THE PEARL NECKLACE

Seidy Gluck	Ghenia Stoian
Raschela Schapira	Sonia Fischler
Leonie Waldman Eliad	Mano Rippel
Abraham Naimark	Mihaela Kreutzer
Rudi Rosenfeld	Samuel Fischler
Beatrice Abramovici	Rudi Bolteanski
Carol Marcovici	Lupi Bercovici
Smil Godrich	Hoisie Segall
Marieta Neuman	Beatrice Naimark

Both programs directed by Franz Auerbach; technical director, Iosis Bolteanski; conductor, Haim Schwartzman; press, Beverly Willis.
The most recent production of record of *The Dybbuk* was the Habimah troupe's, in Hebrew, 2/3/64 for 24 performances on Broadway. *The Pearl Necklace* is a collection of more than 50 numbers, most of them Jewish folk songs, some from a musical *Mazel Tov* which has had a long run in Bucharest. The Jewish State Theater of Bucharest is reputed to be the first professional Yiddish theater troupe, founded in 1976.

We Bombed in New Haven (1). Revival of the play by Joseph Heller; new interpretation conceived by Peter John Bailey. Produced by The Bomb Haven Co. at Circle in the Square. Opened and closed at the evening performance, September 24, 1972.

Directed by Peter John Bailey; scenery, Robert U. Taylor; lighting, Thomas Skelton; sound, Gary Harris; associate producer, Joan Rowe; stage manager, Cleveland Morris; press, John Springer Associates, Ruth Cage, Ted Goldsmith. With Frank Bara, Raina Barrett, Brian Brownlee, Carter Cole, James Doerr, Steven Keats, Rory Kelly, Richard Kline, John Kuhner, Christopher Logan, J.R. Marks, William Preston, Robert Shea, Gary Springer, John Wardwell.

We Bombed in New Haven was previously produced on Broadway 10/16/68 for 85 performances.

New York Shakespeare Festival Public Theater. Schedule of five programs. **Wedding Band** (175). By Alice Childress. Opened September 26, 1972; see note. (Closed February 25, 1973) **The Children** (64). By Michael McGuire. Opened November 28, 1972; see note. (Closed January 21, 1973) **The Cherry Orchard** (86). Revival of the play by Anton Chekhov. Opened December 7, 1972; see note. (Closed February 18, 1973) **Siamese Connections** (64). By Dennis J. Reardon. Opened January 9, 1973; see note. (Closed March 4, 1973) **The Orphan** (53). By David Rabe. Opened March 30, 1973; see note. (Closed May 13, 1973) Produced by the New York Shakespeare Festival Public Theater, Joseph Papp producer, at the Public Theater.

WEDDING BAND

Julia Augustine	Ruby Dee	The Bell Man	Brandon Maggart
Teeta	Calisse Dinwiddie	Princess	Vicky Geyer
Mattie	Juanita Clark	Herman	James Broderick
Lula Green	Hilda Haynes	Annabelle	Polly Holliday
Fanny Johnson	Clarice Taylor	Herman's Mother	Jean David
Nelson Green	Albert Hall		

Directed by Alice Childress and Joseph Papp; scenery, Ming Cho Lee; costumes, Theoni V. Aldredge; lighting, Martin Aronstein; associate producer, Bernard Gersten; production stage manager, Ron Dozier; press, Merle Debuskey, Robert Ullman, Norman L. Berman.

Time: Summer 1918. Place: A city by the sea, South Carolina. Act I, Scene 1: Saturday morning. Scene 2: That evening. Act II: Sunday morning. Act III: Early afternoon, the following day.

Blacks and whites both disapprove of a love affair between a black woman and a white man in the deep South, in a decidedly bigoted era at the closing days of World War I.

Robert Loggia replaced James Broderick 12/19/73.

THE CHILDREN

Kathleen	Fern Sloan	Dan	Kevin McCarthy
Christopher	Bob Balaban	Alexander	George Welbes

Directed by Paul Schneider; scenery, Marsha Eck; costumes, Theoni V. Aldredge; lighting, Arden Fingerhut; production stage manager, Dyanne Hochman.

Time: 19—. Place: The American mid-West, farm country. Act I: An old farmhouse. Act II: An old farmhouse and the country nearby.

Husband, lover and children attend a woman's death bed, in a symbolic and melodramatic construction of family relationships.

THE CHERRY ORCHARD

Lubov Ranevskaya	Gloria Foster	Dunyasha	Verona Barnes
Anya	Suzanne Johnson	Firs	Zakes Mokae
Varya	Ellen Holly	Yasha	Leon Morenzie
Gayev	Earle Hyman	Wayfarer; Police Chief	Paul Benjamin
Lopahin	James Earl Jones	Stationmaster	Clifford Mason
Trofimov	Robert Jackson	Post Office Clerk; Wayfarer	Paul Makgoba
Simeonov-Pishchik	Clark Morgan	Guest	Zaida Coles
Charlotta Ivanovna	Josephine Premice	Violinist	Noel Pointer
Yepidohov	Dennis Tate		

Singing Chorus: Verona Barnes, Zaida Coles, Deloris Gaskins, Paul Makgoba, Leon Morenzie, Clark Morgan, Dennis Tate.

Production conceived by James Earl Jones; directed by Michael Schultz; translation, Avrahm Yarmolinsky; scenery, David Mitchell; costumes, Theoni V. Aldredge; lighting, Ian Calderon; music, John Morris; choreography, Eliot Feld; production stage manager, Lou Rogers.

Time: 1900. Place: Mme. Ranevskaya's estate in Russia. Act I: May—the nursery. Act II: July—the gazebo. Act III: August—the drawing room. Act IV: October—the nursery.

This production of *The Cherry Orchard* was performed by an all-black cast. The Chekhov play was last revived here by ANTA in a regional theater production 5/9/70 for 5 performances and by APA-Phoenix 3/19/68 for 38 performances.

SIAMESE CONNECTIONS

Frank Kroner Sr. .... Roberts Blossom	Grandmother Kroner .... William Hickey
Kate Kroner .... Cathryn Damon	Tom Jensen .... Ralph Roberts
Franklin Kroner Jr. .... David Selby	Gretchen .... Mary Hamill
James Kroner .... James Staley	

Directed by David Schweizer; scenery, Santo Loquasto; costumes, Nancy Adzima, Richard Graziano; lighting, Ian Calderon; music, Cathy MacDonald; production stage manager, Christopher Alden.

Time: The present. Place: An American farm. Scene 1: an afternoon in late autumn. Scene 2: Very early the next morning. Scene 3: Three months later. Scene 4: One month later; a day sometime between winter and spring. The play was presented in two parts.

Ghosts and murder in a farm family which has lost a son in the Vietnam war. Previously produced in the University of Michigan Professional Theater Program.

THE ORPHAN

The Speaker .... Jeanne Hepple	Agamemnon .... W.B. Brydon
Orestes .... Cliff DeYoung	Aegisthus .... John Harkins
Clytemnestra 1 .... Marcia Jean Kurtz	The Girl .... Mariclare Costello
Clytemnestra 2 .... Rae Allen	Apollo .... Richard Lynch
Electra .... Carol Williard	Calchas .... Tom Aldredge
Iphigenia .... Laurie Heineman	Pylades .... Peter Maloney

The Family: Laurie Heineman, Peter Maloney, Joanne Nail, Janet Sarno, Carol Williard, Annemarie Zinn.

Directed by Jeff Bleckner; scenery, Santo Loquasto; costumes, Theoni V. Aldredge; lighting, Tharon Musser; music, Peter Link; production stage manager, David Eidenberg; stage manager, Helaine Head.

Act I: Policymaking. Act II: Flowerchildren. The Oresteia freely adapted as a parable of modern America.

ADDENDA: *Winning Hearts and Minds,* an experimental multimedia play adapted by Paula Kay Pierce from poems by 33 Vietnam war veterans, was produced 8/1/72 under Ms. Pierce's direction, with a cast of Kelly Monaghan, William T. Jones, James Hackett, Carl Crudup, Tucker Smallwood, Robert Cox, Susan Batson, Irma Sandrey and Joanna Rotte, but it was not offered for review or for a run of public performances.

In Joseph Papp's Public Theater there are many separate auditoriums. *Wedding Band* played the Estelle R. Newman Theater, *The Children* played the Other Stage, *The Cherry Orchard* and *The Orphan* played the Florence S. Anspacher Theater, *Siamese Connections* played the Public Theater Annex.

NOTE: In this volume, certain programs of off-Broadway companies like New York Shakespeare Festival Public Theater are exceptions to our rule of counting the number of performances from the date of the press coverage. When the official opening night takes place late in the run of a play's public performances (after previews), we count the first performance of record, not the press date, as opening night. Press date for *Wedding Band* was 10/26/72; for *The Children* 12/17/72; for *The Cherry Orchard* 1/11/73; for *The Siamese Connection* 1/25/73. for *The Orphan* 4/18/73.

City Center Acting Company. Repertory of six revivals. **The School for Scandal** (12). By Richard Brinsley Sheridan. Opened September 27, 1972 matinee. U.S.A.

(3). Dramatic revue adapted by Paul Shyre from the novel by John Dos Passos. Opened October 1, 1972 matinee. **The Hostage** (8). By Brendan Behan. Opened October 9, 1972. **Women Beware Women** (8). By Thomas Middleton. Opened October 16, 1972. **Next Time I'll Sing to You** (2). By James Saunders. Opened October 25, 1972 matinee. **The Lower Depths** (6). By Maxim Gorky; adapted by Alex Szogyi. Opened October 23, 1972. (Repertory closed October 28, 1972) Produced by the City Center Acting Company, John Houseman artistic director, at the Good Shepherd-Faith Church.

PERFORMER	"THE SCHOOL FOR SCANDAL"	"THE HOSTAGE"	"THE LOWER DEPTHS"
Leah Chandler	(Maria)		Anna
Peter Dvorsky			(Policeman)
Benjamin Hendrickson	Rowley	Princess Grace	Kleshch
Tom Henschel			Medvedyev
Cynthia Herman	Mrs. Candour	Miss Gilchrist	Vasilissa
Cindia Huppeler	(Maria)	Ropeen	
Kevin Kline	Charles Surface	IRA Officer	Vaska Pepel
Patti LuPone	Lady Teazle	(Colette); Kathleen	Natasha
Anne McNaughton	Lady Crabtree	(Meg Dillon; Colette)	
Dakin Matthews	(Sir Oliver Surface)	Pat	Bubnov
James Moody		Rio Rita	Tartar
Mary Joan Negro		Theresa	Nastya
Mary Lou Rosato	Lady Sneerwell	(Meg Dillon)	Kvashnya
Jared Sakren	Moses	Volunteer	Kostilyov
David Schramm	Sir Peter Teazle	Police Officer	Luka
Gerald Shaw	Sir Benjamin Backbite	Piano Player	Alyoshka
Norman Snow	(Sir Oliver Surface)	Leslie	Actor
David Ogden Stiers	Joseph Surface	Monsewer	Baron
Sam Tsoutsouvas	Snake; Careless	Mr. Mulleady	Satin

PERFORMER	"U.S.A."	"WOMEN BEWARE" WOMEN"	"NEXT TIME I'LL SING TO YOU"
Leah Chandler	Player E	Isabella	
Benjamin Hendrickson	Player B	Lord Cardinal	Meff
Kevin Kline		Guardiano	
Patty LuPone		(Bianca)	Lizzie
Anne McNaughton		The Widow	
Dakin Matthews		Fabritio	
James Moody	Player C		
Mary Joan Negro	Player D	(Bianca)	
Mary Lou Rosato	Player F	Livia	
Jared Sakren		Sordido	Hermit
David Schramm		Leantio	Rudge
Gerald Shaw	Player G; Piano Player	(The Ward)	
Norman Snow	Player A	(The Ward)	Dust
David Ogden Stiers		Duke of Florence	
Sam Tsoutsouvas		Hippolito	

(Parentheses indicate role in which the performer alternated)

Servants, Gentlemen in *The School for Scandal:* Leah Chandler, Cindia Huppeler, Dakin Mathews, James Moody, Mary Joan Negro, Peter Dvorsky.

Soldiers, Attendants, Masquers in *Women Beware Women:* Peter Dvorsky, Cynthia Herman, Patti LuPone, James Moody, Gerald Shaw.

ALL PLAYS—Producing directors, John Houseman, Margot Harley, Stephen Aaron; lighting, Joe Pacitti; stage manager, Tom Warner; press, Sol Jacobson, Lewis Harmon.

THE SCHOOL FOR SCANDAL—Directed by Gerald Freedman; scenery, Douglas W. Schmidt; costumes supervised by John David Ridge; music, Robert Waldman.

Sheridan's comedy was first performed at the Drury Lane Theater, London, in 1777. Its most recent professional New York production was the APA Repertory revival on Broadway

11/21/66 for 48 performances. In this production by the City Center Acting Company—formerly the Julliard Acting Ensemble—it was presented in three acts.

U.S.A.—Directed by Anne McNaughton; costumes, John David Ridge.

This dramatic reading based on the Dos Passos novel with occasional music, was presented in two parts. It was previously produced in New York 10/28/59 for 256 performances.

THE HOSTAGE—Directed by Gene Lesser; scenery, Douglas W. Schmidt; costumes, Carrie F. Robbins; musical direction, Roland Gagnon; dance consultant, Elizabeth Keen.

Place: A lodging house in Dublin. The play was presented in two parts. Its first production was in London 10/14/58. It was produced in New York 9/20/60 for 127 performances on Broadway and 12/12/61 for 545 performances off Broadway.

WOMEN BEWARE WOMEN—Directed by Michael Kahn; scenery, Douglas W. Schmidt; costumes supervised by John David Ridge; music supervised by Martin Verdrager; choreography, William Burdick.

Place: Florence. The play was presented in three parts. It was first performed by the King's Men in London in 1621. This is reported to be the first professional staging of the Jacobean tragedy—about romance and murder in a self-serving, self-mocking anti-moral society—in the United States.

NEXT TIME I'LL SING TO YOU—Directed by Marian Seldes; costumes, John David Ridge.

Absurdist study of a hermit, first performed in Ealing, England in 1962 and the Arts Theater in London in 1963, presented here in two parts. It was previously produced off Broadway 11/27/63 for 23 performances and was named a Best Play of its season.

THE LOWER DEPTHS—Directed by Boris Tumarin; scenery, Douglas W. Schmidt; costumes, John David Ridge; musical direction, Gerald Shaw; accordion, William Schimmel.

Time: The turn of the century. Place: A flophouse in a provincial town in Russia. The play was presented in two parts. It was first produced by the Moscow Art Theater in 1902. It was last produced in New York in APA Repertory off Broadway 3/30/64 for 32 performances.

Berlin to Broadway With Kurt Weill (152). Musical revue with music by Kurt Weill; lyrics by Maxwell Anderson, Marc Blitzstein, Bertolt Brecht, Jacques Deval, Michael Feingold, Ira Gershwin, Paul Green, Langston Hughes, Alan Jay Lerner, Ogden Nash, George Tabori, Arnold Weinstein. Produced by Hank Kaufman and Gene Lerner in association with Michael Arthur Film Productions at the Theater de Lys. Opened October 1, 1972. (Closed February 11, 1973)

Margery Cohen	Jerry Lanning
Ken Kercheval	Hal Watters
Judy Lander	

Directed by Donald Saddler; musical direction and arrangements, Newton Wayland; text and format, Gene Lerner; production design, Herbert Senn, Helen Pond; costumes, Frank Thompson; lighting, Thomas Skelton; sound, Gary Harris; projections, Lester Polakov; conductor, Robert Rogers; assistant to the director, Richard Landon; production stage manager, Fred Seagraves; press, Saul Richman.

A "musical voyage" through the shows and songs of Kurt Weill, with Ken Kercheval in the role of The Guide on the Voyage.

PART I: *The Threepenny Opera* (lyrics by Bertolt Brecht, English version by Marc Blitzstein): "Morning Anthem"—Margery Cohen, Judy Lander, Jerry Lanning, Hal Watters; "Mack the Knife"—Lanning; "Jealousy Duet"—Misses Cohen, Lander; "Tango Ballad"—Lanning, Miss Lander; "Love Duet"—Lanning, Miss Cohen; "Barbara Song"—Miss Lander; "Useless Song"—Watters; "How to Survive"—Lanning, Watters, Misses Cohen, Lander. *Happy End* (lyrics by Bertolt Brecht): "Bilbao Song" (English version by Michael Feingold)—Lanning, Watters; "Surabaya Johnny" (English version by George Tabori)—Miss Lander. *The Rise and Fall of the City of Mahagonny* (text by Bertolt Brecht, English version by Arnold Weinstein): "Alabama Song" (original English by Brecht)—Miss Cohen with Lanning, Watters, Miss Lander; "Deep in Alaska"—Watters with Lanning, Misses Cohen, Lander; "Oh, Heavenly Salvation"—Watters, Lanning, Misses Cohen, Lander; "As You Make Your Bed"—Company. "Pirate Jenny" from *The Threepenny Opera*—Miss Lander. *Marie Galante* (lyrics by Jacques Deval, English version by Gene Lerner and Alice Baker): "I Wait for a Ship"—Miss Cohen. "Sailor Tango" from *Happy End*—Lanning, Watters, Misses Cohen, Lander.

PART II: *Johnny Johnson* (lyrics by Paul Green): "Songs of Peace and War"—Lanning with Misses Cohen, Lander; "Song of the Guns"—Lanning, Misses Cohen, Lander; "Hymn to

Peace"—Watters; "Johnny's Song"—Watters. *Knickerbocker Holiday* (lyrics by Maxwell Anderson): "How Can You Tell an American?"—Lanning, Watters, Misses Cohen, Lander; "September Song"—Lanning. *Lady in the Dark* (lyrics by Ira Gershwin): "My Ship"—Miss Cohen; "Girl of the Moment"—Lanning, Watters; "The Saga of Jenny"—Miss Lander with Lanning, Watters. *One Touch of Venus* (lyrics by Ogden Nash): "That's Him"—Miss Cohen; "Speak Low"—Lanning, Watters, Misses Cohen, Lander. *Love Life* (lyrics by Alan Jay Lerner): "Progress" (staged by Richard Landon)—Lanning, Watters. *Street Scene* (lyrics by Langston Hughes): "Moon-Faced, Starry-Eyed" (excerpt)—Watters; "Ain't It Awful, the Heat?"— Lanning, Watters, Misses Cohen, Lander; "Lonely House"—Watters; "Lullaby"—Miss Cohen, Lander. *Lost in the Stars* (lyrics by Maxwell Anderson): "Train to Johannesburg"—Watters with Lanning, Misses Cohen, Lander; "Trouble Man"—Miss Lander; "Cry the Beloved Country"—Miss Cohen with Lanning, Watters, Miss Lander; "Lost in the Stars"—Lanning. "Love Song" from *Love Life*—Lanning, Watters, Misses Cohen, Lander. "Happy Ending from *The Threepenny Opera*—Kercheval.

Lady Audley's Secret (7). Musical adapted by Douglas Seale from the novel by Mary Elizabeth Braddon; music by George Goehring; lyrics by John Kuntz. Produced by Haila Stoddard and Arnold H. Levy at the Eastside Playhouse. Opened October 3, 1972 (Closed October 8, 1972)

Directed by Douglas Seale; musical staging, George Bunt; musical direction and arrangements, John Cina; scenery and costumes, Alicia Finkel; lighting Lawrence Metzler; production stage manager, Jan Moerel; press, Betty Lee Hunt Associates. With Lu Ann Post, Danny Sewell, Donna Curtis, Douglas Seale, June Gable, Russell Nype, Richard Curnock, Rick Atwell, Rosalin Ricci, Michael Serrecchia, Jonathan Miele, Virginia Pulos, Dennis Roberts, Joyce Maret.
   Victorian melodrama about the wages of sin, camped and musicalized.

* Oh Coward! (274). Musical revue with words and music by Noel Coward; devised by Roderick Cook. Produced by Wroderick Productions at the New Theater. Opened October 4, 1972.

Barbara Cason   Jamie Ross
Roderick Cook

Directed by Roderick Cook; musical direction and arrangements, Rene Wiegert; scenery, Helen Pond, Herbert Senn; additional musical arrangements, Herbert Helbig, Nicholas Deutsch; production stage manager, Jay Leo Colt; press, Seymour Krawitz.
   Excerpts from Noel Coward's *The Young Idea, Present Laughter, Private Lives, Shadow Play, Not Yet the Dodo* (poems), *Pomp and Circumstance* (novel), *Collected Short Stories* and *Present Indicative* (autobiography), with a collection of Coward songs in shows and other media from 1925 to 1963.

ACT I

Introduction
   The Boy Actor ....Company
Oh Coward!
   "Something to Do With Spring," "Bright Young People," "Poor Little Rich Girl," "Ziegeuner," "Let's Say Goodbye," "This Is a Changing World," "We Were Dancing," "Dance Little Lady," "Room With a View," "Sail Away" ....Company
England
   London Pastoral ....Jamie Ross
   "The End of the News" ....Barbara Cason, Roderick Cook
"The Stately Homes of England" ....Ross, Cook
   London Pride ....Miss Cason
   "I Wonder What Happened to Him?" ....Ross, Cook
Family Album
   Auntie Jessie ....Cook
   "Uncle Harry" ....Miss Cason, Ross
Music Hall
   Introduction ....Cook

"Chase Me Charlie" ....Miss Cason
"Saturday Night at the Rose and Crown" ....Company
"The Island of Bollamazoo" ....Ross
"What Ho, Mrs. Brisket!" ....Cook
"Has Anybody Seen Our Ship?" ....Company
"Men About Town" ....Ross, Cook
"If Love Were All" ....Miss Cason
Travel
Too Early or Too Late ....Cook
"Why Do the Wrong People Travel?" ....Miss Cason, Ross
"The Passenger's Always Right" ....Company
Mrs. Worthington
"Don't Put Your Daughter on the Stage, Mrs. Worthington" ....Company

ACT II

"Mad Dogs and Englishmen" ....Company
A Marvellous Party
"I've Been to a Marvellous Party," "The Party's Over Now" ....Cook
Design for Dancing
"Dance Little Lady" (Reprise) ....Company
You Were There ....Ross
Theater
"Three White Feathers" ....Miss Cason, Ross
The Star ....Ross
The Critic ....Cook
The Elderly Actress ....Miss Cason
Love
Gertie ....Cook
Loving ....Ross
I Am No Good at Love ....Cook
Sex Talk ....Ross
A Question of Lighting ....Ross, Cook
"Mad About the Boy" ....Miss Cason
Women
Introduction ....Cook
"Nina" ....Ross
"A Bar on the Piccola Marina" ....Cook
"Alice Is at It Again" ....Cook
"World Weary" ....Company
"Let's Do It" ....Company
    (Music, Cole Porter; lyrics, Noel Coward)
Finale
"Where Are the Songs We Sung?" ....Ross
"Someday I'll Find You" ....Cook
"I'll Follow My Secret Heart" ....Miss Cason
"If Love Were All" (Reprise) ....Company
"Play Orchestra Play" ....Company
"I'll See You Again" ....Company

The Chelsea Theater Center of Brooklyn. Schedule of four programs. **Lady Day: A Musical Tragedy** (24). By Aishah Rahman; music by Archie Shepp; additional music by Stanley Cowell and Cal Massey. Opened October 17, 1972; see note. (Closed November 5, 1972) **Sunset** (24). By Isaac Babel; translated from the Russian by Mirra Gunsburg and Raymond Rosenthal. Opened December 5, 1972; see note. (Closed December 24, 1972) **Kaspar** (48). By Peter Handke; English version by Michael Roloff. Opened February 6, 1973; see note. (Closed March 17, 1973) **Fly Chelsea to Brooklyn** (58). Mini-festival of limited engagements of guest productions: The New Theater of Palo Alto, Calif., for 16 performances March 20, 1973 through April 1, 1973; Iowa City, Iowa Theater Lab's *The Naming* for

18 performances April 3, 1973 through April 18, 1973; El Teatro Campesino de Azatlán's *La Carpa de Los Rasquachis* (The Tent of the Underdogs) for 10 performances April 19, 1973 through April 29, 1973; San Francisco, Calif.'s Video Free America for 14 performances April 24, 1973 through May 6, 1973. Produced by The Chelsea Theater Center of Brooklyn, Robert Kalfin artistic director, Michael David executive director, Burl Hash productions director, at the Brooklyn Academy of Music.

LADY DAY: A MUSICAL TRAGEDY

Ronnie; Vi-Tone; Wino; Reporter; Guard ..................................R.T. Vessels
Ricky; Vi-Tone; Wino; Buttercup; Waiter ....Don Jay
Sonny; Vi-Tone; Wino; Beware Scat; Reporter ....Joe Lee Wilson
Bullfrog ....Psyche Wanzandae
Flim Flam; Preacher; Freddie Freedom ....Roger Robinson
Mother Horn; Mom ....Rosetta Le Noire
Vi-Tone; Wino; Cameraman; Shelly ....Eugene Riley
Billie ....Cecelia Norfleet
Piano Player; White Club Owner; Judge; Policeman; Newsboy ....Frank Adu
Lester ....Clifford Jordan Jr.
Fanny; Flo ....Madge Sinclair
Anonymous White Woman; Gilly ....Signa Joy
Mort Shazer; Gangster ....Maxwell Glanville
Dan Sugarman; Levitt; Unknown Lover ....Al Kirk
Cellmate; Nurse ....Onike Lee

Directed by Paul Carter Harrison; musical direction, Stanley Cowell; scenery, Robert U. Taylor; costumes, Randy Barcelo; lighting, William Mintzer; sound, Gary Harris; production stage manager, James Doolan; stage manager, Errol Selsby; press, Penny Peters.

Time: Yesterday, today but not tomorrow. Place: In the eye of the Black Nation.

An evokation of the life, times and career of Billie Holiday in a series of episodes and songs.

MUSICAL NUMBERS

First Beat
"My My Darling" ....Ronnie
"Ah Need" ....Ricky
"Tears of This Fool" ....Sonny
"In the Spring of the Year 1915—Raped at 10" ....Flim-Flam, Vi-Tones
"Song of Fate" ....Winos
"Looking for Someone to Love" ....Billie
"Billie's Blues" (arranged by RoMas) ....Mom

Second Beat
"He's Gone" ....Mom, Billie, Fanny, Anonymous White Woman
"Strange Fruit" (arranged by Charles "Majeed" Greenlee) ....Buttercup
"Beware Scat Song" ....Beware Scat
"Blues for the Lady" ....Billie
"Stealin' Gold" ....Vi-Tones
"America on Her Back" ....Company
"Enough" ....Flo

Third Beat
"God Bless the Child" (arranged by Charles "Majeed" Greenlee) ....Flim-Flam, Vi-Tones
"No One Will Help the Lady" ....Winos
"A Year and a Day" ....Winos
"I Know 'Bout the Life" ....Billie, Cellmate
"What Would It Be Without You" ....Billie
"Do You Know What It's Like" ....Waiter
"The Professional Friends Duet" ....Gilly, Shelly
"Lover Man" (arranged by RoMas) ....Freddie Freedom
"I Cried Like a Baby" ....Billie
"Big Daddy" ....Billie
"Song to a Loved One" ....Company

SUNSET

Ayre-Leib ....Martin Garner	Senka Topun ....Frank Anderson
Lekra Krick; 4th Blind Singer;	Russian Sailor ....Christopher Thomas
Talmudist ....Zitto Kazann	Tavern Woman; Neighbor;
Benya Krick ....Andrew Jarkowsky	Pregnant Woman ....Louise Williams
Nechama Krick ....Sonia Zomina	Tavern Woman; Neighbor's Voice;
Dvoira Krick ....Shirley Stoler	Madame Popyatnik ....Blanche Dee
Monsieur Boyarkski; Turk; Jew .Michael Vale	Tavern Woman; Neighbor; Rich
Mendel Krick ....Louis Zorich	Guest ....Ronica Stern
Nikifor; Ryabtsov ....Jerome Raphel	Blacksmith; Talmudist ....Ben Slack
Flute Player, Jew ....Al Secunda	Chorus Leader; Jew ....Martin Siegel
Waiter; 1st Jew; Neighbor;	2d Blind Singer; Cantor Zweiback;
Rich Guest ....Paul Slimak	Rabbi Ben Zcharia ....Jerrold Ziman
Ourussov; Father; Semen; Cattle	3d Blind Singer; Jew; Neighbor;
Merchant ....K. Lype O'Dell	Young Peasant ....Sean Stephens
Eudokia ....Despo	Marusia; Mother ....Ellie George
Fomin; 2d Jew; Bobrinetz ......Arn Weiner	Boy ....Fabian Arnell

Directed by Robert Kalfin; music composed and arranged by Ryan Edwards; scenery, Santo Loquasto; costumes, Carrie F. Robbins; lighting, William Mintzer; production stage manager, Richard Frankel; stage manager, Peggy Peckham; press, Penny Peters, Leslie Gifford.

Time: 1913. Place: Odessa. Scene 1: The dining room in the Krick home. Scene 2: The Kricks' bedroom, night. Scene 3: A tavern on Privosny Square. Scene 4: Potapovna's attic. Scene 5: The Teamster's Synagogue in the Moldavanka district of Odessa, Friday evening service. Scene 6: The Kricks' yard, 7 p.m. Scene 7: The Krick coach house. Scene 8: The Krick dining room, evening.

Conflict between father and son in a Jewish community in Odessa before World War I. The Babel play, written in 1928, was previously produced off Broadway in this translation 5/12/66 for 14 performances.

KASPAR

Kaspar ....Christopher Lloyd

The Prompters and The Other Kaspars: Randy Chicoine, Veronica Castang, Robert Einenkel, Guy Boyd.

Directed by Carl Weber; video conceived and executed by Arthur Ginsberg and Skip Sweeney; design, Wolfgang Roth; production stage manager, Errol Selsby.

Study of an underdeveloped, animal-like youth trying to learn to become part of the human experience. A foreign play previously produced in Germany and elsewhere. The play was presented in two parts.

FLY CHELSEA TO BROOKLYN

The New Theater created, designed, directed and performed by Gerald Hiken and Paul E. Richards. A repertory of short plays informally presented in a so-called "handshake" relationship between the performers and the audience.

The Naming directed by Ric Zank; administrative director, Gillian Richards; sponsored by the Center for New Performing Arts of The University of Iowa. With Kim Allen Bent, Harold Goodman, Deborah Gwinn, George Kon. Described as being "about erotic exaltation and terror."

La Carpa de los Rasquachis (The Tent of the Underdogs) directed by Luis Valdez. With Phil Esparza, Jesus Padron, Olivia Chumacero, Francis Romero, Carlos Acosta, Lily Mejia, Rogelio Rojas, Jose Delgado, Edwardo Robledo, Rosemary Apodaca, Felix Alvarez, Alan Cruz, Roberta Esparza. A farm workers' theater production of a drama about the hardships of a worker's family, told in "Corrido" (traditional Mexican ballad) style, with dialogue in English and the story's running narrative sung in Spanish.

Video Free America created by Arthur Ginsberg. With Skip Sweeney, Sukey Wilder, Bob Klein. A "video tape novel about pornography, sexual identities, the institution of marriage and the effects of living too close to an electronic medium," told in the following episodes:

Prologue, Exposition, Richard, The Argument, Wedding Morn, Wedding Consummation, Interlude, Evanston, Ill., Carel & Ferd, Return to San Francisco, Watching Themselves.

NOTE: In this volume, certain programs of off-Broadway companies like The Chelsea Theater Center are exceptions to our rule of counting the number of performances from the date of the press coverage. When the official opening night takes place late in the run of a play's public performances (after previews), we count the first performance of record, not the press date, as opening night. Press date for *Lady Day: A Musical Tragedy* was 10/25/72; for *Sunset* 12/7/72, for *Kaspar* 2/14/73 matinee.

Yerma (16). Revival of the play by Federico Garcia Lorca in the Spanish language. Produced by the Brooklyn Academy of Music and Ninon T. Karlweis in the Nuria Espert Company Production, Armando Moreno administrator, in a limited engagement at the Brooklyn Academy of Music. Opened October 17, 1972. (Closed October 29, 1972)

Yerma .... Nuria Espert	Maria; 1st Washerwoman ...... Rosa Vicente
Juan .... José Luis Pellicena	3d Washerwoman; Child ...... Conchita Leza
Victor .... Daniel Dicenta	4th Washerwoman;
Old Pagan Woman;	Female Voice .... Gloria Berrocal
6th Washerwoman .... Amparo Valle	5th Washerwoman .... Nuria Moreno
Dolores; 2d Washerwoman;	Male .... Enrique Majo
Child .... Paloma Lorena	Female .... Alicia Day

Sisters-in-Law: Enrique Majo, Eduardo Bea. Men: Antonio Correncia, Angel Sempere, Juan Antonio Hormigon, Javier Macua, Eduardo Bea.

Directed by Victor Garcia; scenery and costumes, Victor Garcia, Fabian Puigserver; lighting, Polo Villasenor; assistant to director, Nuria Espert; stage director, José Maria Labra; production stage manager, Tennent McDaniel; press, Jan Hash, Carol Lawhon, Beverly W. Willis.

This Spanish language production of *Yerma* was previously produced in Madrid and in London as part of the 1972 World Theater Season at the Aldwych. *Yerma's* New York production history includes a staging in English translation by the Repertory Theater of Lincoln Center at the Vivian Beaumont 12/8/66 for 60 performances, and by the Greenwish Mews Spanish Theater in both Spanish and English in the 1970-71 season.

Bil Baird's Marionettes. Schedule of three marionette programs. **Winnie the Pooh** (44). Revival based on the book by A.A. Milne; adapted by A.J. Russell; music by Jack Brooks; lyrics by A.A. Milne and Jack Brooks. And **Bil Baird's Variety.** Opened October 29, 1972. (Closed December 17, 1972). **Davy Jones' Locker** (79). Revival with book by Arthur Birnkrant and Waldo Salt; music and lyrics by Mary Rodgers. And **Bil Baird's Variety.** Opened December 24, 1972. (Closed March 11, 1973). **Band-Wagon** (75). Variety revue. Opened March 16, 1973. (Closed May 20, 1973). Produced by The American Puppet Arts Council, Arthur Cantor executive producer, in the Bil Baird's Marionettes production at the Bil Baird Theater.

PERFORMER	"WINNIE THE POOH"	"DAVY JONES' LOCKER"
Bil Baird	Owl	
Peter Baird	Roo	Billy; Bosun
Pady Blackwood	Kanga; Rabbit	Paddlefoot; Sea Monster
Olga Felgemacher	Christopher Robin	Miranda
John O'Malley	Tigger	Nick
Simon Sisters	Mice	
Frank Sullivan	Winnie-the-Pooh	Mr. Merriweather
William Tost	Eeyore	Capt. Fletcher Scorn
Byron Whiting	Piglet	Davy Jones

BOTH PROGRAMS—Executive director, Bil Baird; artistic associate, Frank Sullivan; directed by Lee Theodore; musical direction and arrangements, Alvy West; production manager, Carl Harms; press, Frank Rowley.

WINNIE THE POOH—Place: In and around the 100 acre wood. This program was last presented by the Baird Marionettes 3/27/71 for 48 performances. The play was presented in two acts.

DAVY JONES' LOCKER—Place: A deserted island in the Bahamas, aboard the ship of Captain Fletcher Scorn and in Davy Jones' locker. The play, presented in two acts, was last presented by the Baird Marionettes in the 1967-68 season.

BIL BAIRD'S VARIETY—Perennial exhibition of "puppet virtuosity embodying many styles and types."

BAND-WAGON—Directed by Lee Theodore; lighting, Peggy Clark. With the Bil Baird's Marionettes company. ACT I: Lift Off!; It's Happening!; Tables; Punch and Judy; The Dance; Toy Bird; The Tale of Caliph Stork; You're My Everything; Spring, Sun and Flowers. ACT II: About Puppets; Bill Bailey; The Dying Swan; Whaddya Read?; The Stars; Rope Dancers; Old MacDonald Had a Farm; Cecilia; Finale.

NOTE: Bil Baird's Marionettes presented an additional program entitled *The Magic Onion,* written by Bil Baird, in 18 special performances for young children 7/11/72-7/21/72.

* **The American Place Theater.** Schedule of four programs. **The Kid** (32). By Robert Coover. Opened November 2, 1972; see note. (Closed December 2, 1972) **Freeman** (37). By Phillip Hayes Dean. Opened January 25, 1973; see note. (Closed February 24, 1973) **The Karl Marx Play** (32). By Rochelle Owens; music by Galt MacDermot; lyrics by Rochelle Owens. Opened March 16, 1973; see note. (Closed April 14, 1973) * **Baba Goya** (22). By Steve Tesich. Opened May 9, 1973; see note. Produced by The American Place Theater, Wynn Handman director, at The American Place Theater.

THE KID

Sheriff	Beeson Carroll	The Kid	Dale Robinette
Deputy	John Coe		

Cowpokes: Albert M. Ottenheimer, George Bamford, Bob Gunton, David Ramsey, James Richardson, Don Plumley, Sy Johnson, Neil Portnow. Belles: Alice Beardsley, Jenny O'Hara, Cherry Davis.

Directed by Jack Gelber; music composed and directed by Stanley Walden; scenery, Kert Lundell; costumes, Joe Aulisi; lighting, Roger Morgan; staged movement, Edward Roll; associate director, Julia Miles; production stage manager, Franklin Keysar; stage manager, Grania M. Hoskins; press, David Roggensack.

Sheriff kills the West's fastest gun and is first idolized, then killed, by the townsfolk, in a dramatization of the love-hate relationship between public and heroes.

FREEMAN

Teresa Aquila	Estelle Evans	Freeman Aquila	Bill Cobbs
Ned Aquila	Dotts Johnson	Rex Coleman	J.A. Preston
Osa Lee Aquila	Marjorie Barnes		

Directed by Lloyd Richards; scenery, Douglas Higgins; costumes, Bernard Johnson; lighting, Shirley Prendergast, music, William S. Fischer.

Time: The recent past. Place: A small industrial city in Michigan. The play was presented in two parts.

Misfit son of black conformist parents is gradually defeated as he strives for a more ambitious, meaningful role in life.

THE KARL MARX PLAY

Shirlee (clarinet)	Linda Mulrean	Karl Marx	Leonard Jackson
Krista (violin)	Deborah Loomis	Frederick Engels	Randy Kim
Elly (cello)	Louie Piday	Jenny von Westphalen	Katherine Helmond
Trinka (guitar)	Zenobia Conkerite	Lenchen	Lizabeth Pritchett
Laurie (autoharp-baritone)	Linda Swenson	Baby Johann	Ralph Carter
Leadbelly	Norman Matlock		

Directed by Mel Shapiro; scenery, Karl Eigsti; lighting, Roger Morgan.

Free representation of Karl Marx as a penurious family man living in London before achieving fame with his writings.

BABA GOYA

Goya	Olympia Dukakis	Adolf	Ken Tigar
Mario	John Randolph	Criminal	Randy Kim
Old Man	Lou Gilbert	Studly	David A. Butler
Bruno	R.A. Dow	Client	James Greene
Sylvia	Peggy Whitton		

Directed by Edwin Sherin; scenery, Karl Eigsti; lighting, Roger Morgan; costumes, Whitney Blausen.

Time: The present. Place: A house in Queens. The play was presented in two parts.

Life in a zany household whose mother has made of it a warm and understanding refuge for orphans and other strangers, and an affectionate one for a series of husbands.

GUEST PRODUCTION: The Eugene O'Neill Memorial Theater Center production of *The Little Theater of the Deaf* played a limited engagement of 12 performances 12/26/72-12/31/72 at The American Place Theater at American Place's invitation and under its auspices. The various works offered by *The Little Theater of the Deaf* (David Hays producing director) were directed by Bernard Bragg, Remy Charlip, David Hays and J. Ranelli; with costumes by Fred Voelpel and scenery by J.C. Hansen and Elliott Joslin; performed by Linda Bove, Julianna Field, Richard Casselman, Timothy Scanlon and Edmund Waterstreet.

NOTE: In this volume, certain programs of off-Broadway companies like The American Place Theater are exceptions to our rule of counting the number of performances from the date of the press coverage. When the official opening night takes place late in the run of a play's public performances (after previews), we count the first performance of record, not the press date, as opening night. Press date for *The Kid* was 11/17/72, for *Freeman* 2/5/73, for *The Karl Marx Play* 4/2/73, for *Baba Goya* 5/21/73.

A Quarter for the Ladies Room (1). Musical revue with lyrics by Ruth Batchelor; music by John Clifton and Arthur Siegel. Produced by Phillip R. Productions at the Village Gate. Opened and closed at the evening performance, November 12, 1972.

Directed by Darwin Knight; musical direction, Karen Gustafson; scenery, David R. Ballou; costumes, Miles White; lighting, Lee Watson; arrangements, Bill Brohn; production stage manager, Robert Bruyr; press, Seymour Krawitz. With Helon Blount, Paula Cinko, Norma Donaldson, Judy MacMurdo, Benay Venuta.

Ladies assembled in a powder room sing of the men in their lives.

Green Julia (147). By Paul Ableman. Produced by Dina and Alexander Racolin at the Sheridan Square Playhouse. Opened November 16, 1972. (Closed March 25, 1973)

Robert "Bradshaw" Lacey .....Fred Grandy   Jacob "Carruthers" Perew .....James Woods

Directed by William E. Hunt; scenery and lighting, David F. Segal; press, Max Eisen, Milly Schoenbaum.

Time: The present, a day in late spring. Place: Untidy "digs" in a university town in England shared by Perew and Lacey. Act I: About 3 p.m. Act II: Twenty minutes later.

Comedy-drama of two graduating college roommates playing roles and games with each other, as though searching for identities suitable for the adult world they are about to enter. A foreign play previously produced in Edinburgh, London and Washington, D.C.

John Pleshette replaced James Woods 12/5/72.

A Best Play; see page 178

The Repertory Theater of Lincoln Center. Festival of two programs of one-act plays (three revivals and one world premiere) by Samuel Beckett, in repertory. **Happy Days** and **Act Without Words 1** (16). Opened November 20, 1972. **Krapp's Last Tape** and **Not I** (world premiere) (15). Opened November 22, 1972. Produced by The Repertory Theater of Lincoln Center, Jules Irving director, at the Forum Theater. (Repertory closed December 17, 1972)

PERFORMER	"HAPPY DAYS"	"ACT WITHOUT WORDS 1"	"KRAPP'S LAST TAPE"	"NOT I"
Hume Cronyn	Willie	The Player	Krapp	
Hendeson Forsythe				Auditor
Jessica Tandy	Winnie			Mouth

Directed by Alan Schneider; scenery, Douglas W. Schmidt; lighting, John Gleason; costumes, Sara Brook; production stage manager, Barbara-Mae Phillips; stage manager, Robert Walter; press, Susan Bloch, William Schelble, Norman J-F. Lombino.

In *Not I*, a mouth speaks words rapidly, sometimes meaninglessly, in a panic effort to stave off death. *Act Without Words 1* was previously produced in New York by the Living Theater and is a wordless pantomime of tantalization. The most recent of numerous New York productions of *Krapp's Last Tape* was by Theater 1969 on Broadway 10/9/68 for 5 performances, and *Happy Days* was last produced off Broadway in French by Le Tréteau de Paris 4/24/70 for 10 performances.

LINCOLN CENTER'S ANNUAL COMMUNITY/STREET THEATER FESTIVAL

In addition to its regular programs, Lincoln Center sponsored outdoor performances in the Lincoln Center Plaza by street theater groups from all boroughs of New York City and various other cities, opening 8/21/72 and continuing through 9/3/72. Here is a list of participating organizations and their programs: Irish Arts Group (folk songs); The Mount Morris Everyman Company, *Everyman and Roach;* Brownsville Lab Theater, *Variations of Freedom;* Brothers and Sisters United from Staten Island, *Being Black;* Harlem Children's Theater; Puerto Rican Traveling Theater, *The Passion of Antigona Perez;* East River Players, *Dark Symphony;* Brownsville Theater Project (variety); New Federal Theater, *Abdal-José Marti;* Bed-Stuy Street Academy, *Nigger Gangs, Nigger;* Inwood People's Performance Company, *Choices;* House of Nilaja; The Street Corner Society, East Lansing, Mich., *The Woman Play;* The Freedom House Players, Madison, Wis., *The Throw-Away Kids;* Artists Collective, Hartford, Conn., *The Many Moods of Black Experience;* Workshops for Careers in the Arts, Washington, D.C., *God Is in the Streets Today;* Theater West, Dayton, Ohio, *The System;* Traveling Players Festival, Lewiston, Me., *Noah* and *The Artisan;* Theater Black, Ltd., *Black Magic;* Brownsville Lab Theater Arts, Inc.; Street Theater, Inc., Ossining, N.Y., *All Junkies* by Miguel Pinero, *In the Park* by Ronald Young and *The Street Corner* by Richard Wesley; Bridgton, Me., Homestead Players, *Little Alice* by Billy Dymond; Black Chants (poetry and music); Everyman Company of Brooklyn, *The Blind Junkie* by Peter Copani; Black Spectrum Theater, *Black Love;* Afro-American Total Theater, *Makin' It* by Jimmy Justice and Holly Hamilton.

Doctor Selavy's Magic Theater (144). Musical conceived by Richard Foreman; music by Stanley Silverman; lyrics by Tom Hendry. Produced by Lyn Austin and Oliver Smith in the Lenox Arts Center production at the Mercer-O'Casey Theater. Opened November 23, 1972. (Closed March 25, 1973)

Fortune Teller	Denise Delapenha	Doctor With Most Hair	Steve Menken
Female Pirate	Mary Delson	Little Girl	Jackie Paris
Patient	Ron Faber	Shortest Male Doctor	Robert Schlee
Jessica Harper	Rock Singer	Shortest Female Doctor	Amy Taubin
Dr. Selavy	George McGrath		

Musicians: Allen Shawn piano, Bill Takas bass, Luther Rix percussion and cello, Harvey Sarch guitar.

Directed by Richard Foreman; vocal director, Cathy MacDonald; assistant producer, Michael Frazier; associate producer, Mary Silverman, production stage manager, Duane Mazey; press, Michael Alpert.

Musical comedy approach to the subject of mental illness and its therapy. First produced at the Lenox, Mass. Arts Center in the summer of 1972.

Barry Primus replaced Ron Faber 11/28/72.

MUSICAL NUMBERS: Introduction—"I Live by My Wits." First Day's Treatment: Facing the Pirates—"Three Menu Songs," "Bankrupt Blues," "Future for Sale," "Life on the Inside." Second Day's Treatment: Living the Good Life—"Strawberry-Blueberry," "The More You Get," "Money in the Bank," "Life on the Inside" (Reprise), "Long Live Free Enterprise," "Doesn't It Bug You," "Dusky Shadows." Third Day's Treatment: Dreaming of Love—"Poor Boy," "Dearest Man." Fourth Day's Treatment: The Symbolic Death and Rebirth—"Where You Been Hiding Till Now," "Fireman's Song," "What are You Proposing," "Party's Gonna End," "Requiem." Fifth Day's Treatment: The Ecstasy and Cure—"Let's Hear It for Daddy Moola," "Life on the Inside" (Reprise).

The Mother of Us All (16). Revival of the opera with text by Gertrude Stein; music by Virgil Thomson. Produced by Lyn Austin, Orin Lehman, Hale Matthews and Oliver Smith at the Guggenheim Museum. Opened November 26, 1972. (Closed December 10, 1972)

(Susan B. Anthony) . . . . Judith Erickson, Phyllis Worthington	Elliot's Brother . . . . Wayne Turnage
Anne; Indiana Elliott . . . . . Lynne Wickenden	(Daniel Webster) . . . . David Wilder, Kenneth F. Bell
Gertrude S.; Angel More;	Jo the Loiterer; Andrew Johnson . . Gene West
Lillian Russell . . . . Olivia Buckley	John Adams . . . . Jon Garrison
Virgil T; Chris the Citizen; Thaddeus Stevens; Ulysses S. Grant; Indiana	Jenny Reefer . . . . Kate Hurney

(Parentheses indicate roles in which the actors alternated)

Directed by Elizabeth Keen and Roland Gagnon; entire production under the artistic direction of Virgil Thomson; musical direction, Roland Gagnon; scenery, Oliver Smith; costumes, Patricia Zipprodt; lighting, Richard Nelson; scenario, Maurice Grosser; associate producer, Mary Silverman; production stage manager, Jonathan Stuart; stage manager, Brian Meister; press, Michael Alpert.

Act I, Scene 1 (Prologue): A room in the house of Susan B. Anthony. Scene 2: A political rally. Scene 3: A village green adjoining the house of Susan B. Anthony. Scene 4: The same. Scene 5: The same. Act II, Scene 1: The drawing room of Susan B. Anthony. Scene 2: The same. Scene 3 (Epilogue): The Congressional Hall.

This Stein-Thomson opera about the life and times of Susan B. Anthony, the pioneer suffragette, was first produced at Columbia University in 1947. The present production was first mounted at the Lenox, Mass. Arts Center in the summer of 1972.

The Contrast (24). Musical based on the play by Royall Tyler; adapted by Anthony Stimac; music by Don Pippin; lyrics by Steve Brown. Produced by Peter Cookson at the Eastside Playhouse. Opened November 28, 1972. (Closed December 13, 1972)

Charlotte . . . . Connie Danese	Dimple . . . . Ty McConnell
Letitia . . . . Elaine Kerr	Colonel Manly . . . . Robert G. Denison
Frank; Van Rough . . . . Gene Kelton	Jessamy . . . . Grady Clarkson
Maria . . . . Patti Perkins	Jonathan . . . . Philip MacKenzie
Jenny . . . . Pamela Adams	

Directed by Anthony Stimac; choreography, Bill Guske; musical direction, Dorothea Freitag; scenery, David Chapman; costumes, Robert Pusilo; lighting, C. Murawski; musical arrangements, Don Pippin; stage manager, Ted Harris; press, Thelma E. Boalby, Howard Atlee, Clarence Allsopp.

Act I, Scene 1: Charlotte's apartment. Scene 2: A room in Van Rough's house. Scene 3: Charlotte's apartment. Scene 4: The Mall. Scene 5: Dimple's room. Act II, Scene 1: The Mall. Scene 2: Charlotte's apartment. Scene 3: A room in Van Rough's House. Scene 4: Dimple's room. Scene 5: Charlotte's apartment.

The Contrast on which the book of this musical is based was the first comedy of record by a native American author. It was performed at the John Street Theater in New York City on April 16, 1787, the year in which it was written, and is a comedy of plain American manners contrasted with the refinements of European manners of its day. Its only previous production in the modern New York theater was 11/11/33 for 6 performances of excerpts on a program of Dorothy Sands sketches.

ACT I

Prologue ....Company
"A Woman Rarely Ever" ....Charlotte, Letitia
"A House Full of People" ....Maria
"Keep Your Little Eye Upon the Main Chance, Mary" ....Van Rough
"So They Call It New York" ....Jonatthan, Jessamy
"Dear Lord Chesterfield" ....Dimple
"Dear Lord Chesterfield" (Reprise) ....Jessamy
"A Sort of Courting Song" ....Jenny, Jonathan
"So Far" ....Company

ACT II

"She Can't Really Be" ....Dimple, Manly
"That Little Monosyllable" ....Charlotte, Maria
"It's Too Much" ....Dimple, Charlotte, Maria, Manly, Letitia
"Keep Your Little Eye Upon the Main Chance, Mary" (Reprise) ....Van Rough
"Wouldn't I" ....Mary, Manly
"A Hundred Thousand Ways" ....Jessamy, Jonathan
"I Was in the Closet" ....Company
"So Far" (Reprise) ....Company

Die Brücke (The Bridge). German Theater Ensemble for Overseas in a schedule of two programs in the German language. **Der Frieden** (Peace) (7). By Aristophanes; adapted by Peter Hacks. Opened November 28, 1972. (Closed December 3, 1972). **Woyzeck** (7). By Georg Büchner. Opened December 5, 1972. (Closed December 10, 1972). Produced by the Goethe Institute of Munich and the Gert von Gontard Foundation at the Barbizon Plaza Theater.

PERFORMER	"DER FRIEDEN"	"WOYZECK"
Eva Böttcher	Trygaios's 1st Daughter	Margaret; Grandmother
Dieter Brammer	Chorus Leader; Hierokles	Captain
Harald Dietl	War	Drum Major
Elisabeth Endriss	Lenzwonne	Marie
Siegfried Fetscher		Sergeant; Innkeeper
Gerhard Friedrich	Hermes	Doctor
Michael Hoffmann		2d Apprentice; Town Idiot
Claudia Lobe	Trygaios's 2d Daughter	Charlatan's Wife; Kathe
Gudrun Mebs	Herbstfleiss; Boy	Girl
Klaus Münster	Tumult; Helmschmied	Old Man; 1st Apprentice
Hans Putz	Trygaios	Charlatan
Joost Siedhoff	2d Slave	Andres; Jew
Wolfgang Reinbacher	1st Slave; Waffenkramer	Woyzeck

Chorus in *Der Frieden:* Siegfried Fetscher, Michael Hoffman, Dieter Steinbrink, Stephan Bastian, Klaus Münster, Joost Siedhoff, Harald Dietl, Gerhard Friedrich, Claudia Lobe. Students in *Woyzeck:* Dieter Steinbrink, Michael Hoffmann. Siegfried Fetscher, Stephan Bastian.
BOTH PLAYS: Makeup and wigs, Ursula Esch; technical director, Holger Christiansen; assistant, Imme Siedhoff; press, Philip C. Rogerson.
DER FRIEDEN directed by Günther Fleckenstein; scenery and costumes, Hans-Walter Lenneweit; music, Eric Tass.
Aristophanes's *Peace* was last presented in New York in the 1968-69 season in a musical version at the Judson Poets Theater and subsequently 1/27/69 off Broadway for 142 performances. This Die Brücke production was presented in two acts.
WOYZECK directed by Hans Joachim Heyse; scenery and costumes, Christian Bussmann; music, Dieter Schönbach.
The Büchner work appeared on Broadway 4/5/66 in the Bavarian State Theater production, in German, for 8 performances. This Die Brücke production was presented without intermission.

F.O.B. (3). By Jeff Weiss. Produced by Placato Enterprises at the Mercer Brecht Theater. Opened November 24, 1972. (Closed November 26, 1972)

Directed by Gaby Rodgers; scenery, Lewis Rosen; production stage manager, Lewis Rosen; press, Samuel J. Friedman. With Jeff Weiss, William Finley.
Virtually a monologue, a playwright's absurdist view of his own problems.

Blue Boys (1). By Allan Knee. Produced by Michael Carson at the Martinique Theater. Opened and closed at the evening performance November 29, 1972.

Directed by Neal Kenyon; scenery and lighting, Tom Munn; costumes, Joan E. Thiel; production stage manager, John Hagan; press, Seymour Krawitz. With Ray Thorne, Tom Lee Jones, Allan Knee, Robert Stattel, Jerry Dodge, Diane Kagan, Ann Sweeny.
Civil War soldiers fighting, dying and remembering their past lives.

The Bar That Never Closes (33). Musical with book by Louisa Rose; sketches by Marco Vassi; music by Tom Mandel; lyrics by Louisa Rose, John Braswell and Tom Mandel. Produced by Albert Poland and Bruce Mailman at the Astor Place Theater. Opened December 3, 1972. (Closed December 31, 1972)

Anybody; Little Woman ....Jennie Mortimer Mistaken Man;	Anybody's Friend's Friend ..Mary Jo Kaplan Homosexual; Elevator Girl;
Mrs. Schneider ....Susan Haviland	Debutante ....Barbara Greca
Old Woman ....Nancy Schwartz	Singing Bar ....Jean Andalman
Michael; Table and Spigot ..Richard Westlein	Nurse; Harry ....Raina Hefner
Mr. & Mrs. Dear ....Mary Jo Kaplan, Kyle Andersen	Doctor ....Christopher Lamal The Libidoes ......Barbara Greca, Bill Eddy
Girl ....Lane Binkley	Riddle's Woman ....Kyle Andersen
God ....Bill Eddy	Butch Medusa ....Camille Tibaldeo
The Lovers .....Ralph Smith, Kyle Andersen	Mad People ....Ensemble
Anybody's Friend ....Sara Parker	

Directed by John Braswell; musical direction and arrangements, Cathy MacDonald, Tom Mandel; associate producer, Ina Lea Meibach; production conceived by John Braswell and Louisa Rose; bar drop painting and logo, Susan Haskins; production stage manager, Gary Weathersbee; press, Saul Richman, Sara Altshul.
Act I, Scene 1: Prologue. Scene 2: The Bar That Never Closes. Scene 3: The Lover. Scene 4: The Kingdom of Come. Scene 5: The Old Woman. Scene 6: The Amethyst Goblet. Act II, Scene 7: Bowel Boogie. Scene 8: The Towers. Scene 9: The Three Riddles. Scene 10: Circus of Jade. Scene 11: The Snow Queen's Mirror. Scene 12: Epilogue. (The Kingdom of Come, Bowel Boogie and Circus of Jade are from *Tales for Heads*.)
Series of sketches and numbers generally on a theme of loneliness.

ACT I

"Walking With You, Two by Two" ....Ensemble
   (Lyrics by Louisa Rose)
"Do It" ....Anybody, Ensemble
   (Lyrics by John Braswell)
"Recipe for Love" ....Old Woman, Ensemble
   (Lyrics by John Braswell)
"Kaleidoscope" ....Anybody's Friend
   (Lyrics by Louisa Rose)

ACT II

"I Don't Think I'll Ever Love You" ....Ensemble
   (Lyrics by John Braswell)
"Dear Dear" ....Riddle's Man
   (Lyrics by Tom Mandel)
"Tears of Ice" ....Singing Bar
   (Lyrics by Louisa Rose)
"Circus of Jade" ....Butch Medusa
   (Lyrics by John Braswell)
"Precious Little Darkness" ....Anybody
   (Lyrics by Louisa Rose)

Say When (7). Musical with book and lyrics by Keith Winter; music by Arnold Goland. Produced by Walter Rosen Scholz at the Plaza 9 Theater. Opened December 4, 1972. (Closed December 9, 1972)

Directed and choreographed by Zoya Leporska; musical direction, Marc Pressel; scenery, William James Wall; costumes, Leila Larmon; lighting, Clarke W. Thornton; production stage manager, Clarke W. Thornton; press, Lynda Wells. With Bill Berrian, Andrea Duda, Michael Miller, Gerrianne Raphael, Anita Darian, Don Kyle, Sharron Miller, Michael Misita, Terrance McKerrs.

Reminiscences of the 1920s from the point of view of the 1970s.

The River Niger (120). By Joseph A. Walker. Produced by The Negro Ensemble Company, Douglas Turner Ward artistic director, Robert Hooks executive director, Frederick Garrett administrative director, at St. Marks Playhouse. Opened December 5, 1972. (Closed March 3, 1973; see note)

Grandma Wilhelmina Brown ..Frances Foster	Mo ....Neville Richen
Johnny Williams ......Douglas Turner Ward	Gail ....Saundra McClain
Dr. Dudley Stanton ....Graham Brown	Skeeter ....Charles Weldon
Ann Vanderguild ....Grenna Whitaker	Al ....Dean Irby
Mattie Williams ....Roxie Roker	Jeff Williams ....Les Roberts
Chips ....Lennal Wainwright	Voice of Lt. Staples ......Morley Morgana

Directed by Douglas Turner Ward; scenery, Gary James Wheeler; costumes, Edna Watson; lighting, Shirley Prendergast; incidental music, Dorothy A. Dinroe; stage manager, Wyatt Davis; press, Howard Atlee, Clarence Allsopp, Charles House.

Time: The present, early February. Place: Harlem, the Williams's brownstone on 133d Street, between Lenox and Seventh Avenues. Act I: Friday—4:30 p.m., midnight, later. Act II: Saturday, the next day—10:45 a.m. Act III: Friday, six days later—early evening, later that same night.

Several members of a courageous Harlem family, headed by a father who is a poet by inclination and a house painter by necessity, come to grips with the central problems of their lives.

NOTE: *The River Niger* transferred to Broadway for a continued run opening 3/27/73. See its entry in the "Plays Produced on Broadway" section of this volume.

A Best Play; see page 211

NEC WORKSHOP PRODUCTIONS

In addition to its professional program of record, The Negro Ensemble Company presented a series of 13 informal programs 1/23/73 through 2/18/73, entitled "Repertory Workshops," with press invited for articles on the overall productions of the plays and for "impressions," but not for reviews, since the productions were works in progress, performed by a repertory company.

Programs were as follows: 1/23-1/26—Works of three black women playwrights, *Laundry* by Gertrude Greenidge, *Wildflowers* by Robbie McCauley and *Indiana Avenue* by Debbie Wood, all directed by Hazel Bryant; 1/27-1/31—*Galavantin'* by Milburn Davis and *The Death of Little Marcus* by Herman Johnson, both directed by Arthur French; 2/1-2/4—*Johnnas* by Bill Gunn and *Playstreet* by Ted Harris, both directed by Michael Fleming; 2/6-2/9—*Crocodiles* and *The Riddle of the Palm Leaf* by Femi Euba, both directed by Sati Jamal; 2/10-2/14—*The Yellow Pillow* by John Perkins; 2/15-2/18—*Funnytime* and *Funnytime, No You Didn't* by Seret Scott and *Buy a Little Tenderness* by Buryel Clay.

Another series of special events scheduled by NEC 5/11/73 through 6/3/73 included two theater programs: Vinie Burrows in *Walk Together Children* 5/26-5/27 and The Demi Gods production of *Yin Yang*, a new play by Joseph A. Walker, with music by Dorothy A. Dinroe, 5/29-5/31.

Please Don't Cry and Say No (15). Program of three one-act plays: *The Brown Overcoat* by Victor Sejour and *The Botany Lesson* by Joachin Maria Machado de Assis, both translated by Townsend Brewster, and the title play by Townsend Brewster. Produced by Sally Sears and Primavera Productions, Ltd. at Circle in the Square. Opened December 6, 1972. (Closed December 17, 1972)

Directed by Philip Taylor; music, Dorothy A. Dinroe; scenery and lighting, Hal Tine; costumes, Jon Haggins; production stage manager, Jerry Laws; press, Dorothy Ross. With Janet League, Lee Kirk, Michael Brassfield, Tyrone Browne, Vanessa K. Gilder, Ethel Ayler, David Downing, Charles Turner, Ronald Dennis, Joseph Mydell, B. Henry Douglass. Guitarist, Leon Atkinson.

The Brown Overcoat, translated from the French, is a 19th century comedy of manners; *The Botany Lesson*, translated from the Brazilian Portuguese, is an early 20th century study of sexual attraction; *Please Don't Cry and Say No* is a modern tale of a busy executive's wife having an affair with a younger man.

Rainbow (48). Musical with book by James and Ted Rado; music and lyrics by James Rado. Produced by James and Ted Rado at the Orpheum Theater. Opened December 18, 1972. (Closed January 28, 1973)

Man	Gregory V. Karliss	President	Dean Compton
Jesus	Philip A.D.	First Lady	Marie Santell
Ms. Friendstrangle; Stripper	Patricia Gaul	President's Child	Stephen Scharf
Dr. Banana	Rudy Brown	President's Child	Marcia MClain
Mother	Camille	Wizard	Bobby C. Ferguson
Father	Michael D. Arian	Girl	Kay Cole
Buddha	Meat Loaf	Twin Girl	Janet Powell
Opera	Elinor Frye		

Rainbow Band: Billy Schwartz electric and acoustic guitar; Herb Bushler bass; Richard D. Pratt drums, percussion; Charles Sullivan trumpet, fluglhorn; William Blount alto, tenor, baritone saxophone, flute, clarinet; Stephen Margoshes piano, five-string banjo.

Directed by Joe Donovan; musical supervision, arrangements, direction, Stephen Margoshes; scenery and lighting, James Tilton; costumes, Nancy Potts; sound, Abe Jacob; associate producer, Richard Osorio; production stage manager, Ronald Schaeffer; press, Solters/Sabinson/Roskin, Inc., Marilynn LeVine.

Corcunopia of rock numbers and pastiches, loosely assembled in a fantasy of a young man killed in Vietnam and now restlessly seeking his place in the universe.

ACT I

"Who Are We"	
"Love Me Love Me Dorothy Lamour La Sarong"	Rainbeams
"Fruits and Vegetables"	Rainbeams
"Welcome Banana"	Rainbeams
"Questions Questions"	Dr. Banana, Rainbeams
"Song to Sing"	Stripper
"My Lungs"	Girl, Rainbeams
"You Got to Be Clever"	Man, Rainbeams
"Tangled Tangents"	Girl, Rainbeams
"What Can I Do for You"	Man, Dr. Banana, Master of Ceremonies
"Oh I Am a Fork"	Twin Girl
"People Stink"	Mother, Father, Rainbeams
"Guinea Piggin"	Father, Rainbeams
"Give Your Heart to Jesus"	Mother, Rainbeams
"Joke a Cola"	Rainbeams
"Mama Loves You"	Rainbeams
"I Want to Make You Cry"	Mother, Father, Man, Jesus, Rainbeams
"I Am a Cloud"	Man, Twin Girl
"A Garden for Two"	Rainbeams
"Starry Cold Night"	Man, Girl, Rainbeams
"Bathroom"	Girl, Twin Girl, Rainbeams
"O.K., Goodbye"	Mother, Father, Man
"Deep in the Dark"	Man, Mother, Father
"You Live in Flowers"	Man, Wizard
"I Don't Hope for Great Things"	Man, Rainbeams

ACT II

"Globligated" ....Girl, Twin Girl, Man
"Be Not Afraid" ....Man, Rainbeams
"Obedience" ....President
"Ten Days Ago" ....President, Rainbeams
"Oh, Oh, Oh" ....First Lady, Jesus
"Moosh, Moosh" ....President, Generals, Business Leaders
"The Man" ....Girl, Twin Girl
"The World Is Round" ....President, Ms. Friendstrangle, Man
"Stars and Bars" ....President, Generals
"Cacophony" ....Man, Rainbeams
"Groovy Green Man Groovy" ....Girl, Twin Girl, Man, President's Children
"Heliopolis" ....Man, Rainbeams
"I Am Not Free" ....Man, President
"We Are the Clouds" ....President's Child, Rainbeams
"How Dreamlike" ....President, Man, Rainbeams
"Somewhere Under the Rainbow" ....Man, Rainbeams
"Star Song" ....Man, Rainbeams

The Trials of Oz (15). By Geoff Robertson; with songs by Buzzy Linehart, Mick Jagger, John Lennon and Yoko Ono. Produced by Richard Scanga and The Friends of Van Wolf, Ivor David Balding executive producer, Cathy Cochran associate producer, at the Anderson Theater. Opened December 19, 1972. (Closed December 31, 1972)

Directed by Jim Sharman; scenery, Mark Ravitz; costumes, Joseph G. Aulisi; lighting, Jules Fisher; music arranged and conducted by Bill Cunningham; production stage manager, Rick Thayer; press, Gifford/Wallace, Inc. With Harry Gold, Cliff DeYoung, Dan Leach, Greg Antonacci, Peter Kybart, Dalas Alinder, Myra Carter, Gabor Morea, Ginny Russell, Alek Primrose.

Play based on the transcript of the Old Bailey obscenity trial of editors of the controversial publication *Oz,* with interpolations of rock music. A foreign play previously produced as a reading by the Royal Shakespeare Company in London.

Shay Duffin as Brendan Behan (89). One-man program based on the works of Brendan Behan; performed, written and adapted by Shay Duffin. Produced by Signature Productions at the Abbey Theater. Opened January 2, 1973. (Closed March 18, 1973)

Directed by Dennis Hayes; New York production director, Marvin Gordon; scenery, Shay Duffin, Joe Behan; lighting, Joe Behan; executive producer, Les Weinstein; stage manager, Joe Behan; press, Bill Doll and Company, Inc.

Collection of excerpts from Behan's work listed below, with the following program note by Mr. Duffin: "The Behan I am playing . . . . . is Brendan giving his last hurrah six months before he died. I could have called it *The Three Phases of Behan,* for I have designed it to deal with the three most important aspects of his life: Behan the talker, Behan the pub entertainer and Behan the rebel."

Each program was assembled from the following: We're here because we're queer, Bells of hell (*The Hostage*); Words of introduction (*Brendan Behan's New York*); Giants of Irish literature, Down by the glenside, Pubs, whisky, whores and porter, Parsnips and Yeats, Popes, pulpits and parish priests (*Brendan Behan's Island*); My father, English spoken in North America, Almost a smuggler, Pimp and pornographer (*Confessions of an Irish Rebel*); The sea, oh the sea, Another martyr for old Ireland, Prison cells, mass, benediction and excommunication, British justice and judges (*Borstal Boy*); Overheard in a bookshop (*Hold Your Hour and Have Another*); The old triangle, Capital punishment (*The Quare Fellow*); "Trust in Drink" (song, author unknown); Reflections (by Shay Duffin, from his own collection of Behanisms).

Mystery Play (14). By Jean-Claude van Itallie. Produced by J. Craig Owens at the Cherry Lane Theater. Opened January 3, 1973. (Closed January 14, 1973)

Directed by Jacques Levy; scenery, Philip Gilliam; costumes, Patricia McGourty, lighting, Judy Rasmuson; original song by Richard Peaslee; production stage manager, Robert J. Bruyr; press, David Roggensack. With Tom Brannum, Rod Browning, Shami Chaikin, Nancy Charney, Rick Friesen, Cynthia Harris, Judd Hirsch, Donald Warfield. Fred Goldrich piano.

Satire on mystery plays, political attitudes, social mores, etc., in a farce in which the characters are murdered one by one.

The Grand Music Hall of Israel (15). Musical revue in the Hebrew and other languages conceived by Jonathon Karmon. Produced by Madison Square Garden Productions and Hy Einhorn at the Felt Forum. Opened January 4, 1973. (Closed January 14, 1973)

Directed and choreographed by Jonathon Karmon; musical direction, Rafi Paz; assistant director, Gavri Levi; press, Max Eisen. With Shoshana Damari, Ron Eliran, Myron Cohen and the Karmon Israeli Dancers and Singers.

Third in a series of world-touring collections of Israeli music and dance mounted by Mr. Karmon and his troupe.

* National Lampoon's Lemmings (145). Musical revue with words and lyrics by David Axlerod, Anne Beatts, Henry Beard, John Boni, Tony Hendra, Sean Kelly, Doug Kenny, P.J. O'Rourke and the cast; music by Paul Jacobs and Christopher Guest. Produced by Tony Hendra at the Village Gate. Opened January 25, 1973.

John Belushi	Paul Jacobs
Chevy Chase	Mary-Jenifer Mitchell
Garry Goodrow	Alice Playten
Christopher Guest	

Directed by Tony Hendra; music directed by Paul Jacobs; lighting, Beverly Emmons; sound, Abe Jacob; arrangements, Paul Jacobs, Christopher Guest; production supervisor, Peter Lavery; press, Lenny Traube, Irving Zussman.

Satire on sex, politics, rock music and other contemporary conceits. The show was presented in two parts (no identification of individual sketches and musical numbers was made).

The White Whore and the Bit Player (18). By Tom Eyen. Produced by the Duo Theater at St. Clement's off off Broadway). Opened February 5, 1973. (Closed February 18, 1973)

Directed by Manuel Martin; choreography, Tony Cantanese; scenery, Jose Erasto Ramirez; costumes, Van Labriola; lighting, Lewis Rosen, Dale Mosher; sound, Felipe Napoles; press, Alan Eichler. With Candy Darling, Hortensia Colorado, Edwing Avila, Antonio Candolfi, Rafael Deligado, Ken Evans, Arturo Gines, Roberto Lopez, Padro Lorca, Carlos Noceda, Rene Troche.

First professional production of a work produced off off Broadway, first in 1964 at Cafe La Mama, and then at The Extension in 1969. It has often been played in Spanish as well as in English and alternated between the two languages in this production.

Welcome to Andromeda and **Variety Obit** (24). Program of two plays by Ron Whyte. Produced by Ruth Kalkstein and Patricia Gray at the Cherry Lane Theater. Opened February 12, 1973. (Closed March 4, 1973)

WELCOME TO ANDROMEDA

The Boy	David Clennon	The Nurse	Bella Jarrett

VARIETY OBIT

Singers	Andrea Marcovicci, Richard Cox	Musicians	Mel Marvin, Gary Mure
The Narrator	David Clennon		

Directed by Tom Moore; scenery, Peter Harvey; lighting, Roger Morgan; costumes, Bruce Harrow; associate producer, Sidney Annis; production stage manager, Robert Keegan; press, David Lipsky.

Welcome to Andromeda, presented in two parts, concerns a bedridden but articulate young man trying to persuade his nurse to kill him while his over-protective mother is out of the house on an errand. *Variety Obit*, a musical one-acter, eulogizes a multi-generation show business family.

* **El Grande de Coca-Cola** (150). Musical revue in the Spanish language written by the cast; based on an idea by Ron House and Diz White. Produced by Jack Temchin, Gil Adler and John A. Vaccaro in The Low Moan Spectacular Production at the Mercer Arts Center. Opened February 13, 1973.

Sr. Don Pepe Hernandez . . . . Ron House	Consuela Hernandez . . . . Diz White
Miguel Hernandez . . . . Alan Shearman	Maria Hernandez . . . . Sally Willis
Juan Rodriguez . . . . John Neville-Andrews	

Choreography, Anna Nygh; production design, Mischa Petrow; musical arrangements, Alan Shearman, John Neville-Andrews; production stage manager, Lary Opitz; press, Lawrence N. Belling.

The play was presented without intermission, and without a formal list of sketches and musical numbers.

Musical comedy in comprehensible pidgin Spanish, about the owner of a second-rate night club in Honduras pretending to put on an internationally star-studded floor show. A foreign (British) play previously produced in various theaters in England and Continental Europe.

Penthouse Legend (30). Revival of the play formerly entitled *Night of January 16th* by Ayn Rand. Produced by P.J. and K. Smith at the McAlpin Rooftop Theater. Opened February 22, 1973. (Closed March 18, 1973)

Bailiff . . . . Edwin Fenton	Homer Van Fleet;
Judge Heath . . . . Don Lochner	James Chandler . . . . Douglas Fisher
Dist. Atty. Flint . . . . Michael Thompson	Elmer Sweeney . . . . Joseph O'Sullivan
Defense Atty. Stevens . . . Robert Fitzsimmons	Magda Svenson . . . . Ruth McCormick
Clerk . . . . Waller Thomas Burns	Nancy Lee Faulkner . . . . Holly Hill
Karen Andre . . . . Kay Gillian	John Graham Whitfield . . . . Bob Allen
Dr. Kirkland . . . . Gerard McLaughlin	Siegurd Jungquist . . . . Robert Keiper
John Hutchins . . . . Merrill E. Joels	"Guts" Regan . . . . Harvey Solin

Directed by Phillip J. Smith; scenery and lighting, David Houston; production stage manager, Arthur Silber; press, Meg Gordean.

Time and place: The three days of Karen Andre's trial. The play was presented in three parts.

Penthouse Legend, a courtroom drama whose "jury" is chosen nightly from the audience and whose ending is adaptable to their verdict, was first presented on Broadway 9/16/35 for 23 performances. It was previously revived off Broadway 4/10/40 at the Cherry Lane Theater.

* **The Tooth of Crime** (75). By Sam Shepard; music by The Performance Group; lyrics by Sam Shepard. Produced by The Performance Group at The Performing Garage (off off Broadway). Opened March 7, 1973.

Galactic Max; Doc . . . . Stephen Borst	Star; Ref . . . . Elizabeth LeCompte
Hoss . . . . Spalding Gray	Becky Lou . . . . Joan MacIntosh
Cheyenne . . . . James Griffiths	Crow . . . . Timothy Shelton

Directed by Richard Schechner; environmentalist, Jerry Rojo; technical director, James Clayburgh; costumes, Franne Lee; musical consultant, Paul Epstein; press, Stephen Borst.

Confrontation between an aging rock star and a young man who challenges him. Previously produced in London (at the Open Space), Vancouver (at the University of British Columbia) and Oswego, N.Y. (at the State University).

You Never Know (8). Musical revival based on a play by Siegfried Geyer and Robert Katscher; adapted by Rowland Leigh; music and lyrics by Cole Porter.

Produced by Stanley H. Handman at the Eastside Playhouse. Opened March 12, 1973. (Closed March 18, 1973)

Directed by Robert Troie; musical direction, Walter Geismar; production design, Robert Troie; production stage manager, Robert J. Bruyr; press, Betty Lee Hunt Associates. With Dan Held, Esteban Chalbaud, Grace Theveny, Lynn Fitzpatrick, Rod Loomis, Jamie Thomas.

You Never Know was first produced 9/21/38 for 78 performances. Its only previous New York revival was by the Stage Directors & Choreographers Workshop in the season of 1969-70.

Brother Gorski (6). By Emanuel Fried. Produced by the Brother Gorski Company at the Astor Place Theater. Opened March 15, 1973. (Closed March 18, 1973)

Directed by Salem Ludwig; scenery, Don Jensen; costumes, Sonia Lowenstein; lighting, Bob Brand; assistant to director, Leonardo Cimino; "Theme From Brother Gorski" by Johnny Brandon; production stage manager, G. Allison Elmer; press, Sol Jacobson, Lewis Harmon. With Ken Chapin, Albert M. Ottenheimer, Louis Quinones, Richard Sisk, John Leighton, Richard Triggs, Clinton Allmon, Clarence P. Jones Jr., Larry Gordon, Dennis McMahon, Leroy Gray, Bari Michaels, Iris Claire Braun, Jean Alexander, Nell Burnside, Robert Riesel.

Comedy-drama of union leadership.

Thoughts (24). Musical by Lamar Alford; additional lyrics by Megan Terry and Jose Tapla. Produced by Arthur Whitelaw, Seth Harrison and Dallas Alinder at the Theater de Lys. Opened March 19, 1973. (Closed April 6, 1973)

Mary Alice	Barbara Montgomery
Jean Andalman	Jeffrey Mylett
Martha Flowers	Howard Porter
Robin Lamont	Sarallen
Baruk Levi	E.H. Wright
Bob Molock	

Orchestra: Ray Bertuglia guitar, Warren Benbow drums, Eustis Guillemet bass.

Directed by Michael Schultz; musical staging, Jan Mickens; scenery, Stuart Wurtzel; costumes, Joseph Thomas; costume supervisor, Stanley Simmons; musical consultant, Joyce Brown; arrangements, David Horowitz; lighting, Ken Billington; produced in association with Peter Kean; presented by special arrangement with Lucille Lortel Productions, Inc.; production stage manager, Martin Herzer; press, Max Eisen, Maurice Turet.

Self-styled "musical celebration" of memories of growing up in the South as the son of a black preacher. Previously produced at Cafe La Mama. The play was presented without intermission.

MUSICAL NUMBERS: Opening (lyrics by Megan Terry)—Martha Flowers; "Blues Was a Pastime"—Barbara Montgomery, Company; "At the Bottom of Your Heart"—Robin Lamont, Jeffrey Mylett; "Ain't That Something"—Company; "Accepting the Tolls" and "One of the Boys"—Howard Porter; "Trying Hard"—Miss Montgomery; "Ain't That Something" (Reprise)—Mary Alice; "Separate but Equal"—Jean Andalman, Baruk Levi, Company; "Gone"—Mary Alice, Company; "Jesus Is My Main Man"—Bob Molock, Miss Flowers, Company; "Bad Whitey"—Misses Lamont, Andalman, Messrs. Mylett, Levi; "Thoughts"—Miss Andalman; "Strange Fruit"—Miss Montgomery; "I Can Do It Myself"—Sarallen, Company; "Walking in Strange and New Places"—Porter; "Music in the Air"—Miss Lamont, Company; "Sunshine"—Mary Alice, Company; "Many Men Like You"—Miss Flowers; "Roofs"—Porter; "Day oh Day"—Miss Flowers, Company.

An Evening With the Poet-Senator (14). By Leslie Weiner. Produced by Joel W. Schenker at Playhouse 2. Opened March 21, 1973. (Closed April 1, 1973)

Directed by Isaiah Sheffer; scenery and lighting, Tom Munn; costumes, Anne de Velder; production stage manager, David Taylor; press, Solters/Sabinson/Roskin, Inc., Milly Schoenbaum. With Peter Brandon, Tandy Cronyn, Henderson Forsythe, Margaret Linn, David Margulies, Thomas A. Stewart, Donald Symington.

Professional and private life of a particularly talented and distinguished former U.S. Senator, now a writer-in-residence and lecturer at a university.

* **The Hot l Baltimore** (80). By Lanford Wilson. Produced by Kermit Bloomgarden and Roger Ailes in The Circle Theater Company production at Circle in the Square. Opened March 22, 1973.

Bill ....Judd Hirsch	Mr. Katz ....Antony Tenuta
Girl ....Trish Hawkins	Suzy ....Stephanie Gordon
Millie ....Helen Stenborg	Suzy's John ....Burke Pearson
Mrs. Billotti ....Henrietta Bagley	Paul Granger III ....Jonathan Hogan
April ....Conchata Ferrell	Mrs. Oxenham ....Louise Clay
Mr. Morse ....Rob Thirkield	Cab Man ....Peter Tripp
Jackie ....Mari Gorman	Delivery Boy ....Marcial Gonzales
Jamie ....Zane Lasky	

Directed by Marshall W. Mason; scenery, Ronald Radice; costume co-ordination, Dina Costa; production stage manager, Andie Wilson Kingwill; press, The Merlin Group, Ltd., Sandra Manley, Cheryl Sue Dolby.

Time: Memorial Day. Place: The lobby of the Hotel Baltimore. Act I: 7 a.m. Act II: Afternoon. Act III: Midnight.

Transients and derelicts tell each other sad stories of the death of their lives in the lobby of a hotel which, much like the people it houses, is soon to suffer complete destruction. Previously produced off off Broadway by The Circle Theater Company in this same production, which was transferred to off-Broadway.

A Best Play; see page 292

Echoes (1). By N. Richard Nash. Produced by Orin Lehman at the Bijou Theater. Opened and closed at the evening performance, March 26, 1973.

Directed by Melvin Bernhardt; scenery, Ed Wittstein; costumes, Sara Brook; lighting, Martin Aronstein; stage manager, Allan Leicht; press, Solters/Sabinson/Roskin, Inc., Ellen Levene. With Lynn Milgrim, David Selby, Paul Tripp.

Dramatic fantasies of two schizophrenics in a psychiatric ward.

Smile, Smile, Smile (7). Musical with book by Robert Russell; music and lyrics by Hugo Peretti, Luigi Creatore and George David Weiss. Produced by Stuart Duncan at the Eastside Playhouse. Opened April 4, 1973. (Closed April 6, 1973)

Directed by Robert Simpson; scenery, Philip Gilliam; costumes, Patricia McGourty; lighting, Barry Arnold; orchestrations, Jack Andrews; dance arrangements, Bob Tartaglia; musical supervision, Joseph Stecko; production stage manager, Michael Massee; press, Max Eisen, Maurice Turet. With Bobby Lee, Rudy Tronto, Carole Joan Macho, Diane Findlay, William Pierson, Chim Zien, Casey Craig, Marilyn Saunders, Joseph Neal, Suellen Estey, Gary Beach, Virginia Pulos, J. Richard Beneville, Geoff Leon, Donna Liggitt Forbes.

An inept ruler tries to turn his undiscovered island into a tourist attraction.

L'Eté (Summer) (10). By Romain Weingarten; translated from the French by Shepperd Strudwick III. Produced by Margaret Barker at the Cherry Lane Theater. Opened April 9, 1973. (Closed April 18, 1973)

Directed by Wendell Phillips; scenery and lighting, William Strom; sound, Susan Ain; production stage manager, Peter von Mayrhauser; press, M.J. Boyer. With Michael Mullins, Michael Higgins, Maureen Mooney, Jerry Mayer.

Comedy about a brother and sister and a pair of cats—played by people—under the hot, romantic sun of summer. A foreign play previously produced in Paris and London.

The Soldier (8). By Nick Bellitto. Produced by the DIApeiron Company at the Provincetown Playhouse. Opened April 10, 1973. (Closed April 18, 1973).

Directed by Eleanore Chapin; scenery, Richard Ferrugio; lighting, O.B. Lewis; sound, George Jacobs; stage manager, Robert Kerman; press, David Lipsky. With Tom Kindle, Megan Hunt, Sam Locante, Richard Ferrugio, Gregory Tigani, Paula Mallandi, Frank Girrardeau, Steve Simpson.

Former athlete and supposed Vietnam hero comes home and is troubled by a mysterious stain on his character.

Le Médecin Malgré Lui (The Doctor in Spite of Himself) (8). Revival of the play by Molière, performed in the French language. Produced by Le Tréteau de Paris in association with Le Jeune Théâtre National, with the patronage of the French Institute-Alliance Française, at the American Place Theater. Opened April 16, 1973. (Closed April 21, 1973)

Sganarelle	Yves Pignot	Jacqueline	Elizabeth Margoni
Martine	Anne-Marie Quentin	Lucinde	Nicole Chausson
Mr. Robert	Philippe Murgier	Leandre	Alain Roland
Valere	Loic Volaro	Thibaut	Jean-Claude Amyl
Lucas	Yves Ferry	Perrin	Alain Foures
Geronte	Michel Baumann		

Directed by Jean-Louis Thamin; scenery and costumes, Francoise Darne; technical director, Francis Charles; press, David Roggensack.

Molière's comedy done by the state-subsidized Paris troupe Le Jeune Théâtre National in honor of the playwright's tercentenary. There is no Broadway production of record, but the play was done off Broadway during the season of 1956-57.

* **What's a Nice Country Like You Doing in a State Like This?** (49). Cabaret revue based on an original concept by Ira Gasman, Cary Hoffman and Bernie Travis; music by Cary Hoffman; lyrics by Ira Gasman. Produced by Budd Friedman at the Upstage at Jimmy's. Opened April 19, 1973.

Betty Lynn Buckley	Priscilla Lopez
Sam Freed	Barry Michlin
Bill La Vallee	

Directed and choreographed by Miriam Ford; musical direction and vocal arrangements, Arnold Goss; scenery, Billy Puzo; costumes, Danny Morgan; orchestrations, Hurbert Arnold; design consultant, Paul Zalon; graphic design, Joe Budne; lighting design and production stage manager, Richard Delehanty; press, The Merlin Group, Ltd.

Topical revue, political satire presented at a time of troubled waters in Washington.

ACT I: "It's a Political-Satirical Revue"—Company; "Liberal's Lament"—Barry Michlin; "I'm in Love With—"—Priscilla Lopez; "Massage a Trois"—Company; "Changing Partners"—Miss Lopez, Michlin, Betty Lynn Buckley; "Crime in the Streets"—Sam Freed, Bill La Vallee, Michlin; "I'm in Love With—" (Reprise)—Miss Lopez; Street Suite ("Street People"—Company, "It's Getting Better"—La Vallee, Company, "I Like Me"—Miss Buckley, Company); "I'm in Love With—" (Reprise)—Miss Lopez; "Male Chauvinist"—Freed, Miss Buckley; "Primary Tango"—Miss Lopez, Company; "Johannesburg"—Michlin; New York Suite ("But I Love New York"—Miss Lopez, Freed, "Why Do I Keep Going to the Theater?—Miss Buckley, Michlin, "I Found the Girl of My Dreams on Broadway"—Freed, "But I Love New York," Reprise—Freed, Misses Buckley, Lopez, "A Mugger's Work Is Never Done"—La Vallee, "But I Love New York," Reprise—Company).

ACT II: "Kissinger und Kleindeinst und Klein"—Company; "Farewell First Amendment"—Company; "Why Johnny?"—Miss Buckley; "The Right Place at the Right Time"—Company; "Love Story"—Freed, Miss Lopez; "I'm Not Myself Any More"—Michlin; Porcupine Suite ("People Are Like Porcupines"—Michlin, La Vallee, Miss Buckley, "On a Scale of One to Ten"—Michlin, Miss Buckley, "Threesome"—La Vallee, Miss Buckley, Michlin); "Come on, Daisy"—Miss Buckley, Company; "Whatever Happened to the Communist Menace?"—Company; Finale—Company.

Crystal and Fox (24). By Brian Friel. Produced by Sheila Conlon at the McAlpin Rooftop Theater. Opened April 23, 1973. (Closed May 13, 1973)

Fox Melarkey	Will Hare	Pedro	Walt Gorney
Tanya	Jo Anne Belanger	Irish Policeman	Pat McNamara
El Cid; Detective	Chet Carlin	Gabriel	Brad Davis
Crystal	Rue McClanahan	Detective	Barry Corbin
Papa	Joseph Boley		

Directed by Patrick Conlon; scenery, Philip Gilliam; costumes, Philip Gilliam, Jennifer von Mayrhauser; lighting, Judy Rasmuson; incidental music, Ted Auletta; associate producer, Carmel Quinn; production stage manager, Ginny Freedman; press, Seymour Krawitz.

Scene 1: Backstage during a performance of the Fox Melarkey Show, Ballybeg, Ireland. Scene 2: Later that night. Scene 3: One week later. Scene 4: Night, one week later. Scene 5: A few hours later. Scene 6: A crossroads—two days later. The play was presented in two parts with an intermission between Scenes 2 and 3.

Self-destructive impulses of the director of a run-down troupe of barnstorming Irish entertainers. A foreign play previously produced in Dublin and Los Angeles.

A Phantasmagoria Historia of D. Johann Fausten Magister, PhD, MD, DD, DL, Etc. (1). By Vasek Simek. Produced by Vaslin Productions at the Truck and Warehouse Theater. Opened and closed at the evening performance, April 24, 1973.

Directed by Vasek Simek; scenery, Clarke Dunham; costumes, Patricia Quinn Stewart; lighting, David F. Segal; electronic sound, John Watts; production stage manager, Richard Husson; press, Max Eisen, Maurice Turet. With Jack Hollander, Barton Heyman, Lilly Noyes, Dennis Tate, Molly McKasson, Jara Kohout, Henry L. Baker, Danny DeVito, Mark Siegel, Muriel Miguel, Ann Miles, Jane Culley, Natalie Gray, Rhea Perlman.

A re-working of the Faust story combining various sources.

The Pilgrim's Progress (14). By John Bunyan; adapted by Orlin Corey. Produced by The Committee for the Theater of the Riverside Church in The Everyman Players production in the Nave of the Riverside Church (off off Broadway). Opened April 24, 1973. (Closed May 6, 1973)

Directed by Orlin Corey; assistant director and choreographer, Wren Terry; designer, Irene Corey; composer, Johan Franco; press, Betty Lee Hunt Associates, Henry Luhrman, Harriett Trachtenberg, Maria C. Pucci. With The Everyman Players: Hal Proske, Orlin Corey, Clay Harris, Michael Zipperlin, Ron Foreman, Charles Merritt, Gary Ballard, Marilee Hebert, Wren Terry, Kathy Parsons, Anna Antaramian, James R. Ray, Richard Barker, Brenda Musgrove, Ken Holamon, Stewart Slater.

Adaptation of the Bunyan novel presented by a touring theatrical troupe.

Whiskey (7). By Terrence McNally. Produced by Theater at St. Clement's at St. Clement's Church (off off Broadway). Opened April 29, 1973. (Closed May 6, 1973)

Directed by Kevin O'Connor; scenery, Kert Lundell; costumes, Lorie Watson; lighting, Charles Cosler; sound, Lewis Rosen; production stage manager, Jimmy Cuomo; press, Alan Eichler. With Kelly Fitzpatrick, Tom Rosqui, Charlotte Rae, Beeson Carroll, Susan Browning, Michael Sacks.

Comic study of a boozy troupe of cowboy actors.

Spoon River Anthology (32). Revival of the dramatic reading of works by Edgar Lee Masters; adapted and arranged by Charles Aidman; music by Naomi Caryl Hirshhorn; lyrics by Charles Aidman. Produced by The Spoon River Company at Stage 73. Opened April 30, 1973. (Closed May 27, 1973)

Robert Elston	Paul Larson
Barbara Gilbert	Ralph Penner
Lori Hillman	Diane Tarlton

Directed by Peter John Bailey; scenery, Henry Scott III; costumes, Vel Riberto; lighting, Barry Arnold; associate producer, Joan Rowe; production stage manager, Cleveland Morris; press, Seymour Krawitz, Robert Larkin.

An Illinois town, Spoon River, at about the turn of the century, as depicted in a collection of songs, poems, sketches, character studies, etc.

ACT I: "He's Gone Away," The Hill, Tom Beatty, Illinois, Mrs. Williams, Dora Williams, Archibald Higbie, Walter Simmons, Deacon Taylor, Emily Sparks, Benjamin Pantier, Mrs.

Pantier, Emily Sparks, Reuben Pantier, Emily Sparks, Margaret Fuller Slack, "Soldier Oh Soldier," Knowlt Hoheimer, Lydia Puckett, Fiddler Jones, Ollie McGee, Fletcher McGee, Hamilton Greene, Elsa Wertman, Hamilton Greene, Rosie Roberts, Russian Sonia, Lucius Atherton, "Times Are Gettin' Hard," Eugene Carmen, "Water Is Wide," William & Emily, "Water Is Wide (2d chorus), Yee Bow, Enoch Dunlap, Mrs. Kessler, Nancy Knapp, George Gray, Harry Wilmans, Nellie Clark, "Paper of Pins," Roscoe Purkapile, Mrs. Purkapile, A.D. Blood, Shack Dye, "Freedom," Hannah Armstrong, Faith Matheny.

ACT II: "3 Nights Drunk," Judge Lively, Zilpha Marsh, Searcy Foote, Mrs. Charles Bliss, "Far Away From Home," Pauline Barrett, Village Atheist, Mabel Osborne, Franklin Jones, Schofield Huxley, "In the Night," Dippold the Optician, "In the Night" (Reprise), Elijah Browning, Mornin's Come, Alexander Throckmorton, Amanda Barker, Willard Fluke, Lois Spears, "Sow Took the Measles," Abel Melveney, Hod Putt, Ida Frickey, Silas Dement, Aner Clute & Daisy Fraser, Indignation Jones, Minerva Jones, Doc Meyers, "Who Knows Where I'm Goin'," The Sibleys, Willie Metcalf, "I Am, I Am," "Barbers Shoulder," "A Horse Named Bill," Batterton Dobyns, Flossie Cabanis, Hortense Robbins, Frank Drummer, Barney Hainsfeather, "Spoon River," Lucinda Matlock, Petit the Poet, Anne Rutledge, "Spoon River" (Reprise), Epilogue (Birthday).

Alpha Beta (14). By E.A. Whitehead. Produced by Max Brown and Robert Victor by arrangement with The Royal Court Theater. Opened May 3, 1973. (Closed May 13, 1973)

Directed by John Berry; scenery, David Chapman; lighting, David F. Segal; stage manager, Patrick Horrigan; press, Max Eisen, Maurice Turet. With Laurence Luckinbill, Kathryn Walker.

Two-character, three-act play describing a corrosive marital relationship over a period of almost a decade. A foreign play previously produced in London.

* Hot and Cold Heros (14). Musical revue conceived by Joe Jakubowitz. Produced by Mama Hare's Tree (Edith O'Hara) at the 13th Street Theater (off off Broadway). Opened May 9, 1973.

Directed by Joe Jakubowitz; musical direction and arrangements, Lee Gillespie, Mark Weiner; choreography, Ivan Todd; scenery, R. Thomas Finch; costumes, Fran Caruso; lighting, Carla Blumberg; production stage manager, Joel Schapira; press, Alan Eichler. With Jehan Clements, Susan Conderman, Damian Leake, Melanie Michelle, Helene Reis, Murray J. Schactman, Ron Zarro, Monica Grigon.

Unstructured collection of musical comments on life in the city.

Owners (2). By Caryl Churchill. Produced by Terese Hayden at the Mercer-Shaw Theater. Opened May 14, 1973. (Closed May 15, 1973)

Directed by Terese Hayden; scenery, Fred Kolouch; production stage manager, John Branon; press, Max Eisen, Maurice Turet. With Stefan Gierasch, Martin Shakar, Jacqueline Brookes, Alir Elias, Sam Schacht.

About possessions, including people as well as property. A foreign play previously produced in London at the Royal Court.

The Children's Mass (7). By Frederick Combs. Produced by Sal Mineo and Robin Archer Moles in association with Serpentine Productions, Ltd., by special arrangement with Lucille Lortel Productions, Inc. at the Theater de Lys. Opened May 16, 1973. (Closed May 20, 1973)

Directed by Richard Altman; scenery and costumes, Peter Harvey; lighting, Roger Morgan; production stage manager, Rock Ralston; press, Betty Lee Hunt Associates. With Kipp Osborne, Gary Sandy, Bruce Howard, Shelley Bruce, Courtney Burr, Elizabeth Farley, Donald Warfield.

The life and death of a transvestite in the New York drug scene.

Some Additional Productions
And Off Off Broadway

Here is a selected listing of off-off-Broadway and other experimental or peripheral New York productions. Producing groups are identified in **bold face type,** and examples of their outstanding 1972-73 programs are listed with play titles in capital letters. In many cases these are works in progress with changing scripts and casts, usually without an engagement of record (but when available, opening dates are included in the entries).

The Actors Studio. This season, the Studio gave public performances of both new and standard works. Among these were:

SIAMESE CONNECTIONS by Dennis J. Reardon, directed by Peter Masterson, June 8, 1972. THE BIRDS by Aristophanes, translated by William Arrowsmith, directed by George Christodoulakis, October 19, 1972. THE MASQUE OF ST. GEORGE AND THE DRAGON, a traditional old English Mummers Play originally presented by Fred Stewart, directed by Anna Strasberg, December 15, 1972. VIRILITY, written and directed by Ed Setrakian, January 11, 1973. OTHELLO by William Shakespeare, directed by Gene Frankel, February 8, 1973. THE EFFECT OF GAMMA RAYS ON MAN-IN-THE-MOON MARIGOLDS by Paul Zindel, directed by Robert H. Livingston, February 18, 1973. A BREAK IN THE SKIN by Ronald Ribman, directed by Arthur Sherman, May 28, 1973.

Afro-American Studio for Acting and Speech. Black theater group.

EXPERIMENTAL DEATH UNIT NO. 1, JUNKIES ARE FULL OF SHHH and GREAT GOODNESS OF LIFE by Imamu Amiri Baraka (LeRoi Jones) presented in repertory beginning October 1, 1972.

American Center for Stanislavski Art. Sonia Moore's acting ensemble in the Stanislavski tradition.

THE CHERRY ORCHARD by Anton Chekhov; DESIRE UNDER THE ELMS by Eugene O'Neill; THE MAN WITH THE FLOWER IN HIS MOUTH by Luigi Pirandello; THE STRONGER by August Strindberg an THE SLAVE by Imamu Amiri Baraka (LeRoi Jones); THE ANNIVERSARY, THE BOOR and THE MARRIAGE PROPOSAL by Anton Chekhov, all plays directed by Sonia Moore.

American Theater Company. This East 14th Street group specializes in works of early American theater, with some new ones included. Among this season's offerings:

FASHION by Anna Cora Mowatt, directed by by Dorothy Chernuck. A MASQUE OF REA- SON and A MASQUE OF MERCY by Robert Frost.

Central Arts Cabaret. A newly-organized theater designed to present both new works and revivals. Among the plays presented this season:

LEMON SKY by Lanford Wilson, directed by Rae Tattenbaum, January 12, 1973. LIGHT-NIN' BUGS 'N' GOD 'N' THINGS by Bruce Peyton, directed by Nyla Lyon, February 16, 1973. GOODBYE TOMORROW, book and lyrics by Sue Brock, music by Carl Friberg, directed by Anthony Stimac, March 23, 1973.

Circle Theater Company. Based in a loft on the Upper West Side, under the artistic direction of Marshall W. Mason, this repertory group presents a varied schedule of full productions and workshops. The major productions of the 1972-1973 season were:

THREE NEW PLAYS BY LANFORD WIL-
SON: GREAT NEBULA IN ORION; IKKE,
IKKE, NYE, NYE, NYE, and THE FAMILY
CONTINUES, directed by Marshall W. Ma-
son, October 12, 1972. A ROAD WHERE
THE WOLVES RUN by Claris Nilson, di-
rected by Marshall W. Mason, November 24,

1972. THE HOT L BALTIMORE by Lanford
Wilson, directed by Marshall W. Mason, January 27, 1973. WHEN WE DEAD AWAKEN
by Henrik Ibsen, directed by Marshall Oglesby,
April 12, 1973. THE TRAGEDY OF
THOMAS ANDROS by Ron Wilcox, directed
by Marshall Oglesby, May 26, 1973.

Clark Center for the Performing Arts. Housed by the Young Women's Christian
Association, presenting a wide variety of programs, this season including:

EMPOROR AND GALILEAN by Henrik
Ibsen, adapted and directed by Barnet Kell-
man, September 30, 1972. THE SECRET
PLACE by Garrett Morris, directed by Bill
Duke, December 16, 1972. BILLY by Fred-

erick Kirwin, directed by Barnet Kellman,
April 18, 1973. THE GIRLS MOST LIKELY
TO SUCCEED by Dennis Anderson, directed
by Russell Treys, May 9, 1973.

CSC Repertory. This troupe presents classic and standard plays in repertory. Included in its 1972-1973 schedule:

THE HOMECOMING by Harold Pinter, di-
rected by Robert Hall, September 7, 1972.
ROSENCRANTZ AND GUILDENSTERN
ARE DEAD by Tom Stoppard, directed by
Christopher Martin, September 14, 1972.
THE TEMPEST by William Shakespeare,
directed by Christopher Martin. MACBETH
by William Shakespeare, directed by Robert
Hall, November 9, 1972. THE DEVILS by
John Whiting, directed by Christopher Martin,
January 28, 1973. RASHOMON by Runosuke

Akutagawa, directed by Christopher Martin,
May 12, 1973. LOOT by Joe Orton, directed
by Robert Hall, May 12, 1973. In addition to
it regular schedule, CSC Repertory presented
a series of new plays, including: THE POOL
HALL OF THE HEART by Joseph Baldwin,
directed by Julianne Boyd, September 28,
1972. ANNA-LUSE by David Mowat, directed
by David Villaire, November 30, 1972. FIRE-
EATER'S ENEMY by Tone Brulin, directed
by Eric Krebs, January 26, 1973.

The Cubiculo and **Cubiculo/Studio III.** Established in 1968, The Cubiculo, the experimental arts club of the National Shakespeare Company, offers two theaters
where playwrights and directors may present new and unusual work before a re-
sponsive audience. Among the plays presented during the 1972-1973 season were:

DEAR JANET ROSENBERG, DEAR MR.
KOONING by Stanley Eveling, directed by
Robert Coston, June 8, 1972. STUMP RE-
MOVAL by Tone Brulin, presented by the
Otrabanda Company, June 22, 1972. HOM-
AGE AT NIGHT by Lars Gustafsson, directed
by Robert Horen, July 12, 1972. ALLIGATOR
MAN by Jack A. Kaplan, directed by Nancy
Rubin, THE PARTY by Slawomir Mrozek,
directed by Robert Weil, July 13, 1972. THE
NANNIES by Yiorgos Skourtis, directed by
John Hourchin and THE STRONG MEN by
Stratis Karras, directed by George Christo-
doulakis, July 26, 1972. BUBBLES by James
Lavin, directed by Harlen Schneider, August
9, 1972. AFTER WE EAT THE APPLE,
WE WHAT? By Henry Fanelli, directed by
Marcia Rodd and Keith Charles, August 10,
1972. PRESS CUTTINGS and THE MUSIC
CURE by George Bernard Shaw, directed by
Maurice Edwards, October 19, 1972. 'OH!' by
Key-Aberg, directed by Robert Horen, Novem-
ber 8, 1972. THE ENTREPRENEURS by
Jack Gilhooley, directed by Clinton Atkinson,

November 9, 1972. DEATHWISH by Frank
Gutswa, directed by James Howe, November
15, 1972. INDIANS by Arthur Kopit, directed
by Michael Tenenbaum, Dec. 7, 1972. NIGHT-
BIRDS, written and directed by Andy Milligan,
January 12, 1973. GARBAGE COLLECTORS
by Frank Steinkellner, directed by Chris
Thomas, January 18, 1973. BRIDEGROOM
OF DEATH by Rock Kenyon, directed by
Richard A. Rubin, February 3, 1973. BUSI-
NESS DAY written and directed by Gershon
Freidlin, February 21, 1973. CASSANDRA
AND AARON by Abigail Quart, directed by
Arthur Pellman, February 8, 1973. THE
SWEET ENEMY by Joyce Carol Oates, di-
rected by Maurice Edwards, March 9,
1973. PIGEONS by Edward Friedman, di-
rected by Alfred Gingold, March 15, 1973.
THE POETRY READING and SHUFFLE
OFF by Stanley Nelson, directed by Larry
Nadell, April 19, 1973. I'M NOT JEWISH
AND I DON'T KNOW WHY I'M SCREAM-
ING by Stanley Lachow, directed by Quinton
Raines, May 3, 1973.

Equity Library Theater. Actors Equity produces a series of revivals each season at the 300-seat Master Theater as showcases for the work of its actor-members, under the managing directorship of George Wojtasik.

THE MAID'S TRAGEDY by Beaumont and Fletcher, directed by Clinton J. Atkinson, October 19, 1972. HOW TO SUCCEED IN BUSINESS WITHOUT REALLY TRYING, book by Abe Burrows, Jack Weinstock and Willie Gilbert, music and lyrics by Frank Loesser, based on the book by Shepherd Mead, directed and choreographed by Joe Davis, November 9, 1972. IN WHITE AMERICA by Martin Duberman, directed by Russell Treyz, December 7, 1972. THE SECRET LIFE OF WALTER MITTY, book by Joe Manchester, music by Leon Carr, lyrics by Earl Shuman, suggested by the James Thurber story, directed by Jerry Grant, January 11, 1973. THUNDER ROCK by Robert Ardrey, directed by Stephen Book, February 8, 1973. OUT OF THIS WORLD, music and lyrics by Cole Porter, book by George Oppenheimer, based on a libretto by Dwight Taylor and Reginald Lawrence, directed by Richard Michaels, March 8, 1973. SUMMER BRAVE by William Inge (final, revised version of Inge's *Picnic*), directed by Ian Wilder, April 5, 1973. RIVERWIND, book, music and lyrics by John Jennings, directed by Jeff Hamlin May 3, 1973.

Gramercy Arts Theater. This organization presents Spanish-language plays in Spanish and English and English-language plays in Spanish. Among this season's productions:

WHO'S AFRAID OF VIRGINIA WOOLF? (in Spanish) by Edward Albee, translated and directed by Rene Burch. BODAS DE SANGRE by Federico Garcia Lorca, directed by Rene Burch. NADA QUE VER by Griselda Gambaro, translated by Charles Pilditch, directed by George Del Lago.

Greenwich Mews Theater. Housed in the basement of a combination church and synagogue in the West Village, this organization plays host to a variety of offerings. In 1972-1973, these included:

THE CONTRAST, adapted and directed by Anthony Stimac, music by Don Pippin, lyrics by Steve Brown, based on a play by Royall Tyler. DOWNTOWN HOLY LADY by Joseph Caldwell, directed by Allan Albert. LADYBUG by Dakota Don Peterson, derected by Patricia Carmichael, November 16, 1972. THE BRIDGE by Oscar Brand, November 28, 1972. THE BUSINESS OF GOOD GOVERNMENT by John Arden, directed by Archie Gresham, December 21, 1972. HOLY MOSES, written and directed by Hal Grego, February 8, 1973. HOW MR. MOCKINPOTT WAS CURED OF HIS SUFFERING by Peter Weiss, directed by Manfred Bormann, May 25, 1973.

Jean Cocteau Theater. A small house in the Bowery presenting experimental productions, this season including:

THE TRAGEDY OF TRAGEDIES, OR THE LIFE AND DEATH OF THE GREAT TOM THUMB by Henry Fielding, directed by Eve Adamson. THE HORRORS OF DOCTOR MOREAU, based on the novel by H.G. Wells, adapted and directed by Joel Stone.

Jones Beach Marine Theater. Every summer Guy Lombardo produces a revival of a musical classic at this huge outdoor theater on Long Island.

THE KING AND I, book and lyrics by Oscar Hammerstein II, music by Richard Rodgers, directed by John Fearnley, June 28, 1972.

The Judson Poets' Theater. Housed in the Judson Memorial Church, the Poets' Theater is home base for Al Carmines who, when not sermonizing from the pulpit, writes and frequently directs and appears in decidedly unconventional musical extravaganzas.

THE LIFE OF A MAN, words, music and direction by Al Carmines, September 29, 1972. THE MAKING OF AMERICANS, libretto adapted by Leon Katz from Gertrude Stein's novel, music by Al Carmines, directed by Lawrence Kornfeld, November 10, 1972. CHRISTMAS RAPPINGS, text from the New Testament, music and direction by Al Carmines, Dec. 15, 1972. THE FAGGOT, words, music and direction by Al Carmines, April 13, 1973.

La Mama Experimental Theater Club. Probably the best known off-off-Broadway theater, La Mama, under the direction of founder Ellen Stewart, housed an eclectic schedule of plays. Among them in 1972-73:

EVERYMAN AT LA MAMA, written and directed by Geraldine Fitzgerald and Brother Jonathan, music by Jimmy Justice, September 7, 1972. EVERYTHING FOR ANYBODY (later THE BAR THAT NEVER CLOSES) by Louisa Rose, with fables by Marco Vassi, music by Tommy Mandel, directed by John Braswell, September 9, 1972. LUNA PARK and TRAMP, conceived, directed and performed by the Théâtre Laboratoire Vicinal, September 27, 1972. LORRIE by Bernard M. Kahn, directed by Henry Hewes, October 4, 1972. FEUNTE OVEHUNA by Lope de Vega, music by Guy Strobel, directed by Alan Holzman, October 12, 1972. SHOW NO. 44, written, directed and performed by the People Show, October 18, 1972. NA HÁAZ'AN written and directed by Robert Shorty and BODY INDIAN by Hanay Geoigamah, music by Ed Wapp, October 25, 1972. POMPEII, written and directed by Ching Yeh, November 1, 1972. AUDITION by Steven Holt, music by John Braden, directed by Suzanna Foster, November 8, 1972. SISSY by Seth Allen, music by Michael Meadows and Seth Allen, directed by John Vaccaro, performed by The Playhouse of the Ridiculous, November 9, 1972. THOUGHTS by Lamar Alford, directed by Jan Mickens, December 6, 1972. PLAY BY PLAY written and directed by Robert Patrick, December 28, 1972. THE BEAUTY AND THE BEAST, adapted and directed by Oswald Rodriguez, music by Joseph Blunt, January 4, 1973. CITY OF LIGHT, conceived and directed by John Dodd, music by John Herbert McDowell and Terence Thomas, January 5, 1973. THE WHITE WHORE AND THE BIT PLAYER by Tom Eyen, directed by Manual Martin, January 17, 1973. BLOOD WEDDING by Federico Garcia Lorca, directed by Patrick Burke, January 18, 1973. CARMILLA, directed by Wilford Leach and John Braswell, music by Ben Johnston, performed by the ETC Company, February 2, 1973. DEMON by John Braswell and RENARD by Igor Stravinsky, performed by the ETC Company, February 7, 1973. MS. NEFERTITI, written and directed by Tom Eyen, music by Ilene Berson and Tom Eyen, performed by the Theater of the Eye, February 9, 1973. SILENT PRAYER, written and directed by Stephen Varble, March 14, 1973. THE MAGIC SHOW OF DR. MAGICO, written and directed by Jen Bernard and John Vaccaro, music by Richard Weinstock, March 15, 1973. OPHELIA, written and directed by Kathleen St. John, March 29, 1973. SILVER QUEEN, written by Paul Foster, music by John Braden, directed by Robert Patrick, April 11, 1973. SACRED GUARD, conceived and directed by Ken Rubenstein, music by John Smead, April 11, 1973. AND THAT'S HOW THE RENT GETS PAID, PART II, written and directed by Jeff Weiss, April 20, 1973. THE MYTHS OF AMERICA SMITH, written by Greg Antonacci, directed by Joel Zwick, May 2, 1973. PLAY MARY PLAY written by Roy Kift, directed by Leland Moss, May 25, 1973.

The Manhattan Theater Club. Uncounted readings, workshops and full productions play here every year. In addition to the selected events listed below, the Club played host to the New York Theater Strategy's first season (see separate listing).

THE BEST IS YET TO BE by Margie Appelman, directed by Roger H. Simon, July 20, 1972. WELL . . . FAIR by Anne Roby with music by Sandy Alpert, directed by David Schweizer, September 27, 1972. THE REVUE by Avery Corman, Edward Kleban, Bobby Paul, Dan Greenburg and Edward Pomerantz, directed by John Pleshette, October 19, 1972. CANADIAN GOTHIC/AMERICAN MODERN by Joanna Glass, directed by Austin Pendleton, November 16, 1972. OFF THE WALL, directed by Michael McGuire, December 7, 1972. I DON'T GENERALLY LIKE POETRY BUT HAVE YOU READ TREES? by Albert Innaurato and Chris Durange, presented by the Yale Cabaret, December 14, 1972. CRUNCH by John Buskin, directed by Alfred L. Gingold, February 1, 1973. THE BIG BROADCAST ON EAST 53d STREET by Dick Brukenfeld, directed by David Vaillaire, March 1, 1973. JESUS AS SEEN BY HIS FRIENDS by Amos Kenan, directed by Sergei Retitov, March 22, 1973. AUTO-DESTRUCT by Jeff Wanshel, directed by John Lion, April 5, 1973. THE COMPLAINT DEPARTMENT CLOSES AT FIVE by Edward M. Cohen, directed by Robert Hendricks Simon, April 12, 1973. THE PETITION by Donald Flynn and A LITTLE SINGING, A LITTLE DANCING by Robert K. Smith, April 19, 1973.

Matinee Theater Series at the Theater de Lys. Under the artistic direction of Lucille Lortel, presented the following plays during its 17th annual series.

MADAME DE SADE by Yukio Mishima, translated by Donald Keene, directed by Herbert Machiz, October 30, 1972. WILDE! by Frederick Gaines, directed by John J. Desmond, December 4, 1972. LOVE GOTTA

COME BY SATURDAY NIGHT by Ronnie Paris, directed by Donald Buka and ORRIN by Don Evans, directed by Earle Hyman, January 8, 1973.

N.Y.U. School of the Arts Theater Program. Under the sponsorship of New York University, veterans of the School of the Arts's theater department have formed professional companies to present new theater pieces. The groups tend to work improvisationally, either creating new material or re-shaping existing texts to their own purposes.

The Manhattan Project, under the direction of Andre Gregory: ENDGAME by Samuel Beckett, February 2, 1973 and ALICE IN WONDERLAND, based on the "Alice" books by Lewis Carroll, April 5 (return production). Section Ten, under the direction of Omar Shapli and Andrea Balis: THE NEW YORK MONSTER SHOW, new version, May 12,

1973 and GREAT HOSS PISTOL, text drawn from historical writings, arranged by Omar Shapli, May 9, 1973. The Shaliko Company: CHILDREN OF THE GODS, a "collage" developed from Aeschylus's *Agamemnon* and Euripedes's *Electra, Orestes* and *Iphigenia in Aulis,* directed by Leonardo Shapiro, May 17, 1973.

The New Dramatists, Inc. An organization devoted to playwrights; member writers may use the facilities for anything from private cold readings of their material to workshop stagings. Among projects receiving stagings this season were:

PASSION AND OTHER PLAYS by Stephen Foreman, directed by Stephen Book, June 7, 1972. RITE OF PASSAGE by Rose Leiman Goldemberg, directed by Ted Weiant, September 20, 1972. HEYDAY written and directed by Herbert Appleman, September 28, 1972. THE ELIZABETHANS, written and directed by Sidney Michaels, November 14, 1972. TODAY WE KILLED MOLLY BLOOM by Eric Thompson, directed by Robert Hendricks Si-

mon, November 30, 1972. IN THE BEGINNING by Edward Greenberg, directed by Seymour Vall, February 1, 1973. DINNER AT THE AMBASSADOR'S by Michael O'Reilly, directed by Charles Maggiore, February 12, 1973. KINDLY OBSERVE THE PEOPLE by Barry Berg, directed by Craig Anderson, March 15, 1973. GHOST DANCE written and directed by Stuart Vaughan, May 15, 1973.

The New Phoenix Repertory Company. In addition to presenting two productions on Broadway this season, this company offered workshop productions of new plays, including:

GAMES/AFTER LIVERPOOL by James Saunders, directed by Michael Montel.

STRIKE HEAVEN by Richard Wesley, directed by Israel Hicks.

New Village Theater. New plays are presented here by a permanent company of actors. This season the plays included:

THE DAY THEY TOOK GRANDFATHER AWAY by Ralph William Scholl and THE LIFE by Cary Pepper, directed by Shan Covey, October 6, 1972. THE HOLY GHOSTLY and ICARUS'S MOTHER by Sam

Shepard, directed by Shan Covey, November 29, 1972. SAFE AT LAST by James V. Hatch and Larry Garvin, directed by Shan Covey, February 16, 1973.

New York Theater Ensemble. Prolific off-off-Broadway organization oriented to the production of new plays in a small but almost continuously active facility. Among this season's productions were:

THUNDERSTORMS, NEW YORK STYLE, written and directed by Hal Craven, July 7, 1972. SIDD-ARTHUR AND HIS PSYCHE'-DAHLIA-NCE by Sheldon Cholst, directed by Mark Jessurun-Lobo, August 11, 1972. A SPECIMEN by Judith Gilhousen, directed by

Will Owen, MAKING IT IN A BAKERY WITHOUT LETTING THE DOUGH FALL by Christopher Mathewson, directed by Bill Kusher, September 29, 1972. BROKEN MIRRORS IN A JUNKYARD by Blance Mednick Olaik, directed by Florence Miller, DRIVE-IN

MOVIE, written and directed by Dallas Mayr, ON-STAGE, written and directed by Walter Tyszka, THE WOMAN WHO PLEASED EVERYBODY, written and directed by Rose Sher, October 20, 1972. STRIPTEASE and LIFE AND DEATH IN DETROIT by David MacLaren, directed by Mark Jessurun-Lobo, YOU CAN'T TELL A COVER BY ITS COLOR by Stanley Zawatsky, directed by Bob Solebello, December 8, 1972. AN EASTER SONG FOR JEANNE DIXON by Christopher Mathewson, directed by Richard Viola, THE POWER MACHINE by Jean Richards, directed by Osi Daljord, and SOMETHING ELSE by Robert Patrick, directed by Osi Daljord, January 19, 1973. I DON'T CARE WHO YOU GIVE IT TO, AS LONG AS YOU GIVE SOME TO ME by Hal Craven, directed by Barbara Bohak, HEY OUT THERE, IS ANYONE OUT THERE by Elaine Denholtz, directed by Rod Carter, EXCHANGES by Walter Tyszka, directed by Rod Carter, THE METAPHYSICAL COP by David Scott Milton, directed by Bill Kushner, February 16, 1973. THIRD RIDE ON A MERRY-GO-ROUND and STRAYS by Blance Mednick Olaik, directed by Alice Rubenstein, I WISH I HAD A NAME LIKE ISABEL by Richard Schuster, directed by Jim Gara, THE GNOME WHO BROUGHT HAPPINESS TO ALL, written and directed by Rose Sher, March 23, 1973.

New York Theater Strategy. Organized by a number of well known "new-wave" playwrights, the Strategy is dedicated to the production of new and revived works by its members. Housed in the Manhattan Theater Club, the organization's first series straddled the dividing line between the 1972-1973 and 1973-1974 seasons. Those plays which opened during the 1972-1973 season included:

EDDIE AND SUSANNA IN LOVE by Leonard Melfi, directed by Robert Burgos; BAD HABITS by Terrence McNally, directed by Robert Drivas; THE FAMILY JOKE, written and directed by David Starkweather; MARY JANE, written and directed by Kenneth Bernard; and THE WHITE WHORE AND THE BIT PLAYER, written and directed by Tom Eyen, May 16, 1973. OLDER PEOPLE, written and directed by John Ford Noonan; SUSAN PERETZ AT THE MANHATTAN THEATER CLUB by Megan Terry, directed by Joanne Schmidman; and THE HAWK by Murray Mednick, Tony Barsha and the Keystone Company, directed by Tony Barsha, May 24, 1973. KITCHENETTE by Ronald Tavel, directed by Harvey Tavel and SOFTLY AND CONSIDER THE NEARNESS by Rosalyn Drexler, directed by Maxine Klein, May 30, 1973.

The Nighthouse. This East Village organization presented the following productions during the 1972-1973 season:

MACBETH by William Shakespeare, directed by Gerald Mast, February 2, 1973. UBU ROI by Alfred Jarry, adapted by Gerald Mast and B.Y. Sitterly, directed by Gerald Mast, February 9, 1973. THE WOMEN'S REPRESENTATIVE by Sun Yu (play from Red China), adapted by David Gaard, directed by Pamela De Sio, May 30, 1973.

Omni Theater Club. This small theater presents new plays in the interest of assisting participating playwrights in the development of their work. Among this season's presentations:

ANIMALS by Betzie Parker and CIRCUS by Ilsa Gilbert, directed by Gladys F. Smith, June 23, 1972. BUNNY BOY by Wallace Hamilton, directed by Viktor Allen, September 29, 1972. LIBERTY SOMETIMES by Martin Ring, directed by Ted Feder, October 7, 1972. APRIL by John Wolfson, directed by Viktor Allen, November 19, 1972. THE BETRAYAL by Steve Press, directed by Bill Dance, March 2, 1973. ANDROID PROJECT by Betzie Parker, director by Larry Crane, May 10, 1973.

Ontological-Hysteric Theater. Richard Foreman writes, directs and designs all of this avant-garde group's works. This season the productions included:

SOPHIA-(WISDOM) PART 3: THE CLIFFS at the Cinematheque, December 8, 1972. PARTICLE THEORY at the Theater for the New City, April 18, 1973.

The Open Theater. Under the direction of Joseph Chaikin, this group has carved out a formidable reputation among experimental theater companies. This season their presentations included:

THE MUTATION SHOW, a collective work by The Open Theater, co-directed by Joseph Chaikin and Roberta Sklar, first presented during the 1971–1972 season. NIGHTWALK, a work-in-progress created by The Open Thea-ter; contributing writers Jean-Claude van Itallie, Sam Shepard and Megan Terry; directed by Joseph Chaikin, first performed April, 1973.

The Other Stage. The experimental space at Joseph Papp's Public Theater housed only two projects this season:

THE CHILDREN by Michael McGuire, directed by Paul Schneider, November 28, 1972. MORE THAN YOU DESERVE by Michael Weller, directed by Kim Friedman, April 13, 1973.

The Performance Group. This season Richard Schechner's experimental theater group presented:

THE TOOTH OF CRIME by Sam Shepard, directed by Richard Schechner, March 8, 1973.

The Playbox. A small house presenting new plays. Included in this year's schedule:

THE EMPRESS REFLECTIONS by J.B. Rise, directed by Joe Donovan, Setember 22, 1972. NIGHT TRAVELERS by Gloria Gonzalez and WE'RE OFF TO SEE THE WIZARD by Edna Schappert, directed by Leonhard Kluge-Britton, October 19, 1972. NOWHERE TO RUN, written and directed by Peter Copani, February 23, 1973.

Players' Workshop. Located in the East Village, this theater housed a festival of black plays, including:

CEREMONIES IN DARK OLD MEN by Lonne Elder III, directed by Bett Howard, October 2, 1972. THE BLACK TERROR by Richard Wesley, October 3, 1972. STREET SOUNDS by Ed Bullins and THE BAPTISM by Imamu Amiri Baraka (LeRoi Jones), October 7, 1972.

The Playwrights Cooperative. This organization of playwrights presents productions of members' works in a variety of houses. Works performed as part of its first festival and opened before June 1, 1973 included:

SURVIVING DEATH IN THREE ACTS by Nancy Fales, music by George Miller, directed by Nancy Fales and Gail Julian, May 2, 1973 at The Active Trading Company. SOLOS presented by and at the Byrd Hoffman School of Byrds, May 7, 1973. TONTO by Guy Gauthier and MAGIC TIME by William Kushner, directed by Frederick Bailey and ROARSHOCK by Chris Mathewson, directed by Chris Mathewson and J. Gulliver, May 17, 1973, at Cubiculo. CONQUEST OF EVEREST and THE HERO by Arthur Kopit, directed by Frank Errante and ADORA by Jean Reavey, directed by Kent Wood and L'HABITAL SPLENDID by Jean Reavey, directed by Jane Odin, May 18, 1973 at the New York Theater Ensemble. MONKEY OF THE INK POT by Helen Duberstein and DRY RUN by Victor Lipton, directed by Ira Zuckerman and LIVING ROOM WITH SIX OPPRESSIONS by Oscar Mandel, directed by Richard Viola, May 19, 1973 at the Actor's Experimental Unit Theater. HONOR, written and directed by Richard Foreman and GO CHILDREN SLOWLY by Arthur Sainer, directed by Marjorie Melnick, May 25, 1973 at Cubiculo. A BLUES TO BE CALLED CRAZY WHEN CRAZY'S ALL THERE IS by Claire Burch, directed by Frank Errante, May 26, 1973 at St. Clement's. KENNEDY'S CHILDREN by Robert Patrick, directed by J. Kevin Hanlon, May 30, 1973 at the Clark Center.

Playwrights' Workshop Club at Bastiano's. Dedicated to the exposure and development of writers, actors and directors, at last report this group was in search of a new home, having left its old house on Cooper Square. Among its presentations this season:

THE BITCH, written and directed by Andy Milligan, September 6, 1972. SPEARS THAT ROAR FOR BLOOD by Pat Hyland, directed by Anthony DeVito, September 27, 1972. IN SEARCH OF THE COBRA JEWELS by Harvey Fierstein, directed by Donald L. Brooks, October 4, 1972. THE POETRY READING by Stanley Nelson, directed by Brian R. Boylan and PRISM CITY by David Garvin, directed by Tim Oppee, November 1, 1972. RAPES by Mario Fratti, LIVING ROOM WITH SIX OPPRESSIONS by Oscar Mandel, and THE TRAP by Henry Salerno, directed by Craig Barish, December 20, 1972. ORESTES, written and directed by Greg Rozakis, February 14, 1973.

The Queens Playhouse. This season marked the attempt to provide Queens with a professional theater company. Originally scheduled to present four plays, the company presented two before closing up shop.

PYGMALION by George Bernard Shaw, directed by Paul Shyre, October 30, 1972. TWELVE ANGRY MEN by Reginald Rose, directed by Martin Fried, December 3, 1972.

The Ridiculous Theatrical Company. Camp theatricals written and directed by Charles Ludlam featuring trans-sexual casting.

CORN, written and directed by Charles Ludlam, music and lyrics by Virgil Young, November 23, 1972. CAMILLE, adapted from Alexandre Dumas and directed by Charles Ludlam, May 2, 1973.

The San Francisco Mime Troupe. Based in San Francisco, this troupe occasionally tours to raise enough money to maintain its operations in its home city. This season, its New York presentation was:

THE DRAGON LADY'S REVENGE, "written, directed, designed, composed, built, costumed, stage, painted, publicized, produced, performed by The San Francisco Mime Troupe," at Washington Square Methodist Church, November 24, 1972.

The Shade Company. Under the direction of Edward Berkeley, this ensemble is devoted to productions of both classics and new plays.

HEARTBREAK HOUSE by George Bernard Shaw, July 13, 1972; MOTHER COURAGE by Bertolt Brecht, October 19, 1972; CASINA by Plautus, December 28, 1972; DR. HERO by Israel Horovitz, March 19, 1973. All plays directed by Edward Berkeley.

The Space. For the most part the Space has served as a rehearsal facility, but changes are afoot. Renovations of two theaters under its roof will signal its transition into a performing arts center. In the meantime, The Space has housed a few productions. The Open Theater played here this season (see separate listing). Other productions from the 1972-1973 season:

IMITATION OF ART, September 1, 1972, and BREAKDOWN AT THE SUPERBOWL, December 26, 1972; both pieces written and directed by Jim Hoberman and Robert Schneider for the Theater of Gibberish. KAP THE KAPPA, written and directed by Betty Jean Lifton, performed by The Jugglers in December, 1972. MEDICINE SHOW, written by Barbara Vann and Richard Schotler and directed by Barbara Vann, May 31, 1973.

Theater at St. Clement's. The former home of the American Place Theater has been reorganized under the artistic direction of Kevin O'Connor into a unit which both presents its own productions and houses presentations from the outside. This, its first full season, included the following:

OF MICE AND MEN by John Steinbeck, directed by Charles Briggs, September 21, 1972. CEREMONY FOR A MURDERED BLACK by Fernando Arrabal, directed by Castulo Guerra, November 9, 1972. MOON MYSTERIES by William Butler Yeats, directed by Jean Erdman, November 17, 1972. TWO BY PAUL AUSTIN, directed by Louis Turenne, November 21, 1972. THAT SIMPLE LIGHT MAY RISE OUT OF COMPLICATED DARKNESS presented by the Bread and Puppet Theater, December 12, 1972. THE GOLDEN DAFFODIL DWARF AND OTHER WORKS by Daniela Gioseffi, directed by Nancy Rubin, January 4, 1973. THE TRINITY: LES MORTS, LES MYSTÈRES ET LE MARASSA presented by the Mokurai, directed by Teijo Ito, January 28, 1973. THE WHITE WHORE AND THE BIT PLAYER by Tom Eyen, directed by Manuel Martin, February 2, 1973. WHISKEY by Terrence McNally, directed by Kevin O'Connor, April 29, 1973. WINGING IT! by Jeff Sweet, directed by Kevin O'Connor, May 29, 1973.

Theater for the New City. Specializing in experimental productions, this West Village house's 1972-1973 season included:

THE ATLANTIC CROSSING by Charles Mingus III, songs by Paul Jeffrey and Charles Mingus III, music by Gunter Hampel, directed by Lee Kissman, July 27, 1972. THE DISCOVERY OF AMERICA by Diane di Prima, directed by John Herbert McDowell, September 21, 1972. UNDER COVER COP and THE SKY SALESMAN by Robert Nichols, directed by Crystal Field, September 9, 1972. THE THING ITSELF by Arthur Sainer, music by Jim Kurtz, Meredith Monk, Robert Cosmo Savage, and David Tice, directed by Crystal Field, November 30, 1972. MONDAY NIGHT VARIETIES by John Ford Noonan, directed by Eve Packer, December 8, 1972. WICKED WOMEN REVUE by the Westbeth Feminist Collective, directed by Kim Friedman, January 13, 1973. WOODEN NICKELS by Susan Yankowitz, directed by Ronald Roston, February 22, 1973. MORNING TO MIDNIGHT by Georg Kaiser, translated and adapted by John Teta and Irma Bartenieff directed by Crystal Field, May 24, 1973.

Theater Genesis. One of the earliest-formed off-off-Broadway companies. This season the Genesis schedule included:

BIGFOOT by Ronald Tavel, directed by Michael Smith, November 9, 1972. O-ZONED, presented by Ralston Farina and Friends, December 15, 1972. BLUE BITCH by Sam Shepard, directed by Murray Mednick and TANGO PALACE by Maria Irene Fornes, directed by Michael Smith, January 18, 1973. ARE YOU LOOKIN'?, written and directed by Murray Mednick, March 21, 1973. WHEELING REDS, written and directed by Walter Hadler, May 24, 1973.

Thirteenth Street Theater. This small West Village house alternately presents its own productions and plays host to outside packages. In addition to housing the Ridiculous Theater Company (see separate listing), this season the 13th Street Theater also presented:

THE UNCLE, written and directed by Philip Lam. HOT AND COLD HEROES conceived and directed by Joe Jakubowitz.

Urban Arts Corps. Vinnette Carroll's experimental theater group this season sponsored:

REQUIEM POR YARINI by Carlos Felipa, directed by Dume, presented by the New York Theater of the Americas, October 14, 1972. SISYPHUS AND THE BLUE-EYED CYCLOPS and PAPA B ON THE DEE TRAIN, written and directed by Garland Lee Thompson, October 30, 1972. RECUERDOS DE TULIPA by Reguera Saumell, directed by Mario Pena, presented by the Latin American Theater Ensemble, November 10, 1972. STEP LIVELY, BOY, adapted and directed by Vinnette Carroll, based on a play by Irwin Shaw, music and lyrics by Micki Grant, February 7, 1973. CROESUS AND THE WITCH, written and directed by Vinnette Carroll, music and lyrics by Micki Grant, March 14, 1973.

Workshop of the Players' Art. An Obie Award saluted the quality and quantity of this off-off-Broadway group. This season, productions included:

THE THREEPENNY OPERA by Bertolt Brecht, music by Kurt Weill, adaptation by Marc Blitzstein, directed by Roger Furman, October 13, 1972. HYPATIA 3 by Michael McGrinder, directed by Craig Barish, October 17, 1972. IN DARKEST AFRICA: A LADIES GUIDE TO THE NILE by Doris Baizley, music by Richard Weinstock, directed by Bob Plunket, November 17, 1972. AND DOROTHY PARKER SAID by William Van Gieson, directed by Terence Quinn, AN ABSENCE OF HEROES by Alex Gotfryd and Bob Herron, directed by Jamie Brown, and AND NO CEREMONY by Tevia Abrams, directed by Paul Meacham November 21, 1972. THE RED PUMPS, written and directed by Jeannine O'Reilly, December 1, 1972. A BOY NAME DOG, written and directed by Joseph Renard, January 12, 1973. A NOONAN NITE! five plays by John Ford Noonan, directed by Jack Marks, January 19, 1973. FUNERAL GAMES by Joe Orton, directed by Warren Monteiro, TEACUPS by Henry Morrison, directed by Jerry Stecher and GETTING READY by Grace Cavalier, directed by Michael D. Moore, January 16, 1973. MERCY DROP by Robert Patrick, music by Richard Weinstock, directed by Hugh

Gittens, and LA TOSCA by Victorian Sardou, translated by Joseph Renard, directed by Martin L.H. Reymart, February 24, 1973. COX AND BOX by F.C. Burnand, music by Arthur S. Sullivan, directed by Robert Barger; TONGUE TIED TALES, written and directed by Nancy Z. Rubin, and THE DANGERS OF GREAT LITERATURE by Gabriele Roepke, directed by Terence Quinn, March 30, 1973. A MODERN HAMLET by John Guenther, music by Dennis Deal, directed by Michael Dennis Moore, April 3, 1973. ANDROMACHE by Jean Racine, translated by Lionel Abel, directed by Martin L.H. Reymart April 27, 1973. REETY IN HELL by Stephen Holt, music by Don Arrington, directed by Peter Schneider, May 8, 1973.

CAST REPLACEMENTS AND TOURING COMPANIES

Compiled by Stanley Green

The following is a list of the more important cast replacements in productions which opened in previous years, but were still playing in New York during a substantial part of the 1972-1973 season; or were still on a first class tour in 1972-73 (casts of first class touring companies of previous seasons which were no longer playing in 1972-73 appear in previous *Best Plays* volumes of appropriate years).

The name of each major role is listed in *italics* beneath the title of the play in the first column. In the second column directly opposite appears the name of the actor who created the role in the original New York production (whose opening date appears in *italics* at the top of the column). Indented immediately beneath the original actor's name are the names of subsequent New York replacements, together with the date of replacement when available.

The third column gives information about first-class touring companies, including London companies (produced under the auspices of their original Broadway managements). When there is more than one roadshow company, #1, #2, #3, etc., appear before the name of the performer who created the role in each company (and the city and date of each company's first performance appears in *italics* at the top of the column). Their subsequent replacements are also listed beneath their names, with dates when available.

A note on bus-truck touring companies appears at the end of this section.

ANNA K.

	New York 5/7/72	
Countess Lydia; Annushka; Countess Vronsky	Eugenie Leontovich	
Kitty; Sapho	Lanna Saunders Leslie Ann Ray 9/19/72	
Karenin	Arthur Roberts Howard Green 10/17/72	

APPLAUSE

	New York 3/30/70	*#1 Toronto 11/29/71* *#2 London 11/16/72*

Margo Channing	Lauren Bacall
	  Anne Baxter 7/19/71
	  Arlene Dahl 5/1/72
		#1 Lauren Bacall
		  Eleanor Parker 6/27/72
		#2 Lauren Bacall

Bill Sampson	Len Cariou
	  Keith Charles 5/3/71
	  John Gabriel 5/1/72
		#1 Don Chastain
		  George McDaniel 6/27/72
		#2 Ken Walsh

Eve Harrington	Penny Fuller
	  Patti Davis 4/16/71
	  Penny Fuller 5/3/71
	  Janice Lynde 11/22/71
		#1 Virginia Sandifur
		  Penny Fuller 4/25/72
		  Janice Lynde 6/27/72
		#2 Angela Richards

Howard Benedict	Robert Mandan
	  Lawrence Weber 4/19/71
	  Franklin Cover 1/17/72
		#1 Norwood Smith
		#2 Basil Hoskins

Karen Richards	Ann Williams
	  Gwyda Donhowe 8/24/70
	  Peggy Hagan 12/13/71
	  (name changed to
	  Phebe Hagan 5/1/72
		#1 Beverly Dixon
		#2 Sarah Marshall

Buzz Richards	Brandon Maggart	#1 Ted Pritchard #2 Rod McLennan

Duane Fox	Lee Roy Reams
	  Tom Rolla 11/22/71
	  Larry Merritt 4/24/72
		#1 Lee Roy Reams
		  Orrin Reiley 6/27/72
		#2 Eric Flynn

*Bonnie**	Bonnie Franklin
	  Carol Petrie 4/29/71
	  Bonnie Franklin 6/21/71
	  Leland Palmer 9/6/71
	  Bonnie Franklin 11/22/71
		#1 Leland Palmer
		  Candy Brown 6/27/72
		#2 Sheila O'Neill

*Except from 4/29/71 to 6/21/71, when character was known as Nancy, the name of this part has always been the first name of the dancer playing it.

THE BEGGAR'S OPERA

Bklyn 3/21/72
New York 5/30/72

Macheath	Stephen D. Newman
	  Timothy Jerome 5/30/72
	  Peter Lombard 9/72

Polly Peachum	Kathleen Widdoes Leila Martin 7/5/72

Mr. Peachum	Gordon Connell
	  Rex Robbins 10/72
	  Jerrold Ziman
	  Tom Batten

Mrs. Peachum	Jeanne Arnold
	  Mary Louise Wilson 7/5/72
	  Charlotte Jones 10/17/72

Lucy Lockit	Marilyn Sokol
	  June Gable
	  June Helmers 9/19/72
	  June Gable 10/24/72

THE FANTASTICKS

New York 5/3/60

El Gallo

Jerry Orbach
  Gene Rupert
  Bert Convy
  John Cunningham
  Don Stewart 1/63
  David Cryer
  Keith Charles 10/63
  John Boni 1/13/65
  Jack Mette 9/14/65
  George Ogee
  Keith Charles
  Tom Urich 8/30/66
  John Boni 10/5/66
  Jack Crowder 6/13/67
  Nils Hedrick 9/19/67
  Keith Charles 10/9/67
  Robert Goss 11/7/67
  Joe Bellomo 3/11/68
  Michael Tartel 7/8/69
  Joe Bellomo 2/15/72
  David Cryer 5/2/72
  Michael Vidnovic 6/12/72
  Joe Bellomo 11/12/72

Luisa

Rita Gardner
  Carla Huston
  Liza Stuart 12/61
  Eileen Fulton
  Alice Cannon 9/62
  Royce Lenelle
  B.J. Ward 12/1/64
  Leta Anderson 7/13/65
  Carole Demas 11/22/66
  Leta Anderson 8/7/67
  Carole Demas 9/4/67
  Anne Kaye 1/23/68
  Carole Demas 2/13/68
  Anne Kaye 5/28/68
  Carolyn Magnini 7/29/69
  Virginia Gregory 7/27/70
  Leta Anderson
  Marty Morris 3/7/72
  Sharon Werner 8/1/72

Matt

Kenneth Nelson
  Gino Conforti
  Jack Blackton 10/63
  Paul Giovanni
  Ty McConnell
  Richard Rothbard
  Gary Krawford
  Bob Spencer 9/5/64
  Erik Howell 6/28/66
  Gary Krawford 12/12/67
  Steve Skiles 2/6/68
  Craig Carnelia 1/69
  Erik Howell 7/18/69
  Samuel D. Ratcliffe 8/5/69
  Michael Glenn-Smith
    5/26/70

Jimmy Dodge 9/20/70
Geoffrey Taylor 8/31/71
Erik Howell 3/14/72
Michael Glenn-Smith 6/13/72
Phil Killian 7/4/72
Michael Glenn-Smith 9/24/72

FOLLIES

	New York 4/4/71	*Los Angeles 7/22/72*
Phyllis Stone	Alexis Smith	Alexis Smith
Sally Plummer	Dorothy Collins	Dorothy Collins Janet Blair 9/72
Buddy Plummer	Gene Nelson	Gene Nelson
Benjamin Stone	John McMartin	John McMartin Edward Winter 9/72
Carlotta Campion	Yvonne DeCarlo	Yvonne DeCarlo
Hattie Walker	Ethel Shutta	Ethel Shutta
Solange LaFitte	Fifi D'Orsay	Fifi D'Orsay
Stella Deems	Mary McCarty	Mary McCarty
Christine Crane	Ethel Barrymore Colt Terry Saunders 7/7/71 Jan Clayton 2/27/72	Jan Clayton
Meredith Lane	Sheila Smith Marion Marlowe 1/29/72 Terry Saunders 4/24/72	Terry Saunders
Young Phyllis	Virginia Sandifur	Suzanne Rogers
Young Sally	Marti Rolph	Marti Rolph

A FUNNY THING HAPPENED ON THE WAY TO THE FORUM

	New York 3/30/72
Pseudolus	Phil Silvers John Bentley 7/24/72 Tom Poston 8/9/72
Hysterium	Larry Blyden

GODSPELL

#1 *London 11/17/71*
#2 *Boston 12/11/71*
#3 *Washington 4/7/72*
#4 *Toronto 6/1/72*
#5 *San Francisco 7/18/72*
#6 *Chicago 9/18/72*
#7 *Toledo 9/21/72*
#8 *Pittsburgh 10/27/72*

	New York 5/17/71	
Jesus	Stephen Nathan Andy Rohrer 6/6/72	#1 David Essex #2 Dan Stone Jeffrey F. Weller 8/'/2

	Don Hamilton	#3 Dean Pitchford
	Ryan Hilliard	Rune Kaptur
	Don Scardino 1/73	#4 Victor Garber
		Don Scardino
		Gordon Thompson
		Eugene Levy 6/1/73
		#5 Stacker Thompson
		Stephen Nathan
		#6 Dan Stone
		Richard Gilliland
		#7 Jeremy Sage
		#8 Mark Shera
Judas	David Haskell	#1 Jeremy Irons
	Bart Braverman 5/72	#2 Lloyd Bremseth
	Lloyd Bremseth	Mark Syers
		#3 Irving Lee
		#4 Jerry Salsberg
		Jim Betts 6/1/73
		#5 Tom Rolsing
		#6 Joe Mantegna
		#7 Michael Hoit
		#8 Mark Ganzel

GREASE

	New York 2/14/72	*New Haven 1/22/73*
Danny Zuko	Barry Bostwick	Jeff Conaway
Sandy Dumbrowski	Carole Demas	Pamela Adams
	Eileen Graff 3/73	
Betty Rizzo	Adrienne Barbeau	Judy Kane
	Elaine Petrokoff 3/73	

HARK!

New York 5/22/72

Sharon Miller
Patti d'Beck 7/25/72

JESUS CHRIST SUPERSTAR

	New York 10/12/71	*London 8/9/72*
Jesus of Nazareth	Jeff Fenholt	Paul Nicholas
	Dennis Cooley 4/2/73	
Judas Iscariot	Ben Vereen	Stephen Tate
	Patrick Jude 7/5/72	
Mary Magdalene	Yvonne Elliman	Dana Gillespie
	Marta Heflin 4/17/72	
	Kathye Dezina 3/12/73	
Pontius Pilate	Barry Dennen	John Parker
	Seth Allen 1/24/72	
	W.P. Dremak 7/24/72	
	George Mansour 4/23/72	

LENNY

New York 5/26/71

Lenny Bruce	Cliff Gorman
	Sandy Baron 6/12/72

NO, NO, NANETTE

	New York 1/19/71	*#1 Cleveland 12/27/71* *#2 Dallas 10/6/72* *#3 London 5/15/73*
Sue Smith	Ruby Keeler Penny Singleton 8/16/71 Ruby Keeler 8/31/71 Ruth Maitland 3/27/72 Ruby Keeler 4/4/72 Ruth Maitland 7/31/72 Ruby Keeler 8/14/72 Ruth Maitland 11/6/72 Joy Hodges 11/13/72	#1 June Allyson Virginia Mayo 10/30/72 #2 Evelyn Keyes #3 Anna Neagle
Jimmy Smith	Jack Gilford Ted Tiller 1/3/72 Benny Baker 1/10/72	#1 Dennis Day Elliott Reid #2 Don Ameche #3 Tony Britton
Billy Early	Bobby Van Anthony S. Teague 4/10/72 Bobby Van 8/1/72	#1 Jerry Antes #2 Swen Swenson #3 Teddy Green
Lucille Early	Helen Gallagher	#1 Sandra Deel Arlene Fontanna 1/73 #2 Lainie Nelson #3 Anne Rogers
Pauline	Patsy Kelly Lillian Hayman 10/30/72 Martha Raye 11/6/72	#1 Judy Canova #2 Ruth Donnelly #3 Thora Hird
Nanette	Susan Watson Barbara Heuman 12/71	#1 Dana Swenson #2 Darlene Anders #3 Susan Maudslay
Tom Trainor	Roger Rathburn	#1 Bill Biskup #2 Tim Heathman #3 Peter Gale
Flora Latham	K.C. Townsend Sandra O'Neill 3/17/71 Sally Cooke 8/71	#1 Laura Waterbury #2 Charlene Mathies #3 Anita Graham
Betty Brown	Loni Zoe Ackerman Jill Jaress Linda Rose 1/73	#1 Connie Danese #2 Elizabeth Kovacs #3 Elaine Holland

ONE FLEW OVER THE CUCKOO'S NEST

New York 3/23/71

Randle Patrick McMurphy	William Devane
	Lane Smith 6/71

George Welbes 12/72
Kevin Conway 5/73

Nurse Ratched   Janet Ward
                         Jane Curtin 6/1/72
                         Jane Cronin 12/72

THE PRISONER OF SECOND AVENUE

	New York 11/11/71	*Los Angeles 10/17/72*
Mel Edison	Peter Falk	Art Carney
	Art Carney 6/5/72	
	Hector Elizondo 10/27/2	
Edna Edison	Lee Grant	Barbara Barrie
	Barbara Barrie 6/5/72	Rosemary Prinz 1/29/73
	Phyllis Newman 10/2/72	
	Barbara Barrie 1/29/73	
Harry Edison	Vincent Gardenia	Jack Somack
	Jack Somack 5/22/72	
	Harry Goz 10/2/72	

THE REAL INSPECTOR HOUND* and AFTER MAGRITTE**

New York 4/23/72

*Cynthia *; Thelma ***   Carrie Nye
                                Lynn Milgrim 7/5/72
                                Catherine McGrath

*Mrs. Drudge *; Mother ***   Jane Connell
                                Catherine McGrath
                                Georgia Heaslip
                                Lizabeth Pritchett
                                Kate Wilkinson

*Simon * Harris ***   Konrad Matthaei
                                Christopher Bernau
                                Donegan Smith 1/73
                                Ted Danson
                                Christopher Bernau

*Magnus *; Foot ***   Remak Ramsay
                                William Bogert
                                John-David Keller

*Inspector Hound *;*
  *Holmes ***   Edmond Genest

*Moon **   David Rounds
                                Lenny Baker

*Birdboot **   Tom Lacy
                                Michael Egan 10/2/72

*Felicity **   Boni Enten
                                Mary Denham 1/11/73

SLEUTH

	New York 11/12/70	*Toronto 10/6/71*
Andrew Wyke	Anthony Quayle	Michael Allinson
	Paul Rogers 9/27/71	

	Patrick Macnee 7/3/72	
	George Rose 4/9/73	
	Patrick Macnee 5/21/73	
Milo Tindle	Keith Baxter	Donal Donnelly
	Donal Donnelly 8/16/71	
	Keith Baxter 9/20/71	
	Brian Murray 3/27/72	
	Jordan Christopher 11/7/72	

THAT CHAMPIONSHIP SEASON

	#1 N.Y. off B'way 5/2/72
	#2 N.Y. B'way 9/14/72
Tom Daley	#1 Walter McGinn
	#2 Walter McGinn
George Sikowski	#1 Charles Durning
	#2 Charles Durning
James Daley	#1 Michael McGuire
	#2 Michael McGuire
Phil Romano	#1 Paul Sorvino
	Joseph Mascolo
	Paul Sorvino 6/27/72
	#2 Paul Sorvino
Coach	#1 Richard A. Dysart
	#2 Richard A. Dysart

TWIGS

	New York 11/14/71	*Detroit 9/6/62*
Emily; Celia; Dorothy; Ma	Sada Thompson	Sada Thompson

TWO GENTLEMEN OF VERONA

	New York 12/1/71	*#1 Toronto 1/22/73* *#2 London 4/26/73*
Sylvia	Jonelle Allen	#1 Jonelle Allen
	Hattie Winston 11/28/72	#2 B.J. Arnau
Julia	Danila Davila	#1 Edith Diaz
		Stockard Channing
		#2 Jean Gilbert
Valentine	Clifton Davis	#1 Clifton Davis
	Samuel E. Wright 11/28/72	#2 Samuel E. Wright
	Joe Morton 3/20/73	
	Larry Marshall 4/10/73	
Proteus	Raul Julia	#1 Larry Kert
	Carlos Cestero 10/23/72	#2 Ray C. Davis
	Chris Sarandon 11/28/72	

BUS-TRUCK TOURS

These are touring productions designed for maximum mobility and ease of handling in one-night and split-week stands (with occasional engagements of a week or more). Among Broadway shows on tour in the season of 1972-73 were the following bus-truck troupes:

Applause with Patrice Munsel, 114 cities, 9/22/72-5/5/73

Sleuth with George Rose and David Haviland, 96 cities, 9/22/72-3/24/73

And Miss Reardon Drinks a Little with Gretchen Wyler and Lillian Roth, 40 cities, 1/25/73-4/8/73

Will Rogers's U.S.A. with Paul Tripp, 14 cities, 1/26/73-2/9/73

Jacques Brel Is Alive and Well and Living in Paris, 14 cities, 12/29/72-4/26/73

Godspell (company #8), 136 cities, 9/21/72 (tour will continue until 8/25/73 and will include 15 more cities)

I Do! I Do! with Don Gilley and Leslie Stewart, 90 cities on two tours, 9/21/72-11/15/72 and 2/25/73-3/27/73

Two by Two with Shelley Berman and Taina Elg, 75 cities, 9/15/72-3/11/73

Story Theater, 53 cities, 12/25/72-4/15/73

No Sex Please, We're British with Maureen O'Sullivan and Tony Tanner, 30 cities (many in prime bookings, some in bus-truck), 10/2/72-1/27/73

FACTS AND
FIGURES

LONG RUNS ON BROADWAY

The following shows have run 500 or more continuous performances in a single production, usually the first, not including previews or extra non-profit performances, allowing for vacation layoffs and special one-booking engagements, but not including return engagements after a show has gone on tour. Where there are title similarities, the production is identified as follows: (p) straight play version, (m) musical version, (r) revival.

THROUGH MAY 31, 1973

(PLAYS MARKED WITH ASTERISK WERE STILL PLAYING JUNE 1, 1973)

Plays	*Number Performances*	Plays	*Number Performances*
Fiddler on the Roof	3,242	The Seven Year Itch	1,141
Life With Father	3,224	Butterflies Are Free	1,128
Tobacco Road	3,182	Pins and Needles	1,108
Hello, Dolly!	2,844	Plaza Suite	1,097
My Fair Lady	2,717	Kiss Me, Kate	1,070
Man of La Mancha	2,328	*Sleuth	1,066
Abie's Irish Rose	2,327	The Pajama Game	1,063
Oklahoma!	2,212	The Teahouse of the August Moon	1,027
South Pacific	1,925	Damn Yankees	1,019
Harvey	1,775	Never Too Late	1,007
Hair	1,750	Any Wednesday	982
Born Yesterday	1,642	A Funny Thing Happened on the Way to the Forum	964
Mary, Mary	1,572	The Odd Couple	964
The Voice of the Turtle	1,557	Anna Lucasta	957
Barefoot in the Park	1,530	Kiss and Tell	956
Mame (m)	1,508	The Moon Is Blue	924
Arsenic and Old Lace	1,444	Bells Are Ringing	924
The Sound of Music	1,443	Luv	901
How To Succeed in Business Without Really Trying	1,417	Applause	896
Hellzapoppin	1,404	Can-Can	892
The Music Man	1,375	Carousel	890
Funny Girl	1,348	Hats Off to Ice	889
Oh! Calcutta!	1,314	Fanny	888
Angel Street	1,295	Follow the Girls	882
Lightnin'	1,291	Camelot	873
Promises, Promises	1,281	The Bat	867
The King and I	1,246	My Sister Eileen	864
Cactus Flower	1,234	No, No, Nanette (r)	861
1776	1,217	Song of Norway	860
Guys and Dolls	1,200	A Streetcar Named Desire	855
Cabaret	1,165	Comedy in Music	849
Mister Roberts	1,157	You Can't Take It With You	837
Annie Get Your Gun	1,147		

419

Plays	Number Performances	Plays	Number Performances
La Plume de Ma Tante	835	The Doughgirls	671
Three Men on a Horse	835	The Impossible Years	670
The Subject Was Roses	832	Irene	670
Inherit the Wind	806	Boy Meets Girl	669
No Time for Sergeants	796	Beyond the Fringe	667
Fiorello!	795	Who's Afraid of Virginia Woolf?	664
Where's Charley?	792	Blithe Spirit	657
The Ladder	789	A Trip to Chinatown	657
Forty Carats	780	The Women	657
Oliver	774	Bloomer Girl	654
State of the Union	765	The Fifth Season	654
The First Year	760	Rain	648
You Know I Can't Hear You When the Water's Running	755	Witness for the Prosecution	645
Two for the Seesaw	750	Call Me Madam	644
Death of a Salesman	742	*The Prisoner of Second Avenue	644
Sons o' Fun	742	Janie	642
Gentlemen Prefer Blondes	740	The Green Pastures	640
The Man Who Came to Dinner	739	Auntie Mame (p)	639
Call Me Mister	734	A Man for All Seasons	637
West Side Story	732	The Fourposter	632
High Button Shoes	727	Two Gentlemen of Verona (m)	627
Finian's Rainbow	725	The Tenth Man	623
Claudia	722	Is Zat So?	618
The Gold Diggers	720	Anniversary Waltz	615
Carnival	719	The Happy Time (p)	614
The Diary of Anne Frank	717	Separate Rooms	613
I Remember Mama	714	Affairs of State	610
Tea and Sympathy	712	Star and Garter	609
Junior Miss	710	The Student Prince	608
Last of the Red Hot Lovers	706	Sweet Charity	608
Company	705	Bye Bye Birdie	607
Seventh Heaven	704	Broadway	603
*Jesus Christ Superstar	703	Adonis	603
Gypsy (m)	702	Street Scene (p)	601
The Miracle Worker	700	Kiki	600
Cat on a Hot Tin Roof	694	Flower Drum Song	600
Li'l Abner	693	Don't Drink the Water	598
Peg o' My Heart	692	Wish You Were Here	598
The Children's Hour	691	A Society Circus	596
Purlie	688	Blossom Time	592
Dead End	687	The Me Nobody Knows	586
The Lion and the Mouse	686	The Two Mrs. Carrolls	585
White Cargo	686	Kismet	583
Dear Ruth	683	Detective Story	581
East Is West	680	Brigadoon	581
Come Blow Your Horn	677	No Strings	580
The Most Happy Fella	676	Brother Rat	577
		Show Boat	572

Plays	Performances Number	Plays	Number Performances
The Show-Off	571	*Grease	535
Sally	570	The Unsinkable Molly Brown	532
Golden Boy (m)	568	The Red Mill (r)	531
One Touch of Venus	567	A Raisin in the Sun	530
Happy Birthday	564	The Solid Gold Cadillac	526
Look Homeward, Angel	564	Irma La Douce	524
The Glass Menagerie	561	The Boomerang	522
I Do! I Do!	560	Follies	521
Wonderful Town	559	Rosalinda	521
Rose Marie	557	The Best Man	520
Strictly Dishonorable	557	Chauve-Souris	520
A Majority of One	556	Blackbirds of 1928	518
The Great White Hope	556	Sunny	517
Toys in the Attic	556	Victoria Regina	517
Sunrise at Campobello	556	Half a Sixpence	511
Jamaica	555	The Vagabond King	511
Stop the World—I Want to Get		The New Moon	509
Off	555	The World of Suzie Wong	508
Florodora	553	The Rothschilds	507
Ziegfeld Follies (1943)	553	Shuffle Along	504
Dial "M" for Murder	552	Up in Central Park	504
Good News	551	Carmen Jones	503
Let's Face It	547	The Member of the Wedding	501
Milk and Honey	543	Panama Hattie	501
Within the Law	541	Personal Appearance	501
The Music Master	540	Bird in Hand	500
Pal Joey (r)	540	Room Service	500
What Makes Sammy Run?	540	Sailor, Beware!	500
What a Life	538	Tomorrow the World	500

LONG RUNS OFF BROADWAY

Plays	Number Performances	Plays	Number Performances
*The Fantasticks	5,443	*One Flew Over the Cuckoo's	
The Threepenny Opera	2,611	Nest	914
Jacques Brel Is Alive and Well		The Mad Show	871
and Living in Paris	1,847	*Godspell	850
You're a Good Man		The Effect of Gamma Rays on	
Charlie Brown	1,597	Man-in-the-Moon Marigolds	819
The Blacks	1,408	A View From the Bridge (r)	780
Little Mary Sunshine	1,143	The Boy Friend (r)	763
The Boys in the Band	1,000	The Pocket Watch	725
Your Own Thing	933	The Connection	722
Curley McDimple	931	Adaptation and Next	707
Leave It to Jane (r)	928	Oh! Calcutta!	704

Plays	Number Performances	Plays	Number Performances
Scuba Duba	692	Dames at Sea	575
The Knack	685	The Crucible (r)	571
The Balcony	672	The Iceman Cometh (r)	565
America Hurrah	634	The Hostage (r)	545
Hogan's Goat	607	Six Characters in Search of an	
The Trojan Women (r)	600	Author (r)	529
Krapp's Last Tape and		The Dirtiest Show in Town	509
The Zoo Story	582	Happy Ending and Day of	
The Dumbwaiter and		Absence	504
The Collection	578	The Boys From Syracuse (r)	500

DRAMA CRITICS CIRCLE VOTING, 1972-73

The New York Drama Critics Circle voted **The Changing Room** the best play of the season by a plurality of 38 points representing the critics' consensus on a weighted second ballot, after no play obtained the majority of first choices (11 of the 20 critics present) needed to win on the first ballot. Other best-play points on the weighted ballot (counting 3 for each critic's first choice, 2 for his second and 1 for his third) were distributed as follows: *The Hot l Baltimore* 18, *The River Niger* 17, *Butley* 17, *The Sunshine Boys* 16, *The Tooth of Crime* 9, *Not I* 4, *Enemies* 1.

Having named a foreign play best, the Critics Circle decided to name a best American play. By the same consensus scoring method weighted as above after the first ballot, **The Hot l Baltimore** won in a close vote with a plurality of 25 points against 21 for *The Sunshine Boys* and 20 for *The River Niger*. Five of the critics present abstained. Other plays which received points in the voting in this category were *The Tooth of Crime* 17, *Baba Goya* 2, *Finishing Touches* 2, *An Evening With the Poet-Senator* 1, *Freeman* 1, *The Karl Marx Play* 1.

In the same manner of weighted consensus on the second ballot, **A Little Night Music** was named best musical of the season by a plurality of 34 points against 27 for *Seesaw* and 24 for *Pippin*. Other musicals named in this voting and their point scores were as follows: *El Grande de Coca-Cola* 15, *Doctor Selavy's Magic Theater* 9, *Much Ado About Nothing* 3, *Oh, Coward!* 2, *Rainbow* 2, *What's a Nice Country Like You Doing in a State Like This?* 2, *The Life of a Man* 1, *Smith* 1.

Here's the way the Circle members' votes were distributed on the weighted second ballots for best play, best American play and best musical:

SECOND BALLOT FOR BEST PLAY

Critic	1st Choice (3 pts.)	2d Choice (2 pts.)	3d Choice (1 pt.)
Clive Barnes *Times*	The Changing Room	The Tooth of Crime	Butley
John Beaufort *Monitor*	The Sunshine Boys	The Changing Room	The River Niger
Harold Clurman *The Nation*	The River Niger	The Hot l Baltimore	The Changing Room
Brendan Gill *New Yorker*	The River Niger	Baltimore	Butley
William H. Glover *AP*	The River Niger	The Sunshine Boys	The Changing Room
Martin Gottfried *Women's Wear*	Baltimore	Not I	The Tooth of Crime
Henry Hewes *Saturday Review*	The River Niger	The Changing Room	The Tooth of Crime
Ted Kalem *Time*	The Changing Room	The Sunshine Boys	Butley
Walter Kerr *Times*	The Changing Room	Butley	The Sunshine Boys
Jack Kroll *Newsweek*	The Changing Room	Baltimore	The Tooth of Crime
John Lahr *Village Voice*	The Tooth of Crime	Baltimore	The Changing Room
Emory Lewis *Bergen Record*	The River Niger	The Changing Room	Baltimore
Hobe Morrison *Variety*	Butley	The Sunshine Boys	The Changing Room
George Oppenheimer *Newsday*	The Changing Room	Baltimore	Butley
William Raidy *Newhouse Papers*	The Changing Room	Butley	The River Niger
John Simon *New York*	Butley	The Changing Room	Enemies
Marilyn Stasio *Cue*	The Changing Room	Baltimore	The Tooth of Crime
Allan Wallach *Newsday*	Butley	The Changing Room	The Sunshine Boys
Douglas Watt *Daily News*	The Sunshine Boys	Not I	Baltimore
Richard Watts Jr. *Post*	The Changing Room	The Sunshine Boys	Baltimore

SECOND BALLOT FOR BEST AMERICAN PLAY

Critic	1st Choice (3 pts.)	2d Choice (2 pts.)	3d Choice (1 pt.)
Clive Barnes	The Tooth of Crime	Baltimore	The Sunshine Boys
John Beaufort	The Sunshine Boys	The River Niger	Baba Goya
Harold Clurman	The River Niger	Baltimore	The Tooth of Crime
Brendan Gill	The River Niger	Baltimore	The Tooth of Crime
William H. Glover	The River Niger	The Sunshine Boys	Freeman
Martin Gottfried	Baltimore	The Tooth of Crime	The Karl Marx Play
Henry Hewes	The River Niger	The Tooth of Crime	An Evening With the Poet-Senator
Ted Kalem	Abstain		
Walter Kerr	Abstain		
Jack Kroll	Baltimore	The Tooth of Crime	The River Niger
John Lahr	The Tooth of Crime	Baltimore	The Sunshine Boys
Emory Lewis	The River Niger	Baltimore	The Sunshine Boys
Hobe Morrison	The Sunshine Boys	The River Niger	Finishing Touches
George Oppenheimer	Abstain		

William Raidy	Abstain		
John Simon	Abstain		
Marilyn Stasio	Baltimore	The Tooth of Crime	The Sunshine Boys
Allan Wallach	The Sunshine Boys	Baltimore	The Tooth of Crime
Douglas Watt	The Sunshine Boys	Baltimore	Baba Goya
Richard Watts Jr.	The Sunshine Boys	Baltimore	Finishing Touches

SECOND BALLOT FOR BEST MUSICAL

Critic	1st Choice (3 pts.)	2d Choice (2 pts.)	3d Choice (1 pt.)
Clive Barnes	A Little Night Music	El Grande de Coca-Cola	Seesaw
John Beaufort	Pippin	Seesaw	A Little Night Music
Harold Clurman	Doctor Selavy's Magic Theater	Seesaw	A Little Night Music
Brendan Gill	A Little Night Music	Seesaw	Pippin
William H. Glover	Seesaw	Pippin	Doctor Selavy
Martin Gottfried	Coca-Cola	Rainbow	Doctor Selavy
Henry Hewes	A Little Night Music	Seesaw	The Life of a Man
Ted Kalem	Pippin	A Little Night Music	Seesaw
Walter Kerr	Seesaw	A Little Night Music	Pippin
Jack Kroll	Coca-Cola	Doctor Selavy	Seesaw
John Lahr	Coca-Cola	Doctor Selavy	Seesaw
Emory Lewis	A Little Night Music	Pippin	Much Ado About Nothing
Hobe Morrison	A Little Night Music	Seesaw	Pippin
George Oppenheimer	Pippin	Seesaw	A Little Night Music
William Raidy	A Little Night Music	Coca-Cola	Seesaw
John Simon	Seesaw	What's a Nice Country Like You Doing in a State Like This?	Coca-Cola
Marilyn Stasio	A Little Night Music	Oh, Coward	Pippin
Allan Wallach	A Little Night Music	Pippin	Coca-Cola
Douglas Watt	Pippin	Much Ado	Seesaw
Richard Watts Jr.	A Little Night Music	Pippin	Smith

First ballot first-choice votes which were changed on the second ballot of the various categories were as follows: for best play, William H. Glover from *Freeman* to *The River Niger*, Richard Watts Jr. from *The Sunshine Boys* to *The Changing Room*; for best musical, John Simon from *What's a Nice Country Like You*, etc. to *Seesaw*.

CHOICES OF SOME OTHER CRITICS

Critic	Best Play	Best Musical
Hobe Morrison *Variety*	The Sunshine Boys	A Little Night Music
Judith Crist "Today"	The Sunshine Boys	A Little Night Music
Leonard Probst NBC-TV	Baltimore	A Little Night Music
Leonard Harris WCBS-TV	The Changing Room	A Little Night Music
Norman Nadel Scripps-Howard	Abstain	A Little Night Music
Alvin Klein WNYC Radio	Baltimore	A Little Night Music
Stewart Klein WNEW-TV	The Changing Room	A Little Night Music
Virgil Scudder WINS Radio	The River Niger	A Little Night Music
Tom Prideaux	The Changing Room	A Little Night Music

NEW YORK DRAMA CRITICS CIRCLE AWARDS

Listed below are the New York Drama Critics Circle Awards from 1935-36 through 1972-73, classified as follows: (1) Best American Play, (2) Best Foreign Play, (3) Best Musical, (4) Best, regardless of category (this category was established by new voting rules in 1962-63 and did not exist prior to that year).

1935-36—(1) Winterset
1936-37—(1) High Tor
1937-38—(1) Of Mice and Men, (2) Shadow and Substance
1938-39—(1) No award, (2) The White Steed
1939-40—(1) The Time of Your Life
1940-41—(1) Watch on the Rhine, (2) The Corn Is Green
1941-42—(1) No award, (2) Blithe Spirit
1942-43—(1) The Patriots
1943-44—(2) Jacobowsky and the Colonel
1944-45—(1) The Glass Menagerie
1945-46—(3) Carousel
1946-47—(1) All My Sons, (2) No Exit, (3) Brigadoon
1947-48—(1) A Streetcar Named Desire, (2) The Winslow Boy
1948-49—(1) Death of a Salesman, (2) The Madwoman of Chaillot, (3) South Pacific
1949-50—(1) The Member of the Wedding, (2) The Cocktail Party, (3) The Consul
1950-51—(1) Darkness at Noon, (2) The Lady's Not for Burning, (3) Guys and Dolls
1951-52—(1) I Am a Camera, (2) Venus Observed, (3) Pal Joey (Special citation to Don Juan in Hell)
1952-53—(1) Picnic, (2) The Love of Four Colonels, (3) Wonderful Town
1953-54—(1) Teahouse of the August Moon, (2) Ondine, (3) The Golden Apple
1954-55—(1) Cat on a Hot Tin Roof, (2) Witness for the Prosecution, (3) The Saint of Bleecker Street
1955-56—(1) The Diary of Ann Frank, (2) Tiger at the Gates, (3) My Fair Lady
1956-57—(1) Long Day's Journey Into Night, (2) The Waltz of the Toreadors, (3) The Most Happy Fella

1957-58—(1) Look Homeward, Angel, (2) Look Back in Anger, (3) The Music Man
1958-59—(1) A Raisin in the Sun, (2) The Visit, (3) La Plume de Ma Tante
1959-60—(1) Toys in the Attic, (2) Five Finger Exercise, (3) Fiorello!
1960-61—(1) All the Way Home, (2) A Taste of Honey, (3) Carnival
1961-62—(1) The Night of the Iguana, (2) A Man for All Seasons, (3) How to Succeed in Business Without Really Trying
1962-63—(4) Who's Afraid of Virginia Woolf? (Special citation to Beyond the Fringe)
1963-64—(4) Luther, (3) Hello, Dolly! (Special citation to The Trojan Women)
1964-65—(4) The Subject Was Roses, (3) Fiddler on the Roof
1965-66—(4) The Persecution and Assassination of Marat as Performed by the Inmates of the Asylum of Charenton Under the Direction of the Marquis de Sade, (3) Man of La Mancha
1966-67—(4) The Homecoming, (3) Cabaret
1967-68—(4) Rosencrantz and Guildenstern Are Dead, (3) Your Own Thing
1968-69—(4) The Great White Hope, (3) 1776
1969-70—(4) Borstal Boy, (1) The Effect of Gamma Rays on Man-in-the-Moon Marigolds, (3) Company
1970-71—(4) Home, (1) The House of Blue Leaves, (3) Follies
1971-72—(4) That Championship Season, (2) The Screens, (3) Two Gentlemen of Verona (Special citations to Sticks and Bones and Old Times)
1972-73—(4) The Changing Room, (1) The Hot 1 Baltimore, (3) A Little Night Music

PULITZER PRIZE WINNERS, 1916-17 TO 1972-73

1916-17—No award
1917-18—Why Marry?, by Jesse Lynch Williams

1918-19—No award
1919-20—Beyond the Horizon, by Eugene O'Neill

1920-21—Miss Lulu Bett, by Zona Gale
1921-22—Anna Christie, by Eugene O'Neill
1922-23—Icebound, by Owen Davis
1923-24—Hell-Bent fer Heaven, by Hatcher Hughes
1924-25—They Knew What They Wanted, by Sidney Howard
1925-26—Craig's Wife, by George Kelly
1926-27—In Abraham's Bosom, by Paul Green
1927-28—Strange Interlude, by Eugene O'Neill
1928-29—Street Scene, by Elmer Rice
1929-30—The Green Pastures, by Marc Connelly
1930-31—Alison's House, by Susan Glaspell
1931-32—Of Thee I Sing, by George S. Kaufman, Morrie Ryskind, Ira and George Gershwin
1932-33—Both Your Houses, by Maxwell Anderson
1933-34—Men in White, by Sidney Kingsley
1934-35—The Old Maid, by Zoë Akins
1935-36—Idiot's Delight, by Robert E. Sherwood
1936-37—You Can't Take It With You, by Moss Hart and George S. Kaufman
1937-38—Our Town, by Thornton Wilder
1938-39—Abe Lincoln in Illinois, by Robert E. Sherwood
1939-40—The Time of Your Life, by William Saroyan
1940-41—There Shall Be No Night, by Robert E. Sherwood
1941-42—No award
1942-43—The Skin of Our Teeth, by Thornton Wilder
1943-44—No award
1944-45—Harvey, by Mary Chase
1945-46—State of the Union, by Howard Lindsay and Russel Crouse
1946-47—No award.
1947-48—A Streetcar Named Desire, by Tennessee Williams
1948-49—Death of a Salesman, by Arthur Miller

1949-50—South Pacific, by Richard Rodgers, Oscar Hammerstein II and Joshua Logan
1950-51—No award
1951-52—The Shrike, by Joseph Kramm
1952-53—Picnic, by William Inge
1953-54—The Teahouse of the August Moon, by John Patrick
1954-55—Cat on a Hot Tin Roof, by Tennessee Williams
1955-56—The Diary of Anne Frank, by Frances Goodrich and Albert Hackett
1956-57—Long Day's Journey Into Night, by Eugene O'Neill
1957-58—Look Homeward, Angel, by Ketti Frings
1958-59—J. B., by Archibald MacLeish
1959-60—Fiorello!, by Jerome Weidman, George Abbott, Sheldon Harnick and Jerry Bock
1960-61—All the Way Home, by Tad Mosel
1961-62—How to Succeed in Business Without Really Trying, by Abe Burrows, Willie Gilbert, Jack Weinstock and Frank Loesser
1962-63—No award
1963-64—No award
1964-65—The Subject Was Roses, by Frank D. Gilroy
1965-66—No award
1966-67—A Delicate Balance, by Edward Albee
1967-68—No award
1968-69—The Great White Hope, by Howard Sackler
1969-70—No Place to Be Somebody, by Charles Gordone
1970-71—The Effect of Gamma Rays on Man-in-the-Moon Marigolds, by Paul Zindel
1971-72—No award
1972-73—That Championship Season, by Jason Miller

ADDITIONAL PRIZES AND AWARDS, 1972-73

The following is a list of major prizes and awards for theatrical achievement. In all cases the names of winners—persons, productions or organizations—appear in **bold face type.**

VILLAGE VOICE OFF-BROADWAY (OBIE) AWARDS for off-Broadway excellence, selected by a committee of judges whose members were Mel Gussow, Michael Smith and Marilyn Stasio. Best plays, *The River Niger, The Hot l Baltimore.* Distinguished plays, *The Tooth of Crime, What if It Had* *Turned Up Heads?, Bigfoot.* Distinguished foreign plays, *Not I, Kaspar.* Distinguished performances, **Hume Cronyn, Mari Gorman, James Hilbrandt, Stacy Keach, Christopher Lloyd, Charles Ludlam, Lola Pashalinski, Alice Playten, Roxie Roker, Jessica Tandy, Douglas Turner Ward, Sam Waterston.**

Distinguished direction, **Jack Gelber, William E. Lathan, Marshall W. Mason.** Special citations: to the **City Center Acting Company** for its "first season of classical repertory," to **Richard Foreman** for his Ontological-Hysteric Theater, to the **Workshop of the Players' Art** for "continuing diversity and imagination," to the **San Francisco Mime Troupe** for *The Dragon Lady's Revenge.*

OUTER CIRCLE AWARDS (voted by critics of out-of-town and foreign periodicals for distinctive achievement in New York theater). **Christopher Plummer** in *Cyrano,* **Michele Lee** in *Seesaw,* **Debbie Reynolds** in *Irene,* **Ellis Rabb** for direction of *A Streetcar Named Desire,* **Bob Fosse** for direction of *Pippin,* **Julie Harris** in *The Last of Mrs. Lincoln,* the **entire cast** of *The Women* for ensemble playing.

THEATER WORLD AWARDS (29th annual awards to the most promising new performers in Broadway and off-Broadway productions). **Patricia Elliott, Laurence Guittard** and **D. Jamin-Bartlett** in *A Little Night Music,* **James Farentino** in *A Streetcar Named Desire,* **Brian Farrell** in *The Last of Mrs. Lincoln,* **Victor Garber** in *Ghosts,* **Kelly Garrett** in *Mother Earth,* **Mari Gorman** and **Trish Hawkins** in *The Hot l Baltimore,* **Monte Markham** in *Irene,* **John Rubinstein** in *Pippin,* **Jennifer Warren** in *6 Rms Riv Vu.* Special award to **Alexander H. Cohen** "for his contribution to cultivating theater audiences by extending Broadway, not only nationally, but internationally, with his exemplary television productions."

ELIZABETH HULL-KATE WARRINER 1972 AWARD (to the playwright whose work produced within each year dealt with controversial subjects involving the fields of political, religious or social mores of the time, selected by the Dramatists Guild Council). **Phillip Hayes Dean** for *The Sty of the Blind Pig.*

STRAWHAT AWARDS (4th annual awards voted for excellence during the 1972 summer theater season by the Council of Stock Theaters). **Eileen Heckart** in *Remember Me,* **Sid Caesar** in *Last of the Red Hot Lovers,* **Hume Cronyn** for direction of *Promenade, All,* **Victor Borge** as best entertainer, **Benjamin Slack** and **Joan Bassie** as best supporting actor and actress in *See How They Run,* **Erin Connor** as most promising newcomer in *Butterflies Are Free, A Conflict of Interest* by Jay Broad as best new play tried out in stock, special achievement award to **Helen Hayes.**

MARGO JONES AWARD (for the most significant contribution to the theater through a continuing policy of producing new plays). **Jules Irving** for the Repertory Theater of Lincoln Center's production program in the Forum Theater.

JOSEPH MAHARAM FOUNDATION AWARDS (for distinguished New York theatrical design). Best 1972-73 scenic design, **Douglas W. Schmidt** for *Enemies* and **Robin Wagner** for *Seesaw.* Best 1972-73 costume design, **Theoni V. Aldredge** for *Much Ado About Nothing.* Special honors for lighting to **Jules Fisher** for *Pippin* and **John Gleason** for the entire Lincoln Center Repertory season.

SAM S. SHUBERT FOUNDATION AWARD (for theatrical achievement). **Robert Whitehead.**

VERNON RICE AWARD (for outstanding contribution to the off-Broadway season, voted by Drama Desk members). **The New York Shakespeare Festival in Central Park.**

THE TONY AWARDS

The Antoinette Perry (Tony) Awards are voted by members of the League of New York Theaters, the governing bodies of the Dramatists Guild, Actors, Equity, the American Theater Wing, the Society of Stage Directors and Choreographers, the United Scenic Artists Union, and members of the first and second night press, from a list of four nominees in each category. Nominations are made by a committee serving at the invitation of the League of New York Theaters, which is in charge of the Tony Awards procedure, with the committee's personnel changing every year. The 1972-73 nominating committee was composed of John Beaufort, Radie Harris, Jack Kroll, Elliot Norton, Allan Wallach, Douglas Watt and Audrey Wood. Their list of nominees follows, with winners listed in **bold face type.**

BEST PLAY. *Butley* by Simon Gray, produced by Lester Osterman and Richard Horner; *That Championship Season* by Jason Miller, produced by Joseph Papp; *The Changing Room* by David Storey, produced by Charles Bowden, Lee Reynolds and Isobel Robins; *The Sunshine Boys* by Neil Simon, produced by Emanuel Azenberg and Eugene V. Wolsk.

BEST MUSICAL. *A Little Night Music* by Hugh Wheeler and Stephen Sondheim, produced by Harold Prince in association with Ruth Mitchell; *Don't Bother Me, I Can't Cope* by Micki Grant, produced by Edward Padula and Arch Lustberg; *Pippin* by Roger O. Hirson and Stephen Schwartz, produced by Stuart Ostrow; *Sugar* by Peter Stone, Jule Styne and Bob Merrill, produced by David Merrick.

BEST BOOK OF A MUSICAL. *A Little Night Music* by **Hugh Wheeler,** *Don't Bother Me, I Can't Cope* by Micki Grant, *Don't Play Us Cheap* by Melvin Van Peebles, *Pippin* by Roger O. Hirson.

BEST SCORE. *A Little Night Music* by **Stephen Sondheim,** *Don't Bother Me, I Can't Cope* by Micki Grant, *Much Ado About Nothing* by Peter Link, *Pippin* by Stephen Schwartz.

BEST ACTOR—PLAY. Jack Albertson in *The Sunshine Boys,* **Alan Bates** in *Butley,* Wilfrid Hyde-White in *The Jockey Club Stakes,* Paul Sorvino in *That Championship Season.*

BEST ACTRESS—PLAY. Jane Alexander in *6 Rms Riv Vu,* Coleen Dewhurst in *Mourning Becomes Electra,* **Julie Harris** in *The Last of Mrs. Lincoln,* Kathleen Widdoes in *Much Ado About Nothing.*

BEST ACTOR—MUSICAL. Len Cariou in *A Little Night Music,* Robert Morse in *Sugar,* Brock Peters in *Lost in the Stars,* **Ben Vereen** in *Pippin.*

BEST ACTRESS—MUSICAL. **Glynis Johns** in *A Little Night Music,* Leland Palmer in *Pippin,* Debbie Reynolds in *Irene,* Marcia Rodd in *Shelter.*

BEST SUPPORTING ACTOR—PLAY. Barnard Hughes in *Much Ado About Nothing,*

John **Lithgow** in *The Changing Room,* John McMartin in *Don Juan,* Hayward Morse in *Butley.*

BEST SUPPORTING ACTRESS—PLAY. Maya Angelou in *Look Away,* **Leora Dana** in *The Last of Mrs. Lincoln,* Katherine Helmond in *The Great God Brown,* Penelope Windust in *Elizabeth I.*

BEST SUPPORTING ACTOR—MUSICAL. Laurence Guittard in *A Little Night Music,* **George S. Irving** in *Irene,* Avon Long in *Don't Play Us Cheap,* Gilbert Price in *Lost in the Stars.*

BEST SUPPORTING ACTRESS—MUSICAL. **Patricia Elliott** and Hermione Gingold in *A Little Night Music,* Patsy Kelly in *Irene,* Irene Ryan in *Pippin.*

BEST DIRECTOR—PLAY. **A.J. Antoon** for *That Championship Season* and *Much Ado About Nothing,* Alan Arkin for *The Sunshine Boys,* Michael Rudman for *The Changing Room.*

BEST DIRECTOR—MUSICAL. Vinnette Carroll for *Don't Bother Me, I Can't Cope,* Gower Champion for *Sugar,* **Bob Fosse** for *Pippin,* Harold Prince for *A Little Night Music.*

BEST SCENIC DESIGNER. Boris Aronson for *A Little Night Music,* David Jenkins for *The Changing Room,* Santo Loquasto for *That Championship Season,* **Tony Walton** for *Pippin.*

BEST COSTUME DESIGNER. Theoni V. Aldredge for *Much Ado About Nothing,* **Florence Klotz** for *A Little Night Music,* Miles White for *Tricks,* Patricia Zipprodt for *Pippin.*

BEST LIGHTING DESIGNER. Martin Aronstein for *Much Ado About Nothing,* Ian Calderon for *That Championship Season,* **Jules Fisher** for *Pippin,* Tharon Musser for *A Little Night Music.*

BEST CHOREOGRAPHER. Gower Champion for *Sugar,* **Bob Fosse** for *Pippin,* Peter Gennaro for *Irene,* Donald Sadler for *Much Ado About Nothing.*

THE DRAMA DESK AWARDS

The Drama Desk Awards for outstanding contribution to the theater season are voted by the critics, editors and reporters who are members of Drama

Desk, a New York organization of theater journalists in all media. Selections are made from a long list of nominees covering Broadway, repertory theater, off Broadway and off off Broadway. In order that work in productions seen only by a portion of the voters can compete fairly with that seen by almost all, the ballots ask each voter to check only those candidates whose work they actually saw. This makes it possible to compute the proportion of those who voted for the show to those who saw the show, determining winners by percentages rather than total votes received.

Winners of 1972-73 Drama Desk Awards are listed below in the order of percentages received. The actual percentage figure is given for those who scored highest in each category. The "most promising playwright" category does list the playwrights in the order of their percentage scores, but no figure is given for those who won the other most promising citations because they were chosen by a committee of Drama Desk (and previous winners of "most promising" awards are not eligible).

OUTSTANDING PERFORMANCES (chosen from 70 nominees). **Mari Gorman** (81.2 per cent) in *The Hot l Baltimore*, **Christopher Plummer** in *Cyrano*, **Alan Bates** in *Butley*, **Julie Harris** in *The Last of Mrs. Lincoln*, **Sam Waterston** in *Much Ado About Nothing*, **Ben Vereen** in *Pippin*, **Jack Albertson** in *The Sunshine Boys*, **John McMartin** in *The Great God Brown* and *Don Juan*, **Stacy Keach** in *Hamlet*, **John Glover** in *The Great God Brown*, **Jessica Tandy** in *Happy Days* and *Not I*, **Christopher Lloyd** in *Kaspar*, **Ruby Dee** in *Wedding Band*, **Michele Lee** in *Seesaw*, **Glynis Johns** in *A Little Night Music*, **Rosemary Harris** in *A Streetcar Named Desire* and *The Merchant of Venice*, **John Lithgow** in *The Changing Room*, **Colleen Dewhurst** in *Mourning Becomes Electra*, **Douglass Watson** in *Much Ado About Nothing*, **James Earl Jones** in *Hamlet* and *The Cherry Orchard*, **Patricia Elliott** in *A Little Night Music*, **Pamela Payton-Wright** in *Mourning Becomes Electra*.

OUTSTANDING DIRECTORS (chosen from 21 nominees). **Michael Rudman** (73.7 per cent) for *The Changing Room*, **Bob Fosse** for *Pippin*, **Victor Garcia** for *Yerma*, **Joseph Chaikin** for *The Mutation Show*, **Harold Prince** for *The Great God Brown* and *A Little Night Music*.

OUTSTANDING SCENE DESIGNERS (chosen from 15 nominees). **Victor Garcia** and **Fabian Puigserver** (66.7 per cent) for *Yerma*, **Tony Walton** for *Pippin* and *Shelter*, **David Jenkins** for *The Changing Room*.

OUTSTANDING COSTUME DESIGNERS (chosen from 7 nominees). **Theoni V. Aldredge** (75 per cent) for *Much Ado About*

Nothing and *Hamlet*, **Patricia Zipprodt** for *Pippin*.

OUTSTANDING COMPOSER (chosen from 12 nominees). **Stephen Sondheim** (80.9 per cent) for *A Little Night Music*.

OUTSTANDING LYRICIST (chosen from 9 nominees). **Stephen Sondheim** (95.5 per cent) for *A Little Night Music*.

OUTSTANDING CHOREOGRAPHER (chosen from 5 nominees). **Bob Fosse** (84.2 per cent) for *Pippin*.

OUTSTANDING BOOK WRITER (chosen from 6 nominees). **Hugh Wheeler** (61.9 per cent) for *A Little Night Music*.

MOST PROMISING PLAYWRIGHTS. **Joseph A. Walker** (79.1 per cent) for *The River Niger*, **Robert Randall** for *6 Rms Riv Vu*, **James Prideaux** for *The Last of Mrs. Lincoln*, **Steve Tesich** for *Baba Goya*.

MOST PROMISING PERFORMERS. **Tom Atkins** in *The Changing Room*, **Ralph Carter** in *Dude*, **Bill Cobbs** in *Freeman* and *What the Wine Sellers Buy*, **Trish Hawkins** in *The Hot l Baltimore*, **D. Jamin-Bartlett** in *A Little Night Music*, **Mary Lou Rosato** in *The School for Scandal*, **Gail Strickland** in *Status Quo Vadis*.

MOST PROMISING SCENE DESIGNER. **Jerry Rojo** for *Endgame*.

MOST PROMISING COSTUME DESIGNER. **Laura Crow** and **Cookie Gluck** for *Warp*.

MOST PROMISING COMPOSER. **Stanley Silverman** for *Doctor Selavy's Magic Theater*.

MOST PROMISING LYRICIST: *National Lampoon* writers for *National Lampoon's Lemmings.*

MOST PROMISING BOOK WRITER. **Ron House** and **Diz White** for *El Grande de Coca-Cola.*

1972-1973 PUBLICATION
OF RECENTLY-PRODUCED PLAYS

American Place Theater, The: Plays. Richard Schotter, Editor. Delta (paperback).
An Evening with Richard Nixon. Gore Vidal. Vintage (paperback).
Basic Training of Pavlo Hummel, The and *Sticks and Bones.* David Rabe. Viking.
Burning, The. Stewart Conn. Calder & Boyars.
Butley. Simon Gray. Viking.
Catch-22. Joseph Heller, Delta (paperback).
Creation of the World and Other Business, The. Arthur Miller. Viking.
Crucificado: Two Plays (The Crucificado and *The Life and Times of J. Walter Smintheus).* Edgar White. Morrow.
Creeps. David Freeman. Univ. of Toronto (paperback).
Dramatization of 365 Days, The. H. Wesley Balk. Univ. of Minnesota (also paperback).
Enter a Free Man. Tom Stoppard, Grove (paperback).
Four Plays by John Osborne. (West of Suez, A Patriot for Me, Time Present, Hotel in Amsterdam). Dodd, Mead.
Grease. Warren Casey and Jim Jacobs. Winter House (paperback).
In the Clap Shack. William Styron. Random House.
In the Heart of the British Museum. John Spurling. Calder & Boyars (paperback).
Incomparable Max, The. Jerome Lawrence and Robert E. Lee. Hill & Wang.
Lay By. Howard Brenton, Brian Clark, Trevor Griffiths, David Hare, Stephen Poliakoff, Hugh Stoddart and Snoo Wilson. Calder & Boyars.
Lear. Edward Bond. Hill & Wang (also paperback).
Lennon Play, The: In His Own Write. John Lennon, Adrienne Kennedy and Victor Spinetti. Simon & Schuster.
Lenny. Julian Barry. Grove.
Les Blancs: The Collected Last Plays of Lorraine Hansberry. Vintage (paperback).
Love Suicide at Schofield Barracks, The and *Democracy and Esther.* Romulus Linney. Harcourt Brace.
More Plays From off off Broadway. Edited by Michael Smith. Bobbs-Merrill (also paperback).
Occupations and *The Big House.* Trevor Griffiths. Calder & Boyars (also paperback).
Off-off-Broadway Book, The. Anthology. Albert Poland and Bruce Mailman. Bobbs-Merrill.
Prisoner of Second Avenue, The. Neil Simon. Random House.
Scripts 7. Collection of playscripts edited by Erika Munk and published by New York Shakespeare Festival and Joseph Papp (paperback) contains *The Meat Rack* by Kathleen Kimball, *The Service for Joseph Axminster* by George Dennison, *Izzy* by Lonnie Carter, *Cop and Blow* by Neil Harris, *Perfection in Black* by China Clark, *Helliocentric World* by Sebastian Clarke, *The Wall* by Ben Caldwell, *One the Two of Us* by William Adell Stevenson III.
Scripts 8. Contains *The Resolution of Mossie Wax* by Stephen H. Foreman, *Audioplay 2— Safe* by Jakov Lind, *On the Eve of Publication* by David Mercer, *Ol-Dopt* by David Dozer, *The Bagman* by John Arden, *The Great Silkie of Sule Skerry* by Lucy Bate.
Scripts 9. Contains *The Ballygombeen Bequest* by John Arden and Margaretta D'Arcy, *Within Two Shadows* by John Haire.
Sleep. Jack Gelber. Hill & Wang (paperback).
Sleuth. Anthony Shaffer. Bantam (paperback).
Small Craft Warnings. Tennessee Williams. New Directions (also paperback).
Solitaire/Double Solitaire. Robert Anderson. Random House.
Spontaneous Combustion. Rochelle Owens, editor (*Sun* by Adrienne Kennedy, *Cinque* by Leonard Melfi, *Dialect Determinism* by Ed Bullins, *Sanibel and Captiva* by Megan Terry, *A Quick Nut Bread to Make Your Mouth Water* by William M. Hoffman, *Schubert's Last Serenade* by Julie Bovasso, *Ba-Ra-Ka* by Imamu Amiri Baraka (LeRoi Jones), *He Wants Shih* by Rochelle Owens. Winter House.

Story Theater. Paul Sills (paperback).
Subject of Scandal and Concern, A. John Osborne. Dramatic Publishing (paperback).
That Championship Season. Jason Miller. Atheneum (paperback).

A SELECTED LIST OF OTHER PLAYS PUBLISHED IN 1972-73

Arise, Arise. Louis Zukofsky. Grossman (also paperback).
Best Short Plays 1972, The. Stanley Richards, editor. Chilton.
Black Theater. Compiled by Lindsay Patterson. New American Library (paperback).
Bertolt Brecht: Collected Plays, Vol. 9. Ralph Manheim and John Willett, editors. Pantheon.
Early Plays of Michael Bulgakov, The. Ellendea Proffer. editor. Indiana Univ. Press.
German Drama Between the Wars. George E. Wellwarth, editor. Dutton.
Oedipus the King. Sophocles; new translation and adaptation by Anthony Burgess. Univ. of Minnesota.
One-Act Plays for Our Times. Francis Griffith, Joseph Mersand, Joseph B. Maggio. Popular Library (paperback).
Performing Arts Books in Print: An Annotated Bibliography. Ralph Newman Schoolcraft, editor (first complete compilation of English-language in-print books on the theater and its allied arts). Drama Book Specialists.
Plays by and About Women. Victoria Sullivan, James Hatch, editors. Random House.
Plays of J.P. Donleavy, The. Delacorte (also paperback).
Plays of the Year: Volume 40 (1970-1971). The Contractor by David Storey, *The Jockey Club Stakes* by William Douglas Home, *Children of the Wolf* by Joan Peacock, *Unaccompanied Cello* by John Harrison. Ungar.
Ten Classic Mystery and Suspense Plays of the Modern Theater. Stanley Richards, editor. Dodd, Mead.
Tropical Madness: Four Plays. Stanislaw Witkiewicz. Winter House.

MUSICAL AND DRAMATIC RECORDINGS
OF NEW YORK SHOWS

Title and publishing company are listed below. Each record is an original New York cast album unless otherwise indicated. An asterisk (*) indicates recording is also available on cassettes. Two asterisks (**) indicate it is available on eight-track cartridges.

Berlin to Broadway With Kurt Weill. Paramount (two records).
Carmilla. Vanguard.
Clown Around. RCA. (*) (**).
Different Times. RCA.
Evening with Richard Nixon, An. Ode.
Grease. MGM. (*) (**).
Irene. Columbia. (*) (**).
Joan. Judson (two records).
Long Day's Journey Into Night. Caedmon (four records).
Man of La Mancha, (Nabors, Horne, Gilford, Tucker). Columbia. (*) (**).
Mourning Becomes Electra. American Shakespeare Festival Theater, Caedmon (four records).
Oh, Coward! Bell. (*) (**).
Pippin. Motown. (*) (**).
School for Wives, The. Phoenix Theater. Caedmon (three records).
Secret Life of Walter Mitty, The. Columbia. (*)
Seesaw. Buddah. (*) (**).
1776 (movie sound track). Columbia.
Sound of Music, The (London cast). Stanyard.
Sugar. United Artists. (*) (**).
Trial of the Catonsville Nine, The. Caedmon (two records).
Where's Charley? (London cast). Monmouth Evergreen.

THE BEST PLAYS, 1894-1972

Listed in alphabetical order below are all those works selected as Best Plays in previous volumes in the *Best Plays* series. Opposite each title is given the volume in which the play appears, its opening date and its total number of performances. Those plays marked with an asterisk (*) were still playing on June 1, 1973 and their number of performances was figured through May 31, 1973. Adaptors and translators are indicated by (ad) and (tr), and the symbols (b), (m) and (l) stand for the author of the book, music and lyrics in the case of musicals.

NOTE: A season-by-season listing, rather than an alphabetical one, of the 500 Best Plays in the first 50 volumes, starting with the yearbook for the season of 1919-1920, appears in *The Best Plays of 1968-69*.

PLAY   VOLUME OPENED PERFS.
DIARY OF ANNE FRANK, THE—Frances Goodrich, Albert Hack-
ett, based on Anne Frank's *The Diary of a Young Girl* ....55-56..Oct.   5, 1955.. 717
DINNER AT EIGHT—George S. Kaufman, Edna Ferber ....32-33..Oct. 22, 1932.. 232
DISENCHANTED, THE—Budd Schulberg, Harvey Breit, based on
Mr. Schulberg's novel ....58-59..Dec.   3, 1958.. 189
DISRAELI—Louis N. Parker ....09-19..Sept. 18, 1911.. 280
DISTAFF SIDE, THE—John van Druten ....34-35..Sept. 25, 1934.. 177
DODSWORTH—Sidney Howard, based on Sinclair Lewis's novel ...33-34..Feb. 24, 1934.. 315
DOUGHGIRLS, THE—Joseph Fields ....42-43..Dec. 30, 1942.. 671
DOVER ROAD, THE—A.A. Milne ....21-22..Dec. 23, 1921.. 324
DREAM GIRL—Elmer Rice ....45-46..Dec. 14, 1945.. 348
DUEL OF ANGELS—Jean Giraudoux's *Pour Lucrèce*, (ad) Chris-
topher Fry ....59-60..Apr. 19, 1960..   51
DULCY—George S. Kaufman, Marc Connelly ....21-22..Aug. 13, 1921.. 246
DYBBUK, THE—S. Ansky, (ad) Henry G. Alsberg ....25-26..Dec. 15, 1925.. 120
DYLAN—Sidney Michaels ....63-64..Jan. 18, 1964.. 153

EASIEST WAY, THE—Eugene Walter ....09-19..Jan. 19, 1909.. 157
EASTWARD IN EDEN—Dorothy Gardner ....47-48..Nov. 18, 1947..   15
EDWARD, MY SON—Robert Morley, Noel Langley ....48-49..Sept. 30, 1948.. 260
EFFECT OF GAMMA RAYS ON MAN-IN-THE-MOON MARIGOLDS,
THE—Paul Zindel ....69-70..Apr.   7. 1970.. 819
EGG, THE—Felicien Marceau, (ad) Robert Schlitt ....61-62..Jan.   8, 1962..   8
ELIZABETH THE QUEEN—Maxwell Anderson ....30-31..Nov.   3, 1930.. 147
EMPEROR JONES, THE—Eugene O'Neill ....20-21..Nov.   1, 1920.. 204
EMPEROR'S CLOTHES, THE—George Tabori ....52-53..Feb.   9, 1953..   16
ENCHANTED, THE—Maurice Valency, based on Jean Girau-
doux's play *Intermezzo*. ....49-50..Jan. 18, 1950..   45
END OF SUMMER—S. N. Behrman ....35-36..Feb. 17, 1936.. 153
ENEMY, THE—Channing Pollock ....25-26..Oct. 20, 1925.. 203
ENTER MADAME—Gilda Varesi, Dolly Byrne ....20-21..Aug. 16, 1920.. 350
ENTERTAINER, THE—John Osborne ....57-58..Feb. 12, 1958..   97
EPITAPH FOR GEORGE DILLON—John Osborne, Anthony Creigh-
ton ....58-59..Nov.   4, 1958..   23
ESCAPE—John Galsworthy ....27-28..Oct. 26, 1927.. 173
ETHAN FROME—Owen and Donald Davis, based on Edith Whar-
ton's novel ....35-36..Jan. 21, 1936.. 120
EVE OF ST. MARK—Maxwell Anderson ....42-43..Oct.   7, 1942.. 307
EXCURSION—Victor Wolfson ....36-37..Apr.   9, 1937.. 116

FALL GUY, THE—James Gleason, George Abbott ....24-25..Mar. 10, 1925.. 176
FAMILY PORTRAIT—Lenore Coffee, William Joyce Cowen ......38-39..May   8, 1939.. 111
FAMOUS MRS. FAIR, THE—James Forbes ....19-29..Dec. 22, 1919.. 344
FAR COUNTRY, A—Henry Denker ....60-61..Apr.   4, 1961.. 271
FARMER TAKES A WIFE, THE—Frank B. Elser, Marc Connelly,
based on Walter Edmonds's novel *Rome Haul* ....34-35..Oct. 30, 1934.. 104
FATAL WEAKNESS, THE—George Kelly ....46-47..Nov. 19, 1946.. 119
FIDDLER ON THE ROOF—(b) Joseph Stein, (l) Sheldon Har- 64-65..Sept. 22, 1964..3,242
nick, (m) Jerry Bock, based on Sholom Aleichem's stories ....
FIORELLO!—(b) Jerome Weidman, George Abbott, (l) Sheldon
Harnick, (m) Jerry Bock ....59-60..Nov. 23, 1959.. 795
FIREBRAND, THE—Edwin Justus Mayer ....24-25..Oct. 15, 1924.. 269
FIRST LADY—Katharine Dayton, George S. Kaufman ....35-36..Nov. 26, 1935.. 246
FIRST MRS. FRASER, THE—St. John Ervine ....29-30..Dec. 28, 1929.. 352
FIRST YEAR, THE—Frank Craven ....20-21..Oct. 20, 1920.. 760
FIVE FINGER EXERCISE—Peter Shaffer ....59-60..Dec.   2, 1959.. 337
FIVE-STAR FINAL—Louis Weitzenkorn ....30-31..Dec. 30, 1930.. 175
FLIGHT TO THE WEST—Elmer Rice ....40-41..Dec. 30, 1940.. 136
FLOWERING PEACH, THE—Clifford Odets ....54-55..Dec. 28, 1954.. 135
FOLLIES—(b) James Goldman, (m, l) Stephen Sondheim ......70-71..Apr.   4, 1971.. 521
FOOL, THE—Channing Pollock ....22-23..Oct. 23, 1922.. 373
FOOLISH NOTION—Philip Barry ....44-45..Mar.   3, 1945.. 104

NECROLOGY

MAY 1972—JUNE 1973

PERFORMERS

Abbott, Michael Ann (44)—November 22, 1972
Adams, Mrs. Francis (86)—October 18, 1972
Adams, William P. (85)—September 29, 1972
Adrian, Max (69)—January 19, 1973
Ahmed, Raju (35)—December 12, 1972
Alban, Jean-Pierre (38)—January 15, 1973
Andersen, Lale (59)—August 29, 1972
Andre, Gaby—August 9, 1972
Andrews, Tod (51)—November 6, 1972
Arbury, Guy (65)—December 26, 1972
Armstrong, Robert (82)—April 20, 1973
Banner, John (63)—January 28, 1973
Barker, Lex (53)—April 11, 1973
Barrett, Ray (65)—January 16, 1973
Barrington, Josephine—February 27, 1973
Barry, Leonard (50)—September 14, 1972
Bauer, David (55)—February 13, 1973
Beems, Patricia Jane (46)—February 2, 1973
Belokurov, Vladimir V. (69)—January 30, 1973
Bernard, James (43)—May 9, 1973
Booth, Nellie (84)—March 29, 1973
Borel, Louis (67)—May 1973
Bourne, William Payne (36)—October 8, 1972
Boyd, William (74)—September 12, 1972
Branch, Phyllis (48)—June 6, 1972
Brannigan Owen (64)—May 9, 1973
Brasseur, Pierre (66)—August 14, 1972
Bravo, Nino (28)—April 16, 1973
Breakston, George P. (53)—May 1973
Brinkley, John D. (65)—August 8, 1972
Brown, Bessie Greenwood (92)—February 13, 1973
Brown, Winifred Colleano (75)—February 22, 1973
Burnett, Al (67)—April 19, 1973
Byal, Carl (83)—September 12, 1972
Call, John (64)—April 3, 1973
Campbell, Webster (79)—August 28, 1972
Caracol, Manolo (62)—February 24, 1973
Carlin, Cynthia—February 23, 1973
Carlson, Ken (53)—January 11, 1973
Carney, Alan (63)—May 2, 1973
Carr, Ginna (35)—July 13, 1972
Carroll, Leo G. (80)—October 16, 1972
Carroll, Jean (63)—July 29, 1972
Chadwick, John (65)—June 28, 1972

Chamberlain, Charlie (61)—June 16, 1972
Church, Esme (79)—May 31, 1972
Cohen, Morris (66)—January 7, 1973
Cooper, Melville (76)—March 29, 1973
Corey, Joseph (45)—August 30, 1972
Correll, Charles J.—September 26, 1972
Cox, Wally (48)—February 15, 1973
Cragen, William (62)—June 29, 1972
Craig, Walter (71)—July 5, 1972
Crooks, Richard (72)—October 1, 1972
Crosse, Rupert (45)—March 5, 1973
Curry, Winnie Garland—April 2, 1973
Dallimore, Maurice (70s)—February 20, 1973
Daniels, Charlotte (44)—May 9, 1973
Danzi, Muriel Chapman (62)—January 8, 1973
De Haven, Rose (91)—July 23, 1972
De Kowa, Victor (69)—April 1973
Devon, Pru—February 1973
Devine, Claire (82)—April 22, 1973
de Wilde, Brandon (30)—July 6, 1972
Dhotre, Damoo (72)—January 24, 1973
Dickson, Donald (61)—September 20, 1972
Difilippi, Arturo (78)—June 27, 1972
Dipaola, Earlamae (44)—October 28, 1972
Dixon, Denver (82)—November 9, 1972
Dombre, Barbara (28)—January 3, 1973
Dominique, Ivan (45)—April 3, 1973
Doonan, George (76)—April 17, 1973
Dorkin, Millie Morgan (77)—September 1, 1972
Droy, Frank (64)—January 1973
Dyer, Deb (69)—April 30, 1973
English, Paul Allen (44)—July 25, 1972
Epperson, Don (35)—March 17, 1973
Essex, Harold (68)—April 11, 1973
Essler, Fred (77)—January 17, 1973
Everett, Ethel (63)—April 2, 1973
Fahey, Myrna (34)—May 6, 1973
Fairhurst Edwin—February 1973
Feldman, Andrea—August 8, 1972
Finney, Mary (68)—February 26, 1973
Fischer, Bob (36)—August 12, 1972
Floyd, Sara Trainor (78)—August 16, 1972
Foster, Dudley (48)—January 8, 1973
Frank, Carl (63)—September 23, 1972
Fraser, Constance (63)—May 1973
Gannon, Charles A. (78)—October 27, 1972
Gary, Sid (72)—April 3, 1973
Gersten, Berta (78)—September 10, 1972

Goetz, Theo (78)—December 29, 1972
Gombell, Minna (81)—April 14, 1973
Gordon, Bobby (69)—February 17, 1973
Gordon, Colin (61)—October 4, 1972
Gordon, Grant (64)—August 6, 1972
Gordon, Riki (38)—January 16, 1973
Granville, Audrey (62)—October 20, 1972
Green, Nigel (48)—May 15, 1972
Gurin, Ellen (24)—June 5, 1972
Guzman, Richard (29)—July 29 1972
Hack, Signe (74)—January 6, 1973
Hackett, Lillian—February 28, 1973
Hall, Cliff (78)—October 6, 1972
Hamer, Gerald (86)—July 6, 1972
Hannen, Nicholas J. (91)—July 1972
Hanson, Gladys (89)—February 24, 1973
Hanson, Harry (77)—November 2, 1972
Harmon, Irving (66)—March 19, 1973
Harmon, Lee (41)—September 20, 1972
Harris, Stacy (54)—March 14, 1973
Healy, Jack (68)—July 14, 1972
Henning, Pat (62)—April 28, 1973
Hinckley, Dorothy—November 23, 1972
Holt, Tim (54)—February 15, 1973
Hopkins, Miriam (69)—October 9, 1972
Houston, Billie (66)—September 30, 1972
Howard, Sam (88)—October 25, 1972
Hughes, David (43)—October 19, 1973
Hulburd, H.L. (Bud)—February 10, 1973
Huley, Pete (80)—February 6, 1973
Husting, Lucille (70s)—June 30, 1972
Hutton, June—May 2, 1973
Jeans, Ursula (66)—April 21, 1973
Jewkes, Penny (22)—December 26, 1972
Johnson, Gertrude (78)—March 28, 1973
Jones, Emrys (56)—July 10, 1972
Jordin, Russ (43)—October 4, 1972
Juveneau, John J. (57)—March 8, 1973
Kammans Louise-Philippe (60)—October 21, 1972
Kapoor, Prithvi Raj (66)—May 29, 1972
Kelly, Flo (68)—September 2, 1972
Kellaway, Cecil (79)—February 28, 1973
Kent, Herbert (96)—March 13, 1973
Ketchum, Robyna Neilson—November 9, 1972
Khoury, Edith Leslie—April 9, 1973
King, Billy—July 19, 1972
King, Hetty (89)—September 1972
Klein, Gordon D. (58)—November 15, 1972
Knapp, Betty (72)—January 22, 1973
Kop, Mila (68)—January 15, 1973
Koralli, Vera (81)—November 1972
Krizman, Lynne Allen (48)—September 3, 1972
Landin, Hope (80)—February 28, 1973
Lanfield, Sidney (74)—June 30, 1972
Lange, Mary (60)—April 20, 1973
Lansing, Joi (37)—August 7, 1972
LaBelle, Rupert (72)—August 9, 1972
LaRose, Rose (59)—July 27, 1972
LaTour, Babe (79)—April 1, 1973
Lee, Bessie (66)—June 28, 1972
Leonard, Jack E. (62)—May 11, 1973

Libby, George A. (86)—January 22, 1973
Lichniavskaia, Alexandra (24)—February 16, 1973
Lisa, Luba (31)—December 15, 1972
Little, Lillian (66)—July 30, 1972
Livanov, Boris N. (68)—September 23, 1972
Logan, John (48)—December 7, 1972
Long, Wesley (72)—March 28, 1973
Lopukhov, Fyodor (86)—February 1973
Lorde, Athena (57)—May 23, 1973
Lorenz, George (52)—May 29, 1972
Lorenz, John A. (85)—April 30, 1972
McCann, Alfred W., Jr. (64)—December 8, 1972
McClelland, Evelyn A. (79)—June 8, 1972
McDowell, Fred (68)—July 3, 1972
McFarlin, Julius R. (85)—May 18, 1973
McLeod, Tex (83)—February 2, 1973
McTurk, David Harvey (67)—August 25, 1972
MacGowran, Jack (54)—January 31, 1973
Mack, Lester (66)—October 11, 1972
Mack, Russell (79)—June 1, 1972
Mackenzie, Donald (92)—July 21, 1972
Marion, Frances (86)—May 12, 1973
Marsh, Della—May 6, 1973
Martin, John F. X. (46)—February 16, 1973
Marum, Marilyn Harvey (44)—March 29, 1973
Maynard, Ken (77)—March 23, 1973
Meikle, Pat (49)—January 18, 1973
Melchior, Lauritz (82)—March 18, 1973
Menninger, Marion K.—January 29, 1973
Miloradovich, Milo (71)—October 27, 1972
Mooney, Rita (69)—January 3, 1973
Moore, Patti (71)—November 26, 1972
Moreland, Peg Leg (84)—January 1973
Moreno, Ascension (86)—August 28, 1972
Morrison, Anna Marie (88)—July 5, 1972
Morrison, George Pete (82)—February 5, 1973
Mulroy, Steve (80)—September 1972
Munro, Janet (38)—December 6, 1972
Mussiere, Lucien (82)—December 23, 1972
Nagy, Bill—January 19, 1973
Naish, J. Carrol (73)—January 24, 1973
Neal, Tom (59)—August 7, 1972
Nedell, Bernard (79)—November 23, 1972
Nielsen, Asta (90)—May 24, 1972
Nosseck, Max (70)—September 29, 1972
Oliver, Larry (93)—January 22, 1973
O'Neill, Eugene F. (84)—August 22, 1972
Otway, Rita (85)—October 25, 1972
Oukrainsky, Serge (86)—November 1, 1972
Owen, Reginald (85)—November 5, 1972
Oya, Ichijiro (78)—May 28, 1972
Palmer, Dawson (35)—September 10, 1972
Parker, Lew (65)—October 27, 1972
Patterson, James (40)—August 19, 1972
Patterson, Burdella (90)—April 13, 1973
Paul, Wauna (61)—March 31, 1973
Paxinou, Katina (72)—February 22, 1973
Pena, Julio (70)—July 22, 1972

Phelps, Lucian (65)—January 10, 1973
Pierpont, Laura (91)—December 11, 1972
Pimley, John (53)—May 17, 1972
Powers, Chris L. (82)—June 12, 1972
Procter, Ivis Goulding (67)—May 14, 1973
Prud'homme, George (71)—June 11, 1972
Purcell, Irene (70)—July 8, 1972
Quong, Rose Lanu (93)—December 14, 1972
Radilak, Charles H. (65)—July 19, 1972
Ramsey, Mary E.—August 17, 1972
Randolph, Isabel (83)—January 11, 1973
Ray, Gabrielle (91)—May 21, 1973
Reeves-Smith, Olive (77)—July 20, 1972
Reid, Carl Benton (79)—March 15, 1973
Rey, Roberto (67)—June 1972
Reynolds, Harold (76)—September 21, 1973
Richman, Harry (77)—November 3, 1972
Riley, George (72)—May 30, 1972
Rios, Lalo (46)—March 7, 1973
Rittenhouse, Mae (88)—October 18, 1972
Robinson, Edward G. (79)—January 26, 1973
Rodriguez, Tito (50)—February 28, 1973
Rogers, Mildred (74)—April 17, 1973
Ross, Larry (65)—April 5, 1973
Rosenberg, Michel (71)—November 18, 1972
Roswaenge, Helge (76)—August 1972
Rutherford, Tom—January 6, 1973
Ryan, Grace M. (82)—October 8, 1972
Ryan, Irene (70)—April 26, 1973
Sahni, Balraj (60)—April 13, 1973
Schulz, Fritz (76)—May 9, 1972
Schwannecke, Ellen—June 16, 1972
Seabury, Ynez (65)—April 11, 1973
Sedgwick, Josie (75)—April 30, 1973
Setterberg, Carl Douglas (54)—April 15, 1973
Sellers, Virginia (51)—March 15, 1973
Seymour, Cy (70)—April 21, 1973
Shannon, William J. (62)—May 25, 1973
Sharpe, Gyda (65)—January 14, 1973
Shaw, Sala (66)—November 3, 1972
Shoji, Taro (73)—October 4, 1972
Short, Antrim (72)—November 23, 1972
Shunmugham, T. K. (61)—March 1973
Smith, Art (73)—February 24, 1973
Smith, Betty Jane (49)—April 25, 1973
Spencer, Lou (56)—November 18, 1972
Stack, James (65)—March 30, 1973
Stanley, Raymond (54)—February 8, 1973
Story, Bob (47)—February 14, 1973
Stossel, Ludwig (89)—January 29, 1973
Stridel, Gene (46)—January 9, 1973
Stuart, Nick (69)—April 7, 1973
Tamiroff, Akim (72)—September 17, 1972
Tarasova, Alla (75)—April 1973
Tassel, Hazel Mae (80)—February 21, 1973
Tazewell, Charles (72)—June 26, 1972
Templeton, C. Mercer (83)—January 9, 1973
Thorndike, Russell (87)—November 7, 1972
Tindall, Loren (52)—May 10, 1973
Tissier, Jean (77)—April 1973
Tordesilla, Jesus (80)—March 24, 1973
Tozere, Frederic (71)—August 5, 1972
Traubel, Helen (69)—July 29, 1972

Tyler, Charles (32)—June 9, 1972
Uggams, Eloise (75)—July 14, 1972
Ulmann, Doris (56)—October 24, 1972
Umann, Olga (57)—October 1, 1972
Van, Samye (61)—July 19, 1972
Vernon, Hilary (52)—March 5, 1973
Votipka, Thelma (74)—October 24, 1972
Wade, Warren (76)—January 14, 1973
Walker, Arlene (54)—April 15, 1973
Wallington, James S. (65)—December 22, 1972
Ward, Clara (48)—January 16, 1973
Warren, Jimmy (50)—October 22, 1972
Webster, Margaret (67)—November 13, 1972
Weede, Robert (69)—July 9, 1972
White, Alfred H. (89)—August 22, 1972
Williams, Billy (62)—October 12, 1972
Williams, Claud (81)—November 4, 1972
Willis, Dave (78)—January 1, 1973
Willis, H. O.—September 1972
Wilmer—Brown, Maisie (80)—February 13, 1973
Wilson, Harvey L. (72)—June 4, 1972
Wilson, Marie (56)—November 23, 1972
Wilson, William Woodrow (60)—July 4, 1972
Windsor, Claire—October 24, 1972
Winston, Helen (40)—August 24, 1972
Wolfson, Billy (75)—January 15, 1973
Yanagiya, Kingoro (71)—October 22, 1972
Yassin, Ismail (60)—June 1972
Yazinsky, Jean (81)—March 11, 1973
Yengibarov, Leonid (30)—August 1972
Zimmermann, Ed (39)—July 6, 1972

PLAYWRIGHTS

Benson, Sally (71)—July 19, 1972
Bowles, Jane (56)—May 4, 1973
Buck, Pearl S. (80)—March 6, 1973
Carlton, Henry F. (80)—April 25, 1973
Cavett, Frank (67)—March 25, 1973
Coward, Noel Pierce (73)—March 26, 1973
de la Torre, Claudio (77)—January 10, 1973
Delderfield, R. F. (60)—June 24, 1972
de Montherlant, Henry (76)—September 21, 1972
Deval, Jacques (82)—December 19, 1972
Flaiano, Ennio (62)—November 20, 1972
Friedberg, Dr. Charles K. (64)—July 14, 1972
Guitton, Jean (86)—April 15, 1973
Guthrie, Lady (67)—July 25, 1972
Herz, Andrew (25)—November 10, 1972
Jeans, Ronald (86)—May 16, 1973
Keedick, Mabel Ferris (89)—April 24, 1973
Kikuta, Kazuo (65)—April 5, 1973
Korneichuk, Aleksandr Y. (66)—May 14, 1972
Laszlo, Miklos (69)—April 19, 1973
Mackenzie, Compton (89)—November 30, 1972
Reeves, Theodore (62)—March 18, 1973
Roberts, Edward Barry (71)—August 6, 1972
Romains, Jules (86)—August 14, 1972

COMPOSERS AND LYRICISTS

Alpaerts, Jef (68)—January 15, 1973
Baxter, Phil (75)—November 21, 1972
Britt, Elton (59)—June 23, 1972
Brown, Lawrence (79)—December 25, 1972
Chase, George Salisbury (62)—August 1, 1972
Clare, Sidney (80)—August 29, 1972
Conn, Chester (77)—April 4, 1973
Dolan, Robert Emmett (64)—September 26, 1972
Erickson, John (74)—June 16, 1972
Evans, Redd L. (60)—August 29, 1972
Fletcher, Robert (87)—November 20, 1972
Foch, Dirk (87)—May 24, 1973
Fort, Hank (59)—January 13, 1973
Frankel, Benjamin (67)—February 11, 1973
Freed, Arthur (78)—April 12, 1973
Friml, Rudolf (92)—November 12, 1972
Golden, John (68)—October 17, 1972
Graff, George (86)—January 24, 1973
Grun, Bernard (71)—December 28, 1972
Haba, Alois (79)—November 1972
Jaffe, Moe (71)—December 2, 1972
Kaminski, Joseph (68)—October 13, 1972
Koehler, Ted (78)—January 17, 1973
Leibowitz, Rene (59)—August 28, 1972
Leplin, Emanuel (55)—December 1, 1972
McBride, Claude E. (36)—February 2, 1973
O'Brien, Havergal (96)—November 28, 1972
Ory, Edward (Kid) (86)—January 23, 1973
Overton, Hall (52)—November 24, 1972
Parenteau, Zoel (89)—September 13, 1972
Perper, Bob—September 2, 1972
Pietrack, Irving (70)—December 19, 1972
Razaf, Andy (77)—February 3, 1973
Rollins, Walter E. (66)—January 1, 1973
Schroder, Friedrich (62)—September 25, 1972
Sherman, Noel (41)—June 4, 1972
Shine, Joe (70)—March 13, 1973
Stalling, Carl W. (84)—November 29, 1972
Usera, Ramon (Moncho) (67)—August 11, 1972
Weeks, William J. (71)—September 8, 1972
Wess, Richard (43)—March 14, 1973

PRODUCERS, DIRECTORS, CHOREOGRAPHERS

Baron, Milton (Mickey) (76)—May 22, 1972
Beaumont, Hugh (64)—March 22, 1973
Bloom, Norton L. (45)—December 6, 1972
Bonfils, Helen G. (82)—June 6, 1972
Bradley, Buddy (70s)—July 17, 1972
Bran, Mary (73)—August 16, 1972
Brucato, Jimmy (55)—March 2, 1973
Buchs, Julio (46)—January 19, 1973
Burrell, John (62)—September 28, 1972
Cash, Don (53)—January 27, 1973
Cooper, Merian C. (78)—April 21, 1973
Czinner, Paul (82)—June 22, 1972
D'Andria, Giorgio (72)—July 5, 1972
Deeter, Jasper (77)—May 31, 1972

Deroisey, Lucien (60)—October 10, 1972
Dieterle, William (79)—December 9, 1972
Ebi, Earl (69)—January 24, 1973
Fedorova, Alexandra (83)—August 20, 1972
Freed, Arthur (78)—April 12, 1973
Freeman, Valdo Lee (72)—December 4, 1972
Fritschy, Walter A. (91)—December 1, 1972
Gallone, Carmine (87)—March 11, 1973
Goldgran, Henry (58)—October 19, 1972
Graf, Herbert (69)—April 5, 1973
Halliday, Richard (67)—March 3, 1973
Hart, Everett L. (51)—January 1, 1973
Hastings, Harold (54)—May 30, 1973
Hill, Jerome (67)—December 21, 1972
Jensen, Howard C. (58)—July 3, 1972
Jonson, William (51)—November 21, 1972
Kalatozow, Mikhail (69)—March 27, 1973
Kerkow, Herbert (68)—August 26, 1972
Kertesz, Istvan (43)—April 17, 1973
Koplan, Harry (53)—May 20, 1973
Kozintsev, Grigory (68)—May 11, 1973
Leisen, Mitchell (74)—October 28, 1972
Levoy, Albert E. (70)—December 21, 1972
Lichine, David (62)—June 26, 1972
Limon, Jose Arcadia (64)—December 3, 1972
Loew, David L. (75)—March 25, 1973
Loper, Don (66)—November 22, 1972
Lovell, James (59)—September 15, 1972
McDonald, Marvin (78)—April 27, 1973
Markas, Gary (42)—October 30, 1972
Migatz, Marshall—May 25, 1973
Nicholson, James (56)—December 10, 1972
Olney, Dorothy McGrayne (73)—April 22, 1973
Paal, Alexander (60s)—November 9, 1972
Patton, Phil (61)—May 28, 1972
Roland, Will (63)—March 30, 1973
Schneiderov, Vladimir A. (72)—January 4, 1973
Scott, Robert Adrian (61)—December 25, 1972
Siodmak, Robert (72)—March 10, 1973
Sorel, Felicia (66)—September 7, 1972
Spier, William H. (66)—May 30, 1973
Stone, Louis H. (76)—June 17, 1972
Taylor, Sylvia (50)—January 1, 1973
Ulmer, Edgar G. (68)—September 30, 1972
Walker, Hal (76)—July 3, 1972
Watts, Peter (72)—December 9, 1972
Woodward, Horace L. (68)—April 20, 1973

CONDUCTORS

Balaban, Emanuel (78)—April 17, 1973
Brusiloff, Leon (73)—April 1, 1973
Chagrin, Francis (67)—November 9, 1972
Denzler, Robert F. (80)—August 25, 1972
Horenstein, Jascha (74)—April 2, 1973
Kertesz, Istvan (43)—April 17, 1973
Kletzki, Paul (72)—March 5, 1973
Roman, Myron (67)—January 11, 1973
Smallens, Alexander (83)—November 24, 1972

Spamon, Kenneth—June 1972
Van Ginneken, Jaap (58)—September 1972

DESIGNERS

Barsacq, Andre (64)—February 4, 1973
Berman, Eugene (73)—December 15, 1972
Dreyhuss, Henry (68)—October 5, 1972
Furse, Roger (68)—August 19, 1972
Sutherland, Alec (35)—May 12, 1973

CRITICS

Archer, Eugene (42)—January 30, 1973
Arneel, Eugen (52)—December 3, 1972
Alexander, David (65)—March 21, 1973
Burke, Cornelius G. (70)—May 18, 1973
Goldberg, B. Z. (78)—December 29, 1972
Carroll, Harrison (71)—August 2, 1972
Chesselet, Robert (70)—October 24, 1972
Coates, Robert M. (75)—February 8, 1973
French, Winsor B. II (68)—March 6, 1973
Gans, Sidney (60)—August 28, 1972
Gardner, Archibald M. (65)—November 1972
Hartley, L. P. (76)—December 13, 1972
Hussey, Dyneley (79)—September 6, 1972
Lejeune, C. A. (76)—April 1, 1973
Lovell, Florence (50)—June 5, 1972
MacDougall, Sally (97)—February 19, 1973
Maher, James P. (78)—March 14, 1973
Mallett, Richard (62)—November 29, 1972
Miller, Paul Eduard (64)—December 16, 1972
Parsons, Louella (91)—December 9, 1972
Rayfield, Fred (49)—June 5, 1972
Reno, Doris—April 18, 1973
Saarinen,, Aline B. (58)—July 13, 1972
Saltzberg, Geraldine (Jerry) (80)—July 25, 1972
Steinfirst, Donald S. (68)—August 22, 1972
Wilson, Edmund (77)—June 12, 1972
Wolf, Louis J. (67)—May 24, 1972

MUSICIANS

Abel, Earl Sr. (73)—February 9, 1973
Alvis, Hayes (65)—December 30, 1972
Apollon, Dave (74)—May 30, 1972
Autier, Vicky (48)—December 23, 1972
Beidel, Richard (69)—January 14, 1973
Blanchard, Edgar V.—October 17, 1972
Bowne, Walter R. (70s)—September 26, 1972
Brown, Lawrence (79)—December 25, 1972
Byas, Don (59)—August 24, 1972
Capocci, Guerino C. (79)—January 17, 1973
Castel, Albert R. (67)—October 9, 1972
Cavan, Jack (64)—December 5, 1972
Cole, Brian (28)—August 2, 1972
Coleman, Cornelius J. (44)—February 20, 1973
Deering, Henri (77)—March 27, 1973
Denny, Dave (51)—August 2, 1972
De Paris, Wilbur (72)—January 3, 1973
Dorham, Kenny (48)—December 5, 1972

Douglas, Walter Johnstone (85)—August 1972
Duques, Augustin (73)—August 14, 1972
Eisenberg, Maurice (72)—December 13, 1972
Forbes, Jean Reti—May 7, 1972
Ganz, Rudolph (95)—August 2, 1972
Gardner, Billy (44)—March 5, 1973
Gillette, Robert F. (70)—September 24, 1972
Hambourg, Clement (72)—February 3, 1973
Hamill, Mel (59)—May 1, 1973
Hanson, James B. (68)—April 3, 1973
Harris, William J. (83)—August 28, 1972
Harrison, Ray (70)—February 24, 1973
Higginbotham, Jay C. (67)—May 26, 1973
Jackson, Jack Everett—June 17, 1972
Kenyon, Clara (61)—January 1973
Kneisel, Frank (68)—May 23, 1973
Knox, Ethel (79)—October 17, 1972
Kuhn, Frank (88)—March 5, 1973
Lake, Martin (62)—April 21, 1973
Legan, William (47)—December 11, 1972
Lennon, Florence (Roxanne) (81)—November 9, 1972
Lesko, Charles (80)—January 15, 1973
Levant, Oscar (65)—August 14, 1972
Lewis, William Hayes (33)—March 1972
Liddell, Arnold (Arny) J. (56)—May 31, 1972
Long, Johnny (56)—October 31, 1972
McKernan, Ron (27)—March 8, 1973
McPhatter, Clyde L. (41)—June 13, 1972
MacGregor, John Chalmers (69)—March 9, 1973
Meroff, Benny (72)—March 1973
Mezzrow, Mezz (73)—August 6, 1972
Minchin, Nina M. (79)—August 27, 1972
Monroe, Vaughn (62)—May 21, 1973
Munn, Worth E. (71)—November 16, 1972
Murcia, Billy (19)—November 6, 1972
Oakley, Berry (20s)—November 11, 1972
Ocko, Bernard (70)—October 15, 1972
O'Craven, Knuckles (71)—February 8, 1973
Oldre, Fred (76)—August 14, 1972
Ory, Kid (86)—January 23, 1973
Papalia, Rosario (Russ) (69)—November 3, 1972
Perryman, Rufus (Speckled Red) (80)—January 2, 1973
Phillips, Sid (65)—May 21, 1973
Provenzano, John (75)—December 27, 1972
Rakos, Julius, Sr. (77)—October 22, 1972
Ramsey, Collie (52)—March 3, 1973
Roberts, Samuel H. (67)—January 23, 1973
Rogosinski, Curt (74)—November 1972
Rushing, Jimmy (68)—June 8, 1972
Sanders, Sigmund (75)—November 18, 1972
Sassone, Frank N. (65)—January 13, 1973
Saunders, Richard (39)—January 22, 1973
Shaffer, Elaine (47)—February 19, 1973
Silverman, Ernest A. (66)—January 19, 1973
Sloan, K. Bert (65)—February 28, 1973
Smith, Joseph M. (78)—January 28, 1973
Smith, Willie (The Lion) (79)—April 18, 1973

Snowden, Elmer (72)—May 14, 1973
Steinhardt, Laurence (59)—March 10, 1973
Stoneman, Scot (40)—March 4, 1973
Storm, Rory (33)—September 28, 1972
Szigeti, Joseph (80)—February 20, 1973
Taylor, Murray (76)—October 18, 1972
Tidona, George (62)—December 18, 1972
Tieber, William R. (Bill) (58)—September 9, 1972
Vaughan, Denny (52)—October 3, 1972
Walton, Jon (50)—May 14, 1972
Weir, Louis (68)—August 27, 1972
Wessel, Mark E. (79)—May 2, 1973
Wolfe, Martin Fred (28)—February 28, 1973
Yahnke, Otto (86)—January 7, 1973

OTHERS

Aba, Marika—November 11, 1972
  Publicist
Abel, Grover Cleveland (79)—July 21, 1972
  Dancing instructor
Abeles, Julian T. (80)—March 6, 1973
  Show business lawyer
Adler, Harry (66)—February 16, 1973
  Personal manager and agent
Adler, Herbert (66)—November 22, 1972
  Hollywood labor leader
Ansley, Edmond (84)—September 26, 1972
  Midget who toured as Buster Brown
Austin, Mrs. Florence Ames (89)—January, 1973. National Assn. of Organists pioneer
Bailey, Joseph (61)—October 1, 1972
  TV producer and theatrical lawyer
Barlow, Seaghan (late 80s)—July 1972
  Last member of National Dramatic Society
Barr, Richard M. (64)—June 13, 1972
  Publicist
Beck, James Montgomery (80)—December 4, 1972. Musical director of RCA Victor
Belcher, Ernest (90)—February 24, 1973
  Reputedly first Hollywood dance director
Berger, Sam (63)—July 5, 1972
  Personal manager and club date producer
Berle, Frank (70)—May 10, 1973
  Brother of Milton, manager of Cort Theater
Berman, Max (88)—November 1, 1972
  British costumer
Blackmar, Mrs. Margaret (89)—March 29, 1973. Exec. sec. to Morton Gould, Vincent Lopez
Blair, Mrs. Helen Bowen (82)—August 9, 1972
  Patron of arts
Blum, Martin A. (36)—November 20, 1972
  Publicist
Bly, Dan (37)—February 2, 1973
  Stage manager
Brandt, Harry N. (75)—June 3, 1972
  Movie industry pioneer
Brandt, Mrs. Harry N. (68)—March 11, 1973
  Co-chairman, Amer. Theater Wing Club
Brannigan, Bob (75)—February 12, 1973
  Stagehand

Briggs, Don (56)—June 26, 1972
  Road manager for Ray Charles
Brockway, Wallace (67)—November 5, 1972
  Editor, author in field of music
Broun, Mrs. Heywood—February 5, 1973
  Widow of columnist
Burkey, Evelyn F. (62)—February 18, 1973
  Exec. director, Writers Guild East
Burns, Joey (68)—December 11, 1972
  Vocal coach and accompanist
Buzzell, Eugene (68)—May 1, 1973
  Public relations director
Calvin, Frank (74)—August 13, 1972
  Researcher for Cecil B. DeMille
Campbell, Mrs. Maria L. (103)—March 31, 1973. Recited "Mary Had a Little Lamb" for Thomas A. Edison's first record in 1877
Cape, Safford (67)—March 26, 1973
  Expert in ancient music
Carmel, Eddie (36)—July 30, 1972
  Circus giant (500 lbs., 9 feet tall)
Cavallero, Gene (84)—June 11, 1972
  Founder of Colony Restaurant
Chanin, Henry (79)—February 25, 1973
  Builder of legitimate theaters
Christenberry, Robert K. (74)—April 14, 1973
  Manager of Astor Hotel
Cleary, Maurice G. (78)—February 17, 1973
  Business manager for actors
Clurman, Edith (55)—March 25, 1973
  Former dancer, wife of Robert Clurman
Cohan, Mrs. George M. (89)—September 9, 1972. Widow of the actor, herself a dancer
Condon, Robert (51)—June 13, 1972
  TV and radio writer
Crandell, Roland (80)—August 14, 1972
  Pioneer of animated cartoons
Culbertson, Ernest H. (86)—July 24, 1972
  Council member, Episcopal Actors Guild
Cullman, Howard S. (80)—June 29, 1972
  Investor in Broadway shows
Denyer, James (46)—October 30, 1972
  Publicist
Dewey, Kenneth S. G. (37)—August 2, 1972
  Founder of Action Theater
Djury, Vladimir (60)—July 2, 1972
  Specialist in music and theater arts
Doulens, Roger B. (57)—September 2, 1972
  Publicist
Downey, James J. (65)—May 31, 1972
  Owner of Downey's Steak House
Dreyer, Lewis A. (57)—September 26, 1972
  Music publishing executive
Dubrawski, Frank (46)—July 14, 1972
  Savoy Theater Complex, Boston
Duffy, James (56)—December 29, 1972
  Circus boss, Duffy's Circus in Ireland
Edwards, Nate (70)—September 12, 1972
  Production manager
Emline, Mrs. Velman (76)—January 14, 1973
  Known as Broadway Billy
Enloe, William G. (70)—November 22, 1972
  Theater manager in Raleigh, N. C.

Escande, Maurice (80)—February 11, 1973
Leading figure in Comédie Française
Fabiani, Aurelio (82)—April 27, 1973
Founder of Philadelphia Lyric Opera
Favorite, Mrs. Harriet Leaf (76)—June 24, 1972. Philadelphia theater patron
Feld, Israel S. (61)—December 15, 1972
Co-owner, Ringling Bros. Circus
Fenner, H. Wolcott (61)—October 14, 1972
Senior vice president, Ringling Bros.
Finnegan, James F. (Jimmy) (64)—October 7, 1972. Publicist.
Flaherty, Frances H. (87)—June 22, 1972
Widow of Robert J. Flaherty
Fleischer, Max (89)—September 11, 1972
Creator of Out of the Inkwell, Popeye
Gage, Richard N. (72)—November 16, 1972
Managing director of Allenberry Playhouse
Galt, William R. (91)—November 1972
Vaudeville agent
Garozzo, Nella (50s)—October 1972
Publicist
Gates, Sylvester G. (71)—November 12, 1972
Chairman of British Film Institute
Gentele, Goeran (54)—July 18, 1972
General manager of Metropolitan Opera
Gilbert, Dr. Benjamin A. (67)—July 9, 1972
House physician
Glaser, Paul (50)—December 8, 1972
Member of Actors' Equity Council
Gooding, Floyd E. (77)—August 14, 1972
Carnival operator
Grady, Billy (87)—March 5, 1973
Dean of Hollywood talent directors
Graf, Herbert (69)—April 3, 1973
Stage director, Metropolitan Opera
Green, Abel (72)—May 10, 1973
Editor of Variety
Grossinger, Jennie (80)—November 20, 1972
Owner of Catskill resort
Hale, Frank (72)—December 20, 1972
Owner of Royal Poinciana Playhouse
Hastings, William T. (65)—August 21, 1972
Theater manager
Heinecke, Paul (87)—December 23, 1972
European leader of authors, composers
Helbock, Joe (76)—January 5, 1973
Founder of Onyx Club
Hiller, Joe (84)—April 14, 1973
Dean of theatrical bookers, Pittsburgh
Hirsch, Mrs. Martin (81)—April 1, 1973
Theater ticket agency owner
Hixon, Frank G. (82)—April 26, 1973
Promoter, box office operator
Hoehn, Hans (48)—October 12, 1972
Variety correspondent in Berlin
Hoffman, Lloyd (62)—May 15, 1973
Publicist
Holzman, Samuel (80)—July 13, 1972
Coney Island amusement operator
Horohan, John (53)—February 4, 1973
A president of IATSE

Hughes, James T. (74)—September 18, 1972
Former board chairman of ATPAM
Ireland, Charles (51)—June 7, 1972
CBS president
Isaac, Lester B.—January 25, 1973
Representative of IATSE
Jacobs, Ray J. (64)—November 20, 1972
Brother of Danny Thomas
Jacoby, Herbert (73)—November 19, 1972
Proprietor of The Blue Angel
Jenner, Caryl (55)—January 29, 1973
Pioneer in children's theater
Judell, Maxson, F. (74)—September 27, 1972
Publicist
Kabos, Ilona (75)—May 27, 1973
Piano teacher at Juilliard
Kanter, Mitchell (68)—June 16, 1972
Treasurer of Winter Garden Theater
Kelley, Lloyd (Handshake) (69)—June 3, 1972. Stage electrician
Kirk, Neil (79)—September 16, 1972
Broadway booking agent
Klein, Jacob (94)—March 9, 1973
Attorney for the Shuberts
Knecht, Karl Kae (88)—July 28, 1972
Variety correspondent
Kopf, Jack (79)—April 26, 1973
Theatrical costumer
Krapp, Herbert J. (86)—February 16, 1973
Theater architect
Landau, Marty W. (74)—February 23, 1973
Artists' manager
Lenihan, Edward T. (89)—October 6, 1972
Theatrical manager
Leyendecker, Frank S. (67)—January 10, 1973
Editorial director, Greater Amusements
Lipman, Ann (32)—July 26, 1972
Publicist
LoCastro, Al (69)—January 27, 1973
Regional director of AGVA
Lofaro, Rocco (60)—December 16, 1972
Retired Times Square traffic patrolman
Lohman, Mrs. Dorothy—May 1, 1973
Child actors' agent
Long, Hubert (48)—September 7, 1972
Talent agent in country music
Lowe, Alva Hovery (80)—December 14, 1972
Booker of theater personalities
Lowenbach, Jan (92)—August 13, 1972
Musicologist
Lurie, Louis (84)—September 6, 1972
Financial angel for Broadway
McCarthy, Neil S. (84)—July 25, 1972
Theatrical lawyer
McClane, John E. (50)—July 10, 1972
Publicist
McCullough, Russell H. (76)—August 31, 1972. Director of theater construction
McKenney, Ruth (60)—July 25, 1972
Author of My Sister Eileen
McLaughlin, Michael J. (83)—April 12, 1973
Recording engineer

Marden, Ben (77)—April 7, 1973
  Showman, theaterowner
Martin, Christina—January 14, 1973
  Broadway dresser
Marx, Milton (75)—March 11, 1973
  Theatrical caricaturist for Newark *News*
Mazzei, Irvin P. (55)—July 24, 1972
  Western director for AGVA
Melling, Ray (72)—August 20, 1972
  Charter member of IATSE
Mercur, William (74)—August 10, 1972
  Publicist
Mullen, Jack (54)—September 23, 1972
  Publicist
Murray, Richard F. (74)—December 12, 1972
  General manager, ASCAP
Murrel, Roger E. (86)—April 24, 1973
  Vaudeville agent
Newsom, Earl (75)—April 11, 1973
  Publicist
Nyren, David (47)—February 3, 1973
  Theatrical agency executive
Ogg, Marguerite (64)—August 22, 1972
  Children's agent
Oshrin, George (69)—May 31, 1972
  Company manager
Parnell, Val (78)—September 22, 1972
  Managing director, Moss Empire Theaters
Parsons, William C. (49)—April 21, 1973
  Representative for Actors Equity
Perrett, Francis L. (73)—November 2, 1972
  Publicist
Podhajsky, Col. Alois (75)—May 23, 1973
  Chief of the Spanish Riding School
Poultney, George—October 10, 1972
  Equity representative in San Francisco
Reade, Walter, Jr. (56)—February 24, 1973
  Theater owner and distributor
Rees, Les (84)—April 27, 1973
  Variety stringer
Reynolds, Patrick J. (59)—August 18, 1972
  Director, Catholic Actors Guild
Ribner, Irving (50)—July 2, 1972
  Shakespearean scholar
Ricketts, Matthew R. (91)—August 7, 1972
  Chairman, Chappell & Co.
Roth, Al (68)—October 30, 1972
  Musical director
Rothschild, Alfred (83)—September 11, 1972
  Editor of Bantam Shakespeare

Sarno, James (62)—June 14, 1972
  Publicist
Schallmann, Sidney M. (82)—July 14, 1972
  Theatrical agent
Shaw, Stan (64)—August 16, 1972
  Originator of "Milkman's Matinee"
Southard, Paul E. (74)—October 8, 1972
  Records division of Columbia, RCA
Stern, Harold (65)—October 14, 1972
  Theatrical lawyer
Suber, Harry (74)—January 7, 1973
  Representative of Local 802
Sullivan, Mrs. Ed. (69)—March 16, 1973
  Wife of columnist
Sweeten, Robert G. (59)—July 29, 1972
  Publicist
Talbot, Slim (77)—January 25, 1973
  Stand-in for Gary Cooper
Taplinger, Dick (62)—February 13, 1973
  President, Taplinger Publishing
Tinayre, Vyes (80)—July 12, 1972
  Musicologist
Towler, Thomas (80)—June 22, 1972
  Publisher of *Town & Country*
Trammell, Niles (78)—March 28, 1973
  Third president of NBC
Van Doren, Mark (78)—December 10, 1972
  Critic, poet, teacher
Vedovelli, Umberto (60)—November 15, 1972
  Assistant conductor, Metropolitan Opera
Volkman, Ivan—October 17, 1972
  Production manager, assistant director
Wadsworth, Jessie (81)—February 21, 1973
  Talent agent
Whisenant, Elijah (62)—January 25, 1973
  Theater manager
Whitney, Art (60)—November 9, 1972
  Stage manager, booking agent
Winscott, Dudley A. (70)—December 15, 1972
  Theater manager
Wunnink, Karel (66)—May 1973
  Manager, Carre Theater in Amsterdam
Wylie, William (44)—April 22, 1973
  Gen. manager, Stratford, Ontario
Yates, Stephen (43)—August 18, 1972
  Theatrical agent
Zirato, Bruno (88)—November 28, 1972
  Private secretary to Enrico Caruso
Zylbercweig, Zalmen (77)—July 25, 1972
  Historian of Yiddish stage

INDEX

Play titles are in **bold face** and **bold face italic** page numbers refer to pages where cast and credit listings may be found.